BRUNNER/MAZEL PSYCHOSOCIAL STRESS SERIES NO. 8

TRAUMA and Its WAKE

VOLUME II: Traumatic Stress Theory, Research, and Intervention

Edited by

Charles R. Figley, Ph.D.

BRUNNER/MAZEL, *Publishers* • New York

Acknowledgment is hereby given for permission received from the Putnam Publishing Group to reprint the excerpts that appear in Chapter 2 from *A Fall of Fortresses* by Elmer Bendiner. Copyright © 1980 by Elmer Bendiner.

Library of Congress Cataloging-in-Publication Data
(Revised for volume 2)

Trauma and its wake.

(v. Brunner/Mazel psychosocial stress series;
no. 8)
Includes bibliographies and indexes.
Contents: [v. 1] The study and treatment of post
traumatic stress disorder — v. 2. Traumatic stress
theory, research, and intervention.
1. Post-traumatic stress disorder—Collected works.
2. Stress (Psychology)—Collected works. I. Figley,
Charles R., 1944-   . II. Series: Brunner/Mazel
psychosocial stress series; no. 8, etc. [DNLM:
1. Stress Disorders, Post-Traumatic. WM 170 T777]
RC552.P67T73   1985   616.85'21   84-29344
ISBN 0-87630-385-8 (v. 1)
ISBN 0-87630-431-5 (v. 2)

Copyright © 1986 by Charles R. Figley

For information and ordering, contact:
Brunner/Mazel
A member of the Taylor & Francis Group
47 Runway Road, Suite G
Levittown, PA 19057-4700
1-800-821-8312

MANUFACTURED IN THE UNITED STATES OF AMERICA

This book is dedicated to the Society for Traumatic Stress Studies, born in 1985, and dedicated to the accumulation, application, and dissemination of knowledge about the immediate and long-term psychosocial consequences of extraordinarily stressful circumstances.

Editorial Note

Trauma and Its Wake, Volume II: Post-Traumatic Stress Disorder Theory, Research, and Treatment is the eighth book in the Psychosocial Stress Book Series. The purpose of the Series is to develop and publish books that in some way make a significant contribution to the understanding and management of the psychosocial stress reaction paradigm. The books are designed to advance the work of clinicians, researchers, and other professionals involved in the varied aspects of human services. The primary readership of this Series includes those practitioners, scholars, and their students who are committed to this purpose.

The Psychosocial Stress Series is among the few that are "refereed." The quality and significance of the Series are guided by a nationally and internationally respected group of scholars who compose the Editorial Board. The Board reviews and approves each book that is published in the Series. Like the readership, the Board represents the fields of general medicine, pediatrics, psychiatry, nursing, psychology, sociology, social work, family therapy, political science, and anthropology.

Collectively, the books and chapters in this Series have focused on the immediate and long-term psychosocial consequences of extraordinary stressors such as war, divorce, parenting, separation, racism, social isolation, acute illness, drug addiction, death, sudden unemployment, rape, natural disasters, incest, crime victimization, and many others.

The first volume in the Series, *Stress Disorders Among Vietnam Veterans*, published in 1978 and edited by this author, focused on the immediate and long-term effects of war. It alerted the nation to the difficulties of coping with one's war experiences long after the war was over. It provided a state-of-the-art source book for scholars and practitioners working in the area of war-related stress reactions and disorders. With the publication of this book and other resources, mental health professionals and policymakers began to recognize the complexity of the postwar readjustment of Vietnam veterans. Soon a national outreach program emerged within the Veterans Administration with storefront Vet Centers in every major city in the country and inpatient treatment programs in many VA Medical Centers across the country to focus on these problems. As a result, thousands of professionals have since become aware of the special circumstances of war veterans.

The next two volumes in the Series, *Stress and the Family, Volume I: Coping With Normative Transitions* and *Stress and the Family, Volume II: Coping With Catastrophe,* edited by Charles R. Figley and Hamilton I. McCubbin, provide a comprehensive summary of the available information about how families cope with psychosocial stress. The former volume attends to the typical and predictable stressors of family life, while the latter volume focuses on how families cope with extraordinary and unpredictable stressors. Each chapter follows the same outline, which first introduces the stressor, then identifies the functional and dysfunctional ways families and family members cope.

The origin of this current book can be traced to Volume #4 in the Series, *Trauma and Its Wake: The Study and Treatment of Post-Traumatic Stress Disorder,* edited by Charles R. Figley. This was the first attempt to generalize research and clinical findings among a wide variety of traumatic or catastrophic events towards a generalized view of traumatic and post-traumatic stress reactions. Chapters focused on the immediate and long-term psychosocial consequences of exposure to one of many types of catastrophic events: war, rape, natural disasters, incest. Other chapters focused on effective methods of treating or preventing stress reactions or disorders. It is the first in a series of books that will review the latest innovations in theory, research, and treatment of post-traumatic stress disorder (PTSD), caused by a wide variety of stressful life events. The book you are reading is the second of this series of annually published volumes on PTSD within the Book Series.

The fifth volume in the Series, *Post-Traumatic Stress Disorder and the War Veteran Patient,* edited by William E. Kelly, focused on war veterans in general, and Vietnam war veterans in particular. Built upon the most important contributions of the past, this volume provides a specific blueprint for conceptualizing and treating war-related post-traumatic stress disorders. In many ways, it serves as an excellent introduction for the volume which follows this editorial note. Both are concerned about the direct aftermath of war on those who fought it, though focusing on significantly different conflicts.

The sixth volume, *The Crime Victim's Book,* written by Morton Bard and Dawn Sangrey, deals with yet another context in which individuals struggle to manage their violent life experiences. This book is written as a primer for those interested in working with victims of crime, particularly violent crime, although the authors hoped that victims themselves would read it. The book provides summaries of two important recent task force reports: one produced by the President's Task Force on Victims of Crime and the other by the American Psychological Association's Task Force on the Victims of Crime and Violence, chaired by the book's senior author.

Stress and Coping in Time of War, edited by Norman Milgram, is the seventh volume, but the first in the Series to focus on an international issue: the special psychosocial stress of war upon not only those who fight, but also the nations, communities, and social systems directly affected. Although the volume looks at the special circumstances faced by one country, Israel, its content has far-reaching implications for any nation that must commit its resources towards an all-out national defense. This book considers the *context* of war and its multilevel impact. It is the first to focus on war-related stress and coping at the levels of the individual, the group, and the nation-state.

The present volume, *Trauma and Its Wake, Volume II*, is the state of the art in theory, research, and treatment associated with the PTSD. And PTSD is the latest and most significant conceptualization of the negative consequences of extraordinary, catastrophic stressors. As with the first volume of *Trauma and Its Wake*, Volume II includes the thoughtful work of scholars—both researchers and clinicians—from all of the major mental health disciplines. They focus on the explication and application of knowledge about the psychosocial impact of traumatic experiences: how the *memories* of extraordinarily stressful life experiences invade the everyday life of those who survived them.

This and subsequent annual volumes are guided by eight fundamental, integrating questions. These include, for example: What constitutes a catastrophe (an extraordinarily stressful experience), one that may be viewed as a "traumatic event"? Who will be traumatized by a catastrophe and who will not? Among the traumatized, who will develop PTSD? What personal and interpersonal attributes most contribute to both resisting and ameliorating PTSD?

The initial three theoretical chapters by leading scholars in the area provide important conceptual insights, followed by five chapters presenting new data on evidence of PTSD among, for example, residents exposed to chemically toxic material, active duty military, and survivors of the Mount St. Helens eruption. The final section of the book includes seven chapters focusing on clinical and judicial intervention on behalf of trauma victims and survivors. They include the clinical application of psychoanalytic principles, inpatient treatment programs, social support network, family therapy, and desensitization. The final two chapters, as the editor's introduction points out, are seemingly antithetical since one emphasizes the denied rights and enormous emotional problems, including PTSD, of families of murdered victims. The next chapter, however, argues that at times the murderer may be a victim of PTSD him/herself, which is partly or entirely responsible for the murderous act. This is, of course, small compensation to the victim's family, as discussed just a chapter earlier.

Together with this most recent volume, the books in this Series form a new orientation for thinking about human behavior under extraordinary conditions. They provide an integrated set of source books for scholars and practitioners interested in how and why some individuals and social systems thrive under stressful situations, while others do not.

Charles R. Figley, Ph.D.
Series Editor
Purdue University
West Lafayette, Indiana

Contents

Acknowledgments

As with every publication of this refereed Book Series, I am indebted to the members of the Editorial Board, who are listed in the front of this book. Most of the members of this elite group are well-known internationally for their many contributions in the area of traumatic stress. I am especially indebted to them for their contribution to this particular volume. Since the *Trauma and Its Wake* series is an annual refereed publication, every chapter must undergo an extensive peer review process. Not only did the Board review and approve the proposal for this volume, but each Board member also reviewed at least one of the chapters in this volume; several reviewed four or more.

In addition to the careful reviews of Editorial Board members, other scholars graciously provided additional and timely reviews of at least one chapter. They include Dr. Talbott Sheely, Dr. Robert McFarland, Dr. James K. Besyner, Dr. Susan Solomon, Vicki Hogancamp, and Rose Sandecki. William Kelly's careful editorial work on several chapters originally selected for his volume in the Series was extremely helpful and effective.

I am especially appreciative of my doctoral students who not only reviewed many of the manuscripts, but also helped shape my thinking regarding traumatic stress. They are: Dr. William Southerly, Dr. Sandra Burge, Shirley Ann Segal, Kathleen Gilbert, C. J. Harris, and Richard Kishur.

Without my cheerful and fastidious secretary, Becky Harshman, the manuscripts' review process and most other aspects of the project would have stalled or collapsed entirely. Indeed, the support of my colleagues—particularly my Department Head, Dr. Robert A. Lewis, and Director of the Marriage and Family Therapy Program, Dr. Douglas Sprenkle, and Director of Clinical Training, Department of Psychological Sciences, Dr. Don Hartsough—provided significant personal, professional, and intellectual support for my work. Also, I am indebted to Purdue University's continuous support of my work since 1974, particularly Purdue's Agricultural Experiment Station research funds, which supported several projects focusing on Post-traumatic Stress Disorder.

My family always sustains me and gives my work meaning and perspective: my sister, Sandra Elliott, and her husband, Michael, and daughter, Amy; my mother, Geni, my wife, Dr. Marilyn Reeves, and daughters, Jessica and Laura.

Contributors

Harriet C. Arnone, Ph.D.
Center for Social Research, Graduate School of the City University of New York.

Morton Bard, Ph.D.
Center for Social Research, Graduate School of the City University of New York.

Andrew Baum, Ph.D.
Uniformed Services University of the Health Sciences, Bethesda, Maryland.

George R. Bowen, Ph.D.
VA Medical Center, Chillicothe, Ohio.

Laura M. Davidson
Uniformed Services University of the Health Sciences, Bethesda, Maryland.

Charles R. Figley, Ph.D.
Professor and Director, Traumatic Stress Research Program, Purdue University, West Lafayette, Indiana.

India Fleming, Ph.D.
Uniformed Services University of the Health Sciences, Bethesda, Maryland.

Angie D. Herndon, Ed.D.
Alabama Vet Cente, Mobile Alabama.

Carmine Iacono, Ph.D.
Department of Psychology, Texas Tech University, Lubbock, Texas.

James A. Lambert, M.Ed.
VA Medical Center, Chillicothe, Ohio.

Joseph G. Law, Jr., Ed.D.
Alabama Vet Center, Mobile, Alabama.

Jacob D. Lindy, M.D.
University of Cincinnati and Cincinnati Psychoanalytic Institute.

Shirley A. Murphy, Ph.D.
Department of Psychosocial Nursing, University of Washington, Seattle.

David Nemiroff, M.A.
Center for Social Research, Graduate School of the City University of New York.

Jenny A. Schnaier, M.A.
Director of Women's Programs, Vietnam Veterans of America, Washington, D.C.

Steven M. Silver, Ph.D.
VA Medical Center, Coatesville, Pennsylvania.

John Russell Smith, Ph.D.
VA Medical Center, Brecksville, Ohio.

Susan D. Solomon, Ph.D.
National Institute of Mental Health, Rockville, Maryland.

Robert H. Stretch, Ph.D.
Captain, USA, Walter Reed Army Institute of Research, Washington, D.C.

James L. Titchener, M.D.
Department of Psychiatry, College of Medicine, University of Cincinnati.

John P. Wilson, Ph.D.
Department of Psychology, Cleveland State University.

Sheldon D. Zigelbaum, M.D.
Director, New Center for Psychotherapy, Boston, Massachusetts.

Introduction

Troubling experiences leave troubling memories. The extent to which we *manage* these memories is associated with how effective we are in overcoming any negative effects and how much we *learn* and potentially benefit from the experience.

The *trauma* created by extraordinarily stressful experiences is like the waves created by a stone cast into a pond. Waves radiate across the surface of the pond from the point of contact, and under certain conditions there is some discernible impact along the shore of the pond. Trauma—the point of penetration—and its wake—the psychosocial repercussions—are normal reactions to extraordinary circumstances.

At some point, however, repercussions transcend normal traumatic stress reactions and become acute or chronic psychological impairments. These impairments, in turn, may lead to other difficulties, such as interpersonal conflicts, drug and alcohol abuse, and other debilitations.

Our ability to discern what is a normal versus an abnormal pattern of reaction to extraordinarily stressful events has increased significantly in recent years, as has our ability to facilitate satisfactory recovery from the events.

Yet the scientific interest in traumatic stress has had a long history (cf. Trimble, 1985). The origin of hysteria, for example, can be traced to the first Egyptian medical writings in 1900 B.C. (Veith, 1965). Since then, a number of concepts have merged that are associated with emotional reactions to environmental stimuli (cf. Trimble, 1982, 1985). These include, in addition to hysteria, rape trauma syndrome, battered wife syndrome, shell shock, split personality, burnout, post-Vietnam syndrome, second wound/injury, couvade, malingering, victimology, child abuse, wife abuse, family violence, sexual violence, child molestation, incest, suicidology, psychosomatic medicine, traumatic neurosis, war neurosis, combat fatigue, melancholia, and phobia.

POST-TRAUMATIC STRESS DISORDER

The most significant surge of scholarly interest in traumatic stress emerged only recently. Most agree that the single most significant factor that stimulated this interest was the development of the concept of post-traumatic stress disorder (PTSD), a new category in the third revision of the American Psychiatric Association's *Diagnostic and Statistical Manual of Mental Disorders (DSM-III)* (1980). Table 1 describes the diagnostic criteria for PTSD. PTSD includes two subtypes: Acute, and Delayed or Chronic.

Acute PTSD occurs when the onset of symptoms is within six months of an extraordinarily stressful event, but the duration of symptoms is less than that. Chronic PTSD applies to cases in which the duration of

TABLE 1
Diagnostic Criteria for
Post-traumatic Stress Disorder*

A. Existence of a recognizable stressor that would evoke significant symptoms of distress in almost anyone

B. Reexperiencing of the trauma as evidenced by at least one of the following:
   (1) recurrent and intrusive recollections of the event
   (2) recurrent dreams of the event
   (3) sudden acting or feeling as if the traumatic event were reoccurring, because of an association with an environmental or ideational stimulus

C. Numbing of responsiveness to or reduced involvement with the external world, beginning some time after the trauma, as shown by at least one of the following:
   (1) markedly diminished interest in one or more significant activities
   (2) feeling of detachment or estrangement from others
   (3) constricted affect

D. At least two of the following symptoms that were not present before the trauma:
   (1) hyperalertness or exaggerated startle response
   (2) sleep disturbance
   (3) guilt about surviving when others have not, or about behavior required for survival
   (4) memory impairment or trouble concentrating
   (5) avoidance of activities that arouse recollection of the traumatic event
   (6) intensification of symptoms by exposure to events that symbolize or resemble the traumatic event

*Reprinted with permission from the American Psychiatric Association. *Diagnostic and Statistical Manual of Mental Disorders*, Third Edition. Washington, D.C.: APA, 1980, p. 238.

symptoms exceeds six months. Delayed PTSD applies to cases in which there was a sudden onset of symptoms six or more months following the event.

Volume 1 of *Trauma and Its Wake* (Figley, 1985) was the first to compile a collection of scientific reports that together transcended the traditional single-stressor approach. The purpose was to publish reports that discuss trauma-related issues having implications generalizable to other victim/survivor groups.

In that volume authors attempted, either directly or indirectly, to address six fundamental questions:

1) What constitutes a catastrophe (an extraordinarily stressful experience), one that may be viewed as a "traumatic event"?
2) Who will be traumatized by a catastrophe and who will not?
3) Among the traumatized, who will develop a post-traumatic stress disorder?
4) Among those diagnosed with this disorder, how can we distinguish among those who are treatable, not treatable, and malingering?
5) Among the treatable, what clinical methods are most effective and why?
6) What are the parameters of societal responsibility to victims?

The final chapter of Volume I attempted to summarize the cumulative efforts of the 33 scholars contributing to that volume to answer these questions. Yet, at the conclusion of Volume I, it became evident that these questions required more than 17 chapters in which to answer. Indeed, these questions served, among other things, as guideposts for this and future volumes in the TRAUMA AND ITS WAKE series. Two additional questions, however, are raised in *this* and subsequent volumes:

7) What personal and interpersonal attributes most contribute to both resisting and ameliorating PTSD?
8) Among families and other victim support systems, what is the process by which the system is traumatized, mobilizes coping resources, and recovers?

This second volume attempts to address these eight fundamental questions. Similar to Volume 1, it is composed of chapters written by scholars from all major areas of the mental health professions: psychiatry, psychology, social work, family therapy, nursing, and sociology. Although

each author attempts to generalize her or his findings to other populations of traumatized groups, chapters generally focus on one or more
traumatic events: natural and "man-made" disasters and accidents, war,
and crime victimization.

These chapters are divided into three sections: Theory, Research, and
Intervention. In the *Theory* section, three chapters attempt to identify
the essence of the traumatic response experience: the general properties
and process of the psychosocial recovery process, and the transactions
among the catastrophe, the individual, and the social network.

Chapter 1, by James Titchener, describes PTSD as an impairment he
defines as "post-traumatic decline," characterized by affective disruption
resulting in self-imposed isolation from and mistrust of human relationships and dissociation from memories of the trauma. "Psychic numbing," a desensitization to stimuli, occurs, according to Titchener, when
the trauma victim's mental systems overload and the victim is unable
to process intrusive memories of the catastrophe. Titchener describes
the characteristic victim experiences that set up conflicts involving attempts to control "destructive drives." Five case studies illustrate personal accounts of post-traumatic decline and its etiology.

Chapter 2 focuses more on the theory of recovery from traumatic
events, specifically the war combat veteran's struggles. John (Jack) Smith
introduces the concept of "sealing over" and "integration" as the key
elements in his recovery theory. The former is defined as a sanctioning
of the veteran's actions, allowing him to manage the stress by fixing
responsibility for his experiences apart from himself. When *societal* sanction is withheld, as in the case of Vietnam veterans, the veteran must
accept personal responsibility and confront his actions—a process defined by Smith as "integration." The final goal is "atonement," when
the individual is at peace with society. Trauma does not emerge directly
from the stressful experiences themselves, according to Smith, but by
the meanings attached to those experiences by the individual. It is these
meanings that can provide the basis for post-traumatic stress.

The final chapter within the theory section, Chapter 3, by Charles R.
Figley, addresses five separate questions concerning the meaning, role,
and consequences of social support for survivors of catastrophe. Social
support is defined as "the degree to which an individual perceives that
he or she may rely on one or more people for assistance with tangible
or emotional aid or both in times of need." Social support provides the
functions of emotional support, encouragement, advice, companionship, and tangible aid to victims of catastrophe. According to Figley, the
family provides social support in the process of promoting emotional

recovery from catastrophes in detection and confrontation of the problem, leading to recapitulation and resolution of the traumatic conflicts. Yet in so doing, the family becomes vulnerable to the consequences of their empathic intervention. Figley emphasizes the importance of incorporating the family/social support system into policy-making and treatment programs for victims of catastrophe.

Section II, *Research,* includes five chapters. The purpose of the section is to present data representing new findings. This new research should, in some significant way, expand our understanding of the immediate or long-term psychosocial consequences of catastrophic events that may evoke traumatic stress.

In the first research chapter, Laura Davidson, India Fleming, and Andrew Baum discuss the relationship between chronic stress and PTSD. In studies conducted with victims of Three Mile Island (near Harrisburg, Pennsylvania) and residents living near a toxic waste site, the authors postulate and report evidence that technological catastrophes (such as the release of hazardous substances into the environment) fall into the category of *cataclysmic* stressors. Their research reveals that residents exposed to these hazards experience more long-lasting and intense symptoms of stress than those *not* exposed to these hazards. Due to the similarity of symptoms of chronic stress and PTSD, research efforts were directed at 1) measuring continued chronic stress in these hazardous areas, 2) documenting PTSD symptoms in the subjects, and 3) examining the relationship between chronic stress and PTSD.

Chapter 5, by Steven Silver and Carmine Iacono, presents the findings of a national study focusing on the relationship between service in Vietnam and particular marital and family functioning. A total of 469 veterans, divided among Vietnam war veterans and non-war veterans, were studied. Part one of the study focused on testing and finding confirmation for the PTSD symptom criteria designated in the current DSM-III (APA, 1980). *Combat veterans showed greater symptoms of aggression, detachment and apprehension and more intense reexperiencing of traumatic events than noncombatants.* The latter part of the chapter described a study that predicted and found support for a statistically significant relationship between severity of PTSD and the quality of family functioning.

Jenny Schnaier, in Chapter 6, discusses her research with female Vietnam veterans. Using a modified version of Wilson and Krauss's (1981) Vietnam-Era Stress Inventory, Schnaier studied 86 women veterans (primarily nurses attached to medical facilities located in Vietnam) to assess the nature and extent of the mental health problems affecting female veterans and if their traumatic stressors were similar to male veterans experiencing symptoms of PTSD. The author reported *a significant correlation between the stressors identified and symptoms associated with PTSD*. The research revealed, among other things, *evidence of 1) current mental health distress among female veterans, 2) personal and professional growth associated with war service, and 3) significant differences with regard to biographic/demographic factors between male and female veterans.* According to Schnaier, this latter finding emphasizes the need for further investigation of the female veteran population. She concludes the chapter with a discussion of the implications of the findings for treating women Vietnam veterans.

Chapter 7, by Shirley Murphy, presents findings from a longitudinal study of victims of the 1980 eruption of Mt. St. Helens, comparing and contrasting her results with those of other disaster studies. The study assessed the stress reactions, coping, and health status of 155 subjects in five groups: disaster victims who suffered presumptive (family member missing) death bereavement, confirmed death bereavement, loss of permanent residence only, loss of recreational residence only, and no disaster-related loss. Using the Life Experience Survey, Hassles Scale, Symptoms Checklist 90-R, and Physical Health Index, Murphy tested two hypotheses: 1) the greater the magnitude of loss experienced, the higher the levels of stress reported; and 2) the higher the level of stress reported, the more negative the impact on health status. *Results confirmed the magnitude of loss hypothesis, with the exception of physical health outcomes, and subjects reported symptoms of both acute and chronic PTSD.*

Robert Stretch, in Chapter 8, reports the results of the first study of the prevalence and etiology of PTSD among active duty military personnel. In this four-phase project, data were collected, using the Vietnam-Era Veterans Adjustment Survey, from 2,700 respondents who served in the U.S. Army during the Vietnam war. Subjects were drawn from active duty, reserve, and Nursing Corps with the Army and a comparable control group of civilian veterans. Stretch hypothesized that 1) a variety of factors will affect the severity of PTSD combat experiences, social support, reentry experiences, and the time period the veteran served in Vietnam; and 2) the prevalence of PTSD would vary according to the current military affiliation of the sampled veterans. *As expected, the results showed the highest prevalence of PTSD among civilian veterans, followed by reserve, active duty, and nurses.*

Section III, *Intervention*, includes eight chapters. The purpose of this section is to present ideas, programs, methods, and policies that effectively *apply* current knowledge about traumatic stress and concepts.

The first chapter of this section, Chapter 9, by Jacob Lindy, discusses his psychoanalytical approach to treating post-traumatic stress disorder. He bases his approach on research conducted by his research group at the University of Cincinnati's Traumatic Stress Study Center. This group has studied survivors of various major traumatic events: fire, flood, and war. Lindy outlines 10 clinical assumptions of psychotherapy for recovery from trauma and loss, while focusing on the patient's intrapsychic or cognitive processing of the trauma. He delineates a three-stage approach to treatment: opening, working through, and termination, exploring the accompanying assumptions of the therapy process for each stage.

Recently the Veterans Administration has developed an impressive inpatient program for war veterans diagnosed with PTSD. In Chapter 10, Steven Silver explicates a model inpatient treatment program. He begins with a brief discussion of the deleterious effects of "sanctuary trauma," a result of mistreatment of an individual who suffered a severe stressor by what is expected to be a supportive and protective environment (e.g., family, friends, fellow citizens, or a VA Medical Center). This mistreatment is often perceived as being even more stressful than the original traumatic event. Silver's exploratory treatment program model includes: an initial stage, gauging the safety of the environment, and the stage where the patient begins to become concerned about the future.

In Chapter 11, Susan Solomon promotes the significance of social support as a significant treatment. Her precis emerges from a review of the extant scientific literature and finds support for the importance of social support networks in the psychosocial recovery from disaster and lessened vulnerability to physical and mental health problems. Disaster victims tend to prefer informal networks of support, with the family supplying the most critical support, supplemented by friends, neighbors, co-workers, and community members. Solomon recommends that professional intervention focus on predisaster preparedness, outreach (e.g., neighborhood service center), consideration of social support in policy making, and identifying ways to involve and build on social support in the treatment of traumatic stress. She suggests that future research should focus on identifying and understanding the dimensions of social support (amount, quality, type, and source), as well as on the concepts of perception of control and learned helplessness.

In Chapter 12, Angie Herndon and Joseph Law present a three-phase approach to counseling war veterans and their families suffering from traumatic stress. Based on their clinical experiences, the authors describe a therapy process using individual and group sessions. The initial phase

Trauma and Its Wake II

of individual counseling allows the veteran to talk about the meaning of his or her war experiences and resultant readjustment problems. The second phase involves group counseling with other veterans. Simultaneously, the families of these patients are encouraged to participate in separate sessions. These sessions are designed to educate them and share their experiences about the Vietnam experience, PTSD, and the various interpersonal and family consequences. In the final stage, the family members and veteran are brought together to bring about a mutual understanding among the family and to begin setting goals for the future.

In the final chapter devoted to treating PTSD (Chapter 13), George Bowen and James Lambert describe and evaluate the effectiveness of systematic desensitization. This approach involves identifying a series of increasingly anxiety-arousing stimuli and training the client in muscle relaxation techniques. In the process patients work through the cognitive conflicts of each of their most traumatic memories in an hierarchical order from least to most troubling. The treatment is complete when all stimuli can be presented without any significant anxiety. In their study Bowen and Lambert evaluated this treatment technique using biofeedback to measure the effects. A sample of Vietnam veterans suffering from combat-related PTSD was administered the technique applied to their traumatic memories of combat situations. The authors found the technique effective in reducing anxiety associated with these memories. The method was particularly effective for outpatient use, where the patient could apply his or her new desensitization skills to other stressful life situations.

The final two chapters of the *Intervention* section focus on *legal intervention*. They address current limitations of the criminal justice system for those who suffer from PTSD. Chapter 14 discusses the maltreatment and deserved rights of the families of murder victims, and the following chapter discusses the criminal behavior of the traumatized and the rights to a fair trial. Though seemingly antithetical, both chapters emphasize the need for proper application of current knowledge about PTSD in the criminal justice system.

In Chapter 14, Morton Bard, Harriet Arnone, and David Nemiroff discuss the nightmarish experiences of the survivors of homicide victims. This chapter is among the few that focus attention on reactions of the family system following a traumatic event, especially one as extraordinary as a family member's murder. Bard (co-author of the celebrated book, *The Crime Victim's Book*), Arnone, and Nemiroff present and discuss two case studies. Both focus on the family member survivors of a murder victim and illustrate how the criminal justice system's focus on the criminal—rather than the survivors—compounds the traumatic stress experience and efforts to find meaning and eventually recover from it. The authors offer some suggestions for improving the criminal justice system and assuring the rights of the survivors of criminal violence.

The final chapter of this section is also devoted in part to sensitizing the criminal justice system to the immediate and long-term consequences of traumatic events. In Chapter 15, John Wilson and Sheldon Zigelbaum theorize that Vietnam veterans on trial for criminal violence are victims of their own wartime experiences. They assert that these defendants have been operating within what they call the "survivor mode" of adaptation to real or perceived threat which first emerged naturally in their role as a combatant. Three patterns of behavior are associated with the survivor mode: dissociative reaction, action addict, and the depression-suicide syndrome. The authors go on to specify a set of forensic assessment procedures to determine the role of PTSD in criminal behavior. A matrix concept is used to assess the attitudes, emotions, and behaviors of the individual before, during, and after the traumatic event. Finally, Wilson and Zigelbaum outline a standard psychiatric/psychological forensic report in cases of PTSD related to criminal behavior.

EPILOGUE

Much has taken place since work on this collection began, in mid-1984. Many of the contributors to this volume have continued their work in the area of traumatic stress; several are expanding the chapters into books of their own. As a result, the efforts represented in this volume are being expanded and improved upon at a greatly accelerated rate.

Perhaps the most significant national and international development, however, is the emergence of an international organization devoted to the study and treatment of traumatic stress and changes in the diagnostic criteria of Post-Traumatic Stress Disorder (PTSD) in the upcoming revised Diagnostic and Statistical Manual (DSM III-R).

The Society for Traumatic Stress Studies

On March 2, 1985, at the Washington Marriott a breakfast meeting was held. At that time the Society for Traumatic Stress Studies was formally established. Those in attendance comprised most of the Founding Board. They included Ann W. Burgess, Arthur Blank, Bernard Mazel, Frank Ochberg, Morton Bard, Marlene Young, Robert Rich, Yael Danieli, Susan Salasin, Scott Sheely, and Charles Figley, who was elected President, with Ann Burgess, Vice-President. Other Board members not in attendance were John Talbott, Robert Jay Lifton, Bonnie L. Green, Peter Erlinder, and John Wilson. It was agreed that the purpose of the Society would be ". . . to advance knowledge about the immediate and long-term human consequences of extraordinarily stressful events and to promote effective methods of preventing or ameliorating the unwanted consequences." Such an organization, we agreed, should have four major objectives: 1) promote the generation of new knowledge in traumatic stress; 2) recognize achievements in knowledge production; 3) disseminate this knowledge through face-to-face contact with colleagues; and 4) through other knowledge transfer media, especially print media.

It was decided to call the group a Society, since the term connotes a small group of like-minded colleagues. The dictionary definition of "society" is "any organized group of people joined together because of some interest in common; as a medical society." The concept of traumatic stress signifies the area that encompasses the entire process of traumatization, the initial and long-term reactions and recovery, including PTSD.

The founding meeting of the Society was held September 22-23 in Atlanta, with Robert Lifton delivering the first annual Society Lecture. Over 450 people attended and became members of the Society. Sessions were devoted to research, policy, treatment, assessment, and diagnosis with a wide range of victim populations: rape victims, victims of crime, police officers and other emergency workers, combat veterans, families of victims, victims and families of intrafamilial abuse.*

Currently there are a number of Society-sponsored efforts to advance and disseminate knowledge about traumatic stress. Examples include the development of professional and scholarly institutes; theoretical, methodological, and psychometric innovations; establishment of professional standards for practitioners; and explication of empirically valid diagnostic criteria for PTSD.

---

*For more information about how to join the Society and the upcoming annual meeting, write the Society for Traumatic Stress Studies, PO Box 2106, Dayton, Ohio 45401–9990.

Revising PTSD

The Society's efforts to suggest revisions to the PTSD criteria are part of a larger effort by a special panel—the Work Group to Revise DSM-III—of the American Psychiatric Association, under way since 1984. This effort has been prompted in part by researchers and practitioners reporting new findings about traumatic stress that run counter to current conceptualizations. Moreover, courts of law, insurance carriers, and agencies disbursing disability benefits (e.g., Social Security and Veterans Administration) are encountering more and more cases of PTSD that require judicious action and, thus, require far more precise, reliable, and valid diagnosis of PTSD than is currently available.

Table 2 is taken from the most recent draft of the diagnostic criteria for PTSD, which will replace the criteria described in Table 1. Not only does this effort represent the latest thinking and research findings regarding traumatic stress, but it is also a significant attempt to eliminate the diagnosis of false positives, incorrectly detecting PTSD when it does not exist, including malingering, and false negatives, misdiagnosing PTSD as some other disorder.

CONCLUSION

As the first volume provided the foundation for discussing traumatic stress and its connections with various symptoms and other outcomes, this second volume provides the direction. This present group of authors is interested in effecting positive change, speeding up the research-in-tervention latency, and promoting effective prevention efforts.

Understanding the patterns associated with the destructive wake of traumatic stress provides the necessary basis for constructing effective methods of action. These actions take the form of verifiable methods of preventing and ameliorating PTSD.

Collectively, these 22 authors not only contribute to answering the eight fundamental questions of the series, but they also set new directions for understanding the immediate and long-term consequences of traumatic events. The roles of cognitive processing, biophysiological reactions, social support, and family systems are emphasized, as are the importance of the stressor situation and the person-environment transaction.

When reading the latest contributions to this growing area of inquiry, the reader of this collection may be impressed, as this writer was, with

TABLE 2
Diagnostic Criteria for Post-traumatic Stress Disorder*

309.89 Post-traumatic Stress Disorder
A: An event that is outside the range of usual human experience and that is psychologically traumatic, e.g., serious threat to one's life or personal physical integrity; serious threat or harm to one's children, spouse, or other close relatives or friends; destruction of one's home or community, or seeing another person who is mutilated, dying or dead, or the victim of physical violence.
B. The traumatic event is persistently reexperienced in at least one of the following ways:
  (1) recurrent and intrusive distressing recollections of the event without any awareness of environmental stimuli that trigger the reaction
  (2) recurrent distressing dreams of the event
  (3) sudden acting or feeling as if the traumatic event were recurring (includes a sense of reliving the experience, illusions, hallucinations, and dissociative [flashback] episodes, even those that occur upon awakening or when intoxicated) (in children, repetitive play in which themes or aspects of the trauma are expressed)
  (4) intense psychological distress or exposure to events that symbolize or resemble an aspect of the traumatic event, including anniversaries of the trauma
C. Persistent avoidance of stimuli associated with the trauma or numbing of responsiveness (not present before the trauma), as indicated by at least two of the following:
  (1) deliberate efforts to avoid thoughts or feelings associated with the trauma
  (2) deliberate efforts to avoid activities or situations that arouse recollections of the trauma
  (3) inability to recall an important aspect of the trauma (psychogenic amnesia)
  (4) markedly diminished interest in significant activities (in young children, loss of recently acquired developmental skills, such as toilet training or language skills)
  (5) feeling of detachment or estrangement from others
  (6) restricted range of affect, e.g., "numbing," unable to have loving feelings
  (7) sense of a foreshortened future, e.g., child does not expect to have a career, marriage or children, or a long life
D. Persistent symptoms of increased arousal (not present before the trauma) as indicated by at least two of the following:
  (1) difficulty falling or staying asleep
  (2) irritability or outburst
  (3) difficulty concentrating
  (4) hypervigilance
  (5) physiologic reactivity at exposure to events that symbolize or resemble an aspect of the traumatic event (e.g., a woman who was raped in an elevator breaks out in a sweat when entering any elevator)
E. "B," "C," and "D" symptoms all were present during the same six-month period of at least one month, although there may be other phases of the illness during which they do not coexist.
Specify if delayed onset if onset of symptoms at least six months after the trauma.

*Reprinted with permission from the Work Group to Revise DSM-III, American Psychiatric Association, DRAFT DSM-III-R IN DEVELOPMENT. Washington, D.C.: American Psychiatric Association, October 5, 1985 and revisions of April, 1986.

the tenacity of the human spirit to struggle and prevail under extraordinary circumstances. The challenge to those who study or facilitate this struggle is to find the precise methods of intervention for the particular situation, and in the process not upset the natural patterns of coping which may have been functioning well prior to intervention.

REFERENCES

American Psychiatric Association (1980). *The diagnostic and statistical manual of mental disorders (DSM-III)* (3rd. ed.). Washington, D.C.: Author.

Figley, C. R. (Ed.) (1985). *Trauma and its wake: The study and treatment of post-traumatic stress disorder*. New York: Brunner/Mazel.

Trimble, M. R. (1982). *Post-traumatic neurosis*. New York: Wiley.

Trimble, M. R. (1985). Post-traumatic stress disorder: History of a concept. In C. R. Figley (ed.), *Trauma and its wake: The study and treatment of post-traumatic stress disorder*. New York: Brunner/Mazel.

Veith, I. (1965). *Hysteria: The history of a disease*. Chicago: University of Chicago Press.

Wilson, J. P., & Krauss, G. E. (1981). *Vietnam era stress inventory*. Cleveland, OH: Cleveland State University.

TRAUMA
and Its
WAKE

VOLUME II: Traumatic Stress
Theory, Research, and
Intervention

SECTION I

Theory

1

Post-Traumatic Decline: A Consequence of Unresolved Destructive Drives

JAMES L. TITCHENER

From our studies of natural and manmade disaster, from clinical work in emergency rooms and surgical wards, from evaluations of victims of rape, assault, housing discrimination, and sexual harassment, our trauma study group in Cincinnati, like many others, has become aware of the probable lifelong course of chronic illnesses that arise too often from the acute and subacute syndromes of post-traumatic stress disorders. We believe it to be an insidious, malignant disease hardly ever recognized by physicians, psychologists, or psychiatrists. We call it post-traumatic decline. In our opinion, it results in deep and extensive impairment, which is highly resistant to change. The aim of this paper is to raise and attempt to answer questions of the etiology of post-traumatic decline and to indicate the urgency of its prevention while providing some suggestions on how it might be done. The syndrome begins with an event in which the individual is threatened with his or her own death or the destruction of an important part of his body, or to such humiliation and manipulation that personal identity may be lost. This traumatic

Presented at the Twenty-fifth Neuropsychiatric Institute, Veterans Administration Medical Center, Coatesville, Pennsylvania, October 21, 1982.

event may last minutes, hours, or days. Almost inevitably, there are associated losses. It may be the loss of persons closely related to the victim, property, a job, the family's way of life, or self-esteem, or an alteration in the network of relationships. Fear and grief are inseparably fused in the dreaded memory of traumatic events.

The acute phase, forerunner of decline, consists of shock effects, fear, inexpressible feelings of loss, disorganization of thinking, impairment of memory, concentration, and judgment, and interference with comfortable regulation of affect. There follow altered attitudes in human relationships consisting of regressive deterioration of trust in others, alternating with unrealistic dependency, and pathetic longings for help from others. This changed sense of the reliability of relationships reflects the sudden cruelty of the catastrophic or traumatic experience causing a drastic change in world view from trust to distrust and failing confidence.

CASE REPORTS

Case 1

After three months of therapeutic work, a young woman was recovering from the effects of a particularly vicious rape, which had led to a brief psychotic episode and then to disabling neurotic symptoms for seven months before treatment was begun. Then she began to receive mysterious phone calls, apparently from her attacker. The therapeutic alliance, which had been building toward a sense of reliability and strength and a positive father transference, changed to mistrust and was infused with bitterness and the feeling of being let down. This changed sense of reliability of relationship was a consequence of the failure of the holding environment in therapy, and it correlated with the dehumanizing effects of the sexual assault. The depth and duration of the misalliance in therapy were determined by our capacity to reinstate a feeling of reliability and trust in men and a revision of her concept of herself as a human being rather than just a terrified and acted-upon dehumanized object.

With the help of treatment, combined with the temporary use of tranquilizers, or through unaided reintegration within the context of stable, communicative relationships, the long course toward recovery begins. It involves a realization of the time and effort needed, both almost always underestimated by the victim and physician. Together they must confront and come to terms with the patient's memories of helplessness, rage, losses sustained, guilt, and shame. We might summarize the recovery process as an internal negotiation in which the person arrives at a new and more realistic acceptance of these frightening memories.

Rage is a reflection of the violence done to the person as well as its infantile origins. For example, the helplessness during the trauma resembles the same affect experienced in infancy when there was a global response to massive intrusion into the boundaries of the self. The memory of helplessness must be articulated verbally and compared with present situations in order to reassess the probability of recurrence of trauma. Most survivors live as though the fire, flood, attack, etc., will recur at any moment. Memories of the trauma and events of the aftermath must be repetitively processed in detail if one is to clarify the feeling and thinking that might otherwise prompt the survivor's guilt and shame. This processing is necessary to overcome the irrational aspects of shame and guilt. The individual must learn to accept his behavior at the time of the trauma as reasonable for the most part, as moral, and as admirable as could have been expected given the conditions of the trauma and period after it. His perception of the trauma and his role in it slowly approaches the reality of the disturbing event. If an individual is unable to accomplish the above tasks, he becomes a wearied, isolated, anhedonic person, disinterested in former gratifications, without ambition, lust, or zest.

Decline has begun. A growing hypochondriasis takes over, and somatic symptoms become the focus of the person's life. Withdrawal from gratifications at work and social life leads to isolation and distrust and preoccupation with the physical self. This amounts to a changed world view and a changed way of life. The medical culture often mistakenly labels this syndrome "compensation neurosis," a projection of the doctor's frustration in not being able to relieve his patient when the process of decline has ensued and the affects of hopelessness, anger, and feelings of incompetence have imbued the patient.

The causes of decline in the aftermath of trauma can be simply stated. Most people believe that accidental horrors happen only to others. When they happen to the self, when the terror and losses of a catastrophic event strike, the infrastructure of the mind is wiped out, washed away, and crumpled. Reparative capacities often are not able to rise to the challenge. So, hollowed out, the victim falls back to a less complex, less stimuli-searching mode of existence, accepting less and trying less. Yet this summary is not enough. There must be more driving the person toward invalidism and invalidation of the self after a trauma. Powerful forces drive him toward becoming a shadow person moving about but hardly participating in the social system, striving only for the space and sustenance required for a shadow's survival.

Case 2

A young man living with his parents and younger siblings in a mobile home was lowering a water tank from a truck by a small crane. The temperature that day was a record high, and some high-tension wires above the trailer, previously well out of reach of the crane, sagged in the heat so that the crane came in contact with them just as his mother emerged from the trailer. With his foot on the control pedal, paralyzed by the electric current, he remembers seeing his mother from the corner of his eye but did not know whether she touched him. He fell back with a burned foot, never knowing whether she died of electric shock transmitted through him or from a coronary occlusion.

Brief psychotherapy during the hospitalization for burn treatment clarified some of the issues involved in the tragedy. But, too soon, he closed off discussion, leaving untouched the nagging problem of the responsibility for his mother's death. In addition, there was an ironic feeling of deserving the inadequacy created by the physical disabilities due to the burn and considered by him a retribution for his carelessness and for leaving his younger siblings without their mother. He could not bear to further explore the question of responsibility for the accident.

Case 3

Surgeons noted that a middle-aged man whom they were treating for minor injuries was "too quiet." While he was driving with his wife and daughter, another car crossed the median strip and smashed into them. When he recovered consciousness, he was lying on the highway and his first sight was the covered bodies of his wife and daughter.

He certainly was "quiet" but cooperative in the hospital when the psychiatrist first visited him and began to see the patient's need to reflect on what had happened. But when the psychiatrist returned for the next interview, the patient had decided that he did not wish to go into the matter further and was quietly adamant about his decision to wall off the traumatic memory.

Case 4

A large man came to the office leaning on a walker, attended by a worried wife and son. Under his clothes he wore a canvas and metal back brace and around his neck he had another. Through the entire hour he writhed with efforts to find a posture to ease the pain in his neck, shoulders, back, and legs. He cooperated in the interview but his participation was limited to descriptions of physical disability and discomfort. He spent his days mostly walking about as it was not possible to remain still for long. His night's sleep was constantly interrupted by the need to change position without causing a painful spasm.

Four years before, working as an air conditioner repairman, he struck an abutment and fell back, losing consciousness for a few seconds. He was able to phone his employers and was told to report to a physician. He went to his truck and later was found a few miles from the scene of the injury, slumped over the steering wheel in a stupor. He was taken to an emergency room, examined, and told to rest at home for a few days. Neither the patient nor his wife remembers well what happened in the next month. Complaining of headaches, poor memory, and pain radiating from the neck into both arms, the patient saw a neurosurgeon, who found an increase of deep reflexes on one side and impairment for recent memory. He told the patient that he had suffered a "concussion with moderate brain damage" but that he would recover and advised another two weeks of rest at home. The patient and his wife feared that the damage to the brain would only become worse and that his memory would continue to deteriorate. He continued to have sleepless nights, increasing headaches, and spreading pain.

Six months after the injury, the patient attempted to return to work, but found that he could not carry out his duties and, after struggling six weeks, gave up. A year later he once again saw the neurosurgeon, who this time diagnosed a ruptured intervertebral disk. It was removed, but this failed to relieve the pain and, in fact, worsened it. The patient originally had been told that he required no surgery. His trust in doctors was all but destroyed. When the neurosurgeon suggested to him a year and a half later that his trouble was a traumatic neurosis, he left the office angrily.

This man, four years after the trauma, talked only about his body. His whole life has become a matter of brooding about physical symptoms. The only feelings he could express were his reactions to pain, doctors, and the limited life he led. During the first days and weeks after the injury, he was angry when there was any, even slight, hint that his mental functioning was not normal. If asked to explain something, he became irritable over the implication that he had not already explained it clearly.

In each of these cases, fear, helplessness, and the shock of a terrible loss were combined with an initial traumatic experience. Several of the victims lost close family members in their accidents. These cases illustrate the dissociation and walling off from the self of intolerable memories of the experience of helplessness along with associated affects and fantasies arising from the traumatic episode. In Case 2, the idea of personal responsibility for the mother's death was dissociated rather than processed cognitively so that a logical and probably benign conclusion about the event could result. In Case 3, the sudden violent death of his wife and daughter could not be accepted by the patient. The psychiatrist would have striven to help this man gradually recognize the initial natural disbelief, the appropriateness of shock, terror, and sadness, and the possibilities of life without his loved ones. Instead the patient suspended thinking about the horror of the experience, became numb, and unconsciously elected a version of the self and a future in which his wife and daughter were simply not there, no more, no less.

In Case 4, concern over declining mental capacity and the expectation of further deterioration in the patient was reinforced by his wife's concerns. These feelings resonated with a bitter distrust of physicians. In his view, while he was deteriorating and his pain increasing, the doctors were merely telling him to rest. Since "they didn't do anything," he became more and more convinced of his decline, and to make matters worse, he found confirmation for his fears in his wife's face. Walling off his despair over the loss of cognitive ability was made possible by substituting the more acceptable pain and spasms in the head, neck, and back. The subsequent diagnosis of a ruptured intervertebral disk and an operation that made him worse was but another episode in the process of decline; i.e., it now seemed inevitable that surgery would not ameliorate but would aggravate his symptoms. The fearful suspicion of mental deterioration, an internal view, was disavowed, split off from the perception of his overall disabilities. This split depended on the patient's unarticulated body-mind duality. He said to the doctors and everyone else, "There *is* something wrong in my body! Find it and fix it!"

Psychic traumata have no basis in wishfulness or fantasy but in dread reality. They often invade preexisting psychoneuroses that have their roots in wishes and fantasies of early life dissociated from the ego as unacceptable. When a traumatic syndrome invades the area of a psychoneurosis, it contaminates the neurotic conflicts, and this become a further obstacle to working them through, because *it* is not rooted in unacceptable desires, wishes, and fantasies but on the frightening memory of a real event. Such "actual neuroses" and the syndrome of depletion that so often becomes their extension require an essential modification in the therapy of the psychoneuroses.

Reports from skilled self-observers, professionals in mental health fields, tell us with some amazement how long it took them to confront and work through the effects of a traumatic experience in their own lives. Our work with the survivors of the Buffalo Creek disaster (Titchener & Kapp, 1976; Titchener, Kapp, & Winget, 1976), at the Beverly Hills Supper Club, at the sites of several tornadoes, and from previous studies of accident victims have shown that the traumatic syndrome is not a derivation or mere elaboration of a preexisting neurosis, but an illness in itself. The problem is the persistence and deepening of the symptoms and the disabling character changes.

Our plan is to review psychoanalytic theory of traumatic neurosis beginning with the one taught to most clinicians, consisting of revisions of Freud's understanding in *Beyond the Pleasure Principle* (Freud, 1954, 1955b; Furst, 1967; Titchener & Ross, 1974; Des Pres, 1971). We look next at Mardi Horowitz's writings (1972, 1975, 1976) and turn then to R. J. Lifton (1974), who proposes some different variables for what he considers a new paradigm for the whole of psychoanalytic theory.

The generally accepted explanation for a traumatic neurosis rests on notions of overloading of the mental systems and functioning, on the implication to the person of the traumatic experience and memories of it, and on the effectiveness of support from the environment after the trauma. Overloading means that massive stimuli or excitation from external events breaks through the stimulus barrier, flooding and disorganizing ego functions.

Ego disorganization from affective flooding may lead to death or psychosis, but usually a spontaneous process of reorganization and restoration of ego functions occurs. We understand this reorganization and return of functioning to be something like the awakening from a nightmare, but this process is taking a much longer period of time with varying degrees of restoration and occasionally with drastic changes in defense systems.

The implication of the traumatic or stressful event at unconscious and conscious levels of understanding and the dreaded memory of the moments of fear and helplessness give it a meaning with widespread effects on individual mental life. Resistances against reexperiencing the event vie with intrusive images of it during the daytime and with dreams of it at night. Conflicts over the guilt of surviving when others did not, neurotic and real guilt about responsibility for the traumatic happening, shame of how one behaved under stress, and the overwhelming feeling of helplessness are all aspects of the psychodynamics of the stress response syndrome.

The capacity to communicate, to share affective responses, and to work over feelings of grief with others constitutes the adaptive factors involved in the nature and severity of the traumatic neurosis.

Horowitz, in describing his experiments on *thought intrusion*, offers possibilities for greater lucidity in thinking about chronicity or delayed recovery from trauma. He aims to clarify psychoanalytic theory by integrating it with information theory, replacing the economic point of view. Thought intrusions and information processing are key concepts in Horowitz's approach. The intrusive thoughts, which are overly active in the aftermath of stress, emerge from memory storage. "Processing" a memory means that it loses its intrusive activism though it is not extinguished. Memories of the traumatic event become less and less intrusive while still recoverable and still retained to be reactivated by external reminders or on anniversaries of the trauma. It is a gradual recycling, a reorganization of information on the meaning of the traumatic event to the person, on how he has changed, on his altered view of the world, his fate and his future, and on how he appears to others and they to him.

If reorganization of information contained in such intrusive memories does not take place, a phase of denial and repetition ensues. Denial, through damping the significance of the experience and reducing the affects aroused by the trauma, attempts to control and manage traumatic intrusions; it appears to be essential for maintaining an integration in the earliest phases of the traumatic aftermath. But soon an unconscious choice is made between more denial or less. If this unconscious choice, based on longing for safety (Sandler, 1960), is toward more denial, then the increase in control of thought, feeling, and conduct of life begins to predominate over processing of the memories. These dissociated memories remain unchanged in content and meaning and are charged with the original affects. Clinicians observe many trauma victims in whom enhancement of control over thought and feeling about the trauma is about all the work that the individual does in his response to the stress situation. In limiting the response to merely a control-and-regulating system, victims enter the path of decline we are describing.

R. J. Lifton has worked with extreme situations as a military psychiatrist in Korea and followed survivors of the Hiroshima atomic bomb (1967), and he has worked with the author on the Buffalo Creek disaster (1976a, 1976b). Recently he has applied similar insights to behavior in day-to-day situations in which man speculates about his own death. Although psychoanalytic theory considers repression and suppression to be the principal control over unacceptable instinctual drives and traumatic memories, Lifton theorizes that in the response to the extreme situation *psychic numbing* predominates. Psychic numbing is a thorough *desensitization* of the mind to all stimuli, either from the environment or from within. Impairment of mental functioning that accompanies *psychic numbing* consists of cessation of the "formative process," i.e., a loss of the ability to form and use symbols. The individual overtaken by psychic numbing cannot feel or confront experiences in which there is evident or implicit arousal or excitation, whether pleasurable or painful, because of "loss of inner forms or imagery that can connect with such experience."

Where have these inner forms gone? Why the disappearance of the imagery that makes life human? In Lifton's concept, it is the loss of symbolic immortality caused by the life-threatening experience which wipes out most of the symbolic forms that give life a sense of meaning and continuity with the world and living humans. Psychic numbing is a stultifying process because the ability to form symbols is blocked and results in less and less capacity to feel experience. According to Lifton, the organization of symbolic immortality forms the basis for the feeling of continuity of life and is necessary for a reasonably serene and energetic life. Psychic numbing destroys this capacity.

Lifton holds that in modern culture psychic numbing is assuming greater emphasis as a control mechanism owing to the unending threats of nuclear and other forms of holocaust. Whether this hypothesis is valid or not, it is an apt description of what can be observed in individuals with stress response syndromes as they turn toward post-traumatic depletion.

The individual manifesting psychic numbing is just that, *numb*. He is feeling hardly any pleasure or pain; his affective and cognitive experiencing and functioning are deadened. Camus' stranger said, "Mother died yesterday; or was it the day before? I do not remember." A defendant jailed for admitted murder of his wife stated, during a pretrial examination, that he thought he had already been tried. His attorneys took this statement to mean that he was insane. The examining psychiatrist realized that it was an example of psychic numbing derived from hopeless indifference.

A THEORY OF POST-TRAUMATIC DECLINE
AND ITS PREVENTION

The Freudian view of traumatic neurosis and recent revisions of it do not seem to account for the chronic, insidious syndrome of post-traumatic decline. The magnitude of this public-health problem is hidden from us because patients in the actue phase flee from psychiatrists and clinics, only to return months, even years, later to become repetitive consumers.

Horowitz (1976) suggests how the traumatic neuroses become chronic and enter a stage of decline, which he terms "frozen overcontrol," and he has devised strategies for modifying it (1975). He conceives of "decision points" at which the patient after psychic trauma may either begin recovery by processing active memories and intrusive thoughts, or turn away from them into the decline syndrome by increasing his denial and numbing of the trauma, entering a phase of overcontrol.

Lifton and Olson (1976a) vividly describe the thoughts and feelings of the psychic trauma victim and offer an antidote to the potentially malignant interference with empathic communication between victim and physician. Their concept fits well with the emotional state of the acutely traumatized person, who may easily slip into a chronic condition of psychic numbness. Yet, not all of the victims do. Is there more driving the traumatized person into a state of decline? Is there a loss of a sense of continuity and of symbol-forming capacity and emptiness of the self after being depleted of the symbols of immortality, as Lifton pointed out? We suggest, however, that these processes are consequences, character symptoms, rather than forces precipitating post-traumatic decline.

We offer a hypothesis for post-traumatic decline based on psychic conflict and the victim's attempts at its resolution. The traumatic experience, almost always combined with some form of object loss, activates and imposes an intrapsychic conflict whose magnitude brings about much devastation of the personality. These conflicts demand extraordinary defensiveness similar to altered adaptation and change in character as described in the survivors of the Buffalo Creek disaster (Titchener & Kapp, 1976; Titchener et al., 1976).

Freud wrote in *Beyond the Pleasure Principle:* "I propose to leave the dark and dismal subject of the traumatic neuroses and pass on to . . . " (1920/1955b, p. 14) [see also Freud, 1919/1955a]. What did he mean? Why are traumatic neuroses dark and dismal? Perhaps the answer may lead to an explanation of post-traumatic decline, a process from which few return once it has taken over, when the adaptive energies of the individual are no longer used to recover but are continually exhausted in the effort to merely stay alive.

In our view, the traumatic neuroses were "dark and dismal" to Freud because he sensed that they were imbued with destructive drives, first given an equal status with libido in that very paper. Destructive drives, emerging after the acute phase of traumatic neurosis, require so much defensive effort and other resources of the ego that the usual capacities for resolving, neutralizing, and taming them are not adequate.

Psychoanalysts and psychiatrists fail to realize the intensity of destructive impulses, hatred, and violence in a trauma victim because clinicians have stimulus barriers, too, especially for *these* impulses. But if one listens to the outcry from the unconscious of these patients in their dreams, associations, and metaphors alluding to rage and aggression and to the terrible struggle to contain them, the therapist can overcome his resistance to an acknowledgment that such frightening affects and impulses occur in another human being.

In short, after serious trauma, the human becomes a reflection of the violence wrought upon him and remains so until there are dynamic changes in adaptive resources modifying and moderating the violent impulses via interactions with others. The common denominator of acute traumatic syndromes turning toward decline is a basic conflict matching the effects it causes. It is a conflict involving destructive aggressive drives, and it may be expressed as follows: rage, hate, and destructive impulses unleashed by the traumatic damage to the self and the losses suffered by the self are opposed by fears of recurrence of the traumatic event as a retaliatory reaction from the environment. Something as destructive or threatening as the original trauma is expected should one's violent impulses exceed the capacity to control them, though raging violence within was stimulated by the trauma itself.

Case 5

A middle-aged man lost his son in the crash of a chartered plane. At an official hearing he perceived that irregularities were being covered up. For years he fought to expose the system, to change regulations, and to obtain enforcement of existing ones. Finally, the fight was over, the battle nearly won. Then physical symptoms of his rage, vented in striving against great forces, began to accumulate, and he became a total invalid, having been an energetic and successful executive a few months before.

This central conflict in the trauma victim arises principally from a *reflexive* rage, an inevitable primitive affect aroused by any trauma. This affect enters into a number of subsidiary conflicts presenting themselves from time to time, depending on the individual, i.e., the particular nature of his traumatic experience and the kinds of events occurring in the aftermath. He may, for example, experience a conflict over guilt because of imagined or real responsibility for the event or the losses of others involved in it. He may have a conflict with regard to shame or personal adequacy over doubts about his behavior during the trying circumstances.

The traumatic experience itself, the memory of helplessness, and the overloading of the ego's resources and functions with temporary disorganization destroy the capacity for neutralization of aggressive drives, leaving them to be held in check only by more primitive defenses such as projection, externalization, denial, and isolation. Therefore, the individual moves into a phase of overcontrol and begins the decline. Helpless to deal adequately with the internal destructive forces excited and loosened from control, the trauma survivor resorts to more primitive defensive styles. Isolated and unable to trust, he makes less and less use of relationships in the outside world, reaching the life-style termed "psychic conservatism" (Titchener et al., 1976), a state of pervasive personality constriction in which all possible irritants and stimuli from within, as well as from outside, are shut out of consciousness. Ambitions, sex, vocational strivings, and recreation are all forsaken for the sake of survival. The aim of life becomes to endure, rather than seeking novelty, excitement, and gratifications beyond those required for existence. The life of the body predominates over the life of the mind, and somatic concerns take the place of interest and pleasures.

Thought intrusions, the experience of mental imagery unpleasantly recalling an aspect of the trauma, represent leakage of anxiety, warning the person that he is not adequate to the task of working through or doing away with the massive influence of the traumatic experience and calling forth greater defensiveness.

Repetition in dreams and symbolic reenactments of the trauma have been explained as attempts at undoing or mastery of the traumatic experience. Perhaps, but it may well be that the dream serves not so much to master the trauma as to act in fantasy as though the trauma had never happened. Everyone has dreamed of frightening happenings and awakened in a cold sweat, relieved that it was "only a dream." So dreams of trauma may be attempts at such a revision of personal history. Symbolic reenactments (subsequent "accidents," fights, counterphobic behavior) may be similar to the dream's function, to erase the trauma by flirting with danger and escaping it. The traumatized person may be striving via such dreams to recreate the pretraumatic feeling of invulnerability.

Resistance to cure is an imposing feature of the post-traumatic decline syndrome. Early intervention is the best hope. However, there are baffling difficulties in victims' recognition and acceptance of psychological illness and in its diagnosis. The sufferer hardly ever complains of mental symptoms. If he does, he alludes to topics remote from the essential problem of fear of recurrence and explosive aggression. We have observed many occasions when the internist, family practitioner, psychiatrist, and psychoanalyst have failed to recognize the depleting fears and anger because of some obstacles to empathic understanding.

In an acute traumatic neurosis, when the defense of denial is initially helpful for the work of reintegration, the doctor is likely to share some of the patient's defensiveness. In a later stage, when the victim has turned toward an overcontrol pattern, the therapist is likely to accept that too, agreeing that everything is "all right" and in many ways participating in the patient's resistances. In such instances, memories, feelings, fantasies, and recurring images of the impact of the traumatic event are not actively elicited by the therapist who, instead, either focuses on childhood experiences or prescribes minor tranquilizers.

Clinicians are likely to conclude that "nothing is wrong" while at the same time the family is impoverished and despairing because the traumatized wage earner is no longer earning and relationships have become distrusting and bitter. Many a professional working with Buffalo Creek disaster survivors (Titchener & Kapp, 1976) was bewildered when he found "nothing wrong" at first glance. His countertransference problem, similar to that of the victims, was with his own conflicts over destructive drives. The clinician is often intimidated by fears that clinical investigation will trigger explosive affects in the patients or, worse, stir up similar ones in himself. Identification with the patient's powerful unconscious conviction of the necessity for control influences the diagnostician–therapist to tread ever so lightly in his work with the traumatized individual, when in truth, at the point when overcontrol has taken over, a persistent, courageous advance toward the traumatic core is desperately needed.

Differences in each individual's conflicts between destructive impulses and counterforces needed to control them are dependent in great part on the survivor's awareness of cause and degrees of responsibility for the cause of the trauma. They form a spectrum from deliberate brutality to self-destruction. The victim must find ways this can be modified and made acceptable. When some humans are so brutal or so uncaring as to cause physical injury, material loss, and psychic damage, the survivor is stripped of the security of trust in other humans. This dehumanizing effect drastically alters attitudes toward the self and object relations. At the other end of the spectrum, destructive drives also predominate but have more to do with self-directed rage, feelings of failure, humiliation, and regression to infantile rage from a perception of a hostile and impersonal environment such as in any natural disaster.

SUMMARY

Massive psychic traumata are capable of devastating even the most secure and mature. These experiences, particularly when they are not worked through after the initial shock, often eventuate in a chronic syndrome we term *post-traumatic decline*, which results in the removal of the person from meaningful participation in family, society, work, and all forms of gratification.

More often than is generally recognized, traumatic events long after childhood become strands in the pathogenesis of psychoneurosis and character disorder, but are often passed over as of little consequence in comparison with infantile and oedipal conflicts. In our view, the development of a transference neurosis and its resolution must wait upon the clearance of these traumatic disruptions.

We believe we have added to Horowitz's and Lifton's understanding of these problems through our concept of the deadening effects of conflicts involving destructive impulses invoked by the trauma and the extraordinary defensive posture adopted to contain them.

REFERENCES

Des Pres, T. (1971). The survivor. *Encounter, 37,* 19.
Freud, S. (1919). Introduction to psychoanalysis and the war neurosis. *Standard edition,* Vol. 17 (pp. 205–210). London: Hogarth, 1955a.
Freud, S. (1920). Beyond the pleasure principle. *Standard edition,* Vol. 18 (pp. 1–64). London: Hogarth, 1955b.
Freud, S. (1954). *The origins of psychoanalysis.* New York: Basic Books.
Furst, S. (Ed.) (1967). *Psychic trauma.* New York: Basic Books.
Horowitz, M. (1976). Psychic trauma: Return of images after a stress response syndrome. In H. Parad, H. Resnik, & L. Parad (Eds.), *Emergency and disaster management: A mental health source book.* Bowie, MD: The Charles Press.

Horowitz, M., & Becker, S. (1972). Cognitive response to stress: Experimental studies of a compulsion to repeat trauma. In R. Hold & E. Peterfreund (Eds.), *Psychoanalysis and contemporary science*, I. New York: Macmillan.
Horowitz, M., & Solomon, G. J. A. (1975). Prediction of delayed stress response syndromes in Vietnam veterans. *Journal of Social Issues, 31*, 67–79.
Lifton, R. J. (1967). *Death in life: Survivors of Hiroshima.* New York: Random House.
Lifton, R. J. (1973). On death and the continuity of life. *American Journal of Psychoanalysis, 33*, 3–15. And (1974) in *History of Childhood Quarterly, 1*, 681–696.
Lifton, R. J., & Olson, E. (1976a). Death imprint in Buffalo Creek. In H. Parad, H. Resnik, & L. Parad (Eds.), *Emergency and disaster management: A mental health source book.* Bowie, MD: The Charles Press.
Lifton, R. J., & Olson, E. (1976b). The human meaning of total disaster: The Buffalo Creek Experience. *Psychiatry, 39*, 1–18.
Sandler, J. (1960). The background of safety. *International Journal of Psychoanalysis, 41*, 352–356.
Titchener, J., & Ross, W. D. (1974). Acute or chronic stress as determinants of behavior, character and neurosis. Chapter in *American handbook of psychiatry* (2nd ed.). New York: Basic Books.
Titchener, J., & Kapp, F. T. (1976). Family and character change at Buffalo Creek. *American Journal of Psychiatry, 133*, 295–299.
Titchener, J., Kapp, F. T., & Winget, C. (1976). The Buffalo Creek syndrome: Symptoms and character change after a major disaster. Chapter in H. J. Parad, H. Resnik, & L. Parad (Eds.), *Emergency and disaster management: A mental health source book.* Bowie, MD: The Charles Press.

2

Sealing Over and Integration: Modes of Resolution in the Post-Traumatic Stress Recovery Process

JOHN RUSSELL SMITH

Powerfully overwhelming events, such as the atomic blast at Hiroshima, concentration camps, and intensive combat, are not easily or quickly handled. And though denial and numbing often afford a seemingly reasonable return to normality, some more substantial form of coping with the trauma of catastrophe must be found.

SEALING OVER*

Throughout the history of warfare, there have been rites and rituals that warriors have used in order to come to terms with the deeds and memories of combat (Radford, 1972). As recently as World War II and the Korean Conflict, American Indian veterans used purification rites

Excerpted from a paper prepared for the Veterans Administration Operation Outreach Training Program, 1980. © 1980 John Russell Smith. Revised 1981.
*The ideas of sealing over and integration as modes of dealing with other psychologically distressing episodes were discussed earlier by McGlasham, Levy, and Carpenter (1975).

in order to reach accommodation with themselves, their deeds, their enemies, and their society.

Rites and rituals after warfare have two functions: one function relates to their purposes for society and will be discussed later under atonement; the purpose of the second function of rites and rituals is to help create a sense of meaning for warfare. The American Indian veterans use their tribal symbols and rituals to develop a systematic rationale for the special events of war (Adair & Vogt, 1949). Following previous wars in America, remnants of those more "primitive" rites and rituals have persisted in parades, medal award ceremonies, uniforms, and veterans' organizations. All these procedures symbolize the ritual of *sanction*, which tribes have traditionally bestowed on their warriors.

Sanction is a process of collective approval; it is also a stamp of communal meaning for the events of war. It provides universal and total meaning for the extraordinary demands of and actions taken during wartime. Sanction fixes in place the background—it sets the values, attitudes, and perceptions against which the actions of the individual, during the catastrophe, are judged. For example, themes of saving the world for democracy, protecting Jews from extermination, and preventing the Japanese takeover of the Pacific were rationales recurrent in movies and books after World War II, which fixed the backdrop of value for that war.

Sanction sets an overall purpose or rationale that grants meaning to and binds up all the undigested elements of the catastrophic event. Subsequently, this sanction promotes a process of sealing over in which responsibility for the action of an individual is fixed by and against that background. The individual need, then, only explain his actions as details expressive of the overall sanction.

As an information specialist in the Pennsylvania Army National Guard, B.—fulfilling a promise he made to himself while lying wounded—urges young men to serve their country. "They ask me if I'd do the same thing. I tell them 'Yes!' No war can justify to a mother the death of her son, but *this little green suit I wear maintains a safe society.*" (*Life Magazine*, October 1979, p. 107)

Like hot wax, which can permeate each strand of a ball of loose ends of string, so, too, in sealing over, sanction permeates the loose ends of experience, giving them meaning and binding them into a unit, immune from the demands of having to be integrated with the view of self and the world, prior to the event.

Thus, after a war, when triggering events begin to propel the individual out of denial into intrusion,* the presence of sanction permits an alternate route, away from denial or disorder, via the process of sealing over.

As Lazarus (1979) has pointed out in his recent work, these processes of denial and sealing over are not to be seen as negative or unhealthy processes, but rather as appropriate and adaptive responses to the event. Sealing over is a further, appropriately adaptive phase. Sealing over has the long-term advantage over denial, because it does not require the energy necessary to keep troublesome, undigested experience out of awareness, nor does it restrict areas of functioning; but rather, sealing over allows for a gentler management of the whole experience as unique and consistent with itself, although separate from other experience.

The stage of sealing over provides an extremely important step toward the management of the extreme actions and reactions demanded in warfare. What the process allows, for the survivors of warfare, is a sharing of responsibility with society for those extraordinary deeds. It permits a gentle and safe respite from the demands of making sense of and taking total individual responsibility for the events as well as from the necessity of incorporating those events into the broader schema of self and world. The sealing over, afforded by sanction, smooths the process out, over years, permitting painful experience either to remain encapsulated or to be incorporated gently, bit by bit, with normal experience.

Thirty-five years after World War II, Elmer Bendiner, a B-17 flyer, wrote his memoirs of the war. A *Newsweek* reviewer pointedly asked why these World War II veterans were still writing memoirs so many years later. Bendiner illustrates the soothing effect of the years and of the sanction on his sealing over.

> Even now, edging past middle age, few of us, I believe, awake in sweat because of the German civilians whom we have blasted. If war dreams disturb us, it is because they replay old fears from which we wake to ward off our own deaths, not the deaths of other. . . .
> World War II has less starry-eyed enchantment than most wars. We were not gulled by slogans. Hitler was real and his victory had to be prevented. For many of us that was the only point of the war. Critics aspiring to the melancholy glamor of membership in a "lost

---

*For a discussion of the stress phases of denial and intrusion see Horowitz (1976).

generation" will grant that truth but nevertheless insist that our means—the setting of fire storms in crowded cities, for example—fatally besmirched our ends.

Yet a question nags me: Suppose our leaders were pure in heart and dedicated solely to the destruction of fascism, undistracted by lesser ambitions, not caring whether the Air Forces or the Navy won the war so long as it was won; and suppose that their minds were as brilliant as their hearts were pure, and that the blasting of cities was in fact the only key to victory; then would not the sacrifice of thousands of lives have been worth it? If one can practice a terrible and Godlike arithmetic, can we say that we were right to kill thousands because they number less than the millions who would have died or lived appallingly if Hitler had won? Could we have dared to refrain from such a sacrifice merely to keep our hands clean? Admittedly this is a dangerous kind of bookkeeping, for if we allow it who can say that any terror is not justified in a cause we believe to be good? And if after the killing discerning critics point out that the strategists were not pure in heart or particularly wise and that therefore some of our victims died needlessly, where can we find absolution? Only in this: that our cause was just. This sets us apart from our enemies. (Bendiner, 1980, p. 238)

By suggesting that the sealing-over process is unitary and encompasses the entire war experience, I want to emphasize that there are some elements of that experience which still can be denied, and, at the same time, there are other aspects of that experience which are incorporated into normal civilian functioning. Overall, the implication of this diversity is that none of these stages is total. Several stages may be in operation at any time; however, one mode will predominate.

The process outlined thus far is a cognitive one. Emotion, or affect, has not been explained. In this cognitive model of the stress recovery process, emotion plays a role in amplification of a particular form of cognitive distress. Emotion is the avenue by which the dissonance of incongruence is expressed. Agony, tears, and rage express the pain of the undigested past. Signaling the distress of incongruence and the pain of intrusion, emotion also serves as a trigger to initiate the avoidance operations that defend against the pain of intrusion. The action of emotion as a trigger often functions unconsciously, possibly apparent, however, to those close to the individual.

Sealing over provides a respite from the emotional fatigue that accompanies denial, intrusion, and disorder. The ultimate objective of the stress recovery process is formulation of individual and collective meaning of the extreme event and incorporation of the personal aspects of the experience into a new schema of self and the world. The disparity between extreme experience and normal views of the world makes sealing over, and the time and relief from the disparity that it affords, significant in quieting the tumult that results from attempting to suddenly make sense of all the incongruity.

INTEGRATION

There have always been veterans for whom the grand rationales, useful for sealing over, have not provided meaning for their experience. (This is the subject of Kormos' chapter in the Figley book [1978].) Generally, though, this is true for isolated soldiers rather than for whole armies. The erosion of meaning, honor, and duty in the first industrialized war, World War I, gave rise to widespread malaise mistakenly named shellshock (Leed, 1979). The loss of meaning in that war gave birth to existentialism, the philosophy of meaninglessness. Even more so during the Vietnam War, the erosion of sanction of the war, the lack of clear purpose, the duplicitous manipulation by political leaders, and the divisive debate among the American people evaporated the meaning of the soldiers' sacrifices.

> A. soon found himself hit by a set of rules that seemed only to reduce his ability to fight. "After four or five months," he says, "we received an order that we were not supposed to fire unless fired upon. And another that said we were supposed to keep ourselves nice and clean out in the field. It was ridiculous! That was when I began to see that it was nothing but a game, that they were playing with our lives to make as much money as they could for DuPont and the munitions makers." (*Life Magazine*, October 1979, p. 112)

> After his return to the U.S., W. encountered little that changed the assessment, "A restaurant in San Diego gave me a free meal, and when I came home to Phoenix, my dad took me to a bar and I got free drinks. That was it. Nobody cared then; nobody cares now. 'Cannon fodder' is overused, but in a sense, that's all we were. We were only there to slow down the spread of Communism. For what? Maybe a couple of years. It's a terrible joke." (*Life Magazine*, October 1979, p. 111)

Unlike veterans of previous wars, most Vietnam veterans have been left without the option of the sealing-over stage. The medals, uniforms, parades, books, and films have a hollow ring for large numbers of these veterans. Closed out from the bridging afforded by sealing over, and largely unable to deny the controversy and reminders of the war constantly around them, these veterans have been forced to the more difficult task of immediate integration.

This more arduous process involves *not* permeating an experience with an overall meaning, but rather, weaving each strand of the experience into the overall fabric of their lives. Rather than having an isolated set of meanings, specific only to that experience, these veterans face the task of integrating their experience with the notions of who they were before, during, and after Vietnam. Integration requires accepting personal responsibility for their actions and recognizing the good and bad aspects of the experiences. In short, the process requires finding personal meaning for *each* aspect of the veterans' military experience, especially their own personal actions.

There is generally an assumption that extreme stress is pathogenic. Locked out of the binding rationales of sealing over, the survivor faces the chasm of loss of meaning. The shattering of the old schema and visions comes hard. For example, Americans, whether soldiers or civilians, found it difficult to believe that My Lai had happened. Despite the many cues, Jews throughout Europe found it impossible to believe what the "final solution" would mean for them. Even in concentration camps, disbelief was pervasive. Such capacity to retain cherished views attests to the powerful resistance of world views to change except under the most extremely compelling circumstances. The shattering of these tightly held perspectives brings agony, outcry, and confusion. Veterans and other survivors, without the prospect of sealing over, can teeter for long periods on the brink of despair and madness. But this agony can also give way to extraordinary acts of courage and integrity.

> At the outset, the living places, the ditches, the mud, the piles of excrement behind the blocks, had appalled me with their horrible filth. . . . And then I saw the light! I saw that it was not a question of disorder or lack of organization but that, on the contrary, a very thoroughly considered conscious idea was in the back of the camp's existence. They had condemned us to die in our own filth, to drown in mud, in our own excrement. They wished to abase us, to destroy our human dignity, to efface every vestige of humanity, to return us to the level of wild animals, to fill us with horror and contempt toward ourselves and our fellows. (Lewinska, 1968, pp. 41–42)

> But from the instant when I grasped the motivating principle . . . it was as if I had been awakened from a dream. . . . I felt under

orders to live. . . . And if I did die in Auschwitz, it would be as a human being, I would hold on to my dignity. I was not going to become the contemptible, disgusting brute my enemy wished me to be. . . . And a terrible struggle began which went on day and night. (Lewinska, 1968, p. 50)

The choice is either a descent into meaninglessness and madness or the slow reconstruction of a whole new sense of meaning. In fact, this crisis of meaning can serve as a catalyst to disrupt old patterns, attempt new responses, and chart a new course.

While some psychiatric observers have focused on the long-term debilitating effects of catastrophic experience, others, like Des Pres (1976), have turned attention to the courageous aspects.

Lifton (1973) speaks of animating guilt and the power of using devastating experience as an opportunity for growth in individuals and contributions to society.

The veterans also make clear that young people, even when considerably confused, can take powerful steps toward new integrity: I think of the My Lai survivor, able to call forth at a crucial moment his idiosyncratically derived ethical forms (from military chivalry, Catholic principles, and the habit of autonomy) to refuse participation in that atrocity. I think of the former grunt whose company was virtually wiped out, appearing at early rap groups in a dissociated state close to breakdown, emerging as a man still highly conflicted but able to mobilize extraordinary sensitivity in furthering his and others' renewal. I think of the former Naval NCO undergoing a series of debilitating personal crises, and through them all evolving a fierce commitment to a vision of integrity new to him and yet so palpable as to provide a nurturing standard for the entire group—and later, through various kinds of writing and consulting, becoming a leading national interpreter of Vietnam veterans' aspirations and needs. (Lifton, 1973, p. 406)

The reconstruction of meaning for the individual is often part of a process of bringing growth to a society. For many survivors of war and catastrophe, their lives have been immeasurably enriched by their experience and especially by their recovery through integration. Though their fabric of meaning previously held has been rent, the remaining strands provide the fundamental threads from which new meaning will be woven.

Rejected by mankind, the condemned do not go so far as to reject it in turn. Their faith in history remains unshaken, and one may well wonder why. They do not despair. The proof: they persist in surviving—not only to survive, but to testify.
The victims elect to become witnesses. (Wiesel, 1972, p. 28)

Thus, from the experience of the war and the preexisting schemata, veterans of Vietnam reconstruct a whole new tapestry of the meaning of the world and a new understanding of their own actions. This process of integration is what the rap groups, in their special way, help to facilitate. As I indicated above, old perspectives die hard. In the process of integration, incongruent and contradictory attitudes may be fiercely held without visible distress. Old views will remain tightly held, and continual attempts will be made to fit new and contradictory experience into them despite the futility of such an exercise. The essential point is that people cling to old and even outmoded patterns of thought and coping until a new system presents itself with terms they can accept. Like an old, worn-out shoe, such perspectives come to fit very comfortably over time. No matter how shiny and attractive a new pair looks, it won't be used regularly until each shoe is broken in and comfortable. Specifically, this means that the period of working through to integration is a time of turmoil and conflict. At times, survivors will seem prophetic and clearly on a new track; at other times, they will seem confused, diffuse, and almost inchoate. When the integrative process is complete, the fragmented bits of traumatic experience will have been reincorporated into an integrative resolution.

Leventman (1978) has repeatedly spoken of the profound loss of illusions—of God, Mom, and apple pie—among Vietnam veterans. It is this erosion of sanction and grand ideals, the roots of sealing over, which has forced Vietnam veterans toward integration. This process of finding individual meaning is a more time-consuming and demanding process. The extraordinary rules, values, and experiences of warfare are not easily compatible with previous civilian values. Sealing over provides an easier interlude in managing that disparity. Integration means confronting it, head on, immediately, without the benefit of a cushion that sealing over provides.

Not all Vietnam veterans, however, have been driven toward integration and forced by experience to give up those rationales of sealing over. Some, like Lieutenant Coker, a POW in Peter Davis' *Hearts and Minds*, still vigorously maintain them. However, this effort is often done with considerable visible energy and at the price of having to deny large portions of experience and the views of many other Vietnam veterans. After Vietnam, neither sealing over nor integration has presented an easy road to healing for the veterans who fought there.

ATONEMENT

Neither sealing over nor integration is a complete resolution. Each of these resolutions must be reached in order to attain a final resolution. Conflict results when veterans or survivors of different generations are locked into opposite poles of the two resolutions, integration and sealing over.

Conflict with Other Veterans

The difficulty of the final resolution process is compounded by the fact that integration and sealing over are at opposite poles of a continuum and these styles of managing traumatic material are not immediately compatible. In sealing over, one does not need to examine individual aspects of the experience, but broadly binds the experience unitarily with the overarching rationale symbolized by the flag, the medals, the parades, and the movies. The intense examination of the strands of experience that occurs among Vietnam veterans can threaten to unravel the sealing over of other generations of veterans and propel those veterans back into the same examination of their own experience. The psychological threat of opening up that isolated experience can often evoke intense reactions among other veterans.

For veterans who are now older and much more sophisticated, this threat can be especially profound, since the sealing-over process froze their experience and perceptions, as they were, thus remaining untouched by later learning. Consequently, the reactions generated in these older men by questioning Vietnam veterans are reactions of 19- and 20-year-olds, frozen years ago, without intense examination, and those reactions are now threatening to demand the same intense examination.

So, too, Vietnam veterans, faced with an experience that has shattered for them the grand rationales, often hear recitations of the binding rationales for previous wars or for national heroes as hollow and simplistic. It is almost as if they resent the loss of those illusions and the grueling process of constructing new meanings. Witness, for example, the eruption of reaction among Vietnam veterans after the return of the Iranian hostages.

This conflict among generations of veterans also becomes embodied in the institutions that cater to them. Policies and regulations of organizations like the Veterans Administration become embodiments of a particular style, like sealing over. For example, the lobby of a VA hospital can become a psychic battleground where a set of military service banners and an American flag and rows of portraits of presidents, VA administrators, and hospital directors become symbolic of an order of affairs that reinforces the binding rationales of the sealing-over process. While soothing for other veterans, for Vietnam veterans, however, these very suggestions of those symbols, those rationales, and the sealing-over process denied them can become offensive affronts and reminders of the turmoil of their loss of meaning and the arduousness of their task of integration.

So, too, some of the antipathy toward Vietnam veterans reflects the personal and institutional response to the threat that these veterans pose to the symbols and values that bind the sealing-over process of previous veterans. Often the projects and outreach centers that Vietnam veterans establish project a style reflecting a determined rejection of those traditional values and symbols which reinforce sealing over. Thus, in a complex way, the VA hospital may be an affront to the psychological coping of a number of Vietnam veterans, while the outreach center profoundly offends the sensibilities of the older veteran.

This discussion of psychological conflicts between veterans of previous wars and veterans of Vietnam is indicative of a larger truth about the readjustment of Vietnam veterans. Homecoming and the readjustment after returning from the war might be as difficult as the actual war experience, if not more so.

The Final Goal: Atonement

The final goal of the stress recovery process is atonement, "making at one." Reaching this goal involves two elements: (1) making at one with the society over the meaning of the event, and (2) integration of the personal aspects of the experience. The sanction, critical for sealing over, accomplishes the first task of arriving at collective meaning. Integration accomplishes the second task, creating the personal meaning for the experience. There are two courses through this process. In the presence of an initial sanction, after the catastrophic event, the course is through a long period of sealing over. Later, undigested bits may be integrated, leading to the final resolution of atonement. In the other course, there is first the difficult process of immediate integration; only later, can there be the formulation of a sanction that leads to sealing over and atonement.

ATONEMENT AFTER SEALING OVER

The Usual Procedure

The usual order of stages followed in the stress recovery process is first to seal over and then to integrate, resulting in an atonement where the individual is at peace with the society and with himself. After years of sealing over, later events propel to the surface the last remaining, undigested bits of experience that cast the veterans momentarily back into intrusion. If the veteran is not yet ready to deal with the remaining experience, those fragments may be moved into denial, or, if disturbing enough, they may propel him, many years after the war, into disorder.

If, however, the sealed-over veteran is prepared to undertake the task, he can begin to integrate those last remaining fragments of experience. This is the task that Bendiner (1980) undertook in writing his memoirs. He attempts to reaffirm his sealing over and then to integrate that significant event which has troubled him for so many years and could not simply be sealed over with a rationale for the war.

> Bendiner recounts his combat missions as a B-17 navigator over Europe with the 8th Air Force. He comes to terms with a pilot afraid to face combat, the loss of three-quarters of his crew and his own near death. He can explain the loss of hundreds of comrades in fiery crashes across Europe and a near tragic ditching in the English Channel. Having completed his 25th mission and freed from combat duty, he faces a more personal adversary—the squadron PR man.
>
> I do not remember a man coming into the bar, but there he was next to me. I have forgotten his name. He was a PR man—an information officer. I had known him slightly, and occasionally given him a bit of color to adorn a press release. He was a mild-mannered man, one of many I had known on the field as I knew the color of the bar or the turn of the road. Until that moment he had been part of the scenery but had not participated in my world. I flew and he walked. I was on familiar terms with death and he

pecked items out on a typewriter as I do now. I was an arrogant snob. I was part of an elite. He was an outsider. Still, I was civil; I made talk.

I believe he bought me a drink, but I am not sure. He had done a squib on my completing my missions, he said, and I nodded appreciatively. His face was a pasty white, as I remember it, but I do not trust myself because I have carried his face so long in my mind that it is the worse for wear.

We were oppressively alone in that bar. The alcohol had diminished me to a point below anything I had known. My spirit had collapsed like a dishrag. Inside my throat I could feel tears drip as from an abscess. Yet we talked to God knows what. We talked until he said quite suddenly, "You made it all the way. Not many of your people stick it out."

I hope to God I did not nod my head or let my hand shake. I know I could not speak. I think he knew I could not speak, and that staggers me with shame thirty-five years later. I put my drink down. That I do remember. I do not think I looked at him. I wish now that I had, that I had seen his face clearly. I cannot tell whether he smiled or smirked or gloated or peered dully at me through his glasses. I will never know. I took my trench coat from the hook on the wall. I recall that I did everything slowly. I put on my crushed airman's hat and walked out.

That is what happened. A plethora of rationalizations followed at once and have continued for thirty-five years. The event came so suddenly upon me, so unexpectedly, that I could not think of any of the thousand witty, savage, blunt things to say or do that have leaped to mind ever since. I was caught completely off guard. I had just been tasting the joys of exclusivity in a bitter time. I had condescended to talk to this paddlefoot, this unprepossessing paper pusher. I had been in and up and he had been down and out. It had been so kind of me to talk to him. Then in the twinkling of an eye he had pulled me down and thrown me out. I walked the dark and rutted roads around Kimbolton, clutching my coat as if caught in a chill wind.

I had always acknowledged my kinship with the Jews of Europe, but it was a watery-thin intellectual nod that I sent them. I had lived in a world—social, political, sexual—where I supposed that others took my Jewishness for granted as I did and made no fuss about it. The crosses of the Klan had burned in the hills near the town I lived in as a child, but they had not referred to me. When we did not laugh at the Klan we hated it because it menaced other people. I loathed anti-Semitism in the same way because it was a scourge for other people though not for me.

Now that stupid little man had stripped the illusion from my war. It was not, then, a game which we played with death in the sky. It was not all gallantry and white contrails against the blue. It was not an aesthetic experience sanctified by an unchallengeable political cause. Hitler was not a dragon with shiny scales to be slain by a shinier knight. There were no dragons, but only savage men and women burning the flesh of other men and women. And I was a Jew with someone's spittle on the face.

I do not pretend that I was a victim of a pogrom. I agree that, living in the same century as Auschwitz, I ought not to mention my little encounter. And it would have left no mark on me if I had not been rendered so vulnerable by a false sense of security derived from the battlefield where death creates the splendid illusion of brotherhood.

None of this was clear to me as I left the bar. It has taken me thirty-five years to begin to understand that nameless PR man. He probably shrugged when I walked out, confirmed in the view that Jews are hypersensitive and unpredictable and that they can't tell a compliment from a kick in the ass. (Bendiner, 1980, pp. 249–251)

If the usual order is followed, sealing over first enables the consolidation of most of the traumatic experience under the canopy of overall meaning. If the remaining segment is successfully integrated, as Bendiner attempts to do above, this phase then leads to the final resolution, atonement in which, now, all of the experience becomes digested.

Responsibility for Personal Actions

As in the Bendiner example above, the final step of integration, in pursuit of atonement, is always the resolution of some personal action or decision, judged harshly in the light of rigid expectations, clouding acceptance of oneself in the experience.

Billy N. joined the Marines with his best friend from high school. They served in the same combat unit in Vietnam. One day, while crossing a swollen stream with their rifles over their heads, Billy was in danger of being swept away. His buddy, who had reached the opposite bank, stretched out a hand to help Billy. Billy handed the rifle, muzzle forward, to his buddy and, while being hauled from the water, accidentally pulled the trigger and killed his lifelong friend. For years after his return, Billy could not forgive himself for the death of his friend. Daily, he made a detour around the town where his buddy was buried. Billy's judgment of that act was

frozen and locked into a value system that allowed him no forgiveness. Several years later, he had come to accept the fact that
he had slipped in a moment of panic, accidentally killing his friend.
It was only when he could drive to the cemetery, kneel in front of
his friend's grave, say he was sorry, and accept forgiveness for
himself that he could go on with his life.

The undigested bits of experience, which cannot be denied or sealed
over, are framed in a value system that was calcified in the war.

Later sophistication and greater flexibility in the judgment of one's
behavior often leave untouched, for years, a single painful act performed
under the strain of combat, as in the following example.

> This Navy corpsman served two tours with the Marines in Vietnam.
> Out on an operation five days before the end of his second tour,
> the corpsman's unit got caught in an ambush. Panicked at all the
> previous close calls he had survived, he hid behind a rock while
> hearing the cries for "corpsman." For 10 years after his discharge,
> he was haunted by his act of "cowardice." It was not until he could
> share the experience with a group of Veterans, who could under-
> stand, that he could begin to accept his own behavior.

Guilt derives from personal actions in the past that are feared will be
reenacted in the future with the same failure. People assume that the
past action is a reflection on their entire character and it forms the essence
of their self-condemnation. The resolution of these secret guilts is the
final task of integration.

> When I was on the battlefield in World War II I was expecting the
> worst, and it didn't bother me at all like this. When my buddies
> got killed I knew I was no part of their getting killed. But when
> the flood came I didn't have time to help that lady and her baby
> who cried for help. (Lifton & Olson, 1975, p. 8)

It is not the traumatic experience of war itself but the meaning that
those events have for the individual which creates trauma. These traumatic experiences, in which there is a core event of personal action or
inaction, often have a precursor in precatastrophe life. Memory of some
small event or loss, long-buried and unresolved, is triggered by and
coupled with action in the catastrophic event.

These earlier, highly personal, and idiosyncratic events are what I
view as predisposition. Many psychiatric observers tend to rush to universal and global factors with which they can locate responsibility clearly

in the individual for their reactions. Thus, they avoid, in analysis and treatment, the social and political factors of the catastrophe that are so central to its meaning.

Each life is likely to contain such personally charged events, which, in themselves, generally produce no major impairment. However, when aroused by a specific event or action in the context of the overwhelming incongruity of the catastrophe, these events become both amplified by and linked with rigid judgments formed in the heat of the catastrophic crisis. It is this linkage of an overall event, which threatens previous meaning, together with critical actions by the individual in the catastrophe, arousing memories of his past action, that forms the trauma central to stress reactions. The road to resolution is reconstructing the outer shell of meaning and sharing that new understanding, thus enabling the uncovering of the critical actions by the individual in the catastrophe. Only then will the precursor, in a prior event, surface for resolution. Attempts to circumvent this process and get directly at the "predisposing" trauma meet with fierce resistance and ignore the cradling role afforded by restructuring the meaning of the catastrophe.

Sealing Over and Natural Disaster

This usual order of procedure, of sealing over followed by integration, is what makes natural disaster easier to handle than man-made disaster. Because society accepts acts of God and nature, there is an implicit sanction enabling sealing over. As with sanctioned combat, this usual order of sealing over first keeps the overall meaning intact and buys time for the more arduous process of integration.

ATONEMENT AFTER PERSONAL INTEGRATION

Blockage of the Usual Procedure

As I noted earlier under integration, there are times when the lack of sanction prevents sealing over and thereby forces the more difficult course of integration to be taken first. This occurs not only in the case of divisive wars like Vietnam but also in man-made disasters such as Buffalo Creek, concentration camps, and the atomic blast at Hiroshima where the constellation of meaning is shattered. Here I will illustrate this more arduous process toward atonement with the example of Vietnam.

Purification Rituals

In the earlier discussion of sanction, I indicated one function of purification rituals. I now wish to explore the other mentioned function. Societies always have difficulties with returning warriors.

> There is a feeling throughout the land that the returned veterans have been engaging in crimes to such an extent as to endanger the very foundation of civil life and safety. Indeed some people have spread before the public a canvas on which the ex-service man is shown bludgeoning all passers-by and after maiming them, robbing them of their possessions. Another canvas portrays armed men walking along the streets and killing, without cause, anyone who dares to venture out and use a public thoroughfare. And while all this happens it must be presumed that the police stand by fearfully and are unable to protect human life and property!
>
> This, it is said, is a consequence of the war training and war experience of those who had to face danger in order to preserve the culture of their country and the safety and independence of their fellow citizens who for one reason or another did not participate in military activities.
>
> It is reasoned that the returning soldier, having engaged in mass movements to vanquish an enemy, returns home with a new code and a new set of morals plus a knowledge of the use of weapons and a desire to continue adventure and to make a living or amass a fortune by expropriating the property of others. (Willbach, 1947, p. 501)

The purification process usually involves a ritual cleansing, a ritual meal, and sexual activity. Other activities are designed not only to purge the warrior but also to reimpose on the warrior the normal constraints of the culture and symbolic restraints on violence. Not only do the symbols of awards, decorations, parades, and uniforms aid the sealing-over process, but they also help protect the civilian society by emphasizing the unique place of the trauma, bloody deeds, and other special demands of war.

Otto Friedrich (1976), in a review of Spear's memoirs of the Third Reich, noted the problem of atonement—the making at one of an individual with a community. He postulated that civilized society could never reaccept Albert Spear into its community, since to do so would have brought the blood and the horror of the Nazis onto the heads of the community. The separation provided by the purification rituals of "primitive tribes," and the rituals' remnants in the metals, victory parades, VFW's, long trips home by ship, extended discharge periods, and the allowance of periods of unemployment during which veterans wore their uniforms in the society, were all part of both the sanction applied to the deeds of war out there and the atonement that enabled the reintegration of soldiers back into the society without the blood of their deeds falling on the heads of society.

After Vietnam, the ambivalence of the society about its sanction for the war, and the rapid discharge of veterans quickly back into society without "purification," threatened to bring responsibility for My Lai and the other events of Vietnam into the homes of America. The presence of Vietnam veterans among the society and the veterans' attempts to find both the good and the bad in their own experience threatened the sealing-over rationales of both the antiwar and the prowar segments of the society. On one level, veterans' examination of their experience threatens the maintenance of certain rationales on the part of both prowar and antiwar segments of the society. Vietnam veterans' adherence to the total reality of their experience threatens the patriotic rationale of the prowar segment; on the other hand, the Vietnam veterans' rejection of the North Vietnamese as "the good guys," innocent of any barbarity in the war, threatens certain cozy rationales of the antiwar movement.

Thus, Vietnam veterans can find themselves cut off from the usual mode of sealing over their war experiences, faced with the more arduous task of integrating, and confronted with an antipathy from both older veterans and the society at large.

These veterans become visible reminders of the society's responsibility as well as impediments to a quick resolution of the society's own sealing over. Segments of the veteran population often find themselves singled out as instigators of society's problems.

> Law enforcement officials in Dade County, Fla. feel that last month's rebellion in Miami was the work of Black Vietnam veterans tightly organized into an "urban guerrilla" force that may be a nationwide phenomena.
>
> They said the Black veterans brought back with them extensive experience in jungle guerrilla warfare and applied the same tactics in Miami's predominantly Black Liberty City district.
>
> "The armed forces trained them to fight and kill," said Capt. Lonnie Lawrence of the Dade County Police Department.
>
> "Many came home to no jobs and no hope, into communities where drugs and racial tensions were serious problems."
>
> Lawrence, an ex-Marine who served in Vietnam, said the guerrilla forces are a new urban development, and Justice Department officials in Miami feel that local officials across the country should

familiarize themselves with the Black veterans' activities "so they will know what to expect." (From the *Milwaukee Courier*, July 1980, quoted in the *Eclipse*, Summer 1980, p. 2)

Thus, Vietnam veterans and other victims of catastrophe become scapegoats of the society's lack of resolution rather than partners in atonement.

Given the forces mitigating against sanction, veterans of Vietnam and often victims of man-made catastrophe are forced to integration as the only solution short of disorder. Despite the fact that Vietnam veterans may, through their process of integration, come to some collective understanding among themselves about their experience, they are, nonetheless, left at odds with the rest of society. The task that survivors, forced to this mode, face when stymied by a lack of sanction, is, in fact, to take their vision to the society in the hope of refashioning a collective understanding.

Thus, veterans of Vietnam who arrive at a resolution of integration are left at odds with the society as a whole. Their task is to take their experience back into intrusion, motivated by the animating guilt of which Lifton speaks (1973), to engage the society in the creation of a new sanction. Through this process, collectively, these veterans and society then seal over their experience and achieve final resolution, atonement. This demands arriving at an understanding where both parties acknowledge the mistakes and arrogant paternalism of the war. The process also allows appreciation to the veterans, for their honest efforts, and honor to the society, for its cherished ideals. Only by undertaking the refashioning of meaning *with* the society can those who are forced to integration first achieve their final resolution of atonement with the society.

REFERENCES

Adair, J., & Vogt, E. (1949). Navajo and Zuni veterans. *American Anthropologist, 51,* 547–561.
American Psychiatric Association (1952). *Diagnostic and statistical manual of mental disorders I* (DSM-I). Washington, DC.
American Psychiatric Association (1968). *Diagnostic and statistical manual of mental disorders* (DSM-II). Washington, DC.
American Psychiatric Association (1980). *Diagnostic and statistical manual of mental disorders* (DSM-III). Washington, DC.
Archibald, H. C., Long, D. M., Miller, C., & Tuddenham, R. D. (1962). Gross stress reaction in combat: Fifteen-year follow-up. *American Journal of Psychiatry, 119,* 317–322.
Archibald, H. C., & Tuddenham, R. D. (1965). Persistent stress reaction following combat: A twenty-year follow-up. *Archives of General Psychiatry, 12,* 475–481.
Bendiner, E. (1980). *A fall of fortresses.* New York: Putnam.
Blank, A. S., Jr. (1979). *Military psychiatric services.* 1st Training Conference Papers. Vietnam

Veterans Operation Outreach. St. Louis, September 1979.

Blank, A. S., Jr. (1985). The unconscious flashback to the war in Vietnam veterans: Clinical mystery, legal defense, and community problem. In S. M. Sonnenberg, A. S. Blank, Jr., & J. A. Talbott (Eds.), *The trauma of war: Stress and recovery in Vietnam veterans.* Washington, DC: American Psychiatric Press.

Davis, P. (1974). *Hearts and minds* (Film). BBS Productions.

Des Pres, T. (1976). *The survivor: An anatomy of life in the death camps.* New York: Oxford University Press.

Friedrich, O. (1976, February 22). Spandau (Review of *Spandau*). *The New York Times Book Review* (Sunday Magazine), p. 1.

Haley, S. A. (1974). When the patient reports atrocities. *Archives of General Psychiatry, 30,* 191–196.

Hall, R. C. W., & Malone, P. T. (1975). Psychiatric residuals of prolonged captivity experience. In H. I. McCubbin, B. B. Dahl, P. J. Metres, & J. A. Plag (Eds.), *Family separation and reunion: Families of prisoners of war and servicemen missing in action.* Washington, DC: US Government Printing Office.

Horowitz, M. J. (1976). *Stress response syndromes.* New York: Aronson.

Horowitz, M. J., Wilner, N., Kaltreider, N., & Alvarez, W. (1980). Signs and symptoms of post-traumatic stress disorder. *Archives of General Psychiatry, 35,* 85–92.

Janet, P. (1923). *Psychological healing* (2 Vols.). New York: Macmillan.

Kormos, H. (1978). The nature of combat stress. In C. Figley (Ed.), *Stress disorders among Vietnam veterans.* New York: Brunner/Mazel.

Lazarus, R. (1979). Positive denial: The case of not facing reality. *Psychology Today, 13,* 4.

Leed, E. J. (1979). *No man's land: Combat and identity in World War I.* New York: Cambridge University Press.

Leventman, S. (1978). Epilogue: Social and historical perspectives on the Vietnam veteran. In C. R. Figley (Ed.), *Stress disorders among Vietnam veterans.*

Lewinska, P. (1968). *Twenty months at Auschwitz.* Translated by Albert Teichner. New York: Lyle Stuart.

Life Magazine (October 1979). Six who came home. 2.

Lifton, R. J. (1954). Home by ship: Reaction patterns of American prisoners of war repatriated from North Korea. *American Journal of Psychiatry, 110,* 732–739.

Lifton, R. J. (1968). *Death in life: Survivors of Hiroshima.* New York: Random House.

Lifton, R. J. (1973). *Home from the war.* New York: Simon and Schuster.

Lifton, R. J., & Olson, E. (1975). The human meaning of total disaster. Paper presented at American Psychiatric Association annual meeting, Anaheim.

McGlasham, T. H., Levy, S. T., & Carpenter, W. T., Jr. (1975). Integration and sealing over. *Archives of General Psychiatry, 32,* 1269–1272.

Piaget, J. (1954). *The construction of reality in the child.* Translated by Margaret Cook. New York: Basic.

Radford, J. (1972). Purification rites: A cross cultural analysis of the reabsorption of warriors back into society after being exposed to war. Illinois Veterans Working Group.

Smith, J. R. (1981). A review of one hundred and twenty years of the psychological literature on reactions to combat from the Civil War through the Vietnam War: 1860–1980. Unpublished manuscript, Duke University.

Tyhurst, J. S. (1951). Individual reactions to community disaster. *American Journal of Psychiatry, 107,* 764–769.

Tyhurst, J. C. (1957a). Psychological and social aspects of civilian disaster. *Canada Medical Association Journal, 76,* 385.

Tyhurst, J. S. (1957b). The role of transition states—including disasters—in mental illness. *Symposium on Preventive and Social Psychiatry* (pp. 149–172). Walter Reed Army Institute of Research, Washington, DC.

Wiesel, E. (1972). *One generation after.* Translated by Lily Edelman & Elie Wiesel. New York: Avon. (1971) London: Weidenfeld and Nicholson.

Willbach, H. (1947). Recent crimes and the veterans. *Journal of Law and Psychiatry, 38:*501.

3

Traumatic Stress: The Role of the Family and Social Support System

CHARLES R. FIGLEY

John and Mary Allen said very little during the 20-minute ride from their home to the Community Hospital. Minutes ago they were telephoned by the City Police Department and informed that their 23-year-old daughter, Paula, had survived a head-on collision with another car that suddenly veered into their lane. Paula's husband, Carl, who was driving her to the airport, was killed, along with the driver of the other car. John and Mary went directly to the reception desk to ask about Paula's condition. Mary was usually the calmer of the two but found herself screaming at the receptionist, who first wanted to know about insurance coverage and home addresses. The initial minutes in the emergency waiting room seemed like hours to John and Mary. Soon, though, they were joined by their other two daughters and several friends and relatives, as the emergency medical team worked to save Paula's life. The friends and family had been together just a week ago to help John and Mary celebrate their silver wedding anniversary. Everyone was so happy then. They waited three hours before receiving word that Paula would survive and, with luck, would recover fully over the next several months. As they waited, there were several more emergency arrivals: an assault victim, a welder injured in an industrial accident, and another auto accident survivor were among the worst of them. Each was joined later by a worried family and friends. The Allens were not alone that night.

Over a month later Paula was released from the hospital to complete her convalescence at her parent's home. The family worried not only about Paula's physical condition, but about her emotional condition as well. During subsequent recovery Paula experienced a collection of symptoms later diagnosed as post-traumatic stress disorder (APA, 1980), a common reaction for victims of catastrophic events. Paula's symptoms included painful recollections of the accident and her initial experiences in the hospital, sleep disturbances, moodiness, emotional withdrawal, jumpiness, crying spells, varying amounts of depression, and guilt associated with surviving Carl. During this recuperative period, Paula's family would be a key factor in her recovery from emotional wounds of her accident. However, they too became affected by the emotional wake of the catastrophic accident. (adapted from Figley, 1983, pp. 3–4)

Today we know more than ever before about the emotional cost to the Allens of this tragic accident as well as the role they play in Paula's recovery. There is little doubt that the family, plus the social support system in general, is the single most important resource to emotional recovery from catastrophe (McCubbin & Figley, 1983; Figley & McCubbin, 1983a). One chapter (Figley, 1983) focuses exclusively on how families, like the Allens, cope with catastrophe. The central thesis of these volumes is that the family is a critical support system to human beings *before, during,* and *after* stressful times and that the *system* and its *members* are also affected, sometimes even more than the victim. In this chapter, I would like to capsulize four years of work by answering five questions:

1. What qualifies as a catastrophe, an event that may result in traumatic or post-traumatic stress reactions?
2. What is the meaning of social support provided by the family?
3. How is this support important in both preventing and abating traumatic and post-traumatic stress impairments?
4. Are the family members of survivors of catastrophe susceptible to being traumatized themselves?
5. What should be done for the families of catastrophe?

CATASTROPHIC LIFE EXPERIENCES

As will be discussed throughout this volume, the third revision of the American Psychiatric Association's (1980) *Diagnostic and Statistical Manual of Mental Disorders* (DSM-III) describes the disorder affecting Paula and others like her: post-traumatic stress disorder (PTSD). The diagnostic criteria for PTSD include three groups of symptoms: (1) evidence of "reexperiencing the trauma," (2) "numbing of responsiveness to or reduced involvement with the external world" following the traumatic event, and (3) a variety of stress reactions. The most unique facet of the disorder, however, is that the client must have survived a "recognizable stressor (event) that would evoke significant symptoms of distress in almost everyone [p. 238], and outside the range of such common experiences as simple bereavement, chronic illness, business losses, or marital conflict [p. 236]." And except for giving examples of such events (e.g., rape, assault, combat, natural disasters, man-made disasters, accidents, and human brutalities) and speculating that those of "human design" may be more traumatic, the manual does not specify what and why certain events induce stress. Thus we consider the first question, *What qualifies as a catastrophe, an event that may result in traumatic or posttraumatic stress reactions?*

Based on reports on victims of a wide variety of catastrophes (Figley, 1975, 1978, 1983, 1985), the characteristics that make these events so troubling is the extent to which they are (1) sudden, (2) dangerous, and (3) overwhelming.

Sudden

Catastrophes are troubling because they happen so suddenly, with very little or no warning to the victims. There is limited or no time to prepare, to devise and rehearse a plan of escape, identify a method of coping, or prevent or avoid the catastrophe. Whereas with normal life changes, there is typically a process of "anticipatory socialization" (Burr, 1973), which enables us to psychologically prepare for new attitudes, values, and behaviors required in a new role, no such process occurs prior to a catastrophe. Behavioral psychologists have noted that fear and general anxiety arousal is decreased as an organism develops repetitious patterns of behavior (Mineka, 1979; Wolpe, 1973); in other words, we become accustomed to various noxious stimuli as we develop a hierarchy of appropriate responses to them. Thus, we are temporarily immobilized when confronted with something which is unexpected and with which we have had little, if any, previous experience. This immobility is especially noxious if associated with the second factor: dangerousness.

Dangerous

Perhaps the most significant element of a catastrophic event which evokes trauma is a perceived sense of danger (Figley, 1979): either for ourselves, or for someone we care about very deeply. Indeed, we may be perfectly safe ourselves, yet still be traumatized when a loved one is in danger. Fear—of death, annihilation, injury, or destruction—is an energizing element of life which has the potential of leaving a clear imprint on the memory of all who experience it, as others have noted (cf. Weisman & Hackett, 1961; Lifton, 1973).

Overwhelming

An event that is sudden and dangerous is usually also emotionally overwhelming. The sense of being "overwhelmed" is often referred to as "sensory overload," "overstimulation," or "role strain," by psychologists and sociologists (Janis, 1969) when referring to relatively mild sources of social stress. These concepts suggest that the individual's attention to the demands of the environment (be it work, family, or some other setting) is so continuously aroused that he or she becomes ineffective in dealing with all of the demands. American scholars since the Civil War have noted that prolonged exposure to highly demanding environments—such as war (Smith, 1981), the Holocaust (Neiderland, 1968), rape (Burgess & Holmstrom, 1979), weather-related (Smith, 1983) and man-made disasters (Gleser, Green, & Winget, 1981)—induces a sense of exhaustion during, but more often immediately following, the exposure. Similar to the parameters of suddenness and dangerousness, being overwhelmed leads to a sense of temporary helplessness, of being out of control (Figley, 1979); which may, in turn, stimulate the survivor to behave in a way (e.g., panic) that is inconsistent with his or her self-concept—something that one may prefer to have relegated to the realm of the forgotten.

MEANING AND FUNCTION OF SOCIAL SUPPORT

Following a catastrophic event the family has a central role to play as a social support system for the victim. Before discussing this role let us first discuss the meaning and nature of social support in general.

Definition

There has been an upsurge in attention recently to the concept of social support. Recently, for example, the *Journal of Social Issues* devoted two entire issues to this topic (see Volume 40:4 and Volume 41:1). Of course, a full discussion of this literature is beyond the scope of this paper. What is important here is a clear delineation of exactly what is social support and the extent to which it is important to the emotional well-being of victims, veterans—survivors—of catastrophe. As a result of this attention, a wide variety of conceptualizations and definitions have emerged, as well as a concomitant increase in confusion about the role of social support in mental health (Thoits, 1982).

For our purposes, social support, provided by both family and close friends, is defined as ". . . the degree to which an individual perceives that he or she may rely on one or more people for assistance with either tangible . . . or emotional . . . aid or both in times of need" (Figley & Burge, 1983, p. 2). Thus we conceptualize social support, as we do with stress and trauma, from the point of view of the person being supported. We, of course, assume that there is little discrepancy between the support a subject claims to have and what he or she either has access to or actually utilizes.

Function

In a recently concluded study at Purdue (Burge, 1982; Burge & Figley, 1982; Figley & Burge, 1983), we isolated five major functions of social support that would be important to anyone in times of need, especially persons with PTSD symptoms. These functions form the basis of a new and powerful research and diagnostic tool titled the *Purdue Social Support Scale* (see p. 44). The functions are: emotional support, encouragement, advice, companionship, and tangible aid, confirming the research findings of others. These functions were noted earlier by Hirsch (1980).

Emotional support is the care, comfort, love, affection, and sympathy shown to the victim. It is the extent to which we are convinced that the supporter is on our side.

Encouragement is the praise and compliments offered by a supporter. It is the extent to which we are inspired by the supporter to feel courage and hope, to prevail.

Advice is useful information for solving a problem. It is the extent to which we feel better informed by interacting with the supporter.

Companionship is simply the time spent with a supporter, doing things that are perceived to be mutually enjoyable. It is the extent to which we don't feel alone.

Tangible aid is a practical resource provided by the supporter, such as helping with various chores, providing transportation, lending money, shopping, or some other form of concrete assistance. It is the extent to which we feel relieved of a burdensome task.

Purdue Social Support Scale

I am interested in knowing where people go when they need social support. Please answer the following questions as well as you can. Answer all questions in each section before moving on.

Your participation in this project is, of course, voluntary. All answers will be held in strict confidence.

PART I: Do not feel that you must fill all of the blanks below, but use as many as you want.

1. In times of need, people generally turn to others for help. In the spaces below, please list those people (first names only) who you would turn to.

2. Next to each name, please indicate each person's relation to you—for example, is he/she a friend, neighbor, spouse, parent, uncle, pastor, physician?

Below are six columns representing different ways in which people may be helpful. They are:

(a) EMOTIONAL SUPPORT .... referring to care, comfort, love, affection, sympathy, being on your side.

(b) ENCOURAGEMENT .... referring to being encouraging, praising, or complimenting you, making you feel important.

(c) ADVICE .... referring to advice as well as providing useful information and help with solving problems.

(d) COMPANIONSHIP .... referring to spending time together, doing things together, visiting each other.

(e) TANGIBLE AID .... referring to help with chores or projects, babysitting, transportation, and/or lending money when needed.

(f) OVERALL HELPFULNESS ...... referring to being generally helpful when needed.

3. Now, I am interested in knowing how satisfied you would expect to be with the support that these people may provide. In the boxes below, consider each person on the previous list according to the six characteristics defined above and rate your EXPECTED SATISFACTION with each person's help.

Use this scale to rate your satisfaction:

"4" means Very Satisfied
"3" means Satisfied
"2" means Dissatisfied
"1" means Very Dissatisfied
"0" means Wouldn't Seek This

Please fill all six boxes for each person listed.

PERSON(S)	(RELATIONSHIP)	EMOTIONAL	ENCOURAGE-MENT	ADVICE	COMPANION-SHIP	TANGIBLE AID	OVERALL HELPFULNESS

These functions are relevant to survivors of catastrophe because over-all social support is clearly linked to the emotional well-being of people in general and to the speed and completeness of recovery of victims in particular (Drabeck, Key, Erickson, & Crowe, 1975). Social support is the essence of family support.

FUNCTION OF THE FAMILY IN PTSD
DEVELOPMENT AND ABATEMENT

"How is this support important in both preventing and abating trau-matic and post-traumatic stress disorders?" I have suggested elsewhere that the family in particular and the entire social support system in general serve as an antidote to PTSD in four separate ways: detecting symptoms, confronting the problem, recapitulating the traumatic events, and resolving the trauma-inducing conflicts associated with the events (Figley, 1983). Let us consider each briefly to illustrate the key role family members play in limiting the emotional upset of traumatic events. First, however, it is important to briefly explicate the typical pattern of recovery from catastrophes apart from the contribution of the family and social support system.

Numerous clinical theorists have speculated on the post-traumatic recovery process of survivors diagnosed as having PTSD (cf., Figley, 1979; Horowitz, 1976; Green, Wilson, & Lindy, 1985). These speculations and the discrete criteria for PTSD specified in DSM-III (APA, 1980) have supported my assertion (Figley, 1980a, 1983) that survivors of catastro-phe are struggling to master the impressions and memories of the ca-tastrophe in toto and the traumatic induction. The traumatic induction is the imprinting of impressions of sensations and affect associated with feeling out of control, helpless, caught off guard. Thus, soon after sur-viving the catastrophe, after experiencing a period of safety (Horowitz, 1976), the survivor attempts to answer five fundamental questions. The answers to these questions, I believe, serve as the antidote to PTSD:

1. What happened to me?
2. How did it happen?
3. Why me?
4. Why did I act as I did?
5. What will I do in another catastrophe?

Recently Figley (1983) has attempted to apply this cognitive struggle to

victims of eight different catastrophes and the ways in which the victims
and their families have attempted to master or cope with the various
stressors (the catastrophes reviewed include chronic childhood diseases,
teen drug abuse, death, unemployment, rape, natural disaster, war, and
captivity by terrorists).

Detection of the Symptoms

The concept of family is derived from the Latin term *familia*, which
means household, including everyone who lives there (slaves, housekeeper, friends, mother-in-law, etc.). Anyone bound by a household—be
they biologically or legally tied—becomes well aware of everyone else
living in that household simply by being in close proximity. Add to this
familiarity the similarities of disposition and temperament and what
emerges in most families is a remarkably sensitive "feel" for the moods
and traits of fellow family members. Thus, when one member is having
a "bad day," we are able to detect it almost immediately and employ
various tactics to help.

For family members who have endured an especially traumatic event
(e.g., war), and who return to the family, there is an excellent chance
that one or more family members will be able to detect emotional upset.

Confrontation of the Problem

In addition to *detecting* a problem, family members are in a key position
to urge and help the victim to confront the problem. Clinicians spend
untold clinical sessions attempting to establish rapport and trust, identify, and *confront* the problems of a client when the victim's own family
is generally better prepared to do it and in less time. On a regular basis
and in an endless variety of ways, family members urge each other to
face and deal with a problem.

Recapitulation of the Catastrophe

A third way that families provide social support to victims which
results in mitigating or abating their traumatic reactions is in assisting
them to reconsider the traumatic events, a process known as recapitulation. Family members are able to help the victim recall additional information useful in viewing the events with greater clarity, correcting
views that have been associated with feelings of guilt, self-hatred, disrespect, and other characteristic signs of PTSD.

Resolution of the Trauma-inducing Conflicts

Finally, the family can be extremely useful in helping the victim "work through" (Horowitz, 1976) his or her traumatic experiences and conflicts. Most important, a family member serves as a facilitator (e.g., passive or active, mutual self-disclosure or one-sided, confrontive or nonconfrontive) for the victim by encouraging him or her to talk about the troubling experiences while at the same time "cleaning up after" the victim by (a) clarifying insights, (b) correcting distortions, (c) placing blame and credit more objectively, and (d) offering or supporting new and more "generous" or accurate perspectives on the event that was originally traumatic. Thus, in this process the victim will find answers to the questions, noted earlier, of all catastrophe victims: "What happened to me?" "How did it happen?" "Why me?" "Why did I act as I did?" and "What will I do in another catastrophe?"

Summary of Functions of the Family

To summarize the natural family support system function in dealing with traumatic reactions, let us return to the Allen family to serve as an illustration. As Paula became more alert and able to recognize and converse with her family, they began to detect various signs and symptoms alerting them to the fact that she was extremely upset by the accident (apart from the grief of a widow and the physical injuries). Slowly and gently Mary began to urge Paula to talk about her experiences. Mary was convinced, based on numerous other traumatic experiences with which she had helped Paula throughout her childhood and adolescence, that Paula would "feel better" if she "talked about it."

Finally, after being released to her parents for additional recuperation, weeks after the accident, Paula revealed something to her mother that she herself had wanted to forget. She had forgotten about it except in brief episodes of recall, which she fought against more and more effectively as time went by. She recalled that she had consumed three glasses of wine the night of the accident and Carl would not let her drive. Instead, they left early so that she could have several cups of coffee at the airport before attempting to drive back. She became enraged with him for forcing her to ride along since she always drove at night, because of Carl's poor night vision. "Had I driven, we may have avoided the other driver altogether. Instead, Carl died only minutes after I screamed at him for forcing me to ride along like a drunk. I killed Carl!" It did not take clever semantic manipulation or therapeutic wizardry on the part of Mrs. Allen to help her daughter adopt an alternate perspective on the event, which she did in a relatively brief period of time. There were other ruminations and resolutions throughout the recovery period, each one dealt with in turn.

Elsewhere Figley (1983) has discussed the functional methods families utilize in managing and coping with catastrophic stress in particular and family-related stress in general. The 11 characteristics identified (acceptance of the stressor, family-centered problem, solution-oriented problem, high tolerance, commitment/affection, communication, cohesion, flexible roles, resource utilization, avoidance of violence, and substance abuse) characterize an ideal family environment for employing the family functions noted above and illustrated by the interactions between Mrs. Allen and her daughter, Paula.

EMPATHY AS THE FAMILY'S ACHILLES' HEEL

For the same reasons the family is extremely effective in helping its traumatized member overcome their highly stressful experiences, the family itself is also susceptible to being traumatized in the process: The reason is love. What may be at the root of both love and effective "therapeutic" intervention is *empathy,* a critical attribute of interpersonal competence and social effectiveness (Guerney, 1978). Thus, just as Achilles was effective as a Greek warrior with his only vulnerability his heel, so family members are extremely effective in helping fellow family members work through their traumatic experiences, yet they are vulnerable to the consequences of their assistance by the very mechanism that makes them so effective: Their strength as well as their Achilles' heel is empathy.

This phenomenon is not unlike that of *couvade* (Taylor, 1965; Hunter & Macalpine, 1963), a custom among some isolated cultures in which the father of the expectant child mimics the pregnancy and labor of the mother. In some cases this simulation includes psychosomatic maladies that match the symptoms of their wives including swollen abdomens, complaints of diarrhea, and vomiting in the absence of medical causes (cf. Rabkin & Struening, 1976). Psychosomatic medicine has reported similar phenomena, such as entire families developing various maladies directly associated with some family-centered upheaval such as residential mobility (Mann, 1972) or divorce (Hetherington, Cox, & Cox, 1976).

In Paula's case, for example, the parents not only suffered from more psychosomatic illnesses (e.g., headaches, skin rashes, colds, coughs) during the recovery period, they also had bouts of sleeplessness and nightmares about the fate of their son-in-law. They were often startled more easily while traveling in an automobile, seemed preoccupied and forgetful at times, and became far more protective of their children, much to the dismay of the children.

Thus, in considering our fourth question—is it possible that those who are most effective in *abating* this emotional stress in others are also more susceptible to being traumatized themselves in the process?—we find that the families of catastrophe are also *victims* of catastrophe—whether they experienced the catastrophe first hand or through a family member—and require the same considerations for treatment that the other victims receive.

INDICATIONS FOR ASSISTING THE FAMILIES OF CATASTROPHE

Our final question, then, is: "What should be done for the families of catastrophe?" This question has consumed a considerable amount of my attention in the last three years since expanding my interest from veterans exclusively to survivors of other traumatic events. This interest assumed new importance when Figley organized a national team of scholars to help the State Department develop a program of assistance for a small but significant group of families of catastrophe (the families of those Americans held hostage in Iran). What was recommended then in a 600-page report (Figley, 1980b; Figley & McCubbin, 1983b) gained considerable importance as that crisis unfolded and is now behind us, since nearly all of our recommendations were followed, including the reentry program and reunion.

Irrespective of the catastrophic event and its circumstances, there are several general principles of policy and practice that should be considered in assisting the families of catastrophe and thereby assisting the immediate victims.

Public Policy

Members of victim families should be viewed as also susceptible to the emotional trauma associated with a catastrophe while at the same time serving as a critical resource for assisting in the recovery. Thus, corporations, governmental entities (including the military), relief organizations, and the media should deal with them accordingly. This should include abandoning the outdated "next of kin" orthodoxy, which suggests that responsibility for the welfare of the families of victims does not extend beyond notification and payment of funds owed.

As a matter of policy, general public-education programs should be initiated to emphasize the importance of the family, its connection to catastrophes and their wake, and the ways and means of helping family members cope with the resulting emotional upset. Such a program, for instance, was initiated at the end of World War II to inform families of the best methods for handling the homecoming and reintegration of their returning servicemen and women. One product, a 15-cent pamphlet, "When He Comes Back and If He Comes Back Nervous" (Rennie & Woodward, 1944), urged family members to:

1. Love him and welcome him.
2. Listen well.
3. Face the reality of the disability—don't ignore it.
4. Treat him as an essentially normal, upstanding, competent person, not as an invalid.
5. Commend his efforts and successes and ignore the slips.
6. Expect him to be different in some ways.
7. Allow him time and freedom in getting acquainted with the old places and in reestablishing his old contacts.
8. Create an atmosphere of expectancy: encourage him to take up his favorite hobby or sport, to go back to work as soon as he is able, and to lead a normal social life; but avoid pushing or regulating him (like the military).
9. Get professional help if it is needed. Don't just muddle through.
10. Let your own faith and beauty of spirit be your chief stock in trade.

The booklet also included an understandable overview of combat-related stress reactions and a guide to community services and other resources.

Similarly, in-service training for all mental health professionals should include the role of the family in catastrophe and its needs. Medical specialists, for example, would benefit from an understanding of the special sources of stress for families of the hospitalized. Such a program is now underway on an experimental basis at Boston City Hospital, linking with nine other medical facilities. While mental health specialists are now receiving more training in the family area, they still receive little regarding the special circumstances of the families of catastrophe. Certainly the Veterans Administration and the Disabled American Veterans outreach programs are far head of their contemporaries in their recognition of the importance of the family.

Indeed, the preliminary results of a national study of victim services in the United States suggest that veterans' centers are not only more educated about catastrophe and its impact, but view the family as a client as well as the veteran and rate "relationship difficulties" as the most significant long-term emotional problem (Rich, 1983).

Moreover, there are thousands of professionals who work directly with families: counselors, therapists, clergy, educators, emergency assistance specialists, the Red Cross, and others. Their guidance to families struggling to cope with catastrophes could be invaluable. Training them in the basics of family stress management would create important resources for families (Figley & McCubbin, 1983b).

Treatment

With regard to clinical intervention, it was implied in earlier writings (Figley, 1976a, 1976b; Figley & Sprenkle, 1978; Stanton & Figley, 1978) and explicitly stated in more recent ones (Figley, 1984, 1985; Hogancamp & Figley, 1983) that a group context—be it family or rap groups—is inefficient for ameliorating PTSD in its more advanced and profound forms. To include the family before the victim has effectively confronted and worked through the traumatic aspects of some of these conflicts would undermine or at least slow the progress and solidify the perception of the victim as the identified patient, rather than the whole family. It is appropriate, however, to see the spouses (and, in rare instances, older children) individually or in groups to explore their special stressors and how to manage them.

Eventually it is important to incorporate the entire family relationship (conjoint therapy). The emphasis in the intervention is on integrating the catastrophic experiences and their wake (impacting both the victim/veteran and his/her family) into the family. This is done by first determining (1) how the catastrophic experiences and the family problem(s) in which it is embedded are affecting each individual family member; (2) how the behavior of family members may be reinforcing or exacerbating the difficulties; (3) whether the family members have any understanding of the immediate and long-term consequences of the catastrophe; and (4) how best to cope with these consequences—through either new strategies, new skills, or both. Most often, the catastrophe-related difficulties fade and are replaced with stressors that have emerged subsequently (e.g., family violence, substance abuse) partly or entirely in an attempt to cope with catastrophe in general or the symptoms of PTSD in particular.

CONCLUSION

War, terrorism, rape, and other violent acts of man and nature rarely result in progress and most often eventuate in countless human tragedies that impact for a lifetime: lost lives, limbs, esteem, confidence, and income, to name only a few. This is the depressive nature of catastrophe: it hurts. However, the *inspiration* that accompanies catastrophes and its wake is equally significant.

Irrespective of the circumstances of the particular catastrophe, of the families it impacts, *families of catastrophe survive*. And more than simply surviving, most go on to lead happy and productive lives. Time does heal the wounds, but only to the extent that with time come perspective and resourceful ways of coping, which most families somehow find and effectively utilize.

By adequate attention to the health and vitality of the family system, victims of catastrophe may rely on a powerful stress-coping resource. And by supplemental consultation to families regarding the functional methods for coping with catastrophic stress, it is possible to more effectively care for the millions of victims of various traumatic events that occur yearly.

REFERENCES

American Psychiatric Association (1980). *Diagnostic and statistical manual of mental disorders* (3rd ed.). Washington, DC: American Psychiatric Association.

Burge, S. K. (1982). The social support scale: Development and initial estimates of reliability and validity of a measure of social support. Unpublished master's thesis, Purdue University.

Burge, S. K., & Figley, C. R. (1982). The social support scale. Unpublished manuscript, Purdue University.

Burgess, A. W., & Holmstrom, L. L. (1979). *Rape: Crisis and recovery*. Bowie, MD: Robert J. Brady.

Burr, W. R. (1973). *Theory construction and the sociology of the family*. New York: Wiley.

Drabeck, T., Key, W., Erickson, P., & Crowe, J. (1975). The impact of disaster on kin relationships. *Journal of Marriage and the Family, 37*(3), 481–494.

Figley, C. R. (1975). The returning veteran and interpersonal adjustment: A review of the research. Paper presented at the annual meeting of the National Council on Family Relations, Salt Lake City, August 1975.

Figley, C. R. (1976a). The Vietnam veteran in family therapy: Implications from the research. Paper presented at the annual meeting of American Personnel and Guidance Association, Chicago, March 1976.

Figley, C. R. (1976b). An overview of the research related to delayed combat stress among Vietnam veterans. Paper presented at the annual meeting of the American Psychological Association, Washington, DC, September 1976.

Figley, C. (Ed.) (1978). *Stress disorders among Vietnam veterans.* New York: Brunner/Mazel.

Figley, C. R. (1979). Combat as disaster: Treating combat veterans as survivors. Invited presentation at the annual meeting of the American Psychiatric Association, Chicago, 1979.

Figley, C. R. (1980a). Overview of the trauma of hostage families. Invited address at the annual meeting of the National Organization for Victim Assistance, Portland, Oregon, October 1980.

Figley, C. R. (Ed.) (1980b). *Mobilization. I: The Iranian crisis: Final report of the Task Force on Families of Catastrophe.* Purdue University, Family Research Institute.

Figley, C. R. (1983). Catastrophe: An overview of family reactions. In C. R. Figley & H. I. McCubbin (Eds.), *Stress and the family, Vol. II: Coping with catastrophe.* New York: Brunner/Mazel.

Figley, C. R. (1984). Treating post-traumatic stress disorder: The algorithmic approach. *The American Academy of Psychiatry and the Law Newsletter,* 9(3).

Figley, C. R. (1985). From victim to survivor: Social responsibility in the wake of catastrophe. In C. R. Figley (Ed.), *Trauma and its wake: The study and treatment of post-traumatic stress disorder.* New York: Brunner/Mazel.

Figley, C. R., & Burge, S. K. (1983). Social support: Theory and measurement. Presented at the Groves Conference on Marriage and the Family, Freeport, Grand Bahama Island, 1983.

Figley, C. R., & McCubbin, H. I. (1983a). Introduction. In C. R. Figley & H. I. McCubbin (Eds.), *Stress and the family, Vol. II: Coping with catastrophe.* New York: Brunner/Mazel.

Figley, C. R., & McCubbin, H. I. (1983b). Looking to the future: Research, education, treatment and policy. In C. R. Figley & H. I. McCubbin (Eds.), *Stress and the family, Vol. II: Coping with catastrophe.* New York: Brunner/Mazel.

Figley, C. R., & Sprenkle, D. H. (1978). Delayed stress response syndrome: Family therapy indications. *Journal of Marriage and Family Counseling,* 4, 53–60.

Gleser, G. C., Green, L., & Winget, C. (1981). *Prolonged psychosocial effects of disaster: A study of Buffalo Creek.* New York: Academic Press.

Green, B. L., Wilson, J. P., & Lindy, J. (1985). Conceptualizing post-traumatic stress disorder: A psychosocial framework. In C. R. Figley (Ed.), *Trauma and its wake: The study and treatment of post-traumatic stress disorder.* New York: Brunner/Mazel.

Guerney, B. (1978). *Relationship enhancement.* San Francisco: Jossey-Bass.

Hetherington, E. M., Cox, M., & Cox, R. (1976). Divorced fathers. *The Family Coordinator,* 25, 417–428.

Hirsch, B. J. (1980). Natural support systems and coping with major life changes. *American Journal of Community Psychology,* 8, 159–171.

Hogancamp, V. E., & Figley, C. R. (1983). War: Bring the battle home. In C. R. Figley & H. I. McCubbin (Eds.), *Stress and the family, Vol. II: Coping with catastrophe.* New York: Brunner/Mazel.

Horowitz, M. J. (1976). *Stress response syndrome.* New York: Aronson, Inc.

Hunter, R., & Macalpine, I. (1963). *Three hundred years of psychiatry 1535–1860.* London: Oxford University Press.

Janis, I. L. (1969). *Stress and frustration.* New York: Harcourt Brace Jovanovich.

Lifton, R. J. (1973). *Home from the war.* New York: Simon & Schuster.

Lifton, R. J. (1978). Advocacy and corruption in the healing profession. In C. R. Figley (Ed.), *Stress disorders among Vietnam veterans: Theory, research and treatment* (pp. 209–230). New York: Brunner/Mazel.

Mann, P. (1972). Residential mobility as an adaptive experience. *Journal of Consulting Clinical Psychology, 39,* 37–42.

McCubbin, H. I., & Figley, C. R. (1983). *Stress and the family, Vol. I: Coping with normative transitions.* New York: Brunner/Mazel.

Mineka, S. (1979). The role of fear in theories of avoidance learning, flooding, and extinction. *Psychological Bulletin, 86,* 985–1010.

Neiderland, W. G. (1968). Clinical observations on the "survivor syndrome." *International Journal of Psychoanalysis, 49,* 313–318.

Rabkin, J. G., & Struening, E. L. (1976). Life events, stress and illness. *Science, 194,* 1013–1020.

Rennie, T. A. C., & Woodward, L. E. (1944). Two talks to families of returning servicemen: "When he comes back and if he comes back nervous," with guide to community resources. New York: New York Rehabilitation Division, National Committee for Mental Hygiene, Inc.

Rich, R. (1983). Providing services to victims: An empirical investigation. Paper presented at the 7th World Congress of Psychiatry, Vienna, 1983.

Smith, J. R. (1981). A review of one hundred and twenty years of the psychological literature on reactions to combat from the Civil War through the Vietnam War: 1860–1980. Unpublished manuscript, Duke University.

Smith, S. M. (1983). Disaster: Family disruption in the wake of natural disaster. In C. R. Figley & H. I. McCubbin (Eds.), *Stress and the family, Vol. II: Coping with Catastrophe.* New York: Brunner/Mazel.

Stanton, M. D., & Figley, C. R. (1978). Treating veterans within the family system. In C. R. Figley (Ed.), *Stress disorders among Vietnam veterans: Theory, research and treatment* (pp. 283–284). New York: Brunner/Mazel.

Taylor, E. B. (1965). Research into the early history of mankind and the development of civilization. In R. Hunter & I. Macalpine (Eds.), *Three hundred years of psychiatry 1535–1860.* London: Oxford University Press.

Thoits, P. A. (1982). Conceptual, methodological, and theoretical problems in studying social support as a buffer against life stress. *Journal of Health and Social Behavior, 23,* 145–159.

Weisman, A., & Hackett, R. (1961). Predilection to death: Death and dying as a psychiatric problem. *Psychosomatic Medicine, 33* (3), 389–393.

Wolpe, J. (1973). *The practice of behavior therapy.* Elmsford, NY: Pergamon.

SECTION II

Research

4

Post-Traumatic Stress as a Function of Chronic Stress and Toxic Exposure

LAURA M. DAVIDSON, INDIA FLEMING,
and ANDREW BAUM

With the increasing prevalence of complex technology in our modern world, the potential for human-made disasters is becoming greater. Of particular significance is the enhanced potential for disasters that involve the release of hazardous substances (e.g., radiation and toxic chemicals) into the environment. When toxicity is involved, catastrophes or accidents appear to cause chronic stress among those who believe they may have been exposed (Baum, Gatchel, & Schaeffer, 1983; Fleming & Baum, 1985). The symptoms of chronic stress found in these victims include some of the complaints or problems used as diagnostic criteria to define post-traumatic stress disorder (PTSD) as noted in the *Diagnostic and Statistical Manual of Mental Disorders*, third edition (APA, 1980), raising questions about the nature of these accidents and the relationship between chronic stress and PTSD. This chapter explores these issues, using data collected from people living near the crippled Three Mile Island (TMI)

This work was supported by the Uniformed Services University of the Health Sciences (Protocol No. C07216) and the National Science Foundation (BNS8317997). The opinions or assertions contained herein are the private ones of the authors and are not to be construed as official or reflecting the views of the Department of Defense or the Uniformed Services University of the Health Sciences.

57

nuclear power plant and from an area near a hazardous toxic waste dump to illustrate these relationships.

Typically, PTSD is viewed as a syndrome caused by a single, extremely threatening, vivid event. Much of the research on PTSD has studied veterans of combat or victims of clearly defined, powerful traumas or accidents (e.g., Wilson, Smith, & Johnson, 1983; Figley, 1978a). It is likely, however, that PTSD-like symptoms may develop following less powerful or immediately threatening events that pose chronic or recurrent danger. The likelihood of low-magnitude chronic stress causing PTSD-like symptoms, the role of duration of a stressor in changing the intensity or impact of an event, and the possibility that persistent stress may be associated with PTSD symptoms have not been adequately considered. Research examining psychobiological responses to living near the site of accidents or mishaps that involve the possibility of exposure to toxic substances may help to clarify these relationships.

POST-TRAUMATIC STRESS

Exposure to stressors can be associated with psychological and physiological sequelae, and PTSD may be one of the most profound psychophysiological outcomes of a stress experience. Post-traumatic stress follows events that are typically considered outside the realm of normal human experience. While major life events like death of a family member, chronic illness, or divorce have been associated with adverse psychological and physiological outcomes (Bartop, Luckhurst, Lazarus, Kiloh, & Penny, 1977; Holmes & Rahe, 1967), they appear less likely to lead to post-traumatic stress states than do cataclysmic events, which severely tax coping abilities and generally overwhelm those involved (Lazarus & Cohen, 1977). Events most often associated with PTSD are of human origin; numerous reports of post-traumatic stress have been documented in former prisoners of war, survivors of concentration camps, and combat veterans. In particular, the Vietnam War seems to have produced an unprecedented number of post-traumatic stress casualties (Figley, 1978b). Other accidents or catastrophes, which are not deliberate, have also been associated with PTSD. However, reports of PTSD are less common following events such as airplane crashes and fires like the ones at the Beverly Hills or Coconut Grove night clubs (e.g., Adler, 1943; Green, 1980) than they are following deliberate acts such as war. Natural disasters such as floods, tornadoes, hurricanes, and blizzards have also been associated with symptoms of PTSD, but the symptoms appear to be less severe than when stressors are planned or are of human origin.

The literature on disasters provides some support for this distinction between the mental health consequences of natural and human-made stressors. Whereas the negative effects of natural disaster appear to be rather short-lived, typically not extending further than the immediate period of impact and recovery, the consequences of technological disasters seem to be more long-lasting and hence more likely to lead to chronic stress (Baum, Fleming, & Davidson, 1983). Although these data suggest that technological disasters are more stressful than natural ones, survivors of these types of events have not typically been assessed for symptoms of PTSD. It is possible that the chronicity of many human-made disasters makes them more potent and increases the likelihood of psychophysiological changes similar to those characterizing post-traumatic stress. These changes may occur even when the precipitating event lacks many of the characteristics common to trauma.

Although the signs and symptoms of PTSD have been observed for centuries, it has only been recently that psychologists and psychiatrists have recognized it as a distinct psychophysiological disorder. Initial cases of postaccident symptoms were thought to be caused by microstructural lesions in the nervous system that resulted from an injury to the spinal cord or brain (Erichsen, 1882). This was quickly challenged, and the importance of psychological factors in the etiology of the syndrome was introduced (Page, 1885). However, the importance of these factors was not immediately accepted. Even today, while some researchers try to understand the pathogenesis of the disorder in terms of physiological changes in systems like the sympathetic nervous system (de la Pena, 1984) or endogenous opioid system (van der Kolk, Boyd, Krystal, & Greenberg, 1984), others focus on psychological factors such as premorbid personality factors and styles of coping and appraisal in their examination of the etiology of PTSD (Hendin & Haas, 1984). A more comprehensive view of PTSD would integrate both physiological and psychological perspectives.

PTSD is typically defined in terms of the diagnostic criteria listed in the DSM-III (APA, 1980). Although a number of symptoms are listed, including guilt and psychic numbing, two of the primary dimensions of the disorder involve intrusive thoughts about the traumatic events and avoidance of stimuli associated with the trauma. Intrusive thoughts include recurrent recollections of the initiating event, dreams, and feeling as if the traumatic events were actually happening again. Avoidance or decreased involvement in the outside world can result in numerous social problems including loss of interest in activities or friends. Constricted affect is also associated with this dimension, and anxiety and depression are common forms of expression. Individuals with PTSD exhibit some symptoms of autonomic changes as well, including hyperalertness, and often report sleep difficulties, memory impairment, and difficulty concentrating.

DEFINING STRESS

As with the development of theories of PTSD, the history of stress research has been marked by the development of separate disciplinary traditions with literatures that have only recently begun to be integrated. Psychological and endocrinological discussion of stress (e.g., Lazarus, 1966; Selye, 1956) developed in isolation from one another resulting in limitation to both perspectives. More recent approaches emphasizing points of interaction between these lines of research have suggested a more comprehensive perspective (e.g., Baum, Singer, & Baum, 1981; Frankenhaeuser, 1975; Mason, 1975a).

Stress may be defined as the process by which environmental events or stressors tax coping abilities or pose a threat to an organism. During stress an organism must find ways of dealing with environmental demands. Thus, the occurrence of a stressor is met by some response designed to remove it or its effects, which continues until the episode subsides. As this process unfolds, there are psychological and physiological changes. Following resolution of a particular situation, additional changes or aftereffects may occur. However, attempts to manipulate or accommodate to environmental demands are not always successful. The success of coping and the persistence and intensity of the demand determine whether negative consequences are likely to occur. These consequences involve integrated sets of biological and psychological changes, which may be mild or severe.

Many different types of events can be stressors, and what is stressful for one person may not be stressful for all people. In an attempt to categorize stressful events, Lazarus and Cohen (1977) divided stressors into three groups—cataclysmic events, personal stressors, and background stressors. Cataclysmic events are powerful and sudden and are likely to have an impact on large numbers of people. War, natural disasters, including earthquakes and storms, and technological disasters such as the one at TMI are examples of these types of events. The stress component of a natural disaster is usually brief, and recovery typically occurs quickly. The consequences of technological events often linger when hazardous substances are involved. For example, as in the case of women given diethylstilbestrol as a prevention for miscarriages who later discovered the delayed effects that this drug can have on female offspring (Herbst, Robboy, Scully, & Poskanzer, 1974), the consequences of exposure to toxic chemicals or radiation may not be evident for years. This chronicity and uncertainty often make coping with technological stressors more difficult. And, according to the DSM-III, cataclysmic events are most often associated with PTSD.

The second type of stressor described by Lazarus and Cohen is personal stressors. They are powerful events that again require adaptive and efficient coping. The main difference between these types of stressors and cataclysmic events is that personal stressors affect fewer people. Background stressors or daily hassles represent the third type of stressor. They are best thought of as low-magnitude events that are persistent or repetitive in daily life, such as commuting and crowding. They may not pose an immediate threat, but their effects appear to be negative and cumulative.

Selye's biological view of the consequences of stressors has dominated the field of stress research for several decades. He described a triad of effects that he found could be caused by any noxious stimulus that he applied. As a result, he believed that these consequences were nonspecifically induced by any threat. The triad included enlargement of the adrenal glands, shrinkage of the thymus, and ulcers. Selye also described the process by which organisms respond to noxious events, referring to it as the "general adaptation syndrome" (GAS). Again, the GAS is triggered by any noxious event and hence is nonspecific. Three stages are involved in the GAS—alarm, resistance, and exhaustion. During the alarm phase the organism readies itself to respond by increasing vital functions like heart rate, blood pressure, respiration, and adrenal activity. When these systems are readied, the stage of resistance is reached. If resistance is low or the stressor is severe enough or is sufficiently long-lasting, adaptive reserves are depleted and exhaustion ensues. During exhaustion, organ systems can be damaged.

In spite of their separate development, there are interesting parallels between theories of stress and theories of PTSD. Notably, Kamman (1951) and Kardiner (1947) conceptualized post-traumatic stress in ways similar to the GAS, noting that PTSD reactions occurred when the adaptive capabilities of an individual were exhausted. Although Selye did not clarify the role or importance of psychological factors in his theory of the GAS, others have. Mason has argued that the physiological changes described by Selye do not occur unless psychological distress is present. Mason (1975b) found that adrenal activity was elicited only under specific psychological conditions. Other studies have provided support for the importance of psychological factors. For example, Symington, Currie, Curran, and Davidson (1955) compared a group of conscious dying patients to a group of comatose dying patients. They found that on autopsy, those in the conscious dying group exhibited greater enlargement of the adrenal gland than did those in the comatose group. These results highlight the importance of psychological mediators in stress responding.

Lazarus (1975) also emphasized the importance of psychological factors in his conceptualization of stress responding. According to Lazarus, only when events are perceived as threatening will stress responding ensue (Lazarus, 1966). His research provided evidence of the importance of psychological factors in stress responding in the same way that psychological factors are necessary to understand symptom formation in PTSD. With the integration of psychological and physiological theories, our understanding of stress responding has become more comprehensive.

Like the symptoms of PTSD, psychological and physiological changes result from chronic stress. Exposure to stressors appears to cause changes in mental status such as anxiety and depression (e.g., Mears & Gatchel, 1979). Stress responding has been associated with increased symptom reporting in general and may also cause cognitive deficits such as performance and motivational decrements (Glass & Singer, 1972). Because people may narrow their attention range in order to avoid a stressor, they may also miss relevant environmental stimuli (Cohen, 1978). Stress also causes alterations in many systems of the body, including the endocrine system, the immune system, the cardiovascular system, the respiratory system, the renal system, and the opioid system (e.g., Baum et al., 1981; Mason, 1975b).

STRESS AND PTSD

There are reasons to believe that exposure to a wide variety of stressors may lead to symptoms of PTSD. Although PTSD and general stress measures are not generally evaluated simultaneously, there are many similarities between them. Under normal conditions, chronic stress appears to be associated with moderate levels of anxiety and depressed affect (Baum, Gatchel, & Schaeffer, 1983), and there is some evidence that sleep problems may also occur during stress episodes (Fleming & Baum, 1983). Changes related to arousal of the sympathetic nervous system also characterize chronic stress, as do alterations in attentiveness to the world and, in some cases, withdrawal and decreased social responsiveness. All of these problems are also characteristic of PTSD, though in more severe form. In addition, PTSD is caused by a stressor that might have resulted in a "normal" stress response or one that did not reach DSM-III criteria. That is, symptoms of PTSD and chronic stress are thought to occur only after adaptive abilities have been exceeded or sorely taxed, and both appear to be integrated sets of physiological and psychological responses. In fact, many stressors that have been associated with PTSD do not appear to cause severe problems for all involved. Some react to these events as if they were manageable stressors and never show symptoms of PTSD. PTSD may reflect the stage of exhaustion that Selye described, and the chronicity of a stressor may contribute to reaching this stage just as intensity does.

Research designed to examine the chronic stress effects of two groups of subjects, one living near the damaged TMI nuclear power station and the other living within one mile of a hazardous toxic dump site, suggests that these residents exhibit symptoms of chronic stress and of post-traumatic stress. Symptoms of hyperarousal have been documented in both groups using urinary catecholamine and cortisol measures (Baum, Gatchel, & Schaeffer, 1983; Fleming & Baum, 1981). Also, sleep disturbances have been noted among TMI area residents (Davidson, Fleming, & Baum, 1984b). Interpersonal problems, alienation, and depression have been found in the two groups, suggesting withdrawal and avoidance (Davidson, Fleming, & Baum, 1984a). Although these symptoms are suggestive of PTSD, we have not assessed other symptoms of the disorder, such as intrusive and avoidance thinking.

Stress at TMI and the Landfill

The accident at TMI occurred in March 1979. During the accident, levels of coolant water dropped in the reactor core, generating extremely high temperatures. These high temperatures caused equipment to fuse and some radiation to be released into the environment, though estimates of how much radiation vary. Following the accident, over 400,000 gallons of radioactive water remained on the floor of the reactor building. Also during the accident, radioactive krypton gas was released and trapped in the containment building of the reactor. After the accident the contaminated gas periodically leaked from the containment building until it was completely released in a series of controlled ventings about 15 months later. Only recently has the radioactive water been treated, and still the damaged reactor core remains.

It is not surprising that researchers found acute stress effects immediately following the accident and two-week emergency period. Stress effects included demoralization, depression, heightened symptom reporting, and increased substance use among people living near the plant (Dohrenwend, Dohrenwend, Kasl, & Warheit, 1979; Houts, Miller, Tokuhata, & Ham, 1980). Others found increased levels of anxiety and depression (Bromet, 1980) and greater symptom reporting up to nine months following the accident.

We began studying TMI residents 15 months after the accident. At this time officials planned to begin controlled venting of the radioactive krypton gas that had been trapped in the containment building. This venting procedure provided the opportunity to study anticipatory effects of the venting, the effects of the actual venting, and postventing effects. Our research has been able to document stress using symptom reporting, task performance, and physiological measures. This began a longitudinal study of stress at TMI, which has continued at six-month intervals over the past five years. This effort has documented elevated stress levels throughout this assessment suggesting the chronic nature of the subjects' responses.

Another group of subjects is composed of people residing within a one-mile radius of a landfill containing toxic waste in a mid-Atlantic state. Although some local residents had been concerned about the landfill previously, virtually all neighborhood residents became aware of the danger in December 1982, when the Environmental Protection Agency (EPA) listed this site among the 10 most potentially hazardous waste sites in the country. At that time the EPA reported the presence of several hazardous chemicals in the soil and some of the water supplies.

Although few studies have examined stress among people living near toxic waste dumps, there is some evidence that there may be stress in these groups. Levine (1982) reported that many residents of the Love Canal neighborhood described themselves as being stressed. Edelstein (1982) reported similar findings from interviews with people living near a toxic dump site in New Jersey. Gibbs (1982) also found that residents living near the New Jersey site had elevated levels of depression. We began studying people living near our toxic waste dump approximately seven months after the EPA ratings. Data collected at this time indicated that stress measures were elevated in this group relative to controls (Fleming, 1985). The present study consists of data from our second assessment about a year after the EPA announcement.

Because of the similarities between PTSD and stress, we decided to evaluate PTSD in these two groups of stressed people.* Thus, research was designed to (1) measure continued chronic stress in the TMI and landfill groups, (2) better document PTSD symptoms in the two groups, and (3) examine the relationship between PTSD and chronic stress.

Measurement of Chronic Stress

Because stress is a "whole-body" response, we have used simultaneous assessments of psychological, behavioral, and biological measures as a composite estimate of stress (cf. Baum, Grunberg, & Singer, 1982). All of these measures can be used as indicators of either acute or chronic stress depending on the duration of the stressors. Because little is known about the nature of chronic stress, a number of measures typically used to study acute stress were initially used. Some, including those reported here, showed long-term change following the accident and are therefore believed to be pertinent to chronic stress. Psychological aspects of stress, including emotional change, somatic distress, concentration problems, and so on, are usually measured by self-reports. In our research, the SCL-90R has been used to measure these self-reported symptoms of stress (Derogatis, 1977). This instrument provides an estimate of overall distress and can be used to measure somatic complaints, problems with concentration and interpersonal relationships, depression, anxiety, anger, fear, suspiciousness, and alienation. Subjects are asked how often they have been bothered by each of the 90 listed symptoms during the previous two weeks. Responses are made on five-point scales ranging from "not at all" bothered by the symptoms to "extremely" bothered by the symptoms.

The Beck Depression Inventory (BDI) was also used as a self-report measure, providing an estimate of depressive symptomatology (Beck, 1967). The scale consists of 21 groups of statements. From each grouping, subjects are asked to choose the response that is most descriptive of him/her.

---

*A third group of subjects was included in this study as controls. Since no preaccident or precontamination variables were present for either the TMI or toxic group, it was particularly important to include a sample of nonvictimized subjects for comparison purposes. Although we will never be able to say for certain whether stress levels were elevated over preaccident baselines, a control group allows us to compare stress levels in our two stressed groups to a matched control group not experiencing any major environmental stressor. Some evidence of preaccident comparability among these groups is presented in Baum, Schaeffer, Lake, Fleming, and Collins (in press). TMI and control area residents exhibited comparable blood pressures during the year before the accident, and during the first postaccident year, TMI area subjects showed a significant increase in blood pressure whereas controls did not.

A behavioral measure of stress was obtained by measuring subjects' performance on a proofreading task (Glass & Singer, 1972). They were given five minutes to circle misspellings, typographical errors, punctuation errors, and grammatical errors that had been systematically inserted in a seven-page passage. Previous research has suggested that the ability to find errors is related to concentration, motivation, and/or tolerance for frustration; the fewer the inserted errors identified, the poorer the concentration, the lower the motivation, and/or the lower the tolerance for frustration. In their studies of noise stress, Glass and Singer (1972) found a relationship between stress and performance decrements on a similar task.

Hormones such as norepinephrine, epinephrine, and cortisol have been found to reflect stress-related arousal (Frankenhaeuser, 1973). For this reason, subjects provided urine samples that were assayed to provide physiological estimates of stress. Subjects were asked to void all urine between the hours of 6 P.M. one evening and 9 A.M. the following morning into a plastic specimen container containing a noncaustic preservative. A 15-hour sample was collected because it provides an overall estimate of adrenal functioning. Once the containers had been retrieved by the experimenters, the volume was measured, and a small sample was saved and frozen for later assay using COMT radioenzymatic procedures. Blood pressure and heart rate were also measured in order to determine cardiovascular arousal.

Assessment of Symptoms of PTSD

Some measures of chronic stress reflect diagnostic criteria for posttraumatic stress. Depression, alienation, interpersonal problems, and indicators of hyperarousal from the catecholamine and blood pressure data all bear on PTSD symptomatology. In addition, the Impact of Events Scale (IES; Horowitz, Wilner, & Alvarez, 1979) was used to assess symptom levels of PTSD. The IES contains two subscales, which are thought to parallel the two primary dimensions of PTSD. One provides a measure of intrusive thinking, including items about dreaming and unwanted images or reminders of the event. The other subscale estimates avoidance thinking. This dimension was measured with questions about staying away from the situation or avoiding reminders of it. While filling out the questionnaire, TMI subjects were first asked to think about the situation at TMI, landfill subjects to think about the toxic dump site, and control area subjects to think about major stressors they had recently experienced. With these events in mind, subjects were then asked to report the frequency of experiencing the symptoms of avoidance and intrusive thoughts over the last seven days. Subjects were able to respond to each item as experienced not at all, rarely, sometimes, or often.

Subjects and Procedures

A total of 114 subjects participated in the study, conducted in January 1984, nearly five years after the TMI accident and 14 months after discovery of the hazards at the toxic waste site. Fifty-three were selected from neighborhoods within five miles of TMI. A second group of subjects consisted of 27 people living within one mile of the toxic waste dump. The control group consisted of 35 subjects living in Frederick, Maryland, an area approximately 80 miles southwest of TMI and west of the dump site. At each site census data were used to target certain streets for evaluation, and every third house was then approached. In this way subjects were randomly sampled from matched areas. Response rates were greater than 70% at all three sites. Informed consent was obtained, and subjects were paid for their participation. Demographic information indicated that all subjects were of comparable age, gender, education, and income.

At all sites, experimenters made appointments to meet with the subjects in their homes. During the session, experimental procedures were explained. Following a brief introduction to the session and an opportunity for subjects to relax, three measurements of heart rate and blood pressure were taken. Next, the proofreading task was administered. Following the completion of the proofreading task, subjects were given directions for collection of the urine samples and for completion of the questionnaires. Before the experimenter left, subjects were given the opportunity to ask questions, and an appointment was made to pick up the urine and completed questionnaires on the following day.

Continuation of Chronic Stress

It was predicted that TMI and landfill residents would exhibit greater evidence of lasting stress than would control area residents. Table 1 summarizes the data from the self-report and performance measures of stress as well as biochemical and physiological measures. One-way analyses of variance were performed comparing the three groups on each of the stress variables. Orthogonal contrasts comparing each possible pairing of groups were also performed in order to determine which groups differed.

TABLE 1
Stress at Three Mile Island, Landfill, and Frederick

	TMI	Landfill	Frederick	P
SCL-90R global distress	34.63[a]	41.78[a]	16.06[b]	0.001
Somatic distress	0.70[a]	0.89[a]	0.21[b]	0.001
Concentration	0.80[a]	0.80[a]	0.24[b]	0.001
Interpersonal	0.56[a]	0.74[a]	0.24[b]	0.001
Depression	0.58[a]	0.89[b]	0.19[c]	0.001
Anxiety	0.67[a]	0.97[b]	0.15[c]	0.001
Anger	0.89[a]	1.14[a]	0.32[b]	0.001
Fear	0.29[a]	0.57[b]	0.05[c]	0.002
Suspiciousness	0.79[a]	1.12[b]	0.42[c]	0.001
Alienation	0.32[a]	0.42[a]	0.13[b]	0.005
Beck Depression Inventory	4.3[a]	8.7[b]	2.9[a]	0.001
Proofreading (% errors found)	35%[a]	38%[a]	60%[b]	0.001
Norepinephrine (ng/hr)	2064[a]	2210[a]	1158[b]	0.001
Epinephrine (ng/hr)	325[a]	449[b]	283[a]	0.1
Cortisol (mcg/hr)	321[a]	520[b]	156[c]	0.002
Systolic blood pressure (mm Hg)	125[a]	125[a]	117[b]	0.08
Diastolic blood pressure (mm Hg)	76[a]	76[a]	71[b]	0.01
Heart rate (beats/min)	76[a]	74[a]	68[b]	0.005

[a,b,c]Groups with different superscripts are significantly different.

Significant between-group differences were found on all of the self-report measures of emotional, somatic, and cognitive distress. This pattern of means was similar on the SCL-90R total symptom distress measure, on each of the subscales, and on the BDI. On each of these measures, TMI and landfill area residents showed elevated levels of distress compared to control subjects. Levels of stress found in the TMI and landfill groups were not usually significantly different, although landfill residents reported higher levels of symptoms on some of these scales.

The pattern of results on the proofreading task was similar to those found for self-report measures. Scores on this task were calculated by computing the percentage of errors found of the total possible errors in the portion of the passage read. A significant between-group difference was found on the proofreading task; residents of the control neighborhood performed significantly better on this task than did residents of either TMI or the landfill neighborhoods (see Table 1).

The physiological measures also suggested greater stress among the TMI and landfill groups. Levels of norepinephrine, epinephrine, and cortisol were calculated by determining the concentration of these hormones in the urine samples and then adjusting this concentration for the volume excreted during the 15-hour collection period. TMI and landfill area residents excreted more norepinephrine and epinephrine than did residents of the control area, but the difference was significant only for norepinephrine. Also, residents of the TMI and landfill neighborhoods had significantly higher levels of cortisol than did residents of the control area. The TMI and landfill groups also had significantly greater systolic and diastolic blood pressures as well as faster heart rates than did the control group (see Table 1). Overall, these data suggest that TMI and landfill area residents were continuing to experience stress-related physiological arousal long after the initial stressor had occurred.

These results show that TMI and landfill area residents were exhibiting self-report, behavioral, and physiological symptoms of stress consistent with our previous findings (Baum, Gatchel, & Schaeffer, 1983; Fleming & Baum, 1985). The results also confirm our hypothesis that victims of disasters involving hazardous substances may continue to experience stress months or years following the onset of these events. Moreover, the symptoms of stress found in the TMI and landfill groups, including anxiety, depression, interpersonal problems, and elevated physiological arousal, may be related to symptoms of PTSD.

Incidence of PTSD Symptoms

The Impact of Events Scale (IES) was used to more directly investigate the relationship between symptoms of stress and symptoms of PTSD. Again, one-way analyses of variance were calculated across the three groups to compare the incidence of avoidance and intrusive thinking. Table 2 summarizes the findings for the IES. Although residents of both the TMI and landfill neighborhoods reported more avoidance thinking, the differences were not significant. However, both TMI and landfill area residents reported experiencing more intrusive thoughts than did

TABLE 2
Impact of Events at Three Mile Island, Landfill, and Frederick

	TMI	Landfill	Frederick	P
Avoidance	8.54[a]	10.48[a]	5.79[b]	0.12
Intrusiveness	10.38[a]	13.00[a]	5.44[b]	0.005

[a,b]Groups with different superscripts are significantly different.

control area residents. These data suggest that victims of these disasters experienced intrusive thoughts about the event and to some extent appeared to have consciously avoided reminders of them, providing evidence for the existence of post-traumatic stress symptomatology in these two groups.

To examine the relationship between symptoms of chronic stress and PTSD, measures of chronic stress were correlated with the intrusion and avoidance subscales of the IES. These correlations are presented in Table 3. Results showed that intrusive thinking correlated positively with total symptom distress as well as somatic distress, difficulty concentrating, interpersonal problems, depression, anxiety, anger, fear, suspiciousness, and alienation. Avoidance thinking also correlated positively with each of these subscales of the SCL-90R. There was a significant negative correlation between the percentage of proofreading errors found and scores on the intrusion and avoidance subscales of the IES, indicating a relationship between concentration and/or motivation deficits and reported symptoms of PTSD. Correlations between the IES subscales and the physiological variables were not as strong, although norepinephrine, epinephrine, and cortisol were positively correlated with both intrusive

TABLE 3
Correlations of Impact of Events with Stress

	Avoidance	Intrusiveness
SCL-90R global distress	0.46[a]	0.61[a]
Somatic distress	0.41[a]	0.57[a]
Concentration	0.36[a]	0.49[a]
Interpersonal problems	0.37[a]	0.49[a]
Depression	0.46[a]	0.57[a]
Anxiety	0.44[a]	0.58[a]
Anger	0.40[a]	0.48[a]
Fear	0.32[a]	0.37[a]
Suspiciousness	0.26[a]	0.45[a]
Alienation	0.44[a]	0.50[a]
Proofreading (% errors found)	−0.23[a]	−0.37[a]
Norepinephrine (ng/hr)	0.40[a]	0.41[a]
Epinephrine (ng/hr)	0.34[a]	0.37[a]
Cortisol (mcg/hr)	0.42[a]	0.43[a]
Systolic blood pressure (mm Hg)	0.15	0.20[a]
Diastolic blood pressure (mm Hg)	0.06	0.08
Heart rate (beats/min)	0.15	0.13

[a]$p < 0.05$.

and avoidance thinking. However, the correlations with the cardiovascular measures showed a different pattern. There was a significant positive correlation between systolic blood pressure and intrusive thinking. Correlations between diastolic blood pressure and heart rate failed to reach significance for either subscale of the IES.

Overall, the correlations between stress symptoms and the IES suggest that symptoms of PTSD are associated with chronic stress. In order to test the hypothesis that TMI and landfill area residents with symptoms of PTSD would show more evidence of chronic stress, median splits were done on the intrusive and avoidance subscales of the IES separately. Subjects scoring above the median were designated as having high levels of intrusive and avoidance thoughts and those scoring below the median were classified as low-level reporters. Separate 2 × 3 analyses of variance were performed crossing level of either intrusive (high, low) *or* avoidance (high, low) thinking with residence (TMI, landfill, control). The measures of chronic stress were used as dependent variables.

The expected interactions of residence with intrusive and avoidance thoughts were found for symptom reporting. Although some of the differences only approached significance, they were in the predicted direction. TMI and landfill residents who reported the most intrusive and avoidance thinking also reported more symptoms than did anyone else. Specifically, TMI and landfill residents who scored high on intrusive and avoidance thinking reported more somatic complaints, concentration difficulties, interpersonal problems, depression, anxiety, anger, fear, suspiciousness, and alienation than did TMI and landfill residents, who were low on intrusive and avoidance thinking, and residents of the control neighborhood (see Table 4).

Although the interaction term failed to reach significance for the proofreading task, the means were in the expected directions. TMI and landfill subjects reporting high levels of PTSD symptoms and both intrusive and avoidance thoughts performed more poorly on the proofreading task than did TMI and landfill residents reporting low levels of PTSD symptoms and residents of the control neighborhood (see Table 4).

Finally, TMI and landfill subjects reporting the most intrusive thinking had significantly more norepinephrine and epinephrine in their urine. The interaction between residence and avoidance thinking was not found for the catecholamines. There were no significant interactions between residence and intrusive or avoidance thinking for cortisol, heart rate, and systolic and diastolic blood pressure, although means were in the appropriate directions (see Table 4).

TABLE 4

Stress as a Function of Residence and
Reporting of Avoidance and Intrusive Imagery

	TMI		Landfill		Frederick	
	Low ($\bar{X}$)	High ($\bar{X}$)	Low ($\bar{X}$)	High ($\bar{X}$)	Low ($\bar{X}$)	High ($\bar{X}$)
Intrusion						
Total symptoms	23.1	43.9	21.5	50.3	14.5	20.3
Somatic complaints	18.0	22.2	18.5	24.5	14.4	15.0
Interpersonal problems	12.9	14.9	11.1	17.6	10.9	11.7
Depression	17.7	23.0	18.6	27.2	15.6	15.4
Anxiety	14.4	18.5	14.8	21.7	11.2	12.3
Alienation	11.4	14.6	10.4	16.3	11.1	11.6
Proofreading (%)	40.5	31.2	53.5	35.3	60.7	59.1
Norepinephrine (ng/hr)	1469.5	2634.7	891.8	2723.5	1390.4	950.6
Cortisol (mcg/hr)	237.5	403.5	216.3	656.3	166.8	188.4
Systolic BP (mm Hg)	120.6	129.7	123.1	126.3	121.2	113.6
Avoidance						
Total symptoms	26.0	42.0	23.2	51.0	15.8	17.7
Somatic complaints	19.0	21.6	18.9	24.7	14.6	14.8
Interpersonal problems	13.0	14.9	12.0	17.5	11.0	11.3
Depression	18.2	22.7	20.56	26.7	15.4	15.33
Anxiety	15.3	17.9	15.1	22.0	11.5	11.7
Alienation	12.1	14.1	10.7	16.4	11.1	11.7
Proofreading (%)	38.5	32.6	41.1	37.3	57.9	64.2
Norepinephrine (ng/hr)	1621.6	2488.9	1172.6	2699.1	1034.7	1973.2
Cortisol (mcg/hr)	259.6	38.06	342.60	615.30	107.50	228.20
Systolic BP (mm Hg)	121.2	129.2	128.6	123.7	120.3	115.9

These results suggest that there is a relationship between chronic stress and symptoms of PTSD. Correlations between intrusive and avoidance thinking and symptom reporting, behavioral deficits, and physiological arousal indicated that measures of chronic stress were related to measures of post-traumatic stress. Analyses of variance indicated that TMI and landfill subjects reporting the most intrusive thinking reported the most symptom distress, were able to find the fewest proofreading errors, and had the highest levels of epinephrine and norepinephrine in their urine. When analyses of variance were performed crossing residence with levels of avoidance thinking, fewer significant interactions were found. In particular, avoidance thinking was less closely related to catecholamine excess in TMI and landfill subjects than was intrusive thinking.

CONCLUSIONS

These results suggest several things. First, the chronicity of stressors may be involved in the formation of post-traumatic stress symptoms. Typically, PTSD is thought to occur following an intense traumatic event of brief duration. According to Lazarus and Cohen's (1977) categorization of stressors, both the TMI and landfill situations could be considered cataclysmic stressors. Cataclysmic events are usually the ones which lead to PTSD, but the TMI and landfill situations are different from other cataclysmic stressors. Although most major events of this type are associated with great physical power, visible destruction, and death or injury, this was not the case at either TMI or the landfill. Instead, these events have remained moderately threatening following an initially higher level during the accident or discovery of danger. No tangible evidence of danger is present. In addition, these events were largely free of the terror and horror that frequently form the basis of intrusive imagery. However, these two events may have been just as threatening for other reasons. Both involved the threat of exposure to toxic chemicals, and few understand the long-term consequences of such exposure. Residents appear to fear the consequences of toxic exposure; not knowing how it might affect them or their offspring, worrying about future exposures, and feeling powerless or helpless to do much about the situation characterize the experience of many victims of these events. Continuing concerns and fears rather than those associated with the initial event could be responsible for both the chronic stress and the symptoms of post-traumatic stress that we have observed. Our results suggest that chronicity may be an important factor in post-traumatic stress symptom formation and should be considered when mental health evaluations are made.

Although there has been no evidence of gross psychopathologies in either the TMI or landfill population, residents are exhibiting many of the symptoms of post-traumatic stress. The symptoms are not as intense as in other reports, but they exist nonetheless. But, given the presence of symptoms of post-traumatic stress and the close relationship between symptoms of PTSD and chronic stress, it follows that PTSD may represent a fairly severe manifestation of psychophysiological consequences associated with chronic stress. Thus, the symptoms of stress may best be viewed on a continuum, with the more typical, low-magnitude symptom reporting, distress, and arousal toward one end, and the more intense manifestation of these changes associated with PTSD toward the other. Movement along the continuum could be explained using a structure similar to Selye's GAS. Under normal conditions, relatively few low-intensity symptoms of stress are experienced. When an organism is threatened, it must resist the stressor, and during exposure to intense or persistent stressors, it becomes more and more difficult for the organism to maintain adequate resistance. Consequently, exhaustion may occur. PTSD may be one possible manifestation of disrupted functioning in the exhausted organism. Considering the GAS, it also becomes clear how both single intense events and chronic events may lead to PTSD; both may deplete adaptive abilities and lead to exhaustion although they may do so in different ways.

Our data do not allow causal inferences regarding symptoms typically associated with stress and those characteristic of PTSD. It is possible that conditioned responses to images associated with the stressors are responsible for distress and arousal. Thus, intrusive imagery could be regarded as an indirect cause, rather than a part of, PTSD and stress response. This does not argue against the notion of PTSD as an integrated form of stress response, but suggests alternatives that require further study.

Finally, with technological or industrial accidents becoming more frequent, it is important to understand the mental health consequences of these types of events. These data suggest a commonality between exposure to different types of industrial-related problems that pose the possibility of toxic exposure. Both the accident at TMI and the improper storage of toxic chemicals in a community led to similar problems. Among these problems were symptoms of PTSD. Knowing that this is a potential consequence of industrial-related accidents may help to facilitate future mental health planning.

In conclusion, traumas that pose long-term threats and require continuing adaptation may be associated with a variety of psychological and physiological outcomes. Thus, the chronicity as well as the intensity of stressors may tax adaptive capabilities. Our data suggest that post-traumatic stress disorder may be a severe manifestation of chronic stress responding. In our world of increasing reliance on technology, exposure to the by-products of this mechanization (e.g., radiation, toxic chemicals) may be one source of chronic stress. Thus, the range of potential sources of post-traumatic stress symptoms may be broader than was originally anticipated. Finally, by conceptualizing post-traumatic stress as a severe manifestation of chronic stress, researchers and clinicians may be able to use the principles of basic stress research to treat and prevent PTSD.

REFERENCES

Adler, A. (1943). Neuropsychiatric complications in victims of Boston's Coconut Grove disaster. *Journal of the American Medical Association, 123,* 1098–1111.

American Psychiatric Association (1980). *Diagnostic and statistical manual of mental disorders* (3rd ed.). Washington, DC: Author.

Bartop, R. W., Luckhurst, E., Lazarus, L., Kiloh, L. G., & Penny, R. (1977). Depressed lymphocyte function after bereavement. *Lancet, 1,* 834–836.

Baum, A., Fleming, R., & Davidson, L. (1983). Natural disaster and technological catastrophe. *Environment and Behavior, 15,* 333–354.

Baum, A., Gatchel, R. J., & Schaeffer, M. A. (1983). Emotional, behavioral and physiological effects of chronic stress at Three Mile Island. *Journal of Consulting and Clinical Psychology, 51,* 565–572.

Baum, A., Grunberg, N. E., & Singer, J. E. (1982). The use of psychological and neuroendocrinological measurements in the study of stress. *Health Psychology, 1*(3), 217–236.

Baum, A., Schaeffer, M. A., Lake, R., Fleming, R., & Collins, D. (In press). Psychological and endocrinological correlates of chronic stress at Three Mile Island. In R. Williams (Ed.), *Perspectives in behavioral medicine* (Vol. 2). New York: Academic Press.

Baum, A., Singer, J. E., & Baum, C. S. (1981). Stress and the environment. *Journal of Social Issues, 37*(1), 4–34.

Beck, A. T. (1967). *Depression: Clinical, experimental, and theoretical aspects.* New York: Hoeber.

Bromet, E. (1980). *Three Mile Island: Mental health findings.* Pittsburgh: Western Psychiatric Institute and Clinic and the University of Pittsburgh.

Cohen, S. (1978). Environmental load and the allocation of attention. In A. Baum, J. E. Singer, & S. Valins (Eds.), *Advances in environmental psychology* (Vol. 1). Hillsdale, NJ: Erlbaum.

Davidson, L. M., Fleming, I., & Baum, A. (1984a). *Chronic stress and TMI: The role of toxic exposure and uncertainty.* Paper presented at the annual meeting of the American Psychological Association, Toronto, Canada.

Davidson, L. M., Fleming, R., & Baum, A. (1984b). *Sleep disturbance and chronic stress.* Unpublished manuscript, Uniformed Services University of the Health Sciences, Bethesda, MD.

de la Pena, A. (1984). Post-traumatic stress disorder in the Vietnam veteran: A brain-modulated compensatory information-augmenting response to information underload in the central nervous system? In B. A. van der Kolk (Ed.), *Post-traumatic stress disorder: Psychological and biological sequelae* (pp. 108–122). Washington, DC: American Psychiatric Press.

Derogatis, L. R. (1977). *SCL-90R: Administration, scoring, and procedures manual I.* Baltimore, MD: Clinical Psychometrics Research.

Dohrenwend, B. P., Dohrenwend, B. S., Kasl, S. V., & Warheit, G. J. (1979). *Report of the Task Group on Behavioral Effects to the President's Commission on the Accident at Three Mile Island.* Washington, DC.

Edelstein, M. R. (1982). *The social and psychological impacts of groundwater contamination in the Legler section of Jackson, NJ.* Mahwah, NJ: Ramapo College, School of Environmental Studies.

Erichsen, J. E. (1882). *On concussion of the spine: Nervous shock and other obscure injuries of the nervous system in their clinical and medico-legal aspects.* London: Longmans, Green and Company.

Figley, C. R. (Ed.). (1978a). *Stress disorders among Vietnam veterans.* New York: Brunner/Mazel.

Figley, C. R. (1978b). Symptoms of delayed combat stress among a college sample of Vietnam veterans. *Military Medicine, 143,* 107–110.

Fleming, I. (1985). *The stress-reducing functions of specific types of social support for victims of a technological catastrophe.* Ph.D. dissertation, University of Maryland, College Park.

Fleming, R., & Baum, A. (1981). *Social support and coping as determinants of stress at Three Mile Island.* Paper presented at the 52nd annual meeting of the Eastern Psychological Association, New York, NY.

Fleming, R., & Baum, A. (1983). *Sleep disturbance at the Three Mile Island nuclear power station.* Unpublished manuscript, Uniformed Services University of the Health Sciences, Bethesda, MD.

Fleming, I., & Baum, A. (1985). *Chronic stress and toxic waste: The role of uncertainty and helplessness.* Unpublished manuscript, Uniformed Services University of the Health Sciences, Bethesda, MD.

Frankenhaeuser, M. (1973). *Experimental approaches to the study of catecholamines and emotion.* Stockholm: University of Stockholm, Reports from the Psychological Laboratories, 392.

Frankenhaeuser, M. (1975). A sympathetic-adrenomedullary activity, behavior and the psychosocial environment. In P. H. Venables & M. J. Christie (Eds.), *Research in psychophysiology.* New York: Wiley.

Gibbs, M. S. (1982). *Psychological dysfunction in the Legler litigation group.* Unpublished manuscript, Fairleigh Dickinson University, Teaneck, NJ.

Glass, D. C., & Singer, J. E. (1972). *Urban stress: Experiments on noise and social stressors.* New York: Academic.

Green, B. L. (1980). *Prediction of long-term psycho-social functioning following the Beverly Hills Fire.* Ph.D. dissertation, University of Cincinnati, Ohio.

Hendin, H., & Haas, A. P. (1984). *Wounds of wars: The psychological aftermath of combat in Vietnam.* New York: Basic Books.

Herbst, A. L., Robboy, S. J., Scully, R. E., & Poskanzer, D. C. (1974). Clear-cell adenocarcinoma of the vagina and cervix in girls: Analysis of 170 registry cases. *American Journal of Obstetrics and Gynecology, 119,* 713–724.

Holmes, T. H., & Rahe, R. H. (1967). The social readjustment rating scale. *Journal of Psychosomatic Research, 28,* 215–228.

Horowitz, M., Wilner, N., & Alvarez, W. (1979). Impact of event scale: A measure of subjective stress. *Psychosomatic Medicine, 41,* 209–218.

Houts, P., Miller, R. W., Tokuhata, G. K., & Ham, K. S. (1980). *Health-related behavioral impact of the Three Mile Island nuclear accident.* Report submitted to the TMI Advisory Panel on health-related studies of the Pennsylvania Department of Health, Hershey, PA.

Kamman, G. R. (1951). Traumatic neurosis: Compensation neurosis or attitude pathosis. *Archives of Neurology and Psychiatry, 65*, 593–601.

Kardiner, A. (1947). *War stress and neurotic illness.* New York: Hoeber.

Lazarus, R. S. (1966). *Psychological stress and the coping process.* New York: McGraw-Hill.

Lazarus, R. S. (1975). Social unrest, stress, and adaptation. In L. Levi (Ed.), *Society, stress, and disease* (Vol. II). London: Oxford University Press.

Lazarus, R. S., & Cohen, J. B. (1977). Environmental stress. In I. Altman & J. F. Wohlwill (Eds.), *Human behavior and the environment: Current theory and research* (Vol. 2). New York: Plenum.

Levine, A. (1982). *Love Canal, science, politics, and people.* New York: Lexington Books.

Mason, J. W. (1975a). A historical view of the stress field. *Journal of Human Stress, 1*(2), 22–36.

Mason, J. W. (1975b). Emotion as reflected in patterns of endocrine integration. In L. Levi (Ed.), *Emotions: Their parameters and measurement.* New York: Raven Press.

Mears, F., & Gatchel, R. J. (1979). *Fundamentals of abnormal psychology.* Chicago: Rand McNally College Publishing Company.

Page, H. (1885). *Injuries of the spine and spinal cord without apparent mechanical lesion.* London: J. and A. Churchill.

Selye, H. (1956). *The stress of life.* New York: McGraw-Hill.

Symington, T., Currie, A. R., Curran, R. S., & Davidson, J. N. (1955). The reaction of the adrenal cortex in conditions of stress. In *CIBA Foundation Colloquia on Endocrinology. Vol. 8: The human adrenal cortex* (pp. 70–91). Boston: Little, Brown, and Company.

van der Kolk, B., Boyd, H., Krystal, J., & Greenberg, M. (1984). Post-traumatic stress disorder as a biologically based disorder: Implications of the animal model of inescapable shock. In B. van der Kolk (Ed.), *Post-traumatic stress disorder: Psychological and biological sequelae.* Washington, DC: American Psychiatric Press.

Wilson, J. P., Smith, W. K., & Johnson, S. K. (1983, October). *A comparative analysis of post-traumatic stress syndrome among survivors exposed to different stressor events.* Paper presented at the second National Conference on the Treatment of Post-traumatic Stress Disorder, Chicago, IL.

5

Symptom Groups and Family Patterns of Vietnam Veterans with Post-Traumatic Stress Disorders

STEVEN M. SILVER and CARMINE IACONO

The criteria for post-traumatic stress disorder (PTSD) in the third edition of the *Diagnostic and Statistical Manual of Mental Disorders* (DSM-III) by the American Psychiatric Association (1980) reflect an emphasis on specificity in diagnosis. Such specificity has gathered particular strength over the past decade, though not without controversy (e.g, Feighner, Robins, & Guze, 1972; McLermore & Benjamin, 1979; Schacht & Nathan, 1977; Spitzer, Endicott, & Robins, 1975).

PTSD requires four criteria: (1) the historical antecedent of a traumatic event; (2) a reexperiencing of the event; (3) a numbing of responsiveness to or withdrawal from the environment; (4) two other symptoms not present prior to the traumatic event, from a group including hyper-alertness or exaggerated startle response, sleep disturbances, survivor guilt, problems with memory or concentration, avoidance of reminders of the trauma event, and an increase in symptom severity when exposed to those reminders (APA, 1980).

These symptoms and others have been associated with veterans of the Vietnam War under various labels, such as post-Vietnam syndrome and delayed stress response as well as PTSD (Cavenar & Nash, 1976; Eisenhart, 1977; Figley, 1978a; Haley, 1978; Horowitz & Solomon, 1975,

Lifton, 1973; Williams, 1980). Not all of the symptoms reported by these and other clinicians found their way into DSM-III.

One immediate question is whether or not DSM-III truly reflects the clinical literature as it relates to PTSD. Specifically, do the respective diagnostic criteria sets of DSM-III reflect an underlying and identifiable symptom structure or are they simply arbitrary groupings of symptoms? Further, are there symptoms that could usefully be included within the criteria sets, but are not?

A further question is raised in seeking to test the criteria themselves. The criteria of numbing of responsiveness and withdrawal reflect early clinical work with Vietnam veterans (Adams & McCloskey, 1974; De-Fazio, 1975; Figley, 1978b; Haley, 1978; Lewis, 1975; Shatan, 1972, 1974) and other trauma survivors. While it would appear logical to expect the manifestation of these particular symptoms in the arena of family functioning, at the start of this decade little research had been done (Figley, 1978a).

The relationship between individual and interpersonal functioning is quite powerful and may be used either to alleviate or to intensify symptoms of a disorder (Minuchin, 1974; Voth & Orth, 1973). Figley and Sprenkle (1978) suggested that PTSD symptoms in particular might become embedded within already existing family pathology. It has been suggested that family events might serve as triggers for PTSD symptoms (Haley, 1978; Stuen & Solberg, 1972)—individual symptomatology has been shown to relate to changes in family structure (Carter & Mc-Goldrick, 1980), such as the addition of a new member.

This research study was developed to address both questions of symptom groupings and family functioning and was one of the first large-scale efforts to do so. It is presented in two parts for the sake of clarity; both parts were conducted with the same sample population.

SUBJECTS

Subjects consisted of a national sample of 406 male Vietnam War veterans who agreed to participate during their first three visits to a Disabled American Veterans' Vietnam Veteran Outreach Center. An additional 63 male veterans who did not serve in Vietnam were drawn from the same source for comparison purposes. All veterans were requesting personal counseling.

Two significant differences existed between the Vietnam and non-Vietnam veterans. At the time of the study, Vietnam veterans averaged

33.0 years old and non-Vietnam veterans averaged 30.7 years old. In pre-service education, Vietnam veterans averaged 11.7 years versus 12.3 for non-Vietnam veterans. A total of 332 (82%) of the Vietnam veterans identified themselves as white; 52 (13%) as black; 12 (3%) as Latin or Hispanic; 9 (2%) as American Indian; none as Oriental. As with the racial breakdowns, there were no significant differences between Vietnam and non-Vietnam veterans in the demographic data for Vietnam veterans shown in Table 1.

Table 1 contains a summary of family data provided by the Vietnam veterans. Closeness to children and to wife or lover used scaled questions similar to those described below. No significant differences existed between Vietnam and non-Vietnam veterans with p set at 0.01. Vietnam veterans tended to have their first child sooner and tended to rate themselves as less close to their wives or lovers.

In the area of Vietnam service, Vietnam veterans had an average age entering Vietnam of 20.7 years ($SD = 3.3$). An average of 14.2 months ($SD = 8.5$) were spent in Vietnam; they departed an average of 133.2 months ($SD = 22.0$) prior to the survey. They reported 69% ($SD = 33$) of their time in Vietnam in combat. Responding to a scaled question

TABLE 1
Additional Descriptive Data of
Surveyed Vietnam Veterans

Variable	M[c]	SD	n[d]
Time since onset of symptoms[a]	84.7	55.2	345
Time since married[a]	92.1	59.9	301
Time since first child's birth[a]	101.1	58.3	252
Number of children	1.7	1.4	252
Closeness to children[b]	2.8	2.0	343
Closeness to wife or lover[b]	3.0	1.7	337
Marital status (total respondents)			404
Married			199
Single, living with someone			29
Separated			45
Divorced			81
Single, living alone			50
PTSR index	51.7	21.6	406

[a]Time in months
[b]Scaled response
[c]Where appropriate
[d]Number of respondents of 406 valid forms

where "0" equaled "not in combat" and "5" equaled "severe," their reported severity of combat was 3.3 (*SD* = 1.6). Using a scaled question ranging from "no friends" to "extremely close," Vietnam veterans rated their closeness to friends in Vietnam at 3.3 (*SD* = 1.6) to an average of 9.1 (*SD* = 10.1) friends. A total of 227 reported being wounded in Vietnam, and 228 claimed a service-connected disability.

PROCEDURE

Thirty copies of a survey instrument, discussed in detail within each part of this study, were sent to each of the Disabled American Veterans Vietnam Outreach Centers and were given to veterans during their first three visits to the centers. Forms were sent to 76 centers in November and December 1980—67 centers proved to be operational during the survey period. Thirty-six (54%) of these centers had responded by the close of the study period, April 1, 1981.

Forms were evaluated for completeness and "faking" by examining patterns of responses. Of 490, 23 (4.7%) were discarded for these reasons. This low number was undoubtedly due to the efforts of the DAV National Service Officers (NSOs). Veterans were free to participate; exact numbers of refusals are not available, but informal contact with participating NSOs indicates that this number was very low, perhaps less than 1%. Again, this probably was due to the efforts of the NSOs, all of whom were veterans and who were able to explain the purpose of the survey and to guarantee anonymity.

THE ISSUE OF COMBAT VERSUS
NONCOMBAT VETERANS

In order to examine the effects of different levels of stress, past convention has been to separate veterans into combatant and noncombatant groups largely on the basis of military occupation—typically, combatants would include those in the infantry, armor, or artillery branches of the Army, but would not include, for example, truck drivers. Given the largely unconventional nature of the Vietnam War, it was decided to rely on the individual's perception of his involvement in combat. Strayer and Ellenhorn (1975) have asserted that self-perception of the extent and degree of combat involvement was a critical variable related to severity of adjustment problems and psychological symptoms. The Vietnam veterans sampled included 371 in traditional combat assignments and 34 in such jobs as truck drivers, medics, engineers, and cooks.

Shatan (1978) noted that the onset of psychological symptoms resulting from combat exposure often did not occur for nine months to five years after leaving the service. At the time of this study, subjects averaged being out of the service 11 years and reported noting symptom onset four years after that.

PART ONE—SYMPTOM GROUPS

Instrument

A symptoms menu was built using items drawn from clinical observations and research results (APA, 1980; Cavenar & Nash, 1976; Eisenhart, 1977; Figley, 1978a, b; Haley, 1978; Horowitz & Solomon, 1975; Lifton, 1973; Williams, 1980). Symptoms were presented in a random sequence, and the participants responded by self-rating each using the following Likert-like scale: not experienced (0), mild (1), moderate (3), severe (5).

Data Analysis

A hypothesized factor structure based on the last three diagnostic criteria sets for PTSD in DSM-III was developed prior to data collection (Comrey, 1978). Factor analysis was based on Product Moment correlations. Factors were extracted using the Principle Factor Method with Varimax rotation. Squared multiple correlations of each variable with all others were used for commonalities. The optimum number of factors was estimated by the Cattell Scree Test (Cattell, 1966); only variables with factor loading of 0.50 or greater were retained.

Results

An unabridged rotated factor matrix is presented in Table 2. Symptoms that met the loading criteria of 0.50 are presented in descending loading order in Table 3. Seven symptoms failed to meet the minimum factor-loading criteria.

TABLE 2
Rotated Factor Matrix with Commonalities (h^2)

Symptoms	I	II	III	IV	h^2
Problems with people in charge*	39[1]	08	38	37	45
Problems with memory	51	27	21	32	47
Suicidal feelings or attempts	53	29	29	24	51
Trouble sleeping*	33	36	43	35	54
Difficulty in relations with others	42	22	29	65	72
Fear of loss of control	40	29	36	52	64
Flashbacks to Vietnam	23	40	62	25	67
Losing temper easily	32	08	44	65	73
Guilt for what I did in Vietnam	15	61	25	15	48
Difficulty in feeling emotions	16	23	17	54	40
Frequently sick*	42	20	25	16	30
Having arguments with others	50	02	38	50	65
Reacting when surprised using military training	16	29	56	31	52
Violent dreams or fantasies	23	33	63	31	66
Jumpiness and hyperalertness	24	33	41	62	72
Difficulty in keeping a job	57	20	26	20	47
Nightmares	31	39	66	16	72
Avoiding places or activities which remind me of the war*	24	42	33	25	41
Feeling separated from others, from country or society	43	41	22	53	68
Feeling emotionally distant from family and others	39	35	12	56	60
Problems with drugs or alcohol*	37	21	10	28	27
Problems talking about the war*	24	46	25	27	41
Trouble concentrating	64	33	18	35	68
Feeling blamed or scapegoated*	27	48	28	37	51
Feeling worthless or unsure about myself	60	36	11	46	72
Feeling angry or irritable	41	22	30	70	80
Mistrust of others or government	33	29	22	63	63
Guilt for surviving Vietnam	23	60	19	14	47
Anxiety	37	42	20	54	65
Grief or sorrow	31	59	22	28	58
Depression	55	36	21	50	73
Low interest in job or other activities	63	23	19	34	60
Painful moods and emotions	38	43	28	54	69

*Symptoms not meeting minimum factor loading of 50
[1]Decimal points omitted

TABLE 3
Rotated Factor Loadings

Symptoms	Loadings
Factor I Depression	
Trouble concentrating	64[1]
Low interest in job or other activities	63
Feeling worthless or unsure about self	60
Difficulty keeping a job	57
Depression	55
Suicidal feelings or attempts	53
Problems with memory	51
Factor II Residual Guilt or Grief	
Guilt about what I did in Vietnam	61
Guilt for surviving Vietnam	60
Grief or sorrow	59
Factor III Reexperiencing the Trauma	
Nightmares	66
Violent dreams or fantasies	63
Flashbacks to Vietnam	62
Reacting when surprised, using military training	56
Factor IV Detachment and Anger	
Feeling angry or irritable	70
Losing temper easily	65
Difficulty in relations with others	65
Mistrust of others or government	63
Jumpiness or hyperalertness	62
Feeling emotionally distant from family and others	56
Anxiety	54
Difficulty feeling emotions	54
Painful moods and emotions	54
Feeling separated from others, from country or society	53
Fear of loss of control	52
Depression	50
Having arguments with others	50

[1]Decimal points omitted

Discussion

The contents of Factor I bear a close resemblance to depression—more specifically, the dysthymic disorder.

Factor II represents symptoms associated with survivor guilt arising specifically from participation in the Vietnam War.

Factor III resembles the DSM-III criterion related to reexperiencing the trauma.

Factor IV included those symptoms indicating an anxious detachment and numbed responsiveness, supporting DSM-III's third criterion. Also found in Factor IV were symptoms reflecting anger and hostility.

These results generally support the DSM-III criteria for PTSD. The primary difference between these results and DSM-III is Factor I, which indicates a depressive reaction as a component of PTSD. In DSM-III this reaction is considered an "associated feature" but is not integral. The role of depression has been discussed by others (Kormos, 1978; Nace, Meyers, O'Brien, Ream, & Mintz, 1977), who have tended to see its importance as greater than that indicated in DSM-III.

The role of anger and hostility as a component in Factor IV is only obliquely addressed in DSM-III as a sense of estrangement. The work of Eisenhart (1975), Egendorf (1975), Howard (1976), Shatan (1978), and others, as well as personal clinical experience, suggests that anger and hostility are endemic to Vietnam veterans having PTSD.

It is our contention that while PTSD defined in DSM-III is a valid diagnosis, it is basically a generic classification. The results presented here are taken from those who experienced the range of traumas relating to war. Given different circumstances of traumatic stressors (or a more rigorous classification system of war-related traumas), it might be possible to examine the role in symptom formation of individual responsibility and perception.

Follow-up Study

A comparison of data from Vietnam and non-Vietnam veterans should have differences if the results are due to service in Vietnam. This assumes that other variables are relatively constant (e.g., demographic, preservice experiences, and so on). Therefore, the non-Vietnam veteran sample was examined for differences on each of the four factors.

Subjects

The non-Vietnam veteran sample (n = 63) was drawn from the same DAV Outreach Centers as the Vietnam veterans. Also requesting personal counseling, none served in Vietnam or in Southeast Asia. They reported first noting symptoms 5.4 years before the study. They had been out of the service an average of eight years.

Procedure and Analysis

The instrument and data-gathering procedure were identical to those for the Vietnam veterans. Both samples were combined (n = 469) and factor-analyzed in the manner described above. Four factors were extracted. Five variables were excluded as being specific to the Vietnam War, which would have resulted in "not experienced—0" ratings by the non-Vietnam veterans. The variables were: "guilt about what I did in Vietnam; flashbacks to Vietnam; avoid places and activities that remind me of the war; problems talking about the war; guilt for surviving Vietnam."

Factor scores were calculated for each subject over the four factors. A one-way MANOVA was made on factor scores for the four factors as the dependent variable and Vietnam versus non-Vietnam as the independent variable.

Results and Discussion

An unabridged factor matrix for the combined sample is presented in Table 4. Six symptoms did not meet the criterion factor loading of 0.50. Symptoms meeting this loading criterion are shown by factor in descending order in Table 5.

A comparison of Tables 3 and 5 shows that Factor II, residual guilt or grief, does not appear in Table 5. This is expected as most of the items comprising this factor were excluded for reasons explained above.

A second difference is that Factor IV (Table 3) split in Table 5 into two factors, Factor III, anger, and Factor IV, detachment.

The F approximation to Wilk's lamda was significant (F 5,463 = 24.93; p < 0.0001). Obligatory univariate ANOVAs revealed a significant difference (p < 0.0001) between Vietnam and non-Vietnam veterans on Factors II through IV. A separate factor analysis of the non-Vietnam veteran sample was not done because of the low number of subjects versus the number of variables.

TABLE 4
Rotated Factor Matrix with Commonalities (h^2) for Combined Vietnam & Non-Vietnam Veterans (n = 469)

Symptoms	I	II	III	IV	h^2
Problems with people in charge*	38[1]	25	49	21	50
Problems with memory	51	22	34	27	50
Suicidal feelings or attempts	53	33	22	28	52
Trouble sleeping	35	53	23	39	60
Difficulty in relations with others	38	29	46	55	74
Fear of loss of control*	41	35	45	44	69
Losing temper easily	29	30	67	37	76
Difficulty in feeling emotions	15	22	37	50	46
Frequently sick*	44	23	34	15	32
Having arguments with others	46	21	62	24	69
Reacting when surprised using military training	19	55	41	20	54
Violent dreams or fantasies	23	71	25	33	73
Jumpiness or hyperalertness	27	45	43	52	73
Difficulty keeping a job	55	26	24	21	47
Nightmares	33	75	17	23	76
Feeling separated from others, from country or society	43	33	28	59	72
Feeling emotionally distant from family and others	35	24	28	63	66
Problems with drugs or alcohol*	36	17	15	34	29
Trouble concentrating	63	25	30	37	68
Feeling blamed or scapegoated*	34	39	26	43	52
Feeling worthless or unsure about myself	61	19	24	50	72
Feeling angry or irritable	37	28	53	57	82
Mistrust of others or government	32	27	41	58	68
Anxiety	41	31	24	60	68
Grief or sorrow*	40	39	11	46	54
Depression	55	31	19	58	77
Low interest in job or other activities	61	20	24	38	61
Painful moods and emotions	42	39	24	57	71

*Symptoms not meeting minimum factor loading of 50
[1]Decimal points omitted

TABLE 5
Rotated Factor Loadings for Combined Vietnam and Non-Vietnam
Veterans (n = 469)

Symptoms by Factor	Loadings
Factor I Depression	
Trouble concentrating	63[1]
Feeling worthless or unsure about self	61
Low interest in job or other activities	60
Difficulty keeping a job	55
Depression	55
Suicidal feelings or attempts	53
Problems with memory	51
Factor II Reexperiencing the Trauma	
Nightmares	75
Violent dreams or fantasies	71
Reacting when surprised, using military training	55
Trouble sleeping	53
Factor III Anger	
Losing temper easily	67
Having arguments with others	62
Feeling angry or irritable	53
Factor IV Detachment	
Feeling emotionally distant from family and others	63
Anxiety	60
Feeling separated from others, country or society	59
Mistrust of others or government	58
Depression	58
Painful moods and emotions	57
Feeling angry or irritable	57
Difficulty in relations with others	55
Jumpiness	52
Difficulty feeling emotions	50

[1]Decimal points omitted

Vietnam and non-Vietnam veterans appear to have quite different outcomes from their service experiences. Vietnam veterans have greater intensity of aggression and detachment and, as to be expected, more intensely reexperienced traumatic events. On the other hand, both groups were quite similar in experiencing a dysthymic reaction as the factor score differences on Factor I were not significant.

These results are in direct contradiction to those who have suggested that Vietnam veterans were not suffering from symptoms uniquely relating to PTSD (Borus, 1973, 1974; Enzie, Sawyer, & Montgomery, 1973; Lee & Elliard, 1973; Strange, 1974; Worthington, 1976). These differences may be due to these investigators' use of elite groups of Vietnam veterans such as college students, failure to make appropriate distinctions between combatants and noncombatants, and use of samples of people still on active duty, which would overlook a possible delayed reaction (Figley, 1978b).

Conclusions

1. Substantial empirical support exists for the symptoms comprising DSM-III's criteria for PTSD.
2. These results suggest that the groupings of these symptoms might be altered to take into account depressive and aggressive behavior as cardinal rather than associated features.
3. The Vietnam veterans showed significantly greater intensity of aggression, detachment, and apprehension, as well as more intense reexperiencing of service-related traumatic stressors. Both groups similarly reported depression.

Further Research

At best, any initial factor analytic study suggesting a certain factor structure for a domain only supplies a preliminary understanding of that domain. The validity of the structure must be determined by methods outside the initial factor analysis (Comrey, 1973). To accomplish this two approaches may be used:
1. A cross-validation study of a new sample of Vietnam veterans having PTSD could be performed.
2. Using the procedures of the follow-up study, one might attempt to replicate its results contrasting other groups of subjects, such as veterans of other wars having PTSD with, for example, patients drawn from a general psychiatric but non-PTSD population.

PART TWO—FAMILY PATTERNS

Hypotheses

It was believed that a significant and meaningful relationship existed between the Vietnam veteran's level of severity of PTSD-related symptoms or reaction and the functioning of his marital family. Specifically, the hypothesis was that when all significant variables were combined, those relating to marital family functioning would account for the greatest amount of variance in the level of the reaction after the war experience itself. An additional hypothesis, derived from Haley (1978), was that the onset of stress reaction symptoms would significantly correlate with marriage date and birth of the first child.

Variable Construction

The dependent variable was a constructed index of post-traumatic stress reaction (PTSR) severity utilizing three of the four diagnostic criteria groups for PTSD in DSM-III. These criteria, reexperiencing the trauma, numbing and withdrawal, hyperalertness, and other problems, were represented by symptoms included in the self-rated menu described earlier.

The symptoms for reexperiencing the trauma were "flashbacks to Vietnam," "reacting when surprised using military training," and "violent dreams or fantasies."

Those relating to numbing or withdrawal were "difficulty in relations with others," "difficulty in feeling emotions," "having arguments with others," "feeling separated from others, from country, or from society," "feeling emotionally distant from family and others," "feeling blamed or scapegoated," "mistrust of others or government," and "low interest in job or other activities."

The final group of DSM-III symptoms was represented by "trouble sleeping," "guilt about what I did in Vietnam," "jumpiness or hyperalertness," "nightmares," "avoiding places or activities which remind me of the war," "problems talking about the war," "trouble concentrating," and "guilt for surviving Vietnam."

The average standard scores of each criterion group were combined and averaged, producing a single standardized score. This was the dependent variable that allowed uniting different symptoms across theoretical boundaries.

The PTSR index had face validity as its gradation corresponded to clinical impressions of PTSD severity among 40 Vietnam veterans interviewed in a pilot study in a DAV Outreach Center. The pilot study established a test-retest reliability of 0.87.

Independent variables were taken from the survey or constructed from information provided in the survey.

Instrument

A survey form evolved from the pilot study and included the cohesion, conflict, and expressiveness subscales of the Family Environment Scale (FES) of Moos, Insel, and Humphrey (1974). As Dreyer (1978) noted, the FES has face validity, and Sines (1978) referred to it as a "psychometrically acceptable instrument for collecting information that may be useful in a practical sense" (p. 822). Intrafamily members tended to have highly correlated scores on the scales of the FES, indicating that, in general, the responses of one family member might be taken as an indication of the perceptions of family functioning by the other family members. Furthermore, for the purposes of this study, it was felt that since the father/husband was being polled, his impression of family functioning was self-fulfilling if not conservative. If he felt there was conflict in his family, there would be.

"Expressiveness" referred to the degree of verbal communication taking place within the family. "Cohesion" reflected family unity. "Conflict" reflected intrafamily antagonism.

Results

Hypotheses were tested using Pearson correlations or stepwise multiple regression. Point biserial correlations were used for dichotomous variables, and dummy coding was used when necessary. Subjects failing to respond on an item were deleted on a pairwise basis, resulting in different numbers of veterans for each analysis. Shrinkage for the regression procedure was estimated using a formula suggested by Kerlinger and Pedhazur (1973). Table 6 summarizes the correlations of significant individual variables with PTSR.

Nonsignificant ($p > 0.05$) variables included race, rank in service, branch of service, months since leaving Vietnam, marital status, and disability incurred in service.

The variable combat experience was an interactive variable consisting

TABLE 6
Significant Variable Correlations with
Post-Traumatic Stress Reaction

Variable	M	SD	r	r²	p	n
Age entering Vietnam	20.7	3.3	−.182	.033	.0001	398
Closeness to friends in Vietnam	3.2	1.6	.200	.040	.00003	404
Combat experience	39.8	38.6	.359	.129	.00001	399
Preservice education	11.8	1.7	−.182	.033	.001	403
Child support system	6.2	6.1	−.196	.038	.00018	327
Closeness to wife or lover	3.0	1.7	−.260	.068	.00001	328
Family dimensions:						
Cohesion	4.7	3.1	−.372	.138	.00001	332
Expressiveness	4.3	2.3	−.268	.072	.00001	332
Conflict	4.2	2.6	.354	.126	.00001	332

of the total time reported in combat multiplied by the severity of that combat. Child support system was likewise an interactive variable combining the number of children with the degree of closeness to them.

No significant relationship was found between time since onset of symptoms and time since marriage or time since first child's birth.

As shown in Table 6, family variables were significantly related to the level of PTSR. The variables of cohesion, expressiveness, and conflict accounted for more variance in PTSR than all other variables except combat experience.

A comparison of Vietnam and non-Vietnam veterans for PTSR cannot be done because of the number of Vietnam-specific items included in the index. However, for all individual non-Vietnam-related symptoms, Vietnam veterans reported significantly ($p < 0.001$) more severe self-ratings. Non-Vietnam veterans reported less conflict ($M = 3.5$, $p = 0.022$) and more cohesion ($M = 6.1$) and expressiveness ($M = 5.7$) with $p < 0.007$.

When these and other family-related variables were combined in a regression procedure with the significant variables of preservice education (which clinical experience indicates is closely related to the probability of drawing a nontechnical military job and hence more likely to be exposed to combat), age entering Vietnam, and closeness to friends in Vietnam, the resultant equation had an r^2 of 0.31, with shrinkage estimated to be 0.02.

Since standard score beta weights permit comparison of relative contributions to dependent variable variance, support for the concept of a marital family relationship to level of PTSR can be found in Table 7. The family variables of conflict, cohesion, and expressiveness ranked high among independent variables.

Discussion

It was hypothesized that marital family variables would significantly relate to the level of PTSR and would, after the combat experience itself, account for the greatest amount of variance in PTSR. Both hypotheses were substantially corroborated.

An implication of this study is that the manner of family system functioning may be of greater importance than the existence of individual components of that system, such as numbers of children and marital state. Perhaps most important, this study draws attention to the relation of the family to trauma responses.

Monitoring of alterations in family system functioning might be used as an indicator of symptom resolution in the individual. Beyond this, there is an implicit endorsement in the usage of family therapy for the treatment of individual trauma responses. The close correlation of family functioning with the severity of the individual's reaction suggests that improvement in such functioning may result in improvement for the individual. This approach could be particularly valuable in cases where the individual veteran is extremely reluctant to reveal war-related ex-

TABLE 7
Summary of Multiple Regression of Significant Variables with Post-Traumatic Stress Reaction

Variable	Step	Beta	r	r^2	F
Combat experience	1	.277	.361	.130	48.10*
Cohesion	2	−.122	.476	.227	46.90*
Conflict	3	.205	.509	.259	37.37*
Closeness to friends in Vietnam	4	.123	.526	.277	30.47*
Child support system	5	−.107	.538	.289	25.86*
Age entering Vietnam	6	−.092	.547	.299	22.59*
Expressiveness	7	−.097	.553	.306	19.89*
Preservice education	8	−.066	.557	.310	17.69*
Closeness to wife or lover	9	−.028	.557	.310	15.71*

*$p < .001$

periences. Family therapy might enable the therapist to have a beneficial impact on both the veteran and the family system without having to give one priority over the other.

The marital subsystem appears to be the primary focus of the inter-relationships of family functioning and PTSR. The correlations of close-ness to wife or lover with cohesion ($r = 0.53$), conflict ($r = -0.18$), and expressiveness ($r = 0.44$) are higher than the correlations of child sup-port system (0.20, -0.01, and 0.15, respectively).

The third hypothesis that family events might relate to onset of PTSR symptoms failed to gain support. Some subjects may simply have had difficulty recalling accurately the date of symptom onset in the sense that such onset may have been relatively gradual. The possibility (Haley, 1978) that the arrival of a spouse or child may trigger associated memories of Vietnamese women or children whom the veteran encountered or even killed during the war may simply not exist. If it does, it may be a sufficiently unique set of circumstances that its occurrence is not de-tectable in an average of a large number of veterans.

The senior author's clinical experience does support the concept that the age of a child may serve as the trigger described above. For a number of veterans, having to perceive children as potential threats made a significant impact. These veterans have no reaction to babies but may report a surfacing of symptoms, particularly intrusive recollections or nightmares, when their own children reach approximately age six.

This study did not attempt to account for large amounts of the variance in post-traumatic stress reactions—its purpose was to justify the ex-penditure of limited resources in more detailed study of the impact of individual trauma on the family. This part of the study has shown poorer family functioning in Vietnam veteran marital families than in non-Viet-nam families. It supports family therapy as an approach not only to help end the agony of the individual Vietnam veteran, but to address the true heart of these results—the impact of Vietnam on veteran families clearly suffering from the widening ripples of the war.

REFERENCES

Adams, C. P., & McCloskey, J. (1974). Twice born men. In A. B. Tuliban, C. L. Attneave, & E. Kingstone (Eds.), *Beyond clinic walls*. University, AL: University of Alabama Press, 1974.

American Psychiatric Association. (1980). *Diagnostic and statistical manual of mental disorders* (3rd edition). Washington, D.C.: American Psychiatric Association.

Borus, J. F. (1973). Re-entry: I. Adjustment issues facing the Vietnam returnee. *Archives of General Psychiatry, 28*, 501–506.

Borus, J. F. (1974). Incident of maladjustment in Vietnam returnees. *Archives of General Psychiatry, 30,* 554–557.

Carter, E. A., & McGoldrick, M. (1980). The family life cycle and family therapy: An overview. In E. A. Carter & M. McGoldrick (Eds.), *The family life cycle: A framework for family therapy.* New York: Gardner.

Cattell, R. B. (1966). The scree test for the number of factors. *Multivariate Behavior Research,* 1, 245–276.

Cavenar, J. C., & Nash, U. L. (1976). The effects of combat on the normal personality: War neurosis in Vietnam returnees. *Comprehensive Psychiatry, 17,* 647–653.

Comrey, A. L. (1973). *A first course in factor analysis.* New York: Academic Press.

Comrey, A. L. (1978). Common methodological problems in factor analytical studies. *Journal of Consulting Clinical Psychology, 46,* 648–659.

DeFazio, V. J. (1975). The Vietnam era veteran: Psychological problems. *Journal of Contemporary Psychiatry, 7,* 9–15.

Dreyer, P. H. (1978). Family environment scale. In O. K. Buros (Ed.), *The eighth mental measurements yearbook (Vol. I).* Highland Park, N.J.: Gryphon.

Egendorf, A. (1975). Vietnam veteran rap groups and themes of postwar life. *Journal of Social Issues: Soldiers in and After Vietnam, 31,* 13–23.

Eisenhart, R. W. (1975). You can't hack it, little girl: A discussion of the covert psychological agenda of modern combat training. *Journal of Social Issues, 31,* 13–23.

Eisenhart, R. W. (1977). Flower of the dragon: An example of applied humanistic psychology. *Journal of Human Psychology, 17,* 3–24.

Enzie, R. F., Sawyer, R. N., & Montgomery, F. A. (1973). Manifest anxiety of Vietnam returnees and undergraduates. *Psychological Reports, 33,* 446.

Feighner, J. P., Robins, E., & Guze, S. B. (1972). Diagnostic criteria for use in psychiatric research. *Archives of General Psychiatry, 26,* 57–63.

Figley, C. R. (1978a). Psychological adjustment among Vietnam veterans: An overview of the research. In C. R. Figley (Ed.), *Stress disorders among Vietnam veterans.* New York: Brunner/Mazel.

Figley, C. R. (1978b). Symptoms of delayed combat stress among a college sample of Vietnam veterans. *Military Medicine, 143,* 107–110.

Figley, C. R., & Sprenkle, D. H. (1978). Delayed stress response syndrome: Family therapy implications. *Journal of Marital and Family Counseling, 4,* 53–60.

Haley, S. A. (1978). Treatment implications of post-combat stress response syndromes for mental health professionals. In C. R. Figley (Ed.), *Stress disorders among Vietnam veterans.* New York: Brunner/Mazel.

Horowitz, M., & Solomon, G. F. (1975). A prediction of delayed stress response in Vietnam veterans. *Journal of Social Issues, 31,* 67–80.

Howard, S. (1976). The Vietnam warrior: His experience and implication for psychotherapy. *American Journal of Psychotherapy, 30,* 121–135.

Kerlinger, F. N., & Pedhazur, E. J. (1973). *Multiple regression in behavioral research.* New York: Holt, Rinehart, & Winston.

Kormos, H. R. (1978). The nature of combat stress. In C. R. Figley (Ed.), *Stress disorders among Vietnam veterans.* New York: Brunner/Mazel.

Lee, R. E., & Elliard, B. (1973). Critical behavior as a function of age. *Newsletter for Research in Mental Health and Behavioral Sciences, 15,* 9–10.

Lewis, C. N. (1975). Memories and alienation in the Vietnam combat veteran. *Bulletin of the Menninger Clinic, 39,* 363–369.

Lifton, R. J. (1973). *Home from the war.* New York: Simon & Schuster.

McLermore, C. W., & Benjamin, L. S. (1979). Whatever happened to interpersonal diagnosis?: A psychological alternative to DSM–III. *American Psychologist, 34,* 17–34.

Minuchin, S. (1974). *Families and family therapy.* Cambridge, MA: Harvard University Press.

Moos, R. H., Insel, P. M., & Humphrey, B. (1974). *Preliminary manual for Family Environment Scale, Work Environment Scale, Group Environment Scale.* Palo Alto: Consulting Psychologist Press.

Nace, E. P., Meyers, A. L., O'Brien, C. P., Ream, N., & Mintz, J. (1977). Depression in veterans two years after Vietnam. *American Journal of Psychiatry, 134*, 167–170.
Schacht, T., & Nathan, P. E. (1977). But is it good for psychologists? Appraisal and status of DSM–III. *American Psychologist, 32*, 1017–1025.
Shatan, C. F. (1972). Soldiers in mourning. *American Journal of Orthopsychiatry, 42*, 300–301.
Shatan, C. F. (1974). Through the membrane of reality: "Impacted grief" and perceptual dissonance in Vietnam combat veterans. *Psychiatric Opinion, 11*, 6–15.
Shatan, C. F. (1978). Stress disorders among Vietnam veterans: The emotional content of combat continues. In C. R. Figley (Ed.), *Stress disorders among Vietnam veterans: Theory, research and treatment*. New York: Brunner/Mazel.
Sines, J. O. (1978). Family Environment Scale. In O. K. Buros (Ed.), *The eighth mental measurements yearbook (Vol. I)*. Highland Park, N.J.: Gryphon.
Spitzer, R. L., Endicott, J., & Robins, E. (1975). Clinical criteria for psychiatric diagnosis and DSM III. *American Journal of Psychiatry, 132*, 1187–1192.
Strange, R. E. (1974). Psychiatric perspectives of the Vietnam veteran. *Mil. Med., 139*, 96–98.
Strayer, R., & Ellenhorn, E. (1975). Vietnam veterans: A study exploring adjustment patterns and attitudes. *Journal of Social Issues, 31*, 81–93.
Stuen, M. R., & Solberg, K. B. (1972). The Vietnam veterans: Characteristics and needs. In C. J. Sherman & E. M. Caffey, Jr. (Eds.), *The Vietnam veteran in contemporary society*. Washington, D.C.: GPO.
Voth, H. M., & Orth, M. H. (1973). *Psychotherapy and the role of the environment*. New York: Behavioral Publications.
Williams, T. (Ed.). (1980). *Post-traumatic stress disorders of the Vietnam veteran*. Cincinnati: Disabled American Veterans.
Worthington, E. R. (1976). The Vietnam era veteran anomie and adjustment. *Military Medicine, 141*, 169–170.

6

A Study of Women Vietnam Veterans and Their Mental Health Adjustment

Jenny A. Schnaier

When I came home, I, too (ME a nurse!!) was asked how many babies I killed—no one asked me how many babies I (we) saved that were VC casualties, no one cared and no one wanted to know the truth . . . it wouldn't jive with the public's already pre-conceived idea of what we were doing in RVN—so I had to deal with people avoiding me for that reason. NOW—with all the emphasis on Delayed Stress Syndrome—I'm having to deal with people that look at me and expect me to go crazy in front of their eyes simply because I'm a Vietnam Vet. Well I'm sick of being typecasted. Sure, many do have problems, but don't cast that shadow on all of us! Please! Before I was proud to be a Viet Vet, now I'm becoming embarrassed to say "I am a Viet Vet." (Quote from a woman Vietnam veteran, 1982)

I would like to thank Dr. Arnold Spokane of the University of Maryland for his thoughtful insights and reviews to both the study and this paper. His contributions and encouragement have been immeasurable. I would also like to express my appreciation to the Vietnam Veterans of America and their staff for their generous support. Finally, I wish to acknowledge the assistance of Dr. John Wilson and Joan Barron, R.N., for their contributions to the instrument used in this study.

The Vietnam War has left its mark on America and on the women and men who fought it. This country's involvement in Vietnam ended more than a decade ago, yet in the past few years the war in Vietnam has reemerged as a topic of "profoundly unfinished moral and psychological business" (Morrow, 1981, p. 20). The personal, social, and historical legacies of the Vietnam war are being conveyed in television documentaries, talk shows, professional conferences, and most recently, in scientific studies. References to, and comparisons with, the Vietnam War are made almost daily in numerous newspapers across the country. Mental health research is also revealing personal consequences for 9 million Americans who served in the armed forces during the Vietnam era (August 5, 1964-May 7, 1975) and 2.8 million who served directly in the Vietnam theater. These consequences include the findings that: of those veterans who were married before going to Vietnam, 38% were divorced within six months after returning from Southeast Asia, and the number of Vietnam veterans hospitalized for alcoholism or drinking problems more than doubled in the years between 1973 and 1980 (DAV, 1980, p. 3).

POST-TRAUMATIC STRESS DISORDER

The most common reaction of veterans to war is called Post-Traumatic Stress Disorder (PTSD). Formerly known as either post-traumatic neurosis or disorder and delayed stress syndrome, this reaction has been linked with "anxiety neuroses of a major sort due to severe and external stress beyond the usual and tolerable experiences of some people" (Veterans Administration, 1981a, p. 1). Figley (1980) notes that these extraordinary events are outside the range of common, normal human experiences such as simple bereavement, chronic illness, business losses, or marital conflict. Rather, PTSD is a reaction to such catastrophic events as explosions, hurricanes, floods, major fires, or airplane accidents. Most specifically it has been linked to stressful military combat experience (Bourne, 1969; Egendorf et al., 1981; Figley, 1978, 1980; Wilson, 1978, 1981). It is not precisely clear how many veterans are suffering from this disorder, but estimates of acute, chronic, or cyclical PTSD incidence range from 700,000 to 800,000 (Wilson, 1980) or about 40 to 60% of all male Vietnam veterans. In a recent comprehensive study of veterans, Veterans Administration findings reveal that the detrimental effects of the Vietnam War are widespread and far from resolved (Egendorf et al., 1981).

Until the 1980 revision of the *Diagnostic and Statistical Manual of Mental Disorders* (DSM-III) of the American Psychiatric Association (1980) appeared, there was no formal diagnostic category for PTSD. It is now, however, classified as a special form of anxiety disorder. The diagnostic criteria for PTSD include (a) existence of a recognizable stressor that would evoke significant symptoms of distress in almost everyone, (b) reexperiencing of the trauma, (c) numbing of responsiveness to or reduced involvement with the external world, beginning some time after the trauma, and (d) various reactive symptoms including excessive autonomic arousal, sleep disturbances, guilt about surviving, memory impairment or trouble concentrating, nonviolent impulsive behavior, and substance abuse. The disorder can range from mild to severe and, in its most extreme forms, can affect nearly every aspect of life (American Psychiatric Association, 1980, pp. 236-238). Although symptoms often occur immediately following the trauma, it is not unusual for emergence to occur after a latency period of several days, many months, or even several years after the original trauma. PTSD can be diagnosed as acute, chronic, or delayed.

THE FEMALE VIETNAM VETERAN

Although several researchers have examined PTSD in the male veteran (Bourne, 1970; Egendorf et al., 1981; Figley, 1978, 1980; Wilson, 1978, 1981) and in so doing have provided a fairly complete picture of this syndrome's impact on those men, space limitations here restrict a thorough discussion of those studies, and the reader is referred to the references for a more in-depth discussion and background. However, a brief summary of the research will illustrate the psychological impact of the war on men. Peter Bourne (1970) explains that although fewer psychiatric casualties occurred in Vietnam, Vietnam veterans have more problems in the readjustment period. He points to the "rapid transit to and from the combat zone," the 12-month tour and rotation that took away group support, the lack of social acceptance, and the psychological impact of ultimately losing the war.

Charles Figley (1978, 1980) has also written extensively on male veterans and PTSD. He has identified some of the unique characteristics of the Vietnam War and studied persons who developed stress reactions in an attempt to discern whether PTSD was linked more with the individual's predisposing factors or was the result of the severity and nature of the external trauma experienced. Figley's data supported the prevalence of PTSD and showed that veterans with combat experience developed more pathology than those without combat experience.

In a large-scale study, John Wilson (1978) has also attempted to look at PTSD symptoms in Vietnam veterans using Erikson's (1963) model of psychosocial development. Wilson's findings provide strong evidence for the prevalence of PTSD. He is among the first to view this syndrome in a broader theoretical framework and to break down the disorder into different types and stages.

The most extensive and comprehensive study of the Vietnam veteran was commissioned by the Veterans Administration and was completed in March 1981 by Arthur Egendorf, Charles Kadushin, Robert Laufer, George Rothbart, and Lee Sloan of the Center for Policy Research, Inc. Designed to look at "comparative adjustment of veterans and their peers," this 900-page, 2 million dollar national study appears to be a statistically sound and thorough evaluation of educational and work careers, postwar trauma, long-term stress reactions, and veterans' coping with the war experience. Investigators found a wealth of specific data supporting the existence of current problems and globally concluded that "those who actually served in Vietnam are plagued by significantly more problems than their peers" (DAV, 1980).

The researchers found that the war was an "undigested experience" far from resolved, pointing out that for some veterans the war's effects dissipate over time, but for others the effects endure. Egendorf et al. (1981) used specific mental health indices such as job status, educational achievement, drug and alcohol use, arrests, and stress-related symptoms and revealed mental health problems that remained pronounced, in spite of the finding that global measures of adjustment had not shown problems. Finally, they found significant variation in the war's detrimental effects on different veteran subgroups such as Hispanics and lower-income veterans.

Not one of the many studies that have been conducted have included women Vietnam veterans for study, and therefore, little if anything is known about their health and well-being.

Although occasional writers have discussed the possible implications of women in the military, they have tended to look only at their possible participation in combat (*Congressional Digest*, 1980; *Newsweek*, 1980; *U.S. News and World Report*, 1981), the historical perspectives of military nursing (*Military Medicine*, 1978; *Nursing Times*, 1977; *Nursing Mirror*, 1981; *Vermont Registered Nurse*, 1979), or the use of V.A. medical services by women (Veterans Administration, 1981d).

Approximately 260,000 women served in the armed forces during the

Vietnam era (Veterans Administration, 1983, p. 2). This statistic was gained only as a result of the 1980 Census in which, for the first time, women were asked if they were veterans. Approximately 10,000 of these female veterans served in the Vietnam theater in front-line combat zones. While most women served in medical positions, others served in such widely varying roles as intelligence and security, air traffic control, aerial reconnaissance photography, supply and legal positions, or clerks and nonmilitary volunteers. Little, if any, data exist on these female veterans, and most of our knowledge about their plight has been gleaned from the popular literature or from self-reports of their mental health problems. The women who have begun to speak out about their experiences recount daily exposure to extreme stressors while in military service and now disclose adjustment problems that they previously had kept hidden. They, like male veterans, appear to have been negatively affected by the Vietnam war in a long-term fashion.

Who are these forgotten females? It is very difficult to say. Current research and available statistics do not cover female veterans. The Department of Defense has no listing of who these women are, or the capacities that they served in. Statistics on gender and military service are not systematically collected. Neither the Bureau of Labor Statistics, the Office of Personnel Management, nor the Census Survey (women were not asked if they were veterans until 1980) collect data on women veterans. Any statistics that do exist are estimates based on various other indicators such as the number of medals awarded. Most of the preliminary and informal studies show that a majority of these women were nurses, and many served on the front lines in combat zones in M.A.S.H.-type facilities.

Despite this lack of formal inquiry, a review of the popular literature on female veterans reveals unrelenting experiences of constant casualties, mangled bodies, 24-hour work shifts, wartime romances ended abruptly, necessity of immediate, God-like medical decisions about treatment, and a daily experience of the death of young boys (the average age of combatants was 19.2 years old [Wilson, 1980]) who were at the prime of their physical development.

One of the first articles about nursing experiences in Vietnam describes the mass casualties, unbearable conditions, poor working facilities, and long stretches of nursing duty (Kirk, 1965). An article about a Navy hospital in Saigon describes nurses frequently making life-and-death decisions in triage, the necessity of making independent professional judgments on medical care, and the nurses' willingness to act as a "sounding board" to soldiers they cared for, allowing them to recount their stories of particularly gruesome or traumatic experiences (Morin, 1966).

As early as 1967, popular articles on nursing in Vietnam began to reveal that nurses often worked and operated under fire and that they began to be haunted by the tragedies they were forced to witness (Martin, 1967). These articles, plus those to follow later (Cribari, 1971; Jones, 1971), shared the common themes that nurses were constantly overworked, exposed to the massive casualties and the extreme injuries characteristic of the Vietnam war, the beginnings of nightmares, and the overall stressful situation that they were involved in daily.

The popular literature on women veterans suggests some possible stressors for women such as: taking care of wounded Vietnamese civilians, women, children, psychiatric casualties, and patients who later died; making decisions about who would receive equipment or personnel if shortages existed; physical and mental exhaustion; patients' death due to lack of equipment, time, or nursing errors; helping patients to wait for their death; and being under direct ground fire.

These identified stressors have also been connected with self-identified symptoms in women veterans including: depression, flashbacks, nightmares, guilt, anxiety attacks, suicidal tendencies, migraine headaches, spontaneous anger, alcohol or drug abuse, inability to sustain relationships, avoidance of intimacy, inability to hold jobs, sleeplessness, and uncontrollable, persisting tears. These symptom patterns suggest the existence of PTSD in female Vietnam veterans.

The unmistakable lack of scientific or empirical research about the mental health status of female veterans magnified the need for the study that is presented here. The purpose of this effort was to assess the nature and extent of mental health problems affecting female Vietnam veterans and to determine whether these experiences and reactions were restricted to a few vocal women, or whether they were similar to those of the male veterans who, previous research has shown, experienced a wide range of psychological problems the most frequent of which was PTSD. This assessment employed a questionnaire designed to ascertain post-traumatic stress disorder symptoms in women veterans. The instrument utilized in this study includes sections covering (a) biographical information, (b) details of the respondent's Vietnam experience, (c) the respondent's current general adjustment, and (d) the respondent's reaction to the Vietnam experience. It was hypothesized that a relationship would be found between stressors experienced in Vietnam and PTSD symptoms experienced subsequently by women veterans.

METHODOLOGY

Subjects

The respondent sample for this study consisted of subjects drawn from the Vietnam Veterans of America (VVA). This group contained women who voluntarily contacted the VVA (a veterans service organization) expressing interest in the experiences of female Vietnam veterans. All of the women sampled were themselves Vietnam veterans and served in various medical positions, the majority of whom were nurses. The respondents were all female and their age ranged from 32 to 67 years. They resided in various areas of the United States representing 31 states and Canada. Preliminary letters were sent to 127 women requesting their participation. An initial return rate of 88.14% was achieved yielding 97 subjects who were willing to participate. Of the 97 surveys mailed out, 89 were returned from nurses who had served in Vietnam, four indicated they were not medical personnel, one had not been stationed in Vietnam, and three surveys were not returned yielding a final return rate of 97%.

The women sampled for this study were similar to one another in several ways. Almost all the women were white, fell within the age group of 34 to 39, and were highly educated both currently and prior to entering the military (84.0% currently hold, at the minimum, a college-level diploma). Slightly less than one-half of the respondents were currently married, one-quarter had been divorced, and few had children (less than 50%).

Almost all women sampled were in the Army and served for one tour of 12 months (although they spent a longer period of time in military service) with approximately 90% holding a military rank of captain or below. Although the women did hold various nursing positions, the majority were related to emergency, intensive care, or surgical procedures.

Very few of these women reported negative feelings about going to Vietnam (see Table 1). Slightly over one-third, however, felt that they either needed more medical training or believed they were under or poorly trained (see Table 2). Almost one-half of the respondents reported having sought professional help for a mental health problem, but less than one-half of those seeking help ever discussed their experiences in Vietnam in counseling (see Table 3).

TABLE 1
Respondents' Attitudes About Going to Vietnam

In general, how did you feel about going to Vietnam?

Response	n	%
Very positive	44	50.6
Somewhat positive	23	26.4
Neutral	5	5.7
Somewhat negative	5	5.7
Very negative	6	6.9
Not sure/don't remember	2	2.3
Other	1	1.1
No response	1	1.1
Total	87	100%

Mean = 2.02
Standard deviation = 1.46

TABLE 2
Respondents' Perceived Adequacy of
Medical Training for Vietnam

How adequately do you feel you were medically trained for your assignment in Vietnam?

Response	n	%
Very well trained	25	28.7
Fairly well trained	32	36.8
Needed some more training	16	18.4
Undertrained	9	10.3
Poorly trained	4	4.6
No response	1	1.1
Total	87	100%

Mean = 2.24
Standard deviation = 1.13

TABLE 3
Respondents Seeking Professional Help for Any Mental Health Problems

Have you ever sought professional help with any mental health problems?

Response	n	%
Yes	42	48.3
No	44	50.6
No response	1	1.1
Total	87	100%

If yes, did you ever discuss your experiences in Vietnam?

Response	n	%
Yes	21	42.9
No	28	57.1
Total	49	100%

Questionnaire

The instrument used was designed for this study to examine Post-Traumatic Stress Disorder and consisted of six parts: Section I—biodemographic data; Section II— (Stressor Scale) identification of stressors in the Vietnam experience; Section III—(Scale 1) stress symptoms and their incidence rates; Section IV—(Scale 2) physical symptoms and their incidence rates; Section V—(Scales 3 and 4) stress symptoms and possible dates of onset and resolution; and Section VI—general questions (see Appendix A).

The general format of the instrument and Sections I, III, IV, and V were adapted with permission from the *Vietnam Era Stress Inventory* by John P. Wilson and Gustave E. Krauss (1981) designed for male veterans. Most of Section II's items were adapted by permission from personal correspondence with Joan Barron, R.N. (VA Medical Center, Dayton, Ohio) from her informal research on female Vietnam nurses. Section V, along with various items in all other sections, was derived empirically as a result of literature review of scientific studies and popular accounts by women veterans. In adapting from these sources, the author attempted to tap both the diagnostic criteria associated with PTSD by the APA's DSM-III and the kinds of experiences medical personnel and women were likely to have that may have differed from, or were in addition to, that which is known about male veterans.

Reliability and Validity

Reliability and validity data for this instrument did not exist at the time of this research effort. Therefore, in the analysis, Cronbach alpha statistics were calculated in order to derive internal consistency data for the subsections of the instrument. The alphas for each of the scales (ranging from 0.87 to 0.98) were judged adequate for research purposes. Earlier versions of similar instruments have been shown to be useful measure of PTSD (Wilson & Krauss, 1981).

Procedures

All female Vietnam veterans on the VVA's mailing list received a letter from the investigator explaining the study's intent and a letter from the National Women's Director of the VVA endorsing this project.

Subjects were kept blind from the investigator and given a code number. This was done to protect individuals who did not wish to participate and to allow for follow-up (via code number) of those who did not respond to the first inquiry. This initial mailing sent by the VVA also included a return postcard addressed to the investigator.

Once permission was secured, each subject received a packet containing: a questionnaire, a return envelope, and a list of professional mental health referrals in the subject's state of residence (compiled by the VVA). If there was no response within two weeks, a follow-up letter was mailed requesting their participation again and reminding them about the questionnaire. After three weeks, a second and final reminder was mailed out. Each participant received a debriefing and a summary of the findings after completion of the study.

Arrangements were made to provide a telephone referral service and debriefing to any woman who wanted it during the time of the survey administration. Subjects were given a telephone number where the experimenter could be reached in the event that completion of the questionnaire elicited anxiety or depressive reactions, or catalyzed the need for mental health services.

RESULTS

In order to summarize the responses, several statistical analyses were computed including descriptive statistics, multiple regression analyses, measures of internal consistency, and item-scale intercorrelations. In addition to this, eight open-ended questions were analyzed through a simple content summary process.

The Stressor Scale surveyed the women's experiences in Vietnam and revealed that a few of the stressors were listed as very high (nursing duties, seeing the mutilation of young bodies, having equipment or personnel shortages, having a continual stream of casualties, feeling tired, and feeling the need to negate emotions). Likewise, a few items were reported very low (participation in death). The majority of responses ranged between "rarely" and "very often."

Scale 1, which ascertains the occurrence of symptoms, showed that those thoughts and feelings that were reported highly concerned anger, fear, feeling different or self-conscious, and feeling cynical about governmental processes and policies. In the categories that account for a problem occurring between 10 and 30 times a month, approximately one-third of the items were endorsed by 25% or more of the subjects.

Scale 2, which tallies physical symptoms that respondents experienced, showed that every item had a frequency of 50% or more in the combined categories of "never" and "1 to 5 times a month." Subjects' responses did extend the full range from 1 to 30 times a month on almost all items.

Scales 3 and 4 together look at possible dates of onset of symptoms and whether or not they are still present today. The symptoms women reported here represent a fairly complete picture of those specific symptoms and experiences associated with PTSD as defined by DSM-III. For those symptoms reported as occurring first between homecoming and one year, approximately 70% were reported as still present today. (For approximately 70% of the items, symptoms were reported as still present today.) (See Appendix B.)

Four stepwise multiple regression analyses were computed regressing specific demographic data on each of the four symptom scales as a method of determining the relationship between the criteria variables of symptom scale scores and various predictor variables. The multiple regression analyses indicated that seeking mental health help, feelings about how adequately medically trained, and the Stressor Scale were statistically significant predictors of the first symptom scale (see Table

4). That is, respondents who experienced symptoms were more likely to seek mental health help, felt they were not well trained medically, and experienced more stressors in Vietnam.

Two F ratios are presented (F and F alone). The first ratio (F) represents a test of significance for each variable when it is included with the rest of the variables in the analysis. The second ratio (F alone) represents a test of significance for each variable when it is used as the only predictor of the dependent variable in this case, Scale 1 (Stressors). The analysis also indicated that seeking mental health help and the Stressor Scale were significant predictors for Scale 2 or physical symptoms. (See Table 5.) Table 6 shows an intercorrelation matrix among all variables.

Pearson correlation coefficients were calculated in order to examine relationships among the variables. The correlations between the Stressor Scale and the first two symptoms scales supported the hypothesis of a strong and linear relationship between stressors experienced in Vietnam and PTSD symptoms experienced subsequently. Correlations among the demographic variables and each of the stress scales did not support the expectation that background or demographic data would have some relation to subsequent reports of symptoms. Four exceptions were: (a) a 0.26 correlation between the Stressor Scale and the respondent's positive response to corresponding with anyone back home during the Vietnam tour, (b) a 0.37 correlation between Scale 1 and a positive response to having sought professional help with any mental health problems, (c) a 0.34 correlation between Scale 2 and a positive response to having suffered a disability or injury in Vietnam were notable (this final correlation is to be expected since Scale 2 measured physical symptoms).

The open-ended questions provided a broader and more subjective context within which to understand the experiences and reactions of women Vietnam veterans. These questions seemed to elicit a great deal of interest from the respondents. It appeared that the women found this section to be an appropriate place to expand on their thoughts and feelings, and many did so by writing additional pages to their questionnaires in order to fully express themselves. The responses were so lengthy and varied that future analyses will be undertaken to garner as much information from these responses as possible. Some observations have been made through a simple summary process.

Insight was gained into subjects' life histories and priorities from the question about important life events that had a major influence in their lives. Respondents seemed to react very positively to the question about gains or benefits from their experiences in Vietnam. They were eager to discuss the positive side of their experiences instead of the usual one-

TABLE 4

Multiple Regression Analysis of Independent Variables on Stress Symptoms and Incidence Rates

Independent variable	Multiple r	r square	r-square change	Simple r	F	F alone
Seeking mental health help	0.3717	0.1381	0.1381	0.3717	9.52	11.86[a]
Number corresponded with	0.3798	0.1443	0.0062	−0.0921	0.63	0.73
Feelings toward going to Vietnam	0.4031	0.1625	0.0182	0.1492	0.86	1.91
How well medically trained	0.4228	0.1787	0.0163	0.2181	0.77	4.08[b]
Stressor Scale	0.5327	0.2837	0.1050	0.3718	11.43	11.87[a]
Number of tours in Vietnam	0.5426	0.2944	0.0107	−0.1439	3.56	1.78
Total months in Vietnam	0.5650	0.3192	0.0248	−0.0747	2.58	0.48
Education prior to military	0.5663	0.3207	0.0015	−0.0077	0.18	0.01
Age in Vietnam	0.5664	0.3208	0.0001	−0.0625	0.01	0.34

[a]$p < 0.01$.
[b]$p < 0.05$.

TABLE 5
Multiple Regression Analysis of Independent Variables on Physical Symptoms and Incidence Rates

Independent variable	Multiple r	r square	r-square change	Simple r	F	F alone
Seeking mental health help	0.3436	0.1181	0.1181	0.3436	7.67	9.62[a]
Number corresponded with	0.3589	0.1288	0.0108	-0.1164	1.19	1.10
Feelings toward going to Vietnam	0.3992	0.1593	0.0305	0.1888	2.23	2.90
How well medically trained	0.4066	0.1653	0.0060	0.1831	0.43	2.73
Stressor Scale	0.4494	0.2020	0.0367	0.2314	3.62	4.36[b]
Number of tours in Vietnam	0.4556	0.2076	0.0056	-0.1117	2.01	1.08
Total months in Vietnam	0.4714	0.2225	0.0150	0.0635	1.64	0.33
Education prior to military	0.4765	0.2271	0.0046	0.0284	0.56	0.06
Age in Vietnam	0.4843	0.2346	0.0075	0.0071	0.75	0.00

[a]$p < 0.01$.
[b]$p < 0.05$.

TABLE 6
Intercorrelation Matrix Among All Variables

Variables	Education prior to military	Number of tours in Vietnam	Total months in Vietnam	Number corresponded with	Feelings toward going to Vietnam	How well medically trained	Seeking mental health help
Education prior to military	1.0000						
Number of tours in Vietnam	0.1444	1.0000					
Total months in Vietnam	-0.1731	-0.5898	1.0000				
Number corresponded with	0.0397	0.0622	0.0076	1.0000			
Feelings toward going to Vietnam	-0.0520	0.1286	-0.1270	-0.0308	1.0000		
How well medically trained	-0.0868	0.1341	-0.0904	0.0249	0.3913	1.0000	
Seeking mental health help	0.0377	0.1893	-0.0745	0.0368	-0.0325	-0.1401	1.0000
Stressor Scale	-0.0636	0.0060	-0.0393	0.0240	0.0398	0.1986	-0.0746
Scale 1	-0.0077	-0.1439	-0.0747	-0.0921	0.1492	0.2181	-0.3717
Scale 2	0.0284	-0.1117	-0.0635	-0.1164	0.1888	0.1831	-0.3436
Scale 3	-0.1066	-0.0547	0.0633	-0.0175	-0.0374	-0.1240	-0.1315
Scale 4	-0.0103	-0.1613	-0.0807	0.0284	0.0938	0.0425	-0.1224
Age in Vietnam	-0.0846	-0.1005	0.2267	0.1378	-0.2108	-0.1725	-0.0367

(Table 6 cont'd)	Stressor Scale	Scale 1	Scale 2	Scale 3	Scale 4	Age in Vietnam
Stressor Scale	1.0000					
Scale 1	0.3718	1.0000				
Scale 2	0.2314	0.7601	1.0000			
Scale 3	-0.1407	0.2206	0.1170	1.0000		
Scale 4	-0.0148	0.5751	0.4760	0.2190	1.0000	
Age in Vietnam	-0.0389	-0.0625	0.0071	0.1118	-0.0172	1.0000

sided inquiry. The answers seemed to indicate the significant gains and growth had occurred for many of the women.

The questions about why subjects volunteered for Vietnam and about their hopes and expectations also provided some insight into what these women's lives were like prior to Vietnam and about what motivated them to go. Once again, responses were varied, but many spoke about idealistic or unreal expectations and beliefs that led them to try to flee a situation or yearn for another. The responses also revealed several women who went to Vietnam knowing the reality of war and what their experiences would be like.

One question showed some of the ways that the Vietnam experience affected the respondents' lives, revealing both positive and negative responses, and also seemed to indicate, for some, a processing through of their experiences and the impact they had. Those who had positive comments about their Vietnam experience (approximately 45% of the responses) wrote such things as: a sifting out of priorities, new insights into self and others, now being tougher, stronger, and more mature, trusting self and realizing strengths, and growing professionally. Comments that were more negative (approximately 32% of the responses) included: finding nursing experiences outside of Vietnam unsatisfactory, being emotionally numb, being impulsive, and being angry and depressive. Very few women responded with comments that were both positive and negative.

The question about specific events that occurred which were especially difficult to deal with also elicited long and involved responses. Many women seemed to hold a specific incident vividly in their memories and used this individual tragedy to globally symbolize the horror and trauma of their entire war experience. Some even responded by saying that there had been an incident to relate, but they would not discuss it because it was still so difficult or painful to deal with.

DISCUSSION

This research has provided evidence that Post-Traumatic Stress Disorder may be applicable to the experiences of women Vietnam veterans. The instrument employed in this study has been found to be both reliable statistically and valid in that there was a significant correlation between stressors and symptom scales for this sample. The highest identified stressors (involving nursing duties, experiencing shortages, continual streams of casualties, negating emotions, and seeing the mutilation of young bodies), together with the types of symptoms identified by the women veterans that are associated with PTSD, support the notion that further studies are indicated and justified to look more closely at women Vietnam veterans and their mental health adjustment.

Second, this research has found that there is evidence of mental health distress among the women sampled. When asked about symptoms during the past six months, the following was observed: 27.6% reported having suicidal thoughts between one and nine times a month, 19.5% reported feeling alienated from other people between 15 and 30 times a month, 19.2% reported feeling depressed between 15 and 30 times a month, 16.1% reported feeling an inability to be close to someone they care about between 15 and 30 times a month, and 10.3% reported feeling numb or nothing inside between 15 and 30 times a month. These are just a few of the examples of the problems that a "significant" minority of women veterans are experiencing and might be applicable to the larger sample of women veterans.

Third, there were positive, growthful aspects associated with the Vietnam experience for many of the women in this sample. Judging from the responses to the open-ended questions, both personal and professional gains were made that need to be more fully explored and understood. This positive aspect is a rarely examined aspect of both women and men veterans' experiences whose influence would be interesting to explore to determine whether the awareness or recognition of growthful aspects of the Vietnam experience has any mediating effects on current adjustment. In addition, attention to this side of the veterans' experience may provide an additional source of pride to the veterans that might allow them and others to accept and view their experience more fully.

Fourth and finally, this sample has indicated that at least as far as biographical-demographic factors are concerned, women Vietnam veterans in this sample were different from men Vietnam veterans in other large-scale studies. This is true for such factors as age in Vietnam, racial background, education level, income level, and for symptoms of substance abuse and survivor guilt, which have been identified by the research on men as important mediating and/or predicting variables but have not stood out in this research as significant predictors of PTSD symptoms. These variables need to be more closely examined to see whether they actually do not serve as predicting or mediating factors in the development or existence of symptoms and, if so, why. One possibility is that the present, limited sample group is too homogeneous to allow these variables to stand out.

There are inherent limitations in this type of research, which is designed as preliminary and descriptive. Some of the limitations are due to a biased, nonrandomized sample group who had previously and voluntarily identified themselves with a veterans' organization, lack of comparison or control groups, no population baseline rates, and a self-report taken many years after the event.

The limitation of a biased sample was dictated by the reality of what population was identified as women veterans and was accessible. Even though 97% of subjects we could locate responded, we do not know how many we could not locate or how representative the present sample is of the whole population of women Vietnam veterans. Research such as this present effort may help to encourage the compilation of a list of women veterans or support the development of a large-scale study similar to the VA's mandated research on male veterans, which will have the person-power and financial resources to select a truly randomized, representative sample of women Vietnam veterans and their peers. For the present, we examined the only available sample of women Vietnam veterans.

Information about the instrument itself was gained by examining the women's responses to it, their comments on the open-ended questions which asked about the questionnaire itself, and the statistical analyses that were computed. One of the findings was that Scale 2, which looked at physical symptoms, was a confusing section to the women and that without a reference to any current medical or physical health problems, the women's responses were difficult to put in context. The inclusion of questions about physical symptoms is supported by the past research findings and should not be dropped, but rather inquired about more clearly and within the context of their general physical health in order to present a more accurate picture of its relationship to PTSD.

It was also indicated that an examination of the response categories used for the items is needed since several women commented that they had difficulty with the numerical representations of categories, citing, for example, that they had difficulty saying "a little bit" when referring to something occurring one to nine times a month. It may be that these categories are too broad and influenced the respondents to respond inaccurately.

A final limitation has to do with additional areas to be explored that were not fully tapped by this questionnaire. These included issues such as sexuality, sexual harassment, and romantic involvements in Vietnam, their possible role change and/or conflicts as women prior, during, and post-Vietnam, and more specific questions about suicidal attempts and feelings. Several women perceived this instrument as "male-oriented" and seemed to indicate that further attempts should be made to more fully address the women's experiences rather than men's.

CONCLUSIONS

Findings from this investigation may provide necessary and useful information for the clinician who works with female veterans in either group or individual counseling. Those mental health professionals who work in VA settings need to be aware of the women veterans' strongly felt cynicism toward governmental agencies and be prepared for the possible distrust, distancing, or anger that might occur. Professionals working outside of VA settings should bear in mind that for the women who have sought mental health help, less than one-half have ever discussed Vietnam with their counselor. While it certainly may be true that the distress is unrelated to the Vietnam experience, clinicians need to be more careful and sensitive to this information and keep in mind that women did serve in Vietnam and that their experiences were probably profound and life-altering in both positive and negative ways.

Counselors may want to use the assessment instrument employed in this study once a therapeutic relationship has begun to be established. The best method would probably involve going over the questions in the instrument face to face while in the counseling session, since many respondents reported reacting strongly to it. Utilization of the instrument would serve several purposes, two of which being that it allows the counselor to demonstrate a knowledge of the kinds of experiences and emotions women Vietnam veterans might have and it allows the veteran to realize that there are other veterans who have similar feelings and reactions. Asking the open-ended, more general questions might be a particularly good way to help the client to begin to open up and share her experiences more fully. Utilizing this type of assessment tool would be especially helpful to nonveteran counselors.

One respondent's comment that seemed to capture the essence of many of the subjects' responses offers particular insight into the female Vietnam veteran. She wrote, " . . . Vietnam was the ultimate of everything good *and* bad. It was, in short, painfully delightful."

This research, then, serves as an indicator that cautions mental health professionals not to treat or view female Vietnam veterans exactly like male veterans when conducting research or in counseling. It substantiates the original conception that women veterans may be suffering mental health problems that appear to be related to their Vietnam experience. Until more is known about women Vietnam veterans, their experiences, and their reactions to them, we as researchers and clinicians have a responsibility to keep an open mind in exploring their lives and experiences.

REFERENCES

American Psychiatric Association (1980). *Diagnostic and statistical manual of mental disorders* (3rd ed.). Washington, DC: American Psychiatric Association.
Bourne, P. G. (1969). *The psychology and physiology of stress.* New York: Academic Press.
Bourne, P. G. (1970). *Men, stress, and Vietnam.* Boston: Little, Brown.
Cribari, M. K. (1971). Trauma—And a four foot giant. *AORN Journal, 13,* 83–88.
Disabled American Veterans (1980). *DAV.* Cincinnati: DAV.
Egendorf, A., Kadushin, C., Laufer, R., Rothbart, G., & Sloan, L. (1981). *Legacies of Vietnam: Comparative adjustment of veterans and their peers.* Center for Policy Research, Inc. (House Committee Print No. 14). Washington, DC: US Government Printing Office.
Erikson, E. (1963). *Childhood and society.* New York: Norton.
Figley, C. R. (1978). *Stress disorders among Vietnam veterans: Theory, research and development.* New York: Brunner/Mazel.
Figley, C. R. (1980). Welcoming back the Vietnam veteran survivor: Review and application of post-traumatic stress disorder. Paper presented at the 133rd annual meeting of the American Psychiatric Association, San Francisco, May 1980.
Figley, C. R., & Leventman, S. (1980). *Strangers at home: Vietnam veterans since the war.* New York: Praeger Publishers.
Fresh doubts about women in armed forces. *U.S. News and World Report, 91*(3), 44, July 20, 1981.
Glass, A. J. (1969). History of psychiatry in Vietnam. In P. Bourne (Ed.), *The psychology and physiology of stress.* New York: Academic Press.
Historical perspectives of armed forces nursing. *Military Medicine, 143*(7), 457–463, July 1978.
History of nursing in the army. *Nursing Mirror, 153*(2), 23–24, July 8, 1981.
Jones, N. (1971). Someday this will end. *American Journal of Nursing, 71,* 1364–1365.
Kirk, D. (1965). It was 2:00 a.m. Saigon time. *American Journal of Nursing, 65*(12), 77–79.
Martin, L. G. (1967). Angels of Vietnam. *Today's Health, 45,* 17–22.
Mary comes marching home. *Los Angeles Herald Examiner,* December 14, 1980.
Morin, A. E. (1966). Navy hospital in Saigon. *American Journal of Nursing, 66,* 1977–1979.
Morrison, D. F. (1976). *Multivariate statistical methods.* New York: McGraw-Hill.
Morrow, L. (1981, July 13). The forgotten warriors. *Time, 118*(2), 18-25.
An overview of nursing's accomplishments in WW I. *Vermont Registered Nurse,* pp. 9–11, December 1979.
Rogers, B. Nurses at war. *Nursing Mirror, 146*(14), 13–16, April 6, 1978.
Veterans Administration (1981a). *Post-traumatic stress syndrome.*
Veterans Administration (1981b). *Professional services letter* (p. 1). Washington, DC: Department of Medicine and Surgery, January 28, 1981.
Veterans Administration (1981c). *Selected characteristics of female veterans.* Washington, DC: Office of Reports and Statistics, Research Division 711.
Veterans Administration (1981d). *Women's use of V.A. hospitals: A profile of the 70's.* Washington, DC: Office of Reports and Statistics, Biometrics Division.
Veterans Administration (1983). *The female veteran population.* Washington, DC: Office of Reports and Statistics, Research Division (711), (RSM 70-84-1).
Williams, T. (1980). *Post-traumatic stress disorders of the Vietnam veteran.* Cincinnati: Disabled American Veterans.

Wilson, J. P. (1978). *Forgotten warrior project*. Cincinnati: Disabled American Veterans.

Wilson, J. P. (1980). Towards an understanding of post-traumatic stress disorders among Vietnam veterans. Testimony before US Senate Subcommittee on Veterans Affairs, Washington, DC, May 21, 1980.

Wilson, J. P. (1981). Cognitive control mechanisms in stress response syndromes and their relation to different forms of the disorder. Panel presentation at Hospital and Community Psychiatry Conference in California, September 15, 1981.

Wilson, J. P., & Krauss, G. E. (1981). *Vietnam era stress inventory*. Cleveland, OH: Cleveland State University.

Women in the military. *Newsweek, 95*(7), 34–42, February 18, 1980.

Women in the U.S. armed forces. *Congressional Digest, 58*(4), 102, April 1980.

Women at war. *Nursing Times, 73*(13), 444–446, March 31, 1977.

APPENDIX A
QUESTIONNAIRE FOR WOMEN VIETNAM
VETERANS*

Instructions

Here is the questionnaire that you have agreed to complete about your experiences and adjustment to your Vietnam experience. The questionnaire contains five parts, and takes about one hour to complete. We believe that you will find this questionnaire to be both interesting and valuable in learning more about yourself.

It is best if you complete the questionnaire in one sitting. However, if it is more convenient for you, you may choose to complete the questionnaire one part at a time being careful not to allow too long a period of time to elapse between parts. Please complete all items on this survey. Each section contains specific instructions, so be sure to read them carefully.

Remember—*DO NOT WRITE YOUR NAME* on the questionnaire. This information will be kept strictly confidential and is being used to learn more about women Vietnam veterans.

Often, other veterans have reported that after filling out a questionnaire such as this, lots of questions and thoughts come to mind about their experiences that they would like to discuss with someone. Therefore, we are enclosing a referral list of possible mental health agencies, veterans groups, and counselors you may wish to contact if you so desire. You may also call me at —————— if you need further assistance.

Once again, we would like to remind you that your participation is entirely voluntary. If at any time you would rather not complete this, you are under no obligation to do so. However, we would greatly appreciate your participation and we thank you for your cooperation and speedy reply in this important endeavor. Please return your completed questionnaire in the enclosed prepaid envelope.

---

*Adapted in part with permission from Vietnam Era Stress Inventory (V.E.S.I.) copyrighted by John P. Wilson and Gustave Krauss, 1981, and parts suggested by Joan Barron, R.N., V.A. Medical center.

After completion you will receive a summary of our findings that will be mailed to all participants through the VVA.

Thank you,

Jenny Schnaier
Graduate Student,
   University of Maryland

1. Date of birth: _____
   Mo Day Yr

2. Race or ethnicity:
   American Indian/Native American   _____
   Black, not of Hispanic origin   _____
   Asian or Pacific Islander   _____
   Hispanic   _____
   White, not of Hispanic origin   _____

3. How much education did you have prior to entering the military?
   Some high school   _____
   Completed high school   _____
   Some college/professional school   _____
   Completed college/professional school   _____
   Some graduate work   _____
   Completed graduate work   _____
   Please specify type of degree(s) held, if any _____

4. How much education do you currently have?
   Some high school   _____
   Completed high school   _____
   Some college/professional school   _____
   Completed college/professional school   _____
   Some graduate work   _____
   Completed graduate work   _____
   Please specify type of degree(s) held, if any _____

5. Since leaving Vietnam, what is your work history? Please list your current job first
   and specify any within job changes (i.e. from surgical to pediatric nurse).

Kind of business or organization	Job Title	Length of Employment	Reason for Leaving

6. What is your approximate present annual gross (before taxes) income?
   0 - 5,000   _____   20,001 - 25,000   _____
   5,001 - 10,000   _____   25,001 - 30,000   _____
   10,001 - 15,000 _____   30,001 or over   _____
   15,001 - 20,000 _____

7. Were you married at the time you entered the military?   Yes _____   No _____

8. If yes, how long had you been married?   _____

9. If no, were you?
   Single _____   Divorced _____   Separated _____   Widowed _____

10. Present marital status?
    Married (never divorced)   _____   Divorced and still single   _____
    Married (previously divorced) _____   Divorced (living with 'lover')   _____
    Married (previously widowed) _____   Living with 'lover'   _____
    Separated   _____   Common law marriage   _____
    Single   _____

11. If divorced, in what year(s) were you divorced?   _____

12. What is your pregnancy history?
    Number of pregnancies   _____   Number of live births   _____
    Number of miscarriages   _____   Number of still births   _____
    Number of abortions   _____   Number of children   _____

13. What branch of the service did you serve in?
    Marines   _____   Navy   _____
    Army   _____   Coast Guard _____
    Air Force _____

14. What was your rank in the military?   _____

120

15. What was your job in the military? (Please list specific jobs)

_____

_____

_____

16. Active service dates?   From: _____   To: _____
                                   Mo Day Yr   Mo Day Yr

17. Type of discharge? (Honorable, general, dishonorable, etc.)

_____

18. Did you ever re-enlist?   Yes _____   No _____

19. How were you sent to Vietnam?
    Routine transfer   _____   Volunteered (willingly)   _____
    Other (specify)   _____   Volunteered (against my will)   _____

20. Did you do more than one tour in Vietnam?   Yes _____   No _____

21. If yes, how did that happen? _____

_____

22. Dates of service in Vietnam?
    From: _____   To: _____
    From: _____   To: _____
    From: _____   To: _____

23. In general how did you feel about going to Vietnam?
    Very positive   _____   Somewhat negative   _____
    Somewhat positive   _____   Very negative   _____
    Neutral   _____   Not sure/don't remember   _____

24. How adequately do you feel you were medically trained for your assignment in Vietnam?
    Very well trained   _____   Undertrained   _____
    Fairly well trained   _____   Poorly trained   _____
    Needed some more training _____

25. Did you correspond with anyone back home continuously during your tour in Vietnam?
    Yes _____   No _____

26. If yes, who?
    Mother   _____   Father   _____
    Brother(s)   _____   Sister(s)   _____
    Husband   _____   Relative   _____
    Boyfriend   _____   Friend   _____
    Other   _____   Child   _____

27. Did you suffer any disability or injuries in Vietnam?
    Yes (please describe) _____
    No _____

28. Have you ever sought professional help with any mental health problems?
    Yes _____   No _____

29. If yes, did you ever discuss your experiences in Vietnam?
    Yes _____   No _____

    Please describe the type of help sought. _____

_____

_____

Below is a list of questions that are about your experiences in Vietnam and what you have thought about them. Please read each one carefully. After you have done so, circle one of the numbered spaces to the right that best describes the frequency that experience happened to you. Circle only one numbered space for each question and do not skip any items.

Frequency for Numbered Spaces

Never - Experience did not occur
Rarely - Experience occurred one time every month
Occasionally - Experience occurred one time every two weeks
Often - Experience occurred one or two times each week
Very Often - Experience occurred three or more times a week

		Never	Rarely	Occasionally	Often	Very Often
30.	Taking care of wounded American soldiers?	0	1	2	3	4
31.	Taking care of wounded Vietnamese soldiers?	0	1	2	3	4
32.	Taking care of wounded civilians?	0	1	2	3	4
33.	Taking care of wounded children and women?	0	1	2	3	4
34.	Taking care of wounded P.O.W.'s?	0	1	2	3	4
35.	Taking care of psychiatric casualties?	0	1	2	3	4
36.	Taking care of a patient who reminded you of someone close to you?	0	1	2	3	4
37.	Taking care of Americans who later died?	0	1	2	3	4
38.	Preparation of American bodies for evacuation?	0	1	2	3	4
39.	Taking care of Vietnamese who died?	0	1	2	3	4
40.	Preparation of Vietnamese bodies for evacuation?	0	1	2	3	4
41.	Having personnel shortages?	0	1	2	3	4
42.	Having equipment and supply shortages?	0	1	2	3	4
43.	Having a continual stream of casualties?	0	1	2	3	4
44.	Having to make decisions about who would receive equipment or personnel if shortages existed?	0	1	2	3	4
45.	Having to make decisions in triage about who would get treatment?	0	1	2	3	4
46.	Having to watch patients die because of equipment or personnel shortages?	0	1	2	3	4
47.	Seeing the mutilation of young bodies?	0	1	2	3	4
48.	Not knowing what happened to a patient after they left your care?	0	1	2	3	4
49.	Feeling underprepared or undertrained to help?	0	1	2	3	4
50.	Feeling tired (lack of sleep) both mentally and physically?	0	1	2	3	4
51.	Having patients die because of medical or nursing errors?	0	1	2	3	4
52.	Making nursing errors due to tiredness and/or overwork, and/or overload?	0	1	2	3	4

Never - Experience did not occur
Rarely - Experience occurred one time every month
Occasionally - Experience occurred one time every two weeks
Often - Experience occurred one or two times each week
Very Often - Experience occurred three or more times a week

		Never	Rarely	Occasionally	Often	Very Often
53.	Actively participating in or aiding in the death of wounded Vietnamese in order to medically assist American soldiers?	0	1	2	3	4
54.	Passively participating in or aiding in the death of wounded Vietnamese in order to medically assist American soldiers?	0	1	2	3	4
55.	Actively participating in helping a patient who requested to be allowed to die?	0	1	2	3	4
56.	Passively participating in helping a patient who requested to be allowed to die?	0	1	2	3	4
57.	Having to use heroic attempts to resuscitate a patient when you felt they would be better off if allowed to die?	0	1	2	3	4
58.	Having to sit with a patient who was waiting for their death?	0	1	2	3	4
59.	Having to communicate with the family and friends of patients who died?	0	1	2	3	4
60.	Being under direct mortar or ground fire?	0	1	2	3	4
61.	Being in situations in which you thought you would not survive?	0	1	2	3	4
62.	Feeling personally responsible for a death?	0	1	2	3	4
63.	Feeling personally responsible for life and death decisions?	0	1	2	3	4
64.	Feeling the need to negate the emotions you experienced at the time in order to get through the experience?	0	1	2	3	4
65.	Feeling like a failure in your job (Unable to provide support, comfort or easing of pain)?	0	1	2	3	4
66.	Adapting to drastic or unexpected role changes both professionally and personally?	0	1	2	3	4
67.	Having to cope with sexual harassment?	0	1	2	3	4

III

INSTRUCTIONS

Below is a list of problems and complaints that some Vietnam Era veterans sometimes have. Please read each one carefully. After you have done so, please
circle one of the numbered spaces to the right that best describes HOW MUCH THAT
PROBLEM HAS BOTHERED OR DISTRESSED YOU DURING THE PAST SIX (6) MONTHS INCLUDING
TODAY. Circle only one numbered space for each problem keeping in mind the
definition of frequency for each numbered space. Do not skip any items.

Frequency for Numbered Spaces

Not at all - Problem does not occur
A little bit - 1 to 9 times a month
Moderately - 10 to 14 times a month
Quite a bit - 15 to 20 times a month
Extremely - 21 to 30 times a month

HOW MUCH WERE YOU BOTHERED BY:	Not at all	A little bit	Moder- ately	Quite a bit	Ex- tremely
68. Feeling anxious or nervous?	0	1	2	3	4
69. Suicidal thoughts?	0	1	2	3	4
70. Problems of concentration?	0	1	2	3	4
71. Feeling depressed (down, bummed out)?	0	1	2	3	4
72. Thoughts of a friend(s) killed in Vietnam?	0	1	2	3	4
73. Asking yourself why others died in Vietnam and not you?	0	1	2	3	4
74. Feeling guilty that you survived the war when others didn't?	0	1	2	3	4
75. Feeling guilty that certain patients survived who you felt probably shouldn't have?	0	1	2	3	4
76. Feeling like isolating or withdrawing yourself from others?	0	1	2	3	4
77. Having problems going to sleep?	0	1	2	3	4
78. Experiencing nightmares of the war?	0	1	2	3	4
79. Experiencing anger?	0	1	2	3	4
80. Experiencing rage?	0	1	2	3	4
81. Experiencing sadness over lost friends that you cannot express?	0	1	2	3	4
82. Experiencing explosive anger?	0	1	2	3	4
83. Trying to get rid of unpleasant thoughts about Vietnam when they come into your head?	0	1	2	3	4
84. Feeling numb or nothing inside?	0	1	2	3	4
85. Feeling that all of your problems are caused by other people doing things to you?	0	1	2	3	4
86. Mistrusting what others say or do?	0	1	2	3	4
87. Memories of Vietnam which just seem to pop into your head in an unpredictable way?	0	1	2	3	4
88. The fear of losing control of your impulses (e.g. feelings, emotions)?	0	1	2	3	4
89. Using alcohol to help you feel better?	0	1	2	3	4

Frequency for Numbered Spaces

Not at all - Problem does not occur
A little bit - 1 to 9 times a month
Moderately - 10 to 14 times a month
Quite a bit - 15 to 20 times a month
Extremely - 21 to 30 times a month

HOW MUCH WERE YOU BOTHERED BY:	Not at all	A little bit	Moderately	Quite a bit	Extremely
90. Using alcohol to help you sleep?	0	1	2	3	4
91. Using hard drugs to help you feel better (e.g. speed, heroin)?	0	1	2	3	4
92. Using hard drugs to help you sleep (e.g. speed, heroin)?	0	1	2	3	4
93. Using marijuana to help you feel better?	0	1	2	3	4
94. Using marijuana to help you sleep?	0	1	2	3	4
95. Responding reflexively, using military-like survival tactics when under stress?	0	1	2	3	4
96. War related thoughts (e.g. memories of Vietnam)?	0	1	2	3	4
97. Taking drugs prescribed by a doctor for your emotional upset?	0	1	2	3	4
98. Feeling an inability to be close to someone you care about?	0	1	2	3	4
99. Experiencing sexual problems?	0	1	2	3	4
100. Feeling alienated from other people?	0	1	2	3	4
101. An inability to talk about the war?	0	1	2	3	4
102. Experiencing a fear of losing loved ones?	0	1	2	3	4
103. Feeling like you lost your romantic, sexual sensitivity in Vietnam?	0	1	2	3	4
104. Getting into fights or conflicts with loved ones?	0	1	2	3	4
105. Getting into fights with others?	0	1	2	3	4
106. Feeling unable to express your real feelings to others?	0	1	2	3	4
107. "Flying off the handle" in frustration when things don't go right?	0	1	2	3	4
108. Losing your temper and getting out of control?	0	1	2	3	4
109. Experiencing problems with your husband or lover?	0	1	2	3	4
110. Arguing with your husband or lover?	0	1	2	3	4
111. Having a problem trusting others for fear of something bad happening to you?	0	1	2	3	4
112. Getting nervous around other people who are not Vietnam veterans?	0	1	2	3	4
113. Experiencing problems being close to your family?	0	1	2	3	4
114. Your husband or lover complaining that Vietnam has messed up the relationship?	0	1	2	3	4
115. Worrying that Vietnam is affecting the way you relate to your children?	0	1	2	3	4
116. Feeling that you are no good and worthless?	0	1	2	3	4

125

Not at all - Problem does not occur
A little bit - 1 to 9 times a month
Moderately - 10 to 14 times a month
Quite a bit - 15 to 20 times a month
Extremely - 21 to 30 times a month

HOW MUCH WERE YOU
BOTHERED BY:

	Not at all	A little bit	Moder- ately	Quite a bit	Ex- tremely
117. Problems remembering things you know you should remember?	0	1	2	3	4
118. Feeling that you have no real goals that matter?	0	1	2	3	4
119. Feeling that you are different than you were before going to Vietnam, (that your sense of identity just won't come together in the right way)?	0	1	2	3	4
120. Feeling self-conscious as a Vietnam veteran?	0	1	2	3	4
121. Experiencing self-doubt and uncertainty?	0	1	2	3	4
122. Feeling that you cannot control the important events in your life?	0	1	2	3	4
123. Feeling like you are just a walking "shell" of your old self?	0	1	2	3	4
124. Not feeling really satisfied with yourself?	0	1	2	3	4
125. Not feeling proud of the kind of person you are?	0	1	2	3	4
126. Feeling that you are not a person of worth?	0	1	2	3	4
127. Feeling that Vietnam took away your "soul" (dehumanized you)?	0	1	2	3	4
128. Feeling that you just cannot get a hold on things?	0	1	2	3	4
129. Feeling like you are still searching for something in your life but just cannot seem to find it?	0	1	2	3	4
130. Feeling like you've been a failure since leaving military service?	0	1	2	3	4
131. Having fantasies of retaliation for what happened to you in Vietnam?	0	1	2	3	4
132. Feeling out of touch (alienated) from the government?	0	1	2	3	4
133. The feeling that you are stigmatized for being a Vietnam veteran?	0	1	2	3	4
134. The feeling that you are stigmatized for being a Vietnam veteran who is a woman?	0	1	2	3	4
135. Feeling cynical about governmental processes, agencies, and policies?	0	1	2	3	4
136. Feeling like you lost your faith in people after Vietnam?	0	1	2	3	4
137. The feeling that you were used by the government for serving in Vietnam?	0	1	2	3	4
138. Having problems with persons in authority positions?	0	1	2	3	4
139. Feeling that your work is menial and below your capabilities?	0	1	2	3	4
140. Feeling uneasy in a crowd such as at a party or movie?	0	1	2	3	4

126

Frequency for Numbered Spaces

Not at all - Problem does not occur
A little bit - 1 to 9 times a month
Moderately - 10 to 14 times a month
Quite a bit - 15 to 20 times a month
Extremely - 21 to 30 times a month

HOW MUCH WERE YOU BOTHERED BY:	Not at all	A little bit	Moder- ately	Quite a bit	Ex-
141. Experiencing conflicts with co-workers?	0	1	2	3	4
142. Legal problems?	0	1	2	3	4
143. The feeling of quitting your job because the work was less than you could do?	0	1	2	3	4
144. Feeling that life has no meaning for you?	0	1	2	3	4
145. Feeling the need to find more purpose in life?	0	1	2	3	4
146. Feeling jumpy or jittery, especially when sudden noises occur?	0	1	2	3	4
147. Having an emotional or physical reaction when you hear a helicopter?	0	1	2	3	4
148. Walking in the woods and listening carefully to the sounds around you?	0	1	2	3	4
149. Thoughts that it is hard to really believe that Vietnam happened to you?	0	1	2	3	4
150. Thoughts that Vietnam is something you still cannot accept in your life?	0	1	2	3	4
151. Thoughts that Vietnam was just one great big nightmare?	0	1	2	3	4
152. Feeling the need to have a weapon on or near you?	0	1	2	3	4
153. Feeling that you drive too fast or recklessly?	0	1	2	3	4
154. Feeling the need to recreate in your work here, the kind of sensations you experienced in your work in Vietnam?	0	1	2	3	4
155. Feeling the need to engage your self in dangerous or highly risky adventures in which you feel that you "live" on the edge"?	0	1	2	3	4
156. The need to seek out high degrees of "sensation" that are inherently risky?	0	1	2	3	4
157. The feeling that you are not free to make your own choices which are important to your life?	0	1	2	3	4
158. The feeling that your personal existence (life) is without meaning?	0	1	2	3	4
159. The feeling that you should be achieving something, but you don't know what?	0	1	2	3	4

HOW MANY TIMES PER MONTH DID YOU EXPERIENCE?

160. Headaches? _____

161. Nervousness or shakiness inside? _____

162. Faintness or dizziness? _____

127

HOW MANY TIMES PER MONTH DID YOU EXPERIENCE?

163. Pains in heart or chest? _____

164. Feeling low in energy or slowed down? _____

165. Trembling? _____

166. Poor appetite? _____

167. Overeating? _____

168. Heart pounding or racing? _____

169. Nausea or upset stomach? _____

170. Trouble getting your breath? _____

171. Hot or cold spells? _____

172. Numbness or tingling in parts of your body? _____

173. A lump in your throat? _____

174. Feeling weak in parts of your body? _____

175. Awakening in the early morning? _____

176. Unable to fall asleep at night? _____

177. Feeling that nothing matters anymore? _____

IV

INSTRUCTIONS

The following list contains symptoms that some Vietnam Era veterans sometimes experience. Read each symptom and if you experienced it, place a check in the year after Vietnam when you FIRST felt it begin. Place a second check if you consider the symptom STILL PRESENT today. If the symptom NEVER occurred, DO NOT check any box. Keep in mind that Homecoming is the first six months after Vietnam.

		Home-Coming to 1 Year	1 to 5 Years	5 to 10 Years	10 Years to Now	Still Present
178.	Emotional numbing?	___	___	___	___	___
179.	Depression - feelings of helplessness, hopelessness, apathy, dejection?	___	___	___	___	___
180.	Anger-rage, hostility (feeling like a walking time bomb)?	___	___	___	___	___
181.	Anxiety-nervousness?	___	___	___	___	___
182.	Emotional constriction and un-responsiveness to self and others?	___	___	___	___	___
183.	Tendency to react under stress with military "survival tactics"?	___	___	___	___	___
184.	Sleep disturbances and recurring nightmares of the war experience?	___	___	___	___	___
185.	Loss of interest in work and activities, fatigue, lethargy?	___	___	___	___	___
186.	Hyper-alertness, startle easily?	___	___	___	___	___
187.	Avoidance of activities that arouse memories of trauma in war zone or medical experiences?	___	___	___	___	___
188.	Seeking out experiences that are risky, dangerous, and exciting in ways similar to Vietnam?	___	___	___	___	___
189.	Seeking out work that tends to recreate your work experiences in Vietnam?	___	___	___	___	___
190.	Suicidal feelings and thoughts; self-destructive behavior tendencies?	___	___	___	___	___
191.	Survivor guilt - wondering why you survived and a friend(s) or patient(s) didn't?	___	___	___	___	___
192.	Flashbacks to traumatic events experienced in war, intrusive thoughts?	___	___	___	___	___
193.	Guilty feelings associated with acts participated in or done in Vietnam?	___	___	___	___	___
194.	Fantasies of retaliation and destruction?	___	___	___	___	___
195.	Ideological changes and confusion in value system?	___	___	___	___	___
196.	Cynicism and mistrust of government and authority?	___	___	___	___	___
197.	Alienation - feeling estranged?	___	___	___	___	___
198.	Feelings of meaninglessness; search for meaning in life?	___	___	___	___	___

	Home-Coming to 1 Year	1 to 5 Years	5 to 10 Years	10 Years to Now	Still Present
199. Negative self-image, low self esteem?	____	____	____	____	____
200. Memory impairment, especially during times of stress?	____	____	____	____	____
201. Hypersensitivity to issues of equity, justice, fairness, equality and legitimacy?	____	____	____	____	____
202. Impulsive - abrupt changes (quick) in lifestyle (job, relocation, etc.)?	____	____	____	____	____
203. Problems in establishing or maintaining intimate relationships?	____	____	____	____	____
204. Tendency to have difficulty with authoritative figures (challenging and testing authority, rules and regulations)?	____	____	____	____	____
205. Emotional distance from children and concern about anger alienating children, husband, and others?	____	____	____	____	____
206. Inability to talk about war experiences and personal emotions?	____	____	____	____	____
207. Fears of loss of others?	____	____	____	____	____
208. Secretly wanting to return to Vietnam?	____	____	____	____	____
209. Tendency to explode in fits of rage and anger especially when disinhibited by drugs/alcohol?	____	____	____	____	____
210. Withdrawal from others, isolation?	____	____	____	____	____
211. Mistrust of others?	____	____	____	____	____
212. Uncontrollable, persisting tears?	____	____	____	____	____
213. Guilt over the inability to heal both physical and psychological wounds?	____	____	____	____	____
214. Reluctance to have children because of the atrocities seen in war?	____	____	____	____	____
215. Fear of having children because of possible exposure to unknown chemicals?	____	____	____	____	____

130

For the following questions, please describe your experiences in your own words. If there is not enough room, you may attach an additional page.

216. Aside from Vietnam, what other important events have had a major influence in your life? Please describe.

_____

_____

_____

217. Do you feel you have gained or benefited anything from your experiences in Vietnam? Please describe.

_____

_____

_____

218. If you volunteered for Vietnam, why did you do so?

_____

_____

_____

219. What were your hopes and expectations about serving in Vietnam? Please describe.

_____

_____

_____

220. How do you think your Vietnam experience has affected your life?

_____

_____

_____

221. Were there any specific events during your tour in Vietnam that were especially difficult for you to cope with emotionally? Please describe.

_____

_____

_____

222. Has this survey stimulated any further thoughts or feelings that may lead you to want to explore these issues further? Please describe.

_____

_____

_____

223. It is often difficult for a form such as this to explore all areas of importance to you. Please feel free to comment on any part of this questionnaire or express any feelings you may have that were not covered by these questions.

APPENDIX B
ITEMS FROM SCALE 3 THAT WERE REPORTED
AS "STILL PRESENT" BY OVER 50% OF THE
RESPONDENTS

178. Emotional numbing.
181. Anxiety-nervousness.
182. Emotional constriction and unresponsiveness to self and others.
186. Hyperalertness, startle easily.
187. Avoidance of activities that arouse memories of trauma in war zone or medical experiences.
192. Flashbacks to traumatic events experienced in war, intrusive thoughts.
193. Guilty feelings associated with acts participated in or done in Vietnam.
195. Ideological changes and confusion in value system.
196. Cynicism and mistrust of government and authority.
197. Alienation—feeling estranged.
198. Feelings of meaninglessness; search for meaning in life.
200. Memory impairment, especially during times of stress.
201. Hypersensitivity to issues of equity, justice, fairness, equality, and legitimacy.
202. Impulsive—abrupt changes (quick) in life-style (job, relocation, etc.).
203. Problems in establishing or maintaining intimate relationships.
204. Tendency to have difficulty with authoritative figures (challenging and testing authority, rules and regulations).
205. Emotional distance from children and concern about anger alienating children, husband, and others.
206. Inability to talk about war experiences and personal emotions.
207. Fears of loss of others.
208. Secretly wanting to return to Vietnam.
209. Tendency to explode in fits of rage and anger especially when disinhibited by drugs/alcohol.
210. Withdrawal from others, isolation.
211. Mistrust of others.
213. Guilt over inability to heal both physical and psychological wounds.
214. Reluctance to have children because of atrocities seen in war.
215. Fear of having children because of possible exposure to unknown chemicals.

7

Health and Recovery Status of Victims One and Three Years Following a Natural Disaster

SHIRLEY A. MURPHY

Being a disaster victim at least once during one's lifetime is more than a remote possibility. Between 1971 and 1980, 326 events were declared major natural disasters by presidential edict and resulted in 2,100 deaths and 72,000 injuries (Gordon, 1982). These figures do not include deaths and injuries resulting from technological (human-error) disasters, such as airplane crashes, fires, and industrial accidents. Although natural disasters are commonly thought to be single episodes, they are more likely to be a series of catastrophic events that include stress-producing warnings, life-threatening impacts, and prolonged traumatic recoveries, including perceived lack of control of future disastrous events.

The recovery period following a disaster involves numerous stressful activities including grieving, adjusting to role changes such as widowhood and single-parent status, moving, cleaning and repairing property,

The data analyses for this study were supported by the American Nurses' Foundation.
Appreciation is expressed to Barbara J. Stewart and Marie Beaudet for statistical consultation, to Susan Miller who assisted with data analysis, and to Julia S. Brown for her helpful comments in the preparation of the manuscript.

133

and preparing lengthy reports associated with loss. A number of past studies have suggested that these stressful activities have led to negative health outcomes, but findings have been controversial, primarily because of the wide range of differences in methodology from study to study (Logue, Melick, & Struening, 1981; Singh & Raphael, 1981; Titchener & Kapp, 1976). To clarify the extent to which health status may be affected by a catastrophic experience, Melick (1985) reviewed 30 studies that reported the presence of illness at least a year following a disaster. Comparisons were made regarding type of disaster (natural versus technological), scope of impact (numbers of victims and extent of damage), sampling, time of measurement, method of data collection, type of health outcome assessed, and results. No two studies were identical on these seven study characteristics. For example, studies included a range of sample sizes varying from 4 to 4,000 subjects and time of measurement varied from 1 to 10 years. One exception to Melick's review is the recent trend toward the use of the Symptom Checklist 90-R to measure the number and severity of psychological symptoms following disasters (Baum, Gatchel, & Schaeffer, 1983; Green, Grace, Lindy, Titchener, & Lindy, 1983; Murphy, 1984).

In addition to the variety of methodologies that have been used to study effects of disasters, there is also little conceptual similarity from study to study, a problem pointed out by others (Berren, Beigel, & Barker, 1982; Green, 1982; Perry & Lindell, 1978). For example, natural and man-made disasters may be conceptually different regarding scope of impact, prolonged threat of recurrence, geographical proximity of those affected, belief of preventability, projected blame, and so forth, but these differences have not been specified by past investigators.

In support of the variability of approaches to studying disasters, Green et al. (1983) point out that it may be impossible or inadvisable to draw conclusions about the effects of disasters, owing to the unique features of each catastrophe. However, it does seem important to identify both similarities and differences among disasters as they occur and are reported.

The purposes of this chapter are twofold. First, findings from a longitudinal study of victims following the 1980 volcanic eruption of Mt. St. Helens in southwestern Washington are reported. Second, the study's conceptual basis, methodology, and findings are compared and contrasted with other disaster findings in an attempt to establish some generic characteristics in the study of victims and post-traumatic stress disorders.

BACKGROUND

Shortly after 8:00 A.M. on May 18, 1980, a series of earthquakes triggered the major volcanic eruption of Mt. St. Helens. Temperatures over 500°F melted snow and released a 50-mph avalanche of earth, timber, and mud into the valley below. More than 200 persons who were working, camping, or sightseeing in the potentially dangerous area that Sunday morning escaped or were rescued, and all but two survived. However, an additional 60 persons died or were reported missing and were presumed to have died. Several hundred residences were either completely destroyed or severely damaged. The volcanic eruption has been studied from a variety of warning, response, and recovery perspectives. Each of the Mt. St. Helens studies reported thus far differs in both purpose and methodology. For example, Perry and Lindell (1978), and Green (1982) studied perceptions of warning. Adams and Adams (1984) reported the effects of volcanic ash on health behaviors in a community 150 miles away. Buist (in progress) is studying forest workers' lung function. Shore, Tatum, and Vollmer (in press) conducted an epidemiological study that compared the disaster-affected community with a nonaffected Oregon community. The current longitudinal study assessed stress, coping, and health outcomes in four groups of disaster victims who suffered mutually exclusive types of loss: presumptive death bereavement, confirmed death bereavement, loss of permanent residence, and loss of recreational residence. Data collected from these four groups of subjects were compared with data collected from a nonloss control group.

A stress/coping/health outcome model served as the conceptual basis for the study (Figure 1). A disaster may produce several levels or magnitudes of loss, such as bereavement, surviving a life-threatening evacuation, and/or property destruction. Losses may vary in both intensity and duration. For example, the death of a significant other is consistently rated the most aversive of stressful events (Holmes & Rahe, 1967; Sarason, Johnson, & Siegel, 1978). There is an argument that mode of death, the cause of death one assigns, the importance of the deceased person, and whether the deceased is confirmed or presumed dead are important differentiating factors in predicting bereavement outcome, although as yet little empirical evidence supports these factors.

Weisman (1973) differentiates timely death, which is expected and accepted, from untimely death, which is premature, unexpected, and violent. Bugen (1977) asserts that if the bereaved believe death was

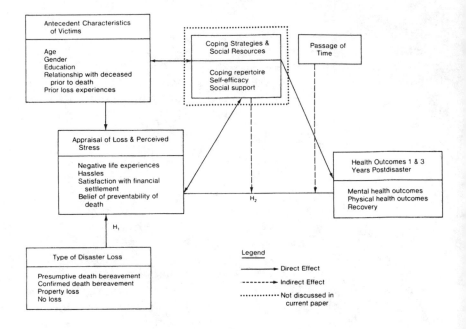

Figure 1. Conceptual model of the disaster study.

preventable, and the deceased/bereaved relationship was central, then grief is likely to be intense and prolonged. Shneidman (1976), discussing the availability of death certificates in the case of confirmed but not presumed death, states, "The impact of the death certificate is considerable. It can affect the fate and fortune of a family, touching both its affluence and mental health" (p. 241). Death certificates are required for claims for life insurance, property rights, and social security benefits for dependent children. Moreover, war experiences suggest that confirmed death, however brutal, contributes to the reality and finality of death (McCubbin, 1976). Alternatively, when a person is missing and therefore presumed dead, relatives and friends continue to hope that the person escaped, will be found alive, or was not in the area at the time, until sufficient contrary evidence surfaces. In addition, there are no generally accepted norms for grieving, nor any legal avenues to financial resolution of presumptive death.

In contrast, loss of one's permanent residence is ranked much lower on life event scales than the death of a significant other (Holmes & Rahe,

1967). However, the prolonged stress associated with moving to temporary housing, and back to one's permanent residence, losing or changing employment, filling out numerous forms, being deprived of community resources, both material and personal, and fear of recurrence of the event, may lead to negative health outcomes (Bolin, 1982). The following propositions were based on the foregoing conceptual relationships: (1) a disastrous event produces losses that differ in severity, (2) appraisal of loss leads to perceptions of stress that vary directly with the severity of loss experienced; and (3) there will be an inverse relationship between the amount of stress experienced and the impact on health. The following hypotheses were tested. Hypothesis 1: The greater the magnitude of loss experienced, the higher the levels of stress reported. Hypothesis 2: The higher the levels of stress reported, the more negative the impact on health status.

The magnitude of loss is here presumed to be greater for individuals whose relative or close friend is *presumed* to have died in the disaster, next greater for individuals whose relative or close friend is *known* to have died; less for individuals who lost permanent homes, still less for individuals losing vacation property, and absent for individuals who suffered *no* disaster loss. Thus, a hierarchical ordering of loss effects was predicted among the five study groups. The hypotheses were unique to this study because the types of loss sustained as a result of the disaster were mutually exclusive among study participants.

METHOD

Subjects

A total of 155 subjects participated in 1981. The follow-up study in 1983 included 101 of these same subjects. To test the hypotheses in 1981, persons were needed to represent each of the five magnitudes of loss: (1) presumed death bereavement, (2) confirmed death bereavement, (3) loss of a permanent residence, (4) loss of a leisure residence, and (5) no disaster-related loss (see Table 1). All losses were officially documented, and bereavement and property losses were mutually exclusive among study participants. Since the study was conducted in a natural setting and followed an uncontrollable event, subjects were recruited in a variety of ways.

The bereaved population was a finite number (60 persons died). Of these, nine were either children or persons whose whereabouts were

TABLE 1
Study Subjects by Group

Magnitude of loss	1981 Participants	1983 "Continuers"	Attrition rates by % between 1981 and 1983
1. Presumed dead bereaved	39	22	29[b]
2. Confirmed dead bereaved[a]	30	27	14
3. Permanent residence	21	18	—
4. Recreational residence loss[c]	15	—	—
5. No-loss comparison subjects	50	34	32
Total	155	101	28

[a]Nine bereaved subjects who had been in the presumed-bereaved group in 1981 were transferred to the confirmed-bereaved group in 1983 to account for bodies found between the two data collection periods.
[b]Bereaved groups 1 and 2 were combined for longitudinal analyses.
[c]Not recontacted in 1983.

not limited to the eruptive area on May 18. No attempts were made to contact their relatives, which left only 51 potential bereaved relatives to recruit as study subjects. To further complicate bereaved subject sampling, only a few of these persons resided in the immediate area, and it was not known when or how provisional death certificates would be processed. As a result, both a close relative and a close friend of each disaster victim were recruited as study subjects. A study participation criterion was that all bereaved subjects score seven or higher on a 1–9 scale regarding centrality of relationship (1 = not close, 9 = very close). This sampling procedure is described in detail in another publication (Murphy & Stewart, 1986). Names of bereaved relatives of those presumed dead were obtained from a list of persons who gave court testimony required for processing provisional death certificates. Names of relatives for the bereaved of the confirmed-dead group were obtained from death certificates. Bereaved relatives were widows, mothers, sons, daughters, and siblings of deceased disaster victims who resided in 10 U.S. cities and two Canadian provinces. Names of friends for both bereaved groups were obtained primarily from relatives, who also confirmed closeness (centrality of the relationship) between these friends and the deceased.

Subjects for the permanent-property-loss group were randomly selected from local telephone listings in 1981. The nature and extent of property loss were verified by tax assessment records. The criterion for inclusion in the study was total destruction of one's permanent residence or severity of damage that necessitated moving at least temporarily. Subjects for the recreational-property-loss group were randomly selected from a recreational homeowner's list.

Finally, the control group was selected by the investigator. These persons had suffered no disaster-related loss, but were similar to the loss subjects in age, gender, occupation, and geographical location. With the exception of the recreational-property-loss group, study subjects' mean age in 1983 was 39 years, with a range from 18 to 69. Ninety-eight subjects were female and 57 were male. The sample could be characterized as white and above average in educational attainment. The majority of subjects had formal post-high-school education and 15 held graduate degrees.

Measures

Measures of stress were the Life Experiences Survey, the Hassles Scale, and investigator-developed items. The mental-health-outcome measure was the Symptom Checklist-90-R. Physical health measures were a physical health index and investigator-developed items. Recovery was measured by investigator-developed items. The independent variable was magnitude of loss, and the dependent variables were mental health, physical health, and recovery. Five levels of loss were distinguished from greater to least: presumptive death bereavement (scored 4), confirmed death bereavement (scored 3), property loss of a permanent residence (scored 2), property loss of a recreational residence (scored 1), and no disaster-related loss (scored 0).

The Life Experiences Survey (LES). This survey, developed by Sarason et al. (1978), is a 47-item, multidimensional scale that permits respondents to indicate stressors experienced and rate events they have experienced during the past year as well as the desirability and impact of those events. The negative-change score has been found to be more predictive than the total-change score. The range of possible scores is -150 to +150. Examples of items are: death of a family member, change in, or loss of, employment, change of residence. Sarason et al. gathered normative data for the LES from 345 undergraduate students. Validity has been shown through significant correlations with other stress-related measures. Test-retest reliability for a five-to-six-week period was 0.56 and 0.88.

The Hassles Scale. Measurement of subjects' daily annoyances were obtained with this scale (Lazarus & Cohen, 1977). The scale consists of 117 items that describe ways in which a person may currently feel distressed. Examples of items are: difficulty making decisions, concerns about owing money, troublesome neighbors, filling out forms. Respondents select and rate hassles for persistence (1 = somewhat, 2 = moderate, 3 = extreme) and irritability (1 = somewhat, 2 = moderate, 3 = extreme). Respondents' levels of stress were scored by multiplying each hassles persistence rating by its irritability rating and then summing across hassles. The total score can range from 0 to 1,053. Normative data were gathered on 100 middle-aged adults who participated in a 12-month study of stress, coping, and emotions. Test-retest correlation coefficients ranged from 0.48 to 0.79 ($p < 0.001$). Construct validity was established by a significant correlation ($r = 0.60$, $p < 0.001$) between frequency of hassles and psychological symptoms measured by the Symptom Checklist-90-R.

Eight items developed by the investigator were additional measures of stress. Included were questions regarding change in and adequacy of income and satisfaction with loss settlement, beliefs regarding preventability of disaster, death, with whom subjects were angry, and whom subjects blamed for their loss.

The Symptom Checklist-90-R. Measures of mental health were obtained by the SCL-90-R, a self-report 90-item checklist. Examples of items are feeling hopeless about the future, nausea, feeling fearful, getting into frequent arguments. Respondents rate each item on a five-point scale of distress from "not at all" (0) to "extremely" (4). Current-point-in-time distress is reflected by scores on three global indices of distress and nine symptom subscales. Derogatis (1977) suggests use of the Global Severity Index (GSI) as the most meaningful single indicator of distress. The GSI score is obtained by adding the score from each item and dividing by 90. The nine subscales are: depression, somatization, anxiety, hostility, interpersonal sensitivity, obsessive-compulsive (lack of concentration), paranoia (suspiciousness), phobic anxiety (fear), and psychoticism (alienation). Subscale scores are obtained by summing the scores for each item on the scale and dividing by the total number of items on the scale. The range of possible scores across all subscales is 0 to 4. The SCL-90-R has an extensive history of psychometric development. Normative data for the SCL reported here were derived from 1,500 subjects from three samples—two psychiatric patient groups and one nonpatient group—and have been widely reported (Derogatis, 1977). Moreover, two measures of reliability for the GSI were established for subjects in the current study for whom longitudinal data were available. The internal consistency reliability for all three study groups was $r = 0.97$. Stability coefficients were $r = 0.66$ for the bereaved group and $r = 0.40$ for both the property loss and control groups ($p \leq 0.01$).

Physical Health Index. Physical health status was assessed in both 1981 and 1983, but by different measures. Consequently, the only longitudinal measure of physical health is a single nine-point item, "as of right now, how do you rate your health?" (1 = extremely poor, 9 = excellent).

Recovery. Subjects were asked to rate recovery on a nine-point Likert scale (1 = not recovered, 9 = completely recovered), and in 1983, those subjects indicating they were completely recovered were asked to rate the length of recovery on a five-point scale.

Procedure

Data collection procedures for both time periods were identical. Letters were mailed to potential subjects to explain the nature and purpose of the study and to assure confidentiality. Written, informed consent was obtained from the potential subjects prior to participation. Questionnaires arranged in three random orders were mailed 11 and 35 months postdisaster to those who agreed to participate.

Personal and telephone interviews were conducted with 44 identical loss subjects, approximately one and three years postdisaster. Widows, adult children, parents, siblings, and friends of the deceased, and persons sustaining property loss comprised the stratified interview sample. The interviews were conducted by the investigator and a nurse with a graduate degree in psychiatric/mental health nursing and followed a standardized, semistructured format that lasted about 60 minutes. Verbatim notes were made at the time of each interview.

RESULTS

Levels of Stress and Health One Year Postdisaster

The hypotheses to be tested specified a hierarchical order of effects based on magnitude of loss: presumed-death bereavement, confirmed-death bereavement, loss of permanent residence, loss of recreational residence, and no loss. Hypotheses were tested by one-way analysis of variance and paired comparisons of each of the stress and health outcome measures. Alpha levels were divided by the number of comparisons to split the level of significance among the comparisons. Moreover, separate variance estimates, rather than pooled, were reported to account for unequal numbers in groups (Kirk, 1968). Nonhypothesized relationships were analyzed by descriptive data. Group means and standard deviations on health outcome measures are presented in Table 2.

The scores on measures of stress (negative Life Experiences and Hassles) and measures of mental distress (SCL-90-R) nine subscales reported by the bereaved of presumed-dead disaster victims were not significantly higher than scores reported by bereaved of confirmed dead or the permanent-property-loss group. However, their scores were significantly higher than those reported by the nonloss comparison group on negative life experiences and depression. In contrast, the bereaved of confirmed dead reported significantly higher scores than the permanent-property-loss group on hassles, overall distress, and depression. Moreover, their scores were significantly higher than the control group on measures of negative life experiences, hassles, overall severity, and four SCL-90 sub-

TABLE 2
Means and Standard Deviations on the SCL 90-R Scales for Groups With and Without Disaster Loss

	Bereaved group (n = 49)				Property-loss group (n = 18)				Control group (n = 34)			
	1981		1983		1981		1983		1981		1983	
Measures	M	SD	M	SD	M	SD	M	SD	M	SD	M	SD
Total no. of symptoms	44.00	21.00	35.00	21.00	42.00	20.00	33.00	22.00	28.00	20.00	25.00	18.00
Global severity index	0.90	0.58	0.59	0.44	0.62	0.39	0.40	0.40	0.55	0.46	0.40	0.37
Somatic complaints	0.81	0.59	0.50	0.45	0.64	0.54	0.54	0.50	0.57	0.63	0.36	0.42
Interpersonal sensitivity	0.80	0.73	0.66	0.66	0.58	0.48	0.43	0.51	0.66	0.60	0.47	0.42
Lack of concentration	1.12	0.86	0.69	0.59	0.82	0.60	0.46	0.55	0.66	0.55	0.54	0.43
Depression	1.34	0.76	0.82	0.66	0.89	0.57	0.50	0.52	0.88	0.72	0.67	0.67
Anxiety	0.96	0.80	0.62	0.57	0.67	0.50	0.41	0.50	0.51	0.56	0.32	0.40
Anger	0.70	0.73	0.58	0.53	0.52	0.64	0.42	0.44	0.42	0.46	0.38	0.47
Suspiciousness	0.86	0.82	0.52	0.52	0.44	0.50	0.31	0.41	0.48	0.52	0.29	0.36
Fear	0.32	0.49	0.22	0.37	0.34	0.44	0.32	0.41	0.15	0.26	0.07	0.16
Alienation	0.54	0.48	0.32	0.36	0.29	0.39	0.16	0.23	0.28	0.35	0.22	0.35

scales. The permanent-property-loss group reported significantly higher scores on negative life experiences when compared to nonvictim controls. The recreational-property-loss group did not differ from controls on any of the measures. There were no statistically significant differences between groups on the physical health measure. In summary, the hierarchical model of magnitude of loss held up when individual loss groups were compared to nonvictim controls on stress and mental health measures. The model did not hold up as predicted in differentiating the two types of bereavement, but did clearly differentiate bereaved of confirmed dead from the permanent property loss group.

Other data. In general, the permanent-property-loss subjects directed their anger and blame toward government officials and insurance companies, whereas the bereaved directed their anger and blame at identification and rescue procedures of their significant others, as well as toward the deceased victims for being in the area, believing they contributed to their own deaths. Some believed that the deaths were unpreventable owing to the unexpected magnitude of the volcanic eruption. However, 11 months postdisaster, 33% of the bereaved believed that the deaths were preventable. Of the three areas of financial status assessed dissatisfaction with financial settlement was the predominant finding, but only among the permanent-property-loss group. Interview data corroborated with statistical findings with the exception of presumptive-versus confirmed-death bereavement.

Among the more stressful aspects of the disaster experience that reportedly led to high rates of mental distress were: multiple deaths in some families, the ages of both the deceased and bereaved, the presumptive death status, the suddenness and magnitude of the event, media coverage, and fear of subsequent eruptions.

Rates of Recovery

Mean rates of recovery for all the loss groups were between 5.00 and 6.00 (1 = not at all recovered, 9 = completely recovered). These findings indicate that the majority of subjects perceived they were only somewhat recovered approximately one year postdisaster.

Follow-up

In 1983, study subjects were recontacted for follow-up study participation. The goal of the second data collection was to examine the differences between short- and long-term disaster effects as they were measured in 1981, one year postdisaster, and in 1983, three years post-disaster. After the initial conceptualization of presumed- versus confirmed-death bereavement and between the two data collection periods, additional bodies of victims were found. To compensate for this phenomenon, appropriate subjects were transferred to the confirmed-bereaved group. Table 1 reflects those changes along with attrition rates between the two data collection periods. Pairwise discriminant function analysis following the one-year postdisaster data analyses confirmed the ANOVA findings regarding the similarities of the two bereaved groups and dissimilarities between the two property-loss groups.

For the bereaved-group comparisons, the overall approximate F (5,62) = 0.99, $p < 0.43$; for the property-loss comparisons, the overall approximate F (5,30) = 4.85, $p < 0.002$. Because of these findings and attrition of subjects, the bereaved groups were combined for the 1983 follow-up study. The recreational property loss group was not recontacted since the two property-loss groups were not similar enough to combine, and the recreational-property-loss group differed on demographic variables when compared to the other loss groups.

Levels of Stress and Health Three Years Postdisaster

Data from both measures of stress, and three scales of the SCL-90-R were analyzed by 3 × 2 repeated measures analysis of variance. The first factor was the three levels (groups) of subjects and the second factor was the two time periods. Table 3 shows mean squares, degrees of freedom, F values, and levels of significance for the sources of variation resulting from the ANOVA computations.

Stress. Significant group × time interactions occurred on both the negative score on the Life Experiences Survey and on the Hassles Scale. Tests of simple main effects on both measures were significant for both the bereaved and property-loss groups (see Table 3 and Figure 2).

SCL-90-R Global Severity Index and Subscales. The ANOVA findings support the magnitude-of-loss hypotheses. Significant main effects occurred for both the group and time factors for two of the mental health outcomes. In general, levels of distress decreased over time, and the distress of the bereaved group was greater than that of the property-loss and control groups. The only significant group × time interaction occurred on the somatization subscale. A test of simple main effects indicated

TABLE 3
Analysis of Variance for Stress and Mental Health Outcomes One and Three Years Postdisaster

Source	df	LES Neg. MS	F	Hassles MS	F	Global severity MS	F	Depression MS	F	Somatization MS	F
Between subjects	*100*										
A (group)	2	575.80	5.92[a]	34760.73	6.31[a]	1.91	5.75[a]	3.84	7.07[b]	0.94	2.23
Ss w. gps.	98	97.19		789348.		0.34		0.55		0.38	
Within subjects	*101*										
B (time)	1	793.17	19.43[b]	38734.	14.78[b]	2.31	24.51[b]	5.69	27.88[b]	1.52	11.71[b]
AB	2	241.14	5.91[a]	5918.77	4.61[a]	0.08		0.54	2.78	3.02	1.36
B × Ss w. gps.	98	40.81		3080.20		0.09		0.20		0.17	

[a] $p < 0.01$.
[b] $p < 0.001$.

that property-loss subjects' scores did not significantly decrease over time as did those of the other two groups (see Table 3 and Figure 2).

Other Data. There were no statistically significant differences between groups on the physical health measure. Descriptive and interview data supported the statistical analyses. Of the 96% of the bereaved subjects who responded to the preventability and blame items, 31% believed the deaths of their loved ones were preventable, only a 2% decrease over the two-year period. Regarding blame for the deaths, 43% of the bereaved blame no one, 15% blamed state and federal officials, 9% blamed the deceased individuals for going to the area, 6% blamed God, and no one blamed those responsible for rescue operations or themselves, a change between the two data collection periods. Feelings of anger among both bereaved and property-loss subjects had greatly subsided 35 months postdisaster, with 62% of those responding stating they were angry with no one. However, 23% continued to be angry with state and

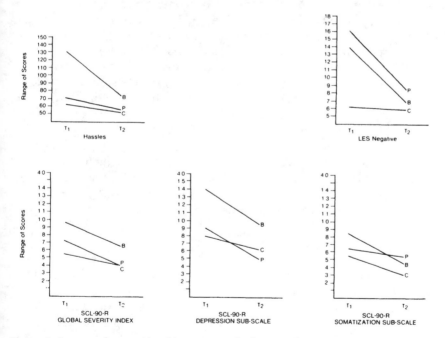

Figure 2. Stress and mental health outcomes for bereaved, property-loss, and nonloss subjects, one and three years postdisaster.
C = control, P = property loss, B = bereaved.

federal officials, and 12% were angry with insurance companies. The questions regarding satisfaction with financial settlement were answered by 64% of the property-loss subjects. Fifty-eight percent of those responding continued to be dissatisfied with financial settlement.

Rate of Recovery

Recovery rose only slightly between the two data collection periods ($M = 6.2$ in 1983 compared to $M = 5.6$ in 1981). Forty-seven percent of all loss subjects rated themselves quite well recovered, 38% somewhat recovered, 9% barely or not at all, and only 6% rated themselves completely recovered. Of those completely recovered, 33% ($n = 2$) were recovered within 6–11 months, 33% ($n = 2$) within 12–17 months, and the two remaining subjects believed it took 24–29 and 30–36 months, respectively, to fully recover.

Interview findings. Several items on the structured interview schedule pertained to appraisal of stress, health outcomes, and recovery. All the bereaved subjects interviewed at both time periods overwhelmingly supported the notion that presumptive-death bereavement would be much worse than confirmed-death bereavement. In contrast, losing one's permanent home presented a very different set of responses that produced three major themes: perceived unfairness, i.e., inconsistent handling of claims by insurance companies and the government; the ongoing stress of living in a potentially dangerous area; and losing a "way of life."

In answer to the question "How have you measured your recovery?" major themes among the bereaved were self-expectations, the passage of time, and change in quality of dreams. The major theme for property-loss subjects was comparison of one's situation with that of other property owners as well as comparison between pre- and postdisaster quality of life among property-loss respondents.

The Relationship Between the Conceptual Model and Study Findings

Path analysis was used to distinguish between the direct and indirect effects of the variables included in the model (Figure 3). At Time 1, the combined measures of stress (LES and Hassles) accounted for 47% of the variance in the proposed model, and the mediating variables (social support and self-efficacy) accounted for 21% of the variance. At Time 2, the combined measures of stress accounted for 40% of the variance, whereas only 6% of the variance was accounted for by mediating vari-

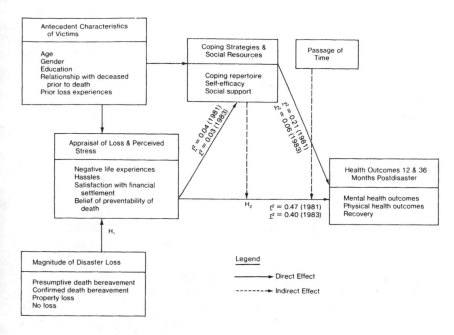

Figure 3. Postanalysis conceptualization including path analysis.

ables. Thus, the overall stress/coping/health outcome model explained 68% of the variance one year postdisaster and 63% three years postdisaster.

DISCUSSION

Results from the cross-sectional data collected one year postdisaster and longitudinal data collected on multiple measures and analyzed three years postdisaster indicated significant differences between the loss and control groups on stress and mental health outcomes, but not physical health outcomes. The 3×2 ANOVA results indicated that even though scores for the bereaved group were significantly lowered with the passage of time, their scores remained significantly higher than those of the control group on all of three mental health outcome measures and significantly higher than those of the property-loss group on all but the somatization measure. Thus, the magnitude-of-loss hypothesis was supported with one exception. Moreover, the results indicate that study subjects reported symptoms of both acute and chronic post-traumatic stress disorder according to DSM-III diagnostic criteria.

What factors may account for the continued mental distress among study subjects three years postdisaster? First, there appeared to be a lack of resolution in both loss groups. For those bereaved as a result of the disaster, the constellation of variables that can be additive and lead to perceptions of stress noted by Hyman and Woog (1982) are high-risk bereavement variables (violent death, multiple deaths in many families, centrality of relationship, belief of preventability, and the ages of both the deceased and bereaved), timing in the life cycle, lack of control, and difficulty finding meaning in the event. These factors are likely to account for the statistically significant levels of mental distress reported on the SCL-90-R.

Property-loss victims experienced lack of financial resolution, concern about the dangers of living near the eruptive area, and incomplete restoration of property to its former beauty and functional status. Some victims had no flood insurance; others who wanted to move could not sell their property; and some property-loss subjects became both plaintiffs and defendants in lawsuits associated with property loss. Similar findings have been reported by other disaster investigators (Singh & Raphael, 1981; Titchener & Kapp, 1976). These factors are likely to account for the high levels of stress and somatic complaints, which may be socially acceptable means of expression of loss and a sense of uncontrollability of future volcanic activity and subsequent threat of flooding.

Several factors may have led to the unpredicted similarities between the two bereaved groups. First, relatives and friends of those presumed dead reported that information regarding the massive destruction of the area and ash asphyxiation of those confirmed dead helped them realize that only those rescued quickly or those outside the eruption zone could have survived. Thus, as time passed, hope for finding loved ones alive lessened.

Another unexpected occurrence that may have led to these similarities was the prompt legal resolution of presumptive-death status. Family members of presumed dead who testified at court hearings received provisional death certificates, canceling the legal seven-year waiting period. These provisional death certificates, made possible by special legislation, hastened the settlement of estates and facilitated the provision of benefits to children under 18 years of age. Thus, by 11 months postdisaster, predicted differences between the groups no longer existed.

Interview data suggest that the bereaved of those presumed dead experienced the most devastating initial effects of the two groups. For instance, the bereaved of presumed dead reported "waiting was agony," "hoping, yet knowing they were dead," family distress in planning and carrying out memorial services, "it's hard to come to terms with no body," and difficulty giving court testimony to verify death.

Finally, measurement is likely to be a factor. Standardized measures with acceptable levels of validity and reliability were selected to offset small numbers. However, these measures did not have items specific to the two types of bereavement.

An unexpected finding was the lack of change between the two data collection periods regarding rates of recovery. Even though 47% were "quite well recovered," the 6% "complete recovery" rate was lower than expected. These findings are consistent with postdisaster and stressful event studies (Burgess & Holmstrom, 1978; Logue et al., 1981; Titchener & Kapp, 1976) but inconsistent with some bereavement literature (Glick et al., 1974; Vachon et al., 1982), although longitudinal data are limited in both disaster and bereavement investigations.

Some positive findings were the absence of physical illness and beneficial effects of the passage of time. Two recent studies (Bartrop, Luckhurst, Lazarus, et al., 1977; Schleifer, Keller, Camerino, et al., 1983) suggest a relationship between major losses that lead to depression, suppression of immunity, and malignancies, which appear not to have occurred in subjects in the current study. Time is also an important variable in disaster research partly because of victims' reluctance to seek help (Lindy et al., 1981). At the first data collection period, only 3 of the 105 loss subjects had sought professional help. Six additional persons had done so between the two data collection periods, but this is indeed a small percentage considering the number of high-risk variables that characterized much of the sample.

Green (1982) suggested that geographical proximity might affect victims' levels of disruption and hence outcomes. Geographical proximity also raises questions regarding who are "victims" and how the provision of crisis and bereavement counseling can be provided. Mt. St. Helens study subjects reside in 10 states and in Canada, but because of their lack of close proximity to the disaster, services provided by funds available via Section 413 of the Federal Disaster Law were not available for many of these persons. The question of whether these persons' health outcomes differ from those of close proximity is an important one that merits future consideration.

Theoretical and Clinical Implications

Findings from the bereaved groups support Bugen's model of grief that suggests that if the relationship between the deceased and bereaved was central (i.e., important) and if the bereaved believe the death(s) could have been prevented, then grief is predicted to be intense and prolonged. These findings merit discussion because they were an attempt to test a "testable" model of grief for its relevance to clinical intervention. It will be recalled that a criterion for subject selection was centrality of relationship, which was measured upon entrance in the study. Even though centrality was not quantitatively measured again three years postdisaster, interview data suggest that closeness between the bereaved and deceased was still apparent. Similarly, only 2% of the bereaved changed their beliefs that the deaths were preventable between the two data collection periods.

According to the model, these attributions can and must be changed in order for resolution to occur. Yet, consistent findings from past disaster studies suggest victims' reluctance to seek help (Lindy et al., 1981), little evidence that treatment helps (Baisden & Quarantelli, 1981), and the tendency of mental health professionals to provide information rather than clinically oriented counseling (Baisden & Quarantelli, 1981). Centrality and preventability appear to impede resolution of grief, yet there are no clear directions regarding intervention.

Another conceptual issue regards the natural versus technological causative agent dichotomy. Green (1982), Logue et al. (1981), and others suggested that guilt, blame, and anger are more commonly associated with technological (human error) disasters. Findings from this study do not support a clear dichotomy between the two etiological classifications of disaster. Blame and anger lessened between the two data collection periods, but were still present three years postdisaster. However, an important difference regards guilt. By three years postdisaster, none of the subjects blamed themselves for the deaths, as they had done one year postdisaster.

Social comparison and relative deprivation theories appear to have potential for developing a theoretical base for responses to property loss following a disaster. Findings reported here support those from past disasters regarding lack of financial resolution, litigation, and accountability for services used (Baisden & Quarantelli, 1981; Titchener & Kapp, 1976).

The results of the path analysis lend support to the conceptual model tested regarding stressful life events and the onset of illness. However, it is disturbing to note the lack of variance accounted for by mediating variables of social support and coping behaviors, which will be addressed in a forthcoming publication. Inasmuch as many stressful life events are beyond personal control, interventions aimed at lessening the impact by strengthening supportive networks and assessing and teaching ways of coping are widespread, yet the cost-benefit ratio of these practices may need to be evaluated.

Findings should be interpreted cautiously owing to the following limitations: (a) Sampling bias is likely to be operating when subjects cannot be randomly selected and assigned to experimental conditions. It is not clear whether more or less impaired individuals participate in disaster studies, even though efforts are made to prevent this phenomenon (Green, 1982). (b) There are no definitions of short- and long-term recovery in the disaster literature. Logue et al. (1981) stated that the recovery period varies from several months to several years and that its termination is probably subjectively defined. Thus, one and three years were arbitrarily chosen for this study with no intent to suggest that these time periods correctly describe short- and long-term recovery.

In summary, the study findings partially support a popular assumption that human beings are resilient and cope with traumatic events that befall them. Moreover, the findings have serious implications for long-term health consequences. Thus, clinical implications include vigorous outreach efforts, early assessment of risk, and active intervention to prolonged mental distress. A general stress/coping/health outcome model used here and by Logue et al. (1981) is recommended as a viable conceptual basis for disaster research. Causal agent, proximity, and uncontrollability models are not comprehensive enough to account for the number of variables that need to be studied to establish a knowledge base for health and recovery outcomes following disasters.

REFERENCES

Adams, P. R., & Adams, G. R. (1984). Mount Saint Helens ashfall: Evidence for a disaster stress reaction. *American Psychologist, 39,* 252–260.

Baisden, B., & Quarantelli, E. (1981). The delivery of mental health services in community disasters: An outline of research findings. *Journal of Community Psychology, 9,* 195–203.

Bartrop, R. W., Luckhurst, E., Lazarus, L., et al. (1977). Depressed lymphocyte function after bereavement. *Lancet, 1,* 834–836.

Baum, A., Gatchel, R. J., & Schaeffer, M. A. (1983). Emotional, behavioral, and physiological effects of chronic stress at Three Mile Island. *Journal of Consulting and Clinical Psychology, 51,* 565–572.

Berren, M., Beigel, A., & Barker, G. (1982). A typology for the classification of disasters: Implications for intervention. *Community Mental Health Journal, 18,* 120–134.

Bolin, R. C. (1982). *Long-term recovery from disaster*. Boulder: University of Colorado Institute of Behavioral Science.
Bugen, L. (1977). Human grief: A model for prediction and intervention. *American Journal of Orthopsychiatry, 47*, 196–206.
Burgess, A. W., & Holmstrom, L. L. (1978). Recovery from rape and prior life stress. *Research in Nursing and Health, 1*, 165–174.
Derogatis, L. (1977). *SCL-90 administration, scoring & procedures manual-I for the revised version and other instruments of the psychopathology rating scale series*. Baltimore, Maryland.
Glick, I., Weiss, R., & Parkes, C. (1974). *The first year of bereavement*. New York: John Wiley & Sons.
Gordon, P. (1982). *Special statistical summary—Deaths, injuries, and property loss by type of disaster, 1970–1980 (A127645)*. Washington, DC: Federal Emergency Management Agency.
Green, B. L. (1982). Assessing levels of psychological impairment following disaster. *Journal of Nervous and Mental Disease, 170*, 544–552.
Green, B. L., Grace, M. C., Lindy, J. D., Titchener, J. L., & Lindy, J. G. (1983). Levels of functional impairment following a civilian disaster: The Beverly Hills Supper Club fire. *Journal of Consulting and Clinical Psychology, 51*, 573–580.
Holmes, T., & Rahe, R. (1967). The social readjustment rating scale. *Journal of Psychosomatic Research, 11*, 213–218.
Hyman, R., & Woog, P. (1982). Stressful life events and illness onset: A review of critical variables. *Research in Nursing and Health, 5*, 155–163.
Kirk, R. (1968). *Experimental design: Procedures for the behavioral sciences*. Belmont, CA: Brooks-Cole.
Lazarus, R., & Cohen, J. (1977). *The hassles scale: Stress and coping project*. University of California, Berkeley, CA.
Lindy, J., Grace, M., & Green, B. (1981). Survivors: Outreach to a reluctant population. *American Journal of Orthopsychiatry, 51*, 468–478.
Logue, J., Melick, M., & Struening, E. (1981). A study of health and mental health status following a major natural disaster. In R. Simmons (Ed.), *Research in community mental health: An annual compilation of research* (Vol. 2, pp. 217–274). Greenwich, CN: JAI Press.
McCubbin, H. (1976). Coping repertoires of families adapting to prolonged war-induced separations. *Journal of Marriage and the Family, 38*, 461–471.
Melick, M. E. (1985). The health of postdisaster populations: A review of literature and case study. In J. Laube & S. A. Murphy (Eds.), *Perspectives on disaster recovery* (pp. 179–209). East Norwalk, CN: Appleton-Century-Crofts.
Murphy, S. A. (1984). Stress levels and health status of victims of a natural disaster. *Research in Nursing and Health, 7*, 205–215.
Murphy, S., & Stewart, B. (1986). Linked pairs of subjects: A method for increasing the sample size in a study of bereavement. *Omega, 16*, 141–153.
Perry, R., & Lindell, M. (1978). The psychological consequences of natural disaster: A review of research on American communities. *Mass Emergencies, 3*, 105–115.
Sarason, I., Johnson, J., & Siegel, J. (1978). Assessing the impact of life changes: Development of the life experiences survey. *Journal of Consulting and Clinical Psychology, 46*, 932–946.
Schleifer, S. J., Keller, S. E., Camerino, M., Thornton, J. L., & Stein, J. (1983). Suppression of lymphocyte stimulation following bereavement. *Journal of the American Medical Association, 250*, 374–377.
Shneidman, E. (1976). *Death: Current perspectives*. Palo Alto, CA: Mayfield.
Shore, J. H., Tatum, E., & Vollmer, W. (In press). Evaluation of mental health effects and adaptation to disaster due to volcanic eruption. In A. Buist and R. Bernstein (Eds.), *Human hazards from volcanic eruptions: Approach to evaluation of an environmental hazard*. (*American Journal of Public Health*, special monograph.)

Singh, B., & Raphael, B. (1981). Post-disaster morbidity of the bereaved. A possible role for preventive psychiatry? *Journal of Nervous and Mental Disease, 169,* 203–212.

Titchener, J., & Kapp, F. (1976). Family and character change at Buffalo Creek. *American Journal of Psychiatry, 133,* 306–312.

Vachon, M., Rogers, J., Lyall, W. A., Lancee, W. J., Sheldon, A. R., & Freeman, S. J. (1982). Predictors and correlates of adaptation to conjugal bereavement. *American Journal of Psychiatry, 139,* 998–1002.

Weisman, A. (1973). Coping with untimely death. *Psychiatry, 36,* 366–379.

8

Post-Traumatic Stress Disorder Among Vietnam and Vietnam-Era Veterans

ROBERT H. STRETCH

Post-traumatic stress disorder (PTSD) results from exposure to trauma that is generally outside the range of usual human experience. It is characterized by symptoms such as recurrent and intrusive dreams and recollections of the traumatic event, a numbing of responsiveness to the external world as evidenced by feelings of detachment from others or constricted affect, and additional symptoms such as sleep disturbance, survivor guilt, and memory impairment or trouble concentrating (APA, 1980).

While PTSD has been studied among survivors of natural disasters such as floods (Newman, 1976; Rangell, 1976; Titchener & Kapp, 1976), a maritime disaster (Carlton, 1980), and a mine disaster (Ploeger, 1977), the majority of research has focused on survivors of the Vietnam War (see Kenton, 1984).

Combat experience remains the variable most often linked to PTSD among Vietnam veterans (Penk, Rabinowitz, Roberts, Patterson, Dolan, & Athers, 1981; Center for Policy Research, 1981; Frye & Stockton, 1982),

---

The opinions expressed herein are those of the author and do not necessarily reflect the views of the department of the Army or the Department of Defense.

but there is no conceptual basis in DSM-III (APA, 1980) for the observation of the apparently higher prevalence of postcombat reactions among Vietnam veterans than among veterans of previous war eras.

With few exceptions (Futterman & Pumpian-Mindlin, 1951; Archibald, Long, Miller, & Tuddenham, 1962), research on veterans of World War II does not document the existence of widespread postcombat reactions. Long-term and/or delayed combat stress reactions appear to be much more common among veterans of Vietnam (Harris & associates, 1980; Schindler, 1980) despite much lower psychiatric casualty rates than experienced during World War II (Datel, 1976).

Several differences exist that serve to set Vietnam apart from previous wars: (1) limited 12- to 13-month tours of duty; (2) lack of clearly defined battle lines; (3) difficulty in discerning friend from foe; (4) political constraints on pursuit of military objectives; (5) lack of popular support at home following the Tet Offensive of 1968; and (6) drug abuse (Renner, 1973). Because of these differences and the apparent lack of widespread long-term stress reactions following previous wars, there exists the possibility that this phenomenon of PTSD among Vietnam veterans may be keyed to events involved in return and reentry to society that serve to either exacerbate or mitigate the negative effects of combat.

An alternate approach to the study of PTSD involves examining factors other than combat experience that may affect the onset of this disorder. One such factor is social support. Many studies have examined personal and psychosocial factors such as coping and social support on the premise that such factors operate to buffer the individual from the negative effects of stress (Brown & Harris, 1978; Johnson & Sarason, 1978; Mitchell, Billings, & Moos, 1982; Pearlin, Lieberman, Menaghan, & Mullan, 1981). PTSD may involve the failure of social support systems to promote the catharsis or abreaction of stressful combat experiences. Without validation or legitimization of these experiences, combat veterans may be unable to cope successfully.

A related factor that may also have influenced the development of PTSD among Vietnam veterans is the time period the veteran served in Vietnam. The history of the Vietnam War is such that it can be viewed in terms of two distinct phases. Until the Tet Offensive of 1968, the war was characterized by the continued buildup of American forces, high morale, popular support at home, a low incidence of drug abuse, and a relatively low neuropsychiatric casualty rate among Army personnel, which ranged from 6.98 hospital diagnoses per 1,000 in 1965 to 12.70 per 1,000 in 1968. These figures are much lower than comparable statistics representing Army personnel during World War II and the Korean War (Datel, 1976).

After the Tet Offensive of 1968, the war in Vietnam was characterized by the gradual disengagement of American forces, low morale, increased antiwar sentiment at home, drug abuse, and a much higher neuropsychiatric casualty rate, which increased to 31.30 hospital diagnoses per 1,000 Army personnel in 1971 and stood at 24.20 per 1,000 in mid-1972 when the bulk of American forces had departed (Datel, 1976). Veterans who served during this second phase of the war are more likely to have received less positive social support for their role in the war given the negative public sentiment prevalent at that time.

A limitation of previous research on PTSD is that several large groups of Vietnam veterans have been ignored. Past studies have focused almost entirely on civilian veterans, yet there are many Vietnam and Vietnam-era veterans who are still affiliated with the military either on active duty or in the Reserves. Little is known about the psychosocial adjustment or prevalence of stress disorders such as PTSD among this population. If social support is indeed an important factor in the development of PTSD, then it is likely that Vietnam veterans still affiliated with the military will differ significantly from their civilian counterparts in the quality of support received. Veterans who maintained a military affiliation most likely received more positive support from friends and peers for their role in the war than did veterans who returned directly to the civilian community given the negative public attitude toward the war at that time.

The prevalence of PTSD among this population of military-affiliated Vietnam veterans is unknown. What little is known concerning prevalence rates of PTSD is limited to reports based on civilian veterans, which are largely speculative. Estimates of PTSD among civilian veterans range from 500,000 out of the 2.8 million military personnel who served in Vietnam (Disabled American Veterans Association, 1980), to 700,000 (Walker & Cavenar, 1982; Mantell & Pilisuk, 1975), to as many as 1.5 million (Harris & associates, 1980; Schindler, 1980). These figures provide an estimate that anywhere from 18% to 54% of the Vietnam veteran population is currently suffering symptoms of PTSD. If social support is an important determinant of PTSD, then the prevalence rate should be significantly less among military-affiliated Vietnam veterans.

Obviously there are difficulties in comparing civilian and military-affiliated veterans. First, veterans still on active duty have gone through a filtering process in which those most likely to have difficulties coping with their experiences in Vietnam either voluntarily left the military or were discharged for various reasons that could be related to readjustment problems.

The Vietnam veterans currently in the Reserves are probably also different in that they have sought to maintain a military identity, which would be unlikely for someone who felt that the military was responsible for any adjustment problems resulting from military experiences. It is also possible that different social support experiences may play an important role in explaining the varied PTSD rates. Veterans who remained in the military following their service in Vietnam returned to a supportive military environment in which they could share their experiences with fellow veterans. The Reservists left active duty but maintained their military affiliation and opportunities for supportive interactions with fellow veterans through their monthly weekend drills and yearly active-duty training.

Since the Reservists are only part-time soldiers, they most likely were exposed to many more of the negative and hostile attitudes and reactions on the part of society than were the active duty veterans. Thus, this group of Reservists may have achieved a "middle-ground" position in terms of social support between their fellow active-duty veterans and those who returned to the civilian community where the chances of experiencing more negative and less positive societal reactions to their service in Vietnam were much greater.

A programmatic research effort into the prevalence of PTSD among Vietnam veterans was launched in the fall of 1981 (Stretch, 1984a, b, c, 1985, in press; Stretch, Vail, & Maloney, 1985). The purpose of the project was to determine the prevalence of PTSD among different groups of Vietnam and Vietnam-era veterans (active duty, Reservists, civilians) as well as to delineate factors having an effect on the development and attenuation of PTSD symptomatology. The major hypothesis tested was that PTSD is affected by several different factors: combat/war zone experiences; social support system validation of experiences both during service in Vietnam and upon reentry (particularly the first year back); and the time period the veterans served in Vietnam (before or after the Tet Offensive of 1968). It was also hypothesized that the prevalence of PTSD would vary according to the current military affiliation of the veterans sampled.

On the basis of a large body of research linking stress to illness in the general population (see Dean & Lin, 1977) and the reported relationship between combat exposure among Vietnam veterans and the prevalence of medical problems during and after military service (Laufer, Yager, Frey-Wouters, & Donnellan, 1981), it was hypothesized that there would be a highly significant positive relationship between perceived physical and psychosocial health among Vietnam veterans.

The project was conducted in four separate phases. Phase 1 studied active-duty Army Vietnam and Vietnam-era veterans. Phase 2 studied U.S. Army Reserve Vietnam and Vietnam-era veterans. Phase 3 studied active-duty Vietnam and Vietnam-era veterans in the Army Nurse Corps, and Phase 4 studied prior-service civilians.

PHASE 1

Method

Subjects. A sample of male veterans who had served in Vietnam was identified through installation personnel data tapes of all personnel assigned to a moderate-sized U.S. Army post on the East Coast. A total of 516 active-duty Vietnam veterans were identified through this procedure. A letter explaining the project along with a questionnaire was mailed to each subject requesting his participation in the study. Seventy questionnaires were returned undelivered because of permanent change of station (PCS) moves or separations from active duty. Completed questionnaires were received from 238 subjects, for a 53% return rate.

A second sample was obtained for purposes of control. This sample consisted of all male personnel at the same post who had entered active duty during the Vietnam era (1963–1972) but who had not served in Vietnam. An examination of the installation personnel data tapes identified 329 Vietnam-era veterans. All subjects were mailed copies of the same letter and questionnaire sent to the Vietnam veterans. Sixty-seven questionnaires were returned undelivered because of PCS moves or separations. Completed questionnaires were received from 85 Vietnam-era veterans, for a 33% return rate. The lower rate of return for the Vietnam-era veterans is thought to be due to the lack of any "emotional stake" involved. It was probably seen as another lengthy form that they were not required to complete.

The mean age of the Vietnam veteran sample was 38.3 years. These veterans are predominantly white (70%), well-educated (68% have had some college experience with 28% holding a degree), volunteered for military service (70%), and have been on active duty over 17 years. Officers comprise over 20.5% of the sample. Seventy-three percent of the Vietnam veterans were married, 15% were remarried, 4% were separated, 5% were divorced, and 3% were single. The primary military assignment of these veterans while in Vietnam was 23% in the combat arms, 33% in direct combat support, and 44% in support (rear echelon).

The hospitalization rate for noncombat injuries was 36.9%, with combat-related injuries accounting for less than 15% of the sample.

The Vietnam-era veterans were very similar to the Vietnam veterans. This group is also predominantly white (67%), well-educated (70% have had some college experience with 36% holding a degree), volunteered for military duty (70%), and have a noncombat rate of hospitalization of 34%. Officers comprise 24% of the sample. The Vietnam-era veterans differ significantly, however, in terms of being younger (M = 33.9, $t[304]$ = −5.99, $p < 0.001$) and having fewer years on active duty (M = 12.2, $t[303]$ = 5.82, $p < 0.001$) than the Vietnam veterans sampled.

Measures. All subjects received copies of the Vietnam-era Veterans Adjustment Survey (VEVAS), a questionnaire based on the Vietnam Veteran Questionnaire (Stretch & Figley, 1984). The VEVAS scales and their reliability coefficients are as follows: combat experience (alpha = 0.93); physical health problems both past (alpha = 0.92) and present (alpha = 0.91); psychosocial health problems during (alpha = 0.91) and after (alpha = 0.93) service in Vietnam; and social support received during (alpha = 0.72) and after (alpha = 0.77) service in Vietnam (scale items and scoring procedures are available on request).

The confidentiality of all subject responses to this and all subsequent phases of the project was guaranteed by Confidentiality Certificate MH-82-14 issued by the National Institute of Mental Health.

Procedure. Using the definition and diagnostic criteria for assessment of PTSD as outlined in DSM-III, responses to six key items in the psychosocial health scale of the VEVAS were examined. These items assess past or current difficulty with the following problems: (1) dealing with bad memories about his Vietnam experiences; (2) sleeping (bad dreams or nightmares); (3) expressing feelings to those cared about; (4) feeling and expressing emotions ("numbness"); (5) concentrating; and (6) dealing with feelings of guilt about having survived Vietnam. The response categories for these items range from *never* (0) to *very often* (4).

For Vietnam veterans, the required existence of a recognizable stressor is assumed to be directly related to experiences in Vietnam, particularly combat experiences. For Vietnam-era veterans, however, the existence of a recognizable stressor would be assumed not related to military service. This is not meant to imply that a Vietnam-era veteran could not suffer symptoms of PTSD as a result of a traumatic event experienced while in the military; it is simply meant that the event would not be of the same type (combat) as experienced by the Vietnam veterans. The assumed stressor for Vietnam-era veterans might be an automobile accident or some other incident not related to combat.

If a Vietnam veteran responded by marking either *occasionally, often,* or *very often* to items 1 plus either of items 3 and 4 plus two of items 2, 5, and 6, then that veteran is considered to be experiencing symptoms of PTSD. Assessment of PTSD among Vietnam-era veterans is slightly different. For these veterans responses to items 2 to 5 only are examined since item 1 necessitates having served in Vietnam and item 6 could be interpreted by some Vietnam-era veterans as asking whether they feel guilty that they survived Vietnam by virtue of not having served there.

Items in the VEVAS that measure combat exposure, social support during Vietnam, and social support the first year back from Vietnam were summed to create three subscale variables called combat, Vietnam social support (VSS), and first-year social support (FYSS). These three variables, together with the year the veteran served in Vietnam, were entered into a stepwise regression equation. Responses to these subscale items were standardized via Z-score transformations. Interaction terms were computed and entered into the regression equation. This procedure allows the regression analysis to test interactions among variables in a manner similar to analysis of variance, but does not require that independent variables be grouped into classes; i.e., the independent variables remain continuous. These variables and interaction terms were regressed against the variable PTSD, the sum of the six items representing the diagnostic criteria of post-traumatic stress disorder.

Results

PTSD prevalence. An examination of the responses to the six PTSD assessment items in the VEVAS revealed that 12 Vietnam veterans (5.1%) could be classified as currently suffering symptoms of PTSD. For the Vietnam-era veterans, the response patterns of two veterans (2.3%) fit the diagnostic criteria for PTSD. The difference in prevalence rates is nonsignificant.

Since the Vietnam veterans were also asked to respond to PTSD items in the VEVAS on the basis of how they felt while they were in Vietnam, responses to the six PTSD items for this time period were also examined. The analysis revealed that 25 Vietnam veterans (10.5%) experienced symptoms of PTSD while in Vietnam. A further breakdown of the data revealed that 17 Vietnam veterans (7.1%) suffered "acute" PTSD (experienced PTSD during Vietnam but are not currently bothered), eight veterans (3.4%) suffer from "chronic" PTSD (experienced PTSD during

Vietnam and are still bothered), and four veterans (1.7%) are suffering from "delayed" PTSD (did not experience PTSD during Vietnam but are currently bothered). This represents an overall PTSD prevalence of 12.2% for the Vietnam veterans in the sample (total PTSD = acute + chronic + delayed).

Regression analysis. The results of the regression analysis on the variable PTSD (r = 0.56) revealed highly significant main effects for combat ($F[1,211]$ = 12.85, $p < 0.01$) and first-year social support ($F[1,211]$ = 34.01, $p < 0.01$), but no statistically significant interactions. The results indicate that as the magnitude of combat experiences increases, so does the severity of PTSD symptoms. Those veterans whose interactions with others since returning home from Vietnam have been primarily critical and nonsupportive (negative) have PTSD symptom levels significantly higher than do those veterans whose interactions with others after returning from Vietnam have been primarily supportive (positive). Combat and first-year social support accounted for 12% and 15%, respectively, of the variance.

Veterans who did not receive positive social support while in Vietnam also have higher PTSD symptom levels than do veterans who received positive social support while in Vietnam, but the differences are not statistically significant. Although the effect for the year the veteran served in Vietnam is also statistically nonsignificant, it is in the predicted direction of higher PTSD symptom levels for veterans who served in the late rather than early stage of the war.

Physical health. Physical health data in the VEVAS consist of responses to a 75-item symptom checklist based on the *Cornell Medical Index* (Cornell University Medical College, 1974) in which the veteran responds by indicating whether he has ever been bothered by a particular illness or ailment in the past and, if so, whether he is still bothered. The items represent six different categories or clusters of health symptoms: respiratory, cardiovascular, gastrointestinal, skin disorders, nervous system problems, and general health. Items within each category are summed to give total scores. In order to assess the validity of the self-report data on physical health, actual military medical records were examined for 50 randomly selected veterans. A comparison of conditions noted in the medical records with those identified in the VEVAS responses indicates an approximate 70% agreement.

The nature of many of the questions in the VEVAS makes it difficult to verify responses. For example, a person may suffer from frequent colds, indigestion, or headaches without seeking treatment from medical facilities. When one considers that military medical records are often incomplete and sometimes difficult to read, the accuracy of the self-report data obtained is sufficiently high to be considered indicative of actual physical health.

Past and current physical health scores for each of the six categories of self-reported health as well as overall health for both the Vietnam and Vietnam-era veterans were compared. After controlling for age differences between the two samples, no significant differences on any measure of past or current health were found. A comparison of the health scores of all Vietnam veterans who had previously been identified as having suffered PTSD symptoms either during or after service in Vietnam with all remaining Vietnam veterans, however, revealed that the PTSD-classified veterans currently have significantly more respiratory and overall health problems than do the non-PTSD-classified Vietnam veterans. PTSD-classified veterans have also had significantly more past problems across all categories of health, including overall health, than have the non-PTSD-classified veterans (see Table 1).

To further demonstrate the relationship between physical and psychosocial health, Pearson Product-Moment correlations were computed between PTSD scores for the Vietnam veterans and all categories of physical health. Results indicate highly significant positive correlations between PTSD symptoms and respiratory ($r = 0.17$, $p < 0.05$), gastrointestinal ($r = 0.28$, $p < 0.01$), nervous system ($r = 0.29$, $p < 0.01$), general health ($r = 0.27$, $p < 0.01$), and overall health ($r = 0.35$, $p < 0.01$).

PHASE 2

Method

Subjects. A stratified random sample of 2,000 male Vietnam and Vietnam-era veterans was identified by the Reserve Component Personnel and Administration Center (RCPAC) in St. Louis. These veterans were selected at random from all Vietnam and Vietnam-era veterans assigned to U.S. Army Reserve troop units nationwide in the spring of 1982. Personnel assigned to troop units perform a minimum of one weekend of duty per month plus at least two weeks of annual training.

In order to ensure adequate representation by both Vietnam and Vietnam-era veterans who served during the early and late stages of the

TABLE 1

Health Scores for Active-Duty PTSD/Non-PTSD Vietnam Veterans

	Vet group	n	Mean	T	DF	Alpha
Current index						
Respiratory health	PTSD	24	3.54	2.21	135	0.02
	Non-PTSD	113	2.36			
Cardiovascular health	PTSD	25	2.52	1.70	118	0.09
	Non-PTSD	95	1.79			
Gastrointestinal health	PTSD	21	3.00	0.98	120	0.33
	Non-PTSD	101	2.48			
Skin disorders	PTSD	16	1.56	1.22	84	0.22
	Non-PTSD	70	1.27			
Nervous system	PTSD	26	3.50	1.37	102	0.17
	Non-PTSD	78	2.64			
General health	PTSD	19	1.47	1.32	93	0.19
	Non-PTSD	76	1.05			
Overall health	PTSD	29	12.24	3.68	187	0.001
	Non-PTSD	209	6.64			
Past index						
Respiratory health	PTSD	29	4.10	4.19	233	0.001
	Non-PTSD	206	1.86			
Cardiovascular health	PTSD	29	3.03	4.50	233	0.001
	Non-PTSD	206	1.29			
Gastrointestinal health	PTSD	29	3.00	2.64	233	0.001
	Non-PTSD	206	1.74			
Skin disorders	PTSD	29	1.03	2.67	233	0.001
	Non-PTSD	206	0.57			
Nervous system	PTSD	29	4.24	5.28	233	0.001
	Non-PTSD	206	1.54			
General health	PTSD	29	1.97	4.36	233	0.001
	Non-PTSD	206	0.74			
Overall health	PTSD	29	17.38	5.43	233	0.001
	Non-PTSD	206	7.74			

war, these 2,000 subjects were selected to represent four distinct groups. Group 1 consisted of 500 Vietnam veterans who had been released from active duty during 1968. Group 2 consisted of 500 Vietnam veterans who had been released from active duty during 1971. Group 3 consisted of 500 Vietnam-era veterans who had been released from active duty during 1968. Group 4 consisted of 500 Vietnam-era veterans who had been released from active duty during 1971. The Vietnam-era veterans in groups 3 and 4 are those who served on active duty in the U.S. Army during the time period American forces were stationed in Vietnam (1963–1973) but did not serve in Vietnam themselves. A cover letter explaining the project, appropriate privacy act/informed consent forms, and a questionnaire (VEVAS) were mailed to each subject using home addresses provided by RCPAC.

Of the 1,000 questionnaires mailed to Vietnam veterans, 88 were returned undelivered owing to moves. Responses were received from 667 veterans, for a 73% rate of return. Of the 1,000 questionnaires mailed to the Vietnam-era veterans, 76 were returned undelivered. Responses were received from 258 subjects, for a 28% return rate.

The lower response rate for the Vietnam-era veterans in this sample is similar to that found among the Vietnam-era veterans in the first phase of the study. Again, lack of emotional stake and length of the questionnaire are probably important factors contributing to this low response rate.

The average age of the Vietnam veteran sample was 36.7 years. These veterans are predominantly white (84%), married (83%), well educated (84% have had some college experience with 27% holding a college degree), volunteered for military duty (61%), and were on active duty an average 42 months. Officers comprise 44% of the sample. The primary military assignment of these veterans in Vietnam was 37% in combat arms, 32% in direct combat support, and 31% in support (rear echelon). The hospitalization rate for noncombat injuries while on active duty was 18% with an additional 16% reporting combat-related hospitalizations.

The Vietnam-era veterans sampled are very similar to the Vietnam veterans demographically. These veterans are also predominantly white (95%), married (83%), well-educated (84% have had some college experience with 30% holding a college degree), volunteered for military duty (68%), and have a noncombat-related hospitalization rate of 15%. Officers comprise 35% of the sample. The Vietnam-era veterans differ, however, from the Vietnam veterans in terms of being significantly younger ($M = 35.8$ $t[915] = 3.28$, $p < 0.01$) and having fewer months of active duty service ($M = 24.4$ $t[916] = 8.27$, $p < 0.01$).

Measures. As in Phase 1, all subjects were sent copies of the VEVAS. All procedures and analyses in Phase 2 were identical to those in Phase 1 with one exception: preliminary *t*-test results indicated some significant differences on the basis of rank (enlisted versus officer). Therefore, the multiple-regression analysis in Phase 2 included the variable rank.

Results

PTSD prevalence. Using the described procedure for assessing PTSD, it was determined that 73 Vietnam veterans (10.9%) had symptoms of PTSD. A breakdown of this figure according to rank revealed that the prevalence of PTSD among enlisted personnel (14.4%) was significantly higher than the prevalence among officers (6.5%, $\chi^2[1,670] = 10.49$, $p = 0.001$).

Four Vietnam-era veterans were identified as having symptoms of PTSD (1.5%). Because this procedure is less precise owing to lack of information on exposure to trauma, it is likely that the rate of PTSD among Vietnam-era veterans is an overestimate of the true rate. Even so, the PTSD rates for the Vietnam and Vietnam-era veterans are still significantly different ($\chi^2[4, n = 925] = 7.18$, $p < 0.01$).

The current PTSD prevalence rate for the Reserve Vietnam veterans (10.9%) is much lower than the estimates for civilian veterans (18%–54%) but is significantly higher than the rate found for active-duty Vietnam veterans (5.1%) in Phase 1 ($\chi^2 [4, n = 908] = 7.18$, $p < 0.01$). Further analyses revealed that 80 veterans (12%) had symptoms of PTSD during their service in Vietnam. A breakdown of the prevalence of PTSD during Vietnam duty according to rank revealed that enlisted veterans had a significantly higher PTSD rate (16.8%) than did officers (5.8%, $\chi^2 [1,670] = 18.74$, $p < 0.001$).

Forty-three Reserve Vietnam veterans (6.5%) were found to have experienced acute PTSD; 37 (5.5%) are suffering from chronic PTSD; and 36 Reservists (5.4%) have developed delayed PTSD. The overall PTSD rate (acute + chronic + delayed) for the Reserve Vietnam veterans is 17.4%. Although the Reserve Vietnam veterans differ significantly from the active-duty Vietnam veterans in terms of current PTSD rates, they do not differ in terms of their PTSD rates while in Vietnam (12% Reserve versus 10.5% active duty). By looking at the rates for acute, chronic, and delayed PTSD for both groups of Vietnam veterans, it is apparent that there is a significantly greater percentage of Reservists (5.4%) than active-duty veterans (1.7%) experiencing delayed PTSD ($\chi^2 [4, n = 145] = 6.39$, $p < 0.02$).

Regression analysis. The results of the regression analysis on the variable PTSD (R = 0.579) revealed highly significant main effects for rank, combat, Vietnam social support, and first-year social support. The greatest proportion of explained variance in the regression equation is accounted for by combat (12%) and first-year social support (12%).

Although no significant main effect was reported for the year the Reservist served in Vietnam, the effect was in the predicted direction of higher PTSD scores among Reservists who served in the late part of the war.

Reserve veterans who served in Vietnam in the enlisted ranks had significantly higher levels of PTSD symptomatology than those who served as officers in Vietnam ($F[1,597]$ = 10.37, $p < 0.01$).

Reserve Vietnam veterans with high combat experience scores also had significantly higher levels of PTSD symptoms than veterans with low combat experience scores ($F[1,597]$ = 55.10, $p < 0.01$).

Veterans who indicated that they had not received positive social support while in Vietnam have significantly higher PTSD scores than do those veterans who reported receiving positive social support while in Vietnam ($F[1,597]$ = 15.92, $p < 0.01$).

Veterans who reported experiencing negative/hostile societal reactions after returning home from Vietnam, particularly the first year back, also have significantly higher PTSD scores than do those veterans who reported receiving positive social support upon return to the United States ($F[1,597]$ = 75.10, $p < 0.01$).

The results of the regression analysis also indicate statistically significant interactions involving combat with first-year social support, first-year social support with Vietnam social support, and rank with first-year social support with Vietnam social support. The amount of variance explained by these interactions (an average 1% each), however, does not merit any further elaboration.

Physical health. Comparisons between Vietnam and Vietnam-era veterans were made on the health scores of each of the six categories of current and past physical health. After controlling for age differences, the Vietnam veterans were found to have significantly higher current self-perceived respiratory ($F[1,509]$ = 10.33, $p < 0.01$), nervous system ($F[1,399]$ = 6.40, $p < 0.01$), and general health scores ($F[1,297]$ = 24.92, $p < 0.01$) than the Vietnam-era veterans. No significant differences in regard to past health exist between the Vietnam and Vietnam-era veterans after controlling for age.

A second comparison was made between those Vietnam veterans who had been identified as having suffered PTSD symptoms either during or after service in Vietnam and those Vietnam veterans who have not had symptoms of PTSD. This analysis revealed that the PTSD-classified Vietnam veterans currently have significantly more self-perceived health problems across all categories (with the exception of skin disorders) than do the non-PTSD-classified Vietnam veterans. The PTSD-classified Vietnam veterans also report significantly more self-perceived health problems across all categories of past health than the non-PTSD-classified Vietnam veterans (see Table 2). The poorer self-perceived health of the PTSD-classified Vietnam veterans cannot be attributed to age differences since this group was significantly younger (35.3 years) than the non-PTSD-classified Vietnam veterans (37.0 years), $t(659) = -4.36, p < 0.01$.

Pearson Product-Moment correlations were computed between current PTSD scores and all categories of current health for the Vietnam veterans in the sample. Results indicate highly significant correlations between PTSD symptoms and present respiratory ($r = 0.38, p < 0.01$), cardiovascular ($r = 0.32, p < 0.01$), gastrointestinal ($r = 0.35, p < 0.01$), nervous system ($r = 0.37, p < 0.01$), general health ($r = 0.25, p < 0.01$), and overall health ($r = 0.50, p < 0.01$).

PHASE 3

The third phase of the project represents an expansion at the request of the Chief of the Army Nurse Corps, who was interested in determining whether PTSD was a problem among active-duty nurses who served in Vietnam. Inclusion of nurses in the project represented an opportunity not only to gain information on the prevalence of PTSD, but also to better understand the nature of war zone trauma as well as determine whether males and females react differently to trauma. While combat has been viewed as the primary stressor in PTSD among Vietnam veterans, the impact of other war zone experiences often associated with combat had not been addressed. For example, combat is often characterized by behaviors such as firing weapons, wounding or killing the enemy, or seeing others in the act of being wounded or killed. Research from World War II indicates that other experiences may also be sufficiently traumatic to produce stress reactions.

In a follow-up study of World War II veterans suffering from traumatic war neuroses, Futterman and Pumpian-Mindlin (1951) observed that these neuroses were more common among certain groups of noncombatants such as soldiers in graves registration units and members of Air

TABLE 2
Health Scores for USAR PTSD/Non-PTSD Vietnam Veterans

	Vet Group	n	Mean	T	DF	Alpha
Current index						
Respiratory health	PTSD	98	4.22	5.28	410	0.001
	Non-PTSD	314	2.66			
Cardiovascular health	PTSD	80	2.55	5.05	309	0.001
	Non-PTSD	231	1.52			
Gastrointestinal health	PTSD	85	3.66	6.55	385	0.001
	Non-PTSD	302	1.98			
Skin disorders	PTSD	64	1.61	1.47	248	0.14
	Non-PTSD	186	1.45			
Nervous system	PTSD	86	4.12	4.88	248	0.001
	Non-PTSD	236	2.50			
General health	PTSD	68	1.66	2.80	237	0.01
	Non-PTSD	171	1.10			
Overall health	PTSD	107	14.01	9.98	564	0.001
	Non-PTSD	459	6.17			
Past index						
Respiratory health	PTSD	113	4.55	9.06	656	0.001
	Non-PTSD	545	1.98			
Cardiovascular health	PTSD	113	2.42	8.34	655	0.001
	Non-PTSD	544	1.03			
Gastrointestinal health	PTSD	113	3.44	8.06	656	0.001
	Non-PTSD	545	1.58			
Skin disorders	PTSD	113	1.06	5.10	655	0.001
	Non-PTSD	544	0.59			
Nervous system	PTSD	112	4.10	9.91	655	0.001
	Non-PTSD	545	1.49			
General health	PTSD	113	1.33	5.71	655	0.001
	Non-PTSD	544	0.59			
Overall health	PTSD	113	16.87	11.08	656	0.001
	Non-PTSD	545	7.35			

Corps emergency fire squad units. Other commonly affected veterans were medical first-aid men who were often in combat situations, but did not carry weapons and were unable to defend themselves or take aggressive action against the enemy. The common link between these veterans is exposure to death and destruction with no effective possibility for retaliation against the enemy.

Nurses in Vietnam also did not carry weapons and were exposed to the brutality and horrors of war on a daily basis. In addition, nurses were not always stationed in safe, secure environs (Tuxon, 1983). Thus, although nurses did not experience combat, daily exposure to the violent aftermath of combat and a sense of pervasive danger may have put them at risk for developing PTSD.

Method

Subjects. A sample of all nurses on active duty in the U.S. Army who had served in Vietnam was identified through personnel data files maintained by the Army Nurse Corps in the spring of 1983. A total of 518 active-duty Vietnam veteran nurses was identified. A letter explaining the project along with a questionnaire was mailed to each subject requesting his/her voluntary participation in the study.

Responses were received from 387 subjects, for a 75% return rate. Of these 387 subjects, 14 were dropped from the sample because they had served in a nonnursing capacity in Vietnam, six were dropped because they indicated that they had not served in Vietnam, five were dropped because they had not served in Vietnam but had served elsewhere in Southeast Asia, and one was dropped because he had already participated in an earlier phase of the study. Data from 361 subjects (141 males, 220 females) were available for analysis.

A second sample was obtained for comparison purposes. This sample consisted of all nurses on active duty during the Vietnam-era (1963–1973) who had not served in Vietnam. A total of 487 Vietnam-era nurses was identified. All subjects were mailed copies of the same letter and questionnaire sent to the Vietnam veteran nurses. Responses were received from 345 subjects, for a 71% rate of return. Together with the six subjects dropped from the Vietnam veteran sample because they had not served in Vietnam, data from 351 Vietnam-era veteran nurses (105 males, 246 females) were available for analysis.

The mean age of the Vietnam veteran nurses was 41.5 years. These veterans are predominantly white (94.7%), female (60.8%), highly educated (53.3% have a master's degree), married (58.6%), and have been on active duty an average of over 17 years. While in Vietnam the primary assignments of these nurses were as follows: administrative (6.4%); anesthetist (10.6%); operating room (18.3%); emergency room (10.8%); ward (22.8%); and intensive care (19.7%). The majority of nurses (53.9%) served in evacuation hospitals in Vietnam while most others served in field units (21.4%) or surgical units/hospitals (10.6%).

The Vietnam-era veteran nurses are similar to the Vietnam veteran nurses in many respects. They are also predominantly white (90.9%), married (61.8%), and highly educated (59% hold a master's degree). They differ from the Vietnam veteran nurses in that they are younger ($M = 38.7$, $t[709] = 6.65$, $p < 0.001$), have fewer years of active duty service ($M = 15.6$, $t[704] = 6.06$, $p < 0.001$), and are more female ($\chi^2[1, n = 712] = 6.20$, $p < 0.01$).

Measures. It was necessary to make some modifications to the VEVAS for use with the nurses. Items in the combat scale assessing active participation in combat activities such as firing weapons and wounding or killing others were deleted. The remaining items assess exposure to the violent aftermath of combat and perceived danger. Scores on this modified scale (alpha = 0.83) were summed to create a subscale variable called combat exposure. Since all the nurses are officers, rank was dropped from the regression analysis and was replaced by the variable sex. A final modification to the VEVAS was the addition of four health scale items assessing gynecological health (alpha = 0.90). All measures of social support and psychosocial health remained identical to the original VEVAS.

Results

PTSD prevalence. An examination of responses to PTSD items in the VEVAS revealed that 12 Vietnam veteran nurses (3.3%) reported symptoms of PTSD. The prevalence among males (3.5%, $n = 5$) was not significantly different than for females (3.2%, $n = 7$). The prevalence rate among the Vietnam-era veteran nurses was found to be less than 1% (0.85%, $n = 3$). Again, because this procedure is less precise for Vietnam-era veterans, this rate is likely to be an overestimate of the true rate. Even so, using Yate's correction for continuity, the PTSD prevalence for Vietnam duty nurses is still significantly higher than the rate for Vietnam-era nurses ($\chi^2 [1, n = 712] = 4.13$, $p < 0.05$). The PTSD rate for Vietnam duty nurses is not significantly different from the rate (5.1%)

reported for other active-duty Army Vietnam veterans in Phase 1 of the study.

The Vietnam veteran nurses in the sample also responded to the same PTSD items in the VEVAS based on their recollection of how they felt while in Vietnam. Using the same PTSD assessment procedure, 33 nurses (9.1%) reported symptoms of PTSD while in Vietnam. This Vietnam duty PTSD rate is also not significantly different from the rate (10.5%) found for other active-duty Army Vietnam veterans in Phase 1. Again, there are no significant differences in PTSD rates among males (7.9%, $n = 11$) and females (9.9%, $n = 22$).

An examination of the number of veterans who reported past PTSD symptoms with those reporting current PTSD symptoms revealed that 26 nurses (7.2%) suffered acute PTSD, seven nurses (1.9%) suffer from chronic PTSD, and five nurses (1.4%) are suffering from delayed PTSD. These figures indicate an overall PTSD prevalence rate of 10.5% (acute + chronic + delayed), which is not significantly different from the overall rate (12.2%) found among other active-duty Army Vietnam veterans.

Regression analysis. The results of the regression analysis on the variable PTSD ($R = 0.50$) revealed highly significant main effects for combat exposure, first-year social support, and Vietnam social support. No significant interactions or main effect for sex were found.

Nurses who experienced the most perceived danger and exposure to violence and combat aftermath had the highest levels of PTSD symptomatology ($F[1,298] = 4.58$, $p < 0.05$). Nurses who indicated that they had experienced positive social support while in Vietnam had significantly lower levels of PTSD than did nurses who reported experiencing negative or hostile reactions from others while in Vietnam ($F[1,298] = 6.59$, $p < 0.05$).

Nurses who reported experiencing reactions from others that were primarily negative or hostile upon return from Vietnam had significantly higher levels of PTSD than did nurses who experienced positive reactions from others ($F[1,298] = 23.654$, $p < 0.01$). Of the 25% total variance explained by the regression equation, first-year social support accounted for over half (14%). Combat exposure and Vietnam social support each accounted for approximately 3% of the explained variance.

The effect for the time period the nurses served in Vietnam was not significant, but was in the predicted direction of higher levels of PTSD symptomatology among nurses who served in the late stages of the war.

Physical health. A comparison of health scores between the Vietnam and Vietnam-era nurses revealed that the Vietnam veteran nurses currently have significantly more cardiovascular, nervous system, and overall health problems than the Vietnam-era veteran nurses. In terms of past health, the Vietnam veteran nurses reported significantly more cardiovascular, nervous system, and overall health problems as well as more skin disorders than the Vietnam-era nurses (see Table 3).

A comparison between health scores of the PTSD-classified Vietnam nurses and the non-PTSD-classified Vietnam nurses revealed that the PTSD-classified Vietnam nurses currently report significantly more cardiovascular, gastrointestinal, and overall health problems than the non-PTSD-classified Vietnam nurses. The PTSD-classified Vietnam nurses also reported significantly more past problems associated with respiratory, cardiovascular, nervous system, general, and overall health than the non-PTSD-classified Vietnam nurses (see Table 4).

The results of Pearson Product-Moment correlations between current PTSD symptoms and current health indices for the Vietnam veteran nurses revealed highly significant correlations for cardiovascular health ($r = 0.28$, $p < 0.01$), general health ($r = 0.21$, $p < 0.01$), nervous system problems ($r = 0.23$, $p < 0.01$), gynecological health ($r = 0.23$, $p < 0.01$), and overall health ($r = 0.37$, $p < 0.001$).

PHASE 4

Method

Subjects. The names and addresses of 2,500 male Vietnam and Vietnam-era veterans selected at random from medical compensation files were provided by the Veterans Administration in the fall of 1983. As before, a cover letter explaining the project, appropriate privacy act/informed consent forms, and a questionnaire were mailed to each subject. Of the 2,500 questionnaires mailed, 160 were returned undelivered owing to moves. Responses were received from 771 veterans, for a 32% return rate. Twenty-three of the questionnaires were excluded because of incomplete responses, leaving 748 questionnaires to be analyzed. These 748 subjects represent 499 Vietnam veterans and 249 Vietnam-era veterans.

Several reasons exist for the low response rate to the questionnaire. The foremost is the suspicion and lack of trust that Vietnam veterans have shown for the Veterans Administration (VA), the military, and the government in general (Stretch & Figley, 1984). Many veterans may have doubted the sincerity of the stated purpose of the project since it involved both the military (which many veterans blame for causing their problems) and the VA (which many veterans blame for not helping to solve their problems).

A second reason might be that many veterans who have had trouble readjusting have dealt with these problems by trying to forget Vietnam and have no desire to relive the war again by answering questions that can stir up painful memories. It is also likely that many Vietnam-era veterans failed to respond because they felt that the questionnaire was not really relevant to them since they had not served in Vietnam. In earlier phases of the project lower response rates among Vietnam-era veterans were observed. It is probable that the response pattern in this phase is similar in that the actual return rate is about 50%, which is more acceptable.

Demographically the Vietnam and Vietnam-era veterans are similar. The two samples differ, however, in that the Vietnam veterans are younger ($M = 39.7$) than the Vietnam-era veterans ($M = 43.6$, $t[740] = -5.14$, $p = 0.001$), more racially diverse (74% white, 12% black, 10% Hispanic) than the Vietnam-era veterans (85% white, 7% black, 6% Hispanic, $\chi^2[4, n = 733] = 12.55$, $p = 0.01$), have fewer children ($M = 2.0$) than the Vietnam-era veterans ($M = 2.3$, $t[661] = -2.09$, $p < 0.05$), were on active duty fewer months ($M = 81.9$) than the Vietnam-era veterans ($M = 125.0$, $t[727] = -5.02$, $p = 0.001$), were younger ($M = 19.5$) when they entered the military than the Vietnam-era veterans ($M = 19.9$, $t[734] = -2.28$, $p < 0.05$), were more likely to have been drafted (32.2%) than the Vietnam-era veterans (21.5%, $\chi^2[5, n = 736] = 17.73$, $p < 0.01$), were more likely to have been in the Army (65.9%) than the Vietnam-era veterans (43.5%, $\chi^2[4, n = 747] = 139.60$, $p < 0.001$), and were more likely to be rated more than 50% disabled by the VA (17.4%) than the Vietnam-era veterans (11.4%, $\chi^2[4, n = 740] = 10.15$, $p < 0.05$).

Educationally, a greater percentage of Vietnam-era veterans (16%) than Vietnam veterans have done postgraduate work (8.1%, $\chi^2[5, n = 736] = 19.79$, $p < 0.001$). This may account for the finding that even though there are no differences in the number of veterans that are employed, a greater percentage of Vietnam-era (58.9%) than Vietnam veterans report earning more than $20,000 per year (47.0%, $\chi^2[4, n = 702] = 11.39$, $p < 0.05$).

TABLE 3
Health Scores for Nurse Corps Vietnam/Vietnam-Era Veterans

Current index	Vet group	n	Mean	T	DF	Alpha
Respiratory health	Vietnam	180	1.85	1.63	342	0.11
	Vietnam-era	164	1.56			
Cardiovascular health	Vietnam	180	1.46	2.42	313	0.01
	Vietnam-era	135	1.08			
Gastrointestinal health	Vietnam	189	1.29	2.42	344	0.80
	Vietnam-era	157	1.24			
Skin disorders	Vietnam	65	1.03	0.81	101	0.42
	Vietnam-era	38	0.92			
Nervous system	Vietnam	158	2.04	2.33	290	0.02
	Vietnam-era	134	1.48			
General health	Vietnam	177	0.91	0.69	337	0.49
	Vietnam-era	162	0.83			
Gynecologic health	Vietnam	100	1.24	2.02	189	0.04ᵃ
	Vietnam-era	91	0.96			
Overall health	Vietnam	312	4.85	2.97	599	0.003
	Vietnam-era	289	3.64			

TABLE 3 (cont'd)

	Vet group	n	Mean	T	DF	Alpha
Past index						
Respiratory health	Vietnam	361	1.43	1.04	709	0.30
	Vietnam-era	350	1.27			
Cardiovascular health	Vietnam	361	1.15	2.96	709	0.003[a]
	Vietnam-era	350	0.82			
Gastrointestinal health	Vietnam	361	1.25	0.88	709	0.38
	Vietnam-era	350	1.13			
Skin disorders	Vietnam	361	0.24	2.03	709	0.04
	Vietnam-era	350	0.16			
Nervous system	Vietnam	361	1.48	2.04	709	0.04
	Vietnam-era	350	1.16			
General health	Vietnam	361	0.99	-0.39	709	0.69
	Vietnam-era	350	1.03			
Gynecologic health	Vietnam	222	0.96	2.63	467	0.009[a]
	Vietnam-era	247	0.68			
Overall health	Vietnam	361	7.11	1.97	709	0.05
	Vietnam-era	350	6.05			

[a]These health symptom differences cannot be attributed solely to service in Vietnam. Results of a stepwise regression analysis reveal that these three health variables are age-related and show up due to the fact that members of the Vietnam veteran sample are significantly older than members of the Vietnam-era sample.

TABLE 4
Health Scores for Nurse Corps PTSD/Non-PTSD Vietnam Veterans

	Vet group	n	Mean	T	DF	Alpha
Current index						
Respiratory health	PTSD	10	2.00	0.26	178	0.79
	Non-PTSD	170	1.84			
Cardiovascular health	PTSD	9	2.66	2.42	178	0.02
	Non-PTSD	171	1.40			
Gastrointestinal health	PTSD	10	0.40	−3.77	187	0.002
	Non-PTSD	179	1.33			
Skin disorders	PTSD	3	0.67	−1.01	63	0.31
	Non-PTSD	62	1.04			
Nervous system	PTSD	11	3.00	1.45	156	0.15
	Non-PTSD	147	1.97			
General health	PTSD	11	1.09	0.69	175	0.51
	Non-PTSD	166	0.90			
Gynecologic health	PTSD	4	1.00	−0.47	98	0.63
	Non-PTSD	96	1.25			
Overall health	PTSD	12	8.25	2.25	310	0.03
	Non-PTSD	300	4.71			

TABLE 4 (cont'd)

	Vet group	n	Mean	T	DF	Alpha
Past index						
Respiratory health	PTSD	12	2.67	1.48	359	0.16
	Non-PTSD	349	1.38			
Cardiovascular health	PTSD	12	2.92	4.05	359	0.001
	Non-PTSD	349	1.22			
Gastrointestinal health	PTSD	12	1.92	1.38	359	0.17
	Non-PTSD	349	1.22			
Skin disorders	PTSD	12	0.33	0.64	359	0.52
	Non-PTSD	349	0.23			
Nervous system	PTSD	12	4.67	3.49	359	0.004
	Non-PTSD	349	1.37			
General health	PTSD	12	2.17	3.09	359	0.002
	Non-PTSD	349	0.95			
Gynecologic health	PTSD	7	1.57	1.31	220	0.45
	Non-PTSD	215	0.94			
Overall health	PTSD	12	15.58	4.15	359	0.001
	Non-PTSD	349	6.82			

Measures. All subjects received copies of the VEVAS. For the civilian subjects three additional questions were added. These questions relate to branch of service, level of VA disability compensation, and employment status. All procedures and subscales utilized in this final phase are identical to those used in earlier phases of the project.

Results

PTSD prevalence. Using the established procedure for assessing PTSD, 160 Vietnam veterans (32.1%) reported current symptoms of PTSD. The prevalence of PTSD among the Vietnam-era veterans was found to be 10% ($n = 25$). This Vietnam-era prevalence rate is higher than expected. Several hypotheses can be presented to explain this high rate. As pointed out earlier, the procedure used for assessing PTSD among Vietnam-era veterans is less precise because no information is available to verify exposure to trauma.

It is possible, however, that the Vietnam-era veterans are experiencing symptoms of PTSD related to noncombat instances of trauma since over 62% of these veterans report having received some type of noncombat injury resulting in hospitalization while in the military. Over 11% of these veterans are also classified as more than 50% disabled by the VA. It may also be that the assessment items are picking up on other symptoms of psychological distress that are related to, but not necessarily indicative of, PTSD.

Several researchers (Domash & Sparr, 1982; Walker & Cavenar, 1982) have pointed out the difficulties involved in differentiating between symptoms of PTSD and those of schizophrenia. Perhaps the less precise nature of the assessment procedure used for the Vietnam-era veterans is identifying veterans suffering from other psychological disorders. In any event, the PTSD rate for the Vietnam-era veterans is over four times as great as that found in earlier phases of the project and should be viewed with caution.

The Vietnam veterans were also asked to respond to the PTSD items on the basis of how they felt while in Vietnam. An examination of their responses revealed that 127 veterans (25.5%) experienced symptoms of PTSD while in Vietnam. A further breakdown of the prevalence data revealed that 41 Vietnam veterans (8.2%) experienced acute PTSD, 86 Vietnam veterans (17.2%) suffer from chronic PTSD, and 74 Vietnam veterans (14.8%) are suffering from delayed PTSD. The overall prevalence rate for the Vietnam veterans in the sample is 40.2% (acute + chronic + delayed).

This overall PTSD prevalence rate is much higher than that reported earlier for active-duty Army (12.2%), active-duty Army nurses (10.5%), and U.S. Army Reserve (17.4%) Vietnam veterans. The largest differences among these groups seems to lie in the much greater percentage of civilian Vietnam veterans suffering from chronic and delayed PTSD. Indeed, the civilian veterans are the only group in which the current PTSD rate is greater than the rate during Vietnam service.

Regression analysis. A preliminary regression analysis was conducted to determine whether the effects of any additional, nonhypothesized variables on PTSD symptoms should be examined. These additional variables included the veteran's rank (officer versus enlisted), race, branch of service, and VA disability level. The results indicated that only rank merited addition to the overall analysis.

The results of the overall regression analysis on the variable PTSD ($R = 0.59$) revealed highly significant main effects for combat and first-year social support with these two variables accounting for 17% and 12%, respectively, of the variance explained. No significant main effect was reported for the year the veteran served in Vietnam, but again, the effect was in the hypothesized direction of higher levels of PTSD among those veterans who served in the late part of the war.

The effect of combat on PTSD was in the direction of significantly higher levels of PTSD symptomatology among veterans with higher combat experience scores ($F[1,446] = 57.36$, $p < 0.001$).

Veterans who reported experiencing negative/hostile societal reactions upon return from Vietnam, particularly the first year back, have significantly higher levels of PTSD symptoms than those veterans who reported receiving positive social support upon return from Vietnam ($F[1,446] = 61.55$, $p < 0.001$).

The results of the regression analysis indicated a statistically significant interaction involving rank with first-year social support with the year served in Vietnam. The amount of variance explained by this interaction (less than 1%), however, does not merit further discussion.

Physical health. Results of comparisons between Vietnam and Vietnam-era veterans on each of the six categories of past and current physical health as well as overall health revealed significantly higher scores among Vietnam veterans for each of the health indices except for general health (see Table 5).

A second comparison of health scores was made between those Vietnam veterans identified as having suffered symptoms of PTSD at some

TABLE 5

Health Scores for Civilian Vietnam/Vietnam-Era Veterans

	Vet group	n	Mean	T	DF	Alpha
Current index						
Respiratory health	Vietnam	384	3.97	4.56	556	0.001
	Vietnam-era	174	2.68			
Cardiovascular health	Vietnam	364	3.19	3.62	519	0.001
	Vietnam-era	157	2.37			
Gastrointestinal health	Vietnam	365	3.68	4.03	531	0.001
	Vietnam-era	168	2.65			
Skin disorders	Vietnam	274	1.68	3.70	349	0.001
	Vietnam-era	77	1.26			
Nervous system	Vietnam	371	5.00	3.15	518	0.001
	Vietnam-era	149	3.80			
General health	Vietnam	358	3.12	2.25	534	0.02
	Vietnam-era	178	2.53			
Overall health	Vietnam	465	16.04	5.62	696	0.001
	Vietnam-era	233	10.29			
Past index						
Respiratory health	Vietnam	497	3.80	4.58	744	0.001
	Vietnam-era	249	2.59			
Cardiovascular health	Vietnam	497	2.86	3.98	744	0.001
	Vietnam-era	249	2.07			
Gastrointestinal health	Vietnam	497	3.49	4.07	744	0.001
	Vietnam-era	249	2.54			
Skin disorders	Vietnam	497	1.05	6.95	744	0.001
	Vietnam-era	249	0.51			
Nervous system	Vietnam	497	4.52	5.03	744	0.001
	Vietnam-era	249	2.92			
General health	Vietnam	497	2.93	1.55	744	0.12
	Vietnam-era	249	2.57			
Overall health	Vietnam	497	18.66	5.11	744	0.001

point in time and those Vietnam veterans who have not experienced PTSD. Results of those comparisons revealed significantly higher scores among the PTSD-classified Vietnam veterans than the non-PTSD-classified Vietnam veterans on all past and present health indices without exception (see Table 6).

Pearson Product-Moment correlations were computed between the PTSD symptom scores of the Vietnam veterans and their current health indices scores. Results indicated highly significant positive correlations as hypothesized between PTSD symptoms and respiratory health ($r = 0.34$, $p < 0.001$), cardiovascular health ($r = 0.30$, $p < 0.001$), gastrointestinal health ($r = 0.36$, $p < 0.001$), skin disorders ($r = 0.29$, $p < .0.001$), nervous system problems ($r = 0.48$, $p < 0.001$), general health ($r = 0.41$, $p < 0.001$), and overall health ($r = 0.53$, $p < 0.001$). These results are very similar to those found among the active-duty and Reserve veterans in earlier phases of the study.

Comparisons with active-duty and reserve veterans. The breakdown of the PTSD prevalence rate into acute, chronic, and delayed PTSD revealed no significant differences in the number of cases of acute PTSD among the civilian, active-duty, and Reserve Vietnam veterans. It is only when one examines the chronic and delayed PTSD rates that one finds significantly greater prevalences among the civilian Vietnam veterans (see Table 7). According to the project hypotheses and results of earlier phases of the study concerning the importance of social support validation of Vietnam experiences upon return to the United States, this would indicate that the civilian Vietnam veterans have not received as much positive social support as have the active-duty and Reserve Vietnam veterans. The observation that the prevalence of PTSD during Vietnam duty was also much higher among the civilian veterans indicates that perhaps their combat experiences or Vietnam social support experiences were also different.

In order to determine whether there were indeed differences in combat experience and/or social support experiences that might account for the PTSD prevalence differences, direct comparisons were made between the combat scores and social support scores of the civilian Vietnam veterans and those of the active-duty (nonnurse) and Reserve Vietnam veterans. The results of comparisons between the civilian and active-duty Vietnam veterans revealed that the civilians did indeed report receiving significantly less positive social support upon return from Vietnam ($M = 9.41$) than did the active-duty veterans ($M = 8.32$, $t[734] = -3.68$, $p < 0.001$). The civilian veterans also reported significantly

TABLE 6
Health Scores for Civilian PTSD/Non-PTSD Vietnam Veterans

	Vet group	n	Mean	T	DF	Alpha
Current index						
Respiratory health	PTSD	169	5.28	7.63	382	0.001
	Non-PTSD	215	2.93			
Cardiovascular health	PTSD	160	4.06	6.36	362	0.001
	Non-PTSD	204	2.51			
Gastrointestinal health	PTSD	163	4.52	5.18	363	0.001
	Non-PTSD	202	3.00			
Skin disorders	PTSD	142	1.93	5.16	272	0.001
	Non-PTSD	132	1.40			
Nervous system	PTSD	176	6.63	8.04	369	0.001
	Non-PTSD	195	3.52			
General health	PTSD	161	4.04	5.81	356	0.001
	Non-PTSD	197	2.37			
Overall health	PTSD	182	24.01	11.68	463	0.001
	Non-PTSD	283	10.92			
Past index						
Respiratory health	PTSD	184	5.73	10.33	495	0.001
	Non-PTSD	313	2.67			
Cardiovascular health	PTSD	184	4. 8	9.32	495	0.001
	Non-PTSD	313	2.08			
Gastrointestinal health	PTSD	184	4.96	8.38	495	0.001
	Non-PTSD	313	2.6			
Skin disorders	PTSD	184	.68	10.98	495	0.001
	Non-PTSD	313	0.68			
Nervous system	PTSD	184	7.4	13.75	495	0.001
	Non-PTSD		2.78			
General health	PTSD	184	4.35	8.83	495	0.001
	Non-PTSD	313	2.09			
Overall health	PTSD	184	8.39	13.58	495	0.001

TABLE 7
PTSD Comparisons among Vietnam/Vietnam-Era Veterans

	Active duty	Army nurses	USAR	Civilian
Vietnam veterans				
Vietnam PTSD rate	10.5%	9.1%	12.0%	25.5%
Current PTSD rate	5.1%	3.3%	10.9%	32.1%
Acute PTSD	7.1%	7.2%	6.5%	8.2%
Chronic PTSD	3.4%	1.9%	5.6%	17.2%
Delayed PTSD	1.7%	1.4%	5.4%	14.8%
Overall PTSD rate	12.2%	10.5%	17.4%	40.2%
Vietnam-era veterans				
Current PTSD rate	2.3%	0.8%	1.5%	10.0%

Acute PTSD is diagnosed for veterans who had PTSD during Vietnam but do not currently have symptoms. Chronic PTSD is diagnosed for veterans who had PTSD during Vietnam and still have symptoms today. Delayed PTSD is diagnosed for veterans who did not have PTSD during Vietnam but are bothered by symptoms currently. Overall PTSD rate consists of acute + chronic + delayed PTSD rates.

higher combat experience scores (M = 22.55) than did the active-duty veterans (M = 17.89, $t[734]$ = −4.87, $p < 0.001$).

A comparison of social support experiences while in Vietnam revealed that the civilians reported receiving significantly less positive social support (M = 12.64) during their Vietnam service than the active-duty veterans (M = 13.71, $t[733]$ = 2.76, $p < 0.01$).

Similar results were found when comparing the civilian Vietnam veterans to the Reserve Vietnam veterans. The civilians again reported receiving significantly less positive social support (M = 9.40) upon return from Vietnam than did the Reserve veterans (M = 8.55, $t[1157]$ = −4.09, $p < 0.001$). The civilians also had significantly higher combat experience scores (M = 22.55) than the Reserve veterans (M = 18.32, $t[1156]$ = −6.05, $p < 0.001$). The civilian veterans also reported receiving less positive social support (M = 12.65) while in Vietnam than the Reserve veterans (M = 14.04, $t[1151]$ = 4.74, $p < 0.001$).

DISCUSSION

Generalizability of Findings

The results of this project deal mainly with the impact of a specific stressor (Vietnam combat/war zone experiences) on the development of PTSD. The data lend support to the notion that traumatic stress is not a unitary concept. There appear to be several components to the trauma of combat such as direct participation, perceived danger, and exposure to the violent aftermath of combat. It is likely that other stressors known to produce PTSD are also multifaceted. For example, tornado victims may be traumatized by the sheer destruction produced, or it is possible that they are also affected by the sheer sense of helplessness to prevent such disasters. The data on the importance of social support in exacerbating or mitigating the symptoms of PTSD are certainly generalizable to rape victims. Rape victims are often viewed as having somehow acted to cause their attack and as a result may not receive the support needed to cope with the resulting trauma. In a similar manner, Vietnam veterans are often viewed as having caused their trauma by participating in the war.

The nature of the sampling procedure used in studying active duty and Reserve Vietnam and Vietnam-era veterans makes the results highly representative of veterans still affiliated with the military. Assessing the generalizability of the findings from the civilians sampled to the entire civilian Vietnam veteran population is more problematic. The finding that the civilian veterans in this study spent an average of almost seven years on active duty raises the possibility of response bias. Many of the Vietnam veterans in the civilian sample served more than one tour of duty since draftees served two years and enlistees served up to four years. It may be that veterans who had more of a commitment to the military as evidenced by the greater amount of time spent on active duty were more likely to respond to the questionnaire than were veterans who served only one tour of duty.

While the reported response rate is approximately 50% for the civilian Vietnam veterans, it may be that because they were willing to respond, they are better adjusted than the veterans who did not respond. The prevalence of PTSD among these veterans, then, may represent an underestimate of the prevalence of PTSD among all Vietnam veterans seeking help from the VA for various physical or mental health problems.

On the other hand, the veterans who responded might be those who have the most problems and possibly see some personal or financial gain in responding. In this case, this study would overestimate the prevalence of PTSD. Thus, while the findings may be representative of Vietnam veterans in the VA system, they may not be representative of other Vietnam veterans in the civilian community who have not sought help from the VA. The direction of the bias (if any) cannot be determined.

Physical Health

The results of this project confirm the hypothesized relationship between physical and psychic manifestations of war zone trauma among Vietnam veterans. Those veterans experiencing the greatest amounts of PTSD symptomatology also had the greatest number of physical health problems. These findings were consistent across all groups of veterans studied. While it is possible that veterans with physical ailments simply report more psychological difficulties than do veterans in better health, it is also possible that these physical health problems are the result of the veterans' inability to handle the stress produced by war-related traumatic experiences. Given this stress-illness relationship, it is possible that treatment programs designed to alleviate psychological adjustment problems of Vietnam veterans may also result in improved physical health as well. In light of the stigma that is often associated with seeking help for psychological problems, physicians should be aware that Vietnam veterans who present physical health problems, particularly respiratory, gastrointestinal, and cardiovascular, may have some type of underlying psychological problem related to PTSD.

Social Support

One of the major findings of this project is the importance of social support on PTSD. Lack of positive social support was consistently associated with high levels of PTSD symptoms for all groups of Vietnam veterans. It appears, however, that this lack of support during or after service in Vietnam has had a more pronounced negative impact on the lives of the civilian veterans. This is reflected in their actual social support scores as well as in the much higher reported prevalence of PTSD among the civilians. It is interesting to note that only among the civilian Vietnam veterans in the project is the prevalence of PTSD significantly greater than it was during Vietnam service. This is also reflected in the significantly higher prevalence of chronic and delayed PTSD among the civilian Vietnam veterans. Veterans suffering from PTSD should be encouraged to seek out other Vietnam veterans and form mutual-support groups as well as participate in "rap groups" sponsored by VA facilities as part of their treatment programs.

Nature of Trauma

The results of comparisons of combat experience and social support experiences among the active duty, Reserve, and civilian veterans, when coupled with the results of the regression analyses, lend further support to the notion that PTSD among Vietnam veterans is a reaction to war zone experiences that is either exacerbated or mitigated by social support system validation of their traumatic experiences. Perhaps more important, however, is the finding that one does not have to be a combatant to be traumatized by war. Data from the study of active-duty nurses demonstrate that simply being in a combat zone with its corresponding elements of perceived danger and exposure to the violent aftermath of combat activities can be just as traumatic as direct participation in combat.

The consistently higher PTSD prevalence rates for civilian Vietnam veterans may be a result of differences in exposure to combat trauma as well as social support experiences. The civilian Vietnam veterans reported significantly higher combat scores than all other veterans sampled. It may be that those veterans who remained affiliated with the military either on active duty or in the Reserves were not as highly traumatized by their combat experiences as were the civilians who may have left active duty because of the traumatic nature of their experiences in Vietnam.

Policy Implications

The findings from this project have many implications for both current and future interventions among veterans traumatized by war. As Berman, Price, and Gusman (1982) propose, a debriefing from military experiences is essential even at this late date. In the future it should be military policy to require that all personnel assigned to a combat theater undergo a period of debriefing and decompression to allow them to work through any unresolved war experiences in the presence of fellow veterans before being sent home or returned to a garrison environment.

The military should discontinue the practice observed in Vietnam of sending soldiers home individually on planes to a military separation center where they were outprocessed and discharged within hours. A better approach would be to send soldiers back as members of a unit on transport ships whereby trained mental health professionals could conduct therapeutic debriefings in a continued military environment over a period of weeks before releasing individuals into the civilian community.

The importance of public support for any armed conflicts on the part of U.S. military forces is obvious. Vietnam has demonstrated the negative consequences of confusing the warrior with the war. The public should be made aware that they have the ability to help heal the psychic wounds of veterans through understanding and acceptance of the sacrifices that have been made on their behalf. Perhaps, in the future, psychiatric casualties can indeed be confined to those which occur on the battlefield and not upon return to society.

Conclusions/Future Research

Overall, the results of this study tend to support those of other researchers with respect to the high prevalence of PTSD among civilian veterans (Disabled American Veterans Association, 1980; Harris & associates, 1980) and document the existence of PTSD among Vietnam veterans still affiliated with the military. While the importance of combat experience in the development of PTSD has been demonstrated by previous studies (Center for Policy Research, 1981; Frye & Stockton, 1982), the results of this study shed additional light on the need to look beyond combat as a unitary concept and recognize that combat trauma is multifaceted. The military experiences of nurses, both male and female, as well as other noncombatants can be highly traumatic and should not be ignored or downplayed. More attention should also be paid to the importance of social support experiences in the attenuation of PTSD symptomatology to which Laufer, Yager, Frey-Wouters, and Donnellan (1981) correctly alluded.

Future research is needed to determine why some people develop PTSD and others exposed to the same trauma do not. Perhaps there are individual factors that predispose a person to PTSD. If these factors can be discovered, then perhaps techniques for strengthening coping abilities can be developed. Because exposure to trauma is often unpredictable, most research studies are retrospective in nature and do not have baseline data prior to exposure to trauma. Longitudinal studies should be conducted using people who are at high risk for future exposure to trauma. Soldiers, police officers, firemen, and persons living in areas known to have high risk of natural disasters such as tornadoes or floods should be studied and baseline date gathered before they are exposed to trauma. Only then can critical information on the causes and potential prevention/treatment of PTSD be gathered.

REFERENCES

American Psychiatric Association (1980). *Diagnostic and statistical manual of mental disorders* (3rd ed.). Washington, DC: Author.

Archibald, H. C., Long, D. M., Miller, D., & Tuddenham, R. D. (1962). Gross stress reactions in combat—A 15 year follow-up. *American Journal of Psychiatry, 119*, 317–322.

Berman, S., Price, S., & Gusman, F. (1982). An inpatient program for Vietnam combat veterans in a Veterans Administration hospital. *Hospital and Community Psychiatry, 33*, 919–922.

Brown, G., & Harris, T. (1978). *Social origins of depression: A study of psychiatric disorder in women.* New York: Free Press.

Carlton, T. G. (1980). Early psychiatric intervention following a maritime disaster. *Military Medicine, 145*, 114–116.

Center for Policy Research (1981). *Legacies of Vietnam: Comparative adjustment of veterans and their peers.* New York: Author.

Cornell University Medical College (1974). *Cornell medical index health questionnaire.* New York: Author.

Datel, W. E. (1976). *A summary of source data in military psychiatric epidemiology* (Report No. A 021 265). Alexandria, VA: Defense Documentation Center.

Dean, A., & Lin, N. (1977). The stress buffering role of social support. *Journal of Nervous and Mental Disease, 165*, 403–417.

Disabled American Veterans Association (1980). *Forgotten warriors: America's Vietnam era veterans.* Washington, DC: Author.

Domash, M. D., & Sparr, L. F. (1982). Post-traumatic stress disorder masquerading as paranoid schizophrenia: Case report. *Military Medicine, 147,* 772–774.

Frye, J. S., & Stockton, R. A. (1982). Discriminant analysis of posttraumatic stress disorder among a group of Vietnam veterans. *American Journal of Psychiatry, 139,* 52–56.

Futterman, S., & Pumpian-Mindlin, E. (1951). Traumatic war neuroses five years later. *American Journal of Psychiatry, 108,* 401–408.

Harris, L., & associates. (1980). *Myths and realities: A study of attitudes toward Vietnam Era veterans.* Submitted by the Veterans Administration to the Committee on Veterans Affairs, US Senate, Senate Committee Print No. 29. Washington, DC: US Government Printing Office.

Johnson, J. H., & Sarason, I. G. (1978). Life stress, depression and anxiety: Internal-external control as a moderator variable. *Journal of Psychosomatic Research, 22,* 205–208.

Kenton, C. (1984). *Posttraumatic stress disorder.* Bethesda, MD: National Library of Medicine.

Laufer, R. S., Yager, T., Frey-Wouters, E., & Donnellan, J. (1981). Post-war trauma: Social and psychological problems of Vietnam veterans in the aftermath of the Vietnam war. In Center for Policy Research (Ed.), *Legacies of Vietnam: Comparative adjustment of veterans and their peers.* New York: Center for Policy Research.

Mantell, D. M., & Pilisuk, M. (1975). Soldiers in and after Vietnam. *Journal of Social Issues, 31,* 4.

Mitchell, R. E., Billings, A. G., & Moos, R. H. (1982). Social support and wellbeing: Implications for prevention programs. *Journal of Primary Prevention, 3,* 77–98.

Newman, C. J. (1976). Children of disaster: Clinical observations at Buffalo Creek. *American Journal of Psychiatry, 133,* 306–312.

Pearlin, L. I., Lieberman, M. A., Menaghan, E. G., & Mullan, J. T. (1981). The stress process. *Journal of Health and Social Behavior, 19,* 2–21.

Penk, W. E., Rabinowitz, R., Roberts, W. R., Patterson, E. T., Dolan, M. P., & Athers, H. G. (1981). Adjustment differences among male substance abusers varying in degree of combat experiences in Vietnam. *Journal of Consulting and Clinical Psychology, 49,* 426–437.

Ploeger, A. (1977). A 10-year follow up of miners trapped for 2 weeks under threatening circumstances. In C. D. Spielberger and I. G. Sarason (Eds.), *Stress and anxiety: IV* (pp. 23–28). Washington, DC: Hemisphere.

Rangell, L. (1976). Discussion of the Buffalo Creek disaster: The course of psychic trauma. *American Journal of Psychiatry, 133,* 313–316.

Renner, J. A. (1973). The changing patterns of problems in Vietnam. *Comprehensive Psychiatry, 14,* 169–181.

Schindler, F. E. (1980). Treatment by systematic desensitization of a recurring nightmare of a real life trauma. *Journal of Behavioral Therapy and Experimental Psychiatry, 2,* 53–54.

Stretch, R. (1984a). *Assessment of psychosocial and physical health among Army Reserve veterans.* Unpublished manuscript.

Stretch, R. (1984b). *Post-traumatic stress disorder among civilian Vietnam and Vietnam-era veterans.* Unpublished manuscript.

Stretch, R. (1984c). *PTSD among Army nurses: Assessment of sex differences.* Unpublished manuscript.

Stretch, R. (1985). Post-traumatic stress disorder among US Army Reserve Vietnam and Vietnam-era veterans. *Journal of Consulting and Clinical Psychology, 53,* 935–936.

Stretch, R. (In press). Incidence and etiology of post-traumatic stress disorder among active duty Army personnel. *Journal of Applied Social Psychology.*

Stretch, R., & Figley, C. R. (1984). Combat and the Vietnam veteran: Assessment of psychosocial adjustment. *Armed Forces and Society, 10,* 311–319.

Stretch, R., Vail, J., & Maloney, J. (1985). Post-traumatic stress disorder among Army Nurse Corps Vietnam veterans. *Journal of Consulting and Clinical Psychology, 53,* 704–708.

Titchener, M. D., & Kapp, F. T. (1976). Family and character change at Buffalo Creek. *American Journal of Psychiatry, 133,* 295–299.

Tuxon, P. (1983). Vietnam veteran nurses speak out on war. Helicopters, heat and holding the hand of the dying. *California Nurse, 79,* 6–8.

Walker, J. I., & Cavenar, J. O. (1982). Vietnam veterans. Their problems continue. *Journal of Nervous and Mental Disease, 170,* 174–180.

SECTION III

Intervention

9

An Outline for the Psychoanalytic Psychotherapy of Post-Traumatic Stress Disorder

JACOB D. LINDY

INTRODUCTION

Historically, psychoanalytic contributions to the treatment of the traumatic neuroses have come from two sources: applications of theory and new clinical generalizations. Concerted attention to the disorder (currently termed post-traumatic stress disorder [PTSD]) tends to be episodic depending on the intermittent nature of catastrophe itself. Thus, one source of psychoanalytic contribution is an updating with regard to more recent theoretical developments in the field. Thus, for example, Abraham (1919) discusses early infantile states and their relationship to the traumatic disorder; Kardiner (1947) observes and applies an adaptive point of view suggested by the ego psychologists; Fox (1974) and Parson (1984) apply some concepts in self-psychology; and Brende (1982) and DeFazio (1984) find useful application of object relations theory.

A report of work carried out through the University of Cincinnati Traumatic Stress Study Center in conjunction with Bonnie Green, Ph.D., Co-director, Mary Grace, M.S., M.Ed., Associate Director, and James Titchener, M.D., Senior Consultant, and the Cincinnati Psychoanalytic Institute.

195

A second source for psychoanalytic contributions to the theory and technique of the treatment of PTSD is, in my view, more experience-near, less theory-bound, and tends to confine itself to observed clinical phenomena. Thus, psychoanalytic observers have offered a series of useful organizing clinical concepts: psychic trauma, the stimulus barrier, and the repetition compulsion (Freud, 1920); the death imprint and survivor guilt (Lifton, 1967); anniversary reactions (Hilgard & Newman, 1959); the intrusion-denial cycle and frozen overcontrol (Horowitz, 1976); and secondary character change (Titchener & Kapp, 1978). In this chapter, we suggest that the "trauma membrane" and the "specific configuration of the traumatic event" be included as clinical organizing concepts with specific application to the conduct of psychotherapy with patients with PTSD.

This chapter outlines some working assumptions of psychoanalytic psychotherapy as they relate to the treatment of PTSD. It describes and discusses an illustrative treatment based on those assumptions and it outlines some methods of such treatment. Ten clinical working assumptions are identified.

While most of the working assumptions are grounded on preexisting psychoanalytic literature, their integration into a stepwise outline for the conduct of focal psychotherapy for survivors, we believe, is new. This outline for psychotherapy is based also on observations on the process of actual therapist-patient interactions during the course of two formal research projects with patients with PTSD: the first deals with survivors of a supper club fire (1978–1979) and the second is a study of combat veterans with PTSD (1982–present).

While the therapeutic process in the case selected in this chapter is that of a Vietnam veteran with PTSD, the specific therapeutic process described is more generic; it is similar to that which we have observed in the successful treatments of survivors of civilian catastrophe as well (Lindy, Green, Grace & Titchener, 1983).

Observations in this chapter are made against a backdrop of ongoing programmatic research regarding clinical and theoretical issues in PTSD being carried out through the University of Cincinnati Traumatic Stress Study Center and in connection with the Cincinnati Psychoanalytic Institute.

This work attends at the intrapsychic level to the individual processing of trauma and loss as this emerges in the clinical dyad. In conjunction with the clinical work, there is group-level programmatic research in disaster. The latter attempts to discriminate, within a given large-scale catastrophe, which elements in the trauma are most likely to lead to psychopathology and which characteristics of the individual and his environment are most likely to mediate recovery (Gleser, Green & Winget, 1981; Green, Grace, & Glesser, in press).

Attending to the intrapsychic and the psychosocial dimensions has led the University of Cincinnati Traumatic Stress Study Center to evolve two interrelated models connecting the nature of the experience of trauma and the development of later pathology (particularly PTSD). Scheme 1 (Green, Wilson, & Lindy, 1985) emphasize how characteristics of the traumatic stressor, characteristics of the individual, and characteristics of the recovery environment are likely to influence the degree and type of prolonged psychiatric impairment following disaster. Scheme 2 (Lindy, Grace, & Green, 1984) includes the same variables but emphasizes a natural history of PTSD including both primary and secondary changes in symptoms, character, and capacities for adaptation and conflict resolution.

The core of either model is termed intrapsychic or "cognitive" processing (Horowitz, 1976). This may lead, on the one hand, to gradual assimilation and growth or, on the other hand, to psychic overload and prolonged psychopathology.

Intrapsychic processing of trauma is the core of the treatment process as well as the model. The therapist strives to occupy a place during the course of therapy poised intrapsychically between the reminder of trauma and the potential for psychic overload. The therapist-patient dyad will hopefully form a unit capable of tolerating and digesting more affect-laden memory than the survivor alone can tolerate. But already we are getting ahead in our story. We must first take a few steps back from our models and review some psychoanalytic working assumptions regarding the natural working through of trauma and loss and some common obstacles in that process before we can appreciate how treatment works.

WORKING ASSUMPTIONS REGARDING TRAUMA AND LOSS

The psychological recovery from the impact of catastrophic events almost always entails, for the survivor, the working through of both "trauma" and "loss." Here, even before we embark on a discussion of these central issues, some definitions are necessary.

"Trauma" is used by some to characterize an external event. We shall try to use the term *traumatic stressor*(s). At times, "trauma" conveys a subjective affect state; we shall use the term *psychic traumatization*. Finally, we have no specific word denoting the process of recovery from the impact of traumatic stressors and must settle for the complex term *working through of trauma*.

In the case of loss and bereavement, our language is more precise. *Loss* is an external event; *grief* is the dominant affect state associated with bereavement; and *mourning* is the intrapsychic process of working through of loss.

With these preliminary remarks, we may then go on to outline some clinical working assumptions regarding intrapsychic recovery from "trauma" and "loss."

a. Affect states associated with the impact of traumatic stressors are naturally occurring phenomena. Within limits, we assume that the psychic organism is capable in its own time of breaking down the impact of traumatic stressors and their associated affect states into manageable amounts that permit gradual intrapsychic processing. We identify this process as the working through of trauma. This task requires (1) the recovery of affect-laden memory traces; (2) the attribution of meaning to these memory traces; and (3) the reestablishment of psychic continuity with the past.

Similarly grief (following loss) is a naturally occurring state. The psychic organism in its own time breaks down the totality of grief into manageable doses of affect-connected memory traces of the lost object. In the case of grief, we are accustomed to terming this process of working through as mourning (Freud, 1917).

b. With trauma, as with grief, the initial metabolizing process is often incomplete. Both anniversary phenomena and other reminders serve the purpose of stimulating the organism to process yet further connections between events and affects (Hilgard & Newman, 1959).

c. The working through of trauma (like the working through involved in mourning) is an exacting task, requiring an intact working ego with sufficient energy available to master the task. In self-psychological terms, there must be a cohesive self before the organism can successfully take on the task (Lindy, 1981).

d. At the time, exposure to traumatic stressors is often occasioned by the internal state of psychic traumatization. This is particularly the case when the duration of the stressor(s) is extended, the intensity is severe and repeated, the capacity to predict is random, and the vulnerability of the individual is high. When psychic traumatization has occurred, there is an overwhelming of the stimulus barrier (Freud, 1920) and the psychic apparatus or, in self-psychological terms, the loss of a cohesive self and traumatic overstimulation (Kohut, 1971).

e. Reminders, then, of traumatic experience may, rather than trigger a metabolizing process, threaten to reinstitute the state of psychic traumatization described above (Horowitz, 1976).

f. In these cases, defenses such as splitting and disavowal are erected to prevent the feared reinstitution of the state of psychic traumatization.

g. Split-off traumatic memories function as hyperactive memory stores (Horowitz, 1976). They press for expression in either motor or cognitive form and set off an intrusion-denial cycle in which the organism expends considerable energy to seek equilibrium.

h. The primary pathological expression of PTSD at a given time is a function of where the pendulum in the intrusion-denial cycle is poised. (1) Intrusive phase: here breakthrough of intrusions in either motor or cognitive form dominates. During the sleep state, breakthroughs occur as night terrors (motor form) or as nightmares (cognitive form), and in the wakeful state, intrusions take the form of reenactments (motor form) or intrusive images (cognitive form). (2) Denial phase: here denial (or, more precisely, disavowal) has taken the upper hand; a state of overcontrol is in existence characterized by psychic numbing, alienation, and estrangement. (3) Hypervigilant phase: here there is an oscillation between intrusion and denial with efforts to ward off intrusive breakthrough dominating the clinical picture. These include hyperarousal, startle reactions, cognitive dysfunction, and irritability. Secondary pathology evolves in chronic PTSD as a result of the consequences of ongoing psychic strain to the organism (from the processes described above). This has been described as overcontrol (Horowitz, 1976) and psychic conservatism (Titchener & Kapp, 1978). Secondary pathology also involves character change where particular efforts to ward off intrusions become structuralized such as the "action junkie" syndrome (Wilson, 1983), the "perimeter" syndrome (Lindy & Titchener, 1983), somatization syndromes (Krystal, 1984), etc. Secondary pathology also includes the ongoing dominance of inappropriate trauma-related affect such as survivor guilt (sometimes with profound suicidal ideation) (Lifton, 1973).

At yet a third level, the long-term pathology from delayed stress may include a developmental arrest taking its origin at the point in time of the psychic trauma and deriving as a result of unavailable energies to invest in phase-appropriate continuing psychological development (epigenesis) (Erikson, 1950; Wilson, 1983; van der Kolk, 1983).

i. As time passes, reminders of the traumatic experience (sensory or special-affect configuration) may take increasingly derivative or more disguised form. Over the years, the patient loses conscious connection between the stimulus and the memory of the trauma itself. Rather, outbursts of symptomatic behavior are characteristically attributed to other causes. In the patient there is a growing sense that something is deeply wrong, which defies comprehension.

j. Finally, the patient has become particularly sensitive to people and relationships unfamiliar with the particular absurd meaning of the trauma and who might serve to stimulate unwanted traumatic memories without a constructive context for healing. He has developed many ways to keep such people outside his "trauma membrane."* Conversely, fellow survivors who truly know the absurd reality of what happened always have a special place of potential closeness within that "membrane" (Lindy, 1981, 1985).

From the patient's point of view, one may conceptualize therapy as a transition from psychiatric casualty to survivor (one who has endured catastrophe and who "lives on" beyond catastrophic events).

From the therapist's point of view, therapy is an effort to remove the blocks to an essentially spontaneous healing process. In order to do this, he must be invited to the boundary of the trauma membrane, be per-

---

*To capture the properties of the survivor's barrier I have introduced the term "trauma membrane" and intend this as the central idea in (j). The properties of this trauma membrane, its relationship at a psychosocial level to Freud's intrapsychic stimulus barrier, its permeability in the therapeutic setting, and relevance for clinical outreach and "survivor networks" are described more fully elsewhere.

mitted entry, and maintain that as healing space, dosing or titrating traumatic memory and its processing.

AN OUTLINE FOR PSYCHOTHERAPY

Treatment reverses the order of the preceding outline.

Opening Phase

The survivor risks allowing the therapist to enter beneath his trauma membrane. (J).* This is an extremely tentative and gradual process, but once complete, it is remarkably enduring.

The therapist, through interpretation, reestablishes the link (I) between derivative reminders, which are currently serving as precipitants of symptoms (H) and the traumatic memories themselves (G), including specific associated affect states (I_2). One such linking interpretation marks the consolidation of the working alliance and the beginning of the working-through phase: this is the identification of a highly salient configuration involving affects and object relations both in the present and within the trauma. We term this a special configuration of the traumatic event.

Working Through Phase

(E, D) The therapist assists the patient in organizing into manageable doses currently experienced pathological reflections of segments of specific traumatic experiences. Toward this end, he utilizes interpretation, reconstruction, transference, signal anxiety, and, in particular, the special configuration of the traumatic event.

(F) The therapist clarifies defenses and underlying affect states such as helplessness, rage, guilt, and shame in the context of the absurd.

(D, C) The therapist-patient unit comes to serve as a temporary cohesive self capable of managing doses of trauma greater than that which the patient himself can tolerate. In this context, the rapid management and interpretation of floating negative transferences are imperative (within the field of trauma) in that uninterpreted, negative transference threatens to disrupt this indispensable therapist-patient bond.

---

*Clinical concepts, as they emerge in process, are designated by capital letters. Each of these clinical concepts is rooted, in turn, in a specific working assumption noted with lower-case letters in the preceding session.

Termination Phase

(B, A) The patient himself begins to experience mastery as he works with new reminders of his trauma. He gains confidence in his capacity to maintain ongoing cohesion in the presence of such threats. Grief now spontaneously surfaces, and the opportunity to work through delayed bereavement connected with the catastrophe becomes central. Mourning is now ready to occur.

As a result of the working through of trauma and the activation of mourning, the patient has reclaimed his disavowed affect, given meaning to the absurd catastrophe, and regained psychic continuity between past, present, and future. He has restored energy for continuing investment in work and in love relationships and is able to resume a posture of continuing developmental growth. He continues to remember, to feel pain, even to value his survivor experience; i.e., there may well still be symptom expression. As trauma and grief are reclaimed by the psychic organism as a whole, the specific meaning of the catastrophe becomes clear as it relates both to the earlier psychogenetic conflicts of the individual and to the capacity to invest the future with energy and ambition.

MEASURING CHANGE IN THE PSYCHOTHERAPY OF POST-TRAUMATIC STRESS DISORDER

The primary pathology of PTSD, as outlined, is a function of the intensity and phase of the intrusion-denial cycle. A measure that quantifies the intensity and phase of that cycle, such as the Impact of Events Scale (Horowitz, Wilner, & Alvarez, 1979), is useful here. Scores here give both an intensity figure and a ratio between the opposing forces of intrusiveness and psychic numbing. Other symptoms included in DSM-III for PTSD are important to include. We are developing a 40-item Cincinnati Traumatic Stress Index, which quantifies intensity of symptoms in the areas of hyperarousal, cognitive dysfunction, hostility, sleep disturbance, suicidal ideation, somatization, and survivor guilt. Since secondary pathology may well include character impairment, we recommend a measure of character pathology such as the Hyler and Rieder Personality Disorder Questionnaire (1980).

The overall level of psychiatric impairment should be observed as an indicator of the degree to which the whole organism is made dysfunctional by the disorder and its many ramifications. Here we have selected a patient-based instrument, the SCL-90 (Derogatis, 1977), and an interviewer-based instrument, the Psychiatric Evaluation Form (Spitzer, Endicott, Mesnikoff, & Cohen, 1968). These instruments are of special value because some previous work with post-disaster populations has utilized them and because they are well standardized. Attention to multiple and differential diagnostic problems on both Axis I and Axis II is important to note in describing a treatment sample at large. In this regard, we prefer to use the SADS-L.

Having noted the above, certain changes hoped for in treatment may occur even while certain symptoms of PTSD persist. As the patient, through psychotherapy, gains a larger repertoire of coping behaviors, there may be an expected shift in the perceived value of new coping strategies and, hence, a measure of coping strategies is recommended (Horowitz, 1980). Furthermore, as the symptoms of PTSD become less consuming and less the entire focus of the organism, there is more energy available for other activities. There is an increased sense of continuity with the past, the reexperiencing of joy, and the integration of meaning of the experience into the subject's world view. The specific vocabulary of the patient as conveyed in metaphor and subjective inference is relevant here. Efforts to observe and measure these are part of the task of an independent interviewer who sees the patient prior to and following psychotherapy. Systematic investigation of these latter constructs should be pursued.

CASE ILLUSTRATION

Tom S., a 35-year-old married machinist, is the father of three children. Tom was a paratrooper in Vietnam.

History of the Present Illness

Tom had been experiencing irritability with outbursts of rage particularly while under the influence of alcohol, affective withdrawal from his wife and children, impaired concentration, and disturbed sleep and nightmares. Outbursts were frequently precipitated by derogatory comments with regard to Vietnam. They seem to have grown worse since he was laid off temporarily from his job.

Precipitating Event

After a bout of drinking, Tom went to the cellar of his house. He began smashing his fists against the basement wall, shouting obscenities. Mrs. S. became frightened and called a neighbor-friend who had, in the past, been able to settle Tom down under these circumstances. Tom could not be restrained by his friend. Continuing to be frightened by the obscenities and the viciousness of his rage, Mrs. S. and the friend called the Vet Center for help. Twenty minutes later, a counselor from the Vet Center, dressed in army fatigues, arrived at the S. house. Tom was behind a desk and had a gun in his hand, which he pointed at the counselor. Tom instructed the counselor not to move. The two remained riveted in that position for one hour. It was with this background, then, that Tom S. was referred for psychotherapy.

Session 1

Mr. S. entered Dr. B.'s office cautiously. He assessed his free access to the door and to the window and then spent much of the remaining time sizing up Dr. B. as to his potential trustworthiness. Dr. B. intuitively sensed Tom's need and confirmed the importance of Tom's testing the environment to see that it was secure and the importance of his testing his possible therapist to see if he were potentially trustworthy. Dr. B. explained to Tom what Dr. B. had been told about the incident that led to the referral. Tom gave a thoughtful, although incomplete, account of the night's events. He had regained only part of his orientation by the time the Vet Center counselor arrived at his home. He was distrustful of who this paramilitary intruder might be and therefore kept him at gunpoint to establish his friendly identity. Often he said his outbursts occurred in rooms like cellars where he felt trapped. He suspected all this had to do with his experience in Vietnam but was not certain how. He was frightened by his behavior, felt it was quite inconsistent with the kind of person he otherwise was, and very much wanted help.

Discussion—Session 1

During the first session, the therapist is interested in assessing diagnostically the presenting picture including the meaning of the patient's violent behavior during the precipitating event (in terms of character, ego function, etc.). Simultaneously, the therapist is assessing whether or not he and the patient will be able to work together. In this regard, he monitors his own fear of violence from the patient as well as the patient's fear of therapeutic engagement. After exploring the events surrounding Tom's holding the counselor at gunpoint and hearing the thoughtful, motivated response, the therapist is more optimistic about a working alliance and arrives at a tentative formulation: that Tom's being laid off from work stirred old feelings of being trapped; these, in turn, in the presence of alcohol led to reenactment of a specific trauma in which the patient was "trapped" and banging against the cellar wall. The doctor is silent at this point about his formulation, but the patient himself is interested in exploring this line of thinking connecting the cellar with Vietnam and seems to convey a beginning rapport with the therapist.

Central to the hour is whether or not the patient is going to allow his doctor within the "trauma membrane" (J). The doctor has been recommended by a combat vet, but the true test of credentials will be how the doctor responds to the affect of the patient's particular war experience.

Finally, it is important to note how readily the patient misreads the intentions of those who are trying to help. For example, the Vet Center counselor's outfit was misperceived and he was seen as the enemy. The possibility of a floating, intense, negative transference, which would negate the potential healing force of the therapist-patient unit, is never far from the work (D,C).

Session 2

In the second session, Tom relayed a dream. He is chained to a floor and can't get loose. There are blank faces who are kicking him in the ribs. Dr. B. said both last week's lashing out in the basement and the dream this week of being kicked while chained are part of memories from Vietnam. Tom agreed; indeed he had been chained to the floor as one of 22 American soldiers when he was held prisoner of war for 17 days in a Vietcong village. The capture lasted 17 days. He knew this for certain because each day one of the prisoners was killed and five were alive when the group was rescued. Tom explained that he had been an airborne paratrooper in Vietnam. On this mission, a wind carried him into a Vietcong area and he was captured. Each day the captors selected one American to be hung on the flag pole in the central square of the village. All prisoners watched this hanging until the prisoner was dead. Selection seemed to be random. The nightmare was a traumatic reliving of the experience of being chained to concrete blocks awaiting probable death. Mr. S. further recounted that this story had remained untold for 13 years. Dr. B. added that Tom had endured an extraordinary experience and it was not surprising that there were consequences 13 years later.

Discussion—Session 2

Tom relates a nightmare of POW captivity. This provides the therapist with the missing link in his formulation toward the end of the second session, connecting the reenactment in the cellar with captivity in Vietnam. The therapist now asserts that there are specific traumatic memories from the past that make comprehensible these intrusive experiences in the present (I) (the reenactment and the nightmare). Given this structure, Tom fills in the outline of his POW experience. This confirms the doctor's silent formulation at the end of the first session and strengthens the tie between patient and doctor. By sharing events that have been hidden for 13 years, the patient is supporting the doctor's entry beneath the trauma membrane (J). But affect is still separated from the narration, and dosage of this affect now becomes a central issue in the subsequent session (H).

Session 3

During the third session, Tom discussed a current incident in which he felt he had behaved irritably and shamefully. It was something about a kitchen table, but it didn't seem particularly important. Dr. B. pursued this incident despite Tom's protest that it was insignificant. Tom's children had a friend over to the house. When they came into the kitchen for a snack, there was one less chair than there were kids. A hassle among the children followed to see who would get chairs and who would be left out. The patient then suddenly felt as if he had totally lost it, screamed at the kids, slammed the door, and returned to his room feeling ashamed of his behavior. In the session, there was a long pause. Dr. B. pointed out the similarity between what Tom described and the childhood game of musical chairs. Tom nodded in agreement. Dr. B. then commented that last week Tom had told him about a very grotesque way in which that game had been played during his prisoner experience. Tom began to cry quietly. Tom was beginning to feel empathy for his own experience and genuine surprise that his attacks of anxiety and rage had a comprehensible cause.

Discussion—Session 3

The patient believes that he is somehow off the topic as he speaks of the mundane events of current life. The therapist views this differently. The therapist is drawn to the incident around the kitchen table because the affect release was qualitatively similar to other outbursts yet of manageable intensity, nearly in the range of signal anxiety. Because it is manageable and current, the doctor, unlike his more contextual frame-of-reference interpretations regarding the reenactment (Session 1) and the nightmare (Session 2), is now active in pursuing more precisely the affective trigger for this event. In this process, the doctor becomes acutely aware of his own associations to the bustle around the kitchen chairs: the picture being described is like the childhood game of musical chairs. The doctor then allows himself to feel (silently, of course) his own unpleasant memories of that game as a child: if you win, you force another out; if you lose, you yourself are out; in Vietnam, the stakes were death. The link to the musical-chair killings in captivity was obvious; furthermore, there was now some empathy in the doctor's voice as he made that link manifest. Following this intervention, Tom's quiet crying is striking; it is the first evidence of beginning "self-empathy" or working through his traumas and the consolidation of the working alliance. Together patient and doctor had discovered the "musical chairs" as condensing a special configuration of Tom's traumatic prisoner-of-war experience (I_2).

Middle Phase—Sessions 4, 5, 6, 7

In the following sessions, Tom recalled in detail each of the incidents that occurred during his 17 days of imprisonment. He remembered the panic of not knowing whether he would be chosen to die, and later, in order to get things over with, his wishes to be chosen to die. He poignantly recalled how each of his fellow prisoners met their death and, in particular, both his disgust at those who degraded themselves by groveling helplessly and the power of seductive impulses to grovel that way himself. He described his phobia of places with limited access and how this symptom was hampering his active functioning at work and at home. For example, he was unable to go to a local steakhouse with his children. In this connection, he drew out the floor plan of his place of imprisonment and the floor plan of the restaurant, pointing out the many disturbing similarities.

Mr. S. reported the beginning of symptomatic improvement. He was now talking more with his wife and children and had more energy for his activities around the house and other projects. He had seen a telephone book and noticed how yellow pages were sandwiched between the white pages. He thought that this was like the period of imprisonment during the Vietnam experience and that he had been turning these yellow pages—each of the 17 of them—over one at a time getting to know them, whereas in the past, he had seen them as something shameful, forbidding, and dangerous. He reported a dream in which he had taken a trip to the city, and while feeling initially lost, he saw a mural on a wall and decided that he had found his way. On awakening, he was able to identify the mural on a building that marked his path from the expressway to the doctor's office. He pointed out that he was now writing down dreams and working on instances in which he found himself particularly irritable and through that method, on his own, recovering forgotten memories in his Vietnam experience.

Tom S. began the seventh session asking Dr. B. what part of the country he came from. Tom suspected that Dr. B. was from the East Coast, perhaps from the New York area, because he had an accent that was not midwestern. There was further discussion in this session about Tom's emotional experience during the moments in which his fellow prisoners were chosen to die. He spoke with pride of his own defiant posture. Prisoners were not allowed to talk during the long hours of being shackled, but he was able to work out a system to communicate with the prisoner next to him, who was from Brooklyn. This particular fellow prisoner shared his value system, and they found a way of communicating with each other even under these terrible circumstances. Both he and his friend had survived.

Discussion of Sessions 4, 5, 6, 7

Here the dosed working through (E, D) of the traumatic experience continues to proceed. The patient's perception that he is on the right track is confirmed in the wall mural dream. The defense of isolation and disavowal (F) are contained in the image of the yellow-page section of the phone book, while the change in this defensive picture is conveyed by the image of opening the book to each of those 17 yellow pages; the meaning of "yellow" would become clear only later in the treatment. That dosage is optimal is further conveyed in the legible print on each of those pages.

The seventh session provides a direct transference reference, which offers a more detailed understanding of the healing or recovery process.

In the treatment an invincible unit has been revived, the bond with the fellow prisoner from Brooklyn. The reactivation of that bond provided a temporary cohesive unit now capable of addressing what otherwise was fearful traumatization (D, C). Here each memory trace may be dissected and processed; each fear can be identified and felt. Finally, 15 years later, the work begun at the time of capture can be completed. The therapist does not interpret this "positive transference" in that the transference is promoting and not impeding the work.

Termination

Mr. S. reported a dream in which a bus exploded. He recounted his association, which related to an experience in the final week before he was sent home from Vietnam. By chance, he was occupied with another task and did not join some of his companions who were also processing out, but the two and a half ton truck that carried them was hit by incoming rocket fire and destroyed. Three of his buddies were killed two days before they were to leave for home. Coincident with his working on these losses, his father-in-law had died. He was surprised by his crying openly at the funeral. During the next session, he spoke of all of the funerals that never took place in Vietnam and that he could not afford affectively to experience the memory of the losses. Tom reported that he was back to his normal functioning, that he had not felt like this for 15 years. He had taken apart a rubic cube, diagrammed its inner workings, and established a method for solving the problem of the rubic cube four or five different ways. He drew these out in diagram form to help Dr. B. in case the doctor wanted to take on the challenge of the rubic cube. Tom was now visiting the Vet Center and attending meetings regularly as well as beginning to become active in other veterans' organizations for the first time. In that context, he was able to put into place the generalizable horror stain (yellow pages) or stigma other soldiers felt with regard to the reminder that any of them could have become prisoner at the hands of the Vietcong. He felt this assisted in providing a dimension for understanding why he had kept the entire experience so secret so long. He also suggested in that session that he and the doctor set a termination date, which they did.

Discussion—Sessions 10–12

The termination phase provided opportunity for mourning (B, A). An intact working ego, which had metabolized so much trauma, could now address the affect and meaning of so many losses of close buddies there.

The mourning phase of treatment began spontaneously, calling only for attentiveness and sensitivity on the part of the therapist.

The patient introduces the rubic cube and his diagrammed solution to the puzzle as confirmation that he has now internalized a method of discovering for himself links between "surface irregularities" or symptoms and further memories related to the trauma. There is an understandable method of proceeding, even though it may at first appear complex and contrary. He suggests that things may yet be difficult as unexpected reminders trigger unexpected reactions, but he is confident that he will be able to sort these out into a comprehensible whole.

Mention of further trauma—and the dream of the bus explosion —surprises the therapist so late in the treatment. This becomes understandable in light of the timing of this trauma just before "termination" from Vietnam.

Follow-up

Six months after termination, the patient's wife, who had known him since childhood, wrote a note confirming the resumption of psychic continuity: "Thanks for giving us back our old Tom, as well as some sense of increased energy. . . . He's alive again."

Let us review. In terms of our psychosocial model Tom was a 19-year-old midwestern American with good premorbid adjustment and solid patriotic ideals who volunteered for service in late adolescence. He was exposed to a prisoner-of-war experience with high degrees of bereavement, life threat, and exposure to the grotesque. During the traumatic events, he was primarily in the role of victim. Social supports in the field were mixed: i.e., he was captured but also rescued. Upon return to his home unit, his experience was disavowed, as it was again when he returned home to the United States. The societal attitudes toward the war were negative, and he anticipated they would be specifically negative toward a prisoner-of-war experience.

For 15 years, the post-traumatic cognitive processing of these traumas had been blocked. The interaction between intrusion and avoidance was on the side of continuing psychopathology. There was both the threat of psychic overload and the fear that no one would understand what he had gone through. In addition, there had long since ceased to be a conscious connection between reminders that were currently causing symptoms and the nature of the original trauma. These were reenactments and intrusions that became life-threatening and prompted referral for treatment.

In terms of the process of psychotherapy, four technical points seemed especially useful in mobilizing successful working through: (1) The therapist, by virtue of his previous contacts with combat veterans, was presented to the patient as someone who could operate within the survivor "trauma membrane." He could be trusted as understanding of the nature of the uniqueness and absurdity of that experience. (2) A strong working alliance was forged, the central purpose of which was to enable dosed amounts of trauma to emerge through the derivatives that were expressing themselves in discomfort in everyday life. (3) The special configuration of the traumatic event, in this case "musical chairs," was clearly identified and became the keystone to the development of that alliance. (4) The specific transference, namely, to his fellow prisoner from Brooklyn, who was chained with him and who also survived, provided a positive transference reference from the field of combat, forging within the treatment a sufficiently strong and cohesive sense of self to withstand traumatic overload and to continue the working-through process that had already begun on the scene as the patient and his friend initially processed their horrendous experience.

REFERENCES

Abraham, K. (1919). *Psychoanalysis of war neuroses*. Leipzig and Vienna: Internationaler Psychoanalytischer Verlag.

Brende, J. O. (1982). Personal communication.

DeFazio, V. J. (1984). Psychoanalytic psychotherapy and the Vietnam veteran. In H. J. Schwartz (Ed.), *Psychotherapy of the combat veteran*. Philadelphia: Spectrum Publications.

Derogatis, L. (1977). *LR SCL-90R Version Manual-I*. Baltimore: Johns Hopkins University.

Erikson, E. (1950). *Childhood and society*. New York: Norton.

Fox, R. (1974). Narcissistic rage and the problem of combat aggression. *Archives of General Psychiatry, 31*, 807–811.

Freud, S. (1917). *Beyond the pleasure principle*, standard ed., Freud's Completed Works, Vol. 19, Mourning and melancholia, J. Strachey, Ed. London: Hogarth Press.

Freud, S. (1920). *Beyond the pleasure principle*, standard ed., Freud's Completed Works, Vol. 18, J. Strachey, Ed. London: Hogarth Press.

Gleser, G. C., Green, B. L., & Winget, C. N. (1981). *Prolonged psychological effects of disaster: A study of Buffalo Creek*. New York: Academic Press.

Green, B. L., Grace, M. C., & Gleser, G. C. (in press). Identifying survivors at risk: Long-term impairment following the Beverly Hills supper club fire. *Journal of Health and Social Behavior*.

Green, B. L., Wilson, J. P., & Lindy, J. D. (1985). Conceptualizing post traumatic stress disorder: A psychosocial framework. In C. Figley (Ed.), *Trauma and its wake* (Vol. 1). New York: Brunner/Mazel.

Hilgard, J. R., & Newman, M. (1959). Anniversaries in mental illness. *Psychiatry, 22*, 113–121.

Horowitz, M. J. (1976). *Stress response syndromes*. New York: Jason Aronson.

Horowitz, M. J. (1980). Life events, stress, and coping. In L. Poon (Ed.), *Aging in the 80's*. Washington, DC: American Psychiatric Association.

Horowitz, M., Wilner, N., & Alvarez, W. (1979). Impact of Events Scale: A measure of subjective stress. *Psychosomatic Medicine, 41*(3), 209–218.

Hyler, S., & Rieder, R. (1980). *Personality Disorder Questionnaire—Biometrics Research Laboratory*. New York: New York State Psychiatric Institute.

Kardiner, A. (1947). *War stress and neurotic Illness*. New York: Paul B. Hoebner.

Kohut, H. (1971). *Analysis of the self* (pp. 235–237). New York: International Universities Press.

Krystal, H. (1984). *Psychoanalytic views on human emotional damages*. In B. A. van der Kolk (Ed.), *Post traumatic stress disorder: Psychological and biological sequelae*. Washington, DC: American Psychiatric Press.

Lifton, R. J. (1967). *Death in life: Survivors of Hiroshima*. New York: Random House.

Lifton, R. J. (1973). *Home from the war*. New York: Simon & Schuster.

Lindy, J. D. (1981). Traumatic loss in oedipal and narcissistic transference (unpublished).

Lindy, J. D. (1985). The trauma membrane and other clinical concepts derived from psychotherapeutic work with survivors of natural disasters. *Psychiatric Annals, 15*(3), 153–160.

Lindy, J. D., Grace, M. C., & Green, B. L. (1984). Building a conceptual bridge between civilian trauma and war trauma. In B. A. van der Kolk (Ed.), *Post traumatic stress disorder: Psychological and biological sequelae*. Washington, DC: American Psychiatric Press.

Lindy, J. D., Green, B. L., Grace, M. C., & Titchener, J. L. (1983). Psychotherapy of survivors of the Beverly Hills fire. *American Journal of Psychotherapy, 27*(4), 593–610.

Lindy, J. D., & Titchener, J. L. (1983). Acts of God and man: Long-term character change in survivors of disaster and the law. *Behavioral Sciences and the Law, 1*(3), 85–96.

Parson, E. R. (1984). The reparation of the self: Clinical and theoretical dimensions in the treatment of the Vietnam combat veteran. *Journal of Contemporary Psychotherapy, 14*(1), 4–56.

Spitzer, R. L., Endicott, J., Mesnikoff, A. M., & Cohen, M. S. (1968). *The psychiatric evaluation form*. New York: Biometrics Research.

Titchener, J. L., & Kapp, F. (1978). Post traumatic decline. Presented at the American Psychoanalytic Association meeting, 1978.

van der Kolk, B. A. (1983). Adolescent turmoil in Vietnam veterans. Presented at American Psychiatric Association meeting, New York, 1983.

Wilson, J. (1983). Personal communication.

10

An Inpatient Program for Post-Traumatic Stress Disorder: Context as Treatment

STEVEN M. SILVER

Treatment-by-environment of post-traumatic stress reaction offers particular strengths not immediately available to clinicians working in a strictly individual therapy setting. The point of view is that of an individual who worked in both out- and inpatient settings but who is now functioning almost entirely on an inpatient program. The program's stated purpose is to treat post-traumatic stress disorder among women and men Vietnam War veterans. While what follows is specifically related to that particular population, it is suggested that the basic principles are applicable to a wide range of severe trauma survivors.

Post-traumatic stress reactions are essentially the reactions of normal people to abnormal stress. A perspective of normalcy offers the therapist a large armory of approaches because the individual is not simply a recipient of treatment. The program described makes the survivor an active participant in treatment of self and others.

The concept of post-traumatic stress reactions as essentially normal is resisted mightily by many mental health professionals. The reasons for this are several, but the greatest single reason for resistance is clinician's fear. The fear is partially the countertransference problem, which Sarah Haley (1974, 1978) has so eloquently discussed. Perhaps the greatest part of the fear comes from the anticipation of confronting the reality of survivorship: anyone at any time is a candidate. The arbitrary nature of trauma is a reality that many find too uncomfortable to maintain in conscious thought. This results in the desire to believe that "you get what you deserve." At worst, this attitude may result in distorting analytical concepts in order to rationalize perceiving the client as flawed. At best, it leads to avoiding the trauma experience in favor of the safer—for the therapist—pretrauma experiences.

SIX O'CLOCK NEWS FIRES: A TRAUMA REACTION MODEL

The evening news offers, with unfortunate regularity, examples of human events that demonstrate the normality of trauma reactions after the trauma experience. These events also offer a convenient model of longer-term reactions as well.

Assume for the moment you are in a tall, burning building with a fairly large number of other people. What we observe is that virtually everyone—barring only the psychotic unable to accurately perceive reality—sees the fire, judges it a threat, and experiences fear. We also notice that most people control the behavioral expression of that fear and, with varying degrees of effectiveness, try to find the means to improve the probability of their survival. A few do not. Their fear overrides their controls and their behavior becomes panicky—they leap from windows, run down smoke-filled hallways, and otherwise decrease the probability of their own survival. Most maintain control. They follow directions, carefully work their way out, and do the things needed to survive. Some of them, by chance, do not survive (for a more complete discussion of reactions to disaster, see Quarantelli & Dynes, 1973).

When you reach the street, someone puts a blanket around your shoulders, hands you a cup of coffee, and helps you find a place to sit down. As you look around you note that other survivors are behaving in some unusual ways. Some are laughing with little cause, some cry, some tremble, one or two may faint, some gregariously try to engage others in loud conversation, and many are still and withdrawn.

You and most other people—and we shall assume that you and "most other people" are normal or the word loses its meaning—deferred your reactions to a severe stressor event. Behaving in this manner is a logical, prosurvival thing to do. Instead of having the building burn for an hour or so, place yourself in a building consumed by fire for 12 to 13 months.

Let us assume when you finally make it to the street, there is no one there to assist you. Rather, someone grabs you by the shirt, tells you not to hang around, and points to a bus pulling away down the block and tells you that is your ride home.

You run down the block and leap on board—it is crowded and you recognize no one else but everyone seems to be looking at you. You are easy to spot. Your clothes are disheveled, reek of smoke, and your face and shirt are smeared with ashes. You get off the bus, alone, outside your family's home. When you enter, dinner is being served. You notice during the meal that people avoid looking at you directly and no one mentions the fire. Indeed, an embarrassing pause occurs when you try to mention where you were for the past year.

While you feel the need to discuss your experiences, it is clear that any attempt to do so will be resisted—for reasons that are not clear—by the people you care most about. Remaining silent about the experience is not initially difficult. After all, you spent the past year developing extremely effective controls to restrain your feelings of fear and confusion. So you go on about your business, or try to, essentially caught up in an internal conflict between expressing and processing your experiences and their suppression. An observer might reasonably predict that this conflict will become more powerful over time as the lack of integration of the experience continues to undercut the processing of new life experiences.

Prolonging the fire for a year sets the stage for understanding one notable source of psychic trauma, the Vietnam War. The qualities that enable ordinary people to function effectively in combat are qualities of deferment. In this somewhat overdrawn model we also have an example of a second trauma source, which is common in the survivor experience.

SANCTUARY TRAUMA

I use the term "sanctuary trauma" to describe what occurs when an individual who suffered a severe stressor next encounters what was expected to be a supportive and protective environment and discovers the environment is not as imagined or expected. It may be that one defense used to deal with the original trauma experience was to build an idealized mental model of what the sanctuary—one's home nation, the hospital, or whatever is viewed as the protective alternative to the trauma environment—would be like. In addition, the defenses raised against the trauma are dropped so thoroughly after leaving the trauma environment that the "normal" and perhaps necessary harshness of the new environment is perceived and experienced as a second trauma. I have encountered sanctuary trauma with survivors of physical assault, rape, sexual abuse, Vietnam and other wars, and other trauma experiences.

The Vietnam War veteran experience is very familiar to students of trauma study. Clinical experience indicates that many others are impacted by this second trauma, often so severely the victims will regard it as or more severe than the original. In my clinical experience, assaulted or raped women often described encountering the police and the hospital emergency room personnel as "a second rape." It is unfortunately true that many members of traditional institutions respond to trauma victims in nontherapeutic, indeed, even stupid, ways, with blaming of the victim clearly in evidence; this is not always the case. People responding to emergency situations tend to be abrupt and brusque, in part owing to the requirements of efficiency and speed and in part as self-protection from the trauma experience of the victim. Distancing by rescuers and other sanctuary personnel encourages continuation of the control mechanisms of trauma survivors by, in effect, convincing them that the trauma is not over.

Because of the survivor's vulnerability and expectations, idealized though they may be, sanctuary trauma may be devastating and is certainly appropriate for consideration and intervention in therapy. This does not always take place. As would be expected, those clinicians who do not accept post-traumatic stress as "real" tend to avoid both the trauma experience and any sanctuary trauma. On the other hand, there are clinicians who work with the original trauma experience but who avoid sanctuary trauma. The phenomenon of avoidance is common enough to suggest that the reasons for its existence may be due to the same reasons other clinicians avoid working with post-traumatic stress reactions. In particular, clinician guilt is a major issue. Members of the helping professions are uncomfortable with evidence suggesting appropriate therapeutic assistance was unavailable or withheld. The temptation is to avoid what makes them uncomfortable.

I have suggested an explanatory model for post-traumatic stress reactions. There deliberately was no attempt to explain post-traumatic stress reaction in terms of a specific school of psychological theory. I take the position that no single theoretical position is complete enough as yet to fully comprehend post-traumatic stress reactions. Furthermore, a single perspective utilizing one of the established theories of human personality and functioning limits the therapeutic tools available to the clinician. It is my observation, one I think many share, that many clinicians work effectively with post-traumatic stress, but contrasting that work with their verbal or written explanations of what they did forces the conclusion that the most effective treatment does not belong to one theoretical position, but draws from many.

This is more than an argument for an eclectic treatment approach. Post-traumatic stress reactions offer a perspective of human functioning suggesting consideration of a unified theory of human functioning. Within post-traumatic stress, therapists typically treat reflexive behaviors requiring deconditioning or modification, altered and sometimes confusing cognitive world views, rigidly controlled and limited emotive processing, powerful new questions of existential values and meaning, and disrupted systemic functioning. Single-theory positions are inadequate to respond to all these areas. The cutting edge of psychology is indicated by our knowledge and, indeed, by our debate about post-traumatic stress.

ASSESSMENT

A critical element in the provision of treatment in a program environment is accurate selection of clients. However, misdiagnosis of post-traumatic stress disorder is a common occurrence even in settings that would be expected to be familiar with particular trauma sources, such as Veterans Administration Medical Centers with combat veterans. One problem is the relatively recent adoption of post-traumatic stress disorder as a recognized disorder by the American Psychiatric Association. The *Diagnostic and Statistical Manual of Mental Disorders*, third edition (APA, 1980) may be unfamiliar to some clinicians and is still debated by others, though current research tends to support DSM-III criteria for post-traumatic stress disorder (Silver & Iacono, 1984).

An additional problem is the tendency for initial interviewers to seize on the presenting symptoms and make the diagnosis with what amounts to incomplete information. For example, an examination of veterans' charts often shows intrusive recollections of combat experiences used as the basis for a diagnosis of obsessive-compulsive disorder. Flashbacks are typically equated with hallucinations resulting from schizophrenia, and, if the veteran felt threatened during the flashback, as paranoid schizophrenia. Withdrawal and a numbing of responsiveness, particularly when accompanied by feelings of estrangement from society and authority, is often regarded as a personality disorder. Potential sources of trauma, such as combat experiences, are typically not examined. In Veterans Administration hospitals, the usual note is the veteran is "Vietnam era," with no further information.

The third problem is resistance to making the diagnosis. This may be due to theoretical disagreements with the concept of post-traumatic stress disorder. However, much of the time the problem resides in the clinician's countertransference reactions when encountering a Vietnam War veteran.

Another problem is the individual's reaction on encountering a mental health professional. The person is often reluctant to fully relate his experiences, particularly trauma experiences. He may see no relationship between current problems and events of many years ago. The trauma events may be such that the person is initially unwilling to share them until a bond of trust is established. Since it is typical in a psychiatric setting for one professional to do the screening and diagnostic interviews while others provide therapy, it is unlikely that the person will have the opportunity to develop a trusting bond with the person who assigns him a diagnostic label.

The psychological instruments used for differential diagnosis are not yet standardized for post-traumatic stress disorder though research is proceeding (e.g., Keane, Malloy, & Fairbank, 1984). In the meantime, this area is still somewhat weak.

There are, of course, a wide variety of scales developed by researchers to assess levels of post-traumatic stress, such as that used by Wilson (1978). A problem with many of these scales is they lack discriminatory items to differentiate between individuals having post-traumatic stress disorder and those "faking bad" for possible secondary gain.

Another part of the problem is the knowledge many Vietnam veterans have of post-traumatic stress disorder. Descriptions of the symptoms are commonly discussed in the media, and information on a relatively technical and sophisticated level is readily available through veterans' organizations such as the Disabled American Veterans (Williams, 1980). This makes it possible for the very few who are seeking government paychecks for a nonexistent disability to recite the diagnostic criteria. A more common situation is the veteran who actually does have post-traumatic stress disorder and who is seeking access to such things as vocational training benefits restricted to those having a disability greater than a certain percentage.

The most common reason for attempting to "fake bad" comes out of a desperate desire to gain help from very limited resources. By 1986, nine years after the fall of Saigon and more than a decade after the pullout of the last major American ground units from South Vietnam, there were only 14 inpatient treatment programs for post-traumatic stress disorder within the nearly 200 Veterans Administration hospitals. Virtually all these programs had waiting lists of several months. It is important to many veterans to convince staff that their problems are real and severe. Many veterans, after years of failed relationships, aching isolation, painful memories, and an ever-increasing sense of hopelessness, use the phrase "This is my last chance." It is not difficult to understand their motivation.

These problems have to be taken into account in the selection of veterans for program treatment. It is important to have as many forms of input as possible. For the program described here, the assessment process involves a review of all available medical and psychiatric records. Psychological tests, records of previous admissions, and observations up to the time of the assessment interview are examined for indications of post-traumatic stress disorder symptoms whether or not they are specifically reported by the individual or previously diagnosed as such. It is common for veterans to regard some symptoms, such as sleep disturbances, as essentially usual and normal and to tend not to report them. Also sought are symptoms not due to post-traumatic stress disorder. This is done to ascertain if a multiple diagnosis is in order or if the symptoms reported as reflecting post-traumatic stress disorder are actually manifestations of some other problem. If substance abuse has been a problem, the pattern of abuse is studied to see it if reflects a self-medication function in response to stress.

In the actual interview, there are four primary areas of emphasis. The first is preservice history and development. The goal is not to find predispositional factors or evidence of preexisting pathology. Instead, this examination is aimed at determining if the person's background is within the relatively broad range of normal limits.

The second area of emphasis is on the military service. Much has been written about this (Scurfield & Blank, 1984), but a major problem here for some clinicians is lack of familiarity with the military in general and the Vietnam War experience in particular. Reviewing medical charts frequently shows that the interviewer only briefly examined the veteran's statements and did not have an accurate picture of the severity of the stressor event(s) for the veteran. Stereotypic views on the part of the interviewer can be introduced. For example, a woman who served as an operating-room nurse had the diagnosis ignored because, being a nurse, she was not in direct combat and therefore could not have post-traumatic stress disorder. This kind of statement reflects ignorance of the kinds of stressor events that can produce post-traumatic stress disorder.

The third area closely examined is functioning since military service. Employment and interpersonal relationships typically reflect a withdrawal from contact with others. It is not unusual to find employment histories reflecting literally dozens of jobs within 10 or 15 years. While conflict with authorities is sometimes the reason for termination of employment, most often the veteran quit while still performing in a satisfactory manner. Often there is difficulty in explaining why the job was left: "I just got restless" and "I was really feeling bored" are typical explanations.

Interpersonal relationships reflect this pattern of withdrawal. Relationships existing prior to military service were not maintained. Continuing and increasing social isolation are common, sometimes manifested by actual physical isolation accomplished by withdrawing to wilderness areas or becoming "lost" within urban areas.

If the person has a history of substance abuse, a check of medical records and personal history is made to determine when the abuse pattern emerged. A veteran with post-traumatic stress disorder may have refrained from substance abuse when out in the field or placed in a critical position where others' lives were at stake. However, once off duty or in a secure area, one might note a heavy utilization of drugs, primarily depressants. The pattern of substance abuse among Vietnam War veterans does not follow the typical style of utilization or response to treatment once back in "the world" (Stanton, 1976).

The final area to be examined is, of course, presenting symptoms. Depression is quite common, but what finally brings a veteran in for help seems to be in one of three broad problem areas. Anger and the fear of its possible and actual consequences if permitted expression is often a major concern. The second is frustration with social isolation and deteriorating interpersonal relationships. The third is the apparently inexplicable emergence (or reemergence) of reexperiencing phenomena, such as dreams, intrusive memories, or "flashbacks." More than one of these problems may surface. Quite often the veteran will deny that there is a link to her or his Vietnam experiences, and a concern will be that insanity is emerging.

Many veterans understand that a link exists between their current difficulty and their war experiences, but they are often uncertain as to its composition. This may be denial, but deliberate avoidance of a confrontation with self is seldom consciously present. Far more often the veteran has a partial or complete amnesia of the trauma event.

This last point, the existence of partial amnesia of the trauma experience, is worth amplification. Complete amnesia may be encountered but it is rare. Partial amnesia is much more likely. By partial amnesia I refer not only to loss of some conscious memories of the experience in terms of its historical chronology. Partial amnesia may also include loss of emotional memories. Frequently Vietnam veterans with post-traumatic stress disorder will be able to rattle off the names, dates, places, and historical sequence of events involved in their trauma experiences. Close questioning often will reveal that this apparently complete memory of the event is actually based on information supplied to the veteran by others after it was over. An indication of this may be that the affect during the presentation is remarkably flat, given the material presented. The veteran's amnesia is not of the history but of the reactive feelings experienced during the trauma. The amnesia serves the purpose of preventing the reexperiencing of these powerful emotions.

More commonly, powerful feelings are stirred during the interview. Sharing feelings requires trust, and the veteran may be hesitant. Silence or the withholding of information may result in misdiagnosis. It is important during the interview that the clinician clearly communicates respect for the veteran and his or her experiences. It is also important that the interviewer does some homework on the war and military service and has an initial understanding of the possible factors involved. This aids in clarifying information from the veteran.

The gathering of all this information is used to substantiate the diagnosis of post-traumatic stress disorder using DSM-III criteria, to determine if other disorders requiring treatment are present, and to assess the level of severity. Severity determines the necessity of using limited inpatient resources.

It is highly likely that additional symptoms will be revealed and further trauma material may become apparent as the veteran is treated. Therefore, reassessment on a regular basis is made to seek out additional information and to make sure that important issues are not neglected. This also permits an evaluation of progress and alerts staff and the veteran to areas needing additional work.

TREATMENT: A CONTEXTUAL APPROACH

The inpatient specialized program described here offers a concentration of treatment to deal with the greatest range and severity of symptoms resulting from post-traumatic stress reactions. Treatment approaches occur concurrently. The philosophy for this is twofold. First, the variety of treatments available tend to reinforce one another. The whole is greater than the sum of its parts. At least some approaches will be effective for some people, and those approaches which do not appear to be effective at one point in the person's process of change may become so later.

The second reason is to build a community—multiple activities to build up group identity, cohesion, and support. This results in isolation and withdrawal being gradually discarded in favor of joining first with those who share similar experiences; this approach provides the veteran with ideas and assistance from others who are dealing with many of the same concerns. This is a very real source of help in the therapeutic process and takes advantage of mutual identification of the veterans with one another. Utilization of the healing power of the group is an example of the perspective that survivors can help heal survivors and, in so doing, help heal themselves.

The treatment program is four months long. Trial-and-error experience found that many veterans spend approximately four weeks developing the bonds of trust needed for effective therapy. The next 12 weeks generally result in major therapeutic gains. Extensions may be granted, though veterans are not kept in the hospital until completely cured. The intent of treatment is for the veteran to function so as to permit a return to "the world" and to continue treatment as needed. Institutionalization is avoided.

Members of various disciplines work as a treatment team for the program. Each member of the clinically trained staff serves as a primary therapist for individual therapy. All participate in at least one of the group therapies offered.

Treatment is continuous and uses four major approaches. Individual, group, family, and milieu therapies are the basic frameworks of the approaches. All are ongoing from the time the veteran enters the program until she or he leaves. The level of therapeutic intensity, then, is very high.

Family therapy may be of critical importance. As noted in Chapter 5, the family is impacted in a major way by the trauma of one of its members, and the family system itself is often in need of aid. The family offers a great deal of power either in therapeutic change or in maintaining the disorder (Figley & Sprenkle, 1978). When a family of procreation still exists and is available, family therapy is indicated. Whether or not the family is accessible, family issues as part of the veteran's history are almost certainly going to be present.

Very frequently the staff person serves as educator as much as therapist. Families are often confused by the veteran's apparently inexplicable emotional reactions, withdrawal, sleep disturbances, and other symptoms. Taking the time to explain post-traumatic stress disorder as a concept often lifts much of the family's concern.

Group therapy is a vital part of treatment and is conducted on a daily basis. Group therapy offers a number of advantages in dealing with post-traumatic stress disorder and is well established as an effective treatment approach for Vietnam veterans (Parson, 1984). Initially, a group of peers offers involvement with people with whom there is identification and trust. Since the group is ongoing with no distinct start or finish, new members meet others who have achieved varying degrees of progress. This is very encouraging to those with a perspective of near hopelessness.

Particular care is taken that group therapy does not degenerate into fruitless "bitch sessions" about wrongs done by society and the government. Such issues are both real and legitimate group material but cannot be permitted to be used as distractors away from treatment issues.

Individual therapy is the third of the four treatment components. There is some variation in therapeutic style among the treatment staff, reflecting a range of theoretical perspectives. Experience and education have developed some commonalities. It is clear that effective treatment requires the surfacing of the trauma material. It is important that the individual comes to understand the relationship between this material and his or her life functioning since.

Ideally, the veteran comes to view the trauma experience as more than a life incident that must, in some way, be endured. A goal is the recognition that there are positives to be gained from it—one veteran referred to this as "diamonds buried in the crap." The emphasis on growth from trauma experiences is not simply a reframing tactic. It is a reality that survivors frequently developed and utilized strengths that might have remained dormant. For war veterans there may be a sharp increase in their compassion and caring. They often have a deep appreciation for what others take for granted. While verbally denying any of these things exist, repeatedly veterans reaching out to help one another display these qualities.

Milieu therapy might be a term to describe this reaching out. Early in the program we saw that the veterans frequently set up their own evening discussion groups to aid one another with particular problems, often of a family nature. We noticed that when one veteran awoke with a nightmare or experienced a flashback, another veteran would help talk her or him down, frequently responding because of proximity faster than the staff.

This recognition led to establishment of a formal therapeutic community. Much of the decision-making power in the program was given to the veterans. Their suggestions for program policies and rules was sought. A number of decisions on day-to-day program functioning are placed in their hands. For people who often felt powerless, this is no small beginning.

Medication is not considered a form of therapy except in the sense of providing some stopgap support during the process of change.

Because of the range of literature available, it is not necessary to discuss at length specific techniques utilized within the therapeutic approaches discussed above. Such tools as desensitization, hypnosis, and others are frequently used, and since the development of these techniques is an ongoing process, it is very important for treatment staff to keep abreast of new research and clinical reports.

The progress of treatment tends to follow several general stages. A veteran's progress through these stages reflects the severity and duration of the disorder. Progress is carefully monitored to judge the rate of therapeutic change and to detect unresolved issues.

The initial stage, on the average lasting four weeks, is marked by the veteran holding her- or himself back from full, active participation in the program's functions. Veterans report that during this time they carefully observe both staff and other patients, trying to determine if the environment is "safe," that is, are the program members willing to be receptive to the veteran and his or her experiences. This stage initially is marked for the veteran by a feeling of relief, and at least initially many presenting symptoms are not present. However, after a few days symptoms return and generally increase in severity as the veteran discovers she or he is in a place where stimulation to recall the trauma is virtually continuous. It becomes impossible to hide from the memories through mental distraction or self-medication. Anxiety increases and morale worsens—the veteran wonders if there is any hope after all.

The point of maximum distress marks the entry into the second and longest stage, which lasts for the next two to three months. The veteran is at a near-crisis point, and it is at this point that the greatest advantage of a specialized inpatient program comes into play. The other veterans, some of whom are "short timers," now actively intervene both to confront and to support the veteran.

The confrontation is directed at the veteran's unrealistic belief or hope in some sort of program magic that will somehow erase the pain of the disorder without further effort. With the staff joining both formally in the various scheduled therapy sessions and informally in community meetings, education classes, and "chance" encounters, the nature of the disorder is explained. A model stressing the need for working through long-buried material and issues is repeatedly described.

While it is true that the staff provides support during entry into the second stage, therapeutic relationships, particularly involving trust, are still embryonic. The most effective support comes from the veteran's peers. The close identification with other survivors has positive value. The veteran may not be willing to take on faith the assurances of staff that the program "works"; however, that same statement from other veterans carries a great deal of weight. A measure of peer support effectiveness is that, though some of the most distressing symptoms (such as flashbacks, nightmares, depression, anxiety, feelings of anger) temporarily increase in severity, only one veteran in over two years opted not to continue the program during entry into the second stage.

The bulk of the second stage is a microcosm of the veteran's history from the war to the present. The initial focus is on the Vietnam experience. Gradually the emphasis shifts to the years since and how the events in them relate to the war. Eventually the veteran's "today" is examined. There often is a going back to address material previously overlooked or avoided. It is very important that effective communication exists among staff so the therapies function in support of one another. Frequently the veteran discusses a particular concern in one forum but not another. This is not a problem as the range of therapeutic approaches allows for individual differences.

The second stage is marked by introduction of family therapy when possible. Obviously, this is precluded for veterans who do not have families or whose families are so distant as to prevent their active participation. In the latter case, family therapy may be possible when the veteran leaves the program. As a general rule of thumb, it has been my clinical experience that, given the availability and willingness of family members, or family equivalents, family therapy should virtually always be considered. Frequently the veteran is into a second marriage and family. Family-specific problems may exist. As the veteran comes to believe in the possibility of improvement, willingness to salvage the family relationships increases. Both in group and in individual therapy staff note an increase in the introduction of family-related concerns.

Overlying the family-specific problems exists the possibility that the veteran's reaction has become embedded in the family functioning. Family functioning in a number of areas may be seriously deteriorated in a manner paralleling the individual veteran's reaction—expressiveness and communication may have deteriorated, conflict and irritability increased, emotions and their expression suppressed, and withdrawal and isolation within the family system by its members may be present. All may have entered into a conspiracy of silence toward the trauma source.

The most significant part of the second stage is the growth of hope. This occurs for two major reasons, according to program veterans. First is the discovery that experiences previously held to be taboo can be approached and explored without utter destruction resulting. The veteran gradually notices an overall decrease in symptoms. Second, the veteran's sense of worth increases. This is due to many reasons, not the least of which is finding some meaning, some value, in the Vietnam experience and its aftermath. Guilt plays a major role in negative self-image and is worth addressing.

The program's approach to guilt avoids direct confrontation. When clarification by religious leaders is of assistance, chaplains are involved. What is avoided are the debates some have encountered with previous therapists. I doubt that it is possible to win such debates and prefer to tell the veterans that their moral code is their own and is of value for it was forged in fire and blood. What is disputed is the consequence of this code. As a response to what they believe to be violations of their own sense of right and wrong, punishment has failed, though it was the first and consistent impulse. It is noted that their moral code, of virtually whatever nature, is based on a concept of right and wrong and simple punishment does nothing to rectify the wrong. The example of medieval knights is often used. When these warriors violated their moral code, be it of chivalry or Church law, their priests clearly understood that assigning punishment was not enough. Trained as knights, experienced in combat, they expected high standards of themselves. Therefore, the priests would require that the knights atone for their guilt by taking on a task contributing to their society, such as guarding travelers from highwaymen or fighting to free the Holy Land. These assignments required sacrifice, utilized the knights' skills and attributes, and improved the lives of others in some way.

The concept of atonement not only responds to feelings of guilt; its emphasis on making a contribution to others aids in reducing isolation. When guilt is a major factor, this approach has met with enthusiasm. Frequently, but not always, the method chosen is one that helps other Vietnam veterans.

During the second stage progress is not a steadily increasing trend. There are fluctuations and plateaus, and some veterans are discouraged by this. The possibility of substance abuse may increase. Random analysis of breath and urine helps provide a structure, albeit one of deterrence and punishment, in addition to support provided by staff and other veterans. Punishment is usually centered on loss of passes; continued substance abuse results in discharge. Fortunately, this is relatively rare.

Overlapping the second stage is the emergence of the third. Many veterans enter the program with literally no hope that their future will be other than the same misery they have endured. The third stage is marked by the birth and development of concern with the future. Family therapy may become critical at this time as the veteran develops a growing desire to improve the family and return to it.

Many of the issues the veteran begins to raise during this time, usually the last month or so, require the pragmatic exploration of employment and education services and opportunities. Most program veterans have had little difficulty in gaining employment but have experienced great difficulty in maintaining it. The issues around this difficulty, such as handling stress and dealing with authority, become more important in therapy.

A caution to be observed is the veteran using future-oriented issues as distractors to avoid more fundamental concerns. If used, this tactic usually is manifested earlier. Nonetheless, the concept of the second and third stages overlapping is important because it emphasizes the need to continue working toward fundamental problem resolution.

From time to time a veteran will request an extension in the program. This may be granted for a variety of reasons. Perhaps the veteran had a greater-than-average amount of material to work through, or was slow to begin for some reason, or may be ultimately returning to an area of the country that has no clearly identifiable, qualified therapeutic resource to continue working. In the latter case, the staff considers it important to gain ground while the opportunity exists. For most it is considered enough to make sufficient progress so the veteran may continue treatment on an outpatient basis.

CASE EXAMPLE

The veteran, Fred, was a 36-year-old white male who was referred for evaluation by the substance abuse treatment unit of the hospital where he had been treated for alcoholism. During the course of his treatment it had been noted that he began to experience difficulty sleeping, complaining of nightmares of Vietnam combat experiences, angry verbal outbursts, and intrusive memories of Vietnam.

His preservice history was unremarkable. He joined the Marine Corps in 1967 to save money and gain educational benefits to enable him to go to college. His family was generally supportive of this decision.

He did well in boot camp and was ordered to Vietnam. He spent 13 months in Vietnam and became a squad leader. Initially in the interview he was reluctant to discuss his war experiences. However, questions about symptoms noted by his alcohol treatment staff, particularly nightmares, led to his revealing several traumatic incidents. One was a decision he made while leading a patrol to take the shorter of two ways to return to his unit.

His patrol was ambushed and many of his friends were killed or wounded. Within a month of this his tour in Vietnam ended and he returned to the United States. Fred was assigned to demonstration troops used in officer training. He was frustrated with the inadequate preparation of the young lieutenants for Vietnam. He drank heavily on weekends but did not permit it to interfere with his work.

After discharge from the Marine Corps, he found that his preservice plans had little attraction. He took a succession of jobs, never staying longer than seven months. Eventually jobs ended owing to his growing use of alcohol. He married but divorced two years later. Fred found it difficult to relate to people except when drinking. By 1982 he had had 27 jobs. He remarried in 1981. When he ceased drinking he experienced violent dreams, which terrified his wife. He realized drinking would destroy his second marriage and he approached a Veterans Administration Vet Center for treatment. They referred him to the alcohol treatment program as a first step. His evaluation for post-traumatic stress disorder placed him on the waiting list, and he came into the program five months later.

At first slow to involve himself, Fred gave the impression of closely watching and testing the staff and other patients. He slowly developed a close relationship with several of the other veterans and, with their support, began to be active in group therapy. His activity in individual therapy also increased.

A number of incidents from Vietnam were troubling Fred, and the ambush of his patrol was not discussed until he was in the program two months. He did some work on this issue by himself by using the ideas discussed in group therapy and in "after-hours" talks with the other veterans. Assistance with guilt came out of talks with the program chaplain and in using hypnosis to rebuild the context of the patrol so he could understand all the variables affecting the decision of that 20-year-old Marine corporal. He welcomed the concept of atonement and that he could use his experiences as a source of strength in helping other veterans of Vietnam.

Family therapy focused on the marital dyad. Emphasis was placed on understanding post-traumatic stress disorder and improving communication skills.

For future planning, Fred took a job as a carpenter and arranged to do volunteer work in a Vet Center. He arranged to be involved in regular outpatient therapy. Follow-up a year later found Fred alcohol-free and running his own roofing business. His marriage was intact with no difficulties. His symptoms had faded, and outpatient therapy was discontinued. He continued to work in the Vet Center.

As a result of Fred's intervention, five other Vietnam veterans were referred to the PTSD program for treatment. Except for his performance as a "referral source," Fred is a typical Vietnam War veteran who has successfully completed our program. His referrals point out the network of communication that exists among many veterans.

OUTCOME RESULTS

In the fall of 1983, 62 Vietnam veterans discharged from the program were contacted—at that time, approximately 90 veterans had been involved in the program. The 62 included those who did not complete the program. The remaining veterans could not be contacted in the time available for the inquiry.

A review of records confirmed 44 (71%) with the diagnosis of post-traumatic stress disorder. The remaining 18 reflect the desire of program staff to provide treatment even when some doubt exists. Also reflected is the "learning curve" of the staff in making the diagnosis—the current non-post-traumatic stress disorder admission rate is estimated to be about half the rate indicated in the study. Inaccurate diagnosis is reflected in the proportion of those who did not complete the program. Among the post-traumatic stress disorder group, 64% completed the program; only 39% of the others stayed for the entire program.

Of the post-traumatic stress disorder veterans who completed the program, only four (14%) returned to an inpatient setting for any reason other than medical—of those who did not complete the program, seven (44%) were readmitted.

Currently, the proportion of post-traumatic stress disorder patients completing the program is estimated to be in excess of 85%. This follow-up study lacks a measure of quality of the veterans' lives. However, informal contact with many indicates that most are much improved.

DISCUSSION

Presented here is not simply an environment in which various treatment methods might be employed. Rather, the context of the program is in itself a treatment modality. Survivors of the same trauma source are brought together to elicit material, provide support and resolution, and break down isolation in an intense manner impossible in other treatment contexts. Virtually any specific treatment method can be utilized within this context.

It is clear that research should be done to determine which ingredients and their interactions in this environment would be most effective.

A contextual or programmatic treatment approach could be applicable to other trauma survivors. Indeed, because the range of Vietnam experiences is so wide it might be argued that the program treats a wider variety of trauma sources than would be encountered in a program working with, for example, raped women. For example, we have worked with Vietnam veterans whose trauma histories include single and multiple traumatic stressors. These stressors range from witnessing massive loss of life to violent personal injury in environments in which the veteran could have been with others or totally isolated. The range of personal control likewise varied enormously. For example, while the common thread of service in Vietnam bonds these veterans together for therapeutic effectiveness, their actual experiences may have been as a triage nurse, a helicopter gunner, a truck driver, a tanker, or a rifleman. There is no such thing as the "typical" Vietnam War experience.

Larger numbers of people are becoming involved with traumatic events—from a resource point of view it might be worthwhile to consider the establishment of trauma treatment centers specializing in certain areas, such as natural disasters and criminal assault.

The final and perhaps most important facet of this programmatic treatment method is its reliance on the strength of the program participants. Working with the results of disaster and trauma can be difficult, even painful. But this is more than balanced by being permitted to be a part of the extraordinary healing that survivors may provide to one another. It is this healing which is uniquely provided by this program.

REFERENCES

American Psychiatric Association (1980). *Diagnostic and statistical manual of mental disorders* (3rd ed.). Washington, DC: Author.

Figley, C. R., & Sprenkle, D. H. (1978). Delayed stress response syndrome: Family therapy implications. *Journal of Marriage and Family Counseling, 4,* 53–60.

Haley, S. A. (1974). When the patient reports atrocities: Specific treatment consideration of the Vietnam veteran. *Archives of General Psychiatry, 30,* 191–196.

Haley, S. A. (1978). Treatment implications of post-combat stress response syndromes for mental health professionals. In C. R. Figley (Ed.), *Stress disorders among Vietnam veterans.* New York: Brunner/Mazel.

Keane, T. M., Malloy, P. F., & Fairbank, J. A. (1984). Empirical development of an MMPI subscale for the assessment of combat-related posttraumatic stress disorder. *Journal of Consulting and Clinical Psychology, 52,* 888–891.

Parson, E. R. (1984). The role of psychodynamic group therapy in the treatment of the combat veteran. In H. J. Schwartz (Ed.), *Psychotherapy of the combat veteran.* New York: Spectrum.

Quarantelli, E. L., & Dynes, R. R. (1973). *Images of disaster behavior: Myths and consequences.* Columbus, OH: Ohio State University.

Scurfield, R. M., & Blank, A. S., Jr. (1984). A guide to the Vietnam veteran military history. In S. M. Sonnenberg, A. S. Blank, & J. Talbott (Eds.), *Psychiatric problems of Vietnam veterans.* Washington, DC: American Psychiatric Press.

Silver, S. M., & Iacono, C. U. (1984). Factor-analytic support for DSM-III's post-traumatic stress disorder for Vietnam veterans. *Journal of Clinical Psychology, 40,* 5–14.

Stanton, M. D. (1976). Drugs, Vietnam, and the Vietnam veteran: An overview. *American Journal of Drug and Alcohol Abuse, 3,* 557–570.

Williams, T. (Ed.) (1980). *Post traumatic stress disorders and the Vietnam veteran.* Cincinnati: Disabled American Veterans.

Wilson, J. P. (1978). *Identity, ideology and crisis: The Vietnam veteran in transition.* Cleveland: Cleveland State University.

11

Mobilizing Social Support Networks in Times of Disaster

SUSAN D. SOLOMON

Most people experienced severe disruptions of their daily routines. Organization activities, conversations, reading, and thinking about Love Canal absorbed their energies. Families who moved in with relatives or to motels exhausted themselves trying to carry on some semblance of their normal routines in unfamiliar settings—some of them unsuitable for daily family living. Some families sorely missed visits from friends and relatives, who were afraid to come into the area. People missed their customary work, hobbies, and recreation—the familiar flow and setting of family life. They missed their neighbors and neighborhood acquaintances—the comforting sense of familiar faces in familiar places.
(Adeline Gordon Levine, *Love Canal: Science, Politics and People,* 1983, p. 185)

Any major disaster carries with it the potential for interfering with the normal functioning of social support networks. Disasters may disrupt social networks in either of two basic ways: through the actual death of

The author would like to thank Dr. Emeline Otey for her helpful comments on an earlier draft of this manuscript.

a primary group member, or through disruptions caused by responses to disaster. Such responses include evacuation, breakdowns in transportation, failure of communication systems, and temporary or permanent relocation (Bolin, 1984). Not only are ties with family and friends affected, but also social ties with the locale. For example, social activities involving voluntary associations, churches, and recreational groups may be jeopardized by the relocation of families and/or the destruction of physical facilities where various activities have been held (Trainer & Bolin, 1976). Ironically, these disruptions of social networks occur at a time when the need for social support is particularly high, since the disaster victim typically experiences many stressful life events at the same time (e.g., disability or death of a family member, material losses, uncomfortable and unfamiliar surroundings, job loss) (Garrison, 1983).

This chapter examines the assumption that the impairment of social support networks affects psychosocial recovery from disaster and increases victim vulnerability to a variety of physical and mental health problems. Following a definition of the terms social support and social network, the discussion briefly summarizes findings from the stress literature on the mental health effects, both positive and negative, of the presence or loss of social support. The chapter then considers ways in which mental health professionals can intervene in the personal network to preserve and enhance social support in times of emergency. It concludes with a discussion of issues in need of further research attention.

Although social support has been defined in many ways, most definitions include the following four components: emotional support, reciprocity of obligation, task-oriented assistance, and provision of information relevant to coping (Mitchell & Trickett, 1980). The first component, emotional support, may include providing information that one is loved, cared for, and respected (Cobb, 1976), and/or providing the opportunity to express one's feelings and beliefs (Lowenthal & Haven, 1968; Wortman & Dunkel-Schetter, 1979). The second kind of support, reciprocity of obligation, involves providing information that one is part of a network or support system of reciprocal help and mutual obligation (Cobb, 1976; Kahn & Antonucci, 1980). Task-oriented assistance, the third type of support, involves the provision of direct aid, including time, information, and materials (Kahn & Antonucci, 1980). Finally, the fourth component of support, coping-related information may be conveyed by providing feedback about the appropriateness of one's fears, beliefs, and opinions (Kahn & Antonucci, 1980; Wortman & Dunkel-Schetter, 1979). (For a more detailed discussion of the construct of social support, see Caplan, 1974; Cobb, 1976; Heller, 1979; Mitchell & Trickett, 1980; Wallston, Alagna, DeVellis, & DeVellis, 1983).

Researchers in this area recognize the need for distinguishing between the concepts of social support and social network (Schaefer, Coyne & Lazarus, 1981). While the former concept tends to be operationalized qualitatively, as in the above definition, the latter is typically operationalized quantitatively, in terms of such factors as the number of relationships one has, the frequency of contact with specific types of others, and the number of linkages between network members (Wallston et al., 1983). The social network may be viewed as the context within which social support functions (Lieberman, 1982); it refers to the individual's personal community of associates with whom s/he interacts on a face-to-face basis (Gottlieb, 1976). More specifically, the social network consists of "a person's relationships with relatives, friends, neighbors, co-workers, and other acquaintances who interact with the person" (Unger & Powell, 1980, p. 566).

EFFECTS OF SOCIAL SUPPORT ON PHYSICAL AND MENTAL HEALTH

A comprehensive review of the literature linking social support with physical and mental health is beyond the scope of this chapter and may be found elsewhere (e.g., Cobb, 1976; Dean & Lin, 1977; Gore, 1978; Haggerty, 1980; Hamburg & Killilea, 1979; Kaplan, Cassel, & Gore, 1977; Lin, Simeone, Ensel, & Kuo, 1979; Mitchell & Trickett, 1980; Silver & Wortman, 1980; Wallston et al., 1983). The present discussion offers illustrative examples of both the positive and negative effects associated with social support and its loss, particularly in the context of exposure to traumatic events.

Positive Effects

It is believed that social supports function as buffers in times of crisis, directly moderating the negative effects of the experience as well as facilitating subsequent coping and adaption (Kahn & Antonucci, 1980). Recent research evidence suggests that adequate social support may function to protect individuals from both physical and mental disorder, following exposure to crisis situations. Along these lines, social support has been shown to reduce the number of psychiatric casualties in combat, the percentage of complications of pregnancy associated with high life change, the amount of child abuse among isolated parents, and the failure to survive shipwreck and other major accidents (Cobb, 1976;

Elliott & Eisdorfer, 1982; Raphael, 1981). In a longitudinal study of responses to job loss following a plant closing, social support from relatives and friends was found to reduce reported distress over the loss (Cobb & Kasl, 1977). Family support has also been associated with recovery of the physically disabled, both in the hospital and in the community (Kelman, Lowenthal, & Muller, 1966; Kemp & Vash, 1971; Litman, 1962; Smits, 1974). One study reports that seeking emotional support was regarded as among the most helpful coping strategies used by patients currently involved in stressful life situations (Horowitz & Wilner, 1980).

The aforementioned studies seem to suggest that social support facilitates adjustment to crisis events. However, most of this research has been correlational in nature, leaving open the possibility of causation in the opposite direction. That is, it may be that those who are more poorly adjusted or in poor health are less likely to have adequate social support, due either to social incompetence or to obvious suffering, which unwittingly creates feelings of vulnerability and inadequacy in others (Heller, 1979; Silver & Wortman, 1980; Wallston et al., 1983). More longitudinal research is needed to assess whether available social support at one point in time is predictive of later mental or physical disorder.

Negative Effects

Researchers in the area of social support tend to emphasize the beneficial effects of support networks. It should be noted, however, that social networks are not always supportive. A distinction was made earlier between the number of relationships a person has (social network) and the person's perception of the supportive value of social interactions (social support). Several studies of the social ties of low-income women have shown that these individuals form informal exchange networks to help one another through crises (Belle, 1982; Jeffers, 1967; Stack, 1974). These studies also found that the prolonged and essentially involuntary interdependence of friends and kin often leads to stress and hostility, and that those financially able to do so tend to opt out of the mutual obligations and dependence such networks entail.

By occupying diverse life roles a woman may extend her social support network, but she also increases her chances of experiencing role conflict. For example, in a disaster situation the relief worker may find herself torn between the obligations of her job and her need to rejoin and protect members of her own family. Along these lines, relief efforts have been found to be less effective when undertaken by individuals who are unsure of the safety of their loved ones, since family welfare tends to be the primary concern of individuals caught in disaster (Smith, 1983). In many cases the conflict may be resolved in favor of loyalty to the family (Dunning & Silva, 1980), although for disaster workers with clearly defined responsibilities the conflict may persist and cause profound emotional distress (Killian, 1952). Killian (1952) suggests that adequate training and/or visibility may be sufficient to predispose rescue workers to perform their community role, without regard for the physical safety of their families. However, little research has been done on the actual nature or difficulty of such decisions for relief workers, or the long-term psychological consequences of a particular choice.

While rescue workers may be faced with role conflict during the impact phase of disaster, others may experience these divided loyalties later in the aftermath. Bates, Fogelman, Parenton, Pittman & Tracy (1963) describe the dilemma faced by members of various relief committees during the reconstruction following Hurricane Audrey. Selected for committee participation by virtue of their leadership positions in the community, these individuals were expected to serve the interests both of the community at large as well as of their relatives, neighbors, and friends. Bates et al. (1963) indicate that these leaders experienced considerable anguish over conflicting expectations, leading to physical and nervous exhaustion in some cases, and withdrawal from participation in others.

When the family unit as a whole is involved in a crisis such as a natural disaster, the process of adaptation may itself become a source of continuing stress (Kellner, 1966). For example, in a study of survivors following the Buffalo Creek flood, a significant relationship was found between parental drinking and/or father's depression level, and delinquency of offspring (Gleser, Green, & Winget, 1981). This study also reported that anxiety and/or depression in one spouse added significantly to the overall severity of the other spouse's response, over and above the contribution made by the stress of the disaster itself. Disasters may inflict injuries that require a protracted recovery period. When the injured person is the head of the household, he/she may find it difficult to relinquish his/her former role for one of dependency; the emotional consequences of this blow to self-esteem may exacerbate the physical problems already being experienced (Croog, 1970). Furthermore, when recovery does occur, the spouse or child may find it difficult to surrender the power and prerogatives s/he experienced while the head of the household was disabled (Visotsky, Hamburg, Goss, & Lebovits, 1961).

Recent research indicates that not only the long-term adaptation but even the initial response to disaster of other family members can heighten the stress experienced by a victim. A study by Handford, Mayes, Mattison, Humphrey, Bagnato, Bixler, and Kales (1983) examined the responses of family members living in the vicinity of Three Mile Island (TMI) during the 1979 nuclear reactor accident. Reactions of children to TMI were not found to relate significantly to the intensity of their parents' response. However, a significant relationship *was* found when parents disagreed in their reaction to the event. Children of single parents, or parents who were consistent with each other in mood or intensity of response (including high distress), were significantly less upset by the incident than were children whose parents had differing reactions to TMI. The above studies as a whole suggest that, in addition to offering social support, the social network also holds the potential for increasing levels of stress.

Attempts to be supportive may fail for a variety of reasons. Reliance on the social support network during rehabilitation can create dependency and low self-esteem, rather than recovery and the development of coping mechanisms (Cobb, 1979; Garrity, 1973; Lewis, 1966). Moreover, statements such as "cheer up" and "it's not as bad as it seems" can impede meaningful communication about the trauma (Wortman & Dunkel-Schetter, 1979). It has been suggested that a more helpful form of support is to provide the distressed individual with an opportunity for the open expression of feelings and concerns (see Silver & Wortman, 1980, for a more thorough discussion of this topic).

The above literature indicates that not enough is known about the maladaptive and adaptive aspects of social support. Further research is needed to determine when too much support, or the wrong kind of support, may be harmful. Furthermore, since the act of providing support can itself produce stress on the family (DiMatteo & Hays, 1981), it may be advantageous to assess the costs and benefits to both receivers and providers in a supportive interaction (Wallston et al., 1983).

Loss of Social Support

Some individuals have been shown to cope well without access to social relationships. For example, Lowenthal (1964) found that old people who had maintained a lifelong pattern of social isolation had higher morale and no greater likelihood of hospitalization than elderly with ongoing personal relationships. She also found that women who had been socially isolated all their lives were less likely to be psychologically impaired or in need of institutionalization than those recently widowed.

As Lowenthal's (1964) work illustrates, the loss of social support may be a source of stress in itself.

Probably the most damaging aspect of disaster is its potential for disrupting existing social support networks. Earthquakes, floods, and tornadoes can destroy whole communities, including neighborhoods, schools, businesses and churches, thereby disrupting all nonkin relationships (Bolin, 1984). Immediately following disaster, communities may pass through "heroic" and "honeymoon" phases in which citizenry band together to help one another. After about two months, however, disillusionment tends to set in and the sense of "shared community" is lost (Farberow, 1978). Disaster victims have often been relocated to temporary or permanent housing, with no attempt to preserve the natural support networks of the individuals involved (Cohen & Ahearn, 1980). A recent study of relocated persons found that the most frequently mentioned source of unhappiness with the move was loss of proximity to friends and relatives (Korsching, Donnermeyers, & Burdge, 1980). Sixty percent visited less often with friends, while 45% visited relatives less often after relocation. Similarly, following the large-scale evacuation caused by a devastating cyclone in Darwin, Australia, the greatest number of psychological problems and highest stress levels were reported by those evacuees who could not return to their homes and neighborhoods (Western & Milne, 1979). These studies indicate that the loss of the support network, when coupled with a new, unfamiliar environment such as a trailer park, can lead to the development of social and emotional problems (Hall & Landreth, 1975).

In addition, exigencies may pit neighbors against one another. For example, the federal 1983 buyout of flood- and dioxin-ridden Times Beach, Missouri, was made contingent on unanimous agreement of all property owners. The few unwilling to sell found themselves stoned by angry fellow residents (Wilson, 1983). In another 1983 disaster, California families were forced by their insurance companies to sue their neighbors, on whose property mudslides originated, for damages (Garaventa, 1983). At Three Mile Island there was considerable disagreement about evacuation, both within families and across friendship groups. A person who had decided to leave would call a normally supportive friend who had decided to stay, and would be rebuked for having panicked. In this instance people were separated not only from their friends but also from the supportive opinion validation that their friends usually offered (Baum, 1984).

In the aftermath of disaster, the natural process of rebuilding can serve to further sever social ties, in that victims feel alone in their troubles and so overwhelmed by the effort of recovery that they dare not expend time or energy engaging in social activities (Garaventa, 1983). Families suffering long-term deprivation in housing and services may feel resentful of others living in undamaged sections of the community (Smith, 1983). Even when no rebuilding is necessary, disasters that pose chronic threats can erode social cohesion. For example, following the evacuation period at Three Mile Island, friends and neighbors continued to disagree about whether the danger had passed. Baum (1984) reports that the differing perceptions often led to acrimonious debates about nuclear power, the TMI receptors, the trustworthiness of the utility, etc. This prolonged disagreement appeared to cast a shift in social networks such that, even four years after the nuclear reactor accident, more social conflict and neighborhood distrust was found at TMI than in the study's comparison community (Baum, 1984).

Family ties are also threatened by disaster, most obviously when a family member is killed or hospitalized for a long period. Probably the most severe loss a family can experience is the death of one of its members (Mileti, Drabek, & Haas, 1975; Osterweis, Solomon, & Green, 1984). Some evidence exists to suggest that young male adults may be particularly devastated by a sudden, unexpected loss. An epidemiological study of mortality rates reported in the 1950 census found that, among young adults (aged 20 to 34), the group with the highest vulnerability was young widowed males. Their death rate was 2-1/2 to 4 times that of married males the same age (Kraus & Lilienfeld, 1959). Although a number of alternative explanations exist for these findings, Heller (1979) speculates that one factor may be that young men have the least developed networks of social ties to access in times of need.

Even without physical trauma, the financial and emotional strains brought about by disaster may lead to marital or familial discord. Although shared catastrophe sometimes strengthens a marriage, couples may undergo severe strain if they were already experiencing difficulties or are unable to comfort one another (Haas, Kates & Bowden, 1977; Hill & Hansen, 1962). As Wilma O'Callahan, chief of the program in charge of disaster relief for the California Department of Mental Health, describes it:

In traditional families the husband is supposed to save the wife. Then all of a sudden the house may be destroyed, he may be out of work, so in this type of relationship he is no longer considered to be fulfilling his role. It is not uncommon to see six months later a rise in child abuse, spouse abuse, alcoholism and suicide among people who simply cannot manage. (Brozan, 1983, p. 85)

Summary

Social supports are believed to buffer some of the stress associated with crisis and to help individuals cope with the effects of exposure to traumatic events. Research indicates that adequate social support may function to protect victims of crisis from both physical and mental disorder. However, social networks are not always supportive. In disaster situations victims may feel torn between the conflicting needs of different network members. The physical and/or mental effects of disaster exposure may linger for some time, contributing to the stress felt by members of the victim's social network. Behaviors intended to be supportive often fail. Furthermore, disaster may be disruptive of support networks, and the loss of support may be a source of stress in itself.

SOURCES OF SOCIAL SUPPORT

Individuals in need of help typically do not contact formal service agencies, even when the agency is designed to assist with their type of difficulty (Cowen, 1982). Instead, victims of disaster first attempt to solve their own problems; if unsuccessful, they then contact members of their social network for support (Booth & Babchuk, 1972; Croog, Lipson, & Levine, 1972; Quarantelli, 1960; Unger & Powell, 1980). A majority of individuals report knowing at least one intimate associate to whom they can turn for help in times of emergency (Wellman, Craven, Whitaker, Dutoit, & Stevens, 1971). A study of clients of a family service agency in Northern California reports that agency clients tended to be more socially isolated—i.e., belonged to fewer voluntary associations, had fewer friends, had fewer local relatives—than were members of the general community (Kammeyer & Bolton, 1968; see also McKinlay, 1973). These findings lend support to the conclusion that formal service agencies are contacted only as a last resort.

A major reason for both the attractiveness and supportive efficacy of social network members is their status as nonprofessionals. Members of the social network do not attempt to maintain objectivity and distance, but rather involve themselves personally with the individual in need. The interaction is voluntary, reciprocal, and mutually beneficial, since members have the opportunity to both give and receive esteem (Caplan, 1974). Heller (1979) notes that reciprocal support provides maximum mutual benefit by allowing the giver and recipient to alternate roles. He contrasts this relationship with that of professional support, which is characterized by asymmetrical "client" and "helper" roles maintained throughout the course of the relationship. Although professional help is usually presumed to be superior to that provided by informal care-givers, Heller and Monahan (1977) suggest that there may be times when informal support is the treatment of choice. They note the need for research that isolates the conditions under which each type of help is more efficacious (see also Gottlieb, 1976).

In addition to reciprocity, the informal support network offers other advantages over professional modes of intervention. Informal supports tend to be more geographically accessible (Cowen, 1982; Gottlieb, 1976); more consistently available (Heller & Monahan, 1977); less stigmatizing (Cowen, 1982; Gottlieb, 1976); less costly (Cowen, 1982; Gottlieb, 1976); more familiar (Cowen, 1982); and more likely to intervene either prior to or at an early point of problem development (Gottlieb, 1976). All these factors contribute to victims' greater reliance on informal rather than professional sources of support following a traumatic event.

Families

A number of studies of disaster indicate that strong kin relationships before disaster may be highly supportive and can promote successful postdisaster recovery among victims (e.g., Bolin, 1976; Cobb, 1976; Drabek, Key, Erickson, & Crowe, 1975; Eaton, 1978). For example, Froland (1978) found that mental health clients who felt able to rely on family members in times of need reported greater physiological health than clients who relied on voluntary or more transient relationships. The support of family members may be of particular importance to disaster workers, who need understanding and comfort from their families in order to remain compassionate under conditions of sustained stress (Raphael, 1981). Indeed, families are probably the most critical source of emotional, informational, and tangible support available to disaster victims and workers alike (see Figley, 1983). In the vast majority of cases this help is voluntarily offered to kin, without the victim needing to request such assistance (Drabek et al., 1975).

One important social support function performed by relatives is the provision of emergency shelter for evacuees from disaster impact zones (e.g., Loizos, 1977). Drabek and Boggs (1968) found that victims are more likely to take refuge with families than with shelters, when forced to evacuate. Bolin (1984) suggests that evacuation to the homes of relatives places victims in a socially supportive context; when families are separated during evacuation or evacuated to the homes of nonkin, negative psychological reactions are significantly more likely to occur (Boyd, 1981; Instituut voor Sociaal Onderzoek, 1955).

The supportive value of even the kin network has its limits, however. Bolin (1984) indicates that beyond a time frame of about one month the relationship between the host family and the evacuee family begins to deteriorate, because of crowding and financial problems. Furthermore, the more socially or geographically distant the kin, the less able they are to fulfill the needs of victim families (Smith, 1983). In addition, kin tend to be less effective when the disaster is widespread and intense, since kinfolk are likely to be victims as well (Hill & Hansen, 1962; Mileti et al., 1975). Despite these limitations, when the needs of disaster victims are long-term, the kinship group seems more able to offer the required commitment of support than are other community members (Drabek & Boggs, 1968).

Nonkin Ties

Although kin supports are likely to be called into operation in acute as well as chronic disaster situations, these supports are often supplemented by the services of friends, co-workers, neighbors, and acquaintances. The number of linkages to nonkin support systems helps determine the victim's ability to recover; the stronger and greater in number these connections, the greater the resources available to the victim (Drabek & Key, 1976). Barton (1969) indicates that the degree of integration into the community (e.g., via participation in community organizations) affected the extent to which people are aware of hazards, the availability of postimpact assistance, and the appropriate means of accessing such aid. And the sooner victims are able to promptly recover lost possessions or begin to redress damages, the less their likelihood of developing mental health problems such as depression and anxiety (Fried, 1964; Haas et al., 1977; Huerta & Horton, 1978).

While kin networks may be the most important in victims' long-range outcome (Drabek & Boggs, 1968), in the short run, or when kin ties are weak or absent, friend supports appear to play a significant role in successful adaption (Perry & Mushkatel, 1983). Barton (1969) suggests that intact friendship networks provide much postimpact aid, since relatives only infrequently live in close proximity to one another.

In addition to friends, other nonkin community members often called upon to provide emotional support are the local professionals, such as teachers, doctors, clergy, nurses, and police officers. These individuals are knowledgeable in their own sphere but tend to be untrained in mental health (Cowen, 1982; Gottlieb, 1976). That people with emotional problems prefer to turn to these "community gatekeepers" rather than to mental health professionals has been documented in a number of large-scale surveys (Eddy, Paap, & Glad, 1970; Gurin, Veroff, & Feld, 1960; Roberts, Prince, Gold, & Shiner, 1966; Rosenblatt & Mayer, 1972; Ryan, 1969). For example, the Roberts et al. (1966) study presented respondents with a hypothetical child psychiatric problem and asked them who they would go to for assistance in such a case. Forty-eight percent of the respondents indicated they would consult their family doctor, 7% cited a clergyman, and 4% a teacher. None of the mental health professions were mentioned in as great a proportion as any of these gatekeepers.

Caplan (1974) describes another type of support member, the "informal caregiver," who may be either a "generalist" or a "specialist." Generalists tend to be gregarious, naturally helpful individuals, known for their understanding of both human nature and the community service system. They tend to have work roles that bring them into repeated contact with a large number of people; for example, they may be hairdressers, dry cleaners, or grocers. In contrast, the specialists are likely to be people known to have suffered and overcome a particular misfortune. They are sought out for their personal experience with the problem by others who find themselves in the same situation.

Summary

Victims of disaster tend to avoid the use of formal agencies, preferring instead to turn to their informal networks for social support. Of all the members of the victims' social network, kin are probably the most crucial sources of support for the disaster victim's long-term needs. In many instances kin resources are supplemented with assistance from friends, neighbors, co-workers, community gatekeepers, and informal caregivers.

IMPLICATIONS FOR PROFESSIONAL
INTERVENTION

How can victims of disaster be helped to preserve or expand their social support networks? Consideration of the support network is important in planning effective policy, outreach, and service efforts, both prior to and following the development of an emergency.

Predisaster Preparation

Some of the negative psychological impact of disaster can be ameliorated by adequate federal, state, and local preparedness planning in advance of the emergency (Zarle, Hartsough, & Ottinger, 1974). Level of preparedness refers to both planning for the management of disaster impact and planning for aftermath reconstruction (Perry & Mushkatel, 1983). The level and type of preparedness planning affect the extent to which social supports remain intact following a disaster.

Policy. Policymakers should be encouraged to attend to social network factors in planning for emergencies. Particular care should be given to preserving existing social support systems. The importance of doing so is suggested by the findings of a study that attempted to assess the long-term consequences of a flash flood through the analysis of public records (Hall & Landreth, 1975). Only a small segment of the population was found to be exhibiting indications of social stress; however, the authors believed that the Federal Disaster Relief Program, more than the flood itself, had greater impact on social dysfunction.

One important area for policymakers to consider in their planning efforts is relocation. Relocation efforts should include the attempt to retain the natural social groupings of the evacuees (Church, 1973). Disaster victims are often settled in temporary housing located away from both the impact zone and established transportation systems (e.g., Davis, 1977). The use of trailers for such housing may be particularly stressful if the trailers are located in camps specifically constructed for disaster victims (Bolin, 1984). Because trailers are typically assigned on a first-come-first-served basis, these temporary camps do not reflect the social patterns of the neighborhoods from which victims come (Gleser et al., 1981). Planners should consider other methods of housing assignment that take into account existing support networks, and attempt to select locations with easy access to functioning public transportation. When permanent relocation is necessary and separation from previous support networks is unavoidable, victims should be guided toward housing designed so that dwellings and walkways maximize opportunities for the formation of new friendships (see Gottlieb, 1976).

Also worthy of policy attention is the importance of adequate communication during the emergency period. The level of community preparedness is positively associated with the likelihood that citizens will receive sufficient warning of an anticipated disaster (Perry & Mushkatel, 1983). Furthermore, breakdown in communication during the emergency period (one to three days postimpact) may be very stressful for victims unable to locate family members or ascertain the well-being of kin, friends, and neighbors (Bolin, 1984).

Since immediate restoration of telephone service may be difficult in some disaster situations, Bolin suggests establishing alternative methods of communication, such as clearinghouses where impacted residents can register and exchange information regarding whereabouts, health status, etc. Availability of effective communication may be of particular importance to emergency workers, who need information about the scope of the impact and reassurance of the safety of family members in order to effectively perform their jobs (Form & Rosow, 1958).

Social policies that emphasize hospital- or clinic-based rather than home-based mental and physical health services should be recognized as disruptive of existing family and social ties. Suggestive in this regard are study findings indicating that acute heart attack victims randomly assigned by their physicians to home care versus hospital care did not differ in mortality, despite the hospital groups' easier access to emergency equipment and trained personnel (Mather, Pearson, Read, Shaw, Steed, Thorne, Jones, Guerrier, Eraut, McHugh, Chorodbury, Jafary, & Wallace, 1971). Bolin (1982) reports that several respondents in his study of Texas tornado victims had to commute over 50 miles to visit hospitalized family members. The need to travel extensively for several weeks impaired the victims' ability to rebuild their homes and obtain aid, and thus added considerably to the stress and disruptiveness of having a family member injured.

More policy attention should also be given to the issue of transportation. Long-term disruption of transportation systems can create difficulties in accessing social support networks (Trainer & Bolin, 1976). Relocation to temporary housing out of the reach of functioning transportation systems can also have this effect (see earlier discussion). Current social policies governing third-party reimbursement for transportation may permit access to a minibus for health purposes, but are likely to exclude its use for social purposes (Snow & Gordon, 1980). It is important that disaster victims have access not only to relief agencies but to members of their social network as well, since it has been shown that individuals unable to use many sources of transportation tend to be among those least able to meet their needs for social interaction (Evans, 1979). Particularly vulnerable in this regard are the elderly and the disabled, for whom transportation poses a problem even without the disruptive effect of disaster.

Outreach. Effective social support mobilization requires an extensive program of outreach and education. Optimally, the bulk of these efforts will occur *prior* to the emergency, as part of a community's preparedness planning. In order for people to be able to quickly mobilize assistance following a traumatic event, they need to have done so in noncrisis situations.

One community model for mobilizing mental health resources is that of the "neighborhood service center" (Riessman, 1967). When such a service program is already in place and meeting community needs in times of nonemergency, the resources for social support are readily available to victims of trauma when disaster does occur. As described by Riessman (1967), the neighborhood service center is staffed largely by indigenous nonprofessionals from the local area, working under the supervision of a professional mental health specialist. Aimed at preventive intervention, one of the goals of such a program is to provide and expedite services relevant to mental health, with an emphasis on outreach and group services that foster the self-help and mutual obligation characteristic of true social support. A second, interrelated goal is to increase social cohesion by developing various types of groups oriented toward meeting community needs. Once so organized, the center is ideally positioned to educate neighborhood residents in the basics of preparedness planning, and to assist them in organizing support networks for both predisaster planning and postdisaster coping.

Riessman (1967) suggests that outreach to the local population is most successfully accomplished by recruiting nonprofessionals directly from the neighborhoods the agency is attempting to serve (see also Heller, 1979; Reiff, 1967; Silverman, 1976). These paid nonprofessionals may be in a position to accomplish social support functions that the professionals cannot, such as establishing a peer relationship and empathizing with the victim's style of life (Reiff and Riessman, 1965). The indigenous nonprofessional workers are encouraged to play the role of the friendly neighbor who listens sympathetically and provides emotional support (Riessman, 1967). This role is of particular value in working with disaster victims, who are known to shun services labeled "mental health" because of the associated stigma. The indigenous nonprofessional not only discovers and/or educates the citizenry about community needs, but also serves as a social model of active participation, influencing other reference group members in the direction of preventive mental health practices and community preparedness planning (cf. Green, 1970). The indigenous worker is also in a position to identify local key activists and opinion leaders so that their support may be enlisted in mobilizing the community for preparedness planning (see Gottlieb, 1976).

In addition to the use of local nonprofessionals, another method of outreach to social support networks is by means of the local media. In their predisaster planning efforts, communities should develop and distribute public service messages that stress family preparedness for possible disasters, with instructions on how to prepare for both physical and psychological survival of such events (Smith, 1983). Similarly, professional newsletters provide a medium for encouraging businesses to develop disaster plans that train employees in their respective areas of responsibility in the event of different types of emergencies (e.g., Red Cross Disaster Resource Center, 1982).

Postdisaster Activities

Although adequate planning in advance of the emergency is extremely important for subsequent psychological recovery, too often communities find themselves unprepared when disaster strikes (e.g., Zarle et al., 1974). Regardless of how much or how little advance planning has taken place, there are a number of ways in which social support systems may be fostered and utilized to enhance recovery in the aftermath of disaster.

Outreach. After disaster strikes a community, informal social networks can be used to disseminate information about an agency and to generate referrals. Indigenous paraprofessionals may be recruited for postdisaster casefinding (Bowman, 1975; Duffy, 1978; Zarle et al., 1974). The efficacy of these indigenous workers stems in part from their status as reference group members who transmit norms sanctioning the use of professional services. This is especially important because experiencing obvious psychological or physical disaster aftereffects may not in itself be sufficient for a victim to seek professional help; she/he must also perceive the symptoms as interfering with effective functioning, and she/he must perceive help-seeking as sanctioned by her/his support group (Zola, 1973; see also Lieberman, 1982; Wallston et al., 1983).

With or without the assistance of indigenous nonprofessionals, mental health professional staff can enhance the effectiveness of their outreach efforts by the use of network analysis (Llamas, Pattison, & Hurd, 1981; McCallister & Fischer, 1978). Staff should be encouraged to develop skills in helping individuals to establish and maintain networks, as well as in the art of linking individuals with community resources (Mitchell & Trickett, 1980). The latter may involve conducting a preliminary needs and resource assessment of the community, to identify problem areas and high-risk groups. Both paid staff and volunteer services workers should be trained to use an information and referral system, in which a directory of available social services is compiled and used to make appropriate referrals (e.g., Mathews & Fawcett, 1979).

Because social networks serve as major sources of information about and referral to professional services, informal community caregivers and neighborhood leaders can be identified and used to publicize mental health programs. For example, a disaster might affect a neighborhood of low-income elderly who are relatively isolated and unaware of existing formal resources. If network analysis suggested frequent church attendance, the clergy could be used as a source for disseminating information about available mental health programs (Mitchell & Trickett, 1980). Along these lines, Leutz (1976) found that providing information about formal resources to informal caregivers (such as clergy, bartenders, and merchants) increased the number of referrals made by these individuals to social service agencies.

For networking strategies to be effective, program staff must learn to identify network leaders and provide them with (1) consultation for the psychological and health problems that come before them, (2) information about existing community resources, and (3) backup services for problems beyond the capacity of the informal support system (Cohen & Sokolovsky, 1979).

As a final approach to outreach, social support networks can be effectively activated through public service announcements by the media. Newspaper, radio, and television personnel should be educated to go beyond fragmented dramatization of a disaster event, to the role of activating citizenry toward creation of support resources for themselves, as well as of helping victims to identify existing formal resources and available options for rebuilding their community. A good example of this approach is the effort undertaken by the Greater Kansas City Mental Health Information Network following the skywalk collapse of the Kansas City Hyatt Regency Hotel in 1981, a major tragedy in which 114 individuals were killed and over 200 others injured (see Hartsough, 1983). The Network immediately formulated a campaign to provide a coordinated flow of therapeutic messages and information to the local media. Four aspects were consistently stressed: (1) certain distressing reactions are to be expected following a disaster; (2) these are normal responses to an abnormal event; (3) it is important for one's well-being to be accepting of one's own as well as other's feelings, and to share one's feelings with others; and (4) help is available.

Services. Postdisaster mobilization of the support network is important not only in outreach but in service intervention as well. The mental health problems experienced by disaster victims tend not to be psychoses but rather stress-induced symptoms precipitated by countless practical problems victims encounter in the aftermath (Smith, 1983). Practitioners advocate that victims be viewed as normal individuals temporarily disrupted by severe stress (Farberow, 1978). Major goals of mental health disaster intervention include restoring the ability of victims to handle the stresses they experience, and assisting victims in reordering their world through social interaction (Cohen & Ahearn, 1980). Disaster victims need both emotional support and material support in this time of crisis; the mental health worker's role is to facilitate victims' contacts with formal and informal support networks to ensure that both kinds of needs are met. Although assistance efforts may include providing concrete types of help for normal problems of living (Farberow, 1978; Riessman, 1967), too much dependency should be discouraged (Cohen & Ahearn, 1980). Instead, the chief aim should be to foster self-sufficiency by helping victims develop their own resources for recovery (Smith, 1983). Among the most important resources available to the victim is the social support network. Because existing social ties may be disrupted by disaster, an important goal for the mental health professional working with victims is to assist in strengthening these ties and building new ones.

Since kinship bonds may be strained, services should be oriented toward fortifying these relationships. Victims need the opportunity to describe their traumatic experiences, often repeatedly (Figley, 1979). They need an opportunity to ventilate their feelings of anger, guilt, and loss (Grossman, 1973). Some victims may experience emotional, psychosomatic, or behavioral problems following impact (Gleser et al., 1981). Smith (1983) suggests that families who are able to accept and encourage these responses and who foster the quick resumption of normal roles and patterns will speed victims' coping processes. When families are unable to provide an effective stress-buffering environment, professional intervention is needed.

Intervention programs most effectively facilitate recovery when services are planned around the victim's natural support system. Professionals and nonprofessionals alike should be trained in the need to deal with families as units, and in the importance of keeping kin together whenever possible so that family support systems remain intact (Smith, 1983). When a client presents a problem, the mental health professional must first determine whether the difficulty can be handled by the client's existing support system. Family members as well as neighbors and friends may then be contacted and encouraged to increase their participation in the problem, voice their concerns, and implement solutions (Unger & Powell, 1980). Since disaster has a traumatic impact on the whole family, therapy might best be provided to the entire family unit, rather than to only the troubled individual (Smith, 1983).

The mental health professional can show families how to provide a supportive environment for their own members by offering a model of empathic listening, concern, and acceptance, as well as an approach for defining problems and establishing recovery priorities. Professionals assist the family in restoring the normal interactions that children need in order to reestablish a sense of security and familiarity (Blaufarb & Levine, 1972). Since parents often find it difficult to give their children the extra attention they need while also taking care of urgent recovery activities, the mental health worker can suggest ways of involving the children in restoration activities (Smith, 1983). She/he can also direct parents toward available day-care services, one of the most salient needs of parents abruptly faced with a search for new living quarters and other immediate tasks (Levine, 1983; Peuler, 1984).

Nonkinship ties are also important sources of support for services providers to foster. One approach is to direct efforts toward strengthening existing networks that have been disrupted by disaster. Along these lines, Smith (1983) recommends encouraging families to keep active their ties with their neighbors and friends, perhaps by establishing a teamwork approach to postdisaster chores. Families should also be encouraged to devote time to purely recreational activities that maintain social contact with their support network.

Alternatively, mental health professionals may direct their efforts toward facilitating the construction of *new* social support networks for the disaster victim. In this regard, the service agency might foster the development of an active mutual aid system among clients sharing similar problems in coping with the effects of exposure to disaster. Lieberman (1982) makes a distinction between informal social resources and the type of resources provided by a self-help group (see also Gottlieb, 1976). Lieberman (1982) describes self-help groups as "highly bounded systems, requiring more formal and specified exchange than is ordinary in kith or kin relationships . . . . (S)elf-help groups . . . provide social linkages to relevant networks of people who can become friends and confidants" (p. 765).

Mental health professionals are in a position to assist in the establishment of this kind of new support system for disaster victims. Attempts have been made to do so in a number of different disasters, with varying degrees of success (e.g., Grossman, 1973; Hartsough, 1983; Peuler, 1984). For example, Grossman (1973) describes a series of support groups composed of survivors, relatives, and staff members that were organized following a Chicago train wreck. Although attendance was poor, the survivors who did attend considered the sessions to be a vital part of their recovery, since they felt that the lasting effects of their trauma could be fully understood only by those who had shared the experience. Practitioners have made several recommendations for maximizing the success of such disaster support groups: leadership by a nonprofessional mental health aide (Riessman, 1967); short-term, topic-oriented discussions (Levin et al., 1980); sessions tailored to subgroups of victims with common problems (e.g., parent groups, women's groups) (Levin et al., 1980); and sessions held within the community rather than within the (stigmatizing) mental health facility (Farberow, 1978; Hartsough, 1983; Peuler, 1984).

Among the individuals most in need of the help offered by a support group are the disaster relief workers (Cohen & Ahearn, 1980; Dunning & Silva, 1980; Hartsough, 1983; Mitchell, 1982; Peuler, 1984). Dunning and Silva (1980) suggest that rescue organizations should implement stress-debriefing programs that provide for the prevention of stress symptoms through early detection and treatment. These programs require organizational prior commitment and immediate action (24 to 48 hours) following disaster to provide information and encourage communication among workers. In these sessions, emergency workers should be trained to offer emotional support to one another, by discouraging unrealistic self-expectations, by acceptance and understanding of other's on-scene or delayed stress responses, and by demonstrating appreciation for the supportive efforts of fellow workers (Mitchell, 1982). Mitchell suggests that, while an operations critique of the disaster may be needed for improved performance, it should take place separately from the stress-debriefing session. A policy of mandatory (but nonpunitive) attendance of these sessions may be useful in overcoming workers' reluctance to seek help (Hartsough, 1983), in that it reduces the stigma associated with seeking mental health care. However, the rescue organization should also assume responsibility for encouraging workers to seek therapy for more severe manifestations of disaster trauma (Dunning & Silva, 1980). Worker support groups that include family members may also be of benefit, since families need to be aware of behavioral disturbances caused by the traumatic experience and may feel cut off when workers' reactions are not shared with them.

Summary

Adequate preparedness planning can do much to alleviate the trauma experienced by disaster victims. Policymakers should consider ways in which existing social support systems can best be preserved, in planning for relocation, communication, health care, and transportation needs following disaster. Communities best prepared for disaster are those whose mental health needs are being successfully met in noncrisis situations. A neighborhood service center staffed with indigenous nonprofessionals may reach those who would otherwise avoid association with a mental health facility; ongoing support groups may be started by this center and encouraged to include disaster preparedness planning in their community problem-solving efforts. Media public service announcements and business newsletters should include messages that stress the importance of family and organizational disaster preparedness planning.

Much can also be done in the aftermath of disaster to strengthen social support systems. Mental health professionals need to be trained to conduct a network analysis of their communities. Indigenous nonprofessional workers and community gatekeepers should be trained to detect the psychological effects of disaster exposure and to refer individuals with problems to the mental health agency. Media should be encouraged to educate the citizenry in how to maximize their social resources and access formal resources after disaster strikes. Service interventions should be oriented toward strengthening existing kith-and-kin ties, as well as toward developing new sources of social support. Self-help groups for both victims and rescue workers may do much to relieve the emotional burdens experienced by those exposed to the trauma of disaster.

RESEARCH IMPLICATIONS AND
CONCLUSIONS

This chapter indicates that the social support network may be an invaluable resource for victims of disaster and suggests a number of ways in which the support network can be mobilized to assist in the recovery of these individuals. However, it should be noted that many of these conclusions are drawn from naturalistic clinical studies and need to be subjected to rigorous experimental or quasi-experimental testing. The following discussion highlights some of the important issues in need of this kind of research attention.

Research on Social Support

With respect to the effects of social support, many studies indicate that social networks can do much to reduce stress and facilitate coping in the wake of trauma. However, as noted earlier, most of the evidence supporting this conclusion comes from naturalistic and correlational studies, leaving the findings open to alternative interpretation. Research on social support tends to view this construct as a property of the environment to which people have varying degree of access. Wallston et al. (1983) suggest that there is need to also examine characteristics of the target persons that allow them to attract and benefit from support. It may be that deficits in social competence are responsible for the poorer adjustment reported for unsupported individuals; such deficits could also account for the lower levels of support they receive (Heller, 1979). Needed are studies that examine qualities of both the person and the environment in order to fully comprehend the basis for the positive effects of social support.

A causal relationship between social support and adjustment could also be determined by studies in which participants are assigned to treatments that augment the support naturally available to them (Silver & Wortman, 1980). A few studies have attempted to do just that for victims of heart attack (Gruen, 1975), cancer surgery (Ferlic, Goldman, & Kennedy, 1979), and bereavement (Raphael, 1977). Each of these studies supplemented existing social networks with either professional or peer support and found that the interventions produced positive medical and/or psychological effects as compared to control groups receiving no treatment. However, because most of these interventions included a number of components in addition to emotional support (e.g., information, psychotherapy) it is unclear which aspects of the supportive interventions were responsible for the positive benefits. Also, because some components were delivered by professionals, these studies do not contribute to our understanding of natural support systems.

The concept of social support network contains within it a number of different dimensions: amount, quality, type (e.g., emotional, material, informational), and source (e.g., kith, kin, professional). Future research should examine which of these dimensions are most important in determining positive adjustment following trauma, and whether results vary according to the target persons and/or assessed outcomes. Clearly, social support is not needed to the same degree by everyone. Gruen (1975), for example, found a subsample of patients in both his supportive intervention and control groups who were so naturally invulnerable to stress that they did not require any treatment. Furthermore, the social network has been found to produce negative effects as well as positive ones and may at times be viewed as a burden. In Lieberman's (1982) studies of stressful transitions, the strongest relationship between social support and stress reduction was found in individuals' *perceptions* that they had a dependable social network available to them, regardless of whether or not this network was actually used. Along these lines, a recent analysis of data from a large-scale national survey showed perceived support to be more important than received support in predicting adjustment to traumatic events (Wethington & Kessler, 1985). Wethington and Kessler suggest that actual supportive behaviors may be consequential primarily because they reinforce cognitions of support availability.

Relation of Perceived Control Theory to Social Support

One body of cognitive theory that may serve to enlighten future research on social support is that related to perceived control and learned helplessness (Abramson, Seligman, & Teasdale, 1978; Dweck & Wortman, 1980; Glass & Singer, 1972; Seligman, 1975; Wortman & Brehm, 1975). Exposure to negative events perceived as uncontrollable and/or unpredictable has been linked to adverse mental and physical outcomes, such as depression and death (Seligman, 1975). Wallston et al. (1983) suggest that the way in which social support networks influence health is by enhancing perceptions of control over the environment. For example, Schulz (1976) randomly assigned institutionalized elderly to groups who received either regular visits, visits at random, or no visits from college students, and found that the elderly patients receiving regular visits were rated healthier and required less medication than the elderly in either of the other two groups. This work indicates that it is not merely the occurrence of interpersonal contact but its predictability/controllability that contributes to recovery. Schulz and Decker (1982) speculate that social support reduces helplessness by fostering internal attributions, providing assurances of environmental stability, directing attention to positive features of a situation, and proving accurate information for problem solving.

The above theoretical framework may help to explain why social networks have at times been associated with adverse outcomes for victims of traumatic events (see earlier discussion). Emergency workers caught in a conflict between their responsibilities to their organization and their responsibilities to their families may perceive the social network as impeding their ability to control their environment. Similarly, a newfound dependency on loved ones may contribute to deterioration rather than to rehabilitation for injured disaster victims (Croog, 1970). Striking evidence for the importance of control is also offered by the Handford et al. (1983) study, which showed that children of parents who disagreed about the seriousness of the Three Mile Island situation were more distressed than children of parents who agreed in their evaluation of the situation as quite dangerous. This study suggests that perception of parents as stable sources of accurate information may be more crucial to children's sense of control over the environment than the substance of the information itself.

Theories of perceived control and learned helplessness may also explain the deleterious effects associated with loss of support. Lowenthal's (1964) work indicated that lifelong isolates were no more prone to illness than those with adequate support systems and were less vulnerable to physical and psychological impairment than the recently widowed. Again, these findings suggest that the predictability/controllability of social support may be of greater importance to well-being than interpersonal contact per se.

Perceptions of control may also account for some intriguing sex differences found in studies of social support and illness. In their epidemiological study of 1950 census data, Kraus and Lilienfeld (1959) found death rates higher for single men than for single women. Similarly, Strole, Langner, Michael, Kirkpatrick, Opler, & Rennie (1962) found that the rate of psychological impairment for bachelors was much higher than for married men or for women regardless of marital status. Finally, Gleser et al. (1981) found that married women victims of the Buffalo Creek disaster showed higher psychopathology than women victims who lived alone; furthermore, married women were more severely distressed by their spouse's anxiety and/or depression than were married men. In general, women tend to be more upset than men by the traumatic life events experienced by members of their social network (Kessler & McLeod, 1984). All of the above studies support Kessler and McLeod's speculation that social networks may be less often supportive and more often burdensome to women than to men, since women are more likely to be perceived (or perceive themselves) as responsible for the emotional welfare of others (see also Belle, 1982). If women do, indeed, feel less control over the (often greater) emotional demands placed upon them, this could account for relatively less positive effects of social support for women than for men.

Intervention and Implementation Research

The above discussion suggests the need for studies that examine both perceived control and social support on mental and physical health outcomes, in order to better understand the process by which social support mediates reactions to traumatic events. If enhanced sense of control proves to be the basis for the supportive value of social networks, it may also explain victims' preference for seeking assistance from selp-help groups and indigenous nonprofessionals rather than from mental health professionals. Because the relationship with professionals is asymmetrical and nonreciprocal, it may be perceived as a greater threat to self-esteem and autonomy (control) than is the mutual self-help relationship. Needed are studies that provide sound evidence recording the relative effectiveness (i.e., actual helpfulness) of informal caregivers as compared to professionals (Cowen, 1982), as well as the kinds of help each group is best suited to provide.

Also needed is a better understanding of how professionals and natural caregivers can be helped to work together more effectively (see Froland, 1980). One model is a relationship in which the professional identifies key informal caregivers and trains these individuals in basic counseling skills. Two problems are potentially associated with the approach: (1) mental health professionals may be wary of encouraging lay agents to take on mental health problems that exceed their training, and (2) the nonprofessional's basic pattern of relationship may be "trained out," so that precisely those features which attract victims to natural support systems are destroyed (Cowen, 1982; Gottlieb, 1976). Research is needed to determine which, if either, of these concerns is well founded. An alternative model is a collaborative relationship of resource exchange, in which professionals provide natural helping agents with information about formal resources and train them to make more accurate referrals. For this model to be successful, ways must be found to better identify key opinion leaders and to improve the rate at which victims follow through with lay referrals. In this regard, research is needed on both variations in influence among referral agents and methods of improving referral accuracy (Gottlieb, 1976).

When the positive features of social support networks have been identified and interventions that maximize efficacy of support systems have been developed, special efforts must then be made to encourage the implementation of these interventions. Active dissemination efforts are needed to overcome community values that work against the institutionalization of social support programs, such as those that emphasize personal initiative and norms of privacy (Heller, 1979).

This chapter suggests that social networks are potentially important sources of information, comfort, advice, and tangible assistance to disaster victims. Policymakers should be encouraged to consider any possibly disruptive effects on support systems prior to implementing a disaster intervention. Human service workers should look for ways to build on existing social supports in designing their outreach and intervention efforts. Researchers should attempt to identify the underlying mechanisms of social networks that account for their positive effects and incorporate these features into models of service intervention. This kind of attention to social support issues can make a major difference in the extent to which disaster victims successfully cope with trauma.

REFERENCES

Abramson, L. Y., Seligman, M. E. P., & Teasdale, J. (1978). Learned helplessness in humans: Critique and reformation. *Journal of Abnormal Psychology, 87*, 49–74.
Barton, A. (1969). *Communities in disaster.* New York: Doubleday.
Bates, F. L., Fogelman, C. W., Parenton, V. J., Pittman, R. H., & Tracy, G. S. (1963). *The social and psychological consequences of a natural disaster: A longitudinal study of Hurricane Audrey* (Publication No. 1081). Washington, DC: NAS/NRC.
Baum, A. (1984, March). *Disruption during disaster.* Working paper for National Institute of Mental Health Workshop entitled "Mental Health Needs Assessment Following Disaster," Bethesda, MD.
Belle, D. (1982). Social ties and social support. In D. Belle (Ed.), *Lives in stress: Women and depression.* Beverly Hills, CA: Sage Publications.
Blaufarb, H., & Levine, J. (1972). Crisis intervention in an earthquake. *Social Work, 17*, 16–19.
Bolin, R. (1976). Family recovery from natural disaster. *Mass Emergencies, 1*, 267–277.
Bolin, R. (1982). *Long-term family recovery from disaster.* Boulder, CO: Institute of Behavioral Science, University of Colorado.
Bolin, R. (1984, March). *Community disruption and psychosocial impacts.* Working paper for National Institute of Mental Health Workshop entitled "Mental Health Needs Assessment Following Disaster," Bethesda, MD.
Booth, A., & Babchuk, N. (1972). Seeking health care from new resources. *Journal of Health and Social Behavior, 13*, 90–99.
Bowman, S. (1975, August). *Disaster intervention from the inside.* Paper presented at the annual meeting of the American Psychological Association, Chicago, IL.
Boyd, S. (1981). Psychological reactions of disaster victims. *South African Medical Journal, 60*, 744–748.
Brozan, N. (June 27, 1983). Natural disaster: Hidden legacy of pain. *The New York Times.*

Caplan, G. (1974). *Support systems and community mental health: Lectures on concept development*. New York: Behavior Publications.

Church, J. (1973, August). The Buffalo Creek disaster: Extent and range of emotional and/or behavioral problems. In *Picking up the pieces: Disaster intervention and human ecology*. Symposium presented at the annual meeting of the American Psychological Association in Montreal, Canada.

Cobb, S. (1976). Social support as a moderator of life stress. *Psychosomatic Medicine, 38,* 300–314.

Cobb, S. (1979). Social support and health through the life course. In M. White Riley (Ed.), *Aging from birth to death: Interdisciplinary perspectives*. Boulder, CO: Westview Press.

Cobb, S., & Kasl, S. (1977). *Termination: The consequences of job loss* (Publication #LR77-224). Washington, DC: DHEW (NIOSH).

Cohen, C. I., & Sokolovsky, J. (1979). Clinical use of network analysis for psychiatric and aged populations. *Community Mental Health Journal, 15*(3), 203–213.

Cohen, R. E., & Ahearn, F. L. (1980). *Handbook for mental health care of disaster victims*. Baltimore: The Johns Hopkins University Press.

Cowen, E. L. (1982). Help is where you find it: Four informal helping groups. *American Psychologist, 37*(4), 385–395.

Croog, S. H. (1970). The family as a source of stress. In S. Levine & N. A. Scotch (Eds.), *Social stress*. Chicago: Aldine Publishing Co.

Croog, S., Lipson, A., & Levine, S. (1972). Help patterns in severe illness: The role of kin network, non-family resources, and institutions. *Journal of Marriage and the Family, 34,* 32–41.

Davis, I. (1977). Emergency shelter. *Disasters, 1*(1), 23–40.

Dean, A., & Lin, D. (1977). The stress-buffering role of social support: Problems and prospects for systematic investigation. *Journal of Nervous and Mental Disease, 165,* 403–417.

DiMatteo, M. R., & Hays, R. (1981). Social support and serious illness. In B. H. Gottlieb (Ed.), *Social networks and social support*. Beverly Hills, CA: Sage.

Drabek, T. E., & Boggs, K. S. (1968). Families in disaster: Reactions and relatives. *Journal of Marriage and the Family, 30,* 443–451.

Drabek, T. E., & Key, W. H. (1976). The impact of disaster on primary group linkages. *Mass Emergencies, 1,* 89–105.

Drabek, T. E., Key, W. H., Erickson, P. E., & Crowe, J. L. (1975). The impact of disaster on kin relationships. *Journal of Marriage and the Family, 37*(3), 481–494.

Duffy, J. C. (1978). Emergency mental health services during and after a major aircraft accident. *Disasters, 2*(213), 159–162.

Dunning, C., & Silva, M. (1980). Disaster-induced trauma in rescue workers. *Victimology: An International Journal, 5*(2–4), 287–297.

Dweck, C. S., & Wortman, C. B. (1980). Achievement, test anxiety and learned helplessness: Adaptive and maladaptive cognitions. In H. W. Krohne & L. Laux (Eds.), *Achievement stress and anxiety*. Washington, DC: Hemisphere.

Eaton, W. W. (1978, June). Life events, social supports and psychiatric symptoms: A reanalysis of the New Haven data. *Journal of Health and Social Service,* 230–234.

Eddy, W. B., Paap, S. M., & Glad, D. D. (1970). Solving problems in living: The citizen's viewpoint. *Mental Hygiene, 54,* 64–72.

Elliott, G. R., & Eisdorfer, C. (Eds.) (1982). *Stress and human health: Analysis and implications of research*. New York: Springer Publishing Company.

Evans, L. K. (1979). *The relationship of need awareness, locus of control, health state, and social support system to social interaction as a form of self-care behavior among elderly residents of public housing*. Unpublished doctoral dissertation.

Farberow, N. L. (1978). *Training manual for human service workers in major disasters*. Rockville, MD: National Institute of Mental Health.

Ferlic, M., Goldman, A., & Kennedy, B. J. (1979). Group counseling in adult patients with advanced cancer. *Cancer, 43*, 760–766.

Figley, C. R. (1979, May). *Combat as disaster: Treating combat veterans as survivors.* Invited presentation at the annual meeting of the American Psychiatric Association, Chicago, IL.

Figley, C. R. (1983). Catastrophes: An overview of family reactions. In C. R. Figley and H. I. McCubbin (Eds.), *Stress and the family, Vol. II: Coping with catastrophe.* New York: Brunner/Mazel.

Form, W. H., & Rosow, S. (1958). *Community in disaster.* New York: Harper.

Fried, M. (1964). Effects of social change on mental health. *American Journal of Orthopsychiatry, 34*, 3–28.

Froland, C. G. (1978). *Improving the social adjustment of mental health clients: The case for social support networks.* Unpublished doctoral dissertation.

Froland, C. (1980). Formal and informal care: Discontinuities in a continuum. *Social Service Review, 54*(4), 572–587.

Garaventa, D. (1983, April). Personal communication, Marin County Community Mental Health Services, San Rafael, CA.

Garrison, J. (1983). *Mental health issues in relocation.* Unpublished manuscript, National Institutes of Mental Health.

Garrity, T. F. (1973). Vocational adjustment after first myocardial infarction; comparative assessment of several variables suggested in the literature. *Social Science and Medicine, 7*, 705–717.

Gerber, I., Weiner, A., Battin, D., & Arkin, A. (1975). Brief therapy to the aged bereaved. In B. Schoenberg, I. Gerber, A. Weiner, A. H. Kutscher, D. Peretz, & A. C. Carr (Eds.), *Bereavement: Its psychosocial aspects.* New York: Columbia University Press, 1975.

Glass, D. C., & Singer, J. R. (1972). *Urban stress: Experiments on noise and social stressors.* New York: Academic Press.

Gleser, G. C., Green, B. L., & Winget, C. (1981). *Prolonged psychosocial effects of disaster: A study of Buffalo Creek.* New York: Academic Press.

Gore, S. (1978). The effect of social support in moderating the health consequences of unemployment. *Journal of Health and Social Behavior, 19*, 157–165.

Gottlieb, B. H. (1976). Lay influences on the utilization and provision of health services: A review. *Canadian Psychological Review, 17*(2), 126–136.

Green, L. W. (1970). Should health education abandon attitude change strategies? Perspectives from recent research. *Health Education Monographs, 30*, 25–48.

Grossman, L. (1973). Train crash: Social work and disaster services. *Social Work, 18*(5), 38–44.

Gruen, W. (1975). Effects of brief psychotherapy during the hospitalization period on the recovery process in heart attacks. *Journal of Consulting and Clinical Psychology, 43*, 225–232.

Gurin, G., Veroff, J., & Feld, S. (1960). *Americans view their mental health: A national survey.* New York: Basic Books.

Haas, J. E., Kates, R. W., & Bowden, M. J. (Eds.) (1977). *Reconstruction following disaster.* Cambridge, MA: MIT Press.

Haggerty, R. H. J. (1980). Life stress, illness and social support. *Developmental Medicine and Child Neurology, 22*, 391–400.

Hall, P. S., & Landreth, P. W. (1975). Assessing some long-term consequences of a natural disaster. *Mass Emergencies, 1*, 55–61.

Hamburg, B. A., & Killilea, M. (1979). Relation of social support, stress, illness, and use of health services. In *Healthy people: The surgeon general's report on health promotion and disease prevention* (Background Papers). Washington, DC: US Government Printing Office.

Handford, H. A., Mayes, S. D., Mattison, R. E., Humphrey, F. J., Bagnato, S., Bixler, E.

O., & Kales, J. D. (1983, December). *Three Mile Island nuclear accident: A disaster study of child and parent reaction.* Paper presented at the "Conference on Methodological Issues involving the Study of Children and their Families Exposed to Disaster," sponsored by the American Academy of Child Psychiatry and the National Institute of Mental Health, Airlie House, VA.

Hartsough, D. (1983). *Mitigating the emotional consequences of disaster work: A guide for training and debriefing.* Unpublished manuscript, Purdue University.

Heller, K. (1979). The effects of social support: Prevention and treatment implications. In A. P. Goldstein & F. H. Kanfer (Eds.), *Maximizing treatment gains: Transfer enhancement in psychotherapy.* New York: Academic Press.

Heller, K., & Monahan, J. (1977). *Psychology and community change.* Homewood, IL: Dorsey Press.

Hill, R., & Hansen, D. (1962). Families in disaster. In G. Baker & D. Chapman (Eds.), *Man and society in disaster.* New York: Basic Books.

Horowitz, M. J., & Wilner, N. (1980). Life events, stress and coping. In L. Poon (Ed.), *Aging in the 1980's: Selected contemporary issues.* Washington, DC: American Psychological Association.

Huerta, F., & Horton, R. (1978). Coping behavior of elderly flood victims. *The Gerontologist, 18*(6), 541–546.

Instituut voor Sociaal Onderzoek van her Nederlandse Volk Amsterdam (1955). *Studies in the Holland flood disaster of 1953* (Vol. I–IV). Washington, DC: NAS/NRC.

Jeffers, C. (1967). *Living poor: A participant observer study of choices and priorities.* Ann Arbor, MI: Ann Arbor Publishing.

Kahn, R. L., & Antonucci, T. (1980). Convoys over the life course: Attachment roles and social support. In P. B. Baltes & O. Brim (Eds.), *Life-span development and behavior* (Vol. 3). Boston: Lexington.

Kammeyer, K. C. W., & Bolton, C. D. (1968). Community and family factors related to the use of a family service agency. *Journal of Marriage and the Family, 30,* 488–498.

Kaplan, B. H., Cassel, J. C., & Gore, S. (1977). Social support and health. *Medical Care, 15,* 47–58.

Kellner, R. (1966). *Family ill health: An investigation in general practice.* Philadelphia: Lippincott.

Kelman, H. R., Lowenthal, M., & Muller, J. N. (1966). Community status of discharged rehabilitational patients: Results of a longitudinal study. *Archives of Physical Medicine and Rehabilitation, 47,* 670–675.

Kemp, B. J., & Vash, C. L. (1971). Productivity after injury in a sample of spinal cord injured persons: A pilot study. *Journal of Chronic Diseases, 24,* 259–275.

Kessler, R., & McLeod, D. (1984, October). Sex differences in vulnerability to undesirable life events. *American Sociological Review, 49,* 620–631.

Killian, L. M. (1952). The significance of multiple group membership in disaster. *American Journal of Sociology, 57*(4), 309–314.

Korsching, P. F., Donnermeyers, J. F., & Burdge, R. J. (1980). Perception of property settlement payments and replacement housing among displaced-persons. *Human Organization, 39*(4), 332–338.

Kraus, A. S., & Lilienfeld, A. M. (1959). Some epidemiologic aspects of the high mortality rate in the young widowed group. *Journal of Chronic Diseases, 10,* 207–217.

Leutz, W. N. (1976). The informal community caregiver: A link between the health care system and local residents. *American Journal of Orthopsychiatry, 46,* 678–688.

Levin, S. S., Groves, A. C., & Lurie, J. D. (1980). Sharing the move—Support groups for relocated women. *Social Work, 25*(4), 323–325.

Levine, A. G. (1983). *Love Canal: Science, politics and people.* Lexington, MA: Lexington Books.

Lewis, C. E. (1966). Factors influencing the return to work of men with congestive heart failure. *Journal of Chronic Diseases, 19,* 1193–1209.

Lieberman, M. A. (1982). The effects of social supports on responses to stress. In L. Goldberger & S. Breznitz (Eds.), *Handbook of stress: Theoretical and clinical aspects.* New York: Free Press.

Lin, N. R., Simeone, S., Ensel, W. M., & Kuo, W. (1979). Social support, stressful life events, and illness: A model and an empirical test. *Journal of Health and Social Behavior, 20,* 108–119.

Litman, T. J. (1962). The influence of self-conception and life orientation factors in the rehabilitation of the orthopedically disabled. *Journal of Health and Human Behavior, 3,* 249–256.

Llamas, R., Pattison, E. M., & Hurd, G. S. (1981). Social networks: A link between psychiatric epidemiology and community mental health. *International Journal of Family Therapy, 3,* 180–193.

Loizos, P. (1977). A struggle for meaning: Reactions to disaster amongst Cypriot refugees. *Disasters, 1*(3), 231–239.

Lowenthal, M. (1964). Social isolation and mental illness in old age. *American Sociological Review, 29,* 54–70.

Lowenthal, M., & Haven, C. (1968). Interaction and adaption: Intimacy as a critical variance. *American Sociological Review, 33,* 20–30.

Mather, H. G., Pearson, N. G., Read, K. L. Q., Shaw, D. B., Steed, G. R., Thorne, M. G., Jones, S., Guerrier, C. J., Eraut, C. D., McHugh, P. M., Chorodbury, N. R., Jafary, M. H., & Wallace, T. J. (1971). Acute myocardial infarction: Home and hospital treatment. *British Medical Journal, 3,* 334–338.

Mathews, R. M., & Fawcett, S. B. (1979). Community information systems: Analysis of an agency referral program. *Journal of Community Psychology, 7,* 281–289.

McCallister, L., & Fischer, C. S. (1978). A procedure for surveying personal networks. *Sociological Methods and Research, 7,* 131–148.

McKinlay, J. B. (1973). Social networks, lay consultation and help-seeking behavior. *Social Forces, 51,* 275–292.

Mileti, D. S., Drabek, T. E., & Haas, J. E. (1975). *Human systems in extreme environments: A sociological perspective* (Monograph #21). Boulder, CO: Institute of Behavioral Science, University of Colorado.

Mitchell, J. T. (fall, 1982). Recovery from rescue. *Response Magazine,* 7–10.

Mitchell, R. E., & Trickett, E. J. (1980). Task force report: Social networks as mediators of social support: An analysis of the effects and determinants of social networks. *Community Mental Health Journal, 16,* 27–44.

Osterweis, M., Solomon, F., & Green, M. (Eds.) (1984). *Bereavement: Reactions, consequences, and care* (ISBN 0-309-03438-8). Washington, DC: National Academy Press.

Perry, R. W., & Mushkatel, A. H. (1983). *Psychosocial consequences of emergencies in the natural environment: The case of volcanic eruptions.* Unpublished manuscript, Arizona State University.

Peuler, J. (1984, May). *Innovations in family and community outreach in times of disaster.* Paper presented at the National Institute of Mental Health symposium on "Innovations in Mental Health Care of Victims," Washington, DC.

Quarentelli, E. L. (1960). A note on the protective function of the family in disaster. *Journal of Marriage and Family Living, 22,* 263–264.

Raphael, B. (1977). Preventive interview with the recently bereaved. *Archives of General Psychiatry, 34,* 1450–1454.

Raphael, B. (1981). Personal disaster. *Australian and New Zealand Journal of Psychiatry, 15*(3), 183–198.

Red Cross Disaster Resource Center (1982). *San Francisco corporate disaster plan.* San Francisco: Red Cross.

Reiff, R. (1967). Mental health manpower and institutional charge. In E. L. Cowen, E. A. Gardner, and M. Zax (Eds.), *Emergent approaches to mental health problems.* New York: Appleton-Century-Crofts.

Reiff, R., & Riessman, F. (1965). The indigenous nonprofessional. *Community Mental Health Journal*, Monograph No. 1.

Riessman, F. (1967). A neighborhood-based mental health approach. In E. L. Cowen, E. A. Gardner, & M. Zax (Eds.), *Emergent approaches to mental health problems*. New York: Appleton-Century-Crofts.

Roberts, J., Prince, R., Gold, B., & Shiner, E. (1966). *Social and mental health survey: Summary report*. Montreal, Quebec: Mental Hygiene Institute.

Rosenblatt, A., & Mayer, J. E. (1972). Help seeking for family problems: A survey of utilization and satisfaction. *American Journal of Psychiatry, 128*(9), 126–130.

Ryan, W. (1969). *Distress in the city: Essays in the design and administration of urban mental health services*. Cleveland: The Press of Case Western Reserve University.

Schaefer, C., Coyne, J. C., & Lazarus, R. S. (1981). The health-related functions of social support. *Journal of Behavioral Medicine, 4*(4), 381–406.

Schulz, R. (1976). Effects of control and predictability on the physical and psychological well-being of the institutionalized aged. *Journal of Personality and Social Psychology, 33*, 562–573.

Schulz, R., & Decker, S. (1982). Social support, adjustment, and the elderly spinal cord injured: A social psychological analysis. In G. Weary & H. L. Mirels (Eds.), *Integrations of clinical and social psychology*. New York: Oxford University Press.

Seligman, M. E. P. (1975). *Helplessness: On depression, development and death*. San Francisco: W. H. Freeman.

Silver, R. L., & Wortman, C. B. (1980). Coping with undesirable life events. In J. Garber & M. E. P. Seligman (Eds.), *Human helplessness: Theory and applications*. New York: Academic Press.

Silverman, P. R. (1976). The widow as caregiver in a problem of preventive intervention with other widows. In G. Caplan & M. Killilea (Eds.), *Support systems and mutual help: Multidisciplinary explorations*. New York: Grune & Stratton.

Smith, S. M. (1983). Disaster: Family disruption in the wake of disaster. In C. R. Figley & H. I. McCubbin (Eds.), *Stress and the family, Volume II: Coping with catastrophe*. New York: Brunner/Mazel.

Smits, S. J. (1974). Variables related to success in a medical rehabilitation setting. *Archives of Physical Medicine and Rehabilitation, 55*, 449–454.

Snow, D. L., & Gordon, J. B. (1980). Social network analysis and intervention with the elderly. *Gerontologist, 20*(4), 463–467.

Stack, C. (1974). *All our kin: Strategies for survival in a black community*. New York: Harper & Row.

Strole, L., Langner, T. S., Michael, S. T., Kirkpatrick, P., Opler, M. K., & Rennie, T. A. C. (1962). *Mental health in the metropolis: The midtown Manhattan study*. New York: McGraw-Hill.

Trainer, P., & Bolin, R. (1976). Persistent effects of disasters on daily activities: A cross-cultural comparison. *Mass Emergencies, 1*, 279–290.

Unger, D. G., & Powell, D. G. (1980). Supporting families under stress: The role of social networks. *Family Relations, 29*, 566–574.

Visotsky, H. M., Hamburg, D. A., Goss, M. E., & Lebovits, B. Z. (1961). Coping behavior under extreme stress. *Archives of General Psychiatry, 5*, 423–448.

Wallston, B. S., Alagna, S. W., DeVellis, B. M., & DeVellis, R. F. (1983). Social support and physical health. *Health Psychology, 2*(4), 367–391.

Wellman, B., Craven, P., Whitaker, M., Dutoit, S., & Stevens, H. (1971). *The uses of community: Community ties and support systems*. Toronto, Ontario: Center for Urban and Community Studies, University of Toronto.

Western, J. S., & Milne, G. (1979). Some social effects of a natural hazard: Darwin residents and Cyclone Tracy. In R. L. Heathcote & B. G. Thom (Eds.), *Natural hazards in Australia*. Canberra: Australia Academy of Science.

Wethington, E., & Kessler, R. (1985). *Perceived support, received support and adjustment to stressful life events.* Unpublished manuscript, University of Michigan.

Wilson, C. (1983, June). Personal communication. Four-County Mental Health Services, St. Louis, MO.

Wortman, C. B., & Brehm, J. W. (1975). Responses to uncontrollable outcomes: An integration of reactance theory and the learned helplessness model. In L. Berkowitz (Ed.), *Advances in experimental social psychology* (Vol. 8). New York: Academic Press.

Wortman, C. B., & Dunkel-Schetter, C. (1979, May). *Dilemmas of social support: Parallels between victimization and aging.* Paper presented at the National Research Council Committee on Aging Workshop entitled "The Future of the Elderly," Annapolis, MD.

Zarle, T. H., Hartsough, D. M., & Ottinger, D. R. (1974). Tornado recovery: The development of a professional-paraprofessional response to a disaster. *Journal of Community Psychology, 2*(4), 311–320.

Zola, I. K. (1973). Pathways to the doctor—From person to patient. *Social Science and Medicine, 7,* 677–689.

12

Post-Traumatic Stress and the Family: A Multimethod Approach to Counseling

ANGIE D. HERNDON and JOSEPH G. LAW, Jr.

There is a growing body of research which indicates that a large number of Vietnam veterans are currently suffering from stress disorders (Frye & Stockton, 1982; Center for Policy Research, 1980). Frye and Stockton surveyed 88 veterans who had served in Vietnam as officers. Using a symptom checklist and DSM-III criteria of post-traumatic stress disorder (PTSD), Frye and Stockton found that 43% of the respondents had symptoms of PTSD. If these data could be generalized to the 2.6 million population of Vietnam veterans, then we would expect 1,118,000 veterans to be in need of professional assistance at some time following their discharge. The Veterans Administration has responded to this extensive need for readjustment counseling by starting Operation Outreach with 136 Vet Centers throughout the country (Blank, 1982). While the Vet Center program also attempts to meet the needs of women Vietnam veterans, this paper will focus only on PTSD and the male veteran and the effect on his family. The aim of this article is to detail some of the techniques that we in the Vet Center program have been using to work with this special population of clients.

When counseling Vietnam veterans, the counselor becomes aware of intense feelings of pain, suffering, isolation, alienation, grief, and loneliness. Many veterans try to block those feelings, but few succeed. They may numb themselves with alcohol, drugs, or by being overachieving workaholics. It is as though the veteran's feelings are encapsulated in airtight bubbles floating around in his psyche, waiting to pop up at some unexpected time and zap him. While there are many issues that need to be explored, it seems that the most painful immediate problems center around relationships. The veterans want to have meaningful and loving relationships, but feel they are not able to love. There seems to be something that won't let them love, care, or be loved by others. They wonder, "What is wrong with me?" "Why can't I be like everybody else?" In attempts to be "normal" many veterans may even be going through the motions of feeling. They get married, have children, and appear to be fitting into what society expects, but they are not receiving meaning or satisfaction from their activities. Many find themselves acting out the form of a role, without the substance. Thus, the give and take of an intimate relationship is acted out, without emotional involvement (Wilson, 1980).

We realize that an emphasis on military experience alone cannot be used as an excuse for family problems with Vietnam veterans. It would be a mistake to assume that a family of a veteran seeking counseling does so because of war experiences alone or that such counseling must deal exclusively with the war experiences. The aim of this chapter is not to disregard other psychological issues but to understand how war experiences may be functioning now in the family dynamics. The counselor should not respond from a fixed notion of a hidden agenda (that all problems are rooted in war experience alone), nor must the sensitive counselor ignore the profound effects of the war experience on family life. A successful program should deal with the stress disorder as part of the family system. However, the "psychic numbing" (Wilson, 1980, p. 148) we have described can contribute significantly to marital disharmony and personal maladjustment. Conversely, successful counseling can have a beneficial impact on marital adjustment. For example, Hendin (1983) has reported a case study of a Vietnam veteran whose improvement from individual counseling carried over into his family life, with increased marital satisfaction an indirect result of the counseling for a stress disorder.

The presenting problems that bring veterans to counseling are usually enmeshed in the veteran's interpersonal network (Figley, 1976). The family often takes on the burden of feelings of guilt, anxiety, alienation, flashbacks, and nightmares. The wives and children of veteran clients have reported quite frequently how preoccupation with Vietnam-generated problems negatively affects family life. For example, vivid flash-backs and nightmares can be terrifying to a veteran's family. When a veteran is preoccupied with guilt or experiencing extreme anxiety, he is unable to interact in a loving and responsive way to his spouse and children. Ameliorating these problems can be a long and involved process that requires utilizing many counseling techniques and modalities.

Some experts in the field of counseling Vietnam veterans believe that group counseling is the preferred mode (Williams, 1980); others place a stronger emphasis on individual sessions (Figley, 1982). To date there has been a paucity of outcome research, and most of the literature is anecdotal in nature. Our experience has been that veterans with moderate or severe stress disorders are extremely reluctant to join a group of engage in much self-disclosure during group sessions. For many, 10 or more individual sessions with a counselor are necessary to develop the ego strength to benefit from a group experience.

We have found a three-phase counseling process to be effective in helping the veteran and the family. In the first phase of counseling, individual sessions are beneficial in helping the client work through the denial phase in processing the painful emotions associated with wartime trauma. In the second phase of counseling a group composed of other combat veterans gives the client an opportunity to rework through the issues discussed in the individual sessions. In addition, the group provides an opportunity for the veterans to learn skills for relating to others' feelings and experiences, to learn skills for listening and understanding others, and offers support as they begin to set goals and try out new behaviors during the readjustment process. Also, during the second phase of counseling a group for significant others is provided to help the family understand something about the trauma of war, the veteran's readjustment process, and how the effects of both are presently functioning in the marriage relationship. In the third phase of counseling a couples' group is formed. The purpose of this group is to focus on specific goals regarding the veteran's relationship to significant others and to serve as a catalyst for readjustment in many areas of the veterans' and their families' lives.

THE VETERAN'S STRUGGLE

Vietnam veterans do have unique concerns that keep them from dealing with their problems. They are different in that they have experienced a deliberate numbing of emotions and feelings that were associated with some traumatic events in their lives that need to be worked through. Since the average age of the Vietnam soldier was 19 years of age, we are basically talking about individuals between the ages of 17 and 21 being exposed to situations for which they did not have well-defined coping techniques or defenses developed. The defenses and techniques that they learned to deal with these situations have now become a part of their character and personality because they did not already have an established identity to fall back on later when these same coping mechanisms were no longer useful or adaptive. They have confused their warrior role with their essence of being. They set their life and approach reality through these role definitions. Trained to block ability to respond to inner promptings both emotionally and psychologically, they mask their feelings about themselves and block off the possibilities of a genuine encounter with another person. The warrior image manifests itself many times indirectly through emotional detachment, interpersonal withdrawal, and passivity in relationships with women. They now experience themselves as individuals who cannot love or trust and that is "Who I am."

This sense of identity centers around the theme of not being able to feel or get close to anyone. They become an emotional ice cube. They also begin to question the whole idea of their identity having any meaning anyway. That is, even if I know who I am, it does not matter. It's not important. Metaphorically they are an ice cube, numb, cold. They've decided that their identity should be something other than what it is; so they create an identity by getting married, having children, and going to work. However, deep down they still feel numb and experience that feeling as one that is not normal. They give off the outward behavior and they may even show what looks like love. It looks like care. It looks like reaching out. There may even be tears when they talk about these feelings. But they say, "I don't feel it inside." They don't experience the emotional involvement. There is a separation of behavior and experience. They don't feel what they are doing. As one veteran described his experience, "I feel like I am standing on the other side of a window looking in, but it's not really me; I'm outside myself; watching what's happening."

Each veteran seems to still be working through the grief cycle as described by Brammer and Abrego (1981). Many have been shocked and immobilized by a traumatic war experience from which they have failed to recover. Many experience strong denial by avoiding anything that reminds them of the war. Despite the denial, large numbers of veterans begin to experience depression, anxiety, loss of self-esteem, and other problems. They need assistance in navigating through the cycle—the emotional letting go, testing of options, and search for meaning described so well by Brammer and Abrego (1981).

INDIVIDUAL SESSIONS

For most veterans 10 or more individual sessions are necessary to develop the ego strength needed to benefit from a group experience. As the veteran's perceptions and feelings regarding his wartime experiences are explored, there are intense emotional reactions and much anxiety. The veteran experiences mood swings from despair to elation. At one session the client may relate utter despair that he will ever feel "normal" again. However, at another session the veteran may be elated and express the feeling that everything is so much better now in his life.

The veteran usually needs 3 to 4 sessions to talk about what happened in Vietnam relative to his combat experiences and the specific stressors he encountered. As the veteran relates the combat experiences and stressors, the counselor helps the veteran become aware of the meanings those experiences have for him.

The next 3 to 4 sessions focus on the veteran's current readjustment and problems. The counselor helps the veteran explore what happened when he first returned from Vietnam and what is going on in his current life. As the veteran talks about his return home after Vietnam and his current life situations he usually expresses much self-doubt about his ability to cope with life and his own sense of being a competent individual. The veteran doubts his own self. Most veterans express extreme concern about their ability to relate to other people, to hold a job, and to enjoy life. They tend to cut themselves off from many relationships and experiences out of a fear of losing control. For instance, many veterans will not go hunting because they do not trust themselves with a gun. Many withdraw from relationships rather than work through interpersonal problems in the relationship out of fear of reacting violently.

During these sessions the counselor becomes aware of initial readjustment problems faced by the veteran on his return home, the processes the veteran has gone through in order to readjust to being home, and the current life situation. The counselor helps the veteran to explore the current life situation in relationship to the meanings the veteran ascribes to his present life-style.

The next 3 to 4 sessions focus on the meanings ascribed to experiences in Vietnam and the meanings ascribed to the veteran's current readjustment problems. The veteran is confronted with how the meanings from Vietnam are functioning in his present life. On relating his combat experiences and stressors while in Vietnam, one veteran kept saying, "It doesn't matter anyway, there is nothing I can do about it." This was the same meaning he attributed to his current life situations and his present way of dealing with the world.

As the veteran begins to realize the effect these past meanings are having in his life, differential approaches are developed to help the veteran deal with the past attributions, feelings, and behaviors that are functioning in his present life.

Some of the treatment techniques that are used are problem solving, learning self-control of aggression, cognitive restructuring, evaluation of belief systems, exposure to guided imagery, systematic desensitization, and flooding.

Through the problem-solving approach, the veteran learns to state his problems in specific and concrete terms, to look at his present ways of dealing with these problems and the consequence of his present ways of responding to the problems, to explore alternative ways of responding to the problem, the possible consequences of the alternative reactions, and results of these responses. The veteran is helped to explore his values: what he really wants out of life, what he considers worthwhile and what he would like to be happening in his life, to develop plans to move toward the values that he accepts, commitment to those values, and to develop priorities so he can in fact reach the goals that he wants to reach.

Self-control of aggression helps the veteran to manage the distress that results in his aggressive acts. This can be developed through learning covert assertion, which involves learning the skills of interruption and substitution and the skill of stress inoculation. At the first hint of a habitual thought that has in the past led to aggression, the client learns to deal with the unpleasant emotions by interrupting the thought by using the word "stop" or some other interruptive technique. He then fills the void left by the interruptive thought by previously prepared positive thoughts that are more realistic, assertive, and constructive. By acquiring these skills he is more able to successfully cope with thoughts that have in the past led to aggressive behavior. The veteran is also taught self-control of aggression by learning stress inoculation techniques. He learns how to prepare for possible provocation, how to confront the provocation successfully, how to cope with the unpleasant arousal by learning relaxation techniques.

Many veterans have developed distorted thinking patterns based on their past attributions, feelings, and behaviors that are no longer successful coping devices. They are encouraged and helped to explore and evaluate their belief systems by describing the painful emotions that these beliefs lead to, describing the situation and events that surround the painful emotion, their thoughts about the situation and emotional experience, and to identify any possible distortion that they may have that has brought about the painful emotion. As the veteran becomes aware of any distorted thinking patterns, he is helped to develop ways to combat those distortions.

The guided imagery techniques can be beneficial to the veteran as he prepares himself to become more effective in functioning in and relating to the world. Through the use of fantasy and imagery rehearsal, the veteran can mentally play through particular behaviors and events and try out new approaches to effectively cope with his world.

For veterans dealing with the problem of an exaggerated startle response or nightmares, systematic desensitization and flooding has been found to be a useful technique. Prolonged and repeated imaginal exposure to the aversive events surrounding the individual's trauma can result in extinction of the exaggerated startle response and nightmares.

The last few individual sessions focus on the veteran's struggles with guilt about what he did in Vietnam, did not do in Vietnam, and loyalty to the dead. The final stages of the individual counseling phase focus on assimilating the past so that it will help propel the client toward finding personal meaning in his experiences and in setting reachable goals to sustain and fulfill that meaning. It is at this phase in the counseling process that a group composed of other combat veterans can be beneficial to the client. The group can offer the needed emotional support to continue to work through the wartime traumas.

RAP GROUPS

There are differences of opinion between experts on the relative merits of group counseling for veterans with post-traumatic stress disorder. Williams (1980) is an enthusiastic supporter of group counseling as the treatment of choice for veterans with PTSD, but Figley (1982) believes that the group method is limited in its utility. Figley believes that a group setting is appropriate only for veterans with mild cases of PTSD and that extensive individual sessions are needed to completely deal with the problems of Vietnam. The approach described in this article is basically a synthesis of many schools of thought and attempts to integrate individual and group approaches.

While our practical experience has been that veterans need individual sessions to begin to deal with war-related trauma, we have found that a group experience is often necessary to complete the healing process. Following individual sessions in which traumatic memories are desensitized, relaxation and stress management techniques are taught, and the veteran begins a search for the meaning of his Vietnam experiences, we talk to the veteran about attending weekly rap groups. Often, the veteran is reluctant to discuss any of his past or present problems in a group environment. However, we explain to him that he will be in a group of fellow combat veterans, many of whom have experienced similar problems. We emphasize to the veteran that his fellow group members will have experienced similar problems and will be understanding of his attempts to cope.

In presenting the topic of group sessions to the veteran, we have found it useful to use the analogy of the World War II transports. We explain to the veteran that following World War II, returning soldiers came home on ocean transports, which often took months to arrive in the United States. We explain that this allowed the veterans to talk among themselves about their experiences and get it all off their chests. It is suggested to the veteran that a rap group will meet this same need and allow him to share his feelings with others, much as his predecessors did following World War II.

In using the terminology rap group, there is an attempt to communicate to the veteran that he will be engaged in a group process that is primarily peer group counseling as opposed to intensive psychotherapy. Using the term rap group is to counter any hesitation the veteran may have about participating in the group. However, it does not mean that the group experience is shallow or superficial. Hopefully, the rap group experience will touch upon and liberate intense feelings and memories. The fact that veterans belong to a rap group does not mean that the group experience is totally unstructured.

In fact, the counselors have a definite agenda of basic items that we attempt to touch upon during group experience. As a general rule, veterans rapidly develop rapport with each other and fairly early in the experience develop a sense of trust and security. We have found it useful to begin a group by asking the veterans to each discuss or tell a little bit about their trip to Vietnam. This discussion frequently stimulates the veteran to talk about feelings of anxiety, fear, or anticipation that he experienced en route to Vietnam. It also helps tremendously to develop a bond among the group members because of a common shared experience.

Often, after they discuss the trip to Vietnam, we ask the veterans to talk about their first week in-country. This enables the veteran to talk about feelings he may have experienced about being a new member of a group (in the Vietnam case, the platoon, artillery battery, or other unit to which he was assigned). During the war, veterans also often were processed through replacement companies and then assigned to units in the field. The veteran was often replacing an individual who had rotated back to the United States or had been killed or wounded in combat. Thus, when first arriving in Vietnam, the veteran was often a stranger within an already established group. The veteran may be having the same feelings in the current rap group that he experienced upon arriving at his new unit in Vietnam. The counselor attempts to facilitate the group member's exploration of the insecurities and anxieties associated with becoming a member of a group both in the past (Vietnam) and in the present (Vet Center rap group). This rapidly develops into a common bond of trust and establishes other members of the rap group as significant others in the life of the veteran. It also eases the transition from discussion of past events to the topic of learning to cope in the here-and-now. As soon as possible, attempts are made to have each veteran discuss current life problems and to ask the group for assistance in solving them. A focus on problems in the present is encouraged. Readers are referred to Williams (1980) for a more thorough coverage of group approaches with Vietnam veterans.

THE VETERAN AND THE FAMILY SYSTEM

In many cases, a focus on the veteran alone is not the complete solution. Carroll, Rueger, Donahoe, and Foy (1983) have reported on the marital adjustment of help-seeking Vietnam veterans with PTSD. They compared Vietnam combat veteran groups with PTSD, combat veterans without PTSD, and noncombat Vietnam era veterans on a variety of measures. They found a significantly higher incidence of dyadic maladjustment in the PTSD group and recommended that individual counseling be supplemented by attempts to improve dyadic communication and anger management.

If counseling is effective, the veteran may markedly increase his self-disclosure about war experiences to significant others. He may change from a reluctance to communicate to an excessive preoccupation with discussing war experiences. The spouse is then faced with the problem of understanding his experiences. For some it is difficult to maintain an attitude of sympathetic understanding in the face of often gruesome stories of death and destruction. Many women feel torn between their needs and conflicts and those of their husbands. The husband usually wants to talk, but the wife is shocked and often wants to avoid the upsetting topic of war.

The family system, and in particular the wife, need to understand her role in helping herself and her husband work through these feelings. The family system has potential for both maintaining and eliminating the disorder (Stanton & Figley, 1978). They need a rationale or purpose to explain the situation that impinges on their relationship. Just as the veteran needs support to promote a rationale or purpose to explain his war experience, the wife needs help to understand the psychological experiences that produce many of her husband's feelings and behaviors that affect their relationship. Both individual and group counseling can provide the understanding and psychological support base to bolster their morale to work through the marriage difficulties. The counseling process can help them integrate and find personal and shared meaning in how the past war experiences affect their relationship now and what they can do to bring about the desired changes in that relationship.

Think of the analogy of a person as warm on the outside, but an insulated ice cube at the core. The warm interpersonal relations in his or her life maintain that person, but fail to completely melt or warm the numb core of ice. At the same time, the numb inner core prevents the person from progressing much beyond the surface manifestations of warmth and intimacy. What kind of problems can this generate for the marriage relationship? While the mate may present a whole list of issues, the most intense concern appears to be that she feels alienated and cut off from her husband's world. He does not communicate feelings of love and care, does not take responsibilities for work, household, child rearing, and her sexual needs. The husband usually agrees with the list of problems presented by the wife but feels hopeless to do anything about them. His usual response is "That's just the way I am."

This attitude leaves the wife with a sense of hopelessness and helplessness. She feels that she is carrying the weight of the relationship and that she cannot continue under such stress. Very often the wives express that they feel they are ready to have a nervous breakdown because they cannot continue to live under the pressure of the relationship. The couple are encouraged to join a group. The husband is asked to join a group of other Vietnam veterans, the wife a group of other wives of Vietnam veterans, and for both a couples' group. The purpose of the group is to provide an emotional support network for the couple. The knowledge of an existing and available support network, either actual or imagined, affects an individual's perception of stress and his or her assessment of his or her capacity to cope with the stress (Lazarus & Launier, 1978).

GROUP COUNSELING PROGRAM FOR SIGNIFICANT OTHERS

Many of the couples that come in for help do so because they believe that the husband has problems related to his Vietnam War experience. Since this is the concern that brings them in for counseling, the first wives' group session is spent educating the wife about what it is like to be in a combat role. The intensity of training and emotional buildup prior to being sent to Vietnam is discussed. It is helpful if a Vietnam combat veteran can relate his experiences in training to demonstrate the psychological reorientation that is necessary for one to go into combat. Films are shown that depict authentic combat situations. This helps the spouse to identify with the role and to begin to have some feelings for what it must have been like. Here again it is helpful to have a combat veteran share some of his own personal experiences and feelings.

The reaction of the wives is usually one of horror, pity, and disbelief. Some of the spouses find it very difficult to watch the films. For instance, one particular scene in one of the films shows a Vietnamese police officer who holds a gun to the head of a young boy, a Viet Cong soldier, and executes him. The wives often express feeling sick and say that things like that just don't happen. The important point is that the wives get the emotional feeling for what it must have been like for their husbands to have experienced and reexperienced the situations that they only know of through the media. It helps the mate understand the intensity of the feelings that are aroused by such wartime experiences. It occurs to the wives even more profoundly that their husbands might have some of the same types of behaviors that are shown in the films but that their husbands have never been willing to talk about those experiences. It is important to define and label the feelings of the wives and how these might also be the same feelings their husbands had at one time, but more intensely.

The second wives' group session revolves around providing educational information relative to understanding post-traumatic stress disorder. The goal of the group is for the wives to understand that although stress syndromes are not uncommon in the general population, for they themselves have all had stressful experiences, there are special features of the Vietnam veterans' experiences that intensify the problem. It is important and helpful to focus on stressful situations in the spouse's life and the feelings that these experiences engendered. By discussing her personal experiences, she is better able to extrapolate those experiences to understanding the feelings and behaviors that her husband may have related to the stress of war. Sharing by the group members, the group leader, and films can be used to facilitate the understanding of stress symptoms and the behaviors that result from unresolved stress.

The understanding created in the two preceding sessions gives the spouse a rationale or conceptualization of the problems that in itself can be therapeutic in that it makes the stress comprehensible. It replaces the belief system of "I can't cope." This provides the wife with some psychological distance for understanding and alleviating some of her anxiety that is engendered in the marital interaction.

The third group meeting involves helping the wife understand how the characteristics of post-traumatic stress disorder function in the marriage relationship. There are some excellent films that depict the pain of the Vietnam veteran as he strives to form close interpersonal relationships. The wives are asked to watch these films and to pick out the areas in the films that apply to their marriage relationship. The areas most often identified include: alienation, guilt, hostile impulses, lack of affection, depression, insomnia, nightmares, and anxiety. It is important to identify and be specific about how each of these areas functions in the marriage now. It is one thing to talk about alienation but another to experience the rejection one feels as a wife when a husband will not show or receive affection. How does one cope with this? How does it make you feel? How have you dealt with this in the past and what are you doing now? The response gives clues to factors that contribute to the problem and potential targets of intervention.

Clarifying the wife's self-statements about the problems helps her to identify the thoughts and images that precede, accompany, and follow the stressful situations in the marriage relationship. This is important because of the close relationship between how the wife interprets the problem and the following interactions that occur between the interpretation of the problem and the response to the situation. The past attributions given to the problem feed the wife's anxiety, self-fulfilling prophecies, and interactions with the husband. The self-statements of the wife may have an aversive consequence making the situation more likely to result in negative consequences for the marriage relationship.

The wives can share and receive support and ideas from others who say, "That's exactly the way my husband acts," or "That's the way he treats me." It is also at this point in the treatment program that the therapist becomes aware of how the war-related problems function in the interpersonal network and what problems may have other psychological roots as their basis of maintenance in the relationship.

The fourth group meeting moves toward the more personal aspects of the relationship from talking in generalities about the combat role and the relationship on the marriage to identifying specific areas of the marriage (i.e., child rearing, social activities, career advancement) that are causing concern within the marriage. This is an important step because it moves the spouse from a feeling of generally being unhappy with the marriage to identifying specific concerns that cause dysfunction in the marriage. The wife may say things like, "He never goes out anywhere with me or the children"; "He never touches the children"; "He won't even spank the children or correct them in any way"; "He moves from job to job and I never know what to expect"; or, even more personal comments like "He never says, 'I love you'."

The fifth group meeting is devoted to helping the wife recognize the areas of the marriage that she would like to see changes in and evaluating them relative to whether or not they can be changed. For instance, she may be able to change the number of times a month they engage in social activities or go out together, but she may not be able to change the number of nightmares the husband has. The goal is for the wife to understand what things may possibly be changed and what she may not have control over to change. Then, it is necessary to discuss how one copes with things one cannot change.

The sixth group meeting is given to helping the wife to set goals to change those things she may be able to change and how to cope with those things she cannot change. It is important to help her to see that she has an element of control and can make things happen in her world. One wife mentioned that her husband was unemployed and they never had money to go out together and that he didn't like to go places where there were many other people around like parties, restaurants, movie theaters, etc. When asked what they used to do together when they dated that was fun, she said they went for walks in the park. When asked if she had talked with her husband about her desire for just the two of them to get off together alone, she said "no." When asked, "What do you think might happen if you told your husband that you would like for just the two of you to go off to the park together?" she said,

"I don't know, maybe we would go." She agreed to ask him and they did go to the park together and had a wonderful day. While this may seem trite or unimportant, it is a good example of how little communication actually occurs between some of the couples. It is important to make them aware that they themselves can do some things, and this begins to give them a sense of control over meeting their needs and not just waiting for somebody else to do it for them.

After the sixth group meeting, a mixed couples' group is held once a month with husbands and wives together. The mixed couples' group focuses on the same issues as the other group meetings. That is, discussions center around war experiences, post-traumatic stress disorder, and the marriage relationship. The advantage of the mixed group is that it provides the opportunity for the couple to communicate their feelings, experiences, and needs and be heard by the marriage partner. Many times an individual in the group may talk about a specific concern (e.g., child rearing) and the marriage partner may not respond, but another member of the group will respond with some points that open up an awareness for everyone in the group. It gives the couple an opportunity to understand that others have some of the same concerns and issues and they are not alone.

COUPLES' GROUP

The mixed group affords the opportunity for the husbands to begin to understand the wives' feelings about being shut out, and the wives gain more understanding of what their husbands are feeling and experienced in Vietnam. For most veterans it is the first time they have talked about Vietnam in front of their wives. The veteran sees and experiences the anxiety of the wife engendered by his excluding her from that part of his life. She feels that there is a territory she is not allowed to enter. Some of the wives in couples' groups state that they feel like at times their husband is still in Vietnam. They feel jealous because the husband seems to savor those experiences more than living in the present in their relationship.

Many of the husbands report that they did not share their war experiences with their wife because they wanted to protect her and not cause her pain. They come to realize that by shutting her out they are in fact hurting her because of the pain of rejection that she feels.

As the husbands begin to experience the feelings of hurt that their wives feel, they begin to open up in the group and share their feelings. One veteran had held in for years his experiences in Vietnam and had not shared them with anyone. He was a medic and harbored many guilt feelings about not being able to save many wounded soldiers. He shared in the couples' group his pain and suffering along with his sense of helplessness and guilt over not being able to save them. His wife reached over and held his hand; they cried together. The beauty of the experience was not only the sharing of pain with other veterans, but the closeness that it brought to the marital relationship. The sharing of the experience made them able to personalize their relationship so that the anonymous feelings that had all along impinged on that relationship were set free to enable them to experience a genuine encounter.

The sharing of the past frees the husband to let go of the past and focus on the present feelings, needs, and goals in the marriage relationship. The emphasis in the couples' group is on the here-and-now as opposed to working through what went on in the past (this is best accomplished in individual sessions or in groups with other veterans). However, in the mixed group the husband is confronted with the reality of how the past feelings and behaviors are presently functioning in the marriage relationship.

The group provides a sense of community for sharing feelings, experiences, and goals. Others can say, "That's what I want out of my marriage too"; "Those are the same needs I have." The group helps the couple form a new basis for interpreting their world and setting goals that will enhance their relationship.

Marriage activities such as: communication, sex, independence, rearing of children, and household responsibilities are discussed. The wants, feelings, and needs of each individual and couple are explored and shared. Mutual goals are set that will meet the needs of the individual and the marriage dyad. The couples are encouraged to set specific goals, to work toward those goals, and to share their successes and failures with one another and the group.

The couples' group facilitates the transition as the veteran moves from preoccupation with unresolved Vietnam issues to an understanding of how that preoccupation affects his marriage. The ultimate goal is to help the veteran and his partner develop a genuine and intimate relationship that is satisfying to both. As the couple explore the dynamics of their relationship, they can look for meaning in life together and explore avenues for meeting their needs and achieving their goals.

REFERENCES

Blank, A. S. (1982). Apocalypse terminable and interminable: Operation outreach for Vietnam veterans. *Hospital and Community Psychiatry, 33*, 11.

Brammer, L. M., & Abrego, P. J. (1981). Intervention strategies for coping with transitions. *The Counseling Psychologist, 9*(2), 19–36.

Carroll, E. M., Rueger, D. B., Donahoe, C. P., & Foy, D. W. (1983). The marital adjustment of help-seeking Vietnam veterans with post-traumatic stress disorder. Paper presented at the annual meeting of the *Western Psychological Association*, San Francisco, CA, April 1983.

Center for Policy Research (1980). *Vietnam Era research project: Preliminary report.* New York: Center for Policy Research.

Erikson, E. (1968). *Identity, youth and crisis.* New York: W. W. Norton.

Figley, C. R. (1976). The Vietnam veteran in family therapy: Implications from the research. Paper presented at the annual meeting of the American Personnel and Guidance Association, Chicago, March 1976.

Figley, C. R. (1982). Post-traumatic stress disorder: Diagnosis and treatment in various contexts. A clinical workshop presented to the Vietnam Veterans Outreach Program's Southeast Region Phase IV training in Nashville, TN, September 1982.

Frye, J. S., & Stockton, R. A. (1982). Discriminant analysis of post-traumatic stress disorder among a group of Vietnam veterans. *American Journal of Psychiatry, 139*(1), 52–56.

Hendin, H. (1983). Psychotherapy for Vietnam Veterans with post-traumatic stress disorders. *American Journal of Psychotherapy, 37*(1), 86–99.

Lazarus, R. S., & Launier, R. (1978). Stress-related transactions between persons and environment. In L. A. Pervin & M. Lewis (Eds.), *Perspectives in interactional psychology.* New York: Plenum Press.

Stanton, M. D., & Figley, C. R. (1978). Treating the Vietnam veteran within the family system. In C. R. Figley (Ed.), *Stress disorders among Vietnam veterans.* New York: Brunner/Mazel.

Williams, T. (1980). *Post-traumatic stress disorders of the Vietnam veteran.* Cincinnati: Disabled American Veterans.

Wilson, J. P. (1980). Conflict, stress, and growth: The effects of war on psychosocial development among Vietnam veterans. In C. R. Figley (Ed.), *Strangers at home: Vietnam veterans since the war.* New York: Praeger.

13

Systematic Desensitization Therapy with Post-Traumatic Stress Disorder Cases

GEORGE R. BOWEN and JAMES A. LAMBERT

The cluster of symptoms involved in post-traumatic stress disorder (PTSD) is delineated in the *Diagnostic and Statistical Manual of Mental Disorders* (American Psychiatric Association, 1980), and its clinical manifestation among combat veterans has been described by various authors, such as Figley (1978) among many others. One central aspect of the symptomatology of PTSD is anxiety arousal. Behavioral approaches in the assessment and treatment of this aspect of post-traumatic stress disorder have been shown to be useful and effective. Malloy, Fairbank, and Keane (1983) and Blanchard, Kolb, Pallmeyer, and Gerardi (1982) found differential patterns of physiological arousal for Vietnam combat veterans and noncombat veterans.

Malloy and his associates established three groups of 10 veterans each. One group (Ptsd) was thoroughly assessed and diagnosed as meeting the standard criteria for PTSD, another group (Psych) included psychiatric inpatients who were not psychotic or organic and who had no combat exposure, and the third group (Normal) was composed of Vet-

We wish to thank Richard Whinery for his consultation on the statistical analysis and Susan Brantley for her assistance on the statistical computations.

erans Administration Medical Center staff members, most of whom had combat experience in Vietnam but who did not meet the standard diagnostic criteria for PTSD and who had never sought psychiatric treatment. Each of these groups was presented with two videotapes with correlated audio background. One consisted of neutral scenes of a family on a trip to a shopping mall, and the other consisted of combat scenes of a platoon preparing for a helicopter assault, landing in a "hot" landing zone, and then being under mortar and small-arms attack. Each subject's heart rate and skin resistance was monitored, and it was found that the Ptsd group had a significant increase in heart rate and skin resistance responses to the combat tape compared to the neutral tape, whereas there were no significant changes for the Psych and Normal control groups. These results showed definite physiological signs of anxiety arousal associated with PTSD, consistent with behavioral and self-report measures of increases in anxiety.

Blanchard and his associates used two groups of 11 subjects each. One group was composed of Vietnam combat veterans who met standard criteria for PTSD and the other of non-Vietnam veterans. Each group was instructed to do several types of mental arithmetic as a neutral stressor and then to listen to an audio tape recording of intervals of "somewhat strident" music, followed by silence, followed by combat sounds (taken from the sound track of the movie *Apocalypse Now*). A final condition presented continuous combat sounds. Each subject's heart rate, blood pressure, fingertip temperature, forehead muscle activity, and skin resistance was monitored. Results indicated that the Vietnam veteran group had significant increases in heart rate, systolic blood pressure, and forehead muscle activity in response to the combat sounds whereas the non-Vietnam veteran group did not. A discriminant function analysis revealed that heart rate was the best single measure for discriminating between the groups. The authors suggest that this physiological responsivity of the veterans shows the "persistence of a conditioned emotional response" (p. 229). Kolb (1984) extends this notion to a conditioned fear response and considers the essential therapeutic effort to be alleviation of this conditioned emotional fear response. He reports little success in this effort by using desensitization, although his methodology is not fully reported and he does acknowledge one report in the literature that appeared to be successful using behavioral techniques.

This report noted by Kolb, i.e., Keane andd Kaloupek (1982), documents the treatment success of imaginal flooding with one Vietnam veteran who had presenting complaints of nightmares, flashbacks, and intrusive thoughts along with other related psychological and behavioral problems. Three specific traumatic events were isolated and treated by imaginal flooding, i.e., the patient mentally recreated the event in detail with assistance by the therapist, who also encouraged the patient to continue imagining the scene even when he became anxious and until it was no longer anxiety provoking. Nineteen treatment sessions were conducted, during which heart rate was continuously monitored. The authors report that at the end of treatment heart rate showed "a definite decrease" compared to pretreatment rates, although exact figures were not provided. Other behavioral and subjective rating measures of anxiety also decreased.

Fairbank and Keane (1982) also report behavioral treatment success using imaginal flooding with two different Vietnam combat veterans. Each veteran identified four specific traumatic events related to combat. After five treatment sessions in which the flooding technique was used for 60 to 120 minutes each session, both subjects subjectively related their anxiety by means of a rating scale to be markedly lower. Furthermore, one subject's anxiety arousal was monitored by means of skin conductance and heart rate, and these measures were found to decrease after treatment.

Kolb's (1984) identification of a conditioned emotional fear response as the essential therapeutic target is consistent with the effort of applying the technique of systematic desensitization to the anxiety-arousal aspects of the PTSD syndrome. Systematic desensitization is a standard behavioral treatment technique to reduce arousal from anxiety-laden stimuli (Wolpe, 1969). It basically involves identifying a series of increasingly anxiety-arousing stimuli or situations, training the patient in muscle relaxation techniques, and then systematically presenting the stimuli to the patient *in vivo* or by imagination while concurrently having the patient actively maintain relaxation. When the patient can imagine the least arousing scene with minimal anxiety, the next scene in the anxiety hierarchy is worked on in the same manner until all stimuli can be presented without significant anxiety. Although this technique has been applied to many phobic stimuli, its application to the treatment of PTSD has not been extensively reported in the research literature, although Kolb does mention that he attempted it.

One of the early studies to use *in vivo* systematic desensitization with combat-related anxiety is reported by Kippler (1977). He used individually self-administered desensitization and desensitization in dyads with Israeli soldiers during the Yom Kippur War in October 1973. In both cases, muscle relaxation skills were taught and then applied by the subjects in the presence of gradually increasing anxiety-arousing situations which were related to their original traumatic event. Three cases were presented which described successful treatment, but overall outcome results were not reported systematically.

In more careful studies, Schindler (1980) and Miller and DiPilato (1983), among others, have successfully used relaxation and desensitization to reduce frequency and intensity of anxiety-arousing nightmares. Schindler reports cessation of a combat-related nightmare occurring in one Vietnam veteran by using relaxation with standard imaginal desensitization techniques for six sessions. Miller and DiPilato used 32 adult subjects (89% females), solicited via news media in a large city, who reported having a frightening dream which awakened them at least once a month. They were randomly assigned to a relaxation only group (taught only relaxation skills), a desensitization group (which included relaxation training plus systematic desensitization to a dream hierarchy), and a waiting list control group (who only recorded their dreams). After 15 weeks, both the relaxation and desensitization groups showed significantly reduced nightmare frequency (but not intensity ratings) compared to the waiting list control group, with no significant differences between treatment groups. However, after a 25-week followup, the desensitization group showed significantly reduced nightmare intensity rating compared to the relaxation group but were still equivalent in terms of nightmare frequency. The authors conclude that behavioral approaches are effective in the treatment of nightmares and that desensitization "showed a modest advantage at long-term followup" (p. 875).

In the use of desensitization and flooding with PTSD cases, acknowledgment should be made of considerable research and some controversy in the previous decade. Comparative studies of the relative efficacy and efficiency of desensitization versus flooding were made, some generally concluding in favor of desensitization (Lang, 1969; Paul, 1969) and some more favorable to flooding or extinction approaches (Marks, 1975), but with both sides acknowledging the presence of mixed outcome results. The specific effective elements of the desensitization process were explored and, while the reciprocal inhibition principle of relaxation as a competing physiological response to anxiety was not consistently supported, and some questioned the necessity of relaxation procedures at all, the importance of the subject remaining in the presence of the arousing stimuli by whatever means until the arousal diminished was generally acknowledged.

It is not within the scope or purpose of this paper to thoroughly review or to recreate the issues of the past decade in this area. The purpose of the present study was to apply individual systematic desensitization techniques to anxiety-arousing memories of military experiences among a group of veterans and to determine the effect of the techniques by means of subjective ratings and physiological monitoring with biofeedback equipment. None of the studies reviewed above have combined all the elements of imaginal desensitization, a group of several veterans with military-related anxiety arousal, and both subjective and physiological treatment effect variables as the present study did. It was hypothesized that the veterans would show decreased physiological arousal to the military memories after a period of treatment and that this decrease would be greater than that for stressful nonmilitary memories which were not specifically treated.

METHOD

Subjects

Ten veterans who were already involved in active psychiatric outpatient therapy at the Veterans Administration Medical Center were included as subjects. Eight of these patients were veterans in their middle thirties in age who served in Vietnam, one was a World War II combat veteran and prisoner of war in his early sixties in age, and one was a post-Vietnam Era veteran in his early twenties in age who witnessed an airplane crash on an aircraft carrier. All but one of the Vietnam veterans experienced extensive combat while serving complete 12- or 13-month tours of duty. The remaining Vietnam veteran served primarily in a base camp but experienced considerable subjective stress by periodic shelling and frequently seeing dead bodies brought in from the field. The World War II (European Theater) veteran experienced six months of combat and was a prisoner of war for five months. The post-Vietnam Era veteran saw no combat but witnessed and assisted in helping after a traumatic airplane crash in which a number of crewmates were killed and injured. After an extensive interview assessment, they all were judged to have experienced a significantly traumatic stressor, required as one element for a diagnosis of PTSD. They all complained of reexperiencing the trauma by current intrusive anxiety-arousing thoughts of their military experiences as one of the major problems for which they sought treatment and thus met another element required for the PTSD diagnosis. Many also experienced nightmares. Many but not all of the veterans met the other symptomatic criteria for PTSD such as guilt, anxiety arousal, and numbing of responsiveness. Thus, not all the veterans in the sample received a diagnosis of PTSD but all were judged to have significant symptoms of delayed stress in the area of focus for this study, namely anxiety arousal from thoughts of traumatic stress they had experienced. This partial symptom picture is quite typical for these kinds of cases in an outpatient psychiatric clinic. All veterans in the sample received individual systematic desensitization therapy. In addition, six of the Vietnam veterans were also in interactive group therapy and eight of the veterans received psychotropic medication, mostly tricyclic antidepressants, except for one veteran who received a minor tranquilizer. While for some veterans there was a mixture of treatment modalities, which often occurs in psychiatric outpatient clinics, the particular mixture remained constant for each veteran during his course of desensitization treatment.

Procedure

Pretreatment. A stress list of combat stress incidents (average number of 8.9) and noncombat stress incidents (average number of 3.2) of increasing severity of stress as presently remembered was developed for each patient. A typical example of mild combat stress was being awakened at night by sirens announcing a mortar attack on the base camp, a moderately stressful combat situation often involved being in a short firefight while on patrol in the jungle but having no personal close call with being hit, and high combat stress situations frequently were those in which the veteran had close-in combat with individual enemy troops or in which he himself or a buddy next to him was wounded in combat action. Typical noncombat stress situations involved marital or girlfriend conflict, witnessing the death or dying of parents or grandparents, and serious accidents in which the veteran was involved. Order of presentation of scenes in a biofeedback monitoring session was determined by a table of random numbers, with combat and noncombat scenes intermingled in order to control for systematic effects due to presentation order.

During this monitoring session in an equipped biofeedback laboratory, all patients were seated in an upright position in an overstuffed chair that provided head and neck support, with their feet flat on the floor. They were instructed to sit quietly in the chair with their head tilted slightly forward, their left arm remaining comfortably still on the arm of the chair, and their eyes closed during the recording. They also were instructed to remove any gum, dental plates, wristwatch, etc., that could confound the recordings. Peripheral nervous system responsivity was measured by electromyogram (EMG) surface electrodes placed on the patient's frontalis muscle area using a Cyborg BL 900 EMG Monitor. Autonomic nervous system responsivity was measured by a heart rate (HR) sensor attached to the radial aspect of the left wrist using a Cyborg BL 907 Pulse Wave Velocity Monitor. These two monitors were inter- faced with a Cyborg Q 880 Data Accumulator.

The sequence of activity in the monitoring session was as follows: (a) period of baseline monitoring until readings were stable, (b) verbal read- ing by the therapist of the stress scene listed as first in order of pre- sentation with the patient told to imagine himself back in the situation as realistically as possible, (c) physiological responsivity monitored for 60-second periods during which responses were automatically averaged every 10 seconds, (d) patient told to open his eyes and rate the subjective stress he felt on a five-point scale, (e) patient told to close his eyes again and relax, (f) physiological state monitored until readings indicated a return to baseline level, and (g) then the second scene was read. This procedure was followed until all scenes were completed.

Treatment. A variable period of several months of individual outpatient treatment for each subject followed the pretreatment assessment phase. The first phase of treatment consisted of muscle relaxation training using a 20-minute audio cassette tape by Hartman (1976). This tape follows standard relaxation training procedures of briefly tensing and releasing each major muscle system in the body and concentrating on the internal physical sensations produced. After becoming familiar with those sen- sations by daily home practice, the patient was encouraged to practice eliciting those sensations covertly while in anxiety-arousing situations during his daily routines.

After the relaxation technique was mastered, the second phase of treatment, i.e., desensitization therapy, was started. During individual clinic treatment sessions, several combat stress scenes were read by the therapist, and the patient imagined himself in the combat setting as realistically as possible but he also actively maintained relaxation with the therapist's verbal guidance. Each scene was slowly repeated several times with encouragement by the therapist to recall all details of the situation as they actually happened. The therapist actively guided this imagery by repeating details the patient had described as having hap- pened, but no new or corrective imagery was included by the therapist, only the periodic instruction to maintain relaxation. The patient was encouraged to practice this procedure at home also. It is important to note that the noncombat stress scenes were not practiced in the clinic or at home in order to provide a comparison between treated and non-treated scenes within each patient. Average time for treatment (relaxation and desensitization) was 5.8 months, with clinic sessions usually every two weeks.

Posttreatment. When all combat scenes could be imagined with subjective comfort, the patient returned to the biofeedback laboratory, and the monitoring procedure previously described was repeated in exactly the same manner and sequence of scene presentation.

RESULTS

Descriptively, the combat stress scenes showed significantly higher readings on both HR and EMG before treatment than did the noncombat stress scenes. This suggests that, while both types of scenes involved psychological stress, the combat scenes tended to be more anxiety arousing than the noncombat scenes. However, following treatment the treated scenes were not significantly different from the nontreated scenes and in fact were slightly lower on the HR measure. Table 1 shows these descriptive relationships.

TABLE 1
Relationship of Dependent Variables Before and After Treatment

Variable	Treated scenes (combat)	Nontreated scenes (noncombat)	Difference	t ratio
Pretreatment				
HR (avg. beats/min.)	86.579	84.829	1.750	3.50[a]
EMG (avg. microvolts)	8.659	7.663	0.996	2.41[b]
Posttreatment				
HR (avg. beats/min.)	78.410	78.707	−0.297	0.25
EMG (avg. microvolts)	5.416	5.172	0.244	0.45

[a]$p < 0.005$.
[b]$p < 0.05$.

The treatment effects were measured by using the *t* test to evaluate the significance of the differences between the pretreatment and post-treatment means on HR and EMG for the treated scenes and the non-treated scenes. The HR data were analyzed separately from the EMG data, and the treated scenes were separated from the nontreated scenes. It should be remembered that the noncombat scenes were not specifically treated by desensitization. As can be seen from Table 2, HR and EMG were significantly decreased after treatment for both treated and non-treated scenes.

The decreased tension arousal of the nontreated scenes could have been due to generalizability of relaxation or to passage of time. To determine if there were specific treatment effects due to the desensitization therapy and not just to these general factors, pretreatment-posttreatment difference scores were compared for the treated scenes versus the non-treated scenes. These difference scores were obtained by subtracting the average posttreatment reading from the average pretreatment reading for each patient for HR and EMG. If the treated scenes show a significantly greater decrease than the nontreated scenes, then specific treatment effects for desensitization would be indicated. As can be seen from Table 3, the difference scores for the treated scenes are significantly greater (i.e., showed greater decrease after treatment) than the non-treated scenes for the HR data. They are in the expected direction but not significantly different for the EMG data.

TABLE 2
Treatment Effects for HR and EMG

Scenes	Pretreatment	Posttreatment	Pre-post difference	*t* ratio
HR (avg. beats/min.)				
Treated (combat)	86.58	78.41	8.17	2.81[a]
Nontreated (noncombat)	84.83	78.71	6.12	2.01[b]
EMG (avg. microvolts)				
Treated (combat)	8.66	5.42	3.24	1.79[b]
Nontreated (noncombat)	7.66	5.17	2.49	1.92[b]

[a]$p < 0.01$.
[b]$p < 0.05$.

TABLE 3
Significance of Difference between Treated and Nontreated Pre-post
Difference Scores

Variable	Treated (combat)	Nontreated (noncombat)	Difference	t ratio
HR	8.17	6.12	2.05	2.38[a]
EMG	3.24	2.49	.75	1.17

[a]$p < 0.05$.

TABLE 4
Subjective Stress Ratings Before and After Treatment

Scene	Pretreatment rating (avg.)	Posttreatment rating (avg.)	Difference	t ratio
Treated scenes (combat)	3.112	2.357	0.755	4.710[a]
Nontreated scenes (noncombat)	2.717	1.617	1.100	3.900[b]

[a]$p < 0.001$.
[b]$p < 0.01$.

A similar procedure was followed to evaluate changes in the subjective five-point stress ratings each patient gave for each scene during the biofeedback monitoring sessions before and after treatment. The ratings for both the treated and nontreated scenes were significantly lower after treatment than before, as shown in Table 4.

However, a difference score analysis, similar to that described previously, showed no significant differences between the changes in the treated scene ratings versus the nontreated scene ratings (t [8] = 1.280, $p = 0.12$).

DISCUSSION

While the sample size is obviously small and some caution is needed in drawing general conclusions until replication studies with larger samples and, preferably, independent groups can be made, the results do suggest the utility of desensitization therapy in reducing physiological arousal (at least autonomic arousal) associated with intrusive thoughts, which are a frequent complaint in PTSD. The treatment reported here focuses on the essential therapeutic effort for this condition as identified by Kolb (1984), i.e., alleviation of a conditioned emotional response. Consistent with that type of response, the study uses physiological (along with subjective) outcome measures to suggest successful intervention using desensitization in contrast to the unsuccessful results Kolb notes. Thus, desensitization therapy could provide the therapist with a specific individual treatment technique to consider for anxiety- or fear-arousing intrusive thoughts. This approach seems particularly appropriate for an outpatient setting, since constant follow-up monitoring of the aftereffects of exposure to the anxiety stimuli on the patient are generally not necessary because the exposure is gradual and not overwhelming. However, it certainly could be used in an inpatient setting as well. After the technique is well learned with therapist guidance, the patient can apply it himself to new stressful thoughts, thus expanding his capacity to deal with stress in a variety of situations. Using relaxation as an active technique allowing the patient to remain (in fantasy) in the presence of the arousing stimuli seems to enhance his feeling of self-control, a notion proposed by Sherman and Plummer (1973).

However, a much broader concept that may apply here is that of self-efficacy, described by Bandura (1982) as "concerned with judgements of how well one can execute courses of action required to deal with prospective situations" (p. 122). Among Bandura's extensive studies of this concept is one study showing that as perceived self-efficacy increases, fear arousal, as measured by blood pressure and heart rate, decreases for subjects with snake phobias (Bandura, 1982). In the current context, as veterans are given active coping techniques such as relaxation training to control their anxiety arousal, it could be the case that their perceived self-efficacy would increase, thus further enhancing their decrease in anxiety.

The possible application of the self-efficacy concept to systematic desensitization is an area for future research efforts. It recently has been applied in a treatment comparison study to another behavioral treatment technique, that of flooding or "exposure," in the description by the authors (Williams, Dooseman, & Kleifield, 1984). They conclude that "mastery-oriented treatment based on self-efficacy theory was more effective than exposure in producing therapeutic changes in severe and intractable phobias" (p. 515), which involved 32 height and driving phobic subjects. Future studies could be directed toward the treatment process issues of a possible self-efficacy component to the active coping skills learned in desensitization procedures and to whether there are unique therapeutic elements in the desensitization procedures that are not accounted for by self-efficacy.

Another direction for future research, in a more treatment outcome orientation, would be to apply desensitization procedures to treatment of victims of trauma other than military combat. The present study, along with many past studies of phobic subjects, suggests desensitization could have treatment value in a variety of traumatic situations in which strong anxiety or fear is aroused.

REFERENCES

American Psychiatric Association (1980). *Diagnostic and statistical manual of mental disorders* (3rd ed.). Washington, DC: Author.

Bandura, A. (1982). Self-efficacy mechanism in human agency. *American Psychologist, 37*(2), 122–147.

Blanchard, E. B., Kolb, L. C., Pallmeyer, T. P., & Gerardi, R. J. (1982). A psychophysiological study of post-traumatic stress disorder in Vietnam veterans. *Psychiatric Quarterly, 54*(4), 220–229.

Fairbank, J. A., & Keane, T. M. (1982). Flooding for combat-related stress disorders: Assessment of anxiety reduction across traumatic memories. *Behavior Therapy, 13*(4), 499–510.

Figley, C. R. (Ed.). (1978). *Stress disorders among Vietnam veterans,* New York: Brunner/Mazel.

Hartman, C. H. (Speaker), 1976. Mixed scanning relaxation training program: Advanced instructions (Cassette Recording No. T-34). New York: Biomonitoring Applications.

Keane, T. M., & Kaloupek, D. G. (1982). Imaginal flooding in the treatment of a post-traumatic stress disorder. *Journal of Consulting and Clinical Psychology, 50*(1), 138–140.

Kipper, D. A. (1977). Behavior therapy for fears brought on by war experiences. *Journal of Consulting and Clinical Psychology, 45*(2), 216–221.

Kolb, L. C. (1984). The post-traumatic stress disorders of combat: A subgroup with a conditioned emotional response. *Military Medicine, 149*(3), 237–243.

Lang, P. J. (1969). The mechanics of desensitization and the laboratory study of human fear. In C. M. Franks (Ed.), *Behavior therapy: Appraisal and status* (pp. 160–191). New York: McGraw-Hill.

Malloy, P. F., Fairbank, J. A., & Keane, T. M. (1983). Validation of a multimethod assessment of posttraumatic stress disorders in Vietnam veterans. *Journal of Consulting and Clinical Psychology, 51*(4), 488–494.

Marks, I. (1975). Behavioral treatments of phobic and obsessive-compulsive disorders: A critical appraisal. In M. Herson, R. M. Eisler, & P. M. Miller (Eds.), *Progress in behavior modification: Vol. 1* (pp. 66–158). New York: Academic Press.

Miller, W. R., & DiPilato, M. (1983). Treatment of nightmares via relaxation and desensitization: A controlled evaluation. *Journal of Consulting and Clinical Psychology, 51*(6), 870–877.

Paul, G. L. (1969). Outcome of systematic desensitization II: Controlled investigations of individual treatment, technique variations, and current status. In C. M. Franks (Ed.), *Behavior therapy: Appraisal and status* (pp. 105–159). New York: McGraw-Hill.

Schindler, F. E. (1980). Treatment by systematic desensitization of a recurring nightmare of a real life trauma. *Journal of Behavior Therapy and Experimental Psychiatry, 11*(1), 53–54.

Sherman, A. R., & Plummer, I. L. (1973). Training in relaxation as a behavioral self-management skill. *Behavior Therapy, 4,* 543–550.

Williams, S. L., Dooseman, G., & Kleifield, E. (1984). Comparative effectiveness of guided mastery and exposure treatments for intractable phobias. *Journal of Consulting and Clinical Psychology, 52*(4), 505–518.

Wolpe, J. (1969). *The practice of behavior therapy.* New York: Pergamon Press.

14

Contextual Influences on the Post-Traumatic Stress Adaptation of Homicide Survivor-Victims

MORTON BARD, HARRIET C. ARNONE, and DAVID NEMIROFF

INTRODUCTION

The number of homicides in the United States has increased steadily over the years and in 1981 reached 22,250 (US Department of Justice, 1983). The impact of this form of violence is usually measured only in the loss of life; the consequences for surviving relatives have been virtually ignored as a matter of social concern, as a matter of public policy, and by the field of mental health. There is convincing epidemiological evidence that in all cultures the loss of a close family member is a traumatically stressful event (Holmes & Masuda, 1974). In homicide, the loss follows the murderous act of another person, a factor which, logic suggests, should influence the adaptation of surviving relatives.

This chapter describes an exploratory study that sought to determine the effects on survivors when a close family member dies violently and suddenly. Its aim was to investigate the adaptive experiences of surviving relatives and to study how their adaptations were influenced by

The research reported in this chapter was supported by the National Institute of Mental Health under grant number R01 MH31685-02.

interactions with formal systems (e.g., medicine, criminal justice, and social services) and informal helping networks (e.g., relatives, friends, and neighbors).

Most interventions with those who suffer from post-traumatic stress reactions focus almost entirely on the circumstances surrounding the precipitating event and the individual's response to it (Horowitz, 1982). It is our impression that little attention is paid to the social contexts that influence the person's feelings and behaviors after the event. In order to adequately plan interventions it would seem logical that these contextual factors be identified.

First, it is important to acknowledge that surviving relatives of homicide have, in fact, no status in law, not even the status of victims (Geis, 1975). Yet following the crime of homicide, it is not the deceased alone who bear the burdens of victimization; they continue to be felt long afterward by those who survive. In this chapter, as in our research, we refer to the relatives of those slain as "survivor-victims." The word "survivor" is used in the sense of "one who outlives another" (Black, 1933), rather than one who has lived through a life-threatening event such as a war or a natural disaster.

In the aftermath of a homicide, most survivor-victims invariably become enmeshed in the criminal justice system (McDonald, 1976). Their experiences can be traced in order to examine the psychological impact of context. In part, the aim of this study was to identify how the system's activities may aggravate the traumatic stress of homicide for survivors.

OVERVIEW OF THE STUDY

Because of the paucity of prior research on the question of homicide-survivor adaptation, there was early concern by the investigators and the funding agency about untoward survivor reaction to research intrusiveness and its possible adverse emotional effects. Accordingly, a decision was made to develop a retrospective design as a first-stage exploratory study rather than to embark initially on full-scale concurrent research.

The Sample

Survivors of homicide victims were identified (two to five years after the death) through records of the New York City Chief Medical Examiner's Manhattan office. A comparison sample of suicide survivors was

drawn to enable us to investigate whether homicide is a special class of
sudden death imposing unique adaptive demands on survivors. From
a sample frame of 392, 40 interviews (10%) were completed. Detailed
comparisons (based on information from records) between the people
interviewed and those who either refused or did not respond showed
no significant differences in demographic characteristics. (A brief sample
description is given in Table 1.) A majority of those interviewed were
female and disproportionately white. The typical subject was the parent
or child of the deceased; a minority were siblings and spouses.

The rate of subject participation in this research was low compared
with other studies of the bereaved, which report a mean participation
rate of 43%, with a range of 36% to 48% (Ball, 1977; Parkes, 1972; Rudestam, 1977; Wallace, 1973). There are at least two factors in the design
that may account for this difference. First, in cases of sudden, violent
death, relocation to a new place of residence may be a significant adaptive mechanism (see Nixon & Pearn, 1977), and this, in turn, may help
to explain the relative difficulty we had in locating survivors. Second,
our retrospective approach may have discouraged participation by some
potential subjects who might have considered an in-depth discussion
of this painful experience in their lives a threat to their hard-won, late-
stage adaptations. Such reluctance has been cited by several authors
(e.g., Lowman, 1979; Stein, 1980).

TABLE 1
Sample Description

	Homicide[a]	Suicide
Sex		
Male	7	6
Female	17	10
Race		
Black	14	2
White	6	12
Hispanic	4	2
Relationship		
Parent	11	8
Child	6	1
Spouse	3	3
Sibling	4	4
	24	16

[a]Includes relatives of six vehicular homicides.

The Interview

All interviews were conducted by two-member teams; the *primary interviewer* had major responsibility for the conduct of the discussion, while the *community interviewer* functioned in a support role, helping to maintain a favorable interview climate, particularly as regards social class and cultural differences that might otherwise affect communication. A "focused interview guide" ensured eliciting uniform data in all interviews.

After obtaining consent, the primary interviewer asked a series of questions about the backgrounds of the subject and the deceased. This was an important time; the matter-of-fact, unemotional nature of the questions allowed the subject to become accustomed to the interview and to become acquainted with the interviewers as nonthreatening.

After this, subjects were ready to provide accounts of the death itself. Once again, we sought objective facts: Where, when, how did it happen? Who was involved? Did the survivor believe that the deceased suffered much? Did the subject believe that the body had been mutilated? There was also exploration of the question of perceived causality. If a person was believed responsible for the death, we asked about the subject's and the decedent's prior relationship to that person. We also inquired about the actions of "officials" after the death.

Following discussion of the death, the interview focused on the subject's experiences immediately afterward. If not a witness, how did the subject learn about the death? What happened next? This portion of the interview explored social and cultural practices, both formal and informal, following the sudden death. We asked how family and friends reacted and how their responses affected the subject. We also inquired about the role (if any) that surviving relatives played in hospital procedures, in criminal justice practices, in funeral and religious rites, and in financial support systems such as life insurance, worker's compensation, welfare, crime victims' compensation, and so forth.

In general, subjects had very little trouble providing us with information on these topics. Although much of the content was unpleasant and sometimes upsetting, subjects seemed to remember it in great detail. Even after long intervals, many continued to have strong feelings about some of the things that happened, including those related to the criminal justice system. For example, a woman whose husband had been murdered told us, leaning forward in her chair, her voice suddenly full of rage, that a police officer had knocked on her door and "he crudely said: 'I think your husband's dead.' "

Finally, the interview focused on the ways in which the subject's own

life was changed by the death. In this connection, we explored the short-
and long-term impact of the death on four major areas: social and occupational functioning, and physical and mental health status. Again,
to guard against undue distress during the interview and afterward, we
took two precautions. First, immediately after the interview both interviewers made sure that the subject was not unduly anxious or upset.
No subjects were found to be distressed. In addition, two days after the
interview all subjects were called by the interviewer or project director
to determine whether there were any adverse consequences. In no case
were any reported, and several subjects even indicated that the interview
had been beneficial.

SUMMARY OF RELEVANT FINDINGS

Post-traumatic Stress Disorder (PTSD)

   In an attempt to identify the presence or absence of PTSD, as defined
in DSM-III (APA, 1980), interview responses were scored for evidence
of it during two time periods: (a) the first year after the death, and (b)
at the time of the interview. More than half of the homicide survivors
(14) showed evidence of PTSD during the first time interval; one did by
the time of the interview, four years after the death.
   Qualitative analysis for subjects with PTSD indicated that adaptive
changes occurred in stages. There was an initial period of numbness,
sleep disorder, disorientation, and confusion. This was followed by a
time of impaired functioning, which included withdrawal, depression,
and anxiety. Finally, a plateau of reorganization was usually achieved.
The boundaries between these three stages seemed to be clear to the
subject, at least in retrospect. They were usually marked by memorable
events: a vacation, a change in residence or job, resumption of social or
recreational activities, and/or interest in new or old friends or lovers.
Usually, several such events occurred within the space of a few weeks
or months and signaled to survivors a change for the better.
   In addition to PTSD, many of the homicide survivors reported two
other conditions that often follow stressful events: somatic disturbances
(other than those relating to sleep) and strong feelings of anger or hatred.

Somatic Disturbances

   Two-thirds (17) of the homicide survivors reported having had somatic
disorders such as digestive problems, physical illness, or severe head-

aches during the first 6 to 12 months after the death, and seven continued to experience these symptoms at the time of the interview. There was no relationship between subjects' reports of these symptoms and the presence or absence of PTSD.

Anger or Hatred

A striking element of subjects' affect was the presence of strong feelings of anger or hatred. During the first year, more than half of the survivors (14) described themselves as feeling angry or as hating the person believed responsible for the death. Revenge fantasies were common; indeed, at the time of the interview, six subjects still referred to them.

It was this affective dimension that called our attention to the similarities between the experiences of the survivors of motor vehicle homicide and those of criminal homicide. Indeed, subjects in these two groups were more alike on most measures than either was like the group of survivors of suicide. Motor vehicle homicide survivors tend to reject "accident" as an explanation for the loss and focus instead, as do criminal homicide survivors, on *intentionality* as the explanation. Both groups show similar patterns of anger at the person "responsible" for the death.

These findings should be viewed with some caution, however, because this homicide sample comprised mainly poor ethnic minority group members (black and Hispanic). Without greater social class and ethnic variability, it is difficult to determine which results should be attributed to the effect of the trauma and which to the influence of socioeconomic status.

CASE EXAMPLES

The evidence presented above suggests that the impact of the loss of a close relative by homicide was traumatic for most of the subjects in our study. It was also apparent from accounts of several of the survivor-victims that they experienced additional stress in dealing with the criminal justice system, and that the nature of this stress might be related to their social class. Specifically, some of the stressful events in the context of the criminal justice system appeared to have been interpreted quite differently by members of lower-class minority groups and members of the white middle class. To describe the kinds of stress encountered, and to contrast the experiences of these two groups, two fairly typical case examples are presented.

Case 1

Mrs. D. is a 33-year-old black woman whose 16-year-old son was slain in an altercation with two men on a city street. The circumstances of his death are anything but clear; the word on the street, however, is that the slaying resulted from a "drug deal that went bad." Mrs. D. knew of no such activity on her son's part, points to the fact that he had no record of arrests, and suspects that it is typical to use "drugs" as an easy way of explaining away violence in a black community.

Mrs. D. gives the impression of a woman struggling to raise her children under extremely difficult circumstances. Abandoned by the father of her four children, she has become almost phobic since the violent death of her oldest son in her efforts to protect the children who survive . . . in constant fear that the same fate may befall them. The remaining children, a son of 14, a daughter of 13, and an 11-year-old boy, are the objects of her vigilance, so much so that she has severely curtailed her social life in an attempt to protect them against the dangers she sees around her. She had worked until the death of her son but now devotes virtually all her energies to guarding her brood. She is now supported entirely by public assistance. Mrs. D. is particularly concerned about the 11-year-old, who has been a behavior problem at school and has been truant a number of times. She now escorts him to school each day and is there to pick him up at the end of the day. The children complain that she is restricting them severely and threaten to run away.

Central to Mrs. D.'s concerns are the rumors in the neighborhood that name the person who killed her son. She knows he was taken in for questioning and released; she has little hope that he will even be charged with the crime, let alone convicted of it. Her frequent telephone calls to the police regarding the investigation met with little response; indeed, most were not even returned. She has given up trying to communicate with the police for two reasons: (1) she feels they are just not interested in "another black kid gone bad," and (2) she is afraid that any communication with the police would somehow get back to the man accused in the rumors and that he would retaliate by harming her other children.

Since the killing, Mrs. D. has suffered a number of other symptoms of post-traumatic stress disorder, most of which were not present before her son's death. She has not slept through the night in over two years. Typically she retires exhausted and is up and alert just an hour or so later. For the remainder of the night Mrs. D. tosses and turns, with dream-filled episodes of sleep interwoven with anxiety attacks evoked by a rapidly beating heart and excessive perspiration. Her thoughts at night are intrusive and invariably involve the moment when she first learned of her son's death. She is obsessed about her callous treatment at the hands of the police and tries to think of a way to break out of the trap she feels her life has become. While she would like to relocate in a different part of the city, even if she could she is reluctant to leave her neighborhood friends who have become her major sources of emotional support.

Case 2

Until his wife was murdered during a subway robbery, Dr. T. had little occasion to even speculate about the workings of the law and the criminal justice system. A successful biochemist, his life had followed a fairly typical course for a white, middle-class professional. At the age of 41 he was in his most productive years, when suddenly his world was turned upside down. The death of his wife sent him into a deep depression, which lasted for about six months. Since her death he has consistently avoided traveling on the subway line where the murder took place.

He required psychiatric assistance but has recovered enough so that today, 2 ½ years after the murder, he is back working long hours but with much less efficiency than before. His work is interrupted with obsessional thoughts of his wife's last moments. In short, he is able to function despite continuing evidence of some PTSD symptoms. His understanding colleagues often have to "cover" for him when the pressure of deadlines is really great. But work is the only activity that gives him any relief from the gnawing anguish of the loss of his wife.

Dr. T.'s two children, girls aged 11 and 8, commute to school each day via public transportation, and this is some source of worry to him. He has been fortunate enough to have acquired the services of a sleep-in housekeeper, but the children do not seem to be doing well. They both seem generally distracted and unlike themselves; the 11-year-old is doing so poorly in school that, he recently learned, she may fail all of her subjects this term.

Dr. T. has become withdrawn, has lost interest in most social activities, and does not go to the theater or vacation as he used to when his wife was alive. He has largely withdrawn from their circle of friends. The only positive growth in relationships has been with his wife's family. The closeness is tempered by the fact that they live some 500 miles away although there has been an increase in visiting.

In the time since his wife's murder Dr. T. has become embittered about the police. He expected that they would be responsive and would find and punish the murderer. He has spent many hours in police offices trying to get their attention. He is preoccupied with both revenge and bitterness about the failure of the police not only to apprehend the killer but also to treat him seriously and with the kind of respect to which he feels he is entitled. This has been a source of great frustration and disappointment to him. He feels let down by society and has left no stone unturned to get the authorities to act. Given his status in his community, he has been able to mobilize influential friends, and yet nothing seems to have changed.

Dr. T. is now depressed most of the time but not so deeply as he was initially. Burying himself in his work has served him well, but he has discovered that he has been drinking too much during the past four or five months. He states that he has little appetite and has lost more than 15 pounds since his wife's death. Mostly he feels sad that such a fate should have befallen a hard-working, "good" person like his wife and feels almost overwhelmed in his disappointment in the inability of the police to "do anything."

In both these cases the victim feels that the criminal justice system fails not only in its explicit task of apprehending and punishing the criminal, but also in its task of restoring the survivor's sense of social order. For both people, the first insult—not providing justice—is great; in Dr. T.'s case there is a second insult—the failure to fulfill positive expectations about the responsiveness to society of people in trouble. The findings of our investigation led us to an analysis of the psychological impact of the criminal justice system and the role it plays in compounding the stress of homicide survivor-victims.

DISCUSSION

The criminal is virtually the sole focus of the criminal justice system, according to several writers (Ziegenhagen, 1976; Bolin, 1980). However, the actions within this sociolegal context also carry important symbolic meanings for society, crime victims in general, and homicide survivor-victims in particular. Specifically, they *acknowledge,* on behalf of society, that a crime has taken place and confirm that the individuals affected are in fact "victims." Then, through actions intended to *set things right,* they provide evidence of a trustworthy social environment. Because these symbolic aspects of legal system practices have received so little attention, we will discuss them in detail. They are central to understanding how the criminal justice system acted as a contextual stressor for most of the homicide survivors in our research.

Social Acknowledgment

To be victimized by crime is to assume a new identity. Being a crime victim adds a new dimension to the definition of self. Following this stressful event, other people may be supportive and helpful, or they may be rejecting and stigmatizing. Whatever its cast, communication from others, especially in certain contexts, reinforces the victim's sense that social identity has been transformed.

Identity is a psychological construct locating people in a world of others. It also enables an enduring sense of self over time, despite changing environments and situations (DeLevita, 1965; Erikson, 1950, 1959; Lynd, 1958). Essential to such continuity is that the behavior of others confirms the individual's self-knowledge of who they are and where they fit in the world. Ordinarily, people take little notice of the identity-confirmation process; it is only when the behavior of others disconfirms identity that its social nature becomes apparent (Goffman, 1959).

When identity undergoes change, a disparity exists between a person's self-knowledge and the perceptions of others. At first, the discrepancy between how victims think others *should* behave and how they actually *do* behave gives them a heightened self-awareness. If the discrepancy persists, it can lead to confusion, to self-doubt, and ultimately to anger and frustration, as in Dr. T.'s treatment by the criminal justice system. In his view, the system simply did not treat him with the respect he felt he deserved as a crime victim. Like many people in his socioeconomic circumstances, his consuming anger is directed almost equally at the criminal justice system and the person who killed his wife. We believe that the reason for his anger at the legal system lies in its failure to meet his expectations that he would be dealt with in a way befitting his status in the community and his identity as a victim of a serious crime.

Agents of the law take on special significance for crime victims or their families in this process of confirming or disconfirming identity. They occupy crucial roles in that they are seen as symbolic representations of society. Moreover, their expertise reinforces their authority in the eyes of victims. Thus it is particularly reassuring when police officers, prosecutors, or judges confirm crime victims' sense of themselves as victims. In contrast, it is especially confusing, alienating, and stressful when they do not.

We have found in our research that, regardless of whether the killer was apprehended and punished, denial of homicide survivor-victims' identities is psychologically stressful. We consider this contextual issue an example of how the criminal justice system aggravates the stress reactions of homicide survivors.

Setting Things Right

A crime can be seen as a breach of the rules that embody society's shared values and morality. Defiance of these rules creates stress for the law-abiding by eroding the expectation that others will not do harm. Through the legal system society reaffirms its rule structure. By pursuing, apprehending, trying, and punishing criminals, the criminal justice system communicates the consequences of threats to social order. Conversely, these actions also communicate standards of *acceptable* behavior, restoring confidence in the predictability of the social environment (Dentler & Erikson, 1959; Garfinkel, 1956; Goffman, 1959, 1971). At times of disorder the violation of rules by those whose function it is to maintain them is particularly stressful.

Following homicide, survivor-victims feel stigmatized by others and isolated from the rest of society (Bard & Sangrey, 1979). They have a strong impulse to do things to prove that they themselves are trustworthy and to test the limits of others' reliability. To counteract their sense of disorder, these victims need to experience social reordering. We believe that this need to set things right is one reason why crime victims and their relatives invoke and pursue the legal process. They report crimes, try to follow the progress of investigations, attend trials, etc. By attempting to participate actively in the response to crime, victims are engaged in self-repair in order to rekindle social trust and thereby reduce stress.

We have observed that especially with homicide-survivors, involvement in the legal process is resisted by the criminal justice system as an unnecessary intrusion. Its commitment seems to be the restoration of social order through a single-minded focus on the source of disorder—the criminal. The victim is incidental to this primary objective and is treated as irrelevant. An unintended consequence is that survivors experience further stress in the context of the very system they hope will reduce it.

Mrs. D.'s case illustrates the effects on survivors of the legal system's criminal-centeréd strategy. She is resigned to the fact that her son's murderer will never be brought to justice, and she is prevented from participating in the legal process that might restore her social trust. Instead, she relies on the tenuous "order" provided by rumors and shows continuing stress symptoms.

Compounding the effects of excluding victims from involvement is the fact that the criminal justice system performs poorly in its primary activity—apprehending and punishing criminals (McDonald, 1976). This additional failure reinforces the victim's sense of disorder in the world and can exacerbate stress reactions. A basic assumption of social existence seems to be the just-world hypothesis, namely, that people get what they deserve: if you do good you are rewarded; if you do harm, you are punished (Lerner & Simmons, 1966). When the legal system fails to accomplish this, which it often did in the cases we studied, stressfulness is perpetuated—the world remains the unpredictable and unjust place it had suddenly become with the crime.

Things are never really "set right."

CONCLUSION

At least one finding of this research should be of interest to those concerned with the impact of traumatic stress. Trauma only *begins* with the event. Following it, there may be predictable sets of *additional, contextual stressors* that have significant impact on the adaptive process.

This notion has a clear implication: those concerned with the prevention and amelioration of PTSD may need to broaden their focus. Many of the stressors we discussed in this report are not inevitable. They are unintended by-products of a social system that narrowly defines its responsibilities along other dimensions, unaware of how its practices compound the difficulties of people already under stress. Mental health professionals, on the other hand, who have little hope of affecting the incidence of primary stressors can substantially reduce secondary ones. It may be that if mental health professionals devoted as much effort to designing corrections in the systems that affect the traumatized as is now devoted to their individual treatment, post-traumatic stress adaptation could be substantially enhanced.

It is our obligation to come to understand the nature of the environmental contexts in which people try to come to terms with trauma. We must identify those aspects of the environment which directly clash with the psychological needs of people suffering traumatic stress reactions, whether they consist of overall system goals, routine procedures, or even the organization of physical space. With this knowledge it may be possible to learn how to approach these systems and design changes in how they operate.

REFERENCES

American Psychiatric Association (1980). *Diagnostic and statistical manual of mental disorders* (3rd ed.). Washington, DC: Author.

Ball, J. (1977). Widow's grief: The impact of age and mode of death. *Omega, 7*(4), 307–333.

Bard, M., & Sangrey, D. (1979). *The crime victim's book.* New York: Basic Books. (2nd. Ed. 1986, New York: Brunner/Mazel.)

Black, H. (1933). *Black's law dictionary* (3rd ed.). St. Paul, MN: West Publishing.

Bolin, D. (1980). Police-victim interactions. Observations from the police foundation. *Evaluation and Change*, Special Issue, 110–115.

DeLevita, D. (1965). *The concept of identity.* New York: Basic Books.

Dentler, R., & Erikson, K. (1959). The functions of deviance in groups. *Social Problems, 7*, 98–107.

Erikson, E. (1950). *Childhood and society.* New Haven, CN: Norton.

Erikson, E. (1959). Identity and the life cycle. *Psychological Issues*, Whole No. 1.

Garfinkel, H. (1956). Conditions of successful degradation ceremonies. *American Journal of Sociology, 61*, 420–424.

Geis, G. (1975). Victims of crimes of violence and the criminal justice system. In D. Chappell & J. Monahan (Eds.), *Violence and criminal justice.* Lexington, MA: Heath & Co.

Goffman, E. (1959). *The presentation of self in everyday life.* Garden City, NY: Doubleday.

Goffman, E. (1971). *Relations in public.* New York: Harper & Row.

Holmes, T., & Masuda, M. (1974). Life change and illness susceptibility. In B. S. Dohrenwend & B. P. Dohrenwend (Eds.), *Stressful life events: Their nature and effects.* New York: Wiley.

Horowitz, M. (1982). Stress response syndromes and their treatment. In L. Goldberger & S. Breznitz (Eds.), *Handbook of stress: Theoretical and clinical aspects.* New York: Free Press.

Lerner, M. J., & Simmons, C. H. (1966). Observer's reaction to the innocent victim: Compassion or rejection? *Journal of Personality and Social Psychology, 4*, 203–210.

Lowman, M. J. (1979). Grief intervention and sudden infant death syndrome. *American Journal of Community Psychology, 7*(6), 665–677.

Lynd, H. M. (1958). *On shame and the search for identity.* New York: Science Editions.

McDonald, W. (Ed.) (1976). *Criminal justice and the victim.* Beverly Hills, CA: Sage.

Nixon, J., & Pearn, J. (1977). Emotional sequelae of parents and siblings following the drowning or near-drowning of a child. *Australian and New Zealand Journal of Psychiatry, 11*, 265–268.

Parkes, C. (1972). *Bereavement: Studies of grief in adult life.* New York: International Universities Press.

Rudestam, K. (1977). Physical and psychological responses to suicide in the family. *Journal of Consulting and Clinical Psychology, 45*(2), 162–170.

Stein, J. (1980). Better services for crime victims: A prescriptive package. *Evaluation and Change*, Special Issue, 108.

US Department of Justice (1983). *Report to the nation on crime and justice: The data.* Washington, DC.

Wallace, S. (1973). *After suicide.* New York: Wiley.

Ziegenhagen, E. (1976). Toward a theory of victim-criminal justice system interaction. In W. McDonald (Ed.), *Criminal justice and the victim.* Beverly Hills, CA: Sage.

15

Post-Traumatic Stress Disorder and the Disposition to Criminal Behavior

JOHN P. WILSON and SHELDON D. ZIGELBAUM

In recent years the study of extremely stressful life events on the psychic functioning of the survivor has emerged as an important area of psychiatry, psychology, and other social sciences (e.g., Figley, 1985; Lifton, 1980; Eitinger & Strom, 1973; Figley & Leventman, 1980). As a result of clinical, epidemiological, and empirical research, there now exists a substantial set of research on post-traumatic stress disorder (PTSD) or what might be termed more broadly as stress response syndromes in survivors and victims (e.g., Horowitz, 1976; Figley, 1985; Gleser, Green, & Winget, 1981).

The third edition of the *Diagnostic and Statistical Manual of Mental Disorders* (DSM-III) of the American Psychiatric Association (1980) has officially classified PTSD as an anxiety disorder that characterizes behavioral adaptation following extraordinary stressful life events. The central feature of PTSD is that the survivor or victim *reexperiences* the original trauma in dreams, uncontrollable and distressing intrusive images, dissociative states of consciousness, and unconscious behavioral reenactments of the traumatic situation. As will be discussed later, the unconscious reliving of a traumatic event may precipitate criminal behavior. However, it is also common for survivors to report symptoms of psychic numbing, a loss of affect, depression, a loss of interest in work and significant activities, survivor and moral guilt, alienation and stigmatization, a loss of capacity for intimate relations, sleep disturbances, anger, rage, mistrust, helplessness, and approach and avoidance tendencies of stimuli with trauma-related associational value (e.g., Figley, 1978; Figley & Leventman, 1980; Horowitz, 1979; Wilson, 1980; Krystal, 1969; Wilson & Zigelbaum, 1983).

As noted in DSM-III, the antecedent stressors that produce the syndrome are likely to "evoke significant symptoms of distress in most people, and [are] generally outside the range of such common experiences as simple bereavement, chronic illness, business losses or marital conflict" (p. 236). We believe that this conceptual distinction is particularly important because it specifically implies that a major cause of the symptoms are the life-threatening or profoundly stressful events which, by themselves or in conjunction with premorbid factors, produce the stress syndrome.

Furthermore, the explicit diagnostic criteria listed in DSM-III note that there must exist after the trauma new symptoms, character traits, or modes of personality functioning that were not evident or typical of the person before being exposed to the stressful experience. Thus, we believe that *PTSD is most accurately conceptualized as a transformative, reactive process that characterizes the pattern of human adaptation to unusually stressful life events*. In addition, as Horowitz (1976) has observed, the survivor typically progresses through a predictable sequence of stages in assimilating the trauma: outcry, denial and avoidance, intrusion, transition, and integration. However, in the early phases of coping with the trauma, which may require many years, it is common for survivors to experience an alternation between the avoidance and intrusion stages of the disorder. This cyclical alternation may generate in the survivor or victim pronounced feelings of depression, anger, episodic rage, and unconscious reenactments of the event in an attempt to master the as-yet-unassimilated trauma. Among the examples of unconscious reenactment of the traumatic episode are: (1) acting-out in nightmare states or other unconscious thoughts in a *dissociative* or a "flashback" state of mind, (2) returning to the site of the trauma, and (3) the conscious or unconscious use of behaviors that were required for survival in the trauma (e.g., hyperalertness, hypervigilance, risky and dangerous actions, numbing of emotions, aggression, and other survival tactics).

It is the purpose of this chapter to explain how both violent and nonviolent behavior may be a symptom of PTSD that leads to criminal behavior. The chapter is organized into three parts. The first part presents a discussion of PTSD and the survivor mode of psychological functioning. The second part discusses the differential diagnosis of PTSD and the criteria for determining its relationship to criminal behavior. The third part discusses the preparation of a forensic report and the role of the expert witness in the legal process.

THE DISPOSITION TO CRIMINAL BEHAVIOR: PTSD AND THE SURVIVOR MODE OF PSYCHOLOGICAL FUNCTIONING

It is a truism to say that not all survivors adapt to trauma in the same way. As previous research has noted (e.g., Green, Wilson, & Lindy, 1985 [see Vol. 1]), there are many classes of variables (e.g., environmental, dispositional, demographic) that affect how an individual assimilates a traumatic event and the subsequent pattern of personality integration that characterizes their coping and ego-defensive mechanisms. Table 1 presents a modification of Wilson's (1981) typology of stress response syndromes associated with PTSD. Although beyond the scope of this chapter, inspection of Table 1 indicates that survivors may possess one or more of the different PTSD syndromes depending on (1) the stage of assimilation of the trauma, (2) the role of the individual in the trauma, (3) the nature of the trauma, and (4) premorbid personality traits and other factors.

The Survivor Mode of Psychological Functioning

The way in which someone with PTSD reexperiences his or her traumatic episodes varies from powerful, "flashback" images and emotional feelings of "being back there again" to more subtle and unconscious expression in restlessness, irritability, sleeplessness, and hyperalertness. However, upon reexperiencing the traumatic event in dreams, distressing intrusive imagery, affective flooding, or physiological hyperactivity, the survivor may feel *trapped in the trauma*, helpless, fearful that it is recurring, overwhelmed by a flood of visual images, thoughts, and emotions, and briefly disoriented as to time and space. In response to this distressing mental state, the survivor or victim typically attempts to remove the painful thoughts from conscious or unconscious awareness by avoidance mechanisms (Horowitz, 1976). Generally, avoidance is a defensive operation that usually involves repression, denial, blocking of the intrusive imagery, perceptual distortion, and projection. When

TABLE 1
A Typology of Stress Response Syndromes Among Survivor Groups

1. *Depression and suicidal syndrome.* Person feels helpless, depressed, hopeless, dejected; a sense of loss of others; may show impacted grief and have suicidal ideations. May manifest other classical signs of depression (e.g., problems sleeping, etc.).
2. *Isolation and withdrawal syndrome.* Person may live in remote, scarcely populated areas, avoids crowds, and prefers to live alone, away from others. Some prefer to live in the "woods" and maintain hyperalertness. Seeks a self-contained life-style that is under personal control.
3. *Sensation-seeking syndrome.* Person fits Zuckerman's criteria of high sensation seeking. May be an "action junkie" who only feels happy, alive, and whole when engaging in thrill- and adventure-seeking activities analogous to those performed in trauma. Generally, high-energy, intense persons who enjoy physical danger, gambling, parachute jumping, sport diving, scuba, motorcycles, and flying. Also, may develop addictive disorder, although most likely to use marijuana and cocaine as psychoactive drugs rather than depressors.
4. *Paranoid state syndrome.* Person tends to be angry, hostile, suspicious, irritable, and has explosive rage. Often feels exploited and persecuted by traumatic agent and is overly suspicious of authority and power. May maintain a hyperalertness state of perception on a chronic basis similar to that employed in trauma.
5. *Profound psychic numbing syndrome.* Person feels numb and has sense of self-continuity broken by catastrophic experience. Feels like a walking shell of former self often accompanied by loss of ego identity. Capacity for basic hope extremely diminished. Person may show catastrophic anxiety or manifest bland, zombielike stare.
6. *Alienation and cynicism syndrome.* Person is alienated and cynical about the law, the "system," the government, and authority figures. Feels outside the conventional mainstream of society. Generally, person is not depressed or preoccupied with intrusive thoughts of trauma but experiences them unconsciously. Although moral and ethical, person typically seeks an antisystem perspective in terms of moral reasoning.
7. *Problems of intimacy syndrome.* Person has strained interpersonal relations (object relations) and is emotionally distant despite strong needs for intimacy. Intimate relations often pose a threat and raise fear of loss of love objects again. When frustrated or under stress, person may react to normal stressors by flight or explosive fits.
8. *Fusion of stress syndromes with premorbid disposition syndrome.* PTSD can aggravate, precipitate, and fuse with other underlying psychiatric disorders. Typically, this includes aggravating premorbid character disorders, causing paranoid state to become predominant and overlay PTSD. In some cases PTSD can manifest classical hysterial components, such as fugue states or amnesia reactions brought on by life stress.
9. *Prosocial-humanitarian syndrome.* Person is altruistic and has *transformed* survivor guilt and other trauma-related symptoms into a nurturing humanist orientation to others and society. Person is intense and creative. Lives with existential need to work toward ends-oriented values that promote life and self-actualization. This is, perhaps, the healthiest form of coping with the stress syndromes.

Source: John P. Wilson (1981).

successful, the avoidance mechanism returns the unassimilated imagery to memory until the threshold of effective coping is weakened by demands that exceed the person's capacity to maintain control over emotionally distressing thoughts. However, as observed by Kardiner (1959), the survivor with PTSD is especially vulnerable to a broad range of stimuli that can intensify the symptoms of PTSD.

In our clinical and forensic work with survivors of profoundly stressful life events, we have observed that because of an ideational or environmental stimulus, the individual with PTSD may enter into a *survivor mode* (Figley, 1978; Wilson & Zigelbaum, 1983) of functioning, which is characterized by some or all of the following qualities: an altered state of consciousness, hyperalertness, hypervigilance, excessive autonomic nervous system arousal, frenetic behavior, paranoid ideation, mistrust, and the use of survivor skills and cognitive capacities learned during the period of the traumatic episode. *In addition, depending on the particular personality characteristics of the survivor-victim and the situational stressors that trigger the onset of the survivor mode, the person may experience an oscillation between the survivor mode of functioning and normal personality functioning. Typically, this occurs in a dissociative reaction, but it can occur in nondissociative survivor modalities.*

Three Major Subtypes of Survivor Mode Functioning

At least three major forms of behavior can be identified as part of the "survivor mode" of adaptation. For example, the survivor mode of functioning may lead to violent behavior if there is present an actual or perceived threat that produces conflict with the self-concept, sense of morality, role obligations, and commitments to significant others. In such a situation, a *dissociative reaction* may occur as a response to the approach-avoid and conflict dilemma that is present in the situation. In the dissociative state of consciousness, the survivor is likely to act similarly to that mode of coping which was employed during the trauma. Among combat veterans, a dissociative reaction to situational stress or environmental stimuli may lead to assaultive and violent actions (e.g., Wilson & Zigelbaum, 1983; Erlinder, 1984).

A second way in which the survivor mode affects the disposition to criminal action is the "action addict" syndrome. In this mode of coping with PTSD the survivor manifests many of the characteristics of the sensation-seeking motive (Zuckerman, 1979). We have found this syndrome to be quite paradoxical in nature since the survivor appears to maintain control over the degree to which he experiences intrusive imagery by *actively* seeking out situations that provide a level of arousal similar to that experienced in the original trauma. In this survivor mode, the survivor reports feeling an optimal level of arousal that is subjectively exciting, exhilarating, and stimulating because it increases the inner state of alertness in much the same way as did the precipitating trauma. We have found that these individuals typically seek out vocations or events that can provide this kind of dangerous, risky, adventuresome, and challenging activity (e.g., parachute jumping, flying, skin diving, gambling, mountain climbing, smuggling, police and fire work).

Psychodynamically, this stress response syndrome seems to achieve at least two aims. First, the motivational pattern generates an optimal level of arousal, which enhances the personal sense of being fully alive and animated by "living on the edge of experience." A second, interrelated function is ego-defensive *since the action-seeking behavioral syndrome can be viewed as a complex form of repetition compulsion (Freud, 1959) that actually blocks the onset of intrusive experience.* In this regard, the sensation-seeking activity can be considered as a defense against PTSD since intense, action-oriented enterprise may function as a natural antidepressant. Moreover, it is possible that this syndrome may have a physiological basis. If high levels of activity generate endorphins in the brain, their existence may provide a powerful neurological reward for the behavior itself.

We have also observed that when the survivor-victim is prevented from engaging in action-oriented behavior, he often becomes fully symptomatic with the disorder. It is theoretically plausible that the sensation-seeking syndrome recreates the psychological elements experienced in the trauma and enables the person to continue striving to master it by responding with self-initiated competencies that lead to successful outcomes (i.e., positive emotional arousal and avoidance of intrusive imagery). In essence, the syndrome serves to confirm to the individual that he or she is still alive. This is especially significant since many of these persons fear, at the deepest levels of consciousness, that to cease behaving in this mode will lead to an actual or symbolic death (see Lifton, 1980, for an extended discussion of symbolic death and psychoformative disintegration).

A third way the survivor mode of functioning can motivate criminal behavior may be seen in the *depression-suicide syndrome of PTSD.* In this syndrome the person feels trapped in the trauma, flooded with painful intrusive imagery, hopeless, despondent, and often reports that he or she is simply "a walking shell of his former self that should have died." In addition, the individual may show impacted grief (Shatan, 1974), survivor guilt, sadness, fear of repeating the trauma, a fear of or desire to merge with the dead, and psychic numbing. In this state the person is low in energy and drive, self-recriminating, lacks meaningful goals, and exhibits the classic symptoms of depression. Furthermore, these persons are likely to believe that they are the victims of fate and mere pawns of the events that caused their psychic and physical wounds (Wilson, Smith, & Johnson, 1985). Thus, when the individual experiences intrusive thoughts, he often fears that he will become vulnerable again to unpredictable and uncontrollable forces in his life just as he was in the trauma. Indeed, what eventually may lead to a suicide attempt is *profound* despair, survivor guilt, and the severe anxiety associated with feelings of helplessness (Seligman & Garber, 1980).

At this point, especially if the individual is subjected to other stresses in life that cannot be easily managed, he or she may attempt to kill himself/herself in order to end the psychic pain and survivor guilt by symbolically reuniting with the dead. Among some survivors such a suicidal wish may then give rise to criminal action if the individual unconsciously acts out his anger and depression in an attempt to get killed. Specifically, the actions leading to a criminal act may include pseudoassault (e.g., threatening or shooting at a police officer with no intent to kill), attempted robbery with the hope of getting shot in the act, and the purposeful verbal abuse of others who are prone to violence.

In our forensic work we have found that these types of criminal acts are poorly planned and executed. Indeed, upon completion of the illegal act, the individual does not enjoy having done it. Rather, it appears that the goal is much more unconscious and multifaceted. First, there is an attempt to get killed or attack and vent rage at the perceived source of the anguish and suffering. Second, the illegal act may be a way of "getting caught" in order to receive help for the PTSD and in the *process* enable the person to bear witness as a survivor-victim of a profound event by revealing an ultimate personal horror (Lifton, 1967). Finally, in some instances the act(s) may be an unconscious reenactment of the original trauma (also see Niederland, 1964, for examples of this tendency among victims of the Nazi persecution).

THE DIFFERENTIAL DIAGNOSIS OF PTSD: DETERMINING THE LINK TO CRIMINAL BEHAVIOR

In the courtroom and at different points in the criminal justice system it is important to employ a set of assessment procedures that will produce a valid and reliable diagnosis of the personality structure of the client. In terms of PTSD, the issue of differential diagnosis is especially important since it is a relatively new diagnostic category in DSM-III (APA, 1980) and commonly misdiagnosed by practitioners who are unfamiliar with or inexperienced in working with survivor-victim syndromes. Indeed, DSM-III makes explicit the need to differentiate PTSD from a major depression, organic brain syndromes, and other forms of psychopathology. Therefore, we will attempt to present a set of procedures that we have used in our clinical and forensic work to reach an unequivocal diagnosis of PTSD and to determine whether or not the disorder is related to a particular criminal act or set of behaviors. We wish to emphasize that many valid alternative methods are currently in use for clinical assessment. Our focus here is primarily on the assessment of PTSD and its relation to criminal behavior.

The Criteria for the Application of PTSD

The explicit diagnostic criteria for PTSD listed in DSM-III make clear two major concepts that are extremely important in terms of assessing a person's mental state in relation to a criminal act. First, the criteria indicate that the person must have been exposed to a "stressor that would evoke significant symptoms of distress in almost everyone." Second, the criteria indicate that there must exist in the person "at least two [of six] symptoms that were not present before the trauma" (p. 238). Thus, these criteria indicate that *after* the trauma the person's adaptive functioning and personality traits were changed in ways that can be measured by psychological assessment. We believe that it is useful to view the behavioral functioning of a survivor in terms of a *matrix concept*, which assesses the individual's attitudes, emotions, and behavior at three intervals: before, during, and after the traumatic event (Table 2). The purpose of this technique of assessment is to (1) determine changes in psychosocial functioning, personality dynamics, and adaptive behavior relative to the time of the trauma; (2) determine whether or not these changes in personality can be attributed to the traumatic event, particularly if PTSD is found to exist; and (3) determine whether or not there is a relationship between PTSD and a criminal act.

The Simple Case

In the simple forensic case, the defendant's history shows excellent premorbid functioning prior to the traumatic event. As culled from

TABLE 2
The Matrix Concept: The Assessment of Cognitive Style, Motivation, and Interpersonal Functioning of Survivors Before, During, and After the Traumatic Event

Personal characteristics	Level of psychosocial functioning (Observable changes in level of adaptive behavior)		
	Pretrauma	Traumatic event	Post-trauma
Cognitive style Affective and motivational state Interpersonal behavior			

Source: John P. Wilson

school records and interviews with a cross-section of family, peers, authority figures, and significant others, the survivor manifests average or above-average adaptive behavior. However, following the traumatic event there is a discernible change in the level of psychosocial functioning, personality, and adaptive behavior. Among individuals with PTSD, this is typically manifest as isolation and withdrawal, emotional constriction, sleep disturbance, depression, hyperalertness, self-medication with alcohol, and a loss of friendships and intimate relations. In addition, there may be a dramatic ideological change in world view (e.g., loss of faith in God) and significant changes in personality and personal interests (e.g., loss of interest in hobbies, sports, and previously enjoyed activities). Thus, in the simple case, the assessment process frequently reveals that the traumatic event was the major life event that occurred between the premorbid personality and the post-traumatic adaptive behavior.

The Complex Case

When a careful psychiatric and forensic assessment establishes a principal diagnosis of PTSD, the "ideal case" presents a clear psychodynamic chain of events that led to a legal difficulty. In these cases the stressors that precipitated the PTSD and the criminal behaviors are readily discernible and recognized by the defendant and significant others. However, in more complex cases there may be either some evidence of a premorbid character disorder or a specific vulnerability that may make an accurate diagnosis of the client's mental state more difficult. For example, in *The State of Louisiana v. Charles Heads (1980)* the defendant was acquitted of murdering his brother-in-law by reason of insanity caused by his PTSD. Briefly, Charles Heads was a former Marine who walked point-man on 38 long-range reconnaissance patrols in Vietnam.

In a dissociative state of consciousness, Heads killed his best friend and in-law with search-and-destroy ambush tactics without much conscious recollection of what happened. Immediately prior to the fatal shooting Heads was under much stress because his wife had left with their children and fled to the victim's home. This stressful event caused Heads to experience a vulnerable mental state since his wife and family constituted the only source of emotional support for him after Vietnam. Moreover, Heads' need for strong emotional support was intensified since at age nine he had witnessed his father shoot and kill his mother in an argument. Subsequently, Heads was raised by a maternal grandmother until joining the Marine Corps, where he experienced many combat episodes including being wounded in a surprise Viet Cong ambush. Interestingly, Heads' shooting of his brother-in-law occurred on a hot, humid August night after several days of rain in weather conditions that directly paralleled the night in which he was wounded after surviving nearly a year of elite reconnaissance work.

In this case, the expert witnesses believed he possessed *a premorbid vulnerability to a dissociative reaction and the survivor mode of functioning* because of the twin stressor events, which occurred nearly 10 years apart. Thus, when threatened by his brother-in-law, who simply wanted "no trouble at his house" but who unfortunately brandished an unloaded pistol, Heads reacted to the combined set of stressors (heat, humidity, loss of children, weapon) by reverting to combat-trained survival skills. He mistook his brother-in-law for a Viet Cong terrorist and proceeded to "search" his "hootch" after fatally shooting him with a rifle.

In other complex cases we have found that there is a full range of premorbid experiences that can either confound or fuse with a post-traumatic stress syndrome. These formative experiences include organic brain damage caused by a forceps delivery at birth; child abuse; feelings of inferiority and inadequacy; and acts of delinquency. In each case, it is important to determine, as far as possible, the precise way in which the premorbid factor has affected the adaptive functioning of the survivor prior to and after the traumatic event. For example, if there is a clear history of antisocial behavior across time intervals in the matrix, it is unlikely that the current legal or psychological problem can be attributed to PTSD as the major causal variable. In other cases, the exposure to stressors in the trauma may seriously aggravate an underlying disposition or character trait. Finally, it is also possible that a premorbid factor may exert very little influence on the survivor's current behavior. This is most likely to occur when one can document a strong relationship between the PTSD symptoms, the antecedent stressor events, and the behavior in question. Clearly, Charles Heads' childhood rendered him vulnerable; he needed loving and caring persons in his life. However, his actions in the shooting were those of a combat soldier, which, in turn, could be directly connected to a 10-year history of undiagnosed and untreated PTSD.

Assessing the Linkage Between PTSD and Criminal Behavior

The matrix concept of assessing PTSD enables the clinician to gather information pertinent to a differential diagnosis of PTSD. However, the central forensic issue concerns the *causal link* between the defendant's mental state and the alleged crime. Thus, assuming that a diagnosis of PTSD has been made, the next task is to demonstrate as scientifically as possible its relation or nonrelation to the criminal act. To determine this it is important to gather as comprehensive a set of documents as possible. In cases involving criminal litigation, it is especially important to analyze information from the following sources: (1) all legal documents (e.g., arrest records, police investigations, criminal indictment, laboratory tests); (2) direct psychiatric interviews and the results of biomedical and psychological testing (e.g., MMPI, blood alchohol level); (3) affidavits and statements made by significant others and witnesses that pertain to significant changes following the traumatic event(s) and specific criminal charges; (4) other records (e.g., medical records, military records, VA records, school records, organizational membership records); and (5) any other documents deemed pertinent to understanding the defendant.

Thus, the information obtained from the above-mentioned sources provides a wealth of material for use in rendering a diagnosis based on the matrix concept presented earlier. Taken as a set, these sources of data help the examiner to gain a clear picture of: childhood and adolescent development, the nature and dynamics of the family, academic and intellectual growth, the adaptive competencies and areas of vulnerability and insecurity, motivational and career goals, sexual development and adjustment, personal health, work performance, and the self-concept of the survivor.

PREPARING THE FORENSIC REPORT

In organizing a psychiatric/psychological document for forensic or clinical purposes, it is important that the central issues or questions to be
answered be stated at the beginning of the report. We believe that this
is particularly important since the report will discuss the different
sources of information that will provide the basis of a differential diagnosis and a psychiatric opinion in regard to a specific set of actions.
Furthermore, in legal cases involving issues of criminal liability it is
imperative that the report explain the psychodynamic chain of events
that led to the criminal act. It is not sufficient to merely form an opinion
that a client has a post-traumatic stress disorder; the linkage of PTSD
and/or other mental disorders to the criminal act must be explained
logically and coherently by the sources of data used to make the diagnosis. Stated somewhat differently, we believe that the disparate sources
of information should combine to reach a valid conclusion that rules out
competing hypotheses or alternative explanations of the data. If this is
done, one can conclude with reasonable medical and scientific certainty
that there is a demonstrable relationship between the survivor's mental
state at a given point in time and the alleged criminal act that is of such
a nature as to exculpate, diminish, or mitigate criminal responsibility.

Since there is no uniform procedure governing the organization of a
psychiatric/psychological document for forensic purposes, we present
below an *outline* of one we have developed during the last six years in
our work together in cases in which the defendant was diagnosed as
suffering from PTSD. This *outline* is not intended to portray a comprehensive report but merely to illustrate the organizational format and
vignettes from selected cases.

A General Outline of the Forensic Report

 1. Psychiatric Report on (name of client)
 2. *Purpose of this assessment:*
    Note that report will attempt to answer three questions: (1)
    Does the defendant suffer from a recognizable psychiatric dis-
    order classified under the American Psychiatric Association
    Diagnostic and Statistical Manual of Mental Disorders, third edi-
    tion? (2) If so, is it of a type that would exculpate the defendant
    from criminal responsibility? (3) Is there a relationship between
    the client's traumatic life experiences and the alleged crime?
 3. *Qualifications of the examiners.*

4. *Persons interviewed:* All persons interviewed for purposes of the report are listed here.
5. *Documents reviewed:* All documents reviewed are listed here.
6. *Assessment process:* In this section is contained a general description of the assessment process used in reaching a diagnosis and opinion. Presented below is an illustration.

    (a) *Psychiatric interviewing:* This is a one-to-one diagnostic interview process between the clinician(s) and the patient exploring the emotional and psychological basis of the patient's emotional response systems and the behavioral expressions of these systems. (b) *Psychological testing:* This is a battery of standardized psychological tests which, when integrated, provide a good picture of the patient's personality structure. (c) *Life and psychological history:* This is a systematic, historical interview that plots out a detailed, chronological overview of the patient's psychological, emotional, medical, and behavioral history. (d) *Case conference:* The various evaluating staff responsible for performing the above components have met in extensive conferences to discuss and integrate the data.
7. *Identifying data:* Indicates the client's name, age, marital status, address, occupation, and referral date and source.
8. (a) *Family background;* (b) *childhood and adolescent development;* (c) *dating and heterosexual history.*
9. *Educational history.*
10. *Criminal/legal history.*
11. *Occupational history.*
12. *Alcohol and drug history.*
13. *Medical and psychiatric history.*
14. *History or chronology of events associated with the traumatic experiences (for combat veterans, this would be history of military experiences).*
15. *Post-traumatic adjustment.*
16. *Results of psychological testing.* (Results of all psychological testing performed with comments on testing performed by the prosecutor if it is available for analysis.)
17. *Review of biomedical and neurological testing.*
18. *Answer to assessment questions.* Based on the presentation of all material in the report, the assessment questions are now answered.
19. *Diagnostic impressions.* (Follow the guidelines in DSM-III for presenting a diagnostic summary, i.e., Axis I-V.)

Mr. X.'s diagnoses, with reasonable medical and psychological certainty, based on the latest definitions of the American Psychiatric Association as stated in the third edition of the *Diagnostic and Statistical Manual of Mental Disorders* (DSM-III) are as follows: [Example]

Axis I: 309.81 Post-traumatic stress disorder, chronic.

         R/O 296.64 Bipolar disorder, mixed with psychotic features.

         R/O 295.30 Schizophrenia, paranoid type.

         R/O 294.80 Atypical or mixed organic brain syndrome.

Axis II: 301.22 Schizotypal personality disorder, provisional.

Axis III: Physical disorders: (1) central nervous system damage, etiology unknown; (2) hearing loss, etiology unknown.

Axis IV: Severity of psychosocial stressors: 7 catastrophic —atrocities witnessed in Vietnam; current incarceration and separation from loved ones.

Axis V: Highest level of adaptive functioning in past year: O unspecified—unable to make determination due to current incarceration.

20. *Differential diagnosis of post-traumatic stress order* (i.e., as distinct from other anxiety disorders, depressive states, organic impairments, and psychoses).

21. *Relationship between client's mental state and criminal charges.* (A discussion of the psychodynamic chain of events that led to the present criminal charges. Specifically, a detailed analysis explains the motivation for the alleged crime by showing the linkage between the mental disorder and the criminal act in question.)

SUMMARY

The purpose of this chapter is to suggest the relevance of PTSD to criminal behavior and its possible use as a legal defense. Moreover, we presented a set of procedures for use in the assessment of PTSD among survivors of traumatic events. It should be apparent by now that in order to arrive at a valid diagnosis of the stress syndrome the mental health professional needs to be familiar with the following:

1. *The nature and dynamics of PTSD. To us PTSD is a transformative reactive process. It characterizes the normal pattern of human adaptation to*

abnormally stressful experiences. Individuals with PTSD move through a predictable sequence of stages from initial denial to gradual assimilation. They reexperience the trauma many times in cycles that vary in frequency, severity, and duration of symptom expression.

2. *The criminal behavior of some individuals may be acts of the survivor mode.* This survivor mode of coping with PTSD is characterized by an altered state of consciousness, hyperalertness, hypervigilance, excessive autonomic nervous system arousal, frenetic behavior, paranoid features, mistrust, and the use of survival skills and cognitive capacities learned during the period of trauma. In the survivor mode the individual may experience an oscillation between normal personality processes and the survivor mode itself.

3. *Combat veterans are especially vulnerable to violent behavior.* If there exists an actual or perceived threat, especially to combat veterans, there is an increased probability of violent behavior since they may revert to survival skills learned in a war to cope with the threat. We have suggested that the three principal types of survivor mode functioning associated with criminal behavior are dissociative states, the depression-suicide syndrome, and the sensation-seeking syndrome.

4. *An effective forensic examination requires several key elements.* To adequately make a differential diagnosis of PTSD it is necessary to document in detail the different antecedent stressor experiences that might be associated with the development of the stress disorder. In addition to the administration of standard forensic and psychological tests to a client, it is also necessary to establish a diagnosis of PTSD. Moreover, if PTSD is diagnosed, it is necessary to determine its relationship to an alleged criminal act by examining the changes in psychosocial functioning in cognitive style, motivation, and interpersonal behavior before, during, and after the trauma. Finally, it is important to analyze the psychodynamic chain of events that are associated with the criminal behavior in question: i.e., the logical relationship between the antecedent stressor events that caused the PTSD and how it affected the subsequent adaptive functioning of the individual.

Today there is a growing recognition in the legal and psychological community that the survivors and victims of extremely stressful life events may struggle for years to integrate a traumatic experience into their self-structure without distressing consequences. Beyond the psychological sequelae of PTSD remain larger philosophical and moral issues. The historical lessons of Hiroshima, the Holocaust, World War II, and more recently the Vietnam War and the Buffalo Creek Dam Disaster have raised critical questions that have profound consequences in terms of the lives and well-being of victims and survivors. For example, what rights to financial compensation and human services are they entitled to have? Should society provide various forms of psychosocial support and assistance to the survivor or victim who has PTSD? If PTSD causes a disability in work, intimate relations, and normal psychological functioning, should it be treated as equivalent to a physical disability? Finally, in terms of criminal litigation, should a defendant with PTSD be given special consideration in terms of sentencing and treatment for PTSD instead of incarceration?

Clearly, the future will see a convergence of philosophical, legal, and psychological insight as our knowledge of survivor syndromes creates new challenges and insights into the nature of humanity and the deeper meaning of justice. To the survivor-victim rests the task of transforming the trauma and finding new meaning and purpose in life. To society rests the task of restoring equity and justice to those who were victimized or traumatized by the confluence of social and historical forces.

REFERENCES

American Psychiatric Association. (1980). *Diagnostic and statistical manual of mental disorders* (3rd ed.). Washington, DC: American Psychiatric Association.

Eitinger, L., & Strom, A. (1973). *Mortality and morbidity following extreme stress.* New York: Humanitas Press.

Erlinder, P. (1984, March). Paying the price for Vietnam: PTSD and criminal behavior. *Boston College Law Review, XXV*(2).

Figley, C. R. (1978). *Stress disorders among Vietnam veterans.* New York: Brunner/Mazel.

Figley, C. R., & Leventman, S. (1980). *Strangers at home: Vietnam veterans since the war.* New York: Praeger.

Figley, C. R. (Ed.). (1985). *Trauma and its wake: The study and treatment of post-traumatic stress disorder.* New York: Brunner/Mazel.

Freud, S. (1959). *Introductory lectures on psychoanalysis.* New York: W. W. Norton.

Gleser, G. C., Green, B. L., & Winget, C. N. (1981). *Buffalo Creek revisited: Prolonged psychosocial effects of disaster.* New York: Simon & Schuster.

Green, B., Wilson, J. P., & Lindy, J. (1985). Conceptualizing post-traumatic stress disorder: A psychosocial framework. In C. R. Figley (Ed.). *Trauma and its wake: The study and treatment of post-traumatic stress disorder* (pp. 53–69). New York: Brunner/Mazel.

Horowitz, M. J. (1976). *Stress response syndromes.* New York: Jason Aronson.

Horowitz, M. J. (1979). Psychological response to serious life events. In V. Hamilton & D. M. Warburton (Eds.), *Human stress and cognition.* New York: Wiley.

Kardiner, A. (1959). Traumatic neuroses of war. In S. Arieti (Ed.), *American handbook of psychiatry* (Vol. 1). New York: Basic Books.

Krystal, H. (1969). *Massive psychic trauma.* New York: International Universities Press.

Lifton, R. J. (1967). *Death in life: Survivors of Hiroshima.* New York: Simon & Schuster.

Lifton, R. J. (1980). *The broken connection.* New York: Simon & Schuster.

Niederland, W. (1964). The problem of the survivor. In H. Krystal (Ed.), *Massive psychic trauma.* New York: International Universities Press.

Seligman, M. E., & Garber, J. (1980). *Human helplessness.* New York: Academic Press.
Shatan, C. F. (1974). Through the membrane of reality: Impacted grief and perceptual dissonance in Vietnam combat veterans. *Psychiatric Opinion, 11,* 6–15.
The State of Louisiana v. Charles Heads (1980). The Vietnam connection: Charles Heads verdict. *Criminal Defense, 1.*
Wilson, J. P. (1980). Conflict, stress and growth: The effects of war on psychosocial development among Vietnam veterans. In C. R. Figley & S. Leventman (Eds.), *Strangers at home: Vietnam veterans since the war.* New York: Praeger.
Wilson, J. P. (1981). *Cognitive control mechanisms in stress response syndromes.* Unpublished manuscript. Cleveland State University.
Wilson, J. P., & Krauss, G. E. (1980). *The Vietnam era stress inventory.* Cleveland State University.
Wilson, J. P., & Krauss, G. E. (1985). Predicting post-traumatic stress syndromes among Vietnam veterans. In W. Kelly (Ed.), *Post-traumatic stress disorder and the war veteran patient.* New York: Brunner/Mazel.
Wilson, J. P., Smith, W. K., & Johnson, S. K. (1985). A comparative analysis of PTSD among various survivor groups. In C. R. Figley (Ed.), *Trauma and its wake: The study and treatment of post-traumatic stress disorder* (pp. 142–172). New York: Brunner/Mazel.
Wilson, J. P., & Zigelbaum, S. D. (1983). The Vietnam veteran on trial: The relation of post-traumatic stress disorder to criminal behavior. *Behavioral Sciences and the Law, 4,* 69–84.
Zuckerman, M. (1979). *Sensation seeking.* Hillsdale, NJ: L. Erlbaum.

Name Index

Subject Index

i

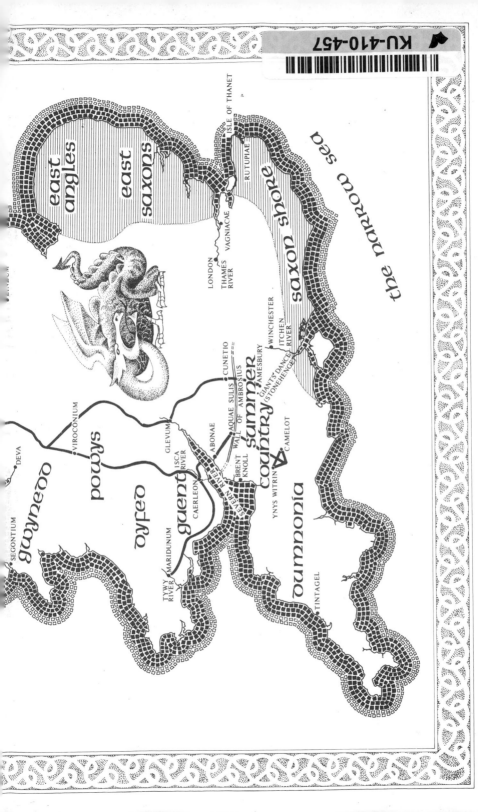

the narrow sea

east angles

east saxons

ISLE OF THANET

RUTUPIAE

VAGNIACAE

saxon shore

LONDON

THAMES RIVER

WINCHESTER

ITCHEN RIVER

AMESBURY

GIANTS DANCE/STONEHENGE

CUNETIO

WALL OF AMBROSIUS

AQUAE SULIS

summer country

GLEVUM

VIROCONIUM

powys

ISCA RIVER

ABONAE

BRENT KNOLL

SEVERN RIVER

CAMELOT

DEVA

gwynedd

dyfed

guent

CAERLEON

YNYS WITRIN

MARIDUNUM

SEGONTIUM

TYWY RIVER

dumnonia

TINTAGEL

The Last Enchantment

Also by Mary Stewart

MADAM, WILL YOU TALK?

WILDFIRE AT MIDNIGHT

THUNDER ON THE RIGHT

NINE COACHES WAITING

MY BROTHER MICHAEL

THE IVY TREE

THE MOONSPINNERS

THIS ROUGH MAGIC

AIRS ABOVE THE GROUND

THE GABRIEL HOUNDS

THE WIND OFF THE SMALL ISLES

THE CRYSTAL CAVE

THE HOLLOW HILLS

TOUCH NOT THE CAT

For Children

THE LITTLE BROOMSTICK

LUDO AND THE STAR HORSE

MARY STEWART

The
Last Enchantment

HODDER AND STOUGHTON
LONDON SYDNEY AUCKLAND TORONTO

British Library Cataloguing in Publication Data
Stewart, Mary, b. 1916
    The last enchantment
    I. Title
    823'.9'1F   PR6069.T46L/

ISBN 0 340 23917 4

CONTENTS

*To one who was dead
and is alive again,
who was lost,
and is found.*

BOOK I

Dunpeldyr

Not every king would care to start his reign with the wholesale massacre of children. This is what they whisper of Arthur, even though in other ways he is held up as the type itself of the noble ruler, the protector alike of high and lowly.

It is harder to kill a whisper than even a shouted calumny. Besides, in the minds of simple men, to whom the High King is the ruler of their lives, and the dispenser of all fates, Arthur would be held accountable for all that happened in his realm, evil and good alike, from a resounding victory in the battlefield to a bad rainstorm or a barren flock.

So, although a witch plotted the massacre, and another king gave the order for it, and though I myself tried to shoulder the blame, the murmur still persists; that in the first year of his reign, Arthur the High King had his troops seek out and destroy some score of newly-born babies in the hope of catching in that bloody net one single boy-child, his bastard by incest with his half-sister Morgause.

"Calumny", I have called it, and it would be good to be able to declare openly that the story is a lie. But it is not quite that. It is a lie that he ordered the slaughter; but his sin was the first cause of it, and, though it would never have occurred to him to murder innocent children, it is true that he wanted his own child killed. So it is just that some of the blame should rest on him; just, too, that some of it should cling to me; for I, Merlin, who am accounted a man of power and vision, had waited idly by while the dangerous child was engendered, and the tragic term set to the peace and freedom which Arthur could win for his people. I can bear the blame, for now I am beyond men's judgment, but Arthur is still young enough to feel the sting of the story, and be haunted by thoughts of atonement; and when it happened he was younger still, in all the first white-and-golden flush of victory and kingship, held up on the love of the people, the acclamation of the soldiers, and the blaze of mystery that surrounded the drawing of the sword from the stone.

It happened like this. King Uther Pendragon lay with his army at Luguvallium in the northern kingdom of Rheged, where he was to face a massive Saxon attack under the brothers Colgrim and Badulf, grandsons of Hengist. The young Arthur, still little more than a boy, was brought to this, his first field, by his foster-father Count Ector of Galava, who presented him to the King. Arthur had been kept in ignorance of his royal birth and parentage, and Uther, though he had kept himself informed of the boy's growth and progress, had never once seen him since he was born. This because, during the wild night of love when Uther had lain with Ygraine, then the wife of Gorlois, Duke of Cornwall and Uther's most faithful commander, the old Duke himself had been killed. His death, though no fault of Uther's, weighed so heavily on the King that he swore never to claim for his own any child born of that night's guilty love. In due course Arthur had been handed to me to rear, and this I had done, at a far remove from both King and Queen. But there had been no other son born to them, and at last King Uther, who had ailed for some time, and who knew the danger of the Saxon threat he faced at Luguvallium, was forced to send for the boy, to acknowledge him publicly as his heir and present him to the assembled nobles and petty kings.

But before he could do so, the Saxons attacked. Uther, though too sick to ride at the head of the troops, took the field in a litter, with Cador, Duke of Cornwall, in command of the right, and on the left King Coel of Rheged, with Caw of Strathclyde and other leaders from the north. Only Lot, King of Lothian and Orkney, failed to take the field. King Lot, a powerful king but a doubtful ally, held his men in reserve, to throw them into the fight where and when they should be needed. It was said that he held back deliberately in the hope that Uther's army would be destroyed, and that in the event the kingdom might fall to him. If so, his hopes were defeated. When, in the fierce fighting around the King's litter in the centre of the field, young Arthur's sword broke in his hand, King Uther threw to his hand his own royal sword, and with it (as men understood it) the leadership of the kingdom. After that he lay back in his litter and watched the boy, ablaze like some comet of victory, lead an attack that put the Saxons to rout.

Afterwards, at the victory feast, Lot headed a faction of rebel lords who opposed Uther's choice of heir. At the height of the brawling, contentious feast, King Uther died, leaving the boy, with myself beside him, to face and win them over.

What happened then has become the stuff of song and story. Enough here to say that, by his own kingly bearing, and through the sign sent from the god, Arthur showed himself undoubted King.

But the evil seed had already been sown. On the previous day, while he was still ignorant of his true parentage, Arthur had met Morgause, Uther's bastard daughter, and his own half-sister. She was very lovely, and he was young, in all the flush of his first victory, so, when she sent her maid for him that night he went eagerly, with no more thought of what the night's pleasure might bring but the cooling of his hot young blood and the loss of his maidenhood.

Hers, you may be sure, had been lost long ago. Nor was she innocent in other ways. She knew who Arthur was, and sinned with him knowingly, in a bid for power. Marriage, of course, she could not hope for, but a bastard born of incest might be a powerful weapon in her hand when the old King, her father, died, and the new young King took the throne.

When Arthur found what he had done, he might have added to his sin by killing her, but for my intervention. I banished her from court, bidding her take horse for York, where Uther's true-born daughter Morgan was lodged with her attendants, awaiting her marriage to the King of Lothian. Morgause, who like everyone else in those days was afraid of me, obeyed me and went, to practise her woman's spells and nourish her bastard in exile. Which she did, as you will hear, at her sister Morgan's expense.

But of that later. It would be better, now, to go back to the time when, in the breaking of a new and auspicious day, with Morgause out of mind and on her way to York, Arthur Pendragon sat in Luguvallium of Rheged to receive homage, and the sun shone.

I was not there. I had already done homage, in the small hours between moonlight and sunrise, in the forest shrine where Arthur had lifted the sword of Maximus from the stone altar, and by that act declared himself the rightful King. Afterwards, when he, with the other princes and nobles, had gone in all the pomp and splendour of triumph, I had stayed alone in the shrine. I had a debt to pay to the gods of the place.

It was called a chapel now – the Perilous Chapel, Arthur had named it – but it had been a holy place long before men had laid stone on stone and raised the altar. It was sacred first to the gods of the land itself, the small spirits that haunt hill and stream and forest, together with the greater gods of air, whose power breathes through cloud and frost and speaking wind. No one knew for whom the chapel had first been built. Later, with the Romans, had come Mithras, the soldiers' god, and an altar was raised to him within it. But the place was still haunted with all its ancient holiness; the older gods received their sacrifices, and the nine-fold lights still burned unquenched by the open doorway.

All through the years when Arthur had been hidden, for his own safety, with Count Ector in the Wild Forest, I had stayed near him, known only as the keeper of the shrine, the hermit of the Chapel in the Green. Here I had finally hidden the great sword of Maximus (whom the Welsh called Macsen), until the boy should come of an age to lift it, and with it drive the kingdom's enemies out and destroy them. The Emperor Maximus himself had done so, a hundred years before, and men thought of the great sword now as a talisman, a god-sent sword of magic, to be wielded only for victory, and only by the man who had the right. I, Merlinus Ambrosius, kin to Macsen, had lifted it from its long hiding-place in the earth, and had laid it aside for the one to come who would be greater than I. I hid it first in a flooded cave below the forest lake, then, finally, on the chapel altar, locked like carving in the stone, and shrouded from common sight and touch in the cold white fire called by my art from heaven.

From this unearthly blaze, to the wonder and terror of all present, Arthur had raised the sword. Afterwards, when the new King and his nobles and captains had gone from the chapel, it could be seen that the wildfire of the new god had scoured the place of all that had formerly been held sacred, leaving only the altar, to be freshly decked for him alone.

I had long known that this god brooked no companions. He was not mine, nor (I suspected) would he ever be Arthur's, but throughout the sweet three corners of Britain he was moving, emptying the ancient shrines, and changing the face of worship. I had seen with awe, and with grief, how his fires had swept away the signs of an older kind of holiness; but he had marked the Perilous Chapel – and perhaps the sword – as his own, beyond denying.

So all through that day I worked to make the shrine clean again and fit for its new tenant. It took a long time; I was stiff from recent hurts, and from a night of sleepless vigil; besides, there are things that must be performed decently and in order. But at length all was done, and when, shortly before sunset, the servant of the shrine came back from the town, I took the horse he had brought, and rode down through the quiet woods.

★   ★   ★

It was late when I came to the gates, but these were open, and no one challenged me as I rode in. The place was still in a roar; the sky was alight with bonfires, the air throbbed with singing, and through the smoke one could smell roasting meats and the reek of wine. Even the presence of the dead King, lying there in the monastery church with his guards around him, could not put a bridle on men's tongues. The times were too full of happening, the town too small: only the very old and the very young found sleep that night.

I found none, certainly. It was well after midnight when my servant came in, and after him Ralf.

He ducked his head for the lintel – he was a tall young man – and waited till the door was shut, regarding me with a look as wary as any he had ever given me in the past when he had been my page, and feared my powers.

"You're still up?"

"As you see." I was sitting in the high-backed chair beside the window. The servant had brought a brazier, kindled against the chill of the September night. I had bathed, and looked to my hurts again, and let the servant put me into a loose bedgown, before I sent him away and composed myself to rest. After the climax of fire and pain and glory that had brought Arthur to the kingship, I, who had lived my life only for that, felt the need for solitude and silence. Sleep would not come yet, but I sat, content and passive, with my eyes on the brazier's idle glow.

Ralf, still armed and jewelled as I had seen him that morning at Arthur's side in the chapel, looked tired and hollow-eyed himself, but he was young, and the night's climax was for him a new beginning, rather than an end. He said, abruptly: "You should be resting. I gather that you were attacked last night on the way up to the chapel. How badly were you hurt?"

"Not mortally, though it feels bad enough! No, no, don't worry, it was bruises rather than wounds, and I've seen to them. But I'm afraid I lamed your horse for you. I'm sorry about that."

"I've seen him. There's no real damage. It will take a week, no more. But you – you look exhausted, Merlin. You should be given time to rest."

"And am I not to be?" As he hesitated, I lifted a brow at him. "Come, out with it. What don't you want to say to me?"

The wary look broke into something like a grin. But his voice, suddenly formal, was quite expressionless, the voice of a courtier who is not quite sure which way, as they say, the deer will run. "Prince Merlin, the King has desired me to bid you to his apartments. He wants to see you as soon as it is convenient for you." As he spoke his eye lingered on the door in the wall opposite the window. Until last night Arthur had slept in that annexe of my chamber, and had come and gone at my bidding. Ralf caught my eye, and the grin became real.

"In other words, straight away," he said. "I'm sorry, Merlin, but that's the message as it came to me through the chamberlain. They might have left it till morning. I was assuming you would be asleep."

"Sorry? For what? Kings have to start somewhere. Has he had any rest yet himself?"

"Not a hope. But he's got rid of the crowd at last, and they cleared the royal rooms while we were up at the shrine. He's there now."

"Attended?"

"Only Bedwyr."

That, I knew, meant, besides his friend Bedwyr, a small host of chamberers and servants, and possibly, even, a few people still waiting in the antechambers.

"Then ask him to excuse me for a few minutes. I'll be there as soon as I've dressed. Will you send Lleu to me, please?"

But this he would not have. The servant was sent with the message, and then, as naturally as he had done in the past when he was a boy, Ralf helped me himself. He took the bedgown from me and folded it, and gently, with care for my stiff limbs, eased me into a day-robe, then knelt to put my sandals on and fasten them.

"Did the day go well?" I asked him.

"Very well. No shadow on it."

"Lot of Lothian?"

He glanced up, grimly amused. "Kept his place. The affair of the chapel has left its brand on him . . . as it has on all of us." The last phrase was muttered, as if to himself, as he bent his head to buckle the second sandal.

"On me, too, Ralf," I said. "I am not immune from the god's fire, either. As you see. How is Arthur?"

"Still on his own high and burning cloud." This time the amusement held affection. He got to his feet. "All the same, I think he's already looking ahead for storms. Now, your girdle. Is this the one?"

"It will do. Thank you. Storms? So soon? I suppose so." I took the girdle from him and knotted it. "Do you intend to stay with him, Ralf, and help him weather them, or do you count your duty done?" Ralf had spent the last nine years in Galava of Rheged, the remote corner of the country where Arthur had lived, unknown, as the ward of Count Ector. He had married a northern girl, and had a young family.

"To tell you the truth I've not thought about that yet," he said. "Too much has happened, all too quickly." He laughed. "One thing, if I stay with him, I can see that I'll look back with longing on the peaceful days when I had nothing to do but ride guard on those young dev— that is, on Bedwyr and the King! And you? You will hardly stay here as the hermit of the Green Chapel now? Will you come out of your fastness, and go with him?"

"I must. I have promised. Besides, it is my place. Not yours, though, unless you wish it. Between us, we made him King, and that is the end of the first part of the story. You have a choice now. But you'll have plenty of time to make it." He opened the door for me, and stood aside to let me pass him. I paused. "We whistled up a strong wind, Ralf. Let us see which way it will blow us."

"You'd let it?"

I laughed. "I have a speaking mind that tells me I may have to. Come, let us start by obeying this summons."

★   ★   ★

There were a few people still in the main antechamber to the King's apartments, but these were mostly servants, clearing and bearing away the remains of a meal which the King had apparently just finished. Guards stood woodenly at the door to the inner rooms. On a low bench near a window a young page lay, fast asleep; I remembered seeing him when I had come this way three days ago to talk with the dying Uther. Ulfin, the King's body-servant and chief chamberlain, was absent. I could guess where he was. He would serve the new King with all the devotion he had given to Uther, but tonight he would be found with his old master in the monastery church. The man who waited by Arthur's door was a stranger to me, as were half the servants there; they were men and women who normally served Rheged's own king in his castle, and who were helping with the extra pressure of work brought by the occasion, and by the High King's presence.

But they all knew me. As I entered the antechamber there was a sudden silence, and a complete cessation of movement, as if a spell had been cast. A servant carrying platters balanced along his arm, froze like someone faced with the Gorgon's head, and the faces that turned to me were frozen similarly, pale and gape-mouthed, full of awe. I caught Ralf's eye on me, sardonic and affectionate. His brow quirked. "You see?" it said to me, and I understood more fully his own hesitation when he came to my room with the King's message.

As my servant and companion he had been close to me in the past, and had many times, in prophecy, and in what men call magic, watched and felt my power at work; but the power that had blazed and blown through the Perilous Chapel last night had been something of quite a different order. I could only guess at the stories that must have run, swift and changing as the wildfire itself, through Luguvallium: it was certain that the humbler folk had talked of nothing else all day. And like all strange tales, it would grow with the telling.

So they stood staring. As for the awe that frosted the air, like the cold wind that comes before a ghost, I was used to that. I walked through the motionless crowd to the King's door, and the guard moved aside without a challenge, but before the chamberlain could lay a hand to the door it opened, and Bedwyr came out.

Bedwyr was a quiet, dark boy, a month or two younger than Arthur. His father was Ban, the King of Benoic, and a cousin of a king of Brittany. The two boys had been close friends since childhood, when Bedwyr had been sent to Galava to learn the arts of war from Ector's master-at-arms, and to share the lessons I gave "Emrys" (as Arthur was then called) at the shrine in the Wild Forest. He was already showing himself to be that strange contradiction, a born fighting man who is also a poet, at home equally with action or with the world of fancy and music. Pure Celt, you might say, where Arthur, like my father the High King Ambrosius, was Roman. I might have expected to see in Bedwyr's face the same awe left by the events of the miraculous night as in the faces of the humbler men present, but I could see only the aftermath of joy, a sort of uncomplicated happiness, and a sturdy trust in the future.

He stood aside for me, smiling. "He's alone now."

"Where will you sleep?"

"My father is lodging in the west tower."

"Goodnight, then, Bedwyr."

But as I moved to pass him he prevented me. He bent quickly and took my hand, then snatched it to him, and kissed it. "I should have known you would see that it all came right. I was afraid, for a few minutes there in the hall, when Lot and his jackals started that treacherous fracas –"

"Hush," I said. He had spoken softly, but there were ears to hear.

"That's over for the present. Leave it. And go straight to your father in the west tower. Do you understand?"

The dark eyes glimmered. "King Lot lodges, they tell me, in the eastern one?"

"Exactly."

"Don't worry. I've already had the same warning from Emrys. Good night, Merlin."

"Good night, and a peaceful sleep to us all. We need it."

He grinned, sketched a half salute, and went. I nodded to the waiting servant, and went in. The door shut behind me.

The royal rooms had been cleared of the apparatus of sickness, and the great bed stripped of its crimson covers. The floor tiles were freshly scoured and polished, and over the bed lay new unbleached sheets, and a rug of wolfskins. The chair with the red cushion and the dragon worked on the back in gold stood there still, with its footstool and the tall tripod lamp beside it. The windows were open to the cool September night, and the air from them sent the lampflames sideways, and made strange shadows on the painted walls.

Arthur was alone. He was over by a window, one knee on a stool that stood there, his elbows on the sill. The window gave, not on the town, but on the strip of garden that edged the river. He gazed out into the dark, and I thought I could see him drinking, as from another river, deep draughts of the fresh and moving air. His hair was damp, as if he had just washed, but he was still in the clothes he had worn for the day's ceremonies; white and silver, with a belt of Welsh gold set with turquoises and buckled with enamel-work. He had taken off his sword-belt, and the great sword Caliburn hung in its sheath on the wall beyond the bed. The lamplight smouldered in the jewels of the hilt; emerald, topaz, sapphire. It flashed, too, from the ring on the boy's hand; Uther's ring, carved with the Dragon crest.

He heard me, and turned. He looked rarefied and light, as if the winds of the day had blown through him and left him weightless. His skin had the stretched pallor of exhaustion, but his eyes were brilliant and alive. About him, already there and unmistakable, was the mystery that falls like a mantle on a king. It was in his high look, and the turn of his head. Never again would "Emrys" be able to lurk in shadow. I wondered afresh how, through all those hidden years, we had kept him safe and secret among lesser men.

"You wanted me," I said.

"I've wanted you all day. You promised to be near me while I went through this business of hatching into a king. Where were you?"

"Within call, if not within reach. I was at the shrine – the chapel – till almost sunset. I thought you'd be busy."

He gave a little crack of laughter. "You call it that? It felt like being eaten alive. Or perhaps like being born . . . and a hard birth, at that. I said 'hatching', didn't I? Suddenly to find oneself a prince is hard enough, but even that is as different from being a king as the egg is from the day-old chick."

"At least make it an eaglet."

"In time, perhaps. That's been the trouble, of course. Time, there's been no time. One moment to be nobody – someone's unacknowledged bastard, and glad to be given the chance to get within shouting distance of a battle, with maybe a glimpse of the King himself in passing; the next – having drawn a couple of breaths as Prince and royal heir – to be High King myself, and with such a flourish as no king can ever have had before. I still feel as if I'd been kicked up the steps of the throne from a kneeling position right down on the floor."

I smiled. "I know how you feel, more or less. I was never kicked half as high, but then I was a great deal lower down to start with. Now, can you slow down sufficiently to get some sleep? Tomorrow will be here soon enough. Do you want a sleeping potion?"

"No, no, when did I ever? I'll sleep as soon as you've gone. Merlin, I'm sorry to ask you to come here at this late hour, but I had to talk to you, and there's been no chance till now. Nor will there be tomorrow."

He came away from the window as he spoke, and crossed to a table where papers and tablets were lying. He picked up a stilus and, with the blunt end, smoothed the wax. He did it absently, his head bent so that the dark hair swung forward, and the lamplight slid over the line of his cheek and touched the black lashes fringing the lowered lids. My eyes blurred. Time ran back. It was Ambrosius my father who stood there, fidgeting with the stilus, and saying to

me: "If a king had you beside him, he could rule the
world . . ."

Well, his dream had come true at last, and the time was now. I
blinked memory away, and waited for the day-old king to speak.

"I've been thinking," he said abruptly. "The Saxon army was not
utterly destroyed, and I have had no firm report yet about Colgrim
himself, or Badulf. I think they both got safely away. We may hear
within the next day or so that they have taken ship and gone, either
home across the sea, or back to the Saxon territories in the south. Or
they may simply have taken refuge in the wild lands north of the
Wall, and be hoping to regroup when they have gathered strength
again." He looked up. "I have no need to pretend to you, Merlin. I
am not a seasoned warrior, and I've no means of judging how
decisive that defeat was, or what the possibilities are of a Saxon
recovery. I've taken advice, of course. I called a quick council at
sunset, when the other business was concluded. I sent for – that is, I
would have liked you to be there, but you were still up at the chapel.
Coel couldn't be there, either . . . You'd know he was wounded,
of course; you probably saw him yourself? What are his chances?"

"Slight. He's an old man, as you know, and he got a nasty slash.
He bled too much before help got to him."

"I was afraid of it. I did go to see him, but was told he was
unconscious, and they were afraid of inflammation of the lungs . . .
Well, Prince Urbgen, his heir, came in his stead, with Cador, and
Caw of Strathclyde. Ector and Ban of Benoic were there, too. I
talked it over with them, and they all say the same thing; someone
will have to follow Colgrim up. Caw has to go north again as soon
as may be; he has his own frontier to hold. Urbgen must stay here in
Rheged, with his father the king at death's door. So the obvious
choice would be Lot or Cador. Well, it cannot be Lot, I think you
will agree there? For all his oath of fealty, there in the chapel, I won't
trust him yet, and certainly not within reach of Colgrim."

"I agree. You'll send Cador, then? You can surely have no more
doubts of him?"

Cador, Duke of Cornwall, was indeed the obvious choice. He
was a man in the prime of his strength, a seasoned fighter, and loyal.
I had once mistakenly thought him Arthur's enemy, and indeed he
had had cause to be; but Cador was a man of sense, judicious and

far-sighted, who could see beyond his hatred of Uther to the larger vision of a Britain united against the Saxon Terror. So he had supported Arthur. And Arthur, up there in the Perilous Chapel, had declared Cador and his sons the heirs to the kingdom.

So Arthur said merely: "How could I?" and scowled for a moment longer at the stilus. Then he dropped it on the table, and straightened. "The thing is, with my own leadership so new –" He looked up then, and saw me smiling. The frown vanished, to be replaced by a look I knew; eager, impetuous, the look of a boy, but with, behind it, a man's will that would burn its way through any opposition. His eyes danced. "Yes, you're right, as usual. I'm going myself."

"And Cador with you?"

"No. I think I must go without him. After what happened, my father's death, and then the" – he hesitated – "then what happened up in the chapel yonder . . . If there is to be more fighting, I must be there myself, to lead the armies, and be seen to finish the work we started."

He paused, as if still expecting question or protest, but I made none.

"I thought you would try to prevent me."

"No. Why? I agree with you. You have to prove yourself to be above luck."

"That's it exactly." He thought for a moment. "It's hard to put it into words, but ever since you brought me to Luguvallium and presented me to the King, it has seemed – not like a dream exactly, but as if something were using me, using all of us . . ."

"Yes. A strong wind blowing, and carrying us all with it."

"And now the wind has died down," he said, soberly, "and we are left to live life by our own strength only. As if – well, as if it had all been magic and miracles, and now they had gone. Have you noticed, Merlin, that not one man has spoken of what happened up yonder in the shrine? Already it's as if it had happened well in the past, in some song or story."

"One can see why. The magic was real, and too strong for many of those who witnessed it, but it has burned down into the memories of all who saw it, and into the memory of the folk who make the songs and legends. Well, that is for the future. But we are here, now, and with the work still to do. And one thing is certain; only you can do it. So you must go ahead and do it in your own way."

The young face relaxed. His hands flattened on the table as he leaned his weight on them. For the first time it could be seen that he was very tired, and that it was a kind of relief to let the weariness sweep over him, and with it the need for sleep.

"I should have known you would understand. So you see why I must go myself, without Cador. He didn't like it, I confess, but he saw the point in the end. And to be honest, I would have liked him with me . . . But this is something I must do alone. You might say it's as much for my own reassurance as for the people's. I can say that to you."

"Do you need reassurance?"

A hint of a smile. "Not really. In the morning I shall probably be able to believe everything that happened on the battlefield, and know it for real, but now it's still like being in the edges of a dream. Tell me, Merlin, can I ask Cador to go south to escort Queen Ygraine, my mother, from Cornwall?"

"There's no reason why not. He is Duke of Cornwall, so since Uther's death her home at Tintagel must fall under his protection. If Cador was able to sink his hatred of Uther into the common weal, he must long ago have been able to forgive Ygraine for her betrayal of his father. And now you have declared his sons your heirs to the High Kingdom, so all scores are paid. Yes, send Cador."

He looked relieved. "Then all's well. I've already sent a courier to her, of course, with the news. Cador should meet her on the road. They will be in Amesbury by the time my father's body arrives there for burial."

"Do I take it, then, that you want me to escort the body to Amesbury?"

"If you will. I cannot possibly go myself, as I should, and it must be royally escorted. Better you, perhaps, who knew him, than I, who am so recently royal. Besides, if he is to lie beside Ambrosius in the Dance of the Hanging Stones, you should be there to see the king-stone shifted and the grave made. You'll do that?"

"Certainly. It should take us, going in a seemly way, about nine days."

"By that time I should be there myself." A sudden flash. "With average luck, that is. I'm expecting word soon, about Colgrim. I'll be going after him in about four hours' time, as soon as it's full light. Bedwyr goes with me," he added, as if that should be a comfort and a reassurance.

"And what of King Lot, since I have gathered he does not go with you?"

At that I got a bland look, and a tone as smooth as any politician's. "He leaves, too, at first light. Not for his own land . . . Not, that is, until I find which way Colgrim went. No, I urged King Lot to go straight to York. I believe Queen Ygraine will go there after the burial, and Lot can receive her. Then, once his marriage with my sister Morgan is celebrated, I suppose I can count him an ally, like it or not. And the rest of the fighting, whatever comes between now and Christmas-time, I can do without him."

"So, I shall see you in Amesbury. And after that?"

"Caerleon," he said, without hesitation. "If the wars allow it, I shall go there. I've never seen it, and from what Cador tells me, it must be my headquarters now."

"Until the Saxons break the treaty and move in from the south."

"As of course they will. Until then. God send there will be time to breathe first."

"And to build another stronghold."

He looked up quickly. "Yes. I was thinking of that. You'll be there to do it?" Then, with sudden urgency: "Merlin, you swear you will always be there?"

"As long as I am needed. Though it seems to me," I added lightly, "that the eaglet is fledging fast enough already." Then, because I knew what lay behind the sudden uncertainty: "I shall wait for you at Amesbury, and I shall be there to present you to your mother."

Amesbury is little more than a village, but since Ambrosius' day it has taken some kind of grandeur to itself, as befits his birthplace, and its nearness to the great monument of the Hanging Stones that stand on the windy Sarum plain. This is a linked circle of vast stones, a gigantic Dance, which was raised first in times beyond men's memory. I had (by what folk persisted in seeing as "magic art") rebuilt the Dance to be Britain's monument of glory, and the burial-place of her kings. Here Uther was to lie beside his brother Ambrosius.

We brought his body without incident to Amesbury, and left it in the monastery there, wrapped in spices and coffined in hollowed oak, under its purple pall before the chapel altar. The King's guard (who had ridden south with his body) stood vigil, and the monks and nuns of Amesbury prayed beside the bier. Queen Ygraine being a Christian, the dead king was to be buried with all the rites and ceremonies of the Christian church, though in life he had barely troubled even to pay lip-service to the Christians' God. Even now he lay with gold coins glinting on his eyelids, to pay the fee of a ferryman who had exacted such toll for centuries longer than Saint Peter of the Gate. The chapel itself had apparently been erected on the site of a Roman shrine; it was little more than an oblong erection of daub and wattle, with wooden shafts holding up a roof of thatch, but it had a floor of fine mosaic work, scrubbed clean and hardly damaged. This, showing scrolls of vine and acanthus, could offend no Christian souls, and a woven rug lay centrally, probably to cover whatever pagan god or goddess floated naked among the grapes.

The monastery reflected something of Amesbury's new prosperity. It was a miscellaneous collection of buildings huddled any-

how around a cobbled yard, but these were in good repair, and the
Abbot's house, which had been vacated for the Queen and her train,
was well built of stone, with wooden flooring, and a big fireplace at
one end with a chimney.

The headman of the village, too, had a good house, which he
made haste to offer me for lodging, but, explaining that the King
would follow me soon, I left him in an uproar of extra preparation,
and betook myself with my servants to the tavern. This was small,
with little pretension to comfort, but it was clean, and fires were
kept burning high against the autumn chills. The innkeeper remembered me from the time I had lodged there during the rebuilding of the Dance; he still showed the awe that the exploit had raised
in him, and made haste to give me the best room, and to promise me
fresh poultry and a mutton pie for supper. He showed relief when I
told him that I had brought two servants with me, who would serve
me in my own chamber, and banished his own staring pot-boys to
their posts at the kitchen burners.

The servants I had brought were two of Arthur's. In recent years,
living alone in the Wild Forest, I had cared for myself, and now had
none of my own. One was a small, lively man from the hills of
Gwynedd; the other was Ulfin, who had been Uther's own servant.
The late King had taken him from a rough servitude, and had
shown him kindness which Ulfin repaid with devotion. This would
now belong to Arthur, but it would have been cruel to deny Ulfin
the chance of following his master's body on its last journey, so I
had asked for him by name. By my orders he had gone to the chapel
with the bier, and I doubted if I would see him before the funeral
was over. Meantime the Welshman, Lleu, unpacked my boxes and
bespoke hot water, and sent the more intelligent of the landlord's
boys across to the monastery with a message from me to be delivered to the Queen on her arrival. In it I bade her welcome, and
offered to wait on her as soon as she should be rested enough to send
for me. News of the happenings in Luguvallium she had had
already; now I added merely that Arthur was not yet in Amesbury,
but was expected in time for the burial.

I was not in Amesbury when her party arrived. I rode out to the
Giants' Dance to see that all was ready for the ceremony, to be told
on my return that the Queen and her escort had arrived shortly after

noon, and that Ygraine with her ladies was settled into the Abbot's house. Her summons to me came just as afternoon dimmed into evening.

The sun had gone down in a clouded sky, and when, refusing the offer of an escort, I walked the short distance to the monastery, it was already almost dark. The night was heavy as a pall, a mourning sky, where no stars shone. I remembered the great king-star that had blazed for Ambrosius' death, and my thoughts went again to the king who lay nearby in the chapel, with monks for mourners, and the guards like statues beside the bier. And Ulfin who, alone of all those who saw him die, had wept for him.

A chamberlain met me at the monastery gate. Not the monks' porter; this was one of the Queen's own servants, a royal chamberlain I recognised from Cornwall. He knew who I was, of course, and bowed very low, but I could see that he did not recall our last meeting. It was the same man, grown greyer and more bent, who had admitted me to the Queen's presence some three months before Arthur's birth, when she had promised to confide the child to my care. I had been disguised then, for fear of Uther's enmity, and it was plain that the chamberlain did not recognise, in the tall prince at the gate, the humble, bearded "doctor" who had called to consult with the Queen.

He led me across the weedy courtyard towards the big, thatched building where the Queen was lodged. Cressets burned outside the door, and here and there along the wall, so that the poverty of the place showed starkly. After the wet summer weeds had sprouted freely between the cobbles, and the corners of the yard were waist high in nettles. Among these the wooden ploughs and mattocks of the working brothers stood, wrapped in sacking. Near one doorway was an anvil, and on a nail driven into the jamb hung a line of horse-shoes. A litter of thin black piglings tumbled squealing out of our way, and were called by a sow's anxious grunting through the broken planks of a half-door. The holy men and women of Amesbury were simple folk. I wondered how the Queen was faring.

I need not have feared for her. Ygraine had always been a lady who knew her own mind, and since her marriage to Uther she had kept a most queenly state, urged to this, possibly, by the very irregularity of that marriage. I remembered the Abbot's house as a humble dwelling, clean and dry, but boasting no comfort. Now in a few short hours the Queen's people had seen to it that it was luxurious. The walls, of undressed stone, had been hidden by hangings of scarlet and green and peacock blue, and one beautiful Eastern carpet that I had brought for her from Byzantium. The wooden floor was scrubbed white, and the benches that stood along the walls were piled with furs and cushions. A great fire of logs burned on the hearth. To one side of this was set a tall chair of gilded wood, cushioned in embroidered wool, with a footstool fringed with gold. Across from this stood another chair with a high back, and arms carved with dragons' heads. The lamp was a five-headed dragon in bronze. The door to the Abbot's austere sleeping-chamber stood open, and beyond it I caught a glimpse of a bed hung with blue, and the sheen of a silver fringe. Three or four women – two of them no more than girls – were busying themselves in the bedchamber, and over the table, which, at the end of the room away from the fire, stood ready for supper. Pages dressed in blue ran with dishes and flagons. Three white greyhounds lay as near to the fire as they dared go.

As I entered, there was a pause in the bustle and chatter. All eyes turned to the doorway. A page bearing a wine-jar, caught within a yard of the door, checked, swerved, and stared, showing the whites of his eyes. Someone at the table dropped a wooden trencher, and the greyhounds pounced on the fallen cakes. The scrabbling of their claws and their munching were the only sounds in the room to be heard through the rustling of the fire.

"Good evening," I said pleasantly. I answered the women's reverences, watched gravely while a boy picked up the fallen trencher and kicked the dogs out of the way, then allowed myself to be ushered by the chamberlain towards the hearth-place.

"The Queen –" he was beginning, when the eyes turned from me to the inner door, and the greyhounds, arched and wagging, danced to meet the woman who came through it.

But for the hounds, and the curtsying women, a stranger might have thought that here was the Abbess of the place come to greet me. The woman who entered was as much a contrast to the rich room as that room had been to the squalid courtyard. She was dressed from head to foot in black, with a white veil covering her

hair, its ends thrown back over her shoulders, and its soft folds
pinned to frame her face like a wimple. The sleeves of her gown
were lined with some grey silken stuff, and there was a cross of
sapphires on her breast, but to the sombre black and white of her
mourning there was no other relief.

It was a long time since I had seen Ygraine, and I expected to find
her changed, but even so I was shocked at what I saw. Beauty was
still there, in the lines of bone and the great dark-blue eyes and the
queenly poise of her body; but grace had given way to dignity, and
there was a thinness about the wrists and hands that I did not like,
and shadows near her eyes almost as blue as the eyes themselves.
This, not the ravages of time, was what shocked me. There were
signs everywhere that a doctor could read all too clearly.

But I was here as prince and emissary, not as physician. I returned
her smile of greeting, bowed over her hand, and led her to the
cushioned chair. At a sign from her the boys ran to collar the
greyhounds and take them aside, and she settled herself, smoothing
her skirt. One of the girls moved a footstool for her, and then, with
lowered eyelids and folded hands, stayed beside her mistress's
chair.

The Queen bade me be seated, and I obeyed her. Someone
brought wine, and across the cups we exchanged the common-
places of the meeting. I asked her how she did, but with purely
formal courtesy, and I knew she could read nothing of my knowledge in my face.

"And the King?" she asked at length. The word came from her as
if forced, with a kind of pain behind it.

"Arthur promised to be here. I expect him tomorrow. There has
been no news from the north, so we have no means of knowing if
there has been more fighting. The lack of news need not alarm you;
it only means that he will be here as soon as any courier he might
have sent."

She nodded, with no sign of anxiety. Either she could not think
much beyond her own loss, or she took my tranquil tone as a
prophet's reassurance. "Did he expect more fighting?"

"He stayed as a cautionary measure, no more. The defeat of
Colgrim's men was decisive, but Colgrim himself escaped, as I
wrote to you. We had no report on where he had gone. Arthur

thought it better to make sure that the scattered Saxon forces could not re-form, at least while he came south for his father's burial."

"He is young," she said, "for such a charge."

I smiled. "But ready for it, and more than able. Believe me, it was like seeing a young falcon take to the air, or a swan to the water. When I took leave of him, he had not slept for the better part of two nights, and was in high heart and excellent health."

"I am glad of it."

She spoke formally, without expression, but I thought it better to qualify. "The death of his father came as a shock and a grief, but as you will understand, Ygraine, it could not come very near his heart, and there was much to be done that crowded out sorrow."

"I have not been so fortunate," she said, very low, and looked down at her hands.

I was silent, understanding. The passion that had driven Uther and this woman together, with a kingdom at stake for it, had not burned out with the years. Uther had been a man who needed women as most men need food and sleep, and when his kingly duties had taken him away from the Queen's bed, his own was rarely empty; but when they were together he had never looked aside, nor given her cause for grief. They had loved each other, King and Queen, in the old high way of love, which had outlasted youth and health and the shifts of compromise and expediency which are the price of kingship. I had come to believe that their son Arthur, deprived as he had been of royal status, and brought up in obscurity, had fared better in his foster-home at Galava than he would have done at his father's court, where, with both King and Queen, he would have come far behind the best.

She looked up at last, her face serene again. "I had your letter, and Arthur's, but there is so much more that I want to hear. Tell me what happened at Luguvallium. When he left to ride north against Colgrim, I knew he was not fit to do so. He swore he must take the field, even if he had to be carried in a litter. Which, I understand, is what happened?"

For Ygraine, the "he" of Luguvallium was certainly not her son. What she wanted was the story of Uther's last days, not the tale of Arthur's miraculous coming into his kingdom. I gave it to her.

"Yes. It was a great fight, and he fought it greatly. They carried him to the battlefield in a chair, and all through the fighting his servants kept him there, in the very thick of the battle. I had Arthur brought down from Galava at his orders, for him to be publicly acknowledged, but Colgrim attacked suddenly, and the King had to take the field without making the proclamation. He kept Arthur near him, and when he saw the boy's sword broken in the fight, threw him his own. I doubt if Arthur, in the heat of the battle, saw the gesture for what it was, but everyone else did who was near. It was a great gesture, made by a great man."

She did not speak, but her eyes rewarded me. Ygraine knew, none better, that Uther and I had never loved one another. Praise from me was something quite other than the flattery of the court.

"And afterwards the King sat back in his chair and watched his son carry the fight through to the enemy, and, untried as he was, bear his part in the rout of the Saxons. So later, when he presented the boy at last to the nobles and the captains, his work was half done. They had seen the sword of kingship handed over, and they had seen how worthily it had been used. But there was, in fact, some opposition . . ."

I hesitated. It was that very opposition that had killed Uther; only a few hours before time, but as surely as the blow from an axe. And King Lot, who had led the opposing faction, was contracted to marry Ygraine's daughter Morgan.

Ygraine said calmly: "Ah, yes. The King of Lothian. I heard something of it. Tell me."

I should have known her. I gave her the whole story, omitting nothing. The roaring opposition, the treachery, the sudden, silencing death of the King. I told her of Arthur's eventual acclamation by the company, though dwelling lightly on my part in that: (*"If he has indeed got the sword of Macsen, he got it by God's gift, and if he has Merlin beside him, then by any god he follows, I follow him!"*) Nor did I dwell on the scene in the chapel, but told her merely of the oath-taking, of Lot's submission, and Arthur's declaration of Gorlois' son Cador as his heir.

At this, for the first time, the beautiful eyes lighted, and she smiled. I could see that this was news to her, and must go some way to assuaging the guilt of her own part in Gorlois' death. Apparently Cador, either through delicacy, or because he and Ygraine still held aloof from one another, had not told her himself. She put out her hand for her wine, and sat sipping it while I finished the tale, the smile still on her mouth.

One other thing, one most important thing, would also have been news to her; but of this I said nothing. But the unspoken part of the tale was loud in my own mind, so that when Ygraine spoke next, I must have jumped like a dog to the whip. "And Morgause?"

"Madam?"

"You have not spoken of her. She must have grieved for her father. It was a fortunate thing that she could be near him. He and I have both had cause to thank God for her skills."

I said, neutrally: "She nursed him with devotion. I am sure that she will miss him bitterly."

"Does she come south with Arthur?"

"No. She has gone to York, to be with her sister Morgan."

To my relief, she asked no more questions about Morgause, but turned the subject, asking where I was lodged.

"In the tavern," I told her. "I know it from the old days, when I was working here. It's a simple kind of place, but they have taken pains to make me comfortable. I shan't be here for long." I glanced round me at the glowing room. "For yourself, do you plan a long stay, Madam?"

"A few days only." If she had noticed my look at the luxury surrounding her, she gave no sign of it. I, who am not normally wise in the ways of women, realised, suddenly, that the richness and beauty of the place was not for Ygraine's own comfort, but had been deliberately contrived as a setting for her first meeting with her son. The scarlet and gold, the scents and waxlights, were this ageing woman's shield and enchanted sword.

"Tell me −" She spoke abruptly, straight out of the preoccupation that, through all else, bound her: "Does he blame me?"

It was the measure of my respect for Ygraine that I answered her directly, with no pretence that the subject was not uppermost in my mind as well. "I think you need have no fear of this meeting. When he first knew of his parentage, and of his inheritance, he wondered why you and the King had seen fit to deny him that birthright. He could not be blamed if, at first, he felt himself wronged. He had already begun to suspect that he was royal, but he assumed that − as in my case – the royalty came sideways . . . When he knew the truth, with the elation came the wondering. But – and I swear that this is true – he gave no hint of bitterness or anger; he was anxious only to know why. When I had told him the story of his birth and fostering, he said – and I will give you his exact words – 'I see it as you say she saw it; that to be a prince one must be ruled always by necessity. She did not give me up for nothing.' "

There was a little silence. Through it I heard echoing, unspoken save in my memory, the words with which he had finished: "I was better in the Wild Forest, thinking myself motherless, and your bastard, Merlin, than waiting yearly in my father's castle for the Queen to bear another child to supplant me."

Her lips relaxed, and I saw her sigh. The soft underlids of her eyes had a faint tremor, which stilled as if a finger had been laid on a thrumming string. Colour came into her face, and she looked at me as she had looked all those years ago, when she had begged me to take the baby away and hide him from Uther's anger. "Tell me . . . what is he like?"

I smiled slightly. "Did they not tell you, when they brought you news of the battle?"

"Oh, yes, they told me. He is as tall as an oak tree and as strong as Fionn, and slew nine hundred men with his own hand alone. He is Ambrosius come again, or Maximus himself, with a sword like the lightning, and the witchlight round him in battle like the pictures of the gods at the fall of Troy. And he is Merlin's shadow and spirit, and a great hound follows him everywhere, to whom he speaks as to a familiar." Her eyes danced. "You may guess from all this that the messengers were black Cornishmen from Cador's troop. They would always rather sing a poem than state a fact. I want fact."

She always had. Like her, Arthur had dealt with facts, even as a child; he left the poetry to Bedwyr. I gave her what she wanted. "The last bit is almost true, but they got it the wrong way round. It is Merlin who is Arthur's shadow and spirit, like the great hound who is real enough; that's Cabal, his dog that his friend Bedwyr gave him. For the rest, what shall I say? You'll see for yourself tomorrow . . . He is tall, and favours Uther rather than you, though he has my father's colouring; his eyes and hair are as dark as mine. He is strong, and full of courage and endurance – all the things your Cornishmen told you, brought down to life-size. He has the hot blood and high temper of youth, and he can be impulsive or arrogant, but under it all he has hard sense and a growing power of control, like any good man of his age. And he has what I consider a very great virtue. He is willing to listen to me."

This won another smile from her, with real warmth in it. "You mean to jest, but I am with you in counting that a virtue! He is lucky to have you. As a Christian, I am not allowed to believe in your magic – indeed, I do not believe in it as the common folk do; but whatever it is, and wherever it comes from, I have seen your power working, and I know that it is good, and that you are wise. I believe that whatever owns and moves you is what I call God. Stay with my son."

"I shall stay as long as he needs me."

Silence fell between us then, while we both looked at the fire. Ygraine's eyes dreamed under their long shadowed lids, and her face grew still once more, and tranquil; but I thought it was the waiting stillness of the forest depth, where overhead the boughs roar in the wind, and the trees feel the storms shaking them to the very root.

A boy came tiptoeing to kneel on the hearth and pile fresh logs on the fire. Flames crept, crackled, leaped into light. I watched them. For me, too, the pause was merely one of waiting; the flames were only flames.

The boy went away quietly. The girl took the goblet from the Queen's relaxed hand, and held her own out, a timid gesture, for my cup. She was a pretty creature, slim as a wand, with grey eyes and light-brown hair. She looked half-scared of me, and was careful, as I gave her the cup, not to touch my hand. She went quickly away with the empty vessels. I said softly: "Ygraine, is your physician here with you?"

Her eyelids fluttered. She did not look at me, but answered as softly. "Yes. He travels with me always."

"Who is it?"

"His name is Melchior. He says he knows you."

"Melchior? A young man I met in Pergamum when I studied medicine there?"

"The same. Not so young now. He was with me when Morgan was born."

"He is a good man," I said, satisfied.

She glanced at me sideways. The girl was still out of hearing, with the rest of the women at the other side of the room. "I should have known I could hide nothing from you. You won't let my son know?"

I promised readily. That she was mortally ill I had known as soon as I saw her, but Arthur, not knowing her, and having no skill in medicine, might notice nothing. Time enough for that later. Now was for beginnings rather than endings.

The girl came and whispered to the Queen, who nodded and stood up. I rose with her. The chamberlain was advancing with some ceremony, lending the borrowed chamber yet another touch of royalty. The Queen half turned to me, her hand lifting to invite me with her to table, when suddenly the scene was interrupted. From somewhere outside came the distant call of a trumpet; then another, nearer, and then, all at once, the clash and excitement of arriving horsemen, somewhere beyond the monastery walls.

Ygraine's head went up, with something of the old lift of youth and courage. She stood very still. "The King?" Her voice was light and quick. Round the listening room, like an echo, went the rustle and murmur of the women. The girl beside the Queen was as taut as a bow string, and I saw a vivid blush of excitement run up clear from neck to forehead.

"He is early," I said. My voice sounded flat and precise. I was subduing a pulse in my own wrist, which had quickened with the swelling hoof-beats. Fool, I told myself, fool. He is about his own business now. You loosed him, and lost him; that is one hawk who will never be hooded again. Stay back in the shadows, king's prophet; see your visions and dream your dreams. Leave life to him, and wait for his need.

A knock at the door, and a servant's quick voice. The chamberlain went bustling, but before him a boy came pelting with the message hurriedly relayed, and stripped of its courtly phrasing:

"With the Queen's leave . . . The King is here and wants Prince Merlin. Now, he says."

As I went I heard the silent room break into hubbub behind me, as the pages were sent scurrying to refurbish the tables, and bring fresh waxlights and scents and wine; and the women, clucking and crooning like a yardful of fowl, bustled after the Queen into the bedchamber.

3

"She's here, they tell me?" Arthur was hindering, rather than helping, a servant drag off his muddied boots. Ulfin had after all come back from the chapel; I could hear him in the adjoining room, directing the servants of the household in the unpacking and bestowing of Arthur's clothes and furnishings. Outside, the town seemed to have burst open with noise and torches and the stamping of horses and the shouting of orders. Now and again one could hear, distinct through the hubbub, the squealing giggle of a girl. Not everyone in Amesbury was in mourning.

The King himself gave little sign of it. He kicked free of his boots at last and shrugged the heavy cloak off his shoulders. His eyes came to me in an exact parody of Ygraine's sidelong look. "Have you spoken with her?"

"Yes. I've just left her. She was about to give me supper, but now I think she plans to feed you instead. She only got here today, and you'll find her tired, but she has had some rest, and she'll rest again all the better for having seen you. We hardly expected you before morning."

" 'Caesar-speed.' " He grinned, quoting one of my father's phrases; no doubt I, as his teacher, had over-used it rather. "Only myself and a handful, of course. We pushed ahead. The rest of them will come up later. I trust they will be here in time for the burial."

"Who is coming?"

"Maelgon of Gwynedd, and his son Maelgon. Urbgen's brother from Rheged – old Coel's third son, his name's Morien, isn't it? Caw couldn't come either, so he's sent Riderch – not Heuil, I'm glad to say, I never could stand that foul-mouthed braggart. Then let me see, Ynyr and Gwilim, Bors . . . and I am told that Ceretic of Elmet is on his way from Loidis."

He went on to name a few others. It seemed that most of the northern kings had sent sons or substitutes; naturally with the remnant of the Saxon armies still haunting the north they would want to stay watching their own borders. So much, indeed, Arthur was saying through the splashing of the water his servant poured for him to wash himself in. "Bedwyr's father went home, too. He pleaded some urgency, but between ourselves I think he wanted to keep an eye for me on Lot's movements."

"And Lot?"

"Headed for York. I took the precaution of having him watched. Sure enough he's on his way. Is Morgan there still, or did she come south to meet the Queen?"

"She's still at York. There is one king you haven't mentioned yet."

The servant gave him a towel, and Arthur disappeared into it, scrubbing his wet hair dry. His voice came muffled. "Who?"

"Colgrim," I said, mildly.

He emerged abruptly from the towel, skin glowing and eyes bright. He looked, I thought, about ten years old. "Need you ask?" The voice was not ten years old; it was a man's, full of mock arrogance, which under the mischief was real. Well, you gods, I thought, you put him there; you cannot count this as hubris. But I caught myself making the sign.

"No, but I am asking."

He was serious at once.

"It was tougher work than we'd expected. You might say that the second half of the battle was still to fight. We broke their strength at Luguvallium, and Badulf has died of wounds, but Colgrim was unhurt, and rallied what was left of his forces some way to the east. It wasn't just a case of hunting down fugitives; they had a formidable force there, and a desperate one. If we had gone in any less strength, they might even have turned the tables on us. I doubt if they would have attacked again – they were making for the east coast, and home, but we caught them halfway there, and they made a stand on the Glein river. Do you know that part of the country?"

"Not well."

"It's wild and hilly, deep in forest, with river glens winding south out of the uplands. Bad fighting country, but that was against them as well as us. Colgrim himself got away again, but there's no chance now that he can pause and remuster any sort of force in the north. He rode east; that's one of the reasons that Ban stayed behind, though he was good enough to let Bedwyr come south with me again." He stood still, obedient now to his servant's hands as he was dressed, a fresh cloak flung over his shoulder and the pin made fast. "I'm glad," he finished, briefly.

"That Bedwyr's here? So I –"

"No. That Colgrim escaped again."

"Yes?"

"He's a brave man."

"Nevertheless, you will have to kill him."

"I know that. Now . . ." The servant stepped back, and the King stood ready. They had dressed him in dark grey, his cloak collared and lined with rich fur. Ulfin came from the bedchamber holding a carved casket lined with embroidery, where Uther's royal circlet lay. The rubies caught the light, answering the flash from the jewels at Arthur's shoulder and breast. But when Ulfin proffered the box he shook his head. "Not now, I think."

Ulfin shut the box, and went from the room, taking the other man with him. The door latched behind them. Arthur looked at me, in another echo of Ygraine's own hesitation. "Am I to understand that she expects me now?"

"Yes."

He fidgeted with the brooch at his shoulder, pricked his finger, and swore. Then, with a half smile at me: "There's not much precedent for this sort of thing, is there? How does one meet the mother who gave one away at birth?"

"How did you greet your father?"

"That's different, you know it is."

"Yes. Do you want me to present you?"

"I was going to ask you to . . . Well, we'd better get on with it. Some situations don't improve with keeping . . . Look, you are sure about the supper? I've eaten nothing since dawn."

"Certain. They were running for fresh meats when I left."

He took a breath, like a swimmer before a deep dive. "Then shall we go?"

* * *

She was waiting beside her chair, standing in the light of the fire. Colour had run up into her cheeks, and the glow of the fire pulsed over her skin and made the white wimple rosy. She looked beautiful, with the shadows purged away, and youth lent back by the firelight and the brilliance of her eyes.

Arthur paused on the threshold. I saw the blue flash of Ygraine's sapphire cross as her breast rose and fell. Her lips parted, as if to speak, but she was silent. Arthur paced forward slowly, so dignified and stiff that he looked even younger than his years. I went with him, rehearsing in my mind the right words to say, but in the end there was no need to say anything. Ygraine the Queen, who had weathered worse moments in her time, took the occasion into her hands. She watched him for a moment, staring at him as if she would look right through his soul, then she curtsied to the ground, and said: "My lord."

He put a hand out quickly, then both hands, and raised her. He gave her the kiss of greeting, brief and formal, and held her hands for a little longer before he dropped them. He said: "Mother?" trying it out. It was what he had always called Drusilla, Count Ector's wife. Then, with relief: "Madam? I am sorry I could not be here in Amesbury to greet you, but there was still danger in the north. Merlin will have told you? But I came as quickly as I could."

"You made better speed than we could have hoped for. I trust you prospered? And that the danger from Colgrim's force is over?"

"For the moment. We have time, at least, to breathe . . . and to do what is to be done here in Amesbury. I am sorry for your grief and loss, Madam. I —" He hesitated, then spoke with a simplicity that, I could see, comforted her and steadied him: "I can't pretend to you that I grieve as perhaps I should. I hardly knew him as a father, but all my life I have known him as a king, and a strong one. His people will mourn him, and I, too, mourn him as one of them."

"You have it in your hands to guard them as he tried to guard them." A pause, while they measured one another again. She was a fraction the taller of the two. Perhaps the same thought touched her; she motioned him towards the chair where I had been sitting, and herself sank back against the embroidered cushions. A page came running with wine, and there was a general breathing and rustle of movement. The Queen began to speak of tomorrow's ceremony; answering her, he relaxed, and soon they were talking more freely. But still behind the courtly exchanges could be felt all the turmoil of what lay between them unspoken, the air so charged, their minds so locked on one another, that they had forgotten my presence as completely as if I had been one of the servants waiting by the laden table. I glanced that way, then at the women and girls beside the Queen; all eyes were on Arthur, devouring him, the men with curiosity and some awe (the stories had reached them soon enough), the women with something added to the curiosity, and the two girls in a dazzled trance of excitement.

The chamberlain was hovering in a doorway. He caught my eye and looked a question. I nodded. He crossed to the Queen's side and murmured something. She assented with a kind of relief, and rose to her feet, the King with her. I noticed that the table was now laid for three, but when the chamberlain came to my elbow I shook my head. After supper their talk would be easier, and they could dismiss the servants. They would be better alone. So I took my leave, ignoring Arthur's glance almost of entreaty, and made my way back to the tavern to see if my fellow-guests there had left any of the supper for me.

★   ★   ★

Next day was bright and sunlit, with the clouds packed away low on the horizon, and a lark singing somewhere as if it were spring. Often a bright day at the end of September brings frost with it, and a searching wind – and nowhere can the winds search more keenly than on the stretches of the Great Plain. But the day of Uther's burial was a day borrowed from spring; a warm wind and a bright sky, and the sun golden on the Dance of the Hanging Stones.

The ceremonial by the grave was long, and the colossal shadows of the Dance moved round with the sun until the light blazed down full in the centre, and it was easier to look at the ground, at the grave itself, at the shadows of clouds massing and moving like armies across the distances, than at the Dance's centre where the priests stood in their robes, and the nobles in mourning white, with jewels flashing against the eyes. A pavilion had been erected for the Queen. She stood in its shade, composed and pale among her ladies, showing no sign of fatigue or illness. Arthur, with me beside him, stood at the foot of the grave.

At last it was done. The priests moved off, and after them the King and the royal party. As we crossed the grass towards the horses and litters, already behind us could be heard the soft thudding of earth on wood. Then from above came another sound to mask it. I looked up. High in the September sky could be seen a stream of birds, swift and black and small, gossiping and calling as they went southwards. The last flock of swallows, taking the summer with them.

"Let us hope," said Arthur, softly, at my elbow, "that the Saxons are taking the hint. I could do with the winter's length, both for the men and for myself, before the fighting starts again. Besides, there's Caerleon. I wish I could go today."

But of course he had to stay, as had we all, as long as the Queen remained in Amesbury. She went straight back to the monastery after the ceremony, and did not appear publicly again, but spent her time resting, or with her son. He was with her as much as his affairs allowed, while her people prepared to make the journey to York as soon as she should feel able to travel.

Arthur hid his impatience, and busied himself with the troops at exercise, or in long hours of talk with his friends and captains. Each day I could see him more and more absorbed in what he was doing, and what he faced. I myself saw little of him or of Ygraine; much of my time was spent out at the Giants' Dance, directing the sinking of the king-stone once more into its bed above the royal grave.

At last, eight days after Uther's burial, the Queen's party set off for the north. Arthur watched them decently out of sight along the road to Cunetio, then gave a great breath of relief, and pulled the fighting men out of Amesbury as neatly and quickly as pulling a stopper from a flask. It was the fifth day of October, and it was raining, and we were bound, as I knew to my cost, for the Severn estuary, and the ferry across to Caerleon, City of Legions.

4

Where the ferry crosses, the Severn estuary is wide, with big tides that come up fast over thick red mud. Boys watch the cattle night and day, for a whole herd can sink in the tidal mud and be lost. And when the spring and autumn tides meet the river's flow a wave builds up like the wave I have seen in Pergamum after the earthquake. On the south side the estuary is bounded by cliffs; the north shore is marshy, but a bowshot from the tide-mark there is well-drained gravel, lifting gently to open woodland of oak and sweet chestnut.

We pitched camp on the rising ground in the lee of the woods. While this was being done, Arthur, with Ynyr and Gwilim, the kings of Guent and Dyfed, went on a tour of exploration, then after supper he sat in his tent to receive the headmen from the settlements nearby. Numbers of the local folk crowded to see the new young King, even the fisherfolk who have no homes but the cliff caves and their frail-skinned coracles. He spoke with them all, accepting homage and complaint alike. After an hour or two of it, I asked leave with a look, got it, and went out into the air. It was a long time since I had smelled the hills of my own country, and besides, there was a place nearby that I had long wanted to visit.

This was the once-famous shrine of Nodens, who is Nuatha of the Silver Hand, known in my country as Llud, or Bilis, King of the Otherworld, whose gates are the hollow hills. He it was who had guarded the sword after I had raised it from its long grave below the floor of Mithras' temple at Segontium. I had left it in his keeping in the lake cave that was known to be sacred to him, before carrying it finally up to the Green Chapel. To Llud, also, I had a debt to pay.

His shrine by the Severn was far older than Mithras' temple, or the chapel in the forest. Its origins had long been lost, even in song or story. It had been a hill fortress first, with maybe a stone or a spring dedicated to the god who cared for the spirits of dead men. Then iron was found, and all through Roman times the place was mined, and mined richly. It may have been the Romans who first called the place the Hill of the Dwarfs, after the small dark men of the west who worked there. The mine had long since been closed, but the name persisted, and so did the stories, of the Old Ones who were seen lurking in the oak woods, or who came thronging out of the earth's depths on nights of storm and starlight to join the train of the dark king, as he rode from his hollow hill with his wild rout of ghosts and enchanted spirits.

I reached the top of the hill behind the camp, and walked down between the scattered oaks towards the stream at the valley's foot. There was a ripe autumn moon that showed me my way. The chestnut leaves, already loosened and drifting, fell here and there quietly to the grass, but the oaks still held their leaves, so that the air was full of rustling as the dry boughs stirred and whispered. The land, after the rain, smelled rich and soft; ploughing weather, nutting weather, the squirrel-time for winter's coming.

Below me on the shadowed slope something moved. There was a stirring of grasses, a pattering, then, like the sound of a hail-storm sweeping past, a herd of deer went by, as swiftly as swallows flying. They were very near. The moonlight struck the dappled coats and the ivory tips of the tines. So close they were that I even saw the liquid shine of their eyes. There were pied deer and white, ghosts of dapple and silver, scudding as lightly as their own shadows, and as swiftly as a sudden squall of wind. They fled by me, down to the valley foot, between the breasts of the rounded hills and up round a curve of oak trees, and were gone.

They say that a white deer is a magical creature. I believe that this is true. I had seen two such in my life, each one the herald of a marvel. These, too, seen in the moonlight, scudding like clouds into the trees' darkness, seemed things of magic. Perhaps, with the Old Ones, they haunted a hill that still held an open gate to the Otherworld.

I crossed the stream, climbed the next hill, and made my way up towards the ruinous walls that crowned it. I picked my way through the debris of what looked like ancient outworks, then climbed the last steep rise of the path. There was a gate set in a high, creeper-covered wall. It was open. I went in.

I found myself in the precinct, a wide courtyard stretching the full width of the flat hilltop. The moonlight, growing stronger every moment, showed a stretch of broken pavement furred with weeds. Two sides of the precinct were enclosed by high walls with broken tops; on the other two there had once been large buildings, of which some portions were still roofed. The place, in that light, was still impressive, roofs and pillars showing whole in the moonlight. Only an owl, flying silently from an upper window, showed that the place had long been deserted, and was crumbling back into the hill.

There was another building set almost in the middle of the court. The gable of its high roof stood up sharply against the moon, but moonlight fell through empty windows. This, I knew, must be the shrine. The buildings that edged the courtyard were what remained of the guest-houses and dormitories where pilgrims and suppliants had lodged; there were cells, walled in, windowless and private, such as I had known at Pergamum, where people slept, hoping for healing dreams, or visions of divination.

I went softly forward over the broken pavement. I knew what I would find; a shrine full of dust and cold air, like the abdicated temple of Mithras at Segontium. But it was possible, I told myself, as I trod up the steps and between the still massive doorposts of the central *cella,* that the old gods who had sprung, like the oak trees and the grass and the rivers themselves – it was possible that these beings made of the air and earth and water of our sweet land, were harder to dislodge than the visiting gods of Rome. Such a one, I had long believed, was mine. He might still be here, where the night air blew through the empty shrine, filling it with the sound of the trees.

The moonlight, falling through the upper windows and the patches of broken roof, lit the place with a pure, fierce light. Some sapling, rooted high up in the masonry, swayed in the breeze, so that shadow and cold light moved and shifted over the dimness within. It was like being at the bottom of a well-shaft; the air, shadow and light, moved like water against the skin, as pure and as cold. The mosaic underfoot, rippled and uneven where the ground had shifted beneath it, glimmered like the floor of the sea, its strange sea-creatures swimming in the swaying light. From beyond the broken walls came the hiss, like foam breaking, of the rustling trees.

I stood there, quite still and silent, for a long time. Long enough for the owl to sail back on hushed wings, drifting to her perch above the dormitory. Long enough for the small wind to drop again, and the water-shadows to fall still. Long enough for the moon to move behind the gable, and the dolphins under my feet to vanish in darkness.

Nothing moved or spoke. No presence there. I told myself, with humility, that this meant nothing. I, once so powerful an enchanter and prophet, had been swept on a mighty tide to God's very gates, and now was dropping back on the ebb to a barren shore. If there were voices here I would not hear them. I was as mortal as the spectral deer.

I turned to leave the place. And smelled smoke.

Not the smoke of sacrifice; ordinary wood-smoke, and with it the faint smells of cooking. It came from somewhere beyond the ruined guest-house of the precinct's north side. I crossed the court-yard, went in through the remains of a massive archway, and, guided by the smell, and then by faint firelight, found my way to a small chamber, where a dog, waking, began to bark, and the two who had been sleeping by the fire got abruptly to their feet.

It was a man and a boy, father and son by the look of them; poor people, to judge by their worn and shabby clothing, but with some look about them of men who are their own masters. In this I was wrong, as it happened.

They moved with the speed of fear. The dog – it was old and stiff, with a grey muzzle and a white eye – did not attack, but stood its ground growling. The man was on his feet more quickly than the dog, with a long knife in his hand; it was honed and bright and looked like a sacrificial weapon. The boy, squaring up to the stranger with all the bravado of twelve or so, held a heavy billet of firewood.

"Peace to you," I said, then repeated it in their own tongue. "I came to say a prayer, but no one answered, so when I smelled the fire I came across to see if the god still kept servants here."

The knife-point sank, but he gripped it still, and the old dog growled. "Who are you?" demanded the man.

"Only a stranger who is passing this place. I had often heard of Nodens' famous shrine, and seized the time to visit it. Are you its guardian, sir?"

"I am. Are you looking for a night's lodging?"

"That was not my intention. Why? Do you still offer it?"

"Sometimes." He was wary. The boy, more trusting, or perhaps seeing that I was unarmed, turned away and placed the billet carefully on the fire. The dog, silent now, edged forward to touch my hand with its greyed muzzle. Its tail moved.

"He's a good dog, and very fierce," said the man, "but old, and deaf." His manner was no longer hostile. At the dog's action the knife had vanished.

"And wise," I said. I smoothed the upraised head. "He's one who can see the wind."

The boy turned, wide-eyed. "See the wind?" asked the man, staring.

"Have you not heard that of a dog with a white eye? And, old and slow as he is, he can see that I come with no intent to hurt you. My name is Myrddin Emrys, and I live west of here, near Maridunum, in Dyfed. I have been travelling, and am on my way home." I gave him my Welsh name; like everyone else, he would have heard of Merlin the enchanter, and awe is a bad hearth-friend. "May I come in and share your fire for a while, and will you tell me about the shrine you guard?"

They made way for me, and the boy pulled a stool out of a corner somewhere. Under my questions, at length, the man relaxed and began to talk. His name was Mog: it is not really a name, meaning, as it does, merely "a servant", but there was a king once who did not disdain to call himself Mog Nuatha, and the man's son was called, even more grandly, after an emperor. "Constant will be the servant after me," said Mog, and went on to talk with pride and longing of the great period of the shrine, when the pagan emperor rebuilt and re-equipped it only half a century before the last of the legions left Britain. From long before this time, he told me, a "Mog Nuatha" had served the shrine with all his family. But now there were only himself and his son; his wife was from home, having gone down that morning to market, and to spend the night with her ailing sister in the village.

"If there's room left, with all that's there now," the man grumbled. "You can see the river from the wall yonder, and when we saw the boats crossing I sent the boy to have a look. The army, he says it is, along with the young King –" He broke off, peering through the firelight at my plain robe and cloak. "You're no soldier, are you? Are you with them?"

"Yes to the last, and no to the first. As you can see, I am no soldier, but I am with the King."

"What are you, then? A secretary?"

"Of a sort."

He nodded. The boy, listening and absorbed, sat cross-legged beside the dog at my feet. His father asked: "What's he like, this youngster that they say King Uther handed the sword to?"

"He is young, but a man turned, and a good soldier. He can lead men, and he has enough sense to listen to his elders."

He nodded again. Not for these folk the tales and hopes of power and glory. They lived all their lives on this secluded hilltop, with this one direction to their days; what happened beyond the oak trees did not concern them. Since the start of time no one had stormed the holy place. He asked the only question that, to these two, mattered: "Is he a Christian, this young Arthur? Will he knock down the temple, in the name of this new-fangled god, or will he respect what's gone before?"

I answered him tranquilly, and as truly as I knew how: "He will be crowned by the Christian bishops, and bend his knees to his parents' God. But he is a man of this land, and he knows the gods of this land, and the people who still serve those gods on the hills and by the springs and fording-places." My eye had caught, on a broad shelf opposite the fire, a crowd of objects, carefully arranged. I had seen similar things in Pergamum and other places of divine healing; they were offerings to the gods; models of parts of the human body, or carved statues of animals or fish, that carried some message of supplication or gratitude. "You will find," I told Mog, "that his armies will pass by without harm, and that if he ever comes here himself he will say a prayer to the god, and make an offering. As I did, and as I will."

"That's good talking," said the boy suddenly, and showed a white-toothed grin.

I smiled at him, and dropped two coins into the outstretched palm. "For the shrine, and for its servants."

Mog grunted something, and the boy Constant slid to his feet and went to a cupboard in the corner. He came back with a leather bottle, and a chipped cup for me. Mog lifted his own cup up off the floor and the boy tipped the liquor in. "Your health," said Mog. I answered, and we drank. The stuff was mead, sweet and strong.

Mog drank again, and drew his sleeve across his mouth. "You've been asking about times long past, and we've told you as best we may. Now do you, sir, tell us what's been happening up there in the north. All we heard down here were stories of battles, and kings dying and being made. Is it true the Saxons have gone? Is it true that King Uther Pendragon kept this prince hidden all this time, and brought him out, sudden as a thunderclap, there in the battlefield, and he killed four hundred of the Saxon beasts with a magic sword that sang and drank blood?"

So once more I told the story, while the boy quietly fed the fire, and the flames spat and leaped and shone on the carefully polished offerings ranged on the shelf. The dog slept again, its head on my foot, the fire hot on its rough coat. As I talked the bottle passed and the mead went down in it, and at last the fire dwindled and the logs fell to ash, and I finished my tale with Uther's burial and Arthur's plans to hold Caerleon in readiness for the spring campaigning.

My host upended the bottle, and shook it. "It's out. And a better night's work it never did. Thank you, sir, for your news. We live our own ways up here, but you'll know, being down in the press of affairs, that even things happening out yonder in Britain" (he spoke of it as if of a foreign land, a hundred miles from his quiet refuge) "can have their echoes, in pain and trouble sometimes, in the small and lonely places. We'll pray you're right about the new King. You can tell him, if ever you get near enough to have speech with him, that as long as he's loyal to the true land, he has two men here who are his servants, too."

"I shall tell him." I rose. "Thank you for the welcome, and the drink. I'm sorry I disturbed your sleep. I'll go and leave you to it now."

"Go now? Why, it's getting on for the dawning. They'll have locked you out of your lodging, that's for sure. Or were you in the camp down yonder? Then no sentry'll let you through, without you've got the King's own token. You'd best stay here. No" – as I started some sort of protest – "there's a room still kept, just as it was in the old days, when they came here from far and wide to have the dreams. The bed's good, and the place is kept dry. You'd fare worse in many a tavern. Do us the favour, and stay."

I hesitated. The boy nodded at me, eyes bright, and the dog, which had risen when I rose, wagged its tail and gave a wide, whining yawn, stretching the stiff forepaws.

"Yes. Stay," begged the boy.

I could see that it would mean something to them if I complied. To stay would be to bring back some of the ancient sanctity of the place; a guest in the guest-house, so carefully swept and aired and kept for the guests who no longer came.

"I shall be glad to," I said.

Constant, beaming, thrust a torch into the ashes and held it till it kindled. "Then come this way."

As I followed him his father, settling himself once more in his blankets by the hearth, said the time-honoured words of the healing-place.

"Sleep soundly, friend, and may the god send you a dream."

★   ★   ★

Whoever sent it, the dream came, and it was a true one.

I dreamed of Morgause, whom I had driven from Uther's court at Luguvallium, with an escort detailed to take her with safe ceremony across the high Pennines, and then south-east to York, where her half-sister Morgan lay.

The dream came fitfully, like those hilltop glimpses one gets through blowing cloud on a dark day. Which, in the dream, it was. I saw the party first on the evening of a wet and windy day, when fine rain blowing down-wind turned the gravel of the road into a slippery track of mud. They had paused on the bank of a river, swollen by rain. I did not recognise the place. The road led down into the river, in what should have been a shallow ford, but now showed as a racing tumble of white water which broke and foamed round an island that split the flood like a ship sailing. There was no house in sight, not even a cave. Beyond the ford the road twisted eastward among its sodden trees, and up through rolling foothills towards the high fells.

With dusk falling fast, it seemed that the party would have to spend the night here, and wait for the river to go down. The officer in command of the party seemed to be explaining as much to Morgause; I could not hear what was said, but he looked angry, and his horse, tired though it was, kept on the fret. I guessed that the choice of route had not been his: the normal way from Luguvallium is by the high moorland road that leaves the west highway at Brocavum and crosses the mountains by Verterae. This last, kept fortified and in fine repair, would have offered the party a staging post, and would have been the obvious choice for a soldier. Instead, they must have taken the old hill road which branches south-east from the five-way crossing near the camp on the River Lune. I had never been that way. It was not a road that had been kept in any kind of order. It led up the valley of the Dubglas and across the high moors, and thence through the mountains by the pass formed by the Tribuit and the Isara rivers. Men call this pass the Pennine Gap, and in past time the Romans kept it fortified and the roads open and patrolled. It is wild country – and still, among the remote summits and cliffs above the tree line, are caves where the Old Ones live. If this was indeed the road Morgause was taking, I could only wonder why.

Cloud and mist; rain in long grey showers; the swollen river piling its white bow-waves against the driftwood and bending willows of the river island. Then darkness and a gap of time hid the scene from me.

Next time I saw them they were halted, somewhere high in the pass, with tree-hung cliffs to the right of the road, and to the left a wide, falling prospect of forest, with a winding river at the foot of the valley, and hills beyond. They had halted by a milestone near the crest of the pass. Here a track branched off downhill to where, in a distant hollow of the valley, lights showed. Morgause was pointing towards these, and it seemed that there was an argument in progress.

Still I could hear nothing, but the cause of the dispute was obvious. The officer had thrust forward to Morgause's side, and was leaning forward in his saddle, arguing fiercely, pointing first at the milestone and then at the road ahead. A late gleam from the west showed, etched by shadow on the stone, the name OLICANA. I could not see the mileage, but what the officer said was clear; that it would be folly to forgo the known comforts that awaited them in Olicana, for the chance that the distant house (if such it was) could accommodate the party. His men, crowding near, were openly supporting him. Beside her, Morgause's women watched her anxiously, one might have said beseechingly.

After a while, with a resigned gesture, Morgause gave way. The escort reformed. The women closed up beside her, smiling. But before the party had gone ten paces one of the women called out sharply, and then Morgause herself, loosing the reins on her horse's neck, put out a hand delicately into the air, as if groping for support, and swayed in her saddle. Someone cried out again. The women crowded to hold her. The officer, turning back, spurred his horse alongside hers and stretched an arm to support her drooping form. She collapsed against him, and lay inert.

There was nothing for it but to accept defeat. Within minutes the party was slithering and thudding down the track towards the distant light in the valley. Morgause, shrouded fast in her big cloak, lay motionless and fainting in the officer's arms.

But I knew, whom am wary of witches, that within the shelter of the rich furred hood she was awake, and smiling her small triumphant smile, as Arthur's men carried her to the house to which, for her own reasons, she had led them, and where she planned to stay.

When the mists of vision parted next, I saw a bedchamber finely appointed, with a gilded bed and crimson covers, and a brazier burning red, throwing its light on the woman who lay there against the pillows. Morgause's women were there, the same who had attended her in Luguvallium, the young maid called Lind who had led Arthur to her mistress's bed, and the old woman who had slept the night through in a drugged slumber. The girl Lind looked pale and tired; I remembered that Morgause, in her rage with me, had had her whipped. She served her mistress warily, with shut lips and downcast eyes, while the old woman, stiff from the long, damp ride, went slowly about her tasks, grumbling as she went, but with sidelong glances to make sure her mistress did not heed her. As for Morgause, she showed no sign of sickness or even fatigue. I had expected none. She lay back on the crimson pillows, the narrow green-gilt eyes staring out through the chamber walls at something far away and pleasurable, and smiling the same smile I had seen on her lips as Arthur lay beside her sleeping.

I must have woken here, shaken out of the dream by hatred and distress, but the god's hand was still on me, because I went back into sleep and into the same room. It must have been later, after some span of time; days, even; however long it had taken Lot, King of Lothian, to wait through the ceremonies at Luguvallium, then gather his troops together and head south and eastwards, by the same devious route, for York. No doubt his main force had gone directly, but he, with a small party of fast horsemen, had hastened to the meeting place with Morgause.

For that it had been prearranged was now clear. She must have got a message to him before she herself left the court, then she had forced her escort to ride slowly, taking time, and finally had contrived, by her feigned illness, to seek shelter in the privacy of a friend's house. I thought I saw her plan. Having failed in her bid for power through her seduction of Arthur, she had somehow persuaded Lot to this tryst, and now with her witch's wiles she would be set on winning his favour, to find a position of some sort at the court of her sister, Lot's future queen.

Next moment, as the dream changed, I saw the sort of wiles that she was using; witchcraft of a kind, I suppose, but the kind that any woman knows how to use. There was the bedchamber again, with the brazier dealing out a glow of warmth, and beside it, on a low table, food and wine in silver dishes. Morgause stood beside the brazier, the rosy glow playing on the white gown and creamy skin, and glimmering on the long shining hair that fell to her waist in rivulets of apricot light. Even I, who loathed her, had to admit that she was very lovely. The long green-gold eyes, thickly fringed by their golden lashes, watched the door. She was alone.

The door opened and Lot came in. The King of Lothian was a big dark man, with powerful shoulders and hot eyes. He favoured jewels, and glittered with arm-rings and finger rings and a chain on his breast set with citrine and amethyst. At his shoulder, where the long black hair touched his cloak, was a magnificent pin of garnet and worked gold, in the Saxon style. Fine enough, I thought grimly, to have been a guest-gift from Colgrim himself. There was rain on his hair and cloak.

Morgause was speaking. I could hear nothing. It was a vision of movement and colour only. She made no move of welcome, nor did he seem to expect it. He showed no surprise at seeing her. He spoke once, briefly, then stooped to the table, and, picking up the silver jug, splashed wine from it into a cup with such haste and carelessness that the crimson stuff slopped over the table and on to the floor. Morgause laughed. There was no answering smile from Lot. He drank the wine down, deeply as if he needed it, then threw the cup to the floor, strode past the brazier, and with his big hands, still marked and muddied from the ride, laid hold of the two sides of her gown at the neck, and ripped it apart, baring her body to the navel. Then he had hold of her, and his mouth was on hers, devouring her. He had not troubled to shut the door. I saw it shift wider, and the girl Lind, scared doubtless by the crash of the fallen cup, peer in, white-faced. Like Lot, she showed no surprise at what she saw, but, frightened perhaps by the man's violence, she hesi-tated, as if about to run to her mistress's aid. But then she saw, as I had seen, the half-naked body melt, clinging, against the man's, and the woman's hands sliding up into the black wet hair. The torn gown slipped down to lie in a huddle on the floor. Morgause said something, and laughed. The man's grip on her shifted. Lind shrank back, and the door closed. Lot swung Morgause up and took four long strides to the bed.

Witch's wiles indeed. Even for a rape it would have been precipi-tate: for a seduction it was a record. Call me innocent, or stupid, or what you will, but at first I could only think, held there in the clouds of dreaming, that some spell had been at work. I believe I thought hazily of drugged wine, Circe's cup, and men turned into rutting swine. It was not until some time later, when the man reached a hand from the bed-covers and turned up the wick of the lamp, and the woman, dazed with sex and sleep, sat up smiling against the crimson pillows and drew the furs up to cover herself, that I began to suspect the truth. He padded across the floor, through the fallen wreck of his own clothes, poured another cupful of wine, drained it, then refilled it and took it back to Morgause. Then he heaved himself back into the bed beside her, sat back himself against the bed-head, and began to talk. She, half-sitting, half-lying against him, nodded and answered, seriously and at length. As they talked, his hand slid down to fondle her breasts; he did it half absently, as was natural enough in a man like Lot, who was used to women. But Morgause, the maiden with the unbound hair and demure little voice? Morgause noticed the gesture no more than the man. Only then, with a jar like an arrow thudding deep into a shield, did I see the truth. They had been here before. They were familiar. Even before she had lain with Arthur, Lot had had her, and many times. They were so used to one another that they could lie twined naked on a bed, and, busily and earnestly, talk . . . About what?

Treachery. That was, naturally, my first thought. Treachery against the High King, whom both, for differing reasons, had cause to hate. Morgause, long jealous of the half-sister who must always take precedence of her, had laid siege to Lot and taken him to her bed. There had, it was to be supposed, been other lovers, too. Then came Lot's bid for power at Luguvallium. It failed, and Morgause, not guessing at the strength and clemency that would make Arthur accept him back among his allies, turned to Arthur himself in her own desperate play for power.

And now? She had magic of a kind. It was possible that she knew, as I knew, that in that night's incest with Arthur she had conceived. A husband she must have, and who better than Lot? If he could be persuaded that the child was his, she might cheat the hated young sister of marriage and kingdom, and build a nest where the cuckoo could hatch out in safety.

It looked as if she would succeed. When next I saw through the dream-smoke they were laughing together, and she had freed her body of the covers and was seated high on the furs against the crimson curtains of the bed-head, with the rose-gold hair streaming down behind her shoulders like a mantle of silk. The front of her body was bare, and on her head was Lot's royal circlet of white gold, glimmering with citrines and the milk-blue pearls of the northern rivers. Her eyes shone bright and narrow as a purring cat's, and the man was laughing with her as he lifted the cup and drank what looked like a toast to her. As he lifted it the cup rocked, and wine slopped over the brim to spill down her breasts like blood. She smiled, not stirring, and the king leaned forward laughing, and sucked it off.

The smoke thickened. I could smell it, as if I was there in the room, close by the brazier. Then mercifully I was awake in the cool and tranquil night, but with the nightmare still crawling like sweat on the skin.

To anyone but me, knowing them as I knew them, the scene would have offered no offence. The girl was lovely, and the man fine enough, and if they were lovers, why, then, she had the right to look towards his crown. There should have been nothing to flinch at in the scene, any more than in a dozen such that one sees on any summer evening along the hedgerows, or in the midnight hall. But about a crown, even such a one as Lot's, there is something sacred; it is a symbol of that mystery, the link between god and king, king and people. So to see the crown on that wanton head, with the king's own head, bared of its royalty, bent below it like a beast's pasturing, was profanity, like spittle on an altar.

So I rose, and plunged my head in water, and washed the sight away.

5

When we reached Caerleon at noon next day, a bright October sun was drying the ground, and frost lay indigo-blue in the lee of walls and buildings. The alders along the river bank, their black boughs hung with yellow coins of leaves, looked bright and still, like stitchery against the background of pale sky. Dead leaves, still rimmed with frost, crunched and rustled under our horses' hoofs. The smells of new bread and roasting meat wound through the air from the camp kitchens, and brought sharply to mind my visit here with Tremorinus, the master engineer who had rebuilt the camp for Ambrosius, and included in his plans the finest kitchens in the country.

I said as much to my companion – it was Caius Valerius, my friend of old – and he grunted appreciatively.

"Let us hope the King takes due time for a meal before he starts his inspection."

"I think we can trust him for that."

"Oh, aye, he's a growing boy." It was said with a sort of indulgent pride, with no faintest hint of patronage. From Valerius it came well; he was a veteran who had fought with Ambrosius at Kaerconan and since then with Uther: he was also one of the captains who had been with Arthur at the battle on the river Glein. If men of this stamp could accept the young King with respect, and trust him for leadership, then my task was indeed done. The thought came unmixed with any sense of loss or declining, but with a calm relief that was new to me. I thought: I am growing old.

I became conscious that Valerius had asked me something. "I'm sorry. I was thinking. You said?"

"I asked if you were going to stay here till the crowning?"

"I think not. He may need me here for a while, if he's set on rebuilding. I'm hoping I shall have leave to go after Christmas, but I'll come back for the crowning."

"If the Saxons give us leave to hold it."

"As you say. To leave it till Pentecost would seem to be a little risky, but it's the bishops' choice, and the King would be wiser not to gainsay them."

Valerius grunted. "Maybe if they put their minds to it, and do some serious praying, God will hold the spring offensive back for them. Pentecost, eh? Do you suppose they're hoping for fire from heaven again . . . theirs, this time, perhaps?" He eyed me sideways. "What do you say?"

As it happened, I knew the legend to which he referred. Since the coming of the white fire into the Perilous Chapel, the Christians had been wont to refer to their own story, that once, at Pentecost, fire had fallen from heaven on their god's chosen servants. I saw no reason to quarrel with such an interpretation of what had happened at the Chapel: it was necessary that the Christians, with their growing power, should accept Arthur as their God-appointed leader. Besides, for all I knew, they were right.

Valerius was still waiting for me to answer. I smiled. "Only that if they know from whose hand the fire falls, they know more than I do."

"Oh, aye, that's likely." His tone was faintly derisive. Valerius had been on garrison duty in Luguvallium on the night when Arthur lifted the sword from the fire in the Perilous Chapel, but, like everyone else, he had heard the tale. And, like everyone else, he shied away from what had happened there. "So you're leaving us after Christmas? Are we to know where for?"

"I'm going home to Maridunum. It's five – no, six years since I was there. Too long. I'd like to see that all is well."

"Then see that you do get back for the crowning. There will be great doings here at Pentecost. It would be a pity to miss them."

By then, I thought, she would be near her time. I said aloud: "Oh, yes. With or without the Saxons, we shall have great doings at Pentecost."

Then we spoke of other things until our quarters were reached,
and we were bidden to join the King and his officers for meat.

★   ★   ★

Caerleon, the old Roman City of the Legions, had been rebuilt
by Ambrosius, and since then kept garrisoned and in good repair.
Arthur now set himself to enlarge it almost to its original capacity,
and make it, besides, a king's stronghold and dwelling-place as well
as a fortress. The old royal city of Winchester was reckoned now to
be too near the borders of the Saxon federated territory, and too
vulnerable, besides, to new invasion, situated as it is on the Itchen
river where longboats had landed before now. London was still
safely held by the British, nor had any Saxon attempted to thrust up
into the Thames valley, but in Uther's time the longboats had
penetrated as far as Vagniacae, and Rutupiae and the Isle of Thanet
had long been securely in Saxon hands. The threat was felt to be
there, and growing yearly, and since Uther's accession London had
begun – imperceptibly at first, and then with increasing
speed – to show decay. Now it was a city fallen on evil days; many
of its buildings had collapsed through age and neglect; poverty
showed itself everywhere, as markets moved away, and those who
could afford to do so, left for safer places. It would never, men said,
be a capital city again.

So, until his new stronghold should be ready to counter any
serious invasion from the Saxon Shore, Arthur planned to make
Caerleon his headquarters. It was the obvious choice. Within eight
miles of it was Ynyr's capital of Guent, and the fortress itself, lying
in a loop of the river but beyond the danger of flood, had mountains
at its back, and was additionally protected on the east by marshes at
the watersmeet of the Isca and the little Afon Lwyd. Of course
Caerleon's very strength restricted it; it could defend only a small
portion of the territory under Arthur's shield. But for the present it
could provide the headquarters for his policy of mobile defence.

I was with him all through that first winter. He did ask me once,
with a smiling lift of the brows, if I was not going to leave him for
my cave in the hills, but I said merely: "Later," and let it be.

I told him nothing about the dream I had had that night at

Nodens' shrine. He had enough to think about, and I was only too thankful that he seemed to have forgotten the possible conse- quences of that night with Morgause. Time enough to talk to him when the news came from York about the wedding.

Which it did, in good time to stop the court's preparation to go north for the celebrations at Christmas. A long letter came first, from Queen Ygraine to the King; one came for me with the same courier, and was brought to me where I walked by the river. All morning I had been watching the laying of a conduit, but for the moment work had ceased, as the men went for their midday bread and wine. The troops drilling on the parade ground near the old amphitheatre had dispersed, and the winter day was still and bright, with a pearled mist.

I thanked the man, waiting, letter in hand, until he had gone. Then I broke the seal.

The dream had been a true one. Lot and Morgause were married. Before ever Queen Ygraine and her party reached York, the news had gone before them, that the lovers were handfast. Morgause – I was reading between the lines here – had ridden into the city with Lot, flushed with triumph and decked with his jewels, and the city, preparing for a royal wedding, with a sight of the High King himself, made the best of its disappointment, and, with northern thrift, held the wedding feast just the same. The King of Lothian, said Ygraine, had borne himself meekly to her, and had made gifts to the chief men of the city, so his welcome had been warm enough. And Morgan – I could read the relief in the plain words – Morgan had showed neither anger nor humiliation; she had laughed aloud, and then wept with what appeared to be sheer relief. She had gone to the feasting in a gay red gown, and no girl had been merrier, even though (finished Ygraine with the touch of acid that I remembered) Morgause had worn her new crown from rising to bed- time . . .

As for the Queen's own reaction, I thought that this, too, was one of relief. Morgause, understandably, had never been dear to her, whereas Morgan was the only child she had had by her to rear. It was clear that, while prepared to obey King Uther, both she and Morgan had disliked the marriage with the black northern wolf. I did, indeed, wonder if Morgan knew more about him than she had told her mother. It was even possible that Morgause, being what she was, had boasted that she and Lot had already lain together.

Ygraine herself showed no suspicion of this, nor of the bride's pregnancy as a possible reason for the hasty marriage. It was to be hoped that there was no hint, either, in the letter she had sent to Arthur. He had too much on his mind now: there would be time yet for the anger and the distress. He must be crowned first, and then be free to go about his formidable task of war without being shackled by what was women's business – and would, all too soon, be mine.

★   ★   ★

Arthur flung the letter down. He was angry, that was plain, but holding it on the rein.

"Well? I take it you know?"

"Yes."

"How long have you known?"

"The Queen your mother wrote to me. I have just read the letter. I imagine it carries the same news as yours."

"That is not what I asked you."

I said mildly: "If you are asking me, did I know this was going to happen, the answer is yes."

The angry dark gaze kindled. "*You did*? Why did you not tell me?"

"For two reasons. Because you were occupied with things that matter more, and because I was not quite sure."

"You? Not sure? Come, Merlin! This from you?"

"Arthur, all that I knew or suspected of this came to me in a dream, one night some weeks ago. It came, not like a dream of power, or divination, but like a nightmare brought on by too much wine, or by too much thinking about that hellcat and her works and ways. King Lot had been in my mind, and so had she. I dreamed I saw them together, and she was trying on his crown. Was that enough, do you think, for me to make you a report that would have set the court by the ears, and you, maybe, racing up to York to quarrel with him?"

"It would have been enough, once." His mouth showed a stubborn and still angry line. I saw that the anger sprang from anxiety, striking at the wrong time about Lot's intentions.

"That," I said, "was when I was the King's prophet. No" – at his quick movement – "I belong to no man else. I am yours, as always. But I am a prophet no longer, Arthur. I thought you understood."

"How could I? What do you mean?"

"I mean that the night at Luguvallium, when you drew the sword I had hidden for you in the fire, was the last time that the power visited me. You did not see the place afterwards, when the fire was gone and the chapel empty. It had broken the stone where the sword lay, and destroyed the sacred relics. Me, it did not destroy, but I think the power was burned out of me, perhaps for ever. Fires fade to ash, Arthur. I thought you must surely have guessed."

"How could I?" he said again, but his tone had changed. It was no longer angry and abrupt, but slow and thinking. As I, after Luguvallium, had felt myself ageing, then Arthur had, for good and all, left his boyhood. "You've seemed the same as always. Clear-headed, and so sure of yourself that it's like asking advice of an oracle."

I laughed. "They were not always so clear, by all accounts! Old women, or witless girls mumbling in the smoke. If I've been sure of myself during these past weeks, it's because the advice I have been asked for concerns my professional skills, no more."

" 'No more?' Enough, one would think, for any king to call on, if that were all he had known from you . . . But yes, I think I see. It's the same for you as for me; the dreams and visions have gone, and now we have a life to live by the rules of men. I should have understood. You did, when I went myself after Colgrim." He walked over to the table where Ygraine's letter lay, and rested a fist on the marble. He leaned on it, frowning downwards, but seeing nothing. Then he looked up. "And what of the years that are to come? The fighting will be bitter, and it will not be over this year, or the next. Are you telling me that I shall have nothing from you now? I'm not talking about your engines of war, or your know-ledge of medicine; I'm asking you if I am not to have the 'magic' that the soldiers tell me about, the help that you gave to Ambrosius and to my father?"

I smiled. "That, surely." He was thinking, I knew, of the effect my prophecies, and sometimes my presence, had had on the fight-

ing troops. "What the armies think of me now, they will go on
thinking. And where is the need for further prophecies concerning
the wars you are embarked on? Neither you nor your troops will
need reminding at every turn. They know what I have said. Out
there in the field, the length and width of Britain, there is glory for
you, and for them. You will have success, and success again, and in
the end – I do not know how far ahead – you will have victory.
That is what I said to you, and it is still true. It is the work you were
trained for: go and do it, and leave me to find a way to do mine."

"Which is, now that you've flown your eagle chick, and yourself
stay earthborne? To wait for victory, then help me build again?"

"In time." I indicated the crumpled letter. "But more immediately, to deal with such things as this. After Pentecost, with your
leave, I shall go north to Lothian."

A moment of stillness, while I saw the flush of relief colour his
face. He did not ask what I meant to do there, but said merely: "I
shall be glad. You know that. I doubt if we need to discuss why this
happened?"

"No."

"You were right before, of course. As ever. What she wanted
was power, and it did not matter to her how she took it. Or indeed,
where she looked for it. I can see that now. I can only be glad to feel
myself absolved of any claim she might make on me." A small
movement of his hand brushed Morgause and her plots aside. "But
two things remain. The most important is that I still need Lot as an
ally. You were right – again! – in not telling me of your dream. I
would certainly have quarrelled with him. As it is –"

He paused, with a lift of the shoulders. I nodded.

"As it is you can accept Lot's marriage to your half-sister, and
count it as sufficient alliance to hold him to your banner. Queen
Ygraine, it seems, has acted wisely, and so has Morgan, your sister.
This is, after all, the match that King Uther originally proposed. We
may safely ignore the reasons for it now."

"All the more easily," he said, "because it seems that Morgan is
not ill pleased. If she had shown herself slighted . . . That was the
second problem I spoke of. But it seems to be no problem after all.
Did the Queen tell you in her letter that Morgan showed nothing
but relief?"

"Yes. And I have questioned the courier who brought the letters from York. He tells me that Urbgen of Rheged was at York for the wedding, and that Morgan hardly saw Lot for watching him."

Urbgen was now King in Rheged, old King Coel having died soon after the battle at Luguvallium. The new King was a man in his late forties, a notable warrior, and still a vigorous and handsome man. He had been widowed two or three years ago.

Arthur's look quickened with interest. "Urbgen of Rheged? Now, that would be a match! It's the one I'd have preferred all along, but when the match was made with Lot, Urbgen's wife was still living. Urbgen, yes . . . Along with Maelgon of Gwynedd, he's the best fighting man in the north, and there has never been any doubt of his loyalty. Between those two, the north would be held firmly . . ."

I finished it for him. "And let Lot and his queen do what they will?"

"Exactly. Would Urbgen take her, do you think?"

"He will count himself lucky. And I believe she will fare better than she could ever have done with the other. Depend upon it, you'll be receiving another courier soon. And that is an informed guess, not a prophecy."

"Merlin, do you mind?"

It was the King who asked me, a man as old and wise as myself; a man who could see past his own crowding problems, and guess what it might mean to me, to walk in dead air where once the world had been a god-filled garden.

I thought for a little before I answered him. "I'm not sure. There have been times like this before, passive times, ebb after flood; but never when we were still on the threshold of great events. I am not used to feeling helpless, and I own that I cannot like it. But if I have learned one thing during the years when the god has been with me, it is to trust him. I am old enough now to walk tranquilly, and when I look at you I know that I have been fulfilled. Why should I grieve? I shall sit on the hilltops and watch you doing the work for me. That is the guerdon of age."

"Age? You talk as if you were a greybeard! What are you?"

"Old enough. I'm nearly forty."

"Well, then, for God's sake —?"

And so, in laughter, we passed the narrow corner. He drew me then to the window table where my scale models of the new Caerleon stood, and plunged into a discussion of them. He did not speak of Morgause again, and I thought: I spoke of trust, what sort of trust is this? If I fail him, then I shall indeed be only a shadow and a name, and my hand on the sword of Britain was a mockery.

When I asked leave to go to Maridunum after Twelfth Night, he gave it half absently, his mind already on the next task to hand for the morning.

★   ★   ★

The cave I had inherited from Galapas the hermit lay some six miles east of Maridunum, the town that guards the mouth of the River Tywy. My grandfather, the King of Dyfed, had lived there, and I, brought up as a neglected bastard in the royal household, had been allowed by a lazy tutor to run wild. I had made friends with the wise old recluse who lived in the cave on Bryn Myrddin, a hill sacred to the sky-god Myrddin, he of the light and the wild air. Galapas had died long ago, but in time I made the place my home, and the folk still came to visit Myrddin's healing spring, and to receive treatment and remedies from me. Soon my skill as a doctor surpassed even the old man's, and with it my reputation for the power that men call magic, so now the place was known familiarly as Merlin's Hill. I believe that the simpler folk even thought that I was Myrddin himself, the guardian of the spring.

There is a mill set on the Tywy, just where the track for Bryn Myrddin leaves the road. When I reached it I found that a barge had come up-river, and was moored there. Its great bay horse grazed where it could on the winter herbage, while a young man unloaded sacks onto the wharf. He worked single-handed; the barge master must be withindoors slaking his thirst; but it was only one man's job to lift the half-score of grain sacks that had been sent up for grinding from some winter store. A child of perhaps five years old trotted to and fro, hindering the work, and talking ceaselessly in a weird mixture of Welsh and some other tongue familiar but so distorted – and lisping besides – that I could not catch it. Then the young man answered in the same tongue, and I recognised it, and him. I drew rein.

"Stilicho!" I called. As he set the sack down and turned, I added in his own tongue: "I should have let you know, but time was short, and I hardly expected to be here so soon. How are you?"

"My lord!" He stood amazed for a moment, then came running across the weedy yard to the road's edge, wiped his hands down his breeches, reached for my hand, and kissed it. I saw tears in his eyes, and was touched. He was a Sicilian who had been my slave on my travels abroad. In Constantinople I had freed him, but he had chosen to stay with me and return to Britain, and had been my servant while I had lived on Bryn Myrddin. When I went north he married the miller's daughter, Mai, and moved down the valley to live at the mill.

He was bidding me welcome, talking in the same excited, broken tongue as the child. What Welsh he had learned seemed to have deserted him for the moment. The child came up and stood, finger in mouth, staring.

"Yours?" I asked him. "He's a fine boy."

"My eldest," he said with pride. "They are all boys."

" 'All?' " I asked, raising a brow at him.

"Only three," he said, with the limpid look I remembered, "and another soon."

I laughed and congratulated him, and hoped for another strong boy. These Sicilians breed like mice, and at least he would not, like his own father, be forced to sell children into slavery to buy food for the rest. Mai was the miller's only daughter, and would have a fat patrimony.

Had already, I found. The miller had died two years back; he had suffered from the stone, and would take neither care nor medicine. Now he was gone, and Stilicho was miller in his stead.

"But your home is cared for, my lord. Either I or the lad who works for me ride up every day to make sure all is well. There's no fear that anyone would dare go inside; you'll find your things just as you left them, and the place clean and aired . . . but of course there'll be no food there. So if you were wanting to go up there now . . ." He hesitated. I could see he was afraid of presuming. "Will you not honour us, lord, by sleeping here for tonight? It'll be cold up yonder, and damp with it, for all that we've had the brazier lit every week through the winter, like you told me, to keep the books sweet. Let you stay here, my lord, and the lad will ride up now to light the brazier, and in the morning Mai and I can go up –"

"It's good of you," I said, "but I shan't feel the cold, and perhaps I can get the fires going myself . . . more quickly, even, than your lad, perhaps?" I smiled at his expression; he had not forgotten some of the things he had seen when he served the enchanter. "So thank you, but I'll not trouble Mai, except perhaps for some food? If I might rest here for a while, and talk to you, and see your family, then ride up into the hill before dark? I can carry all I shall need until tomorrow."

"Of course, of course . . . I'll tell Mai. She'll be honoured . . . delighted . . ." I had already caught a glimpse of a pale face and wide eyes at a window. She would be delighted, I knew, when the awesome Prince Merlin rode away again; but I was tired from the long ride, and had, besides, smelled the savoury stew cooking, which no doubt could easily be made to go one further. So much, indeed, Stilicho was naïvely explaining: "There's a fat fowl on the boil now, so all will be well. Come you in, and warm yourself, and rest till supper time. Bran will see to your horse, while I get the last sacks off the barge, and it away back to town. So come your ways, lord, and welcome back to Bryn Myrddin."

★   ★   ★

Of all the many times I had ridden up the high valley-side towards my home on Bryn Myrddin, I do not quite know why I should remember this one so clearly. There was nothing special to mark it; it was a home-coming, no more.

But up to this moment, so much later, when I write of it, every detail of that ride remains vivid. The hollow sound of the horse's hoofs on the iron ground of winter; the crunch of leaves underfoot, and snap of brittle twigs; the flight of a woodcock and the clap of a startled pigeon. Then the sun, falling ripe and level as it does just before candle-time, lighting the fallen oak-leaves where they lay in shadow, edged with rime like powdered diamond; the holly boughs rattling and ringing with the birds I disturbed from feeding on the fruit; the smell of damp juniper as my horse pushed through; the sight of a single spray of whin flowers struck to gold by the sunlight, with the night's frost already crisping the ground and making the air pure and thin as chiming crystal.

I stabled my horse in the shed below the cliff, and climbed the path to the little alp of turf before the cave. And there was the cave itself, with its silence, and the familiar scents, and the still air stirring only to the faint movement of velvet on velvet, where the bats in the high lantern of the rock heard my familiar step, and stayed where they were, waiting for the dark.

Stilicho had told me the truth; the place was well cared for, dry and aired, and, though it was colder by a cloak's thickness even than the frosty air outside, that would soon mend. The brazier stood ready for kindling, and fresh dry logs were set on the open hearth near the cave's entrance. There was tinder and flint on the usual shelf: in the past I had rarely troubled to use them, but this time I took them down, and soon had a flame going. It may be that, remembering a former, tragic home-coming, I was half-afraid to test (even in this tranquil after-time) the least of my powers: but I believe that the decision was made through caution rather than through fear. If I still had power to call on, I would save it for greater things than the making of a flame to warm me. It is easier to call the storm from the empty sky, than to manipulate the heart of a man; and soon, if my bones did not lie to me, I should be needing all the power I could muster, to pit against a woman; and this is harder to do than anything concerning men, as air is harder to see than a mountain.

So I lit the brazier in my sleeping-chamber, and kindled the logs at the doorway, then unpacked my saddle-bags and went out with the pitcher to draw water from the spring. This trickled out of a ferny rock beside the cave-mouth, and lisped through the hanging lace of rime, to drip into a round stone basin. Above it, among the mosses, and crowned with icy glitter, stood the image of the god Myrddin, who keeps the roads of the sky. I poured a libation to him, then went in to look to my books and medicines.

Nothing had taken harm. Even the jars of herbs, sealed and tied as I had taught Stilicho to do it, seemed fresh and good. I uncovered the great harp that stood at the back of the cave, and carried it near the fire to tune it. Then, having made my bed ready, I mulled some wine and drank it, sitting by the leaping fire of logs. Finally, I unwrapped the small knee-harp that had been with me on all my travels, and carried it back to its place in the crystal cave. This was a small inner cave, with its opening set high in the rear wall of the main cavern, and so placed behind a jut of rock that in the normal way the shadows hid it from sight. When I was a boy it had been my gate of vision. Here, in the inner silence of the hill, folded deep in darkness and in solitude, no sense could play except the eye of the mind, and no sound come.

Except, as now, the murmur of the harp as I set it down. It was the one I had made as a boy, so finely strung that the very air could set it whispering. The sounds were weird and sometimes beautiful, but somehow outside the run of music as we know it, as the song of the grey seal on the rocks is beautiful, but is the sound of the wind and the waves rather than of a beast. The harp sang to itself as I set it down, with a kind of slumbrous humming, like a cat purring to be back on its own hearthstone.

"Rest you there," I told it, and at the sound of my voice running round the crystal walls it hummed again.

I went back to the bright fire, and the stars gemming the black sky outside. I lifted the great harp to me and – hesitating at first, and then more easily – made music.

> *Rest you here, enchanter, while the light fades.*
> *Vision narrows, and the far* •
> *Sky-edge is gone with the sun.*
> *Be content with the small spark*
> *Of the coal, the smell*
> *Of food, and the breath*
> *Of frost beyond the shut door.*
> *Home is here, and familiar things;*
> *A cup, a wooden bowl, a blanket,*
> *Prayer, a gift for the god, and sleep.*
>
> *(And music, says the harp,*
> *And music.)*

6

With the spring came, inevitably, trouble. Colgrim, sniffing his way cautiously back along the eastern coasts, landed within the old federated territories, and set about raising a new force to replace the one defeated at Luguvallium and the Glein.

I was back in Caerleon by that time, busy with Arthur's plans for the establishment there of his new mobile cavalry force.

The idea, though startling, was not altogether new. With Saxon Federates already settled, and by treaty, in the south-eastern districts of the island, and with the whole eastern seaboard continually at risk, it was impossible to set up and effectively maintain a fixed line of defence. There were, of course, certain defensive ramparts already in existence, of which Ambrosius' Wall was the greatest. (I omit Hadrian's Great Wall here; it was never a purely defensive structure, and had been, even in the Emperor Macsen's time, impossible to keep. Now it was breached in a score of places; and besides, the enemy was no longer the Celt from the wild country to the north; he came from the sea. Or he was already, as I have explained, within the gates of south-east Britain.) The others, Arthur set himself to extend and refurbish, notably the Black Dyke of Northumbria, which protects Rheged and Strathclyde, and the older Wall which the Romans originally built across the high chalk downlands south of the Sarum plain. The King planned to extend this wall northward. The roads through it were to be left open, but could be shut fast if any attempt was made by the enemy to move towards the Summer Country to the west. Other defensive works were planned, soon to be under way. Meanwhile, all the King could hope to do was fortify and man certain key positions, establish signal stations between these, and keep open the communicating roads. The kings and chiefs of the British would keep each his own territory, while the High King's work would be to maintain a fighting force that could be taken at need to help any of them, or be thrown into whatever breach was made in our defences. It was the old plan with which Rome had successfully defended her province for some time before the withdrawal of the legions: the Count of the Saxon Shore had commanded just such a mobile force, and indeed Ambrosius, more recently, had done the same.

But Arthur planned to go further. "Caesar-speed", as he saw it, could be made ten times as speedy if the whole force were mounted. Nowadays, when one sees cavalry troops daily on the roads and in the parade grounds, this seems a normal enough thing; but then, when he first thought of it and put it to me, it came with all the force of the surprise attack he hoped to achieve with it. It would take time, of course; the beginnings, perforce, would be modest. Until enough of the troops were trained to fight from horseback, it would have to be a smallish, picked force drawn from among the officers and his own friends. This granted, the plan was feasible. But no such plan could be put into being without the right horses, and of these we could command relatively few. The cobby little native beasts, though hardy, were neither speedy enough nor big enough to carry an armed man into battle.

We talked it over for days and nights, going into every detail, before Arthur would put the idea before his commanders. There are those – the best, too, often among them – who are opposed to any kind of change; and unless every argument can be met, the waverers are drawn to cast with the noes. Between them Arthur and Cador, along with Gwilim of Dyfed and Ynyr from Caer Guent, hammered the thing out over the map-tables. I could contribute little to the war-talk, but I did solve the problem of the horses.

There is a race of horses which are said to be the best in the world. Certainly they are the most beautiful. I had seen them in the East, where the men of the desert prize them more than their gold or their women; but they could be found, I knew, nearer than that. The Romans had brought some of these creatures back from North Africa into Iberia, where they interbred with the thicker-bodied horses from Europe. The result was a splendid animal, fast and fiery, but strong with it, and supple, and biddable as a war-horse should be. If Arthur would send across to see what might be bought, then as soon as the weather would allow safe transportation, the makings of a mounted force could be his by the following summer.

So when I got back to Caerleon in the spring, it was to put in motion the building of big new stable-blocks, while Bedwyr was dispatched overseas to do the horse-trading.

Caerleon was already transformed. Work on the fortress itself had gone quickly and well, and now other buildings were springing up nearby, of sufficient comfort and grandeur to grace a temporary capital. Though Arthur would use the commandant's house inside the walls as battle headquarters, another house (which the folk called "the palace") was being built outside, in the lovely curve of the Isca River, by the Roman bridge. When finished this would be a large house, with several courtyards for guests and their servants. It was well built, of stone and brickwork, with painted plaster and carved pillars at the doors. Its roof was gilded, like that of the new Christian church, which was on the site of the old Mithras temple. Between these two buildings and the parade ground to the west of them, houses and shops were springing up, making a bustling township where before there had only been a small village settlement. The folk, proud of Arthur's choice of Caerleon, and willing to ignore the reasons for it, worked with a will to make the place worthy of a new reign, and a king who would bring peace.

He brought peace of a sort by Pentecost. Colgrim, with his new army, had broken bounds in the eastern regions. Arthur fought him twice, once not far south of the Humber, the second time nearer the Saxon boundary, in the reedy fields of Linnuis. In the second of these battles Colgrim was killed. Then, with the Saxon Shore uneasily recoiling into quiet once more, Arthur came back to us, in time to meet Bedwyr disembarking with the first contingent of the promised horses.

Valerius, who had been to help disembark them, was enthusiastic.

"High as your breast, and strong with it, and as gentle as maidens. Some maidens, that is. And fast, they say, as greyhounds, though they're still stiff from the voyage, and it'll take time before they get their land-legs again. And beautiful! There's many a maiden, gentle or otherwise, who'd sacrifice to Hecate for eyes as big and dark, or skins as silken . . ."

"How many did he bring? Mares as well? When I was in the East they parted only with the stallions."

"Mares as well. A hundred stallions in this first lot, and thirty mares. Better off than the army on campaign, but still fierce competition, eh?"

"You've been at war too long," I told him.

He grinned and went, and I called my assistants and went up through the new cavalry lines to make sure that all would be ready to receive the horses, and to check yet again the new, light field-harness that the saddlers' workshops had made for them.

As I went, the bells began to ring from the gilded towers. The High King was home, and preparations for the crowning could begin.

★   ★   ★

Since I had watched Uther crowned I had travelled abroad, and seen splendours – in Rome, Antioch, Byzantium – beside which anything that Britain could do was like the mumming of gaudy tumblers: but there was about the ceremony at Caerleon a young and springtime glory that none of the riches of the East could have procured. The bishops and priests were splendid in scarlet and purple and white, set off the more brilliantly by the browns and sables of the holy men and women who attended them. The kings, each with his following of nobles and fighting men, glittered with jewels and gilded arms. The walls of the fortress, crested with the shifting and craning heads of the people, stirred with bright hangings, and rang with cheering. The ladies of the court were gay as kingfishers: even Queen Ygraine, in a glow of pride and happiness, had put aside her mourning robes, and shone like the rest. Morgan, beside her, had certainly none of the air of a rejected bride; she was only a little less richly dressed than her mother, and showed the same smiling, royal composure. It was difficult to remember how young she was. The two royal ladies kept their places among the women, not coming to Arthur's side. I heard, here and there, murmurs among the ladies, and perhaps even more among the matrons, who had their eyes on the empty side of the throne; but to me it was fitting that there should be no one yet to share his glory. He stood alone in the centre of the church, with the light from the long windows kindling the rubies to a blaze, and laying panels of gold and sapphire along the white of his robe, and on the fur that trimmed the scarlet mantle.

I had wondered if Lot would come. Gossip had gathered, like a boil, to bursting-point before we knew; but come, in the end, he did. Perhaps he felt that he would lose more by staying away than by braving the King and Queen and his slighted princess, for, a few days before the ceremony, his spears were seen, along with those of Urien of Gore, and Aguisel of Bremenium, and Tydwal who kept Dunpeldyr for him, flouting the sky to the north-east. This train of northern lords stayed encamped together a little beyond the township, but they came crowding in to join the celebrations as if nothing untoward had ever happened at Luguvallium or York. Lot himself showed a confidence too easy to be called bravado; he was relying, perhaps, on the fact that he was now hand-kin to Arthur. Arthur said as much, privately, to me; in public he received Lot's ceremonious courtesies blandly. I wondered, with fear, if Lot yet suspected that he had the King's unborn child at his mercy.

At least Morgause had not come. Knowing the lady as I did, I thought she might have come and faced even me, for the pleasure of flaunting her crown in front of Ygraine, and her swollen belly in front of Arthur and myself. But whether for fear of me, or whether Lot's nerve had failed him and he had forbidden it, she stayed away, with her pregnancy as the plea. I was beside Arthur when Lot gave his queen's excuses; there was no hint of any extra knowledge in his face or voice, and if he saw Arthur's sudden glance at me, or the slight paling of his cheeks, he gave no sign. Then the King had himself in hand again, and the moment passed.

So the day wore through its brilliant, exhausting hours. The bishops spared no touch of holy ceremonial, and, for the pagans present, the omens were good. I had seen signs other than that of the Cross being made in the street as the procession passed, and at the street corners fortunes were told with bones and dice and gazing, while pedlars did a brisk trade with every kind of charm and luck-piece. Black cockerels had been killed at dawning, and offer-

ings made at ford and crossroads, where the old Herm used to wait
for travellers' gifts. Outside the city, in mountain and valley and
forest, the small dark folk of the upper hills would be watching their
own omens and petitioning their own gods. But in the city centre,
on church and palace and fortress alike, the Cross caught the sun. As
for Arthur, he went through the long day with calm and pale-faced
dignity, stiff with jewels and embroidery, and rigid with ceremony, a puppet for the priests to sanctify. If this was needed to
declare his authority finally in the eyes of the people, then this
was what he would do. But I, who knew him, and who stood at his
side all through that endless day, could sense neither dedication or
prayer in that still composure. He was probably, I thought, planning the next fighting foray to the east. For him, as for all who had
seen it, the kingdom had been taken into his hand when he lifted the
great sword of Maximus from its long oblivion, and made his vow
to the listening forests. The crown of Caerleon was only the public
seal of what he had held in his hand then, and would hold until he
died.

Then, after the ceremony, the feast. One feast is much like
another, and this one was remarkable only for the fact that Arthur,
who loved his food, ate very little, but glanced about him from time
to time as if he could hardly wait for the feasting to stop, and the
time of affairs to come back.

He had told me that he would want to talk with me that night, but
he was kept till late, with the press of people around him, so I saw
Ygraine first. She retired early from the feasting, and when her page
came to me with a whispered message, I caught a nod from Arthur,
and followed him.

Her rooms were in the King's house. Here, the sounds of the
revelry could be heard only faintly, against the more distant noise of
the town's rejoicing. The door was opened to me by the same girl
who had been with her at Amesbury; she was slender in green, with
pearls in the light-brown hair, and eyes showing green as her gown:
not the gleaming witch-colour of Morgause, but a clear grey-green,
making one think of sunlight on a forest stream reflecting the young
leaves of spring. Her skin was flushed with excitement and the
feasting, and she smiled at me, showing a dimple and excellent
teeth, as she curtsied me towards the Queen.

Ygraine gave me a hand. She looked tired, and the magnificent gown of purple, with its shimmer of pearls and silver, showed up her pallor, and the shadows at mouth and eyes. But her manner, composed and cool as always, betrayed no trace of fatigue.

She came straight to the point. "So, he got her pregnant."

Even as the knife-twist of fear went through me, I saw that she had no suspicion of the truth; she was referring to Lot, and to what she took to be the reason for his rejection of her daughter Morgan in favour of Morgause.

"It seems so." I was equally blunt. "At least it saves Morgan's face, which is all that need concern us."

"It's the best thing that could have happened," said Ygraine flatly. She smiled faintly at my look. "I never liked that marriage. I favoured Uther's first idea, when he offered Morgause to Lot years ago. That would have been enough for him, and honour for her. But Lot was ambitious, one way or another, even then, and nothing would please him but Morgan herself. So Uther agreed. At that time he would have agreed to anything that sealed the northern kingdoms against the Saxons; but while for policy's sake I saw that it had to be done, I am too fond of my daughter to want her shackled to that wayward and greedy traitor."

I put up my brows at her. "Strong words, Madam."

"Do you deny the facts?"

"Far from it. I was there at Luguvallium."

"Then you will know how much, in loyalty, Lot's betrothal to Morgan bound him to Arthur, and how much marriage would have bound him, if profit pointed another way."

"Yes. I agree. I'm only glad that you yourself see it like that. I was afraid that the slight to Morgan would anger you and distress her."

"She was angry at first, rather than distressed. Lot is among the foremost of the petty kings, and, like him or not, she would have been queen of a wide realm, and her children would have had a great heritage. She could not like being displaced by a bastard, and one, besides, who has not shown her kindness."

"And when the bethrothal was first mooted, Urbgen of Rheged still had a wife."

The long lids lifted, and her eyes studied my impassive face. "Just so," was all she said, without surprise. It was said as if at the end of a discussion, rather than the beginning.

It was no surprise that Ygraine had been thinking along the same lines as Arthur and myself. Like his father Coel, Urbgen had shown himself staunch to the High King. "Rheged's" deeds in the past, and more recently at Luguvallium, were chronicled along with those of Ambrosius and Arthur, as the sky accepts the light of the setting and the rising sun.

Ygraine was saying, thoughtfully: "It might answer, at that. There's no need to ensure Urbgen's loyalty, of course, but for Morgan it would be power of the kind that I think she can manage, and for her sons . . ." She paused. "Well, Urbgen has two already, both young men grown, and fighters like their sire. Who is to say that they will ever reach his crown? And the king of a realm as wide as Rheged cannot breed too many sons."

"He is past his best years, and she is still very young." I made it a statement, but she answered calmly:

"And so? I was not much older than Morgan, when Gorlois of Cornwall married me."

For the moment, I believe, she had forgotten what that marriage had meant; the caging of a young creature avid to spread her wings and fly; the fatal passion of King Uther for Gorlois' lovely duchess; the death of the old duke, and then the new life, with all its love and pain.

"She will do her duty," said Ygraine, and now I saw that she had remembered, but her eyes did not falter. "If she was willing to accept Lot, whom she feared, she will take Urbgen willingly, should Arthur suggest it. It's a pity that Cador is too nearly related for her to have him. I would have liked to see her settled near to me in Cornwall."

"They are not blood kin." Cador was the son, by his first wife, of Ygraine's husband Gorlois.

"Too close," said Ygraine. "Men forget things too quickly, and there would be whispers of incest. It would not do, even to hint at a crime so shocking."

"No. I see that." My voice sounded level and cool.

"And besides, Cador is to wed, come summer, when he gets back to Cornwall. The King approves." She turned a hand over in

her lap, admiring, apparently, the glint of the rings on it. "So perhaps it would be as well to speak of Urbgen to the King, just as soon
as some portion of his mind is free to think of his sister?"

"He has already thought of her. He discussed it with me. I believe
he will send to Urbgen very soon."

"Ah! And then –" For the first time a purely human and female
satisfaction warmed her voice with something uncommonly like
spite. "And then we shall see Morgan take what is due to her in
wealth and precedence over that red-haired witch, and may Lot of
Lothian deserve the snares she set for him!"

"You think she trapped him deliberately?"

"How else? You know her. She wove her spells for this."

"A very common kind of spell," I said drily.

"Oh, yes. But Lot has never lacked women, and no one can deny
that Morgan is the better match, and as pretty a lass besides. And for
all the arts Morgause boasts, Morgan is better able to be queen of a
great kingdom. She was bred for it, as the bastard was not."

I watched her curiously. Beside her chair the brown-haired girl
sat on her stool half asleep. Ygraine seemed careless of what she
might overhear. "Ygraine, what harm did Morgause ever do to
you, that makes you so bitter against her?"

The red came up in her face like a flag, and for a moment I
thought she would try to set me down, but we were neither of us
young any more, or needing the armour of self-love. She spoke
simply: "If you are thinking that I hated having a lovely young girl
always near me, and near to Uther, with a right to him that went
back beyond my own, it is true. But it was more than that. Even
when she was a young girl, twelve, thirteen, no more, I thought of
her as corrupt. That is one reason why I welcomed the match with
Lot. I wanted her away from court."

This was straighter than I had expected. "Corrupt?" I asked.

The Queen's glance slid momentarily to the girl on the stool
beside her. The brown head was nodding, the eyelids closed.
Ygraine lowered her voice, but spoke clearly and carefully. "I am
not suggesting that there was anything evil in her relationship with
the King, though she never behaved to him like a daughter; nor was
she fond of him as a daughter should be; she cajoled favours from
him, no more than that. When I called her corrupt, I spoke of her

practice of witchcraft. She was drawn to it always, and haunted the wise women and the charlatans, and any talk of magic brought her staring awake like an owl at night-time. And she tried to teach Morgan, when the princess was only a child. That is what I cannot forgive. I have no time for such things, and in the hands of such as Morgause . . ."

She broke off. Vehemence had made her raise her voice, and I saw that the girl, like the owl, was also staring awake. Ygraine, recollecting herself, bent her head, a touch of colour in her face again.

"Prince Merlin, you must pardon me. I meant no disrespect."

I laughed. I saw, to my amusement, that the girl must have heard; she was laughing too, but silently, dimpling at me from beyond her mistress's shoulder. I said: "I am too proud to think of myself in the same breath as girls dabbling with spells. I am sorry about Morgan. It is true that Morgause has power of a sort, and it is also true that such things can be dangerous. Any power is hard to hold, and power misused recoils on the user."

"Perhaps some day, if you get the chance, you will tell Morgan so." She smiled, trying for a lighter tone. "She will listen to you, where she would shrug her shoulders at me."

"Willingly." I tried to sound willing, like a grandfather called in to lecture the young.

"It may be that when she finds herself a queen with real power, she will cease to hanker for another sort." She turned the subject. "So now that Lot has a daughter of Uther's, even if only a bastard, will he consider himself bound to Arthur's banner?"

"That I cannot tell you. But unless the Saxons make heavy enough gains to make it worth Lot's while to try another betrayal, I think he will keep what power he has, and fight for his own land, if not for the High King's sake. I see no trouble there." I did not add: "Not of that kind." I finished merely: "When you go back to Cornwall, Madam, I will send letters if you like."

"I should be grateful. Your letters were a great comfort to me · before, when my son was at Galava."

We talked for a while longer, mainly of the day's events. When I would have asked after her health, she put the query aside with a smile that told me she knew as much as I, so I let it be, asking instead about Duke Cador's projected marriage. "Arthur hasn't mentioned it. Who is it to be?"

"The daughter of Dinas. Did you know him? Her name is Mariona. The marriage was arranged, alas, when they were both children. Now Mariona is of age, so when the Duke is home again they will be wed."

"I knew her father, yes. Why did you say 'alas'?"

Ygraine looked, with a fond smile, at the girl by her chair. "Because otherwise there would have been no difficulty in finding a match for my little Guenever."

"I am sure," I said, "that that will prove more than easy."

"But such a match," said the Queen, and the girl made a smiling mouth and lowered her lashes.

"If I dared used divination in your presence, Madam," I said, smiling, "I would predict that one as splendid will present itself, and soon."

I spoke lightly, in formal courtesy, and was startled to hear in my voice an echo, though faint and soon lost, of the cadences of prophecy.

Neither of them heard it. The Queen was holding a hand to me, bidding me good night, and the girl Guenever held the door for me, sinking, as I passed, into a smiling curtsy of humility and grace.

7

"It's mine!" said Arthur, violently. "You only have to count! I heard the men talking about it in the guard-room. They didn't know I was near enough to hear them. They said she was big-bellied by Twelfth Night, and lucky to catch Lot so early, they could pass it off as a seven-month child. Merlin, you know as well as I do that he never came near her at Luguvallium! He wasn't there until the very night of the battle, and that night – that was the night –" He stopped, choking on it, and turned with a swirl of robes to pace the floor again.

It was well after midnight. The sounds of revelry from the town were fainter now, muted with the chill of the hour before dawn. In the King's room the candles had burned low into a welter of honeyed wax. Their scent mingled with the sharp smoke from a lamp that needed trimming.

Arthur turned sharply on his heel and came back to stand in front of me. He had taken off the crown and jewelled chain, and laid his sword aside, but he still wore the splendid coronation robe. The furred cloak lay across the table like a stream of blood in the lamplight. Through the open door of his bedchamber I could see the covers turned back ready on the great bed, but, late though the hour was, Arthur showed no sign of fatigue. His every movement was infused with a kind of nervous fury.

He controlled it, speaking quietly. "Merlin, when we spoke that night of what had happened –" A breathing pause, then he changed course with ferocious directness: "When I lay incestuously with Morgause, I asked you what would happen if she should conceive. I remember what you said. I remember it well. Do you?"

"Yes," I said, unwillingly, "I remember it."

"You said to me, 'The gods are jealous, and they insure against too much glory. Every man carries the seeds of his own death, and there must come a term to every life. All that has happened tonight is that you yourself have set that term.' "

I said nothing. He faced me with the straight, uncompromising look that I was to come to know so well.

"When you spoke to me like that, were you telling me the truth? Was the prophecy a sure one, or were you finding words of comfort for me, so that I could face what was to come next day?"

"It was the truth."

"You meant that, if she bore a child to me, you could foresee that he – she? – would be my death?"

"Arthur," I said, "prophecy does not work like that. I neither knew, in the way most men think of 'knowing', that Morgause would conceive, nor that the child would be a mortal danger for you. I only knew, all the time you were with the woman, that the birds of death were on my shoulders, weighing me down and stinking of carrion. My heart was heavy with dread, and I could see death, as I thought, linking the two of you together. Death and treachery. But how, I did not know. By the time I understood it, the thing was done, and all that was left was to await what the gods chose to send."

He paced away from me again, over towards the bedchamber door. He leaned there in silence, his shoulder to the jamb, his face away from me, then thrust himself off and turned. He crossed to the chair behind the big table, sat down, and regarded me, chin on fist. His movements were controlled and smooth, as always, but I, who knew him, could hear the curb-chain ring. He still spoke quietly. "And now we know the carrion-birds were right. She did conceive. You told me something else that night, when I admitted my fault. You said I had sinned unknowingly, and was innocent. Is innocence, then, to be punished?"

"It's not uncommon."

" 'The sins of the fathers'?"

I recognised the phrase as a quotation from the Christian scriptures. "Uther's sin," I said, "visited on you."

"And mine, now, on the child?"

I said nothing. I did not like the way the interview was going. For the first time, talking with Arthur, I did not seem able to take control. I told myself I was weary, that I was still in the ebb-tide of power, that my time would come again; but the truth is I was feeling a little like the fisherman in the Eastern tale who unstoppered a bottle and let out a genie many times more powerful than himself.

"Very well," said the King. "My sin and hers must be visited on the child. It must not be allowed to live. You will go north and tell Morgause so. Or if you prefer, I shall give you a letter telling her so myself."

I took breath, but he swept on without giving me time to speak.

"Quite apart from your forebodings – which God knows I would be a fool not to respect – can you not see how dangerous this thing could be now, if Lot should find out about it? It's plain enough what has happened. She feared she might be pregnant, and to save her shame she set herself to snare a husband. Who better than Lot? She had been offered to him before: for all we know she had wanted him, and now saw a chance to outshine her sister and give herself a place and a name, which she would lack after her father's death." His lips thinned. "And who knows better than I, that if she set herself to get a man, any man, he would go to her for the whistle?"

"Arthur, you talk of her 'shame'. You don't think you were the first she took to her bed, do you?"

He said, a little too quickly: "I never did think so."

"Then how do you know she had not lain with Lot before you? That she was not already pregnant to him, and took *you* in the hope of snaring some kind of power and favour to herself? She knew Uther was dying; she feared that Lot, by his action at Luguvallium, had forfeited the King's favour. If she could father Lot's child on you . . ."

"This is guesswork. This is not what you said that night."

"No. But think back. It would fit the facts of my foreboding equally well."

"But not the force of them," he said sharply. "If the danger from this child is real, then what does it matter who fathered it? Guesswork won't help us."

"I'm not guessing when I tell you that she and Lot were lovers before ever you went to her bed. I told you I had had a dream that night at Nodens' shrine. I saw them meet at a house some way off an ill-frequented road. It must have been by pre-arrangement. They met like people who have been lovers for a long time. This child may in fact be Lot's, and not yours."

"And we've got it the wrong way round? I was the one she whistled up to save her shame?"

"It's possible. You had come from nowhere, eclipsing Lot as you would soon eclipse Uther. She made her bid to father Lot's child on you, but then had to abandon the attempt, for fear of me."

He was silent, thinking. "Well," he said at length, "time will tell us. But are we to wait for it? No matter whose child this is, it is a danger; and it doesn't take a prophet to see how that could be . . . or a god to act on it. If Lot ever knows – or believes – that his eldest child is fathered by me, how long do you think this chary loyalty of his will last? Lothian is a key point, you know that. I need that loyalty; I have to have it. Even if he had wedded my own sister Morgan, I could hardly have trusted him, whereas now . . ." He threw out a hand, palm up. "Merlin, it's done every day, in every village in the kingdom. Why not in a king's house? Go north for me, and talk to Morgause."

"You think she would listen? If she had not wanted the child, she would not have scrupled to get rid of it long since. She didn't take you for love, Arthur, and she bears you no friendship for letting her be driven from court. And to me" – I smiled sourly – "she bears a most emphatic and justified ill-will. She would laugh in my face. More than that: she would listen, and laugh at the power her action had given her over us, and then she would do whatever she thought would hurt us most."

"But –"

"You thought she might have persuaded Lot into marriage merely for her own sake, or to score from her sister. No. She took him because I foiled her plans to corrupt and own you, and be-cause at heart, whatever the time may force him to do now, Lot is your enemy and mine, and through him she may one day do you harm."

A sharpening silence. "Do you believe this?"

"Yes."

He stirred. "Then I am still right. She must not bear the child."

"What are you going to do? Pay someone to bake her bread with ergot?"

"You will find some way. You will go –"

"I will do nothing in the matter."

He came to his feet, like a bow snapping upright when the string breaks. His eyes glittered in the candle-light. "You told me you were my servant. You made me King, you said by the god's wish. Now I am King, and you will obey me."

I was taller than he, by two fingers' breadth. I had outfaced kings before, and he was very young. I gave it just long enough, then said, gently:

"I am your servant, Arthur, but I serve the god first. Do not make me choose. I have to let him work the way he wills."

He held my eyes a moment longer, then drew a long breath, and released it as if it had been a weight he was holding. "To do this? To destroy, perhaps, the very kingdom you said he had sent me to build?"

"If he sent you to build it, then it will be built. Arthur, I don't pretend to understand this. I can only tell you to trust the time, as I do, and wait. Now, do as you did before, put it aside and try to forget it. Leave it with me."

"What will you do?"

"Go north."

A moment of quickening stillness, then he said: "To Lothian? But you said you would not go."

"No. I said I would do nothing about killing the child. But I can watch Morgause, and perhaps, in time, judge better what we must do. I will send to tell you what happens."

There was another silence. Then the tension went out of him, and he turned away, beginning to loosen the clasp of his belt. "Very well." He started to ask some question, then bit it back and smiled at me. Having shown the whip, it seemed that he was now concerned to retreat on the old trust and affection. "But you will stay for the rest of the feasting? If the wars allow, I have to stay here myself for eight days before I can take horse again."

"No. I think I must be gone. Better perhaps while Lot is still here with you. That way I can melt into the countryside before ever he gets home, and watch and wait, and take what action I can. With your leave, I'll go tomorrow morning."

"Who goes with you?"

"Nobody. I can travel alone."

"You must take someone. It's not like riding home to Maridunum. Besides, you may need a messenger."

"I'll use your couriers."

"All the same . . ." He had got the belt undone. He threw it over a chair. "Ulfin!"

A sound from the next room, then discreet footsteps. Ulfin, carrying a long bedgown over one arm, came in from the bedchamber, stifling a yawn. "My lord?"

"Have you been in there all the while?" I asked sharply.

Ulfin, wooden-faced, reached to undo the clasps at the King's shoulder. He held the long outer robe as the King stepped out of it. "I was asleep, my lord."

Arthur sat down and thrust out a foot. Ulfin kneeled to ease the shoe from it. "Ulfin, my cousin Prince Merlin goes north tomorrow, on what may prove a long and hard journey. I shall dislike losing you, but I want you to go with him."

Ulfin, shoe in hand, looked up at me and smiled. "Willingly."

"Should you not stay with the King?" I protested. "This week of all weeks –"

"I do as he tells me," said Ulfin simply, and stooped to the other foot.

As you do, in the end. Arthur did not say the words aloud, but they were there in the quick glance he gave me as he stood again for Ulfin to gird the bedgown round him.

I gave up. "Very well. I shall be glad to have you. We leave tomorrow, and I should warn you that we may be away for some considerable time." I gave him what instructions I could, then turned back to Arthur. "Now, I had better go. I doubt if I shall see you before I set off. I'll send you word as soon as I can. No doubt I shall know where you are."

"No doubt." He sounded all at once grim, very much the warleader. "Can you spare a moment or two more? Thank you, Ulfin, leave us now. You'll have your own preparations to make . . . Merlin, come and see my new toy."

"Another?"

"Another? Oh, you're thinking about the cavalry. Have you seen the horses Bedwyr brought?"

"Not yet. Valerius told me about them."

His eyes kindled. "They are splendid! Fast, fiery, and gentle. I am told they can live on hard rations if they have to, and that their hearts are so high that they will gallop all day, and then fight with you to the death. Bedwyr brought grooms with them. If everything they say is true, then surely we shall have a cavalry force to conquer the world! There are two trained stallions, white ones, that are real beauties, even finer than my Canrith. Bedwyr chose them especially for me. Over here . . . ." As he spoke he led the way across the room towards a pillared archway closed by a curtain. "I haven't had time to try them yet, but surely I can throw off my chains for an hour or two tomorrow?"

His voice was that of a restive boy. I laughed. "I hope so. I am more fortunate than the King: I shall be on my way."

"On your old black gelding, no doubt."

"Not even that. A mule."

"A mule? – Ah, of course. You go disguised?"

"I must. I can hardly ride into Lothian's stronghold as Prince Merlin."

"Well, take care. You're certain you don't want an escort, at least for the first part of the way?"

"Certain. I shall be safe. What's this you are going to show me?"

"Only a map. Here."

He pulled the curtain back. Beyond it was a kind of anteroom, little more than a broad portico giving on a small private courtyard. Torchlight winked on the spears of the guards on duty there, but otherwise the place was empty, bare even of furniture except for a huge table, rough-adzed out of oak. It was a map-table, but instead of the usual sand-tray it held, I saw, a map made of clay, with mountains and valleys, coasts and rivers, modelled by some clever sculptor, so that there, plain to see, lay the land of Britain as a high-flying bird might view it from the heavens.

Arthur was plainly delighted at my praise. "I knew you would be interested! They only finished setting it up yesterday. Splendid, isn't it? Do you remember teaching me to make maps in the dust?

This is better than scraping the sand into hills and valleys that change when you breathe on them. Of course, it can still be re-modelled as we find out more. North of Strathclyde is anybody's guess . . . But then, by God's mercy, nothing north of Strathclyde need concern me. Not yet, anyway." He fingered a peg, carved and coloured like a red dragon, that stood over "Caerleon". "Now, which way do you plan to go tomorrow?"

"I thought, by the west road through Deva and Bremet. I have a call to make at Vindolanda."

His finger followed the route northward till it reached Bremeten-nacum (which is commonly spoken of now as Bremet), and paused. "Will you do something for me?"

"Willingly."

"Go by the east. It's not so much further, and the road is better for most of the way. Here, see? If you turn off at Bremet, you'll take this road through the mountain gap." His finger traced it out; east from Bremetennacum, up the old road following the Tribuit River, then over the pass and down through Olicana into the Vale of York. There Dere Street runs, a good, fast highway still, up through Corstopitum and the Wall and thence still north, right into Manau Guotodin, where lies Lot's capital of Dunpeldyr.

"You'll have to retrace your steps for Vindolanda," said Arthur, "but not far. You'll lose nothing in time, I believe. It's the road through the Pennine Gap that I want you to take. I've never been that way myself. I've had reports that it's quite feasible – you should have no difficulty, just the two of you – but it's too broken in places for a troop of cavalry. I shall be sending parties up to repair it. I shall have to fortify it, too . . . You agree? With parts of the eastern seaboard so open to the enemy, if they should get a grip on the easterly plains this will be their way into our British heartland in the west. There are two forts there already; I am told they could be made good. I want you to look at them for me. Don't take time over it; I can get detailed reports from the surveyors; but if you can go that way, I would like to have your thoughts about it."

"You shall have them."

As he straightened from the map, a cock crowed outside some-where. The courtyard was grey. He said quietly: "For the other matter we spoke of, I am in your hands. God knows I should be thankful to be so." He smiled. "Now we had better get to our beds. You have a journey to face, and I another day of pleasure. I envy you! Good night, and God go with you."

8

Next day, furnished with food for two days' journey, and three good mules from one of the baggage trains, Ulfin and I set off on the journey northwards.

I had made journeys before in circumstances as dangerous as this, when to be recognised would be to court disaster, or even death. I had, perforce, become adept at disguise; this had given rise to yet another legend about "the enchanter", that he could vanish at will into thin air to escape his enemies. I had certainly perfected the art of melting into a landscape: what I did in fact was to assume the tools of some trade, and then to frequent places where no one would expect a prince to be. Men's eyes are focused on what, not who a traveller is, who goes labelled with his skill. I had travelled as a singer, when I needed access to a prince's court as well as a humble tavern, but more often I went as a travelling physician or eye-doctor. This was the guise I liked best. It allowed me to practise my skill where it was most needed, among the poor, and it gave me access to any kind of house except the noblest.

This was the disguise I chose now. I took my small harp, but only for my private use: I dared not risk my skill as a singer earning me a summons to Lot's court. So the harp, muffled and wrapped into anonymity, hung on the baggage-mule's shabby saddle, while my boxes of unguents and roll of implements were carried plain to be seen.

The first part of our way I knew well, but after we reached Bremetennacum, and turned towards the Pennine Gap, the country was unfamiliar.

The Gap is formed by the valleys of three great rivers. Two of these, the Wharfe and the Isara, spring from the limestone on the

Pennine tops and flow, meandering, eastwards. The other, an important stream with countless smaller tributaries, lapses towards the west. It is called the Tribuit. Once through the Gap and into the valley of the Tribuit, an enemy's way would be clear to the west coast, and the last embattled corners of Britain.

Arthur had spoken of two forts lying within the Gap itself. I had gathered from seemingly idle questions put to local men in the tavern at Bremetennacum, that in times past there had been a third fort guarding the western mouth of the pass, where the Tribuit valley widens out towards the lowlands and the coast. It had been built by the Romans as a temporary marching camp, so much of the turf and timber structure would have decayed and vanished, but it occurred to me that the road serving it would stand a survey, and, if it were still in reasonable condition, could provide a quick corner-cut for cavalry coming down from Rheged to defend the Gap.

From Rheged to Olicana, and York. The road Morgause must have taken to meet with Lot.

That settled it. I would take the same road, the road of my dream at Nodens' shrine. If the dream had been a true one – and I had no doubt of it – there were things I wished to learn.

We left the main road just beyond Bremetannacum, and headed up the Tribuit valley on the gravel of a neglected Roman road. A day's ride brought us to the marching camp.

As I had suspected, little was left of it but the banks and ditches, and some rotting timber where the gateways had once stood. But, like all such camps, it was cleverly placed, on a flank of moorland that looked in every direction over clear country. The hillside had a tributary stream at foot, and to the south the river flowed through flat lands towards the sea. Placed as the camp was, so far west, we might hope that it would not be needed for defence; but, as a staging-camp for cavalry, or as a temporary base for a swift foray through the Gap it was ideal.

I had been unable to find anyone who knew its name. When I wrote my report to Arthur that night, I called it merely "Tribuit".

Next day we struck out across country towards the first of the forts of which Arthur had spoken. This lay in the arm of a marshy stream, near the beginning of the pass. The stream spread out beside it into a lake, from which the place took its name. Though ruinous, it could, I judged, be speedily brought into repair. There was abundant timber in the valley, and plenty of stone and deep moorland turf available.

We reached it towards late afternoon, and, the air being balmy and dry, and the fortress walls promising sufficient shelter, we made camp there. Next morning we began the climb across the ridge towards Olicana.

Well before midday we had climbed clear of the forest and onto heathland. It was a fine day, with mist drawing back from the sparkling sedges, and the song of water bubbling from every crevice in the rock, where the rills tumbled down to fill the young river. Rippling, too, with sound, was the morning sky, where curlews slanted down on ringing streams of song towards their nests in the grass. We saw a she-wolf, heavy with milk, slink across the road ahead, with a hare in her mouth. She gave us a brief, indifferent glance, then slipped into the shelter of the mist.

It was a wild way, a Wolf Road such as the Old Ones love. I kept my eye on the rocks that crowned the screes, but saw no sign that I could recognise, of their remote and comfortless eyries. I had no doubt, though, that we were watched every step of the way. No doubt, either, that news had gone north on the winds, that Merlin the enchanter was on the road, and secretly. It did not trouble me. It is not possible to keep secrets from the Old Ones; they know all that comes or goes in forest and hill. They and I had come to an understanding long since, and Arthur had their trust.

We halted on the summit of the moor. I looked around me. The mist had lifted now, dispersing under the steadily strengthening sun. All around us stretched the moor, broken with grey rock and bracken, with, in the distance, the still misty heights of fell and mountain. To the left of the road the ground fell away into the wide Isara valley, where water glinted among crowding trees.

It could not have looked more unlike the rain-dimmed vision of Nodens' shrine, but there was the milestone with its legend, OLICANA; and there, to the left, the track plunging steeply down towards the valley trees. Among them, only just visible through the leafage, showed the walls of a considerable house.

Ulfin, ranging his mule alongside mine, was pointing.

"If only we had known, we might have found better lodging there."

I said, slowly: "I doubt it. I think we were better under the sky."

He shot me a curious glance. "I thought you had never been this way, sir? Do you know the place?"

"Shall we say that I know of it? And would like to know more. Next time we pass a village, or if we see a shepherd on the hill, find out who owns that villa, will you?"

He threw me another look, but said no more, and we rode on.

Olicana, the second of Arthur's two forts, lay only ten miles or so to the east. To my surprise the road, heading steeply downward, then crossing a considerable stretch of boggy moorland, was in first-class condition. Ditches and embankments alike looked to have been recently repaired. There was a good timber bridge across the Isara itself, and the ford of the next tributary was cleared and paved. We made good speed in consequence, and came in the early evening into settled country. At Olicana there is a sizable township. We found lodgings in a tavern that stood near the fortress walls, to serve the men of the garrison.

From what I had seen of the road, and the orderly appointments of the town's streets and square, it came as no surprise that the walls of the fortress itself were in the same good order. Gates and bridges were sound and stout, and the ironwork looked fire-new. By carefully idle questions, and by listening to the talk in the tavern at supper-time, I was able to gather that a skeleton garrison had been placed here in Uther's time, to watch the road into the Gap, and to keep an eye on the signal towers to the east. It had been an emergency measure, taken hastily during the worst years of the Saxon Terror, but the same men were still here, despairing of recall, bored to distraction, but kept to a tingling pitch of efficiency by a garrison commander who deserved something better (one gathered) than this dismal outpost of inaction.

The simplest way to gather the information I needed was to make myself known to this officer, who could then see that my report was sent straight back to the King. Accordingly, leaving Ulfin in the tavern, I presented myself at the guard-room with the pass Arthur had supplied.

From the speed with which I was passed through, and the lack of surprise at my shabby appearance, and refusal even to state my name or my business to anyone but the commander himself, it could be judged that messengers were frequent here. Secret messengers, at that. If this really was a forgotten outpost (and admittedly nor I nor the King's advisers had known of it) then the only messengers who would come and go so assiduously were spies. I began to look forward all the more to meeting the commander.

I was searched before being taken in, which was only to be expected. Then a couple of the guards escorted me through the fort to the headquarters building. I looked about me. The place was well lighted, and as far as I could see, roads, courtyards, wells, exercise ground, workshops, barracks, were in mint repair. We passed carpenters' shops, harness-makers, smithies. From the padlocks on the granary doors, I deduced that the barns were fully stocked. The place was not large but was still, I reckoned, undermanned. There could be accommodation for Arthur's cavalry almost before the force could be formed.

My pass was taken through, then I was shown into the commander's room, and the guards withdrew, with a neatness that told its own story. This was where the spies came; and usually, I supposed, as late as this.

The commander received me standing; a tribute not to me, but to the King's seal. The first thing that struck me was his youth. He could not have been more than twenty-two. The second thing was that he was tired. Lines of strain were scored into his face: his youth, the solitary post up here, in charge of a bored and hardbitten contingent of men; the constant watchfulness as the tides of invasion flowed and ebbed along the eastern coasts; all this, winter and summer, without help and without backing. It seemed true that, after Uther had sent him here four years ago – four years – he had forgotten all about him.

"You have news for me?" The flat tone disguised no eagerness; that had long since been dissipated by frustration.

"I can give you what news there is when my main business is done. I have been sent, rather, to get information from you, if you will be good enough to supply it. I have a report to send to the High King. I would be glad if a messenger could take it to him as soon as it is completed."

"That can be arranged. Now? A man can be ready within the half hour."

"No. It's not so urgent. If we might talk first, please?"

He sat down, motioning me to a chair. For the first time a spark of interest showed. "Do you mean that the report concerns Olicana? Am I to know why?"

"I shall tell you, of course. The King asked me to find out all I could about this place, and also about the ruined fortress in the pass, the one they call Lake Fort."

He nodded. "I know it. It's been a wreck for nearly two hundred years. It was destroyed in the Brigantian rebellion, and left to rot. This place suffered the same fate, but Ambrosius had it rebuilt. He had plans for Lake Fort, too, so I have been told. If I had had a mandate, I might have –" He checked himself. "Ah, well . . . You came from Bremet? Then you'll know that a couple of miles north of that road there is another fort – nothing there, only the site – but I would have thought it equally vital to any strategy involving the Gap. Ambrosius saw it so, they tell me. He saw that the Gap could be a key point of his strategy." There was no perceptible emphasis on the "he", but the inference was clear. Uther had not only forgotten the existence of Olicana and its garrison, he had either ignored or misunderstood the importance of the road through the Pennine Gap. As this young man, in his helpless isolation, had not.

I said quickly: "And now the new King sees it, too. He wants to refortify the Gap, not only with a view to closing and holding it against penetration from the east, if that becomes necessary, but also to using the pass as a quick line of attack. He has charged me to see what there is to be done. I think you can expect the surveyors up after my reports have been studied. This place is in a state of readiness that I know the King did not expect. He will be pleased."

I told him something then about Arthur's plans for the formation of the cavalry force. He listened eagerly, his weary boredom forgotten, and the questions he put showed that he knew a great deal about affairs on the eastern seaboard. He assumed, besides, a surprisingly intimate knowledge of Saxon movements and strategy.

I left that aside for the moment, and began to put my own questions about Olicana's accommodation and supplies. After little more than a minute of it he got to his feet, and, crossing to a chest locked with another of the great padlocks, opened it, and brought out tablets and rolls on which, it transpired, were lists, fully detailed, of all I wanted to know.

I studied these for a few minutes, then became conscious that he was waiting, watching me, with other lists in his hand.

"I think," he began, then hesitated. In a moment he made up his mind to continue. "I don't think that King Uther, in the last years, ever quite appreciated what the road through the Gap might mean in the coming struggle. When I was sent here – when I was young – I saw it as an outpost only, a place, you might say, to practise on. It was better than Lake Fort then, but only just . . . It took quite a time to get it into working shape . . . Well, you know what happened, sir. The war moved north and south; King Uther was sick, and the country divided; we seemed to be forgotten. I sent couriers from time to time, with information, but got no acknowledgment. So for my own instruction, and, I admit, entertainment, I began to send out men – not soldiers, but boys from the town mostly, with a taste for adventure – and gathered information. I am at fault, I know, but . . ." He stopped.

"You kept it to yourself?" I prompted him.

"With no wrong motive," he said hastily. "I did send one courier, with some information I judged to be of value, but heard no more of him nor of the papers he carried. So I no longer wanted to commit anything to messengers who might not be received by the King."

"I can assure you that anything I send to the King, has only to reach him safely to get his immediate attention."

While we had been talking he had been studying me covertly, comparing, I suppose, my shabby appearance with the manner I had made no attempt, with him, to disguise. He said slowly, glancing down at the lists he held: "I have the King's pass and seal, so I am to trust you. Am I to know your name?"

"If you wish. It is for you only. I have your promise?"

"Of course," he said, a shade impatiently.

"Then I am Myrddin Emrys, commonly known as Merlin. As you will gather, I am on a private journey, so I am known as Emrys, a travelling doctor."

"Sir –"

"No," I said quickly, "sit down again. I only told you so that you could be sure your information will reach the King's ear, and quickly. May I see it now?"

He laid the lists down in front of me. I studied them. More information; plans of fortified settlements, numbers of troops and armaments; troop movements carefully chronicled; supplies; ships . . .

I looked up, startled. "But these are plans of *Saxon* dispositions?"

He nodded. "Recent, too, sir. I had a stroke of fortune last summer. I was put in touch – it doesn't matter how – with a Saxon, a third-generation federate. Like a lot of the old federates, he wants to keep to the old order. These Saxons hold their pledged word sacred, and besides," a glimmer of a smile on the grim young mouth, "they mistrust the incomers. Some of these new adventurers want to displace the wealthy federates just as much as they want to drive out the British."

"And this information comes from him. Can you trust it?"

"I think so. The parts I could check I have found to be true. I don't know how good, or how recent the King's own information is, but I think you should draw his attention to the section – here – about Elesa, and Cerdic Elesing. That means –"

"Elesa's son. Yes. Elesa being our old friend Eosa?"

"That's right, Horsa's son. You would know that after he and his kinsman Octa escaped from Uther's prison, Octa died, at Rutupiae, but Eosa made for Germany and drummed up Octa's sons Colgrim and Badulf to make the attack in the north . . . Well, what you may not have known was that, before he died, Octa was claiming the title of "king" here in Britain. It didn't amount to much more than the chieftainship he had had before, as Hengist's son: neither Colgrim nor Badulf seems to have set much store by it; but now they are dead, too, and, as you see . . ."

"Eosa makes the same claim. Yes. With any more success?"

"It seems so. King of the West Saxons, he calls himself, and his young son Cerdic is known as "the Aetheling". They claim descent from some far-back hero or demigod. That's usual, of course, but the point is that his people believe in it. You can see that this gives a new kind of colour to the Saxon invasions."

"It could alter what you were saying about the old-established federates."

"Indeed. Eosa and Cerdic have that sort of standing, you see. This talk of a 'kingdom' . . . He's promising stability – *and rights* – to the old federates, and a quick killing to the incomers. He's genuine, too. I mean, he's shown himself to be more than a clever adventurer; he's established the legend of a heroic kingship, he's accepted as a law-giver, and powerful enough to enforce new customs. Changed the grave-customs, even . . . they don't burn their dead now, I'm told, or even bury them with their arms and grave-goods in the old way. According to Cerdic the Aetheling, it's wasteful." That grim little smile again. "They get their priests to cleanse the dead man's weapons ritually, and then they re-use them. They now believe that a spear once used by a good fighter will make its next owner as good, or better . . . and a weapon taken from a defeated warrior will fight the harder for being given a second chance. I tell you, a dangerous man. The most dangerous, perhaps, since Hengist himself."

I was impressed, and said so. "The King shall see this as soon as I can get it to him. It will be brought to his attention straight away, I promise you that. You must know how valuable it is. How soon can you have copies made?"

"I already have copies. These can go straight away."

"Good. Now, if you'll allow me, I'll add a word to your report, and put my own report on Lake Fort in with them."

He brought writing materials and set them in front of me, then made for the door. "I'll arrange for a courier."

"Thank you. A moment, though –"

He paused. We had been speaking in Latin, but there was something about his use of it that told me he came from the West Country. I said: "They told me in the tavern that your name was Gerontius. Do I hazard a guess that it was once Gereint?"

He smiled. It took years off him. "It still is, sir."

"It's a name that Arthur will be glad to know," I said, and turned to my writing.

He stood still for a moment, then went to the door, opened it, and spoke with someone outside. He came back, and crossing to a table in the corner, poured wine and set a goblet by me. I heard him draw breath once, as if to speak, but he was silent.

At last I was finished. He went to the door again, and came back, followed this time by a man, a wiry fellow, looking as if he had just wakened up, but dressed ready for the road. He carried a leather pouch with a strong lock. He was ready to go, he said, putting away the packages Gereint handed to him; he would eat on the way.

Gereint's terse instructions to him showed once more how good his information was. "You'll do best to go by Lindum. The King will have left Caerleon by now, and be heading back towards Linnuis. By the time you reach Lindum you'll get news of him."

The man nodded briefly, and went. So, within a few hours of my reaching Olicana, my report, with how much more, was on its way back. Now I was free to turn my thoughts towards Dunpeldyr and what I would find there.

But first, to pay Gereint for his service. He poured more wine, and settled, with an eagerness that must have been foreign to him for a long time, to ply me with questions about Arthur's accession at Luguvallium, and the activities since then at Caerleon. He deserved good measure, and I gave it. Only when the midnight rounds were almost due did I get to my own questions.

"Soon after Luguvallium, did Lot of Lothian ride this way?"

"Yes, but not through Olicana itself. There's a road – it's little more than a track now – that cuts aside from the main road, and leads due east. It's a bad road, and skirts some dangerous bogland, so, though it's the quickest way for anyone heading north, it is very little used."

"But Lot used it, even though he was heading south for York? To avoid being seen in Olicana, do you suppose?"

"That did not occur to me," said Gereint. "Not, that is, until later . . . He has a house on that road. He would go there to lodge, rather than come into the town here."

"His own house? I see. Yes, I saw it from the pass. A snug place, but lonely."

"As to that," he said, "he uses it very little."

"But you knew he was there?"

"I know most things that go on hereabouts." A gesture at the padlocked chest. "Like an old wife at the cottage door, I have little else to do but observe my neighbours."

"I have reason to be grateful for it. Then you must know who met Lot at his house in the hills?"

His eyes held mine for a full ten seconds. Then he smiled. "A certain semi-royal lady. They arrived separately, and they left separately, but they reached York together." His brows lifted. "But how did *you* know this, sir?"

"I have my own ways of spying."

He said calmly: "So I believe. Well, now all is settled and correct in the sight of God and mankind. The King of Lothian has gone with Arthur from Caerleon into Linnuis, while his new queen waits at Dunpeldyr to bear the child. You knew, of course, about the child?"

"Yes."

"They have met here before," said Gereint, with a nod that added, plainly, "and now we see the results of that meeting."

"Have they indeed? Often? And since when?"

"Since I came here, perhaps three or four times." His tone was not that of one passing on tavern gossip, but merely briskly informative. "Once they were here for as much as a month together, but they kept themselves close. It was a matter of report only; we saw nothing of them."

I thought of the bedchamber with its regal crimson and gold. I had been right. Long-time lovers, indeed. If only I could believe what I had suggested to Arthur, that the child could, in fact, be Lot's own. At least, from the neutral tone that Gereint had used, that was what most men assumed as yet.

"And now," he said, "love has had its way, in spite of policy. Is it presumptuous in me to ask if the High King is angry?"

He had earned an honest answer, so I gave him one.

"He was angry, naturally, at the way the marriage was made, but now he sees that it will serve as well as the other. Morgause is his half-sister, so the alliance with King Lot must still hold. And Morgan is free for whatever other marriage may suggest itself."

"Rheged," he said, immediately.

"Possibly."

He smiled, and let the subject drop. We talked for a little longer, then I rose to go.

"Tell me something," I asked him. "Did your information run to a knowledge of Merlin's whereabouts?"

"No. Two travellers were reported, but there was no hint of who they might be."

"Or where they were bound?"

"No, sir."

I was satisfied. "Need I insist that no one is to know who I am? You will not include this interview in your report."

"That's understood. Sir –"

"What is it?"

"About this report of yours on Tribuit and Lake Fort. You said that surveyors would be coming up. It occurs to me that I could save them a good deal of time if I sent working parties over immediately. They could start on the preliminaries – clearing, gathering turf and timber, quarrying, digging the ditches . . . If you would authorise the work?"

"I? I have no authority."

"No authority?" He repeated, blankly, then began to laugh. "No, I see. I can hardly start quoting Merlin's authority, or people might ask how it came my way. And they might remember a certain humble traveller who peddled herbs and simples . . . Well, since that same traveller brought me a letter from the High King, my own authority will doubtless suffice."

"It's had to do so for long enough," I agreed, and took my leave, well satisfied.

9

So we journeyed north. Once we had joined the main road north from York, the way they call Dere Street, going was easy, and we made fair speed. Sometimes we lodged in taverns, but, the weather being fine and hot, more often than not we would ride on as long as the light lasted, then make camp in some flowering brake near the road. Then after supper I would make music for myself, and Ulfin would listen, dreaming his own dreams while the fire died to white ash, and the stars came out.

He was a good companion. We had known one another since we were boys, I with Ambrosius in Brittany where he gathered the army that was to conquer Vortigern and take Britain, Ulfin as servant – slave-boy – to my tutor Belasius. His life had been a hard one with that strange and cruel man, but after Belasius' death Uther had taken the boy into his service, and there Ulfin had soon risen to a place of trust. He was now about five and thirty years old, brown haired and grey eyed, very quiet, and self-contained in the way of men who know they must live their lives out alone, or as the companions of other men. The years as Belasius' catamite had left their mark.

One evening I made a song, and sang it to the low hills north of Vinovia, where the busy small rivers wind deep in their forested valleys, but the great road strides across the higher land, through leagues of whin and bracken, and over the long heather moorlands where the only trees are pine and alder and groves of silver birch.

We were camped in one such coppice, where the ground was dry underfoot, and the slender birch boughs hung still in the warm evening, tenting us with silk.

This was the song. I called it a song of exile, and I have heard versions of it since, elaborated by some famous Saxon singer, but the first was my own:

> *He who is companionless*
> *Seeks oftentimes the mercy*
> *The grace*
> *Of the creator, God.*
> *Sad, sad the faithful man*
> *Who outlives his lord.*
> *He sees the world stand waste*
> *As a wall blown on by the wind,*
> *As an empty castle, where the snow*
> *Sifts through the window-frames,*
> *Drifts on the broken bed*
> *And the black hearth-stone.*
>
> *Alas, the bright cup!*
> *Alas, the hall of feasting!*
> *Alas the sword that kept*
> *The sheep-fold and the apple-orchard*
> *Safe from the claw of the wolf!*
> *The wolf-slayer is dead.*
> *The law-giver, the law-upholder is dead,*
> *While the sad wolf's self, with the eagle,*
>   *and the raven,*
> *Come as kings, instead.*

I was lost in the music, and when at length I laid the last note to rest and looked up, I was taken aback to see two things; one that Ulfin, sitting on the other side of the fire, was listening rapt, with tears on his face; the other, that we had company. Neither Ulfin nor I, enclosed in the music, had noticed the two travellers approaching us over the soft mosses of the moorland way.

Ulfin saw them in the same moment that I did, and was on his feet, knife ready. But it was obvious that there was no harm in them, and the knife was back in its sheath before I said, "Put up," or the foremost of the intruders smiled, and showed a placating hand.

"No harm, masters, no harm. I've always been fond of a bit of music, and you've got quite a talent there, you have indeed."

I thanked him, and, as if the words had been an invitation, he came nearer to the fire and sat, while the boy who was with him thankfully humped the packs off his shoulders and sank down likewise. He stayed in the background, away from the fire, though with the darkness of late evening a cool little breeze had sprung up, making the warmth of the burning logs welcome.

The newcomer was a smallish man, elderly, with a neat greying beard and unruly brows over myopic brown eyes. His dress was travel-worn but neat, the cloak of good cloth, the sandals and belt of soft-cured leather. Surprisingly, his belt buckle was of gold – or else thickly gilded – and worked in an elaborate pattern. His cloak was fastened with a heavy disk brooch, also gilded, with a design beautifully worked, a curling triskele set in filigree within a deeply fluted rim. The boy, whom at first I took to be his grandson, was similarly dressed, but his only jewel was something that looked like a charm worn on a thin chain at his neck. Then he reached forward to unroll the blankets for the night, and as his sleeve slid back I saw on his forearm the puckered scar of an old brand. A slave, then; and, from the way he stayed back from the fire's warmth, and silently busied himself unpacking the bags, he was one still. The old man was a man of property.

"You don't mind?" The latter was addressing me. Our own simple clothes and simpler way of life – the bedding rolls under the birches, the plain plates and drinking horns, and the worn saddle-bags we used for pillows – had told him that here were travellers no more than his equals, if that. "We got out of our way a few miles back, and were thankful to hear your singing and see the light of the fire. We guessed you might not be too far from the road, and now the boy tells me it lies just over yonder, thanks be to Vulcan's fires! The moorlands are all very well by daylight, but after dark treacherous for man or beast . . ."

He talked on, while Ulfin, at a nod from me, rose to fetch the wine flask, and offer it to him. But the newcomer demurred, with a hint of complacency.

"No, no. Thank you, my good sir, but we have food. We need not trouble you – except, if you will allow it, to share your fire and company for the night? My name is Beltane, and my servant here is called Ninian."

"We are Emrys and Ulfin. Please be welcome. Will you not take wine? We carry enough."

"I also. In fact, I shall take it ill if you don't both join me in a drink of it. Remarkable stuff, I hope you'll agree . . ." Then, over his shoulder: "Food, boy, quickly, and offer these gentlemen some of the wine that the commandant gave me."

"Have you come far?" I asked him. The etiquette of the road does not allow you to ask a man directly where he has come from nor whither he is bound, but equally it is etiquette for him to tell you, even though his tale may be patently untrue.

Beltane answered without hesitation, through the chicken leg the boy had handed him.

"From York. Spent the winter there. Usually get out before this onto the road, but waited there . . . Town very full . . ." He chewed and swallowed, adding, more clearly: "It was a propitious time. Business was good, so I stayed on."

"You came by Catraeth?" He had spoken in the British tongue, so, following suit, I gave the place its old name. The Romans called it Cataracta.

"No. By the road east of the plain. I do not advise it, sir. We were glad to turn onto the moor tracks to strike across for Dere Street at Vinovia. But this fool" – a hitch of a shoulder at the slave – "missed the milestone. I have to depend on him; my sight is poor, except for things as near to me as this bit of fowl. Well, Ninian was counting the clouds, as usual, instead of watching the way, and by duskfall we had no idea where we were, or if we had passed the town already. Are we past it now? I fear we must be."

"I'm afraid so, yes. We passed through it late in the afternoon. I'm sorry. You had business there?"

"My business lies in every town."

He sounded remarkably unworried. I was glad of this, for the boy's sake. The latter was at my elbow with the wine-flask, pouring with grave concentration; Beltane, I judged, was all bark and bustle; Ninian showed no trace of fear. I thanked him, and he glanced up and smiled. I saw then that I had misjudged Beltane; his strictures, indeed, looked to be justified; it was obvious that the boy's thoughts, in spite of the seeming concentration on his tasks, were leagues away; the sweet, cloudy smile came from a dream that held him. His eyes, in the shadow-light of moon and fire, were grey, rimmed with darkness like smoke. Something about them, and about the absent grace of his movements, was surely familiar . . . I felt the night air breathing on my back, and the hairs on my nape lifted like the fur of a night-prowling cat.

Then he had turned away without speaking, and was stooping beside Ulfin with the flask.

"Try it, sir," Beltane urged me. "It's good stuff. I got it from one of the garrison officers at Ebor . . . God knows where *he* laid hands on it, but it's better not to ask, eh?" The ghost of a wink, as he chewed once more at his chicken.

The wine was certainly good, rich, smooth and dark, a rival to any I had tasted even in Gaul or Italy. I complimented Beltane on it, wondering as I spoke what service could have elicited payment like this.

"Aha!" he said, with that same complacency. "You're wondering what I could have done to chisel stuff like this out of him, eh?"

"Well, yes, I was," I admitted, smiling. "Are you a magician, that you can read thoughts?"

He chuckled. "Not that kind. But I know what you're thinking now, too."

"Yes?"

"You're busy wondering if I'm the King's enchanter in disguise, I'll warrant! You'd think it might take his kind of magic to charm a wine like that out of Vitruvius . . . And Merlin travels the roads the same as I do; a simple tradesman you'd take him for, they say, with maybe one slave for company, maybe not even that. Am I right?"

"About the wine, yes, indeed. I take it, then, that you are more than just a 'simple tradesman'?"

"You could say so." Nodding, self-important. "But about Merlin, now. I hear he's left Caerleon. No one knew where he was bound, or on what errand, but that's always the way with him. They were saying in York that the High King would be back in Linnuis before the turn of the moon, but Merlin disappeared the day after the crowning." He looked from me to Ulfin. "Have you had any news of what's afoot?"

His curiosity was no more than the natural newsmongering of

the travelling tradesman. Such folk are great bringers and ex-
changers of news: they are made welcome for it everywhere, and
reckon on it as a valuable stock-in-trade.

Ulfin shook his head. His face was wooden. The boy Ninian was
not even listening. His head was turned away towards the scented
dark of the moorlands. I could hear the broken, bubbling call of
some late bird stirring on its nest; joy came and went in the boy's
face, a flying gleam as evanescent as starlight on the moving leaves
above us. Ninian had his refuge, it seemed, from a garrulous master
and the day's drudgery.

"We came from the west, yes, from Deva," I said, giving Beltane
the information he angled for. "But what news I have is old. We
travel slowly. I am a doctor, and can never move far without
work."

"So? Ah, well," said Beltane, biting with relish into a barley
bannock, "no doubt we will hear something when we get to the
Cor Bridge. You're bound that way, too? Good, good. But you
needn't fear to travel with me! I'm no enchanter, in disguise or
otherwise, and even if Queen Morgause's men were to promise
gold, or threaten death by fire, I could make shift to prove it!"

Ulfin looked up sharply, but I said merely: "How?"

"By my trade. I have my own brand of magic. And for all they
say Merlin is master of so much, mine is one skill you can't pretend
to if you haven't had the training. And that" – with the same
cheerful complacency – "takes a lifetime."

"May we know what it is?" The question was mere courtesy.
This, patently, was the moment of revelation he had been working
for.

"I'll show you." He swallowed the last crumb of bannock, wiped
his mouth delicately, and took another drink of wine. "Ninian!
Ninian! You'll have time for your dreaming soon! Get the pack out,
and feed the fire. We want light."

Ulfin reached behind him and threw a fresh faggot on. The
flames leaped high. The boy fetched a bulky roll of soft leather, and
knelt beside me. He undid the ties, and unrolled the thing along the
ground in the firelight.

It went with a flash and a shimmer. Gold caught the rich and
dancing light, enamels in black and scarlet, pearly shell, garnet and

blue glass – bedded or pinned along the kidskin were pieces of jewellery, beautifully made. I saw brooches, pins, necklaces, amulets, buckles for sandals or belts, and one little nest of enchanting silver acorns for a lady's girdle. The brooches were mostly of the round sort he was wearing, but one or two were of the old bow design, and I saw some animals, and one very elaborate curly dragonlike creature done with great skill in garnet set with cellwork and filigree.

I looked up to see Beltane watching me eagerly. I gave him what he wanted. "This is splendid work. Beautiful. It is as fine as any I have seen."

He glowed with simple pleasure. Now that I had placed him, I could let myself be easy. He was an artist, and artists live on praise as bees on nectar. Nor do they much concern themselves in anything beyond their own art; Beltane had been barely interested in my own calling. His questions were harmless enough, a travelling salesman probing for news; and with the events at Luguvallium still a story for every fireside, what finer morsel of news could there be than some hint of Merlin's whereabouts? It was certain that he had no idea who he was talking to. I asked a few questions about the work; these out of genuine interest; I have always learned where I could about any man's skills. His answers soon showed me that he had certainly made the jewels himself; so the service for which the wine had been a reward was also explained.

"Your eyesight," I said. "You spoiled it with this work?"

"No, no. My eyesight is poor, but it is good for close work. In fact, it has been my blessing as an artist. Even now, when I am no longer young, I can see details very finely, but your face, my good sir, is by no means clear; and as for these trees around us, for such I take them to be . . ." He smiled and shrugged. "Hence my keeping this idle dreamer of a boy. He is my eyes. Without him I could hardly travel as I do, and indeed, I am lucky to have got here safely, even with his eyes, the little fool. This is no country to leave the roads and venture across bog-land."

His sharpness was a matter of routine. The boy Ninian ignored it; he had taken the chance of showing me the jewellery to stay near the fire.

"And now?" I asked the goldsmith. "You have shown me work

fit for kings' courts. Too good, surely, for the market-place? Where are you taking it?"

"Need you ask? To Dunpeldyr, in Lothian. With the king newly wed, and the queen as lovely as mayflowers and sorrel-buds, there will surely be trade for such as I."

I stretched my hand to the warmth of the blaze. "Ah, yes," I said. "He married Morgause in the end. Pledged to one princess and married to another. I heard something of that. You were there?"

"I was indeed. And small blame to King Lot, that's what everyone was saying. The Princess Morgan is fair enough, and right enough a king's daughter, but the other one — well, you know how the talk goes. No man, let alone a man like Lot of Lothian, could come within arm's length of that lady, and not lust to bed her."

"Your eyesight was good enough for that?" I asked him. I saw Ulfin smile.

"I didn't need eyesight." He laughed robustly. "I have ears, and I hear the talk that goes around, and once I got near enough to smell the scent she uses, and catch the colour of her hair in the sunlight, and hear her pretty voice. So I got my boy to tell me what she looked like, and I made this chain for her. Do you think her lord will buy.it of me?"

I fingered the lovely thing; it was of gold, each link as delicate as floss, holding flowers of pearl and citrine set in filigree. "He would be a fool if he did not. And if the lady sees it first, he certainly will."

"I reckon on that," he said, smiling. "By the time I get to Dunpeldyr, she should be well again, and thinking of finery. You knew, did you? She was brought to bed two full weeks ago, before her time."

Ulfin's sudden stillness made a pause of silence as loud as a shout. Ninian looked up. I felt my own nerves tighten. The goldsmith sensed the sharpening of the attention he was getting, and looked pleased. "Had you not heard?"

"No. Since we passed Isurium we have not lodged in towns. Two weeks ago? This is certain?"

"Certain, sir. Too certain, maybe, for some folks' comfort." He laughed. "Never have I seen so many folk counting on their fingers that never counted before! And count as they may, with the best will in the world, they make it September for the child's conceiving. That," said the little gossip, "would be at Luguvallium, when King Uther died."

"I suppose so," I said, indifferently. "And King Lot? The last I heard, he was gone to Linnuis, to join Arthur there."

"He did, that's true. He'll hardly have got the news yet. We got it ourselves when we lay for a night at Elfete, on the east road. That was the way her courier took. He had some tale of avoiding trouble by going that way, but it's my belief he'd been told to take his time. By the time King Lot gets news of the birthing, it'll be a more decent interval since the wedding day."

"And the child?" I asked it idly. "A boy?"

"Aye, and from all accounts a sickly one, so with all his haste, Lot still may not have got himself an heir."

"Ah, well," I said, "he has time." I turned the subject. "Are you not afraid to travel as you do, with so much valuable cargo?"

"I confess I have had fears about it," he admitted. "Yes, yes, indeed. You must understand that commonly, when I shut my workshop, and take to the roads for summer, I carry with me only such stuff as the folks like to buy in the markets, or at best, gauds for merchants' wives. But luck was against me, and I could not get these jewels done in time to show them to Queen Morgause before she went north, so needs must I carry them after her. Now my luck is to fall in with an honest man like yourself; I don't need to be a Merlin to tell such things . . . I can see you're honest, and a gentleman like myself. Tell me, will my luck hold tomorrow? May we have your company, my good sir, as far as Cor Bridge?"

I had made up my mind already about that. "As far as Dunpeldyr if you will. I'm bound there. And if you stop by the way to sell your wares, that suits me, too. I recently had a piece of news that tells me there is no haste for me to be there."

He was delighted, and fortunately did not see Ulfin's look of surprise. I had already decided that the goldsmith might be useful to me. I judged that he would hardly have outstayed the spring weather in York, making up the rich jewels he had shown me, without some sort of assurance that Morgause would at least look at them. As he talked cheerfully on, needing very little encouragement to tell me more about the happenings in York, I found that I had been right. Somehow he had managed to engage the interest of

Lind, Morgause's young handmaid, and had persuaded her, in return for a pretty trinket or two, to speak of his wares to the Queen. Beltane himself had not been sent for, but Lind had taken one or two of his pieces to show her mistress, and had assured the goldsmith of Morgause's interest. He told me all about it at some length. For a while I let him talk on, then said, casually: "You said something about Morgause and Merlin. Did I understand that she had soldiers out looking for him? Why?"

"No, you misunderstood me. I was speaking in jest. When I was in York, listening as I do to the talk of the place, I heard someone say that Merlin and she had quarrelled at Luguvallium, and that she spoke of him now with hatred, where before she had spoken with envy of his art. And lately, of course, everyone was wondering where he had gone. Queen or no, little harm could she do a man like that!"

And you, I thought, are luckily short of sight, otherwise I should have to be wary of a perceptive and garrulous little man. As it was, I was glad I had fallen in with him. I was still thinking about it, but idly, as finally even he decided it was time to sleep, and we let the fire go low and rolled ourselves in our blankets under the trees. His presence would give credence to my disguise, and he could be, if not my eyes, my ears and information at the court of Morgause. And Ninian, who acted as his "eyes"? The cold breeze stirred my nape again, and my idle calculations dislimned like a shadow when the sun goes in. What was this? Foreknowledge, the half-forgotten stirring of a kind of power? But even that speculation died as the night breeze hushed through the delicate birch boughs and the last faggot sank to ash. The dreamless night closed in. About the sickly child at Dunpeldyr I would not think at all, except to hope that it would not thrive, and so leave me no problem.

But I knew that the hope was vain.

10

It is barely thirty miles from Vinovia to the town at the Cor Bridge, but it took us six days' journeying. We did not keep to the road, but travelled by circuitous and sometimes rough ways, visiting every village and farmstead, however humble, that lay between us and the Bridge.

With no reason for haste, the journey passed pleasantly. Beltane obviously took great pleasure in our company, and Ninian's lot was made easier by the use of the mules to carry his awkward packs. The goldsmith was as garrulous as ever, but he was a good-hearted man, and moreover a meticulous and honest craftsman, which is something to respect. Our wandering progress was made slower than ever by the time he took over his work – repair-work, mostly, in the poorer places; in the bigger villages, or at taverns, he was of course occupied all the time.

So was the boy, but on the journeys between settlements, and in the evenings by the camp fire, we struck up a strange kind of friendship. He was always quiet, but after he found that I knew the ways of birds and beasts, that a detailed knowledge of plants went with my physician's skill, and that I could, at night, even read the map of the stars, he kept near me whenever he could, and even brought himself to question me. Music he loved, and his ear was true, so I began to teach him how to tune my harp. He could neither read nor write, but showed, once his interest was engaged, a ready intelligence that, given time and the right teacher, could be made to blossom. By the time we reached Cor Bridge I was beginning to wonder if I could be that teacher, and if Ninian could be brought – his master permitting – to serve me. With this in mind, I kept my eyes open whenever we passed some quarry or farmstead, in case

there might be some likely slave I could buy to serve Beltane, and
persuade him to release the boy.

From time to time the small cloud oppressed me still, the hovering chill of some vague foreboding that made me restless and
apprehensive; trouble was there at my whistle, looking for somewhere to strike. After a while I gave up trying to see where that
stroke might fall. I was certain that it could not concern Arthur, and
if it was to concern Morgause, then there would be time enough to
let it worry me. Even in Dunpeldyr I thought I should be safe
enough: Morgause would have other things on her mind, not least
the return of her lord, who could count on his fingers as well as any
man.

And the trouble might be no deep matter, but the trivial
annoyance of a day, soon forgotten. It is hard to tell, when the gods
trail the shadows of foreknowledge across the light, whether the
cloud is one that will blot out a king's realm, or make a child cry in
its sleep.

At length we came to Cor Bridge, in the rolling country just
south of the Great Wall. In Roman times the place was called
Corstopitum. There was a strong fort there, well placed where Dere
Street, from the south, crossed the great east-west road of Agricola.
In time a civilian settlement sprang up in this favoured spot, and
soon became a thriving township, accepting all the traffic, civil and
military, from the four quarters of Britain. Nowadays the fort is a
tumbledown affair, much of its stone having been pillaged for new
buildings, but west of it, on a curve of rising ground edged by the
Cor Burn, the new town still grows and prospers, with houses, inns
and shops, and a thriving market which is the liveliest relic of its
prosperity in Roman times.

The fine Roman bridge, that gives the place its modern name,
still stands, spanning the Tyne at the point where the Cor Burn runs
into it from the north. There is a mill there, and the bridge's timbers
groan all day under the loads of grain. Below the mill is a wharf where
shallow-draught barges can tie up. The Cor is little more than a
stream, relying on its steep tumble of water to drive the mill wheel,
but the great River Tyne is wide and fast, flowing here over bright
shingle between its gracious banks of trees. Its valley is broad and
fertile, full of fruit trees standing deep in growing corn. From this

flowery and winding tract of green the land rises towards the north
to rolling moorland, where, under the windy stretches of sky,
sudden blue lakes wink in the sun. In winter it is a bleak country,
where wolves and wild men roam the heights, and come sometimes
over-close to the houses; but in summer it is a lovely land, with
forests full of deer, and fleets of swans sailing the waters. The air
over the moors sparkles with bird-song, and the valleys are alive
with skimming swallows and the bright flash of kingfishers. And
along the edge of the whinstone runs the Great Wall of the Emperor
Hadrian, rising and dipping as the rock rises and dips. It commands
the country from its long cliff-top, so that from any point of it fold
upon fold of blue distance fades away east or westward, till the eye
loses the land in the misty edge of the sky.

It was not country I had known before. I had come this way, as I
had told Arthur, because I had a call to make. One of my father's
secretaries, whom I had known first in Brittany, and thereafter in
Winchester and Caerleon, had come north after Ambrosius' death,
to retirement of a sort here in Northumbria. The pension he received from my father had let him buy a holding near Vindolanda,
in a sheltered spot beside the Agricolan Road, with a couple of
strong slaves to work it. There he had settled, growing rare plants
in his favoured garden, and writing, so I had been told, a history of
the times he had lived through. His name was Blaise.

We lodged in the old part of the town, at a tavern within the
purlieus of the original fortress. Beltane, with sudden, immovable
obstinacy, had refused to pay the toll exacted at the bridge, so we
crossed at the ford some half mile down-stream, then turned along
the river past the forge, coming into the town by its old east gate.

Night was falling when we got there, so we put up at the first
tavern we found. This was a respectable place not far from the main
market square. Late though the hour was, there was still plenty of
coming and going. Servants were gossiping at the cistern while
they filled their water jars; through the laughter and talk came the
cool splash of a fountain; in some house nearby a woman was
singing a weaving-song. Beltane was in high glee at the prospects
for trading on the morrow, and in fact started business that same
night, when the tavern filled up after supper-time. I did not stay to
see how he did. Ulfin reported a bath-house still in commission

near the old west wall, so I spent the evening there and then retired, refreshed, to bed.

Next morning Ulfin and I breakfasted together in the shade of the huge plane tree which grew beside the inn. It promised to be a hot day. '

Early as we were, Beltane and the boy were before us. The goldsmith had already set up his stall in a strategic place near the cistern; which meant merely that he, or rather Ninian, had spread some rush matting on the ground, and on that had laid out such gauds as might appeal to the eyes and purses of ordinary folk. The fine work was carefully hidden away in the lining of the bags.

Beltane was in his element, talking incessantly to any passer-by who paused even for a moment to look at the goods: a complete lesson in jewelcraft was given away, so to speak, with every piece. The boy, as usual, was silent. He patiently rearranged the items which had been handled and carelessly dropped back on the matting, and he took the money, or sometimes exchange-goods such as food or cloth. Between times he sat cross-legged, stitching at the frayed straps of his sandals, which had given a lot of trouble on the road.

"Or this one, madam?" Beltane was saying, to a round-faced woman with a basket of cakes on her arm. "This we call cellwork, or inclosed work, very beautiful, isn't it? I learned the art in Byzantium, and believe me, even in Byzantium itself you'd never see finer . . . And this very same design, I've seen it done in gold, worn by the finest ladies in the land. This one? Why, it's copper, madam – and priced accordingly, but it's every bit as good – the same work in it, as you can well see . . . Look at those colours. Hold it up to the light, Ninian. How bright and clear they are, and see how the bands of copper shine, holding the colours apart . . . Yes, copper wire, very delicate; you have to lay it in pattern, and then you run the colours in, and the wire acts as a wall, you might say, to contain the pattern. Oh, no, madam, not jewels, not at that price! It's glass, but I'll warrant you've never seen jewels with colours finer. I make the glass myself, and very skilled work it is, too, in my little 'etna' there – that's what I call my smelting stove – but you've no time this morning, I can see that, madam. Show her the little hen, Ninian, or maybe you prefer the horse

. . . that's it, Ninian . . . Now, madam, are the colours not beautiful? I doubt if anywhere in the length and breadth of the land you would find work to equal this, and all for a copper penny. Why, there's as much copper, nearly, in the brooch, as there is in the penny you'll give me for it . . ."

Ulfin appeared then, leading the mules. It had been arranged that he and I would make the short journey to Vindolanda, and return on the morrow, while Beltane and the boy pursued their trade in the town. I paid for the breakfast, then, rising, went across to take leave of them.

"You're going now?" Beltane spoke without taking his eyes off the woman, who was turning a brooch over in her hand. "Then a good journey to you, Master Emrys, and we hope to see you back tomorrow night . . . No, no, madam, we have no need of your cakes, delicious though they look. A copper penny is the price today. Ah, I thank you. You will not regret it. Ninian, pin the brooch on for the lady . . . Like a queen, madam, I do assure you. Indeed, Queen Ygraine herself, that's the highest in the land, might envy you. Ninian" – this as the woman moved away, his voice changing to the habitual nagging tone he used to the boy – "don't stand there with your mouth watering! Take the penny now and get yourself a pair of new shoes. When we go north I cannot have you hobbling and lagging with flapping soles as you did all the way –"

"No!" I did not even realise that I had spoken, till I saw them staring. Even then I did not know what impelled me to add: "Let the boy have his cakes, Beltane. The sandals will suffice, and see, he is hungry, and the sun is shining."

The goldsmith's short-sighted eyes were puckered as he stared up at me against the light. At length, a little to my surprise, he nodded, with a gruff, "All right, get along," to the boy. Ninian gave me a shining look, then ran off into the crowd after the market-woman. I thought Beltane was going to question me, but he did not. He began to set the goods straight again, saying merely: "You're right, I have no doubt. Boys are always starving, and he's a good lad and faithful. He can go barefoot if he has to, but at least let him have his belly full. It isn't often we get sweet stuff, and the cakes smelled like a feast, so they did."

As we rode west along the river-side Ulfin asked, with sharp concern in his voice:

"What is it, my lord? Is something ailing you?"

I shook my head, and he said no more, but he must have known I was lying, because I myself could feel the tears cold on my cheeks in the summer wind.

★ ★ ★

Master Blaise received us in a snug little house of sand-coloured stone, built round a small courtyard with apple trees trained up the walls, and roses hiding the squared modern pillars.

The house had once, long ago, belonged to a miller; a stream ran past, its steep fall controlled by shallow water-steps, its walled banks set with little ferns and flowers. Some hundred paces below the house, the stream vanished under a hanging canopy of beech and hazel. Above this woodland, on the steep slope behind the house, full in the sun, was the walled garden that held the old man's treasured plants.

He knew me straight away, though it was many years since we had met. He lived alone, but for his two gardeners and a woman who, with her daughter, cared for the house and cooked for him. She was bidden to get beds ready, and bustled off to do some scolding over the kitchen braziers. Ulfin went to see our mules stabled, and Blaise and I were free to talk.

Light lingers late in the north, so after supper we went out to the terrace over the stream. The warmth of the day breathed still from the stones, and the evening air smelled of cypress and rosemary. Here and there in the tree-hung shadows the pale shape of a statue glimmered. A thrush sang somewhere, a richer echo of the nightingale. At my elbow the old man (*magister artii,* as he now liked to style himself) was talking of the past, in a pure Roman Latin with no trace of accent. It was an evening borrowed from Italy: I might have been a young man again, on my youthful travels.

I said as much, and he beamed with pleasure.

"I like to think so. One tries to hold to the civilised values of one's prime. You knew I studied there as a young man, before I was privileged to enter your father's service? *Those* years, ah, yes, those were the great years, but as one grows older, perhaps one tends to look back too much, too much."

I said something civil about this being of advantage to an historian, and asked if he would honour me with a reading from his work. I had noticed the lighted lamp standing on a stone table by the cypresses, and the rolls lying handily beside it.

"Would you really care to hear it?" He moved that way readily. "Some parts of it, I am sure, would interest you enormously. And it is a part that you can help me to add to, I believe. As it chances, I have it here with me, this roll, yes, this is the one . . . Shall we sit? The stone is dry, and the evening tolerably mild. I think we shall come to no harm out here by the roses . . ."

The section he chose to read was his account of the events after Ambrosius returned to Greater Britain; he had been close to my father for most of that time, while I had been involved elsewhere. After he had finished reading he put his questions, and I was able to supply details of the final battle with Hengist at Kaerconan and the subsequent siege of York, and the work of settlement and rebuilding that came after. I filled in for him, too, the campaign that Uther had waged against Gilloman in Ireland. I had gone with Uther, while Ambrosius stayed in Winchester; Blaise had been with him there, and it was to Blaise that I had owed the account of my father's death while I was overseas.

He told me about it again. "I can still see it, that great bedchamber at Winchester, with the doctors, and the nobles standing there, and your father lying against the pillows, near to death, but sensible, and talking to you as if you were there in the room. I was beside him, ready to write down anything that was needed, and more than once I glanced down to the foot of the King's bed, half thinking to see you there. And all the while you were voyaging back from the Irish wars, bringing the great stone to lay on his grave."

He fell to nodding then, as old men do, as if he would go back for ever to the stories of times gone by. I brought him back to the present. "And how far have you gone, with your account of the times?"

"Oh, I try to set down all that passes. But now that I am out of the centre of affairs, and have to depend on the talk from the town, or on anyone who calls to see me, it is hard to know how much I miss.

I have correspondents, but sometimes they are lax, yes, the young men are not what they were . . . It's a great chance that brings you here, Merlin, a great day for me. You will stay? As long as you wish, dear boy; you'll have seen that we live simply, but it's a good life, and there is still so much to talk about, so much . . . And you must see my vines. Yes, a fine white grape, that ripens to a marvellous sweetness if the year is a good one. Figs do well here, and peaches, and I have even had some success with a pomegranate tree from Italy."

"I can't stay this time, I'm afraid." I spoke with genuine regret. "I have to go north in the morning. But if I may, I'll come back before long – and with plenty to tell you, too, I promise you! There are great things afoot now, and you will be doing men a service if you will put them down. Meantime, if I can, would you like me to send letters from time to time? I hope to be back at Arthur's side before winter, and it will keep you in touch."

His delight was patent. We talked for a little longer, then, as the night-flying insects began to crowd to the lamp, we carried it indoors, and parted for the night.

My bedchamber window looked out over the terrace where we had been sitting. For a long time before I lay down to sleep I leaned my elbows on the sill, looking out and breathing the night scents that came in wave after wave on the breeze. The thrush had stopped singing, and now the soft *hush* of falling water filled the night. A new moon lay on its back, and stars were out. Here, away from lights and sounds of town or village, the night was deep, the black sky stretching, fathomless, away between the spheres, to some unimaginable world where gods walked, and suns and moons showered down like petals falling. Some power there is that draws men's eyes and hearts up and outwards, beyond the heavy clay that fastens them to earth. Music can take them, and the moon's light, and, I suppose, love, though I had not known it then, except in worship.

The tears were there again, and I let them fall. I knew now what cloud it was that had lain over my horizon ever since that chance meeting on the moorland road. How, I did not know, but the boy Ninian, so young and quiet, and with a grace in look and motion that gave the lie to the ugly slave-burn on his arm – he had had about him the mark of a coming death. This, once seeing, any man might have wept for, but I was weeping, too, for myself; for Merlin the enchanter, who saw, and could do nothing; who walked his own lonely heights where it seemed that none would ever come near to him. In the boy's still face and listening eyes, that night on the moor when the birds had called, I had caught a glimpse of what might have been. For the first time, since those days long ago when I had sat at Galapas' feet to learn the arts of magic, I had seen someone who might have learned worthily from me. Not as others had wanted to learn, for power or excitement, nor for the prosecution of some enmity or private greed; but because he had seen, darkly with a child's eyes, how the gods move with the winds and speak with the sea and sleep in the gentle herbs; and how God himself is the sum of all that is on the face of the lovely earth. Magic is the door through which mortal man may sometimes step, to find the gates in the hollow hills, and let himself through into the halls of that other world. I could, but for that shining edge of doom, have opened those gates for him, and, when I needed it no longer, have left him the key.

And now he was dead. I had known it, I think, after I had spoken in the market-place. My sharp, unthinking protest had been made for no reason that I knew: the knowledge came later. And always, when I spoke like that, men did unquestioningly as I bade them. So at least the boy had had his cakes, and the day's sunshine.

I turned away from the thin, brightening moon, and lay down.

★   ★   ★

"At least he had the cakes, and the day's sunshine." Beltane the goldsmith told us about it as we shared supper at the town's tavern the next evening. He was unusually silent, for him, and seemed stunned, clinging to our company as, in spite of his sharp tongue, he must have clung to the boy's.

"But – drowned." Ulfin said it on a disbelieving note, but I caught a glance from him that told me he had begun to put events together and understand them. "How did it happen?"

"That evening, at supper-time, he brought me back here and packed the things away. It had been a good day, and the take was heavy; we were sure of eating well. He had worked hard, and so when he saw some boys off down to bathe in the river, he asked if he might join them. He was a great one for washing himself . . . and it had been a hot day, and people's feet kick up a lot of dust, and dung besides, in the market-places. I let him go. The next thing was the boys came back, running, with the story. He must have trodden into a hole, and slipped out of his depth. It's a bad river, they tell me . . . How was I to know that? How could I know? When we came over yesterday the ford seemed so shallow, and so safe . . ."

"The body?" asked Ulfin, after a pause when he could see that I was not going to speak.

"Gone. Gone downstream, the boys said, like a log on the flood. He came up half a league down-river, but none of them could come near him, and then he vanished. It's a bad death, a puppy's death. He should be found, and buried like a man."

Ulfin said something kind, and after a while the little man's lamentations ran out, and the supper came, and he made shift to eat and drink, and was the better for it.

Next morning the sun shone again, and we went north, the three of us together, and four days later reached the country of the Votadini, which is called in the British tongue Manau Guotodin.

11

Some ten days later, with due stops for trading, we reached Lot's city of Dunpeldyr. It was late afternoon of a cloudy day, and it was raining. We were lucky enough to find suitable lodgings in a tavern near the south gate.

The town was little more than a close huddle of houses and shops near the foot of a great crag on which the castle was built. In times past the crag had contained the whole stronghold, but now the houses crowd, haphazard, between cliffs and river, and on the slopes of the crag itself, right up to the castle wall. The river (another Tyne) curves round the roots of the cliff, then runs in a wide meander across a mile or so of flat land to its sandy estuary. Along its banks the houses cluster, and boats are pulled up on the shingle. There are two bridges, a heavy wooden one set on stone piers, that holds the road to the main castle gate above; and another narrow span of planking which leads to a steep path serving the side gate of the castle. There had been no road-building here; the place had grown without plan, and certainly without beauty or amenity. The town is a mean one, of mud brick houses with turfed roofs, and steep alleys which in stormy weather become torrents of foul water. The river, so fair only a short distance away, is here full of weed and debris. Between the crag and the river to the east is the market-place, where on the morrow Beltane would set out his wares.

One thing I knew I must do without delay. If, ironically enough, Beltane were to be my "eyes" inside the castle, neither Ulfin nor I must be seen to go about with him; so, dependent as he was on a servant, someone must be found to replace the drowned boy. Beltane had made no move to do this himself on our journey north, and now was only too grateful when I offered to do it for him.

A short way out of the town gates I had noticed a quarry; not much of a place, but still working. Next morning, carefully anonymous in a shabby cloak of rusty brown, I went there and sought out the quarry-master, a big, genial-looking ruffian who was strolling around among the half-derelict workings, and the equally derelict workmen, like a lord taking the summer air in his country demesne.

He looked me up and down with a fine air of disdain. "Able-bodied servants come expensive, my good sir." I could see him assessing me as he spoke, and coming up with a poor enough answer. "Nor have I one to spare. One gets all the riffraff in a place like this . . . prisoners, criminals, the lot. No one who'd ever be a decent house slave, or be trusted on a farm, or with any kind of skilled job. And muscle comes expensive. You'd best wait for the fair. All sorts come then, hiring themselves and their families, or selling themselves or their brats for food – though, come to that, you'd have to wait for winter and sharp weather to get the cheap market."

"I don't wish to wait. I can pay. I am travelling, and I need a man or a boy. He need have no skills, except to keep himself clean, and be faithful to his master, and have enough strength to travel even in winter, when the roads are foul."

As I spoke his manner grew more civil, and the assessment moved up a notch or two. "Travel? So, what is your business?"

I saw no reason to tell him that the servant was not for myself. "I am a doctor."

My answer had the effect it has nine times out of ten. He started eagerly to tell me of all his various ailments, of which, since he was more than forty years old, he had plenty.

"Well," I said, when he had finished, "I can help you, I think, but it had better be mutual. If you have a likely hand you can let me have as a servant – and he should be cheap enough, since it's just the riffraff you get here – then perhaps we can do a deal? One more thing. As you will understand, in my trade there are secrets to be kept. I want no blabbermouth; he must be sparing of speech."

At that the rogue stared, then slapped his thigh and laughed, as if at the greatest joke in the world. He turned his head and bellowed a name. "Casso! Come here! Quickly, you oaf! Here's luck for you, lad, and a new master, and a fine new life adventuring!"

A lanky youth detached himself from a gang which was labouring on stone-breaking under an overhang that looked to me to be ready to collapse. He straightened slowly, and stared, before dropping his pick-helve and starting towards us.

"I'll spare you this one, master doctor," said the quarry-master genially. "He's everything you ask for." And he went off into fits of mirth once more.

The youth came up and stood, arms hanging, eyes on the ground. At a guess, he was about eighteen or nineteen. He looked strong enough – he would have to be, to survive that life for more than six months – but stupid to the point of idiocy.

"Casso?" I said. He looked up, and I saw that he was merely exhausted. In a life without hope or pleasure there was little point in spending energy on thought.

His master was laughing again. "It's no use talking to him. Anything you want to know you'll have to ask me, or look for yourself." He seized the lad's wrist and held up the arm. "See? Strong as a mule, and sound in wind and limb. And discreet enough, even for you. Discreet as hell, is our Casso. He's dumb."

The youth noticed the handling no more than would a mule, but at the last sentence he met my eyes again, briefly. I had been wrong. There was thought there, and with it hope; I saw the hope die.

"But not deaf with it, I gather?" I said. "What caused it, do you know?"

"You might say his own silly tongue." He started his great laugh again, caught my look, and cleared his throat instead. "You'll make no cure there, master doctor, his tongue's out. I never got the rights of it, but he used to be in service down in Bremenium, and the way I heard it, he opened his mouth too wide once too often. Not one to have patience with insolence, isn't the Lord Aguisel . . . Ah, well, but he's learned his lesson. I got him with a job lot of labour after the town bridges were repaired. He's given me no trouble. And for all I know it was house service he was in before, so you'll be getting a bargain with a fine, young – *Hey there!*"

While we had been talking his eye had gone, from time to time, to the gang at work on the stone. Now he started over that way, with some shouted abuse at the "idle scum" who had seized the chance to work more slowly.

I looked thoughtfully at Casso. I had caught the look in his face, and the quick, involuntary shake of the head at the quarry-master's mention of "insolence". "You were in Aguisel's household?" I asked him.

A nod.

"I see." I thought I did, indeed. Aguisel was a man of evil reputation, a jackal to Lot's wolf, who laired in the hilltop remains of Bremenium fortress to the south. Things happened there which a decent man could only guess at. I had heard rumours of his trick of using dumb or blinded slaves.

"Am I right in thinking that you saw what you could not be allowed to report on?"

Another nod. This time his eyes remained fixed on me. It must have been long enough since anyone had tried even this sort of limited communication.

"I thought as much. I have heard stories, myself, of my lord Aguisel. Can you read or write, Casso?"

A shake of the head.

"Be thankful," I said, drily. "If you could, then by this time you would be dead."

The quarry-master had got his gang working again to his satisfaction. He was on his way back to us. I thought quickly.

The youth's dumbness might be no disadvantage to Beltane, who was more than able to do his own talking; but I had been working on the assumption that the new slave must act as his master's "eyes" while we were in Dunpeldyr. Now I saw that there was no need of this: whatever transpired in Lot's stronghold, Beltane was quite able to report on it himself. His sight was not strong, but his hearing was, and he could tell us what was said: what the place looked like would hardly matter. When we left Dunpeldyr, if the goldsmith needed a different servant, no doubt we could find one. But now time pressed, and here I could certainly purchase discretion, even if enforced, and, I thought, the loyalty that went with gratitude.

"Well?" asked the quarry-master.

I said: "Anyone who has survived service in Bremenium is

certainly strong enough for anything I might require. Very well. I'll take him."

"Splendid, splendid!" The fellow waxed loud in his praise of my judgment and Casso's various excellences, so much so that I began to wonder if the slaves were in fact his own to dispose of, or if he was seeing a way to fill his own purse, and would perhaps report the youth's death to his employers. When he began to haggle about price, I sent Casso to collect whatever possessions he had, with instructions to wait for me on the road. I have never seen why, because a man is your captive, or a purchase, he should be stripped of an elementary self-respect. Even a horse or a hound works the better for retaining a pride in itself.

After he had gone I turned back to the quarry-master. "Now, we agreed, if you remember, that I would pay some part of the price in medicines. You will find me at the tavern by the south gate. If you come tonight, or send someone to ask for Master Emrys, I will have the medicines ready for you, and leave them to be picked up. And now, about the rest of the price . . ."

In the end we were agreed, and, followed by my new purchase, I made my way back to the tavern.

Casso's face fell when he heard that he was not to serve me, but to go with Beltane; but by the time the evening was through, with the warmth and good food and the lively company that crowded into the tavern, he looked like a plant which, dying in darkness, has been plunged suddenly into sunlit water. Beltane was outspokenly grateful to me, and embarked almost straight away on a long and happy exposition of his craft for Casso's sake. The latter could hardly have found a place in which his mutilation would have mattered less. I suspected that, as the evening wore through, Beltane began to find it a positive advantage to have a dumb servant. Ninian had hardly spoken at all, but neither had he listened. Casso drank it all in, fingering the pieces with his calloused hands, his brain waking from the numbness of hopeless exhaustion, and expanding into pleasure as one watched.

The tavern was too small – and we were ostensibly too poor – to have a private chamber, but at the end of the hall, away from the fire, there was a deep alcove with a table and twin settles where we could be private enough. No one took much notice of us, and we

stayed in our corner all evening, listening to the gossip that came
into the tavern. Facts there were none, but there were plenty of
rumours, the most important being that Arthur had fought and
won two more engagements, and that the Saxons had accepted
terms. The High King was to be in Linnuis for some time longer,
but Lot, it was said, could be expected home any day now.

In fact he did not come for four more days.

I spent the days withindoors, writing to Ygraine and Arthur, and
the evenings in familiarising myself with the town and its environment. The town was small, and did not attract many strangers, so,
since I wanted to avoid attention, I went out at dusk, when folk
would mostly be at supper. For the same reason I did not advertise
my trade: anyone who approached our party had his full attention
claimed by Beltane, and did not think to look further. They took
me, I imagine, for a poor scribe of some sort. Ulfin haunted the
town gates, picking up what news he could, and waiting for tidings
of Lot's approach. Beltane, innocent and unsuspicious, plied his
trade. He set up his stove in the square near the tavern, and began to
teach Casso the elements of the repairer's art. Inevitably, this drew
interest, and then custom, and soon the goldsmith was doing a
roaring trade.

This, on the third day, brought just the result we all hoped for.
The girl Lind, passing through the market square one day and
seeing Beltane, approached and made herself known. Beltane sent
her back to her mistress with a message, and a new buckle for
herself, and soon got his reward. Next day he was sent for to the
castle, and went off triumphantly, with a laden Casso in his wake.

Even had he not been dumb, Casso could have reported nothing.
When the two were passed in through the postern gate, Casso was
detained to wait in the porter's kennel, while an upper servant
conducted the goldsmith to the queen's chambers.

He came back to the tavern at dusk, bubbling with his news. For
all his talk of great people, this was the first king's house he had been
in, and Morgause the first queen who would wear his jewels. The
admiration he had conceived for her in York had soared now to the
point of worship; at close quarters, even on him, her rose and gold
beauty acted like a drug. He poured his story out over supper,
obviously never thinking for a moment that I would not be

absorbed in any item of gossip he might retail. Casso and I (Ulfin was still out) were given a word by word account of all that was said, of her graces, her praise of his work, her generosity in buying three pieces and accepting a fourth; even of the scent she wore. He did his best, too, with a description of her beauty, and of the splendours of the room where she received him, but here we were dealing with impressions 'only: the picture he conveyed was a perfumed haze of light and colour; the cool brightness from a window running along the sheen of an amber robe, and lighting the wonderful rose-gold hair; the rustle of silk and the glow and crackle of logs lit against the grey day. And music, too; a girl's voice whispering a lullaby.

"So the child was there?"

"Indeed. Asleep in a high cradle near the fire. I could see it, oh, clearly, outlined against the flames; and the girl rocking it and singing. The cradle was canopied with silk and gauze, with a little bell that chimed as she rocked it, and glinted in the firelight. A royal cradle. Such a pretty sight! I could have wished my old eyes different, for that alone."

"And did you see the child itself?"

It appeared that he had not. The baby had woken once, and cried a little, and the nurse had hushed him without lifting him from the blankets. The queen had been trying a necklet at the time, and without looking round had taken the mirror from the girl's hand, and bidden her sing to the baby.

"A pretty voice," said Beltane, "but such a sad little song. And indeed, I would hardly have recognised the maiden herself, if she had not come to speak to me yesterday. So thin and creeping, like a mouse, and her voice gone thin, too, like something pining. Lind, her name is, did I tell you? A strange name for a maiden, surely? Does it not mean a snake?"

"I believe so. Did you hear the child's name?"

"They called him Mordred."

Beltane showed a tendency, here, to go back to his description of the cradle, and of the pretty picture the girl had made, rocking it and singing, but I brought him back to the point.

"Was anything said about King Lot's coming home?"

Beltane, that single-minded artist, did not even see the implica-

tions of the question. They were expecting him, he told me cheerfully, at any time. The queen had seemed as excited as a young girl.
Indeed, she could talk of nothing else. Would her lord like the
necklet? Did the earrings make her eyes look brighter? Why, added
Beltane, he owed half the sale to the king's coming.

"She did not seem afraid at all?"

"Afraid?" He looked blank. "No. Why should she? She was
happy and excited. 'Just wait,' she was saying to the ladies, just like
any young mother with her lord away at the wars, 'just wait till my
lord sees the fine son I bore him, and as like his father as one wolf to
another.' And she laughed and laughed. It was a jest, you understand, Master Emrys. They call Lot the Wolf in these parts, and take
pride in him, which is only natural among savage folks like these of
the north. Only a jest. Why should she be afraid?"

"I was thinking of the rumours you spoke of once before. You
told me of things you heard in York, and then, you said, there were
looks and whispers here among the common folk in the market-
place."

"Oh, those, yes . . . Well, but that was only talk. I know what
you're getting at, Master Emrys, the wicked stories that have been
going about. You know that always happens when a birth comes
before its time, and there's bound to be more talk in a king's house,
because, you might say, more hangs on it."

"So it was before its time?"

"Yes, so they say. It took them all by surprise. It was born before
even the king's own doctors could get here, that were sent north
from the army to tend to the queen. It was the women delivered
her, but safely, by God's mercy. You remember we were told it was
a sickly child? And indeed, I could tell as much from the way he
cried. But now he thrives and puts on weight. The maid Lind told
me so, when I spoke to her on the way back to the gate. 'And is it
true he's the image of King Lot?' I said to her. She gives me a look,
as much as to say, that will silence the gossip, but all she says aloud
is, 'Yes, as like as can be.' "

He leaned across the table, nodding with cheerful emphasis. "So
you see it was all lies, Master Emrys. And indeed, one only has to
talk to her. That pretty creature deceive her lord? Why, she was like
a bride again at the thought of him coming home. And she would

laugh that pretty laugh, like the silver bell on the cradle. Oh, yes, you can be sure the stories were all lies. Put around in York, they would be, by those that had cause to be jealous . . . You know who I mean, eh? And the child the image of him. They were all saying the same, 'King Lot will see himself in a mirror, just as sure as you see yourself, Madam. Look at him, the image, the little lamb . . .' You know how women talk, Master Emrys. 'The very image of his royal father.' "

. So he talked on, while Casso, busying himself with polishing some cheap buckles, listened and smiled, and I, only a little less silent, let the talk go by me while I thought my own thoughts.

Like his father? Dark hair, dark eyes, the description could fit both Lot and Arthur. Was there some faintest chance that fate was on Arthur's side? That she had conceived by Lot, and then seduced Arthur in an attempt to shackle him to her?

Reluctantly, I put the hope aside. When, at Luguvallium, I had felt doom impending, it had been in a time of power. And it did not need even that to tell me to mistrust Morgause. I had come north to watch her, and now the new fragment of information I had just heard from Beltane might well have told me what to watch for.

Ulfin came in then, shaking a fine rain from his cloak. He looked across, saw us, and gave a barely perceptible sign to me. I got to my feet, and, with a word to Beltane, went over to him.

He spoke softly. "There's news. The queen's messenger rode in just now. I saw him. The horse was hard ridden, almost foundered. I told you I was on terms with one of the gatehouse guards? He says King Lot's on his way home. He's travelling fast. They're expecting him tonight or tomorrow."

"Thank you," I said. "Now, you've been out all day. Get yourself into dry clothes, and get something to eat. I've just heard something from Beltane that persuades me that a watch on the postern gate might be profitable. I'll tell you about it later. When you've eaten, come down and join me. I'll find somewhere dry to wait, where we won't be seen." We rejoined the others, and I asked: "Beltane, can you spare Casso to me for half an hour?"

"Of course, of course. But I shall need him later on. I was bidden back there tomorrow, with this buckle mended for the chamberlain, and I need Casso's help for that."

"I shan't keep him. Casso?"

The slave was already on his feet. Ulfin said, with a shade of apprehension: "So you know what to do now?"

"I am guessing," I said. "I have no power in this, as I told you." I spoke softly, and above the tavern's roar Beltane could not hear me, but Casso did, and looked quickly from me to Ulfin and back again. I smiled at him. "Don't let it concern you. Ulfin and I have affairs here which will not touch you or your master. Come with me now."

"I could come myself," said Ulfin, quickly.

"No. Do as I told you, and eat first. It could be a long watch. Casso . . ."

We went through the maze of dirty streets. The rain, steady now, made muddy puddles, and splashed the dung into stinking pools. Where lights showed at all in the houses, they were feeble, smoking glints of flame, curtained from the wet night by hides or sacking. Nothing interfered with our night-sight, and presently we could pick our way cleanly across the gleaming runnels. After a while the tree-banked slope of the castle rock loomed above us. A lantern hung high in the blackness, marking the postern gate.

Casso, who had been following me, touched my arm and pointed where a narrow alley, little more than a funnel for rainwater, led steeply downwards. It was not a way I had been before. At the bottom I could hear, loud above the steady hissing of the rain, the noise of the river.

"A short cut to the footbridge?" I asked.

He nodded vigorously.

We picked our way down over the filthy cobbles. The roar of the river grew louder. I could see the white water of the lasher, and against it the great wheel of a mill. Beyond this, outlined by the reflected glimmer of the foam, was the footbridge.

No one was about. The mill was not running; the miller probably lived above it, but he had locked his doors and no light showed. A narrow path, deep in mud, led past the shuttered mill and along the soaked grasses of the river-side towards the bridge.

I wondered, half irritably, why Casso had chosen this way. He must have grasped some need for secrecy, though the main street was, surely, in this weather and at this time, deserted. But then voices and the swinging light of a lantern brought me up short in the shelter of the miller's doorway.

Three men were coming down the street. They were hurrying, talking together in undertones. I saw a bottle passed from hand to hand. Castle servants, no doubt, on their way back from the tavern. They stopped at the end of the bridge, and looked back. Now something furtive could be seen in their movements. One of them said something, and there was a laugh, quickly stifled. They moved on, but not before I had seen them, clearly enough, in the lantern's glow: they were armed, and they were sober.

Casso was close beside me, pressed back in the dark doorway. The men had not glanced our way. They went quickly across the bridge, their footsteps sounding hollow on the wet planks.

Something else the passing light had showed me. Just beyond the mill, at the corner of the alley, another doorway stood open. From the pile of timber stocks and sawn felloes outside in the weedy strip of yard, I took it to be a wheelwright's shop. It was deserted for the night, but inside the main shed the remains of a fire still glowed. From that sheltering darkness I should be able to hear and see all who approached the bridge.

Casso ran ahead of me into the warm cave of the shop, and lifted a couple of faggots. Taking them to the fire, he made the motion of throwing them on the ashes.

"Only one," I said softly. "Good man. Now, if you will go back and get Ulfin, and bring him here to me, you can get yourself dried and warm, and then forget all about us."

A nod, then, smiling, a pantomime to show me that my secret, whatever it was, would be safe with him. God knew what he thought I was doing; an assignation, perhaps, or spy's work. Even at that, he knew about as much as I knew myself.

"Casso. Would you like to learn to read and write?"

Stillness. The smile vanished. In the growing flicker of the fire I saw him rigid, all eyes, unbelieving, like the lost traveller who has the clue, against all hope, thrust into his hand. He nodded, once, jerkily.

"I shall see that you are taught. Go now, and thanks. Good night."

He went, running, as if the stinking alley were as light as day.

Halfway up it I saw him jump and spring, like a young animal suddenly let out of its pen on a fine morning. I went quietly back into the shop, picking my way past the wheel-pit and the heavy sledge left leaning by the pile of spokes. Near the fireplace was the stool where the boy sat who kept the bellows going. I sat down to wait, spreading my wet cloak to the warmth of the fire.

Outside, drowning the soft sounds of the rain, the lasher roared. A loose paddle of the great wheel, hammered by the water, clacked and thudded. A pair of starving dogs raced by, wrangling over something unspeakable from a midden. The wheelwright's shop smelled of fresh wood, and sap drying, and the knots of burning elm. The faint tick of the fire was clearly audible in the warm darkness against the water-noises outside. Time went by.

Once before I had sat like this, by a fire, alone, with my mind on a birth-chamber, and a child's fate revealed to me by the god. That had been a night of stars, with a wind blowing over the clean sea, and the great king-star shining. I had been young then, sure of myself, and of the god who drove me. Now I was sure of nothing, save that I had as much hope of diverting whatever evil Morgause was planning, as a dry bough had of damming the force of the lasher.

But what power there was in knowledge, I would have. Human guesswork had brought me here, and we should see if I had read the witch aright. And though my god had deserted me, I still had more power than is granted to common men: I had a king at my call.

And now here was Ulfin, to share this vigil with me as he had shared it in Tintagel. I heard nothing, only saw when his body blocked the dim sky in the doorway.

"Here," I said, and he came in, groping his way over to the glow.

"Nothing yet, my lord?"

"Nothing."

"What are you expecting?"

"I'm not quite sure, but I think someone will come this way tonight, from the queen."

I felt him turn to peer at me in the darkness. "Because Lot is due home?"

"Yes. Is there any more news of that?"

"Only what I told you before. They expect him to press hard for home. He could be here very soon."

"I think so, too. In any case, Morgause will have to make sure."

"Sure of what, my lord?"

"Sure of the High King's son."

A pause. "You mean you think they will smuggle him out, in case Lot believes the rumours and kills the child? But in that case —"

"Yes? In that case?"

"Nothing, my lord. I wondered, that's all . . . You think they will bring him this way?"

"No. I think they have already brought him."

"*They have*? Did you see which way?"

"Not since I have been here. I meant that I am certain that the baby in the castle is not Arthur's child. They have exchanged it."

A long breath beside me in the darkness. "For fear of Lot?"

"Of course. Think about it, Ulfin. Whatever Morgause may tell Lot, he must have heard what everyone is saying, ever since it became known that she was with child. She has tried to persuade him that the child is his, but premature; and he may believe her. But do you think he will take the risk that she is lying, and that some other man's son, let alone Arthur's, lies there in that cradle, and will grow up heir to Lothian? Whatever he believes, there's a possibility that he may kill the boy. And Morgause knows it."

"You think he has heard the rumours that it may be the High King's?"

"He could hardly help it. Arthur made no secret of his visit to Morgause that night, and nor did she. She wanted it so. Afterwards, when I forced her to change her plans, she might persuade or terrify her women into secrecy, but the guards saw him, and by morning every man in Luguvallium would know of it. So what can Lot do? He would not tolerate a bastard of any man's; but Arthur's could be dangerous."

He was silent for a while. "It puts me in mind of Tintagel. Not the night we took King Uther in, but the other time, when Queen Ygraine gave Arthur to you, to hide him out of King Uther's way."

"Yes."

"My lord, are you planning to take this child as well, to save him from Lot?"

His voice, softly pitched as it was, sounded thin with some kind of strain. I hardly attended; far out somewhere in the night, beyond the noise of the weir, I had heard a beat of hoofs; not a sound, so much as a vibration under our feet as the earth carried it. Then the faint pulse was gone, and the water's roar came back.

"What did you say?"

"I wondered, my lord, how sure you were about the child up at the castle."

"Sure of what the facts say, no more. Look at them. She lied about the date of birth, so that it could be put about that the birth was premature. Very well; that could be a face-saver, no more; it's done all the time. But look how it was done. She contrived that no doctor was present, and then alleged that the birth was unexpected, and so quick that no witnesses could be called into the chamber, as is the custom with a royal birthing. Only her women, who are her creatures."

"Well, why, my lord? What more was there to gain?"

"Only this, a child to show Lot that he could kill if he would, while Arthur's son and hers goes scatheless."

A gasp of silence. "You mean – ?"

"It fits, doesn't it? She could already have arranged an exchange with some other woman due to bear at the same time, some poor woman, who would take the money and hold her tongue, and be glad of the chance to suckle the royal baby. We can only guess what Morgause told her: the woman can have no inkling that her own child might be at risk. So the changeling lies there in the castle, while Arthur's son, Morgause's tool of power, is hidden near by. At my guess, not too far away. They will want news of him from time to time."

"And if what you say is true, then when Lot gets here –"

"Some move will be made. If he does harm the changeling, Morgause will have to see that the mother hears nothing of it. She may even have to find another home for Mordred."

"But –"

"Ulfin, there is nothing we can do to save the changeling. Only Morgause could save it, if she would. It's not even certain that it will be in danger; Lot is not quite a savage, after all. But you and I would only run on death ourselves, and the child with us."

"I know. But what about all the talk up there in the castle? Beltane would tell you about it. He was talking while I got my supper. I mean, the baby being so like King Lot, the living image, they were all saying. Could this of yours just be a guess, sir? And the child be Lot's own, after all? The date could even have been right. They said it was a sickly child, and small."

"It could be. I told you I was guessing. But we do know that Queen Morgause has no truth in her – and that she is Arthur's enemy. Her actions, and Lot's, bear watching. Arthur himself will have to know, beyond doubt, what the truth is."

"Of course. I see that. One thing we could do, is find out who bore a male child at about the same time as the queen. I could ask around the place tomorrow. I've made a useful wine-friend or two already."

"In a town this size it could be one of a score. And we have no time. Listen!"

Up through the ground, clear now, the beat of hoofs. A troop, riding hard. Then the sound of them, close and coming closer, clear above the river-noises, and, soon, the town noises as people crowded out to see. Men shouting; the crash of wood on stonework as the gates were flung open; the jingle of bits and the clash of armour; the snorting of hard-ridden horses. More shouting, and an echo from the castle rock high above us, then the sound of a trumpet.

The main bridge thundered. The heavy gates creaked and slammed. The sounds dwindled towards the inner courtyard, and were lost in the other, nearer noises.

I stood up and walked to the doorway of the wheelwright's shop, and looked up to where, beyond the mill roof, the castle towered against the clouded night. The rain had stopped. Lights were moving. Windows flared and darkened as the king's servants lighted him through the castle. To the west side were two windows bright with soft light. The moving lights went there, and stayed.

"Lot comes home," I said.

12

Somewhere a bell clanged from the castle. Midnight. Leaning in the doorway of the wheelwright's shop I stretched shoulders aching with the damp of the night. Behind me, Ulfin fed another faggot to the fire, carefully, so that no spurt of flame should attract the attention of anyone who might be waking. The town, sunk back into its night-time stupor, was silent, but for the barking of curs and now and again the scritch of an owl among the trees on the steep crag-side.

I moved silently out from the door's shelter into the street near the end of the bridge. I looked up at the black bulk of the crag. The high windows of the castle still showed light, and light from the troopers' torches, red and smoking, moved behind the walls that masked the courtyard below.

Ulfin, at my elbow, drew breath for a question.

It was never asked. Someone, running chin on shoulder across the footbridge, ran headlong into me, gasped, gave a broken cry, and twisted to dodge past.

Equally startled, I was slow to react, but Ulfin jumped, grasped an arm, and clapped a hand tightly to stifle the next cry. The new-comer twisted and fought in his grip, but was held with ease.

"A girl," said Ulfin, surprised.

"Into the shop," I said quickly, and led the way.

Once there, I threw another piece of elm on the fire. The flames leaped. Ulfin brought his captive, still writhing and kicking, into the light. The hood had fallen from her face and head, and I recognised her, with satisfaction.

"Lind."

She stiffened in Ulfin's grip. I saw the gleam of frightened eyes staring at me above the stifling hand. Then they widened, and she went quite still, as a partridge does before a stoat. She knew me, too.

"Yes," I said. "I am Merlin. I was waiting for you, Lind. Now, if Ulfin looses you, you will make no sound."

Her head moved, assenting. He took his hand from her mouth, but kept his grip on her arm.

"Let her go," I said.

He obeyed me, moving back to get between her and the door-way, but he need not have troubled. As soon as he released her she ran towards me, and flung herself to her knees in the litter of shavings. She clung to my robe. Her body shook with her terrified weeping.

"Oh, my lord, my lord! Help me!"

"I am not here to harm you, or the child." To calm her, I spoke coldly. "The High King sent me here to get news of his son. You know I cannot come to the queen herself, so I waited here for you. What has happened up at the castle?"

But she would not speak. I think she could not. She clung, and shook, and cried.

I spoke more gently. "Whatever has happened, Lind, I cannot help you if I do not know. Come near the fire, and compose yourself, and tell me."

But when I tried to draw my robe from her clutches she clung the harder. Her sobs were violent. "Don't keep me here, lord, let me go! Or else help me! You have the power – you are Arthur's man – you are not afraid of my lady –"

"I will help you if you will talk to me. I want news of King Arthur's son. Was that King Lot who arrived just now?"

"Yes. Oh, yes! He came home an hour ago. He is mad, mad, I tell you! And she did not even try to stop him. She laughed, and let him do it."

"Let him do what?"

"Kill the baby."

"He killed the child Morgause has at the castle?"

She was too distraught to see anything strange about the form of the question. "Yes, yes!" She gulped. "And all the while it was his own son, his very own son. I was there at the birth, and I swear it by my own hearth-gods. It was – "

"What's that?" This, sharply, from Ulfin, on watch in the door-way.

"Lind!" I stooped, pulled her to her feet, and held her steady. "This is no time for riddles. Go on. Tell me all that happened."

She pressed the back of one wrist to her mouth, and in a moment or two managed to speak with some sort of composure. "When he came, he was angry. We had been expecting it, but nothing like this. He had heard what people were saying, that the High King had lain with her. You knew that, lord, you knew it was true . . . So King Lot stormed and raved at her, calling her whore, adulteress . . . We were all there, her women, but he cared nothing for that. And she – if she had talked sweetly to him, lied, even . . ." She swallowed. "It would have calmed him. He would have believed her. He never could resist her. That's what we all thought she would do, but she did not. She laughed in his face, and said, 'But do you not see how like you he is? Do you really think a boy like Arthur could get such a son?' He said, 'So it's true? You lay with him?' She said, 'Why not? You would not wed me. You took that little honey-miss, Morgan, instead of me. I was not yours, not then.' It made him angrier." She shivered. "If you had seen him then, even you would have been afraid."

"No doubt. Was she?"

"No. She never moved, just sat there, with the green gown and jewels, and smiled. You would have thought she was trying to make him angry."

"As she was," I said. "Go on, Lind, quickly."

She had control of herself now. I loosed her, and she stood, still trembling, but with her arms crossed on her breast, the way women stand when grieving. "He tore the hangings off the cradle. The baby started to cry. He said, 'Like me? The Pendragon brat is dark and I am dark. No more than that.' Then he turned on us – the women – and sent us away. We ran. He looked like a mad wolf. The others ran away, but I hid behind the curtains in the outer chamber. I thought – I thought –"

"You thought?"

She shook her head. Tears splashed, glinting, in the firelight. "That was when he did it. The baby stopped crying. There was a crash, as if the cradle fell over. The queen said, as calm as milk, 'You should have believed me. It was your own, by some slut you tumbled in the town. I told you there was a likeness.' And she laughed. He didn't speak for a bit. I could hear his breathing. Then he said, 'Dark hair, eyes turning dark. The brat *his* slut threw would be the same. Where is he, then, this bastard?' She said, 'He was a sickly child. He died.' The king said, 'You're lying still.' Then she said, very slowly, 'Yes, I am lying. I told the midwife to take him away, and find me a son I dared to show you. Perhaps I did wrong. I did it to save my name, and your honour. I hated the child. How could I want to bear any man's child but yours? I had hoped it was your son, not his, but it was his. It is true that he was sickly. Let us hope that he is dead, too, by this.' The king said, 'Let us do more than that. Let us make sure.' "

It was Ulfin this time who said quickly: "Yes? Go on."

The girl drew a shuddering breath. "She waited a moment, then she said – in a light, slighting sort of way, the way you dare a man to do something dangerous – 'And how could you do that, King of Lothian, except by killing every child born in this town since May-Day? I've told you I don't know where they took him.' He didn't even stop to think. He was breathing hard, like someone running. He said, 'Then that is just what I shall do. Yes, boys and girls alike. How else shall I know the truth of this accursed child-bed?' I would have run then, but I could not. The queen started to say something about the people, but he put her aside and came to the door and shouted for his captains. They came running. He shouted it at them, the same. Just those orders, every young baby in the town . . . I don't remember what was said. I thought I would faint, and fall, and they would see me. But I did hear the queen call out something in a weeping voice, something about orders from the High King, and how King Arthur would not brook the talk there had been since Luguvallium. Then the soldiers went. And the queen was not weeping at all, my lord, but laughing again, and she had her arms around King Lot. From the way she talked to him then, you would have thought he had done some noble deed. He began to laugh, too. He said, 'Yes, let them say it of Arthur, not of me. It will blacken his name more surely than anything I could ever do.' They went into her bedchamber then, and shut the door. I heard her call me, but I left her, and ran. She is evil, evil! I always hated her, but she is a witch, and she put me in fear."

"Nobody will hold you to blame for what your mistress did," I told her. "And now you can redeem it. Take me to where the High King's son is hidden."

She shrank and stared at that, with a wild look over her shoulder, as if she would run again.

"Come, Lind. If you feared Morgause, how much more should you fear me? You ran this way to protect him, did you not? You cannot do so alone. You cannot even protect yourself. But if you help me now, I shall protect you. You will need it. Listen."

Above us, the main gates of the castle opened with a crash. Through the thick boughs could be seen the movement of torches, bobbing down towards the main bridge. With the torches came the beat and clatter of hoofs and the shouting of orders.

Ulfin said sharply: "They're out. It's too late."

"No!" cried the girl. "Macha's cottage is the other way. They will come there last! I will show you, lord. This way."

Without another word she made for the door, with myself and Ulfin hard behind her.

Up the way we had come, across an open space, down another steep lane that twisted back towards the river, then along a river path deep in nettles where nothing moved but the rats a-scurry from the middens. It was very dark here, and we could not hurry, though the night breathed horror on the nape like a coursing hound. Behind us, away on the far side of the town, the sounds began. The barking of dogs first, the shouting of soldiers, the tramp of hoofs. Then doors slamming, women screaming, men shouting; and now and again the sharp clash of weapons. I have been in sacked cities, but this was different.

"Here!" gasped Lind, and turned into another twisting lane that led away from the river. From beyond the houses the dreadful sounds still made the night foul. We ran along the slippery mud of the lane, then up a flight of broken steps and out again into a narrow street. Here, all was quiet still, though I saw the glimmer of a light where some scared householder had waked to wonder at the sounds. We ran out from the end of the street into the grass of a field where a donkey was tethered, past an orchard of tended trees and the gaping door of a smithy, and reached a decent cottage that stood away from the rest behind a quickthorn hedge, with a strip of garden in front, and a dovecote, and a kennel beside the door.

The cottage door was wide open and swinging. The dog, at the end of his chain, raved and leaped like a mad thing. The doves were out of the cote and winnowing the dim air. There was no light in the cottage; no sound at all.

Lind ran through the garden, and stopped in the black doorway, peering in.

"Macha? Macha?"

A lantern stood on a ledge beside the door. No time to search for flint and tinder. I put the girl gently aside. "Take her outside," I said to Ulfin, and, as he obeyed me, picked up the lantern and swung it high. The flame tore up hissing from the wick, vivid and alive. I heard Lind gasp, then the sound caught in her throat. The brilliant light showed every corner of the cottage; the bed against the wall, the heavy table and bench; the crocks for food and oil; the stool, with the distaff flung down beside it and the wool unspinning; the clean hearth and the stone floor scrubbed white, except where the woman's body lay sprawled in the blood that had poured from her slit throat. The cradle by the bed was empty.

★   ★   ★

Lind and Ulfin waited at the edge of the orchard. The girl was silent now, shocked even out of her weeping; in the lantern's light her face showed blanched and sick. Ulfin had an arm round her, supporting her. He was very pale. The dog whined once, then sat back on his haunches and lifted his nose in a long, keening howl. It was echoed from the clashing, screaming darkness three streets away. And then again, nearer.

I shut the cottage door behind me. "I'm sorry, Lind. There's nothing to be done here. We should go. You know the tavern at the south gate? Will you lead us there? Avoid the middle of the town where the noise is. Try not to be afraid; I said I would protect you, and I will. For the time being you had better stay with us. Come now."

She did not move. "They've taken him! The baby, they got the baby. And they killed Macha!" She turned blind-eyed to me. "Why did they kill Macha? The king would never have ordered that. She was his leman!"

I looked at her thoughtfully. "Why, indeed?" Then, briskly, taking her by the shoulder and giving her a gentle shake: "Come now, child, we must not stay here. The men won't come this way again, but while you are in the streets you could be in danger. Take us to the south gate."

"*She* must have told them the way!" cried Lind. I might not even have spoken. "They came here first! I was too late! If you hadn't stopped me at the bridge –"

"Then you would be dead, too," said Ulfin crisply. He sounded quite normal, as if the night's horrors touched him not at all. "What could you have done, you and Macha? They'd have found you, and cut you down before you'd run to the end of the orchard yonder. Now, you'd best do as my lord says. That is, unless you want to go back to the queen and tell her what's happened here? You can depend on it, she's guessed where you went. They'll be looking for you soon."

It was brutal, but it worked. At the mention of Morgause she came to herself. She threw a last look of horror at the cottage, then pulled her hood about her face, and started back through the orchard trees.

I paused by the grieving dog and stooped to lay a hand on him. The dreadful howling stopped. He sat shivering. I drew my dagger and cut through the rope collar that bound him. He did not move, and I left him there.

Some score of children were taken that night. Someone – wise-woman or midwife – must have told the troopers where to look. By the time we got back to the tavern, by a roundabout route through the deserted outskirts of the town, the horror was over, the troopers gone. No one accosted us, nor even seemed to notice us. The streets were full and clamorous. People ran aimlessly about, or peered in terror from dark doorways. Crowds gathered here and there, centred on some wailing woman, and stunned or angry man. These were poor folk, with no way of withstanding their king's will. His royal anger had swept through the town, and left them nothing to do but grieve.

And curse. I heard Lot's name: they had after all been his

troopers. But with Lot's name came Arthur's. The lie was already at work, and with time, one could guess, would supersede the truth. Arthur was High King, and the mainspring of good and evil.

One thing they had been spared; there had been no holocaust of blood. Macha's was the only death. The soldiers had lifted the babies from their beds, and ridden off with them into the darkness. Except for a broken head or two, where a father had resisted them, they had done no violence.

So Beltane told me, gasping it out. He met us in the tavern doorway, fully clothed, and trembling with agitation. He seemed not even to notice Lind's presence. He seized me by the arm and poured out his story of the night's happenings. The clearest thing to emerge from it was that the troopers had not long ridden by with the infants.

"Alive still, and crying you may imagine, Master Emrys!" He wrung his hands, lamenting. "Terrible, terrible, these are savage times indeed. All the talk of Arthur's orders, who is to believe such a tale? But hush, say nothing! The sooner we are on the road, the better. This is no place for honest traders. I would have gone before this, Master Emrys, but I stayed for you. I thought you might have been called on to help, some of the men were hurt, they say. They will drown the children, did you know? Dear gods, and to think that only today . . . Ah, Casso, good lad! I took the liberty of saddling your beasts, Master Emrys. I made sure you would agree with me. We should go now. I have paid the landlord, all's done, you may settle with me on the road . . . And you'll see I bought mules for ourselves. I have meant to for so long, and today with the good fortune at the castle . . . What a mercy, what a mercy! But that pretty lady, who could have thought – but no more of that here! Walls have ears, and these are dreadful times. Who is this?" He was peering short-sightedly at Lind, who clung to Ulfin's arm, half fainting. "Why, surely – is it not the young damsel – ?"

"Later," I said quickly. "No questions now. She is coming with us. Meantime, Master Beltane, thank you. You are a good friend. Yes, we should go without delay. Casso, shift the baggage, will you, please? The girl will ride on the pack-mule. Ulfin, you say you have a friend in the guard-house. Ride ahead, and talk us through. Find which way the troopers went. Bribe the guards if you have to."

As it happened, there was no need. The gates were just being closed when we got there, but the guards made no difficulty about letting us through. Indeed, from the muttered talk that could be overheard, they were as shocked as the townspeople at what had happened, and found it quite understandable that peaceful traders should pack up hurriedly and leave the town in the middle of the night.

A short way down the road, out of earshot of the guard-house, I drew rein.

"Master Beltane, I have business to see to. No, not back in the town, so have no fear for me. I'll join you later. Do you ride on to the tavern we stayed at on our way north, the one with the bush of broom outside – remember? Wait for us there. Lind, you will be safe with these men. Don't be afraid, but you will do well to keep silent till I return. Do you understand?" She nodded dumbly. "At the Bush of Broom, then, Master Beltane?"

"Of course, of course. I cannot say I understand, but perhaps in the morning –"

"In the morning, I hope, all will be made clear. For now, good night."

They clattered off. I brought my mule's head up hard. "Ulfin?"

"They took the east road, my lord."

So by the east road we went.

★   ★   ★

Indifferently mounted as we were, we would not normally have expected to catch up with hard-riding troops. But our mounts were rested, while Lot's men must needs, I thought, still be using the poor beasts that had borne them from the battlefields in the south.

So when, after half an hour's riding, we caught no glimpse, nor heard any sound of them, I drew rein, and turned in the saddle.

"Ulfin. A word with you."

He nudged his mule alongside. In that windy darkness I could not see his face, but something came from him that I could sense. He was afraid.

He had not been afraid before, even at Macha's cottage. And here there could only be one source of fear: myself.

I said to him: "Why did you lie to me?"

"My lord –"

"The troopers did not come this way, did they?"

I heard him swallow. "No, my lord."

"Then which way?"

"To the sea. I think – it was thought they were going to put the children into a boat, and set it adrift. The king had said he would put them into God's hands, so that the innocent ones –"

"Pah!" I said. "Lot speak of God's hands? He feared what the people might do if they saw the babies' throats cut, that is all. No doubt he'll have it put about that Arthur ordered the slaughter, but that he himself mitigated the sentence, and gave the babes their chance. The shore. Where?"

"I don't know."

"Is that true?"

"Indeed, indeed it is. There are several ways. No one knew for sure. This is the truth, my lord."

"Yes. If anyone had known, some of the menfolk might have tried to follow. So we go back and take the first road to the shore. We can ride along the beach to look for them. Come."

But as I swung my mule's head round, his hand came down on the rein. It was something he would hardly have dared to do, except in desperation. "My lord – forgive me. What are you going to do? After all this . . . Are you still trying to find the child?"

"What do you think? Arthur's son?"

"But Arthur himself wants him dead!"

So that was it. I should have guessed long since. My mule jibbed as the reins jerked in my hands. "So you were listening at Caerleon. You heard what he said to me that night."

"Yes." This time I could hardly hear him. "To refuse to murder a child, lord, that is one thing. But when the murder is done for you –"

"There is no need to struggle to prevent it? Perhaps not. But since you were eavesdropping that night, you may also have heard me tell the King that I take orders from an authority beyond his own. And so far my gods have told or shown me nothing. Do you imagine they want us to emulate Lot, and his bitch of a queen? And you have heard the calumny they have thrown upon Arthur. For his honour's sake, even just for his peace of mind, he has to know the truth. I am here for him, to watch and to report. Whatever is to be done, I shall do it. Now take your hand off my rein."

He obeyed. I kicked the mule to a gallop. We pounded back along the road.

This was the way we had originally come to Dunpeldyr by daylight. I tried to remember what we had seen then of the coast-line. It is a coast of high cliffs, with wide sandy bays between them. One great headland jutted out about a mile from the town, and even at low tide it seemed unlikely that a man could ride round it. But just beyond the headland was a track leading towards the sea. From there – and the tide, I reckoned, was well out now – we could ride the whole way back along the shore to the mouth of the Tyne.

Faintly, but perceptibly, the night was slackening towards dawn. It was possible to see our way.

Now a cairn of stones loomed on our right. On a flat slab at its base a bundle of feathers stirred in the wind, and the mules showed the whites of their eyes; I supposed they could smell the blood. And here was the track, leading off across rough grassland towards the sea. We swung into it. Presently the track sloped downhill, and there before us was the shore, and the grey murmur of the sea.

The vast headland loomed on our right; to the left the sand stretched level and grey. We turned that way, and struck once more to a gallop.

The tide was out, the rippled sand packed hard. To our right the sea threw a kind of grey light up to the cloudy sky. Some way to the north, set back in the midst of that luminous grey, was the mass of the great rock where the lighthouse stands. The light was red and steady. Soon, I thought, as our mules pounded along, we should be able to distinguish the looming shape of Dunpeldyr's crag to land-ward, and the level reaches of the bay where the river meets the sea.

Ahead of us a low headland jutted out, its seaward end black and broken, with the water whitening at its edge. We rounded it, the mules splashing fetlock deep through the creaming surf. Now we could see Dunpeldyr, a mile or two away inland, still alive with lights. Ahead of us lay the last stretch of sand. Shadowy trees marked the river's course, and the ashen glimmer where its waters spread out to meet the sea. And along the river's edge, where the sea-road ran, bobbed the torches of horsemen heading back at a steady canter for the town. The work was done.

My mule came willingly to a halt. Ulfin's stopped, blowing, half a length to the rear. Under their hoofs the ebbtide dragged at the grating sand.

After a while I spoke. "You have your wish, it seems."

"My lord, forgive me. All I could think of –"

"What do I forgive? Am I to bear you a grudge for serving your master rather than me?"

"I should have trusted you to know what you were doing."

"When I have not known myself? For all I know, you have been wiser than I. At least, since the thing is done, and it seems Arthur will bear some part of the blame for it, we can be forgiven for hoping that Morgause's child is dead with the rest."

"You mean – you think it may not be? Ah, look, my lord."

I swung round to look where he pointed.

Away out to sea, beyond a low reef of rocks at the edge of the bay, a sail showed, a pale crescent, glimmering faintly in the sea-light. Then it cleared the reef, and the boat moved out to sea. The wind, steadily off-shore, filled the sail, taking the boat out with the speed of a gliding gull. Herod's mercy for the innocents lay there, in the movement of wind and sea, as the drifting boat dipped and skimmed, carrying its hapless cargo fast away from shore.

The sail melted into the grey and vanished. The sea sighed and murmured under the wind. The little waves lapped on the rock and dragged the sand and broken shells seaward past the mules' feet. On the ridge beside us the bent-grass whistled in the wind. Then, above these sounds, I heard it, very faintly, carried to us over the water in a lull of the wind; a thin, keening wail, as unhuman as the song of the grey seals at their meeting-haunts. It dwindled as we listened; then suddenly came again, piercingly loud, straight over us, as if some soul, already leaving the doomed boat, had flown homing for the shore. Ulfin shied as if from a ghost, and made the sign against evil; but it was only a gull sweeping over us, high in the wind.

Ulfin did not speak again, and I sat my mule in silence. Something was there in the dark; something that weighed me down with grief. Not the children's fate only; certainly not the presumed death of Arthur's child. But the dim sight of that sail moving away over the grey water, and the sorrowful sounds that came out of the dark, found an echo somewhere in the very core of my soul.

I sat there without moving, while the wind dwindled to silence, and the water lapped on the rock, and on the sea the wailing died away.

BOOK 2

Camelot

Much as I would have liked to do so, I did not leave Dunpeldyr straight away. Arthur was still in Linnuis, and would want my report, not only on the massacre itself but on what happened afterwards. Ulfin, I think, expected to be dismissed, but, reckoning that to lodge in Dunpeldyr itself would hardly be safe, I stayed on at the Bush of Broom, and so kept Ulfin with me to act as messenger and connecting-file. Beltane, who had been understandably shaken by the night's events, went south straight away with Casso. I kept my promise to the latter: it had been a promise made on impulse, but I have found that such impulses commonly have a source which should not be denied. So I talked with the goldsmith, and easily persuaded him of the advantages of a servant who could read and write; I made it clear, besides, that I was letting Casso go to him for less than his cost to me on condition that my wish was met. I found I had not needed to insist; Beltane, that kindly man, promised with pleasure to teach Casso himself, and then they both took leave of me and went south, aiming once more for York. With them went Lind, who, it seemed, had met a man in York who might protect her; he was a small merchant, a respectable fellow who had spoken of marriage, but whom, for fear of the queen, she had rejected. I took leave of them, and settled down to see what the next few days would bring.

Some two or three days after the terrible night of Lot's return, the wreckage of the boat began to come ashore, and with it the bodies. It was apparent that the boat had driven on rock somewhere and had been broken up by the tide. The poor women who went down to the beach fell to a kind of dreadful squabbling as to which baby was which. The shore was haunted by these wretched women. They wept a great deal and said very little; it was apparent that they were accustomed, like beasts, to take what their lords handed out to them, whether alms or blows. It was also apparent to me, sitting in the alehouse shadows and listening, that, in spite of the tale about Arthur's responsibility for the massacre, most folk laid the blame squarely where it belonged, with Morgause, and with Lot, befooled and angry about it. And, because men are men everywhere, they were inclined not to blame their king overmuch for his hasty reaction to that anger. Any man, they were soon saying, would have done the same. Come home to find your wife delivered of another man's boy, and small blame to you if you lost your temper. And as for the wholesale slaughter, well, a king was a king, and had a throne to consider as well as his bed. And speaking of kings, had he not made kingly reparation? For this, wisely, Lot had done; and however much the women might still weep and mourn, the men on the whole accepted Lot's deed, along with the golden recompense that followed it, as the natural action of a wronged and angry king.

And Arthur? I put the question one evening, casually, into one such conversation. If the rumours that were being put about were true, of the High King's involvement in the killing, was not Arthur himself similarly justified? If the child Mordred was indeed his bastard by his half-sister, and a hostage to fortune with King Lot (who had not always been his keenest friend), surely it could be said that policy could justify the deed? What more likely way could Arthur find of keeping the great King of Lothian his friend, than to ensure the death of the cuckoo in the nest, and take the responsibility for its killing?

At this there were murmurs and head-shakings, which resolved at length into a sort of qualified assent. So I threw in another thought. Everyone knew that in matters like this of policy – and high and secret policy, with a great country like Lothian concerned – everyone knew it was not the young Arthur who made the civil decisions; it was his chief adviser, Merlin. Depend upon it, this was the decision of a ruthless and tortuous mind, not of a brave young soldier who spent his every waking moment in the field against Britain's enemies, and who had little time for bedroom politics – except, naturally, those that every man could find time for . . .

So, like a seed of grass, the idea was sown, and as quickly as the grass it spread and grew; so that by the time the news came of Arthur's next victorious engagement the facts of the massacre had been accepted, and the guilt for it, whether of Merlin, Arthur or Lot, almost condoned. It was plain that the High King – may God preserve him against the enemy – had had little to do with it except see its necessity. Besides, the babies, most of them, would have died in infancy of one thing or another, and that without any gifts of gold such as Lot had handed to the bereaved fathers. Moreover, most of the women were soon bearing again, and had perforce to forget their tears.

The queen, also. King Lot was now seen to have behaved in a truly kingly fashion. He had swept home in anger, removed the bastard (whether by Arthur's orders or his own), then got a true heir in the dead boy's place, and ridden off again, his loyalty to the High King undiminished. Some of the bereaved fathers, being offered places in the troop, rode with him, confirmed in their own loyalty. Morgause herself, far from appearing cowed by her lord's violence, or apprehensive of the people's anger, looked (on the one or two occasions when I saw her riding out) sleek and pleased with herself. Whatever the people may have believed about her part in the massacre, she was safe from their illwill now that she was said to be carrying the kingdom's true heir.

If she grieved for her lost son, she gave no sign of it. It showed, the people said, that she had in truth been seduced by Arthur, and could never have wanted the bastard she had been made to bear. But to me, watching and waiting in drab anonymity, it began to mean something quite different. I did not believe that the child Mordred had been in that boat-load of slaughtered innocents at all. I re-membered the three armed men, sober and purposeful, who had gone back into the castle by the postern entrance just before Lot's return – and after the coming of Morgause's messenger from the south. The woman Macha, too, lying dead in her cottage beside the empty cradle with her throat cut. And Lind, running out into the dark without Morgause's knowledge or sanction, to warn Macha and take the child Mordred to safety.

Piecing it together, I thought I knew what had happened. Macha had been chosen to foster Mordred because she had borne Lot a bastard boy; it might even have pleased Morgause to watch the baby killed; she had laughed, Lind had told us. So, with Mordred safe, and the changeling ready for the slaughter, Morgause had waited for Lot's return. As soon as she had news of it, her men-at-arms had been sent with orders to dispatch Mordred to yet another safe foster-home, and to kill Macha, who, if her own baby were to suffer, might be tempted to betray the queen. And now Lot was pacified, the town was quiet, and somewhere, I was sure, the child who was Morgause's weapon of power, grew in safety.

After Lot had ridden to rejoin Arthur, I sent Ulfin south again, but myself stayed on in Lothian, watching and waiting. With Lot out of the way, I moved back into Dunpeldyr, and tried, in every way I could, to find some clue to where Mordred could now be hidden. What I would have done if I had found him, I do not know, but the god did not lay that burden on me. So I waited for fully four months in that squalid little town, and though I walked on the shore by starlight and sunlight and spoke to my god in every tongue and with every way I knew, I saw nothing, either by daylight or in dream, to guide me to Arthur's son.

In time I came to believe that I might have been wrong; that even Morgause could not be so evil, and that Mordred had perished with the other innocents in that midnight sea.

So at length, as autumn slid into the first chills of winter, and news came that the fighting in Linnuis was done, and Lot would soon be on his way home once more, I thankfully left Dunpeldyr. Arthur would be at Caerleon for Christmas, and would look for me there. I paused only once on my journey, to spend a few nights with Blaise in Northumbria and give him the news, then I travelled south, to be there when the King came home.

★   ★   ★

He came back in the second week of December, with frost on the ground, and the children out gathering the holly and ivy for decking the Christmas feast. He barely waited to bathe and change from the ride before he sent for me. He received me in the room where we had talked before we parted. This time the door to the bedroom was shut, and he was alone.

He had changed a good deal in the months since Pentecost. Taller, yes, by half a head – it is an age when youths shoot up like barley-stalks – and with breadth to go with it, and the hard lean brownness got from the soldier's life he was leading. But this was not the real change. That was in authority. His manner showed now that he knew what he was doing and where he was going.

But for that, the interview might have been an echo of the one I had had with the younger Arthur, on the night of Mordred's begetting.

"They say that I ordered this abominable thing!" He had hardly troubled to greet me. He strode about the room, the same strong, light, lion's-prowl of a walk, but the strides were a hand-span longer. The room was a cage restraining him. "When you know yourself how, in this very room, I said, no, leave it to the god. And now this!"

"It's what you wanted, isn't it?"

"All those deaths? Don't be a fool, would I have done it like that? Or would you?"

The question needed no reply, and got none. I said merely: "Lot was never remarkable for his wisdom and restraint, and besides, he was in a rage. You might say the action was suggested to him, or at least encouraged, from without."

He threw me a quick, smouldering look. "By Morgause? So I understand."

"I gather Ulfin has told you all the story? Did he also tell you of his own services in the matter?"

"That he tried to mislead you, and let fate overtake the children? Yes, he told me that." A brief pause. "It was wrong, and I said so, but it's hard to be angry at devotion. He thought – he knew that I would have been easy at the baby's death. But those other children . . . Within a month of the vows I made to protect the people, and my name a hissing in the streets . . ."

"I think you can comfort yourself. I doubt if many men believe that you had anything to do with it."

"No matter." He almost snapped it over his shoulder. "Some will, and that is enough. As for Lot, he had an excuse of a kind; an excuse, that is, that common men can understand. But I? Can I publish it abroad that Merlin the prophet told me the child might be a danger to me, so I had it murdered, and others along with it for fear it should escape the net? What sort of king does this make of me? Lot's sort?"

"I can only repeat that I doubt if you are held to blame. Morgause's women were there within hearing, remember, and the guards knew where their orders came from. Lot's escort, too – they would know he was riding home bent on revenge, and I cannot imagine that Lot remained silent as to his intentions. I don't know what Ulfin has told you, but when I left Dunpeldyr most people were quoting Lot's orders as responsible for the massacre, and those who thought you ordered it, think you did so on my advice."

"So?" he said. He really was very angry. "I am the kind of king who cannot even decide for myself? If there is to be blame allotted for this between us, then I should take it, and not you. You know that well enough. You remember as well as I do exactly what was said."

There was no reply to that, either, and I made none. He prowled up the room and back again before he went on:

"Whoever gave the order, you can say if you like that I feel guilt in this. You would be right. But, by all the gods in heaven and hell, I would not have acted like that! This is the kind of thing that lives with you, and after you! I shall not be remembered as the king who beat the Saxons out of Britain, but as the man who played Herod in Dunpeldyr and murdered the children!" He stopped. "What is there in that to smile at?"

"I doubt if you need trouble yourself about the name you will leave behind you."

"So you say."

"So I said." The change in tense, or something about my tone, arrested him. I met his look, and held it. "Yes, I, Merlin, said so. I said so when I had power, and it is true. You are right to be distressed at this abomination, and you are right, too, to take some of the blame to yourself. But if this thing goes down in story as your act, you will still be absolved of blame. You can believe me. What else is to come will absolve you of anything."

The anger had died, and he was thinking. He spoke slowly. "Do you mean that some danger will come of the child's birth and death?

Something so terrible that men will see the murder as justified?"

"I did not mean that, no –"

"You made another prophecy, remember. You hinted to me – no, you told me – that Morgause's child might be a danger to me. Well, now the child is dead. Could this have been the danger? This smear on my name?" He paused, struck. "Or perhaps some day one of the men whose sons were murdered will wait for me with a knife in the dark? Is that the kind of thing you had in mind?"

"I told you, I had nothing specific in mind. I did not say that the child 'might' be a danger to you, Arthur. I said he would. And, if my word is to be trusted, directly so, and not by a knife in another man's hand."

He was as still, now, as he had been restless before. He scowled at me, intent. "You mean that the massacre failed of its purpose? That the child – Mordred, did you say? – is still alive?"

"I have come to think so."

He drew a quick breath. "Then he was saved, somehow, from that wreck?"

"It's possible. Either he was saved by chance, and is living somewhere, unknowing and unknown, as you did through your childhood – in which case you may encounter him some day, as Laius did Oedipus, and fall to him in all ignorance."

"I'll risk that. Everyone falls to someone, sometime. Or?"

"Or he was never in the boat at all."

He gave a slow nod. "Morgause, yes. It would fit. What do you know?"

I told him the little I knew, and the conclusions I had drawn. "She must have known," I finished, "that Lot's reactions would be violent. We know she wanted to keep the child, and why. She would hardly have put her own child at risk on Lot's return. It's clear enough that she engineered the whole thing. Lind gave us more details later on. We know that she goaded Lot into the furious anger that dictated the massacre; we know, too, that she started the rumour that you were to blame. So what has she done? She has put Lot's fears to rest, and made her own position secure. And I believe, from watching her, and from what I know of her, that at the same time she has contrived –"

"To keep her hostage to fortune." The flush had died from his skin. He looked cold, his eyes like slates with cold rain on them. This was an Arthur that other men had seen, but never I. How many Saxons had seen those eyes just before they died? He said, bitterly: "I have been well paid already for that night of lust. I wish you had let me kill her then. That is one lady who had better never come near me again, unless she comes on her knees, and in sack-cloth." His tone made a vow of it. Then it changed. "When did you get back from the north?"

"Yesterday."

"*Yesterday*? I thought . . . I understood that this abomination took place months ago."

"Yes. I stayed to watch events. Then after I began to make my guesses, I waited to see if Morgause might make some move to show me where the child was hidden. If Lind had been able to go back to her, and had dared to help me . . . but that was impossible. So I stayed until the news came that you had left Linnuis, and that Lot would soon be on his way home again. I knew that once he came home I could do nothing, so I came away."

"I see. All that way, and now I keep you on your feet and rail at you as if you were a guard caught sleeping on duty. Will you forgive me?"

"There's nothing to forgive. I have rested. But I should be glad to sit now. Thank you."

This as he pulled a chair for me, and then sat himself in the big chair beyond the massive table. "You've said nothing in your reports about this idea that Mordred was still alive. And Ulfin never mentioned it as a possibility."

"I don't think it crossed his mind. It was mainly after he had gone, and I had time to think and watch, myself, that I thought back and reached my own conclusion. There's still no proof, of course, that I am right. And nothing but the memory of an old foreboding to tell me whether or not it matters. But I can tell you one thing; from the idle contentment that the King's prophet feels in his bones these days, any threat from Mordred, direct or otherwise, will not show itself for a long time to come."

He gave me a look where no shadow of anger remained. A smile sparked deep in his eyes. "So, I have time."

"You have time. This was bad, and you were right to be angry;

but it is already barely remembered, and soon will be forgotten in the blaze of your victories. Concerning them, I hear talk of nothing else. So put this aside now, and think about the next. Time spent looking back in anger is time wasted."

The tension broke up at last in the familiar smile. "I know. A maker, never a breaker. How often have you told me? Well, I'm only mortal. I break first, to make room . . . All right, I'll forget it. There is plenty to think about and plan for, without wasting time on what is done. In fact" – the smile deepened – "I heard that King Lot is planning a move northward to his kingdom there. Perhaps, in spite of laying the blame on me, he feels uncomfortable in Dun-peldyr . . . ? The Orkneys are fertile islands, they tell me, and fine in the summer months, but tend to be cut off from the main all winter?"

"Unless the sea freezes."

"And that," he said, with most unkingly satisfaction, "will surely be beyond even Morgause's powers. So distance will help us to forget Lot and his works . . ."

His hand moved among the papers and tablets on the table. I was thinking that I should have looked further afield for Mordred: if Lot had told his queen his plans for taking the court northward, she might have made some arrangement for sending the child there. But Arthur was speaking again.

"Do you know anything about dreams?"

I was startled. "Dreams? Well, I have had them."

A glint of amusement. "Yes, that was a foolish question, wasn't it? I meant, can you tell me what they mean, other men's dreams?"

"I doubt it. When my own mean something, they are clear beyond doubt. Why, has your sleep been troubled?"

"For many nights now." He hesitated, shifting the things on the table. "It seems a trivial thing to trouble over, but the dream is so vivid, and it's always the same . . ."

"Tell me."

"I am alone, and out hunting. No hounds, just myself and my horse, hard on the track of a stag. This part varies a bit, but I always know that the chase has been going on for many hours. Then, just as we seem to be catching up with the stag, it leaps into a brake of trees and vanishes. At the same moment my horse falls dead beneath me. I am thrown to the turf. Sometimes I wake there, but when I go back to sleep again, I am still lying on the turf, by the bank of a stream, with the dead horse beside me. Then suddenly I hear hounds coming, a whole pack of them, and I sit up and look about me. Now, I have had the dream so many times that, even while dreaming, I know what to expect, and I am afraid . . . It is not a pack of hounds that comes, but one beast – a strange beast, which, though I have seen it so many times, I can't describe. It comes crashing through the bracken and underbrush, and the noise it makes is like thirty couple of hounds questing. It takes no heed of me or my horse, but stops at the stream and drinks, and then goes on and is lost in the forest."

"Is that the end?" I asked, as he paused.

"No. The end varies, too, but always, after the questing beast, comes a knight, alone and on foot, who tells me that he, too, has killed a horse under him in the quest. Each time – each night it happens – I try to ask him what the beast is, and what is the quest, but just as he is about to tell me, my groom comes up with a fresh horse for me, and the knight, seizing it without courtesy, mounts and prepares to ride away. And I find myself laying hands on his rein to stop him, and begging him to let me undertake the quest, 'for,' I say, 'I am the High King, and it is for me to undertake any quest of danger.' But he strikes my hand aside, saying, 'Later. Later, when you need to, you may find me here, and I shall answer for what I have done.' And he rides away, leaving me alone in the forest. Then I wake, still with this sense of fear. Merlin, what does it mean?"

I shook my head. "That I can't tell you. I might be glib with you, and say that this was a lesson in humility: that even the High King does not need to take all responsibility –"

"You mean stand back and let you take the blame for the massacre? No, that's too clever by half, Merlin!'

"I said I was being glib, didn't I? I have no idea what your dream meant. Probably nothing more than a mixture of worry and indigestion. But one thing I can tell you, and it's the same one that I keep repeating; what dangers lie in front of you, you will surmount, and reach glory; and whatever has happened, whatever you have done, or will do, you will die a worshipful death. I shall fade and vanish

like music when the harp is dead, and men will call my end shameful. But you will live on, in men's imagination and hearts.
Meanwhile, you have years, and time enough. So tell me what
happened in Linnuis."

We talked for a long time. Eventually he came back to the
immediate future.

"Until the ways open with spring, we can get on with the work
here at Caerleon. You'll stay here for that. But in the spring I want
you to start work on my new headquarters." I looked a query, and
he nodded. "Yes, we spoke of this before. What was right in
Vortigern's time, or even in Ambrosius', will not serve in a year or
so from this. The picture is changing, over to the east. Come to the
map and let me show you . . . That man of yours now, Gereint,
there's a find. I've sent for him. He's the kind of man I need by me.
The information he sent to Linnuis was beyond price. He told you
about Eosa and Cerdic? We're gathering what information we can,
but I'm sure he is right. The latest news is that Eosa is back in
Germany, and he's promising the sun, moon and stars, as well as a
settled Saxon kingdom, to any who will join him . . ."

For a while we discussed Gereint's information, and Arthur told
me what had newly come from those sources. Then he went on:
"He's right about the Gap, too, of course. We started work up there
as soon as I got your reports. I sent Torre up . . . I believe the next
push will come from the north. I'm expecting word from Caw and
from Urbgen. But in the long run it will be here, in the south-west,
that we have to make the stand for good and all. With Rutupiae as
their base, and the Shore behind them, call it 'kingdom' or not, the
big threat must come this way, here and here . . ." His finger was
moving on the relief map of clay. "We came back this way from
Linnuis. I got an idea of the lie of the land. But no more now,
Merlin. They're making new maps for me, and we can sit over
them later. Do you know the country thereabouts?"

"No. I have travelled that road, but my mind was on other
things."

"There's little haste yet. If we can start in April, or May, and you
work your usual miracle, that should be soon enough. Think about
it for me, and then go and look when the time comes. Will you do
that?"

"Willingly. I have already looked . . . No, I meant in my mind. I've remembered something. There's a hill that commands this whole tract of country here . . . As far as I remember, it's flat-topped, and big enough to house an army, or a city, or whatever you want of it. And high enough. You can see Ynys Witrin from it — the Isle of Glass — and all the signal chain, and again clear for many miles both to south and west."

"Show me," he said sharply.

"Somewhere here." I placed a finger. "I can't be exact, and I don't think the map is, either. But I think this must be the stream it lies on."

"Its name?"

"I don't know its name. It's a hill with the stream curling round it, and the stream is called, I think, the Camel. The hill was a fortress before the Romans ever came to Britain, so even the early Britons must have seen it as a strategic point. They held it against the Romans."

"Who took it?"

"Eventually. Then they fortified it in their turn and held it."

"Ah. Then there is a road."

"Surely. This one, perhaps, that runs past the Lake from the Glass Isle."

So I showed him on the map, and he looked, and talked, and went on the prowl again, and then the servants brought supper and lights and he straightened, pushing the hair back out of his eyes, and came up out of his planning as a diver comes up out of water.

"Well, it will have to wait till Christmas is past. But go as soon as you can, Merlin, and tell me what you think. You shall have what help you need, you know that. And now sup with me, and I'll tell you all about the fight at the Blackwater. I've told it already so many times that it's grown till I hardly recognise it myself. But once more, to you, is not unseemly."

"Obligatory. And I promise you that I shall believe every word."

He laughed. "I always knew I could rely on you."

2

It was on a sweet, still day of spring when I turned aside from the
road and saw the hill called Camelot.

That was its name later; now it was known as Caer Camel, after
the small stream that wound through the level lands surrounding it,
and curved around near its base. It was, as I had told Arthur, a
flat-topped hill, not high, but high enough over the surrounding
flatlands to give a clear view on every hand, and steep-sided enough
to allow for formidable defences. It was easy to see why the Celts,
and after them the Romans, had chosen it as a stronghold. From its
highest point the view in almost every direction is tremendous. To
the east a few rolling hills block the vision, but to south and west the
eye can travel for miles, and northwards, also, as far as the coast.
On the north-west side the sea comes within eight miles or
so, the tides spreading and filtering through the marshy flatlands
that feed the great Lake where stands the Isle of Glass. This island,
or group of islands, lies on its glassy water like a recumbent goddess; indeed it has from time immemorial been dedicated to the
Goddess herself, and her shrine stands close beside the king's palace.
Above it the great beacon top of the Tor is plainly visible, and,
many miles beyond that, right on the coast of the Severn Channel,
may be seen the next beacon point of Brent Knoll.

The hills of the Glass Isle, with the low and waterlogged levels
surrounding them, are known as the Summer Country. The king
was a man called Melwas, young, and a staunch supporter of
Arthur; he gave me lodging during my first surveys of Caer Camel,
and seemed pleased that the High King should plan to form his main
stronghold at the edge of his territory. He was deeply interested in
the maps I showed him, and promised help of every kind, from the

loan of local workmen to a pledge of defence, should that be needed, while the work was in progress.

King Melwas had offered to show me the place himself, but for my first survey I preferred to be alone, so managed to put him off with civilities of some kind. He and his young men rode with me for the first part of the way, then turned aside into a track that was little more than a causeway through the marshlands, and went cheerfully off to their day's sport. That is great country for hunting; it teems with wildfowl of every kind. I saw a lucky omen in the fact that, almost as soon as they left me, King Melwas flew his falcon at a flock of immigrant birds coming in from the south-east, and, within seconds, the hawk had killed cleanly and come straight back to the master's fist. Then, with shouting and laughter, the band of young men rode off among the willows, and I went on my way alone.

I had been right in supposing that a road would lead to the once-Roman fortress of Caer Camel. The road leaves Ynys Witrin by a causeway which skirts the base of the Tor, spans a narrow arm of the Lake, and reaches a strip of dry, hard land stretching towards the east. There it joins the old Fosse Way, then after a while turns south again for the village at the foot of Caer Camel. This had originally been a Celtic settlement, then the *vicus* to the Roman fortress, its occupants scraping some sort of living from the soil, and retiring uphill within walls in times of danger. Since the fortress had decayed, their lives had been hard indeed. As well as the ever-present danger to the south and east, they even had, in bad years, to beat off the people of the Summer Country, when the wetlands around Ynys Witrin ceased to provide anything but fish and marsh birds, and the young men craved excitement beyond the confines of their own territory. There was little to be seen as I rode between the tumbledown huts with their rotting thatch; here and there eyes watched me from a dark doorway, or a woman's voice called shrilly to her child. My horse splashed through the mud and dung, forded the Camel knee-deep, then at last I turned him uphill through the trees, and took the steep curve of the chariot-way at a plunging canter.

Even though I knew what to expect, I was amazed at the size of the summit. I came up through the ruins of the south-west gateway into a great field, tilted to southward, but sloping sharply ahead of me towards a ridge with a high point west of centre. I walked my horse slowly up towards this. The field, or rather plateau, was scarred and pitted with the remains of buildings, and surrounded on all sides by deep ditching, and the relics of revetments and fortified walls. Whins and brambles matted the broken walls, and mole-hills had heaved up the cracked paving-stones. Stone lay everywhere, good Roman stone, squared in some local quarry. Beyond the ruined outworks the sides of the hill went down steeply, and on them trees, once lopped to ground level, had put out saplings and thickets of suckers. Between these the scarps were quilted with a winter network of bramble and thorn. A beaten pathway through sprouting fern and nettle led to a gap in the north wall. Following this, I could see where, half down the northern hillside, a spring lay deep among the trees. This must be the Lady's Well, the good spring dedicated to the Goddess. The other spring, the main water supply for the fortress, lay halfway up the steep road to the north-east gateway, at the hill's opposite corner from the chariot road I had taken. It seemed that cattle were still watered there: as I watched, I saw a herd, slow-moving, come up through the steep gap, and spread out to graze in the sunshine, with a faint, off-note chiming of bells. Their shepherd followed them, a slight figure whom at first I took for a boy, then saw, from the way he moved, using his staff to lean upon, that it was an old man.

I turned my horse's head that way, and walked him carefully through the tumble of stonework. A magpie got up and flew, scolding. The old man looked up. He stopped short, startled, and, I thought, apprehensive. I raised a hand to him in a sign of greeting. Something about the solitary and unarmed horseman must have reassured him, for after a moment he moved to a low wall that lay full in the sun, and sat down to wait for me.

I dismounted, letting my horse graze.

"Greetings, father."

"And to you." It was not much more than a mumble, in the strong burring accent of the district. He peered at me suspiciously, through eyes clouded with cataract. "You're a stranger to these parts."

"I come from the west."

This was no reassurance. It seemed that the folk hereabouts had

had too long a history of war. "Why'd you leave the road, then? What do you want up here?"

"I came on the King's behalf, to look at the fortress walls."

"Again?"

As I stared at him in surprise, he drove his stick into the turf, as if making a claim, and spoke with a kind of quavering anger. "This was our land before the king came, and it's ours again in spite of him. Why don't 'ee let us keep it so?"

"I don't think –" I began, then stopped, on a sudden thought. "You speak of a king. Which king?"

"I don't know his name."

"Melwas? Or Arthur?"

"Maybe. I tell you I don't know. What do you want here?"

"I am the King's man. I come from him –"

"Aye. To raise the fortress walls again, then take away our cattle and kill our children and rape our women."

"No. To build a stronghold here to protect your cattle and children and women."

"It did not protect them before."

There was silence. The old man's hand shook on his stick. The sun was hot on the grass. My horse grazed delicately round a thistle head growing low and circular, like a splayed wheel. An early butterfly alighted on a purple head of clover. A lark rose, singing.

"Old man," I said gently, "there has been no fortress here in your lifetime, nor in your father's. What walls stood here and looked south and north and westward over the waters? What king came to storm them?"

He looked at me for a few moments, his head shaking with the tremor of age. "It's a story, only a story, master. My granda told it to me, how the folk lived here with cattle and goats and sweet grazing, and wove the cloth and tilled the high field, until the king came and drove them down through yon road into the valley bottom, and there was a grave for them all that day, as wide as a river and as deep as the hollow hill, where they laid the king himself to rest, and his time coming soon after."

"Which hill was that? Ynys Witrin?"

"What? How should they carry him there? It's a foreign country there. They call it the Summer Country, for all it's a sheet of lake water all the year round save through the dry time of midsummer. No, they made a way into the cave and laid him there, and with him the ones who were drowned with him." A sudden, high cackle. "Drowned in the Lake, and the folk watched and made no move to save him. It was the Goddess took him, and his fine captains along with him. Who could have stopped her? They say it was three days before she gave him back, and then he came naked, without either crown or sword." The cackling laugh again, as he nodded. "Your king had best make his peace with her, tell him that."

"He will. When did this happen?"

"A hundred years ago. Two hundred. How would I know?"

Another silence, while I assessed it. What I was hearing, I knew, was a folk memory that had come down tongue to tongue in a winter's tale by some peasant's hearth. But it confirmed what I had been told. The place must have been fortified time out of mind. "The king" could have been any one of the Celtic rulers, driven eventually from the hilltop by the Romans, or the Roman general himself who had stayed here to invest the captured strongpoint.

I said suddenly: "Where is the way into the hill?"

"What way?"

"The door to the king's tomb, where they made the way for his grave."

"How do I know? It's there, that's all I know. And sometimes, on a night, they ride out again. I have seen them. They come wi' the summer moon, and go back into the hill at dawning. And whiles, on a stormy night, when dawn surprises them, one comes late, and finds the gate shut. So he is doomed for the next moon to wander the hilltop alone, till . . ." His voice faltered. He ducked his head fearfully, peering. "A king's man, you said you were?"

I laughed. "Don't be afraid of me, father. I'm not one of them. I'm a king's man, yes, but I have come for a living king, who will build the fortress up again, and take you and your cattle, and your children, and their children, into his hand, and keep you safely against the Saxon enemy from the south. And you will still get sweet grazing for your herd. I promise you this."

He said nothing to that, but sat for a while, nid-nodding in the sun. I could see that he was simple. "Why should I be afraid? There has always been a king here, and always will be. A king is no new thing."

"This one will be."

His attention was leaving me. He chirrupped to the cows. "Come up Blackberry, come up Dewdrop. A king, and tend the cattle for me? Do you take me for a fool? But the Goddess looks after her own. He'd best tend to the Goddess." And he subsided, mumbling his stick, and muttering.

I gave him a silver coin, as one gives a singer the guerdon for his tale, then led my horse off towards the ridge that marked the summit of the plateau.

3

Some days later the first party of surveyors arrived, to begin their measuring and pacing, while their leader was closeted with me in the temporary headquarters that had been made for us on the site.

Tremorinus, the master engineer who had taught me so much of his trade when I was a boy in Brittany, had died some time ago. Arthur's chief engineer now was a man called Derwen, whom I had first met years back, over the rebuilding of Caerleon in Ambrosius' time. He was a red-bearded, high-coloured man, but without the temper that often goes with that colouring; indeed, he was silent to the point of surliness, and could prove sullen as a mule when pressed. But I knew him to be competent and experienced, and he had the trick of getting men to work fast and willingly for him. Moreover, he had taken pains to be master himself of all trades, and was never above rolling up his sleeves and doing a heavy job himself if time demanded. Nor did he appear to mind taking direction from me. He seemed to hold my skills in the most flattering respect: this was not, I knew, because of any especial brilliance I had shown at Caerleon or Segontium – they were built to pattern on the Roman model, on lines laid down through time, and familiar to every builder – but Derwen had been an apprentice in Ireland when I had moved the massive king-stone of Killare, and subsequently at Amesbury, at the rebuilding of the Giants' Dance. So we got along tolerably well together, and understood each what the other was good for.

Arthur's forecast of trouble in the north had come true, and he had gone up in early March. But during the winter months he and I, with Derwen, had spent many hours together over the plans for the new stronghold. Driven by my persistence, and Arthur's enthusiasm, Derwen had finally been brought to accept what he obviously thought of as my wild ideas about the rebuilding of Caer Camel. Strength and speed – I wanted the place ready for Arthur by the time the campaign in the north should near its close, and I also wanted it to last. Its size and force had to fit his state.

The size was there; the hill's summit was vast, some eight acres in area. But the strength . . . I had had lists made of what material was already there, and, as best I could among the ruins, I had studied how the place had been built before, the Roman stonework on top of layer after layer of earlier Celtic wall and ditching. As I worked I kept in mind some of the fortifications I had seen on my travels abroad, strongpoints thrown up in wilder places than this, and on terrain as difficult. To rebuild on the Roman model would have been a formidable, if not impossible, task: even if Derwen's masons had had the knack of the Roman type of stonework, the sheer size of Caer Camel would have forbidden it. But the masons were all expert at their own dry-stone kind of building, and there was plenty of dressed stone to hand, and a quarry nearby. We had the oak-woods and the carpenters, and the sawyers' yards between Caer Camel and the Lake had been packed all winter with maturing timber. So I had made my final plans.

That they were carried out magnificently everyone can see. The steep, ditched sides of the place they now call Camelot stand crowned with massive walls of stone and timber. Sentries patrol the battlements, and stand guard over the great gates. To the northerly gate a waggon-road climbs between its guarded banks, while to the gate at the south-west corner – the one they call King's Gate – a chariot-way curves up, true-cambered to the fastest wheels, and wide enough for a galloping troop of horses.

Within those walls now, as well kept in these times of peace as in the troubled days I built them for, a city has arisen, gay with gilding and the fluttering of banners, and fresh with gardens and orchard trees. On the paved terraces walk women in rich dresses, and children play in the gardens. The streets are crowded with folk, and full of talk and laughter, the chaffering of the market-place, the quick hoofs of Arthur's fleet and glossy horses, the shouts of the young men, and the clamour of the church bells. It has grown rich with peaceful commerce, and splendid with the arts of peace.

Camelot is a marvellous sight, and one which is familiar now to travellers from the four corners of the world.

But then, on that raw hilltop, and among the mess of abandoned buildings, it was no more than an idea, and an idea sprung out of the hard necessities of war. We would start, of course, with the outer walls, and here I planned to use the broken stuff that lay about; tiles from the old hypocausts, flagstones, bedding from the floors, even from the old roadwork that had been laid in the Roman fortress. With these we would throw up a revetment of hard rubble which would retain the outer wall, and at the same time support a broad fighting platform laid along the inner side of the battlement. The wall itself would, on the outer side, rise straight out of the steep hillside, like a crown on a king's head. The hillside we stripped of its trees, and seamed with ditches, so that it became, in effect, a steep of breakneck minor crags, to be topped with a great wall faced with stone. For this we would use the dressed tufa found on site, along with materials quarried afresh by Melwas' masons and our own. Above this again I planned to set a massively smooth wall of wood, tied into the stonework and the rubble of the revetment by a strong timber frame. At the gateways, where the approach-roads ran uphill sunk between rocky banks, I designed a kind of tunnel which would pierce the fortified wall, and allow the fighting platform to run unbroken across, above the gates. These gated tunnels, high and wide enough to let horse-drawn traffic through, or riders three abreast, would be hung with huge gates which could fold back against the oak-lined walls. To do this we would have to sink the roadways still further.

This, and much else besides, I had explained to Derwen. He had been sceptical at first, and only his respect for me had kept him, I could tell, from flat and mulish disagreement – especially about the gates, for which he could see no precedent; and most engineers and architects work, reasonably enough, from well-proved precedent, especially in matters of war and defence. At first he could see no reason to abandon the well-tried model of twin turrets and guard-rooms. But in time, sitting hour by hour over my plans, and conning the lists I had had drawn up of the materials already available on the site, he came to a qualified acceptance of my amalgam of stone and woodworking, and thence to a sort of guarded enthusiasm over all. He was enough of a professional to find excitement in new ideas, especially since any blame for failure would be mine and not his.

Not that blame was likely. Arthur, taking part in the planning sessions, was enthusiastic,but – as he pointed out when deferred to over some technical point – he knew his own business, and he would trust us to know ours. We all knew what the place's function would be; it was up to us to build it accordingly. Once we had built it (he concluded with the brevity of total and unconscious arrogance), he would know how to keep it.

Now, on site at last, and with good weather come early and looking settled, Derwen started work with keenness and despatch, and, before the old herdsman had called the cows home for the first evening's milking, the pegs were driven in, trenches had been started, and the first waggon-load of supplies was groaning uphill behind its straining oxen.

Caer Camel was rising again. The King was coming back.

*   *   *

He came on a bright day of June. He rode up from the village on his grey mare Amrei, accompanied by Bedwyr, and his foster-brother Cei, and perhaps a dozen others of his cavalry captains. These were now commonly known as the *equites* or knights: Arthur himself called them his "companions". They rode without armour, like a hunting-party. Arthur swung from his mare's back, threw the reins to Bedwyr, and while the others dismounted and let their horses graze, he trod up the slope of blowing grass alone.

He saw me, and lifted a hand, but did not hurry. He paused by the outer revetment, and spoke to the men working there, then walked out onto the planking that bridged a trench, while the labourers straightened from their tasks to answer his questions. I saw one of them point something out to him; he looked that way, and then all about him, before he left them to mount the central ridge where the foundations for his headquarters had been dug. From there, he could command the whole area, and make some sense, perhaps, out of the maze of trenching and foundations, half hidden as it was beneath the web of ropes and scaffolding.

He turned slowly on his heel, until he had taken in the full circle. Then he came swiftly over to where I stood, drawings in hand.

"Yes," was all he said, but with a glowing satisfaction. And then: "When?"

"There will be something here for you by winter."

He sent his eyes round again, a look of pride and vision that could have been my own. I knew that he was seeing, as I could see, the finished walls, the proud towers, the stone and timber and iron that would enclose this space of golden summer air, and make it his first creation. It was the look, too, of a warrior who sees a strong weapon being offered to his hand. His eyes, full of this high and fierce satisfaction, came back to me.

"I told you to use a miracle, and I think you have. That is how I see it. Perhaps you are too much of a professional to feel that way, when you see what was only a drawing on clay, or even a thought in your mind, being built into something real that will last for ever?"

"I believe all makers feel this way. I, certainly."

"How fast it has moved! Did you build it with music, like the Giants' Dance?"

"I used the same miracle here. You can see it. The men."

A quick glance at me, then his gaze went across the mess of churned ground and toiling labourers to where, as orderly as in an old, walled city, the workshops of the carpenters and smiths and masons rang with hammering and voices. His eyes took a faraway and yet inward look. He spoke softly. "I'll remember that. God knows every commander should. I use the same miracle myself." Then, back to me: "And by next winter?"

"By next winter you shall have it complete inside, as well as safe to fight from. The place is everything we had hoped for. Later, when the wars are done, there will be space and time to build for other things, comfort and grace and splendour, worthy of you and your victories. We'll make you a veritable eagle's eyrie, hung on a lovely hill. A stronghold to hunt from in war, and a home to breed in in times of peace."

He had half turned from me, to make a sign to the watching Bedwyr. The young men mounted, and Bedwyr approached us, leading Arthur's mare. Arthur swung back to me, brows up.

"So you know? I might have known I could keep no secrets from you."

"Secrets? I know nothing. What secret were you trying to keep?"

"None. What would be the use? I would have told you straight away, but this came first . . . Though she wouldn't like to hear me say so." I must have gaped at him like a fool. His eyes danced. "Yes, I'm sorry, Merlin. But I really was about to tell you. I am to marry. Come, don't be angry. That is something in which you could hardly guide me to my own satisfaction."

"I am not angry. What right have I? This is one thing you must decide for yourself. It seems you have, and I'm glad. Is it concluded?"

"No, how could it be? I was waiting to talk to you first. So far it's only been a matter of letters between Queen Ygraine and myself. The suggestion came from her, and I suppose there'll be a lot of talking to do first. But I warn you –" a glint – "my mind is made up." Bedwyr slipped from his saddle beside us, and Arthur took the mare's reins from him. I looked a query, and he nodded. "Yes, Bedwyr knows."

"Then will you tell me who she is?"

"Her father was March, who fought under Duke Cador and was killed in a skirmish on the Irish Shore. Her mother died at her birth, and, since her father's death, she has been under Queen Ygraine's protection. You must have seen her, but you would not notice her, I expect. She was in waiting at Amesbury, and then again at the crowning."

"I remember her. Did I hear her name? I forget."

"Guenever."

A plover winged overhead, tumbling in the sun. Its shadow floated over the grass between us. Something plucked at the chords of memory; something from that other life of power and terror and bright vision. But it eluded me. The mood of tranquil achievement was unruffled as the Lake.

"What is it, Merlin?"

His voice was anxious, like a boy's who fears censure. I looked up. Bedwyr, beside him, was watching me with the same worried look.

"Nothing at all. She's a lovely girl, and bears a lovely name. Be sure the gods will bless the marriage when the time comes."

The young faces relaxed. Bedwyr said something quick and teasing, then followed it with some excited comment about the building work, and the two of them plunged into a discussion in which marriage plans had no part. I caught sight of Derwen over near the gateway, so we walked that way to talk with him. Then Arthur and Bedwyr took their leave, and mounted, and the other young men turned their fretting horses to ride downhill after their King towards the road.

They did not get far. As the little cavalcade entered the sunken gateway they came head on against Blackberry and Dewdrop and their sisters, making their slow way uphill. The old herdsman, tenacious as goosegrass, still clung to his grazing rights on Caer Camel, and brought the herd daily up towards the part of the field as yet unspoiled by the workings.

I saw the grey mare pause, veer, and start to curvet. The cattle, stolidly chewing, shouldered by, udders swinging. From some-where among them, as suddenly as a puff of smoke from the ground, the old man appeared, leaning on his staff. The mare reared, hoofs flailing. Arthur pulled her aside, and she turned back hard against the shoulder of Bedwyr's black colt, which promptly lashed out, missing Dewdrop by inches. Bedwyr was laughing, but Cei shouted out angrily:

"Make way, you old fool! Can't you see it's the King? And get your damned cattle out of the way. They've no business here now!"

"As good business as yourself, young master, if not better," said the old man tartly. "Getting the good of the land, they are, which you and your likes can do nought but spoil! So it's you should take your horses off and get your hunting done in the Summer Country, and let honest folks be!"

Cei was never one to know when he should curb his anger, or even save his breath. He pushed his horse past Arthur's mare, and thrust his red face down towards the old man. "Are you deaf, old fool, or just stupid? Hunting? We are the King's fighting captains, and this is the King!"

Arthur, half-laughing, began, "Oh, leave it, Cei," then had to control the mare sharply once more as the old goblin bobbed up again at his bridle-hand. The dim eyes peered upwards.

"King? Nay, but you can't fool me, masters. 'Tis only a bit of a lad. The king's a man grown. Besides, 'tis not yet his time. He'll come at midsummer, wi' the full moon. Seen him, I have, with all his fighting men." A gesture with his staff that set the horses' heads tossing again. "These, fighting captains? Boys, that's all they be! Kings' fighting men have armour, and spears as long as ash trees, and plumes on them like the manes on their horses. Seen them, I have, alone here on a summer's night. Oh, aye, I know the King."

Cei opened his mouth again, but Arthur put up a hand. He spoke as if he and the old man were alone in the field. "A king who came here in the summer? What are you telling us, father? What men were they?"

Something in his manner, perhaps, got through to the other. He looked uncertain. Then he caught sight of me, and pointed. "Told him, I did. Yes. King's man, he said he was, and spoke me soft. A king was coming, he said, who would tend my cows for me, and give me the grazing for them . . ." He looked about him, as if taking in for the first time the splendid horses and gay trappings, and the assured, laughing looks of the young men. His voice faltered, and he slid off into his mumbling. Arthur looked at me.

"Do you know what he's talking about?"

"A legend of the past, and a troop of ghosts that he says come riding out of their grave in the hill on a summer's midnight. It's my guess that he's telling an old tale of the Celtic rulers here, or the Romans, or maybe both. Nothing to trouble you."

"Not trouble us?" said someone, sounding uneasy; I think it was Lamorak, a brave and high-strung gentleman who watched the stars for signs, and whose horse's trappings rang with charms. "Ghosts, and not trouble us?"

"And he has seen them himself, on this very spot?" said someone else. Then others, murmuring, "Spears and horsehair plumes? Why, they sound like Saxons." And Lamorak again, fingering a piece of coral on his breast, "Ghosts of dead men, killed here and buried under the very hill where you plan to build a stronghold and a safe city? Arthur, did you know?"

There are few men more superstitious than soldiers. They are, after all, the men who live closest to death. All laughter had vanished, quenched, and a shiver went across the bright day, as surely as if a cloud had passed between us and the sun.

Arthur was frowning. He was a soldier, too, but he was also a king, and, like the King his father before him, dealt in facts. He said, with noticeable briskness: "And what of it? Show me any strong fortress as good as this which has not been defended by brave men, and founded on their blood! Are we children, to fear the ghosts of men who have died here before us, to keep this land? If they linger here at all, they will be on our side, gentlemen!" Then, to the herdsman: "Well? Tell us your story, father. Who was this king?"

The old man hesitated, confused. Then he asked, suddenly: "Did you ever hear of Merlin, the enchanter?"

"*Merlin*?" This was Bedwyr. "Why, do you not know – ?"

He caught my eye, and stopped. No one else spoke. Arthur, without a glance in my direction, asked, into the silence: "What of Merlin?"

The filmed eyes went round as if they could see every man clearly, every listening face. Even the horses stood quiet. The herdsman seemed to take courage from the attentive silence. He became suddenly lucid. "There was a king once, who set out to build a stronghold. And, like the kings of old, who were strong men and merciless, he looked for a hero, to kill and bury beneath the foundations, and hold them firm. So he caught and took Merlin, who was the greatest man in all Britain, and would have killed him; but Merlin called up his dragons, and flew away through the heavens, safely, and called a new king into Britain, who burned the other one to ashes in his tower, and his queen with him. Had you heard that tale, master?"

"Yes."

"And is it true that you are a king, and these your captains?"

"Yes."

"Then ask Merlin. They say he still lives. Ask him what king should fear to have a hero's grave beneath his threshold. Don't you know what he did? He put the great Dragon King himself under the Hanging Stones, that he did, and called it the safe castle of all Britain. Or so they say."

"They say the truth," said Arthur. He looked about him, to see where relief had already overlaid uneasiness. He turned back to the herdsman. "And the strong king who lies with his men within the hill?"

But here he got no further. When pressed, the old man became vague, and then unintelligible. A word could be caught here and there; helmets, plumes, round shields, and small horses, and yet again long spears "like ash trees", and cloaks blowing in the wind "when no wind blows".

I said coolly, to interrupt these new ghostly visions: "You should ask Merlin about that, too, my lord King. I believe I know what he would say."

Arthur smiled. "What, then?"

I turned to the old man. "You told me that the Goddess slew this king and his men, and that they were buried here. You told me, too, that the new young king would have to make his peace with the Goddess, or she would reject him. Now see what she has done. He knew nothing of this story, but he has come here with her guidance, to build his stronghold on the very spot where the Goddess herself slew and buried a troop of strong fighters and their leader, to be the king-stone of his threshold. And she gave him the sword and the crown. So tell your people this, and tell them that the new king comes, with the Goddess's sanction, to build a fortress of his own, and to protect you and your children, and let your cattle graze in peace."

I heard Lamorak draw in his breath. "By the Goddess herself, you have it, Merlin!"

"Merlin?" You would have thought the old man was hearing the name for the first time. "Aye, that's what he would say . . . and I've heard tell how he took the sword himself from the depths of the water and gave it to the King . . ." For a few minutes then, as the others crowded close, talking again among themselves, relieved and smiling, he went back to his mumbling. But then, my final, incautious sentence having got through, he came suddenly, and with the utmost clarity of speech, back to the matter of his cows, and the iniquity of kings who interfered with their grazing. Arthur, with one swift, charged glance at me, listened gravely, while the young men held in their laughter, and the last wisps of trouble vanished in mirth. In the end, with gentle courtesy, the King promised to let him keep the grazing for as long as the sweet grass grew on Caer Camel, and when it did no longer, to find a pasture for him elsewhere.

"On my word as High King," he finished.

It was not clear whether, even now, the old herdsman believed him. "Well, call yourself king or not," he said, "for a lad you show some sort of sense. You listen to them that knows, not like some" – this with a malevolent glance in Cei's direction – "that's all noise and wind. Fighting men, indeed! Anyone who knows ought about fighting and the like, knows there's no man can fight with an empty belly. You give my cows the grass, and we'll fill your bellies for you."

"I have said you shall have it."

"And when yon builder" – this was myself – "has got Caer Camel spoiled, what land will you give me then?"

Arthur had perhaps not meant to be taken so quickly at his word, but he hesitated only for a moment. "I saw good green stretches down by the river yonder, beyond the village. If I can –"

"That's no manner of good for beasts. Goats, maybe, and geese, but not cattle. That's sour grass, that is, and full of buttercups. That's poison to grazing."

"Indeed? I didn't know that. Where would be good land, then?"

"Over to the badgers' hill. That's yonder." He pointed. "Butter-cups!" He cackled. "King or not, young master, however much folks know, there's always someone as knows more."

Arthur said, gravely: "That is something else I shall remember. Very well. If I can come by the badgers' hill, it shall be yours."

Then he reined back to let the old man by, and, with a salute to me, rode away downhill, with his knights behind him. Derwen was waiting for me by the foundations of the south-west tower. I walked that way. A plover – the same, perhaps – tilted and side-slipped, calling, in the breezy air. Memory came back, halting me . . .

. . . The Green Chapel above Galava. The same two young faces, Arthur's and Bedwyr's, watching me as I told them stories of battles and far-off places. And across the room, thrown by the lamplight, the shadow of a bird floating – the white owl that lived in the roof – *guenhwyvar*, the white shadow, at whose name I had felt a creeping of the flesh, a moment of troubled prevision which now I could scarcely recall, except for the fear that the name Guenever was somehow a doom for him.

I had felt no such warning today. I did not expect it. I knew just what was left of the power I had once had to warn and to protect. Today I was no more than the old herdsman had called me, a builder.

"No more?" I recalled the pride and awe in the King's eyes as he surveyed the groundwork of the "miracle" I was working for him now. I looked down at the plans in my hand, and felt the familiar, purely human excitement of the maker stir in me. The shadow fled and vanished into sunshine, and I hurried to meet Derwen. At least I still possessed skill enough to build my boy a safe stronghold.

4

Three months later Arthur married Guenever at Caerleon. He had had no chance to see the bride again; indeed, I believe he had had no more speech with her than what slight formalities had passed between them at the crowning. He himself had to go north again early in July, so could spare no time to travel into Cornwall to escort her to Guent. In any case, since he was High King, it was proper that his bride should be brought to him. So he spared Bedwyr for one precious month to ride down to Tintagel and bring the bride to Caerleon.

All through that summer there was sporadic fighting in the north, mostly a business (in that forested hill country) of ambush and running skirmish, but late in July Arthur forced a battle by a crossing on the River Bassas. This he won so decisively as to create a welcome lull that prolonged itself into a truce through harvest-time, and allowed him at length to travel to Caerleon with a quiet mind. For all that, his was a garrison wedding; he could afford to sacrifice no sort of readiness, so the bridal was fitted in, so to speak, among his other preoccupations. The bride seemed to expect it, taking everything as happily as if it had been some great festive occasion in London, and there was as much gaiety and gorgeousness about the ceremony as I have ever seen on such occasions, even though men kept their spears stacked outside the hall of feasting, and their swords laid ready to lift, and the King himself spent every available moment in counsel with his officers, or out in the exercise grounds, or – late into the night sometimes – poring over his maps, with his spies' reports on the table beside him.

I left Caer Camel in the first week of September, and rode across country to Caerleon. The work on the fortress was going well, and could be left to Derwen to carry out. I went with a light heart. All I had been able to find out about the girl was in her favour; she was young, healthy, and of good stock, and it was time Arthur was married and thinking of getting himself sons. I thought about her no further than that.

I was in Caerleon in time to see the wedding party arrive. They did not use the ferry-crossing, but came riding up the road from Glevum, their horses gay with gilded leather and coloured tassels, and the women's litters bright with fresh paint. The younger of the ladies wore mantles of every colour, and had flowers plaited into their horses' manes.

The bride herself disdained a litter; she rode a pretty cream-coloured horse, a gift from Arthur's stables. Bedwyr, in a new cloak of russet, kept close by her bridle-hand, and on his other side rode the Princess Morgan, Arthur's sister. Her mount was as fiery as Guenever's was gentle, but she controlled it without effort. She appeared to be in excellent spirits, as excited, one gathered, over her own approaching marriage as over the other, more important wedding. Nor did she seem to grudge Guenever her central role in the festivities, or the deference she received for her new state. Morgan herself had state and to spare: she had come, in Ygraine's absence, to represent the Queen, and, with the Duke of Cornwall, to place Guenever's hand in that of the High King.

Arthur, being still ignorant of the seriousness of Ygraine's illness, had expected her to come. Bedwyr had a quiet word with him on arrival, and I saw a shadow touch the King's face, then he banished it to greet Guenever. His greeting was public and formal, but with a smile behind it that she answered with a demure dimple. The ladies rustled and cooed and eyed him, and the men looked on indulgently, the older ones approving her youth and freshness, their thoughts already turning towards an heir to the kingdom. The young men watched with the same approval, coloured with simple envy.

Guenever was fifteen now. She was a shade taller than when I had last seen her, and more womanly, but she was still a little creature, with fresh skin and merry eyes, patently delighted with the fortune that had brought her out of Cornwall as bride of the land's darling, Arthur the young King.

She gave the Queen's excuses prettily, with no hint that Ygraine suffered from anything other than a passing ailment, and the King accepted them smoothly, then gave her his arm, and himself escorted her, with Morgan, to the house prepared for them and their ladies. This was the best of the town houses outside the fortress walls, where they could rest and make ready for the marriage.

He came back to his rooms soon after, and while he was still some way down the corridor I could hear him talking busily to Bedwyr. Nor was the talk of weddings and women. He came into the room already shedding his finery, and Ulfin, who knew his ways, was there ready to catch the splendid cloak as it was flung off, and to lift the heavy sword-belt and lay it aside. Arthur greeted me gaily.

"Well? What do you think? Has she not grown lovely?"

"She is very fair. She will be a match for you."

"And she isn't shy or mim-mouthed, thank God. I've no time for that."

I saw Bedwyr smiling. We both knew he meant it literally. He had no time to trouble with wooing a delicate bride; he wanted marriage and bedding, and then, with the elder nobles satisfied at last, and his own mind free, he could get back to the unfinished business in the north.

So much he was saying now, as he led the way into the anteroom where the map-table stood.

"But we'll talk of that in a moment, when the rest of the Council comes. I've sent for them. There was fresh news last night, by courier. Incidentally, Merlin, I told you, didn't I, that I was sending for your young man Gereint, from Olicana? He got here last night – have you seen him yet? No? Well he'll be coming with the rest. I'm grateful to you; he's a find, and has proved his value already three times over. He brought news from Elmet . . . But leave that now. Before they come, I want to ask you about Queen Ygraine. Bedwyr tells me there was no question of her coming north for the wedding. Did you know she was ill?"

"I knew at Amesbury that she was ailing, but she would not talk about it, then or later, and she never consulted me. Why, Bedwyr, what's the news of her now?"

"I'm no judge," said Bedwyr, "but she looked gravely ill to me. Even since the crowning I could see a change in her, thin as a ghost, and spending most of her time in bed. She sent a letter to Arthur, and she would have written to you, she said, but it was beyond her strength. I was to give you her greetings, and to thank you for your letters, and your thought of her. She watches for them."

Arthur looked at me. "Did you suspect anything like this, when you saw her? Is this a mortal sickness?"

"I would guess so. When I saw her at Amesbury, the seeds of the sickness were already sown. And when I spoke to her again at the crowning, I think she knew herself to be failing. But to guess at how long . . . Even had I been her own physician, I doubt if I could have judged of that."

He might have been expected to ask why I had kept my suspicions from him, but the reasons were obvious enough so he wasted no breath on them. He merely nodded, looking troubled. "I cannot . . . You know that I must go north again as soon as this business is done." He spoke as if the wedding were a Council, or a battle. "I cannot go down into Cornwall. Ought I to send you?"

"It would be useless. Besides, her own physician is as good a man as you could wish for. I knew him when he was a young student in Pergamum."

"Well," he said, accepting it, and then again, "Well . . ."

But he moved restlessly, fidgeting with the pins that were stuck here and there in the clay map. "The trouble is, one always feels there is something one should be doing. I like to load the dice, not sit waiting for someone else to throw them. Oh, yes, I know what you will say – that the essence of wisdom is to know when to be doing, and when it is useless even to try. But I sometimes think I shall never be old enough to be wise."

"Perhaps the best thing you can do, both for Queen Ygraine and for yourself, is to get this marriage consummated, and see your sister Morgan crowned Queen of Rheged," I said, and Bedwyr nodded.

"I agree. From the way she spoke about it, I got the impression that she lives only to see both marriage-bonds safely tied."

"That is what she says in her letter to me," said the King. He turned his head. Faintly, from the corridor, came the sound of challenge and answer. "Well, Merlin, I could ill have spared you for a journey into Cornwall. I want to send you north again. Can

Derwen be left in charge at Caer Camel?"

"If you wish it, of course. He will do very well, though I should like to be back myself in good time for the spring weather."

"There's no reason why you shouldn't be."

"Is it Morgan's wedding? Or – perhaps I should have been more cautious? Is it Morgause again? . . . I warn you, if it's a trip to Orkney, I shall refuse."

He laughed. He certainly neither looked nor spoke as if Morgause or her bastard had been on his mind. "I wouldn't put you at such risk, either from Morgause or the northern seas. No, it is Morgan. I want you to take her to Rheged."

"That will be a pleasure." It would, indeed. The years I had spent in Rheged, in the Wild Forest which is part of the great tract of land they call the Caledonian Forest, had been the crest of my life; they had been the years when I had guided and taught Arthur as a boy. "I trust I'll be able to see Ector?"

"Why not, once you've seen Morgan safely wedded? I must admit it will ease my mind, as well as the Queen's, to see her settled there in Rheged. It's possible that by spring-time there will be war in the north again."

Put like that, it sounded strange, but in the context of those times it made sense. Those were years of winter weddings; men left home in spring to fight, and it was as well to leave a secure hearth behind them. For a man like Urbgen of Rheged, no longer young, lord of great domains, and a keen fighting man, it would be foolish to put off the proposed marriage any longer. I said: "Of course I will take her there. How soon?"

"As soon as things are done here, and before winter sets in."

"Will you be there?"

"If I can. We'll speak of this again. I'll give you messages, and of course you will carry my gifts to Urbgen." He signed to Ulfin, who went to the door. The others came in then – his knights and the men of the Council and certain of the petty kings who had come to Caerleon for the wedding. Cador was there, and Gwilim, and others from Powys and Dyfed and Dumnonia, but no one from Elmet, or the north. This was understandable. It was a relief not to see Lot. Among the younger men I saw Gereint. He greeted me with a smiling gesture, but there was no time for talk. The King

spoke, and we sat over our counsels until sunset, when food was
brought in, and after that the company took their leave, and I with
them.

As I made my way back to my own quarters, Bedwyr fell in
beside me, and with him Gereint. The two young men seemed to
know one another tolerably well. Gereint greeted me warmly. "It
was a good day for me," he said, smiling, "when that travelling
doctor came to Olicana."

"And, I believe, for Arthur," I replied. "How is the work going
in the Gap?"

He told me about it. There was, it seemed, no immediate danger
from the east. Arthur had made a clean sweep in Linnuis, and
meantime the King of Elmet held watch and ward for him. The
road through the Gap had been rebuilt, right through from Olicana
to Tribuit, and both the western forts had been brought to readiness. From talking about this he came to Caer Camel, and here
Bedwyr joined him in plying me with questions. Presently we came
to where our ways parted.

"I leave you here," said Gereint. He glanced back the way we had
come, towards the King's apartments. "Behold," he said, "the
half was not told me." He spoke as if quoting from something,
but it was something I had not heard. "These are great days for
us all."

"And will be greater."

Then we said good night, and Bedwyr and I walked on together.
The boy with the torch was a few paces ahead. At first we talked,
with lowered voices, about Ygraine. He was able to tell me more
than he had said in front of Arthur. Her physician, not wishing to
commit anything to writing, had entrusted Bedwyr with information for me, but nothing about it was new. The Queen was dying,
waiting only – this was from Bedwyr himself – until the two
young women, crowned and in due splendour, had taken their
places, and thereafter it would be a strange thing (Melchior had
said) if she lasted till Christmas. She had sent me a message of
goodwill, and a token to be given to Arthur after her death. This
latter was a brooch, finely made of gold and blue enamel, with an
image of the mother-goddess of the Christians, and the name,
MARIA, inscribed around the edge. She had already given jewels

both to her daughter Morgan and to Guenever; these had come in the guise of wedding gifts, though Morgan already knew the truth. Guenever, it seemed, did not. The girl had been as dear, and lately almost dearer, to Ygraine than her own daughter, and the Queen had carefully instructed Bedwyr that nothing must spoil the marriage celebrations. Not that the Queen, said Bedwyr (who obviously held Ygraine in the greatest respect) had any illusions about Arthur's grief for her; she had sacrificed his love for that of Uther and the kingdom's future, and she herself was resigned to death, secure in her faith; but she was aware how much the girl had come to love her.

"And Guenever herself?" I asked at length. "You must have come to know her well on the journey. And you know Arthur, none better. How will they suit? What is she like?"

"Delightful. She's full of life – in her own way as full as he is – and she is clever. She plied me with questions about the wars, and they were not idle ones. She understands what he is doing, and has followed every move he has made. She was head over ears in love with him from the first moment she saw him in Amesbury . . . in fact, it's my belief that she was in love with him even before that, like every other girl in Britain. But she has humour and sense with it; she's no greensick girl with a dream of a crown and a bedding; she knows where her duty will lie. I know that Queen Ygraine planned this and hoped for it. She has been schooling the girl all this while."

"There could hardly be a better preceptress."

"I agree. But Guenever has gentleness, and she is full of laughter, too. I am glad," he finished, simply.

We spoke of Morgan then, and the other marriage.

"Let us hope it suits as well," I said. "It's certainly what Arthur wants. And Morgan? She seems willing, even happy about it."

"Oh, yes," he said, and then, with a smiling shrug, "you'd think it was a love-match, and that all the business with Lot had never been. You always say, Merlin, that you know nothing of women, and can't even guess at what moves them. Well, no more can I, and I'm not a born hermit, like you. I've known plenty, and now I've spent a month or so in daily attendance on them – and I still don't begin to understand them. They crave for marriage, which for them is a kind of slavery – and dangerous at that. You could understand it with those who have nothing of their own; but here's Morgan: she has wealth and position, and the freedom they give her, and she has the protection of the High King. Yet she would have gone to Lot, whose reputation you know, and now goes, eagerly, to Urbgen of Rheged, who is more than three times her age, and whom she has hardly seen. Why?"

"I suspect because of Morgause."

He shot me a look. "That's possible. I spoke to Guenever about it. She says that, since news came of Morgause's latest lying-in, and her letters about the state she keeps –"

"In Orkney?"

"She says so. It does seem true that she rules the kingdom. Who else? Lot has been with Arthur . . . Well, Guenever told me that lately Morgan's temper had been growing sharp, and she had begun to speak of Morgause with hatred. Also, she had begun to practise what the Queen called her 'dark arts' again. Guenever seems afraid of them." He hesitated. "They speak of it as magic, Merlin, but it is nothing like your power. It is something smoky, in a closed room."

"If Morgause taught her, then it must be dark indeed. Well, so the sooner Morgan is a queen in Rheged, with a family of her own, the better. And what of yourself, Bedwyr? Have you had thoughts of marriage?"

"None, yet," he said, cheerfully. "I have no time."

On which we laughed, and went our ways.

★　　★　　★

So the next day, with a fine sun blazing, and all the pomp and music and revelry that a joyous crowd could conjure up, Arthur married Guenever. And after the feasting, when torches had burned low, and men and women had eaten and laughed and drunk deep, the bride was led away; and later, escorted by his companion knights, the bridegroom went to her.

That night I dreamed a dream. It was brief and cloudy, a glimmer only of something that might be true vision. There were curtains drawn and blowing, and a place full of cold shadows, and a woman lying in bed. I could not see her clearly, nor tell who she was. I thought at first that it was Ygraine, then, with a shift of the blowing light, it might have been Guenever. And she lay as if she were dead, or as if she were sleeping soundly after a night of love.

5

So once again I headed northward, keeping this time to the west road all the way to Luguvallium. It was truly a wedding journey. The good weather held all through that month, the lovely September month of gold that is best for travellers, since Hermes, the god of going, claims it for his own.

His hand was over us through all that journey. The road, Arthur's main way up the west, was repaired and sound, and even on the moors the land was dry, so that we did not need to time our journey to seek for stopping-places to suit the women. If, at sunset, no town or village was near, we made camp where we halted, and ate by some stream with trees for shelter, while plovers called in the dusk, and the herons flapped overhead back from their fishing-grounds. For me, it would have been an idyllic journey, but for two things. The first was the memory of my last journey northward. Like all sensible men, I had put regret out of my mind, or thought I had; but when one night someone petitioned me to sing, and my servant brought the harp to me, it seemed suddenly as if I only had to look up from the strings to see them coming into the firelight, Beltane the goldmsith, smiling, with Ninian behind him. And after that the boy was there nightly, in memory or in dreams, and with him the most poignant of all sorrows, the regret for what might have been, and was gone for ever. It was more than simple grief for a disciple lost who might have done my work for me after I was gone. There was with it a wounding self-contempt for the helpless way I had let him go. Surely I should have known, in that moment of stinging, involuntary protest at Cor Bridge, why the protest was made? The truth was, that the loss of the boy went far deeper than the failure to win an heir and a disciple: his loss was the very symbol of my own. Because I was no longer Merlin, Ninian had died.

The second wasp in the honey of that journey was Morgan herself.

I had never known her well. She had been born at Tintagel, and had grown up there through the years when I had lived in hiding in Rheged, watching over Arthur's boyhood. Since then I had only seen her twice, at her brother's crowning, and at his marriage, and had barely spoken with her on either occasion.

She resembled her brother in that she was tall for her age and dark-haired, with the dark eyes that came, I think, from the Spanish blood brought by the Emperor Maximus into the family of the Ambrosii; but in feature she resembled Ygraine, where Arthur favoured Uther. Her skin was pale, and she was as quiet as Arthur was ebullient. For all this I could sense in her something of the same kind of force, a power controlled, fire banked under cool ash. There was something, too, of the subtlety that Morgause, her half-sister, showed in such abundance, and Arthur not at all. But this is mostly a woman's quality; they all have it in some degree or another; it is too often their only weapon and their only shield.

Morgan refused to use the litter provided for her, and rode beside me for some part of each day. I suppose that when she was with the women, or among the younger men, the talk must have turned on the coming wedding, and the times to come; but when she was by me she spoke mostly of the past. Again and again she led me to talk of those of my deeds which had passed into legend, the story of the dragons at Dinas Emrys, the raising of the king-stone at Killare, the lifting of the sword of Macsen from the stone. I answered her questions willingly enough, keeping to the facts of the stories, and (remembering what I had learned of Morgan from her mother and Bedwyr) trying to convey to her something of what "magic" meant. As these girls see it, it is an affair of philtres, and whispers in darkened rooms, spells to bind a man's heart, or bring the vision of a lover on Midsummer Eve. Their main concern, understandably, is the aphrodisian lore – how to bring, or to prevent, pregnancy, charms for safety in childbirth, predictions about the sex of a child. These matters, to do her justice, Morgan never broached with me; it was to be expected that she was versed in them already. Nor did she seem interested, as the young Morgause had been, in medicine and the healing arts. Her questions turned all on the greater power, and mainly as it had touched Arthur. All that had passed from Uther's first wooing of her mother, and Arthur's conception, to the raising of the great sword of Macsen, she was avid to know. I answered her civilly, and fully enough; she was, I reckoned, entitled to the facts, and (since she was going to be Queen of Rheged, and would almost certainly outlive her husband, and live to guide the future king of that powerful province) I tried to show her what Arthur's aims were for the settled times after the war, and to imbue her with the same ambitions.

It was hard to tell what sort of success I had. After a time I noticed that her talk turned more and more frequently to the hows and wherefores of the power I had owned. I put her questions aside, but she persisted, at length even suggesting, with an assurance as cool as Arthur's own, that I should show some demonstration of it, for all the world as if I were an old wife mixing spells and simples over the fire, or a soothsayer crystal-gazing on market day. At this last impertinence my answer was, I imagine, too cold for her to stomach. Soon afterwards she drew rein and let her palfrey lag back, and thereafter rode the rest of the way with the young people.

Like her sister, Morgan was rarely content with the company of women. Her most constant companion was one Accolon, a splendidly dressed, florid young man with a loud laugh and a high colour. She never let herself be alone with him more than was decent, though he made no secret of his feelings; he followed her everywhere with his eyes, and, whenever he could, touched her hand, or brought his horse sidling so close to her that his thigh brushed hers, and their horses' manes tangled together. She never seemed to notice, and never once, that I could see, gave him other than the same cool looks and answers that she gave to everyone. I had, of course, a duty to bring her unharmed and virgin (if virgin she still was) to Urbgen's bed, but I could have no present fears for her honour. A lover would have been hard put to it to come to her on that journey, even if she had beckoned him. Most nights when we camped, Morgan was attended by all her ladies to her pavilion, which was shared by her two elderly waiting women, as well as her younger companions. She gave no hint that she wished it otherwise. She acted and spoke like any royal bride on her way to a welcome bride-bed, and if Accolon's handsome face and eager courtship moved her she made no sign.

We halted for the last time just short of the limits that are governed by Caer-luel, as the British call Luguvallium. Here we rested the horses, while the servants busied themselves over the burnishing of the harness and the washing of the painted litters, and – among the women – some furbishing of clothes and hair and complexions. Then the cavalcade re-formed, and we went on to meet the welcoming party, which met us well beyond the city limits.

It was headed by King Urbgen himself, on a splendid horse which had been a gift from Arthur, a bay stallion decked with crimson and cloth of gold. Beside it a servant led a white mare, bridled with silver and tasselled with blue, for the princess. Urbgen was as splendid as his steed, a vigorous man, broad-chested and strong-armed, and as active as any warrior half his age. He had been a sandy-coloured man, and now his hair and beard, as is the way with sand-fair men, had gone quite white, thick and fine. His face had been weathered by the summers of warfare and the winters of riding his cold marches. I knew him for a strong man, a stout ally, and a clever ruler.

He greeted me as civilly as if I had been the High King himself, and then I presented Morgan. She had dressed herself in primrose and white, and plaited the long dark hair with gold. She gave him a hand, a deep curtsy, and a cool cheek to kiss, then mounted the white mare and rode on beside him, meeting the stares of his retinue, and his own assessing looks, with unruffled composure. I saw Accolon drop back with a hot, sulky look, as Urbgen's party closed round the three of us, and we rode on at a gentle pace to the meeting of the three rivers where Luguvallium lay among the reddening trees of autumn.

★   ★   ★

The journey had been a good one, but its end was bad indeed, fulfilling the worst of my fears. Morgause came to the wedding.

Three days before the ceremony a messenger came galloping

with the news that a ship had been sighted in the estuary, with the black sail and the badge of the Orcadians. King Urbgen rode to meet it at the harbour. I sent my own servant for news, and he was back with it, hot-foot, before the Orkney party could well have disembarked. King Lot was not there, he told me, but Queen Morgause had come, and in some state. I sent him south to Arthur with a warning; it would not be hard for him to find some excuse not to be present. Mercifully, I myself had no need to look far for a similar excuse: I had already arranged, at Urbgen's own request some days before, to ride out and inspect the signal stations along the estuary shore. With some dispatch, and perhaps a slight lack of dignity, I was gone from the city before Morgause's party arrived, nor did I return until the very eve of the wedding. Later I heard that Morgan, too, had avoided meeting her sister, but then it had hardly been expected of a bride so deep in preparations for a royal wedding.

So I was there to see the sisters meet, at the very gate of the church where, with the Christian rites, Morgan was to be married. Each of them, queen and princess, was splendidly dressed and magnifi-cently attended. They met, spoke, and embraced, with smiles as pretty as pictures, and as fixedly painted on their mouths. Morgan, I thought, won the encounter, since she was dressed for her wed-ding, and shone as the bright centre-piece to the feast-day. Her gown was magnificent, with its train of purple sewn with silver. She wore a crown on her dark hair, and among the magnificent jewels that Urbgen had given her, I recognised some that Uther had given Ygraine in the early days of their passion. Her slim body was erect under the weight of her rich robes, her face pale and composed and very beautiful. To me she recalled the young Ygraine, full of power and grace. I hoped, with fervour, that the reports of the sisters' dislike of one another were true, and that Morgause would not manage to ingratiate herself, now that her sister stood on the threshold of position and power. But I was uneasy; I could see no other reason for the witch to have come to see her sister's triumph and be outshone by her both in consequence and beauty.

Nothing could take from Morgause the rose-gold beauty which, with her maturity, was, if anything, richer than ever. But it could be seen that she was once again with child, and she had brought with her, besides, another child, a boy. This was an infant, still in his nurse's arms. Lot's son; not the one for whom, half in hope, half in apprehension, I was looking.

Morgause had seen me looking. She smiled that little smile of hers as she made her reverence, then swept on into the church with her train. I, as Arthur's vicar in this, waited to present the bride. Obedient to my message, the High King was busying himself elsewhere.

Any hopes I had had of being able to avoid Morgause further were dashed at the wedding-feast. She and I, as the two princes nearest to the bride, were placed side by side at the high table. The hall was the same one where Uther had held the victory feast that led to his death. In a room of this same castle she had lain with Arthur to conceive the child Mordred, and the next morning, in a bitter clash of wills, I had destroyed her hopes, and driven her away from Arthur's side. That, as far as she knew, had been our last encounter. She was still in ignorance – or so I hoped – of my journey to Dunpeldyr, and my vigil there.

I saw her watching me sideways, under the long white lids. I wondered suddenly, with misgiving, if she could be aware of my lack of defence against her now. Last time we had met she had tried her witch's tricks on me, and I had felt their potency, closing on the mind like a limed web. But she could no more have harmed me then than a she-spider could have hoped to trap a falcon. I had turned her spells back on herself, bearing her fury down by the sheer authority of power. That, now, had left me. It was possible that she could gauge my weakness. I could not tell. I had never underrated Morgause, and would not now.

I spoke with smooth civility. "You have a fine son, Morgause. What is he called?"

"Gawain."

"He has a strong look of his father."

Her lids drooped. "Both my sons," she said, gently, "have a strong look of their father."

"Both?"

"Come, Merlin, where is your art? Did you believe the dreadful news when you heard it? You must have known it was not true."

"I knew it was not true that Arthur had ordered the killing, in spite of the calumny you laid on him."

"I?" The lovely eyes were wide and innocent.

"Yes, you. The massacre may have been Lot's doing, the hot fool, and it was certainly Lot's men who threw the babies into the boat and sent them out with the tide. But who provoked him to it? It was your plan from the first, was it not, even to the murder of that poor child in the cradle? And it was not Lot who killed Macha, and lifted the other child out of the blood and carried him into hiding." I echoed her own half-mocking tone. "Come, Morgause, where is your art? You should know better than to play the innocent with me."

At the mention of Macha's name I saw fear, like a green spark, leap in her eyes, but she gave no other sign. She sat still and straight, one hand curved round the stem of her goblet, turning it gently, so that the gold burned in the hot torchlight. I could see the pulse beating fast in the hollow of her throat.

It was a sour satisfaction, at best. I had been right. Mordred was alive, hidden, I guessed, somewhere in the cluster of islands called the Orkneys, where Morgause's writ ran, and where I, without the Sight, had no power to find him. Or, I reminded myself, the mandate to kill him if found.

"You saw?" Her voice was low.

"Of course I saw. When could you hide things from me? You must know that everything is quite clear to me, and also, let me remind you, to the High King."

She sat still, and apparently composed, except for that rapid beat under the creamy flesh. I wondered if I had managed to convince her that I was still someone to be feared. It had not occurred to her that Lind might have come to me; and why should she ever re-member Beltane? The necklet he had made for her jumped and sparkled on her throat. She swallowed, and said, in a thin voice that hardly carried through the hubbub of the hall: "Then you will know that, even though I saved him from Lot, I don't know where he is. Perhaps you will tell me?"

"Do you expect me to believe that?"

"You must believe it, because it is true. I don't know where he is." She turned her head, looking full at me. "Do you?"

I made no reply. I merely smiled, picked up my goblet, and drank from it. But, without looking at her, I sensed in her a sudden relaxation, and wondered, with a chill creeping of the skin, if I had made a mistake.

"Even if I knew," she said, "how could I have him by me, and he as like to *his* father as one drop of wine to another?" She drank, set the goblet down, then sat back in her chair, folding her hands over her gown so that the thickening of her belly showed. She smiled at me, malice and hatred with no trace of fear. "Prophesy about this, then, Merlin the enchanter, if you won't about the other. Will this be another son to take the place of the one I lost?"

"I have no doubt of it," I said shortly, and she laughed aloud.

"I'm glad to hear it. I have no use for girls." Her eyes went to the bride, sitting composed and straight beside Urbgen. He had drunk a good deal, and the red stood in his cheeks, but he kept his dignity, even though his eyes caressed his bride, and he leaned close to her chair. Morgause watched, then said, with contempt: "So my little sister got her king in the end. A kingdom, yes, and a fine city and wide lands. But an old man, rising fifty, with sons already . . ." Her hand smoothed the front of her gown. "Lot may be a hot fool, as you termed him, but he is a man."

It was bait, but I did not rise to it. I said: "Where is he, that he could not come to the wedding?"

To my surprise she answered quite normally, apparently abandoning the malicious game of chess. Lot, it seemed, had gone east again into Northumbria with Urien, his sister's husband, and was busying himself there overseeing the extension to the Black Dyke. I have written of this before. It runs inland from the northern sea, and provides some sort of defence against incursions along the north-eastern seaboard. Morgause spoke of it with knowledge, and in spite of myself I was interested, and in the talk that followed the atmosphere lightened; and then someone asked me a question about Arthur's wedding and the new young Queen, and Morgause laughed and said, quite naturally:

"What's the use of asking Merlin? He may know everything in the world, but ask him to describe a bridal, and I'll wager he doesn't even know the colour of the girl's hair or her gown!"

Then talk around us became general, with a lot of laughter, and

speeches were made, and pledges given, and I must have drunk far
more than I was accustomed to, because I well remember how the
torchlight beat and swelled, bright and dark alternately, while talk
and laughter surged and broke in gusts, and with it the woman's
scent, a thick sweetness like honeysuckle, catching and trapping
the sense as a limed twig holds a bee. The fumes of wine rose
through it. A gold jug tilted, and my goblet brimmed again.
Someone said, smiling, "Drink, my lord." There was a taste of
apricots in my mouth, sweet and sharp; the skin had a texture like
the fur of a bee, or a wasp dying in sunlight on a garden wall
. . . And all the while eyes watching me, in excitement and wary
hope, then in contempt, and in triumph . . . Then servants were
beside me, helping me from my chair, and I saw that the bride had
gone already, and King Urbgen, impatience barely held on a tight
rein, was watching the door for the sign that it was time to follow
her to bed.

The chair beside me was empty. Round my own the servants
crowded, smiling, to help me back to my rooms.

6

Next morning I had a headache as bad as anything that the after-math of magic used to inflict on me. I kept to my rooms all day. On the day following I took leave of Urbgen and his queen. We had sat through a series of formal discussions before Morgause's arrival, and now I could leave the city – how thankfully, it may be guessed – and make my way south-west through the Wild Forest, at the heart of which stood Count Ector's castle of Galava. I took no leave of Morgause.

It was good to be out again, and this time with two companions only. Morgan's escort had been formed mainly of her own people from Cornwall, who had remained with her in Luguvallium. The two men who rode with me were deputed into my service by Urbgen; they would go with me as far as Galava, then return. It was vain for me to protest that I would rather go alone, and would be safe; King Urbgen merely repeated, smiling, that not even my magic would avail against wolves, or autumn fogs, or the sudden on-slaught of early snow, which in that mountainous country can trap the traveller very quickly among the steep valley-passes, and bring him to his death. His words were a reminder to me that, armed as I was now with only the reputation of past power, and not the thing itself, I was as subject to outrage from thieves and desperate men as any solitary traveller in that wild country; so I accepted the escort with thanks, and in so doing I suppose I saved my life.

We rode out over the bridge, and along the pleasant green valley where the river winds, bordered with alder and willow. Though my headache had gone, and I felt well enough, a certain lassitude still hung about me, and I breathed the sweet, familiar air, full of pine scents and bracken scents, with gratitude.

One small incident I remember. As we left the city gates, and crossed the river bridge, I heard a shrill cry, which at first I took to be a bird's, one of the gulls that wheeled about the refuse on the river's banks. Then a movement caught my eye, and I glanced down to see a woman, carrying a child, walking on the shingle by the river's edge below the bridge. The child was crying, and she hushed it. She saw me, and stood quite still, staring upward. I recognised Morgause's nurse. Then my horse clattered off the bridge, and the willows hid woman and child from view.

I thought nothing of the incident, and in a short while had forgotten it. We rode on, through villages and farms rich in grazing cattle. The willows were golden, and the hazel groves a-scamper with squirrels. Late swallows gathered along the rooftops, and as we approached that nest of mountains and lakes that marks the southern limits of the great forest, the lower hills flamed in the sun with ripe bracken, rusty-gold between the rocks. Elsewhere the forest, scattered oaks and pines, was gold and dark. Soon we came to the edge of the Wild Forest itself, where the trees crowd so thickly in the valleys that they shut out the sun. Before long we crossed the track that led up to the Green Chapel. I would have liked to revisit the place, but this would have added some hours to the journey, and besides, the visit could be made more easily from Galava. So we held on our way, staying with the road as far as Petrianae.

Today this hardly deserves the name of town, though in Roman times it was a prosperous market centre. There is still a market, where a few cattle and sheep and goods exchange hands, but Petrianae itself is a poor cluster of daub-and-wattle huts, its only shrine a mere shell of stonework holding a ruinous altar to Mars, in his person of the local god Cocidius. I saw no offering there, except, on the mossed step, a leathern sling, such as shepherds use, and a pile of sling-stones. I wondered what escape, from wolf or wild man, the shepherd was giving thanks for.

Beyond Petrianae we left the road and took to the hill tracks, which my escort knew well. We travelled at ease, enjoying the warmth of the late autumn sun. As we climbed higher the warmth still lingered, and the air was soft, but with a tingle to it that meant the first frosts were not far away.

We stopped to rest the horses in one high, lonely corrie where a small tarn lay cupped in stony turf, and here we came across a shepherd, one of those hardy hillmen who lodge all summer out on the fell tops with the little blue-fleeced sheep of Rheged. Wars and battles may move and clash below them, but they look up, rather than down, for danger, and at the first onslaught of winter take to the caves, faring thinly on black bread and raisins, and meal-cakes made on a turf fire. They drive their flocks for safety into pens built between the rocky outcrops on the hillsides. Sometimes they do not hear another man's voice from lamb-time to clipping, and then on to autumn's end.

This lad was so little used to talking that he found speech hard, and what he did say came in an accent so thick that even the troopers, who were local men, could make nothing of it, and I, who have the gift of tongues, was hard put to it to understand him. He had, it seemed, had speech with the Old Ones, and was ready enough to pass on his news. It was negative, and none the worse for that. Arthur had stayed in Caerleon for almost a month after his wedding, then had ridden, with his knights, up through the Pennine Gap, heading apparently for Olicana and the Plain of York, where he would meet with the King of Elmet. This was hardly news to me, but at least it was confirmation that there had been no new war-move during the late autumn's peace. The shepherd had saved his best titbit till last. The High King (he called him "young Emrys", with such a mixture of pride and familiarity that I guessed that Arthur's path must have crossed his in times past) had left his queen with child. At this, the troopers were openly sceptical; maybe he had, was their verdict, but how, in a scant month, could anyone know for sure? I, when appealed to, was more credulous. As I have said, the Old Ones have ways of knowing that cannot be understood, but deserve to be respected. If the lad had heard this through them . . . ?

He had. That was all he knew. Young Emrys had gone into Elmet, and the lass he'd wedded was with child. The word he used was "yeaning", at which the troopers were disposed to be merry, but I thanked him and gave him a coin, and he turned back to his sheep well satisfied, with only a lingering look at me, half-recognising, I suppose, the hermit of the Green Chapel.

That night we were still well away from the roads, or any hope of a lodging, so when the dusk came down early and dim with mist, we made our camp under tall pines at the forest's edge, and the men cooked supper. I had been drinking water on the journey, as I like to do in mountain country where it is pure and good, but in celebration of the shepherd's news I broke open a new flask of the wine I had been supplied with from Urbgen's cellars. I planned to share this with my companions, but they refused, preferring their own thin ration-wine, which tasted of the skins they carried it in. So I ate and drank alone, and lay down to sleep.

★   ★   ★

I cannot write of what happened next. The Old Ones know the story, and it is possible that somewhere else some other man has set it down, but I remember it only dimly, as if I were watching a vision in a dark and smoking glass.

But it was no vision; they stay with me more vividly, even, than memory. This was a kind of madness that took me, brought on, as I now know, by some drug in the wine I had taken. Twice before, when Morgause and I had come face to face, she had tried her witch's tricks on me, but her novice's magic had glanced off me like a child's pebble off a rock. But this last time . . . I was to recall how, at the wedding feast, the light thickened and beat around me, while the smell of honeysuckle loaded memory with treachery, and the taste of apricots brought back murder. And how I, who am frugal with food and wine, was carried drunken to bed. I remembered, too, the voice saying, "Drink, my lord," and the green, watching eyes. She must have tried her wiles again, and found that now her magic was strong enough to trap me in its sticky threads. It may be that the seeds of the madness were sown then, at the wedding feast, and left to develop later, when I was far enough away for there to be no blame cast on her. Her servant had been there at the river bridge to see me safely out of the city. Later, the witch had implemented the drug with some other poison, slipped into one of the flasks I carried. There she had been lucky. If I had not heard the news of Guenever's pregnancy, I might never have broached the poisoned flask. As it was, we were well away from Luguvallium when I drank the poison. If the men with me had shared it, so much the worse for them. Morgause would have swept a hundred such aside, to harm Merlin her enemy. There was no need to look further for her motive in coming to her sister's marriage.

Whatever the poison, my frugal ways cheated her of my death. What happened after I had drunk and lain down I can only piece together from what I have since been told, and from the whirling fragments of memory.

It seems that the troopers, alarmed in the night by my groans, hurried to my bed-place, where they were horrified to find me obviously sick and in great pain, twisting on the ground, and moaning, apparently too far gone to be sensible. They did what they could, which was not much, but their rough help saved me as nothing could have done, had I been alone. They made me vomit, then brought their own blankets to augment mine, and wrapped me up warmly and made up the fire. Then one of them stayed beside me while the other set off down the valley to find help or lodging. He was to send help back to us, and a guide, then ride on himself down to Galava with the news.

When he had gone the other fellow did what he could, and after an hour or two I sank into a sort of sleep. He hardly liked the look of it, but when at last he dared leave me, and took a step or two away among the trees to relieve himself, I neither moved nor made a sound, so he decided to take the chance to fetch water from the brook. This was a scant twenty paces off, downhill over silent mosses. Once there, he bethought himself of the fire, which had burned low again, so he crossed the brook and went a bit further – thirty paces, no more, he swore it – to gather more wood. There was plenty lying about, and he was gone only a few minutes. When he got back to the camping-place I had vanished, and, scour the place as he might, he could find no trace of me. It was no blame to him that after an hour or so spent wandering and calling through the echoing darkness of the great forest, he took horse and galloped after his fellow. Merlin the enchanter had too many strange vanishings to his name to leave the simple trooper in any doubt as to what had happened.

The enchanter had disappeared, and all they could do was make their report, and wait for his return.

*   *   *

It was a long dream. I remember nothing about the beginning of it, but I suppose that, buoyed up by some kind of delirious strength, I crept from my bed-place and wandered off across the deep mosses of the forest, then lay, perhaps, where I fell, deep in some ditch or thicket where the trooper could not find me. I must have recovered in time to take shelter from the weather, and of course I must have found food, and possibly even made fire, during the weeks of storm that followed, but of this I remember nothing. All I can recall now is a series of pictures, a kind of bright and silent dream through which I moved like a spirit, weightless and bodiless, borne up by the air as a heavy body is borne up by water. The pictures, though vivid, are diminished into an emotionless distance, as if I were looking on at a world that hardly concerns me. So, I sometimes imagine, must the bodiless dead watch over the world they have left.

So I drifted, deep in the autumn forest, unheeded as a wraith of the forest mist. Straining back now in memory, the pictures come to me. Deep aisles of beech, thick with mast, where the wild boar rooted, and the badger dug for food, and the stags clashed and wrestled, roaring, with never a glance at me. Wolves too; the way through those high woods is known as the Wolf Road, but though I would have been easy meat they had had a good summer, and let me be. Then, with the first real chill of winter, came the hoar glitter of icy mornings, with the reeds standing stiff and black out of curded ice, and the forest deserted, badger in lair and deer down in the valley-bottom, and the wild geese gone and the skies empty.

Then the snow. A brief vision this, of the silent, whirling air, warm after the frost; of the forest receding into mist, into dimness, breaking into whirling flakes of white and grey, and then a blinding, silent cold . . .

A cave, with cave-smells, and turf burning, and the taste of cordial, and voices, gruffly uncouth in the harsh tongue of the Old Ones, speaking just out of hearing. The reek of badly cured wolf-skins, the hot itch of verminous wrappings, and, once, a nightmare of bound limbs and a weight holding me down . . .

There is a long gap of darkness here, but afterwards sunlight, new green, the first bird-song, and a vision, sharp as a child's first sight of the spring, of a bank of celandines, glossy as licked gold. And life stirring again in the forest; the thin foxes padding out, the earth heaving in the badger-setts, stags trotting by unarmed and gentle, and the wild boar again, out foraging. And an absurd, dim dream of finding a pigling still with the stripes and long silky hair of babyhood, that hobbled about on a broken leg, deserted by its kind.

Then suddenly, one grey dawn, the sound of horses galloping, filling the forest, and the clash of swords and the whirl of bright axes, the yelling and the screams of wounded beasts and men, and, like a flashing, intermittent dream of violence, a day-long storm of fighting that ended with a groaning quiet and the smell of blood and crushed bracken.

Silence then, and the scent of apple-trees, and the nightmare sense of grief that comes when a man wakes again to feel a loss he has forgotten in sleep.

7

"Merlin!" said Arthur in my ear. "*Merlin!*"

I opened my eyes. I was lying in bed in a room which seemed to
be built high up. The bright sunlight of early morning poured in,
falling on dressed stone walls, with a curve in them that told of a
tower. At the level of the sill I caught a glimpse of treetops moving
against cloud. The air eddied, and was cool, but within the room a
brazier burned, and I was snug in blankets, and good linen fragrant
with cedarwood. Some sort of herb had been thrown into the
charcoal of the brazier; the thin smoke smelled clean and resinous.
There were no hangings on the walls, but thick slate-grey sheep-
skins lay on the floor, and there was a plain cross of olive-wood
hanging on the wall facing the bed. A Christian household and, by
the appointments, a wealthy one. Beside the bed, on a stand of
gilded wood, stood a jug and goblet of Samian ware, and a bowl of
beaten silver. There was a cross-legged stool nearby, where a
servant must have been sitting to watch me: now he was standing,
backed up against the wall, with his eyes, not on me, but on the
King.

Arthur let out a long breath, and some of the colour came back
into his face. He looked as I had never seen him look before. His eyes
were shadowed with fatigue, and the flesh had fallen in below his
cheekbones. The last of his youth had vanished; here was a hard-
living man, sustained by a will that daily pushed himself and his
followers to their very limits and beyond.

He was kneeling beside the bed. As I moved my eyes to look at
him, his hand fell across my wrist in a quick grip. I could feel the
callouses on his palm.

"Merlin? Do you know me? Can you speak?"

I tried to form a word, but could not. My lips were cracked and dry. My mind felt clear enough, but my body would not obey me. The King's arm came round me, lifting me, and at a sign from him the servant came forward and filled the goblet. Arthur took it from him and held it to my mouth. The stuff was a cordial, sweet and strong. He took a napkin from the man, wiped my lips with it, and lowered me back against the pillows.

I smiled at him. It must have shown as little more than a faint movement of muscles. I tried his name, "Emrys." I could hear no sound. I fancy that it came as a breath, no more.

His hand came down again over mine. "Don't try to speak. I was wrong to make you. You are alive, that's all that matters. Rest now."

My eye, wandering, fell on something beyond him; my harp, set on a chair beside the wall. I said, still without a thread of sound, "You found my harp," and relief and joy went through me, as if, in some way, all must now be well.

He followed my glance. "Yes, we found it. It's unharmed. Rest now, my dear. All is well. All is well, indeed . . ."

I tried his name again, and failing, slid back into darkness. Faintly, like movements from the Otherworld of dream, I remember swift commands, softly spoken, the servants hurrying, slippered footsteps and the rustle of women's garments, cool hands, soft voices. Then the comfort of oblivion.

★　★　★

When I awoke again, it was to full consciousness, as if from a long, refreshing sleep. My brain was clear, my body very weak, but my own. I was conscious, gratefully, of hunger. I moved my head experimentally, then my hands. They felt stiff and heavy, but they belonged to me. Wherever I had been wandering, I had come back to my body. I had quitted the world of dream.

I could see, from the change in the light, that it was evening. A servant – a different one – waited near the door. But one thing was the same; Arthur was still there. He had pulled the stool forward, and was sitting by the bed. He turned his head and saw me watching him, and his face changed. He made a quick movement forward, and his hand came down on mine again, a gentle touch like a doctor's, feeling for the pulse in the wrist.

"By God," he said, "you frightened us! What happened? No, no, forget that. Later you'll tell us all you can remember . . . Now it's enough to know that you are safe, and living. You look better. How do you feel?"

"I have been dreaming." My voice was not my own; it seemed to come from somewhere else, away in the air, almost outside my control. It was as feeble as the pigling's pipe when I mended its broken leg. "I have been ill, I think."

"Ill?" He gave a crack of laughter that held nothing of mirth. "You have been stark crazy, my dear king's prophet. I thought you were gone clean out of your wits, and that we should never have you back with us again."

"It must have been a fever of a kind. I hardly remember . . ." I knitted my brows, thinking back. "Yes. I was travelling to Galava with two of Urbgen's men. We made camp up near the Wolf Road, and . . . Where am I now?"

"Galava itself. This is Ector's castle. You're home."

It had been Arthur's home, rather than mine; for reasons of secrecy I had never lived in the castle myself, but had spent the hidden years in the forest, up at the Green Chapel. But as I turned my head and caught the familiar scents of pine forest and lake water, and the smell of the rich tilled soil of Drusilla's garden below the tower, reassurance came, like the sight of a known light through the fog.

"The battle I saw," I said. "Was that real, or did I imagine it?"

"Oh, that was real enough. But don't try to talk about it yet. Take it from me, all is well. Now, you should rest again. How do you feel?"

"Hungry."

This, of course, started up a new bustling. Servants brought broth, and bread, and more cordials, and the Countess Drusilla herself helped me to eat, and then, once more, disposed me for welcome and dreamless sleep.

★　★　★

Morning again, and the bright, clean light to which I had first woken. I felt weak still, but in command of myself. It seemed that the King had given orders that he was to be fetched as soon as I woke, but this I would not allow until I had been bathed and shaved and had eaten.

When he came at length he looked quite different. The strained look about his eyes had lessened, and there was colour in his face under the brown of weather. Something of his own especial quality had come back, too; the young strength that men could drink from, as at a spring, and be strengthened themselves.

I had to reassure him about my own recovery, before he would let me talk, but he eventually settled down to give me news. "The last I heard," I told him, "was that you had gone into Elmet . . . But that's past history now, it seems. I gather that the truce was broken? What was the battle I saw? It must have been up these parts, in the Caledonian Forest? Who was involved?"

He eyed me, I thought strangely, but answered readily enough. "Urbgen called me in. The enemy broke across country into Strathclyde, and Caw didn't manage to hold them. They would have forced their way down through the Forest to the road. I came up with them, and broke them up and drove them back. The remnants fled south. I should have followed straight away, but then we found you, and I had to stay .,. . How could I leave again, till I knew you were home, and cared for?"

"So I really did see the fighting? I wondered if it was part of the dream."

"You must have seen it all. We fought through the forest, along the river there. You know what it's like, good open ground with thin woodland, birch and alder, just the place for a surprise with fast cavalry. We had the hill at our backs, and took them as they reached the ford. The river was full; easy for horsemen, but for foot-soldiers a trap . . . Afterwards, when we came back from the first pursuit, people came running to tell me that you were there. You'd been found wandering among the dead and wounded and giving directions to the doctors . . . Nobody recognised you at first, but then the whispers started that Merlin's ghost was there." A wry little smile. "I gather that the ghost's advice was good, as often as not. But of course the whispers set up a scare, and some fools started throwing stones to drive you away. It was one of the orderlies, a man called Paulus, who recognised you, and put a stop to the ghost stories. He followed you back to where you were living, and then sent to me."

"Paulus. Yes, of course. A good man. I've worked with him often. And where was I living?"

"In a ruined turret, with an ancient orchard round it. You don't remember that?"

"No. But something is coming back. A turret, yes, ruinous, all ivy and owls. And apple trees?"

"Yes. It was little more than a pile of stones, with bracken for bedding, and piles of apples rotting, and a store of nuts, and rags hung to dry on the apple boughs." He paused to clear something from his throat. "They thought at first you were one of those wild hermits, and indeed, when I first saw you myself . . ." His smile twisted. "You looked the part better than you ever looked it at the Green Chapel."

"I can imagine that." And so I could. My beard, before they had shaved me, had grown long and grey, and my hands, lying weakly on the bright blankets, looked thin and old, bones held together with a net of knotted veins.

"So we brought you here. I had to go south again soon after. We caught them up at Caer Guinnion, and fought a bloody engagement there. All went well, but then a messenger came down from Galava with more news of you. When we found you and brought you here, you were strong enough on your feet, but crazy; you didn't know anyone, and you talked about things that made no kind of sense; but once here, and in the women's care, you relapsed into sleep and silence. Well, the messenger came after the battle to tell me that you had never woken. You seemed to fall into a high fever, still talking in the same wild way, then finally lay so long unconscious that they took you for dead, and sent the courier to tell me. I came as soon as I could."

I narrowed my eyes at him. The light from the window was strong. He saw this, and signed to the slave, who pulled a curtain across. "Let me get this clear. After you had found me in the forest and brought me to Galava, you went south. And there was another battle? Arthur, how long have I been here?"

"It is three weeks since we found you. But it is fully seven months since you wandered off into the forest and lost yourself. You were gone all winter. Is it any wonder that we thought you were dead?"

"*Seven months?*" Often, as a doctor, I have had to give this kind of news to patients who have been long feverish, or lying in coma, and I always see the same sort of incredulous, groping shock. I felt it now, myself. To know that half a year had dropped out of time, and such a half year . . . What, in those months, might not have happened to a country as torn and as embattled as mine? And to her King? Other things, forgotten till now in the mists of illness, began to come back to me.

Looking at him, I saw again, with fear, the hollowed cheekbones and the smudge of sleepless nights beneath his eyes: Arthur, who ate like a young wolf and slept like a child; who was the creature of gaiety and strength. There had been no defeat in the field; his glory there had not suffered even the smear of a shadow. Nor could his anxiety for me have brought him to this pass. There remained his home.

"Emrys, what has happened?"

Once more, in that place, the childhood name came naturally. I saw his face twist as if the memory were a pain. He bent his head and stared down at the blankets.

"My mother, the Queen. She died."

Memory stirred. The woman lying in the great bed hung with rich stuffs? I had known, then. "I am sorry," I said.

"I heard just before we fought the battle at Caer Guinnion. Lucan brought the news, with the token you had left with him. You remember it, a brooch with the Christian symbol? Her death came as no surprise. We had expected it. But I believe that grief helped to hasten her death."

"Grief? Why, has there been – ?" I stopped dead. It had come back clearly now, the night in the forest, and the flask of wine I had opened to share with the troopers. And why. The vision stirred again, the moonlit chamber and the blowing curtains and the dead woman. Something closed my throat. I said, hardly: "Guenever?"

He nodded, not looking up.

I asked, knowing the answer: "And the child?"

He looked up quickly. "You knew? Yes, of course you

would . . . It never came to term. They said she was with child, but shortly before Christmas she began to bleed, and then, at the New Year, died in great pain. If you had been there –" He stopped, swallowed, and was silent.

"I am sorry," I said again.

He went on, in a voice so hard that it sounded angry: "We thought you were dead, too. Then, after the battle, there you were, filthy and old and crazy, but the field surgeons said you might recover. That, at least, I had saved from the shambles of the winter . . . Then I had to leave you to go to Caer Guinnion. I won it, yes, but lost some good men. Then on the heels of the action Ector's courier came to tell me you were dead. When I got here at dawn yesterday I expected to find your body already burned or buried."

He stopped, put his forehead hard down on a clenched fist, and stayed so. The servant, rigid by the window, caught my eye, and went, softly. In a moment or two Arthur raised his head and spoke in his normal voice.

"Forgive me. All the time I was riding north, I kept remembering what you said about dying a shameful death. It was hard to bear."

"But here I am, clean and whole, with my wits clear, and ready to become clearer when you tell me all that has happened in the last six months. Now, of your kindness, pour me some of that wine, and go back, if you will, to your journey into Elmet."

He obeyed me, and in a while talk became easier. He spoke of his journey through the Gap to Olicana, and what he had found there, and of his meeting with the King of Elmet. Then of his return to Caerleon, and of the Queen's miscarriage and death. This time, when I questioned him, he was able to answer me, and in the end I could give him the chilly comfort of knowing that my presence at court beside the young Queen could have been no help. Her doctors were skilled with drugs, and had saved her the worst of the pain; I could have done no more. The child was ill-conceived; nothing could have saved it, or its mother.

When he had heard what I had to tell him, he accepted this, and himself turned the subject. He was eager to hear what had happened to me, and impatient of the fact that I could remember little after the marriage feast at Luguvallium.

"Can you not remember anything of how you came to the turret where we found you?"

"A little. It comes clear bit by bit. I must have wandered about in the forest and kept myself alive somehow until winter. Then it seems to me as if some rude folk of the hill forest must have taken me in and cared for me. Without that, I doubt if I could have survived the snow. I thought they might be some of Mab's people, the Old Ones of the mountain country, but if so, they would surely have sent word to you."

"They did. Word came, but only after you had vanished again. As is usual, the Old Ones were snowed up in their high caves all winter, and you with them. They went hunting when the snow melted, and came back to their caves to find you gone. It was from them that I first heard that you had run mad. They had had to tie you, they said, but afterwards, at such times, you would be calm and very weak, and so it was at the time when they left you. When they got home, you had gone."

"I remember being bound. Yes. So after that I must have made my way downhill, and ended up in the ruin near the ford. I suppose, in my crazed way, still making for Galava. It was spring; I remember a little of it. Then the battle must have overtaken me, and you found me there in the Forest. I recall nothing of that."

He told me again how I had been found, thin and filthy and talking no kind of sense, hiding in the ruined turret, with a kind of squirrel's hoard of acorns and beechnuts, and dried windfall apples put by, and a pigling with a splinted leg for company.

"So that part of it was real!" I said, smiling. "I can remember finding the creature, and healing the leg, but not much else. If I was as sharp set as you say, it was good of me not to eat Master Piglet. What happened to it?"

"It's here in Ector's sties." The first glimmer of humour touched his mouth. "And marked, I think, for a long and dishonourable life. There's not one of the boys would dare lay a hand on the enchanter's personal pig, which looks like growing up into a good fighting boar, so it will end up as king of the sty, which is only proper. Merlin, you've told me all you can remember of what happened after making camp up there on the Wolf Road; what do you remember before that? What made you ill? Urbgen's men said it came on suddenly. They thought it was poison, and so did I. I wondered if the witch had had you followed, after the wedding feast, and one of her creatures had dragged you from your bed that night while the trooper's back was turned. But if that had happened, surely they would have killed you? There was no suspicion of foul play from those two men; they were Urbgen's own, hand-picked."

"None at all. They were good fellows, and I owe them my life."

"They told me that you drank wine that night, from your own flask. They did not share it. They say, too, that you were drunk at the marriage feast. You? I have never seen you the worse for wine. And you sat beside Morgause. Have you any reason to believe that she drugged your wine?"

I opened my mouth to answer him, and to this day I swear that the word on my lips was "Yes." This, as far as I knew it, was the truth. But some god must have forestalled me. Instead of the "Yes" that my mind had framed, my lips said, "No."

I must have spoken strangely, because I saw him staring, arrested with narrowed eyes. It was a discomforting look, and I found myself elaborating. "How can I tell? But I don't think so. I have told you that I have no power now, but the witch would not know that. She is still afraid of me. She has tried before, not once but twice, to snare me with her woman's spells. Both times she failed, and I think she would not have dared try again."

He was silent for a while. Then he said, shortly: "When my Queen died, there was talk of poison. I wondered."

At this I could protest truthfully. "There always is, but I beg you will not regard it! From what you have told me, I am certain there was no such thing. Besides, how?" I added, as convincingly as I could: "Believe me, Arthur. If she were guilty, can you see any reason why I should want to protect Morgause from you?"

He still looked doubtful, but did not pursue it further. "Well," was all he said. "She'll find her wings clipped now for a while. She is back in Orkney, and Lot is dead."

I took this in silently. It was another shock. In these few months, how much had changed. "How?" I asked him. "And when?"

"In the Forest battle. I can't say that I mourn him, except that he had that rat Aguisel under his fist, and I believe that I shall have trouble there soon."

I said slowly: "I have remembered something else. During the fighting in the Forest I heard them calling to one another that the king was dead. It struck me with helpless grief. For me, there is only one king . . . But they must have been speaking of Lot. Well, yes, at least Lot was a known evil. Now, I suppose, Urien will have it all his own way in the north-east, and Aguisel with him . . . But there's time enough for that. Meanwhile, what of Morgause? She was carrying a child at Luguvallium, and should have been delivered by now. A boy?"

"Two. Twin sons, born at Dunpeldyr. She joined Lot there after Morgan's wedding. Witch or no witch," he said, with a trace of bitterness, "she is a good breeder of sons. By the time Lot rejoined us here in Rheged, he was bragging that he had left yet another in her before he quitted Dunpeldyr." He looked down at his hands. "You must have had speech with her at the wedding. Did you find anything out about the other boy?"

There was no need to ask which boy he meant. It seemed that he could not bring himself to say "my son".

"Only that he is alive."

His eyes came up quickly to mine. There was a flash in them, suppressed instantly. But I was sure that it was one of joy. So short a time ago, and he had looked for the child only to kill it.

I said, schooling my voice to hide the pity I felt: "She tells me that she does not know where he is to be found. She may be lying, I'm not sure of that. It must be true that she kept him hidden away from Lot. But she may bring him into the open now. What has she to fear, now that Lot has gone? Except, perhaps, from you?"

He was looking at his hands again. "She need not fear me now on that score," he said, woodenly.

That is all I can remember of that interview. I heard someone saying, but the words seemed to go round the curved tower walls like a whispered echo, or like words in my head alone: "She is the falsest lady at this time alive, but she must live to rear her four sons by the King of Orkney, for they will be your faithful servants, and the bravest of your Companions."

I must have shut my eyes then, against the wave of exhaustion that broke over me, for when I opened them again it was dark, and Arthur had gone, and the servant knelt beside the bed, offering me a bowl of soup.

8

I am a strong man, and heal fast. I was on my feet again soon after this, and, some two or three weeks later, thought myself fit enough to ride south in Arthur's wake. He had gone the next morning, riding down to Caerleon. Since then a courier had brought news that longships had been sighted in the Severn estuary, so it looked as if the King would soon have another battle on his hands.

I would have liked to stay a while longer at Galava, perhaps to pass the summer in that familiar country, and revisit my old haunts in the Forest. But after the courier's visit, though Ector and Drusilla tried to keep me, I thought it high time to be gone. The battle now imminent would be fought from Caerleon: indeed, it was possible (the dispatch had said) that the invaders were attempting in force to destroy the war-leader's main stronghold and supply centre. I had no doubt that Arthur would hold Caerleon, but it was time I got back to Caer Camel to see how Derwen had been doing in my absence.

It was high summer when I saw the place again, and Derwen's team had done wonders. There it stood on its steep, flat-topped hill, the vision made real. The outer works were complete, the great double wall, of dressed stone topped with timber, running along the rim of the slope to crown the whole crest of the hill. Piercing it at their two opposing corners, the vast gateways were finished, and impressive. Great double doors of oak, studded with iron, stood open, pulled back to wall the tunnels that led in through the thick rampart. Above them went the sentry-way behind its battlements.

Moreover, there were sentries there. Since winter, Derwen told me, the King had had the place invested, so that the work of finishing could proceed inside defended walls. And finished it soon would be. Arthur had sent word that, come July or August, he wanted to be there with the knights-companions and all his cavalry.

Derwen was all for pressing on with the headquarters buildings, and with the King's own rooms, but I knew Arthur's mind better than that. I had given instructions that the men's barracks, and the horse-lines, the kitchens and service quarters must be completed first, and this had been done. A good start had been made, too, on the central buildings: the King, certainly, must lodge under skins and temporary timber, as if he were still in the field, but his great hall was built and roofed, and carpenters were at work on the long tables and benches within.

There had been no lack of local help. The folk who lived nearby, thankful to see a strong place going up near their settlements, had come whenever they could to fetch and carry, or to lend their skills to our own workmen. With them came many who were willing, but too old or too young to labour. Derwen would have sent them away, but I set them to clearing the nettle-grown trenches of a site not far from headquarters where formerly there must have been a shrine. I did not know, and nor did they, to what god it had been consecrated; but I know soldiers, and all fighting men need some centre-point, with a light and an offering, to tempt their god down among them for a moment of communion, when strength can be received in return for hope and faith.

Similarly, the spring on the northern embankment, which was enclosed within the outer works of the fortification, I set the women to clearing. This they did eagerly, for it was known that, time out of mind, the spring had been dedicated to the Goddess herself. For many years now it had been neglected, and sunk in a tangle of thorny growth that prevented them from making their offerings and sending up the sort of prayers that women send. Now the woodmen had hacked the thickets down, so I let the women make their own shrine. They sang as they worked; they had been afraid, I think, that their sacred place would be shut away in an enclave of men. I told them not so: when once the Saxon power was broken, it was the High King's plan that men and women should come and go in peace, and Caer Camel would be a fair city set on a hill, rather than a camp of fighting men.

Finally, on the lowest part of the field, near the north-east gate, we cleared a place for the people and their cattle, where they could take refuge, and live, if need be, till danger was past.

Then Arthur came. In the night the Tor flamed suddenly, and beyond the flame could be seen the point of light that was the beacon hill behind. In the early morning sunlight he came riding along the Lake's edge, at the head of his knights. White was still his colour; he rode his white war-horse; his banner was white, and his shield also, too proud for a device such as the others wore. He shone out of the misty landscape like a swan on the pearled reaches of the Lake. Then the cavalcade was lost to sight beyond the trees that crowded the base of the hill, and presently the beat of hoofs came steadily on, and up the new curling road to the King's Gate.

The double gates stood open to receive him. Inside them, lining the newly paved road, waited all those who had built the place for him. So for the first time Arthur, duke of battles, High King among the other kings of Britain, entered the stronghold which was to be his own fair city of Camelot.

★ ★ ★

Of course he was pleased with it, and that night a feast was held, to which everyone, man, woman or child, who had lent a hand to the work, was bidden. He and his knights, with Derwen and myself and a few others, sat in the hall, at the long table so newly sanded that the dust still hung in the air and made haloes round the torches. It was a joyous occasion, without form or solemnity, like a feast on a victory field. He made some kind of speech of welcome – of which I now remember no single word – pitching his voice so that the people pressing outside the doors could hear him; then, once we in the hall had started eating, he left his place at the table's head, and, with a mutton bone in one hand and a goblet in the other, went the rounds of the place, sitting with this group or that, dipping into a pot with the masons or letting the carpenters ply him from the mead-barrel, all the time looking, questioning, praising, with all his old, shining way. In a short while, their awe of him melting, they pelted their questions like snowballs. What had happened at Caerleon? In Linnuis? In Rheged? When would he settle here? Was it likely that the Saxons could press this far and get across the downs? What was Eosa's strength? Were the stories – of this, that and the other thing – true? All of which he answered patiently: what men knew they must face, they would face: it was the fear of surprise and the arrow in the dark that unmanned the hardiest.

It was all in the style of the old Arthur, the young King I knew. His looks matched it, too. The fatigue and despair had gone; grief had been laid aside; this was once again the King who held all men's eyes, and whose strength they felt they could draw on for ever, and never weaken him. By morning there would be no one there who would not willingly die in his service. That he knew this, and was fully aware of the effect he made, did not detract one whit from his greatness.

As usually happened, we had a word together before sleep. He was housed simply, but better than in a field tent. A roof of leather had been stretched across the beams of his half-finished sleeping chamber, and rugs laid. His own camp bed had been put against a wall, with the table and reading lamp he worked with, and a pair of chairs and the clothes chest and the stand with the silver bowl and water-jug.

We had not spoken privately since Galava. He asked after my health, and spoke of the work I had done at Caer Camel, and then of what still remained to do. What had happened in the Caerleon fighting I had heard already, in the talk at table. I said something about the change in him. He looked at me for a moment or two, then, apparently, came to a decision.

"There's something I wanted to say to you, Merlin. I don't know if I have any right, but I shall say it all the same. When you last saw me, at Galava, sick as you were, you must have seen something of what I was feeling. In fact, how could you help it? As usual, I laid all my troubles on you, regardless of whether you were fit to bear them, or not."

"I don't remember that. We talked, yes. I asked you what had happened, and you told me."

"I did indeed. Now I am asking you to bear with me again. This time, I hope, I am laying nothing on you, but . . ." A brief pause, to gather his thoughts. He seemed oddly hesitant. I wondered what was coming. He went on: "You once said to me that life divided itself into light and dark, just as time does into day and night. It's true. One misfortune seems to breed another; and so it was with me. That was a time of darkness – the first I had suffered. When I came to you I was half broken with weariness, and with the weight of losses coming one on the other, as if the world had turned sour, and my luck was dead. The loss of my mother, by itself, could be no great grief to me; you know my heart about that, and to tell you the truth, I would grieve more over Drusilla's death, or Ector's. But the death of my Queen, little Guenever . . . It could have been a good marriage, Merlin. We could, I believe, have come to love. What made that grief so bitter was the loss of the child, and the waste of her young life in pain, and with it, besides, the fear that she had been murdered, and by my enemies. Added to that – and I can admit this to you – was the weary prospect of having to start all over again to look for a suitable match, and going once more through all the ritual of mating, when so much else lies waiting for me to do."

I said quickly: "You surely do not still believe that she was murdered?"

"No. You have set my mind at rest there, as you have about your own sickness. I had the same fear about you, that your death had been my fault." He paused, and then said flatly: "And that was the worst. It came as the final loss, overtopping all the others." A gesture, half shame-faced, half resigned. "You have told me, not once but many times, that when I looked for you in need, you would be there. And always, until then, it was true. Then suddenly, at the dark time, you were gone. And with so much still to do. Caer Camel just begun, and more fighting expected, and after that, the settlements and the lawgiving, and the making of civil order . . . But you were gone – murdered, I thought, through my fault, like my little Queen. I could not think past it. I did not kill the children at Dunpeldyr, but by God, I could have killed the Queen of Orkney, had she crossed my path during those months!"

"I understand this. I think I knew it. Go on."

"You have heard, now, about my victories in the field during this time. To other men it must have seemed as if my fortunes were rising to their peak. But to me, mainly because of your loss, I felt life at its blackest depth. Not only for grief at the loss of what lies between us, the long friendship – guardianship – I would say love – but for a reason I don't have to remind you of again. You know that I have been used to turn to you for everything, except in matters of warfare."

I waited, but he did not go on. I said: "Well, that is my function.

No one man, even a High King, can do it all. You are young still, Arthur. Even my father Ambrosius, with all his years behind him, took advice at every turn. There is no weakness in this. Forgive me, but it is a sign of youth to think so."

"I know. I don't think it. This is not what I am trying to say. I want to tell you of something that happened while you were sick. After the battle in Rheged, I took hostages. The Saxons fled into a thick wood on a hill – above the turret where we found you just after. We surrounded the hill, and then drove in on all sides, killing, until the few who were left, surrendered. I believe they might have yielded sooner, but I gave them no chance. I wanted to kill. At the last, those few who were left threw down their arms and came out. We took them. One of them was Colgrim's former second-in-command, Cynewulf. I would have killed him then and there, but he had yielded his arms. I loosed him on the promise to take his ships and go; and I took hostages."

"Yes? It was a wise try. We know it did not work." I said it without expression. I guessed what was coming. I had heard the tale already, from others.

"Merlin, when I heard that, instead of going back to Germany, Cynewulf had turned in again to our coasts, and was burning villages, I had the hostages killed."

"It was not your choice. Cynewulf knew. It was what he would have done."

"He is a barbarian, and an outlander. I am not. Granted Cynewulf knew. He may have thought I would not carry out the threat. Some of them were no more than boys. The youngest was thirteen, younger than I was when I first fought. They were brought to me, and I ordered it."

"Rightly. Now forget it."

"How? They were brave. But I had threatened it and so I did it. You spoke of the change in me. You were right. I am not the man I was before this past winter-time. This was the first thing I have done in war that I knew to be evil."

I thought of Ambrosius at Doward: of myself at Tintagel. I said: "We have all done things that we would like to forget. It may be that war itself is evil."

"How could it be?" He spoke impatiently. "But I'm not telling you about it now because I want either your advice or your comfort." I waited, at a loss. He went on, picking his words: "It was the worst thing I have had to do. I did it, and I will abide by it. What I have to say now is this: if you had been there, I would have turned to you, as always, and asked for your counsel. And though you have said that you no longer have the power of prophecy, I would still have hoped – been sure – that you could see what the future held, and would guide me in the path I ought to take."

"But this time your prophet was dead, so you chose your own path?"

"Just so."

"I understand. You offer me this as comfort, that both act and decision can be safely left to you, even though I am here again? Knowing, as we both do, that your 'prophet' is still dead?"

"No." He spoke quickly, strongly. "You have mistaken me. I am offering you comfort, yes, but of a different kind. Do you think I don't know that it has been a dark time with you, too, ever since the raising of the sword? Forgive me if I am meddling in matters I don't understand, but looking back at what has passed, I think . . . Merlin, what I am trying to tell you is this, that I believe your god is with you still."

There was silence. Through it came the flutter of the flame in the bronze lamp, and, infinitely far away, the noises of the camp outside. We looked at one another, he still in early manhood, myself aged and (as I knew) sorely weakened by my recent sickness. And subtly, between us, the balance was changing; had, perhaps, already changed. He, to offer me strength and comfort. *Your god is with you still.* How could he think so? He had only to recall my lack of anything but the most trivial tricks of magic, my want of defence against Morgause, my inability to find out anything about Mordred. But he had spoken, not with the passionate conviction of youth, but with the calm certainty of a judge.

I thought back, for the first time pushing aside the apathy that, since my sickness, had succeeded the earlier mood of tranquil acceptance. I began to see which way his thoughts had gone. One could say they were the thoughts of a general who can lift a victory out of a planned retreat. Or a leader of men who is able, with a word, to give or withhold confidence.

Your god is with you, he had said. With me, perhaps, in the poisoned cup, and the suffering months that had withdrawn me from Arthur's side, and forced him into solitary power? With me (though this he did not know) in the still whisper that had led me to deny the poisoning, and so save from his vengeance Morgause, the mother of those four sons . . . ? With me in the losing of Mordred, whose survival had brought that glow of joy to Arthur's eye? As he would be with me, even, when at length I went to the living burial I feared, and left Arthur alone on middle-earth, with Mordred his fate still at large?

Like the first breath of living wind to the sailor becalmed and starving, I felt hope stir. It was, then, not enough to accept, to wait on the god's return in all his light and strength. In the dark ebbtide, as much as in the flow, could be felt the full power of the sea.

I bowed my head, like a man accepting a king's gift. There was no need to speak. We read one another's minds. He said, with an abrupt change of tone: "How long before this place is complete?"

"In full fighting order, another month. It is virtually ready now."

"So I judged. I can transfer now from Caerleon, foot, horse and baggage?"

"Whenever you please."

"And then? What have you planned for yourself, until you are needed again to build for peace?"

"I've made no plans. Go home, perhaps."

"No. Stay here."

It sounded like an order. I raised my brows.

"Merlin, I mean it. I want you here. We need not split the High King's power in two before the time comes when we must. Do you understand me?"

"Yes."

"Then stay. Make a place for yourself here, and stay away from your marvellous Welsh cave for a while longer."

"For a while longer," I promised him, smiling. "But not here, Arthur. I need silence and solitude, things hard to come by within reach of such a city as this will become, once you are here as High King. May I look for a place, and build a house? By the time you are ready to hang your sword up on the wall over your chair of state, my marvellous cave will be here, near by, and the hermit installed, ready to join your counsels. If, by that time, you remember to need him."

He laughed at that, and seemed content, and we went to our beds. Next day Arthur and his Companions rode back to Ynys Witrin, and I went with them. We were going by invitation of King Melwas and his mother, the queen, to attend a ceremony of thanks for the King's recent victories.

Now, although there was a Christian church on Ynys Witrin, and a monastic settlement on the hill near the holy well, the ruling deity of that ancient island was still the Goddess herself, the Mother whose shrine has been there time out of mind, and who is served still by her priestesses, the *ancillae*. It is a cult similar to, but I believe older than the keeping of the Vestal fire of old Rome. King Melwas, along with most of his people, was a follower of the older gods; and – which was more important – his mother, a formidable old woman, worshipped the Goddess, and had been generous to her priestesses. The present Lady of the shrine (the high priestess, as representing the Goddess, took this title) was related to her.

Though Arthur himself had been brought up in a Christian household, I was not surprised when he accepted Melwas' invitation. But there were those who were. As we assembled near the King's Gate, ready for the ride, I caught one or two looks thrown at him by his Companions, with, here and there, a hint of uneasiness.

Arthur caught my eye – we were waiting while Bedwyr had some word with the guard at the gate – and grinned. He spoke softly. "Do I have to explain to *you?*"

"By no means. You have bethought yourself that Melwas is to be your near neighbour, and has helped you considerably in the building here. You also see the wisdom of pleasing the old queen. And naturally you are remembering Dewdrop and Blackberry, and what you were told about placating the Goddess."

"Dewdrop and –? Oh, the old man's cows! Yes, of course! I might have known you would get straight to it! As a matter of fact I had a message from the Lady herself. The folk of the island want to give thanks for the year's victories, and call a blessing on Caer Camel. I'm living in fear in case someone tells them that I wore Ygraine's token through the fighting at Caer Guinnion!"

He was speaking of the brooch with the name MARIA engraved around the rim. This is the name of the Christians' goddess. I said: "I doubt if it need trouble you. That shrine is as old as the earth it stands on, and whichever Lady you speak to there, the same one will hear you. There is only one, from the beginning. Or so I think . . . But what will the bishops say?"

"I am High King," said Arthur, and left it at that. Bedwyr joined us then, and we rode out through the gateway.

It was a gentle, grey day, with the promise of summer rain somewhere in the clouds. We were soon clear of the woodland, and into the marsh country. To either side of the road the water stretched, grey and ruffled, as the lynx-paws of the breeze crossed and recrossed it. Poplars whitened in the wayward gusts, and the willows dipped, trailing, in the shallows. Islets and willow-groves and tracts of marshland lay seemingly afloat on the silver surface, their images blurred with the breeze. The paved road, mantled with moss and fern as most roads soon are in that low-lying land, led through this wilderness of reeds and water towards the ridge of higher ground that lay like an arm half-encircling one end of the Island. Hoofs rang suddenly on stone, and the road topped a gentle rise. Ahead now was the Lake itself, lying like a sea moating the Island, its waters unbroken save for the narrow causeway that led the road across, and here and there the boats of fishermen, or the barges of the marsh-dwellers.

From this shining sheet of water rose the hill called the Tor, shaped like a giant cone, as symmetrical as if handbuilt by men. It was flanked by a gentler, rounded hill, and beyond that by another, a long, low ridge, like a limb drawn up in the water. Here lay the wharfs; one could see masts like reeds beyond a dip in the green. Beyond the Island's triple hill, stretching into the distance, was a great shining level of water, sown with sedge and bulrush and the clusters of reed thatch among the willows where the marsh-people lived. It was all one long, shifting moving glimmer, as far as the sea. One could see why the Island was called Ynys Witrin, the Isle of Glass. Sometimes, now, men call it Avalon.

There were orchards everywhere on Ynys Witrin. The trees crowded so thickly along the harbour ridge and up the lower slopes of the Tor that only the plumes of wood-smoke, rising between the boughs, showed where the village lay. (King's capital though it was, it could earn no grander title.) A short way up the hill, above the trees, could be seen the cluster of huts, like hives, where the Christian hermits lived, and the holy women. Melwas left them alone; they even had their own church, built near the Goddess' shrine. The church was a humble affair made of wattle and mud, and roofed with thatch. It looked as if the first bad storm would blow it clean out of the ground.

Far different was the shrine of the Goddess. It was said that, with the centuries, the land itself had slowly grown up around it, and possessed it, so that now it lay beneath the level of men's footing, like a crypt. I had never seen it. Men were not normally received within its precincts, but today the Lady herself, with the veiled and white-clad women and girls behind her, all bearing flowers, waited to welcome the High King. The old woman beside her, with the rich mantle, and the royal circlet on her grey hair, must be Melwas' mother, the queen. Here, she took precedence of her son. Melwas himself stood off to one side, among his captains and young men. He was a thickset, handsome fellow, with a curled cap of brown hair, and a glossy beard. He had never married: rumour had it that no woman had ever passed the test of his mother's judgment.

The Lady greeted Arthur, and two of the youngest maidens came forward and hung his neck with flowers. There was singing, all women's voices, high and sweet. The grey sky parted and let through a glint of sunlight. It was seen as an omen; people smiled and looked at one another, and the singing grew more joyous. The Lady turned, and, with her women, led the way down the long flight of shallow steps into the shrine. The old queen followed, and after her Arthur, with the rest of us. Lastly Melwas came, with his followers. The common folk stayed outside. All through the ceremony we could hear the muttering and shifting, as they waited to catch another look at the legendary Arthur of the nine battles.

The shrine was not large; our company filled it to capacity. It was dimly lit, with no more than half a dozen scented lamps, grouped to either side of the archway that led to the inner sanctuary. In the smoky light the white robes of the women shone ghostly. Veils hid their faces and covered their hair and floated, cloudy, to the ground. Of them all, only the Lady herself could be seen clearly: she stood full in the lamplight, stoled with silver, and wearing a diadem that caught what light there was. She was a queenly figure; one could well believe that she came of royal stock.

Veiled, too, was the inner sanctuary; no one save the initiated – not even the old queen herself – would ever see beyond that curtain. The ceremony that we saw (though it would not be seemly to write of it here) would not be the customary one sacred to the Goddess. It was certainly lengthy; we endured two hours of it, standing crowded together; but I suspect that the Lady wanted to make the most of the occasion, and who was to blame her if thoughts of future patronage were in her mind? But it came to an end at last. The Lady accepted Arthur's gift, presented it with the appropriate prayer, and we emerged in due order into the daylight, to receive the shouts of the people.

It was a small incident, which might have left no mark in my memory, but for what came later. As it is, I can still recall the soft, lively feel of the day, the first drops of rain that blew in our faces as we left the shrine, and the thrush's song from the thorn tree standing deep in summer grass spiked with pale orchis and thick with the gold of the small flower they call the Lady's Slipper. The way to Melwas' palace lay through precincts of summer lawn, where among the apple trees grew flowers that could not have come there in nature, all with their uses, as well I knew, in medicine or magic. The *ancillae* practised healing, and had planted the virtuous herbs. (I saw no other kind. The Goddess is not the same whose bloody knife was thrown, once, from the Green Chapel.) At least, I thought, if I have to live hereabouts, the country is a better garden for my plants than the open hillside at home.

With that, we came to the palace, and were welcomed by Melwas into his hall of feasting.

The feast was much like any other, except (as was natural in that place) for the excellence and variety of the fish dishes. The old queen occupied the central position at the high table, with Arthur to one side of her and Melwas to the other. None of the women from the shrine, not even the Lady herself, was present. What women there were, I noticed with some amusement, were far from being beauties, and were none of them young. Rumour had perhaps been right about the queen. I recalled a glance and a smile passing between Melwas and a girl in the crowd: well, the old woman could not watch him all the time. His other appetites were well enough; the food was plentiful and well cooked, though nothing fanciful, and there was a singer with a pleasant voice. The wine, which was good, came (we were told) from a vineyard forty miles off, on the chalk. It had recently been destroyed by one of the sharp incursions of the Saxons, who had begun to come closer this summer.

Once this was said, it was inevitable which way the talk would go. Between dissection of the past, and discussion of the future, time passed quickly, with Arthur and Melwas in accord, which augured well.

We left before midnight. A moon coming towards the full gave a clear light. She hung low and close behind the beacon at the summit of the Tor, marking with sharp shadows the walls of Melwas' stronghold, a fort rebuilt on the site of some ancient hilltop fastness. It was a place for retreat in times of trouble: his palace, where we had been entertained, stood below, on the level near the water.

We were none too soon. A mist was rising from the Lake. Pale wreaths of it eddied across the grass, below the trees, smoking to our horses' knees. Soon the causeway would be hidden. Melwas, escorting us with his torch-bearers, guided us across the pale fog that was the Lake, and up into clear air, onto the ringing stone of the ridge. Then he made his farewells, and set off for home.

I drew rein, looking back. From here, of the three hills that made the island, only the Tor was visible, rising from a lake of cloud. From the shrouding mist near its foot could be seen the red torchlit glow of the palace, not yet quenched for the night. The moon had sailed clear of the Tor into a dark sky. Near the beacon tower, on the rising spiral of the road to the high fortress, a light flickered and moved.

My flesh crept, like a dog's at the sight of a spectre. A wisp of mist lay there, high, and across it a shadow strode, like a giant's. The Tor was a known gate to the Otherworld; for a flash I wondered if, with the Sight come back to me, I was watching one of the guardians of the place, one of the fiery spirits who keep the gate. Then my sight cleared, and I saw that it was a man with a torch, running up the steep of the Tor to light the beacon fire.

As I set spurs to my horse I heard Arthur's voice, lifted in quick command. A rider detached himself from the cavalcade and leaped forward at a stretched gallop. The others, silent all at once, followed him, fast but collected, while behind us the flames went up into the night, calling Arthur of the nine battles to yet another fight.

10

The investing of Caer Camel saw the start of the new campaign. Four more years it took: siege and skirmish, flying attack and ambush – except during the midwinter months he was never at rest. And twice more, towards the end of that time, he triumphed over the enemy in a major engagement.

The first of these battles was joined in response to a call from Elmet. Eosa himself had landed from Germany, at the head of fresh Saxon war-bands, to be joined by the East Saxons already established north of the Thames. Cerdic added a third point to the spear with a force brought by longboat from Rutupiae. It was the worst threat since Luguvallium. The invaders came swarming in force up the Vale, and were threatening what Arthur had long foreseen, to break through the barrier of the mountains by the Gap. Surprised and (no doubt) disconcerted by the readiness of the fort at Olicana, they were checked and held there, while the message was sent flashing south for Arthur. The East Saxon force, which was considerable, was concentrated on Olicana; the King of Elmet held them there, but the others streamed westwards through the Gap. Arthur, heading fast up the west road, reached the Tribuit fort before them, and, re-forming there in strength, caught them at Nappa Ford. He vanquished them there, in a bloody struggle, then threw his fast cavalry up through the Gap to Olicana, and, side by side with the King of Elmet, drove the enemy back into the Vale. From there a movement beyond countering, right back, east and south, until the old frontiers contained them, and the Saxon "king", looking round on his bleeding and depleted forces, admitted defeat.

A defeat, as it turned out, all but final. Such was Arthur's name now, that its very mention had come to mean victory, and "the coming of Arthur" a synonym for salvation. The next time he was called for – it was the clearing-up operation of the long campaign – no sooner had the dreaded cavalry with the white horse at its head and the Dragon glinting over the helmets, showed in the mountain pass of Agned, than the enemy fell into the disarray of near panic, so that the action was a pursuit rather than a battle, a clearing of territory after the main action. Through all this fighting, Gereint (who knew every foot of the territory) was with the cavalry, with a command worthy of him. So Arthur rewarded service.

Eosa himself had received a wound in the fighting at Nappa. He never took the field again. It was the young Cerdic, the Aetheling, who led the Saxons at Agned, and did his best to hold them against the terror of Arthur's onslaught. It was said that afterwards, as he withdrew – in creditable order – to the waiting longboats, he made a vow that, when he next set foot on British territory, he would stay, and not even Arthur should prevent him.

For that, as I could have told him, he would have to wait till Arthur was no longer there.

★   ★   ★

It was never my intention here to give details of the years of battle. This is a chronicle of a different kind. Besides, everyone knows now about his campaign to free Britain and cleanse her shores of the Terror. It was all written down in that house up in Vindolanda, by Blaise, and the solemn, quiet clerk who came from time to time to help him. Here I will only repeat that never once during the years it took him to fight the Saxons to a standstill was I able to bring prophecy or magic to his aid. The story of those years is one of human bravery, of endurance and of dedication. It took twelve major engagements, and some seven years' hard work, before the young King could count the country safe at last for husbandry and the arts of peace.

It is not true, as the poets and singers would have it, that Arthur drove all the Saxons from the shores of Britain. He had come to recognise, as Ambrosius did, that it was impossible to clear lands that stretched for miles of difficult country, and which had, moreover, the easy retreat of the seas behind. Since the time of Vortigern, who first invited the Saxons into Britain as his allies, the south-east shore of our country had been settled Saxon territory, with its own rulers and its own laws. There was some justification for Eosa's assumption of the title of king. Even had it been possible for Arthur to clear the Saxon Shore, he would have had to drive out settlers of perhaps the third generation, who had been born and bred within these shores, and make them take ship back to their grandfathers' country, where they might meet as harsh a welcome as here. Men fight desperately for their homes when the alternative is to be homeless. And, while it was one thing to win the great pitched battles, he knew that to drive men into the hills and forests and waste places, whence they could never be dislodged, or even pinned down and fought, was to invite a long war which could have no victory. He had before him the example of the Old Ones; they had been dispossessed by the Romans and had fled into the waste places of the hills; four hundred years later they were still there, in their remote mountain fastnesses, and the Romans themselves had gone. So, accepting the fact that there must be still Saxon kingdoms lodged within the shores of Britain, Arthur set himself to see that their boundaries were secure, and that for very fear their kings would hold to them.

So he passed his twentieth year. He came back to Camelot at the end of October, and plunged straight away into council. I was there, appealed to sometimes, but in the main watching and listening only: the counsel I gave him, I gave in private, behind closed doors. In the public sight, the decisions were his. Indeed, they were his as often as mine, and as time went on I was content to let his judgment have its way. He was impulsive sometimes, and in many matters still lacked experience or precedent; but he never let his judgment be ridden by impulse, and he maintained, in spite of the arrogance that success might be expected to bring with it, the habit of letting men talk their fill, so that when finally the King's decision was announced, each man thought that he had had a say in it.

One of the things that was brought up at length was the question of a new marriage. I could see he had not expected this; but he kept silent, and after a while grew easier, and listened to the older men. They were the ones who had names and pedigrees and land-claims

by heart. It came to me also, watching, that they were the ones
who, when Arthur was first proclaimed, would have nothing to do
with the claim. Now not even his own companion knights could
show more loyal. He had won the elders, as he had won all else.
You would have thought each one of them had discovered him
unknown in the Wild Forest, and handed him the sword of the
Kingdom.

You would also have thought that each man was discussing the
marriage of a favourite son. There was much beard-stroking and
head-wagging, and names were suggested and discussed, and even
wrangled over, but none met with general acclaim, until one day a
man from Gwynedd, who had fought right through the wars with
Arthur, and was a kinsman of Maelgon himself, got to his feet and
made a speech about his home country.

Now when you get a black Welshman on his feet and ready to
talk, it is like inviting a bard; the thing is done in order, in cadence,
and at very great length: but such was this man's way, and such the
beauty of his speaking voice, that after the first few minutes men
settled back comfortably to listen, as they might have listened at a
feast.

His subject seemed to be his country, the loveliness of its valleys
and hills, the blue lakes, the creaming seas, the deer and eagles and
the small singing-birds, the bravery of the men and the beauty of
the women. Then we heard of the poets and singers, the orchards
and flowery meadows, the riches of sheep and cattle and the veined
minerals in the rock. From this there followed the brave history of
the land, battles and victories, courage in defeat, the tragedy of
young death and the fecund beauty of young love.

He was getting near his point. I saw Arthur stir in his great chair.

And, said the speaker, the country's wealth and beauty and
bravery were all there invested in the family of its kings, a family
which (I had ceased to listen closely; I was watching Arthur through
the light of a badly flaring lamp, and my head ached) – a family
which seemed to have a genealogy as ancient and twice as long as
Noah's . . .

There was, of course, a princess. Young, lovely, sprung from a
line of ancient Welsh kings joined with a noble Roman clan. Arthur
himself came from no higher stock . . . And now one saw why the

long-drawn panegyric, and the eye slightly askance at the young King.

Her name, it seemed, was Guinevere.

*   *   *

I saw them again, the two of them. Bedwyr, dark and eager, with eyes of love fixed on the other boy; Arthur-Emrys, at twelve years old the leader, full of energy and the high fire of living. And the white shadow of the owl drifting overhead between them; the *guenhwyvar* of a passion and a grief, of high endeavour and a quest that would take Bedwyr into a world of spirit and leave Arthur lonely, waiting there at the centre of glory to become himself a legend and himself a grail . . .

*   *   *

I came back to the hall. The pain in my head was fierce. The fitful, dazzling light struck like a spear against my eyes. I could feel the sweat trickling down beneath my robe. My hands slipped on the carved arms of the chair. I fought to steady my breathing, and the hammer-beat of my heart.

No one had noticed me. Time had passed. The formality of the council had broken up. Arthur was the centre now of a group, talking and laughing; about the table the older men sat still, relaxed and easy, chatting among themselves. Servants had come in, and wine was being poured. The talk was all around me, like water rising. In it could be heard the notes of triumph and release. It was done; there would be a new queen, and a new succession. The wars were over, and Britain, alone of Rome's old subject lands, was safe behind her royal ramparts for the next span of sunlit time.

Arthur turned his head and met my eyes. I neither moved nor spoke, but the laughter died out of his face, and he got to his feet. He came over as quickly as a spear starting for the mark, waving his companions back out of earshot.

"Merlin, what is it? This wedding? You cannot surely think that it —"

I shook my head. The pain went through it like a saw. I think I cried out. At the King's move there had been a hush; now there was complete silence in the hall. Silence, and eyes, and the unsteady dazzle of the flames.

He leaned forward, as if to take my hand. "What is it? Are you ill? Merlin, can you speak?"

His voice swelled, echoed, was whirled away. It did not concern me. Nothing concerned me but the necessity of speech. The lamp-flames were burning somewhere in my breast, their hot oil spilling in bubbles through my blood. Breath came thick and piercing, like smoke in the lungs. When I found words at last they surprised me. I had seen nothing beyond the chamber long ago in the Perilous Chapel, and the vision which might or might not have meant anything. What I heard myself saying, in a harsh and ringing voice that brought Arthur up like a blow, and startled every man to his feet, had a very different burden.

"It is not over yet, King! Get you to horse, and ride! They have broken the peace, and soon they will be at Badon! Men and women are dying in their blood, and children cry, before they are spitted like chickens. There is no king near to protect them. Get you there now, duke of the kings! This is for you alone, when the people themselves cry out for you! Go with your Companions, and put a finish to this thing! For, by the Light, Arthur of Britain, this is the last time, and the last victory! Go now!"

The words went ringing into total silence. Those who had never before heard me speak with power were pale: all made the sign. My breathing was loud in the hush, like that of an old man fighting to stave off death.

Then from the crowd of younger men came sounds of disbelief, even scoffing. It was not to be wondered at. They had heard stories of my past deeds, but so many of these were patently poets' work, and all, having gone already into song, had taken the high colour of legend. Last time I had spoken so had been at Luguvallium, before the raising of the sword, and some of them had been children then. These knew me only as engineer and man of medicine, the quiet councillor whom the King favoured.

The muttering was all around me, wind in the trees.

"There has been no signal; what is he talking about? As if the High King could go off on his bare word, for a scare like this!

Arthur has done enough, and so have we; the peace is settled, anyone can see that! Badon? Where is it? Well, but no Saxon would attack there, not now . . . Yes, but if they did, there is no force there to hold them, he was right about that . . . No, it's nonsense, the old man has lost his senses again. Remember, up there in the Forest, what he was like? Crazy, and that's the truth . . . and now moon-mad again, with the same malady?"

Arthur had not taken his eyes off me. The whispers blew to and fro. Someone called for a doctor, and there was coming and going in the hall. He ignored it. He and I were alone together. His hand came out and took me by the wrist. I felt, through the whirling pain, his young strength forcing me gently back into my chair. I had not even known I was standing. His other hand went out, and someone put a goblet into it. He held the wine to my lips.

I turned my head aside. "No. Leave me. Go now. Trust me."

"By all the gods there are," he said, from the back of his throat, "I trust you." He swung on his heel, and spoke. "You, and you, and you, give the orders. We ride now. See to it."

Then back to me, but speaking so that all could hear: "Victory, you said?"

"Victory. Can you doubt it?"

For a moment, through the stresses of pain, I saw his look; the look of the boy who had braved the white flame at my word, and lifted the enchanted sword. "I doubt nothing," said Arthur.

Then he laughed, leaned forward and kissed me on the cheek, and, with his Companions following, went swiftly out of the hall.

The pain lifted. I could breathe and see. I got up and walked after them, out into the air. Those left in the hall drew back and let me through. No one spoke to me, or dared to question. I mounted the rampart and looked outwards. The sentry on duty there moved away, not like a soldier, but sidling. The whites of his eyes showed. Word had gone round fast. I hunched my cloak against the wind and stayed where I was.

They had gone, so small a troop to throw against the might of the final Saxon bid for Britain. The gallop dwindled into the night and was gone. Somewhere in that darkness to the north the Tor was standing up into the black sky. No light, nothing. Beyond it, no light. Nor south, nor east; no light anywhere, or warning fires. Only my word.

A sound somewhere in the blowing darkness. For a moment I took it for an echo of that distant gallop; then, hearing in it, faintly, the cry and clash of armies, I thought that vision had returned to me. But my head was clear, and the night, with all its sounds and shadows, was mortal night.

Then the sounds wheeled closer, and went streaming overhead, high in the black air. It was the wild geese, the pack of heaven's hounds, the Wild Hunt that courses the skies with Llud, King of the Otherworld, in time of war and storm. They had risen from the Lake waters, and now came overhead, flighting the dark. Straight from the silent Tor they came, to wheel over Caer Camel, then back across the slumbering Island, the noise of their voices and the galloping wings lost at length down the reaches of the night towards Badon.

With the dawn, beacon lights blazed across the land. But whoever led the Saxon hordes to Badon, must hardly have set foot on its bloody soil when, out of the dark, more swiftly even than birds could have flown or fire signalled, the High King Arthur and his own picked knights fell on them and destroyed them, smashing the barbarian power utterly, for his day, and for the rest of his generation.

So the god came back to me, Merlin his servant. Next day I left Caer Camel, and rode out to look for a place where I could build myself a house.

BOOK 3

Applegarth

1

To the east of Caer Camel the land is rolling and wooded, ridges and hills of gentle green, with here and there, among the bushes and ferns of the summits, traces of old dwelling-places or fortifications of past time.

One such place I had noticed before, and now, casting about among the hills and valleys, I looked at it once more, and found it good. It was a solitary spot, in a fold between two hills, where a spring welled from the turf and sent a tiny brook tumbling down to meet a valley stream. A long time ago men had lived there. When the sun fell aright you could see the soft outline of ancient walls beneath the turf. That settlement had vanished long since, but since then some other settler, in harder times, had built himself a tower, the main part of which still stood. It had been built, moreover, with Roman stone taken from Caer Camel. The squared shapes of the chiselled stone showed still clean-edged beneath the encroaching saplings and those stinging ghosts that cluster wherever man has been, the nettles. Even these weeds were not unwelcome; they are sovereign for many ailments, and I intended, as soon as the house was done, to plant a garden, which is the chief of the arts of peace.

And peace we had at last. The news of the victory at Badon reached me even before I had paced out the dimensions of my new home. From the account Arthur sent me of the battle it seemed certain that this must be the final victory of the campaign, and now the King was imposing terms, being set on the decisive fixing of his kingdom's boundaries. There was no reason to suppose, his message ran, that there would be any further attack or even resistance for some time to come. I, not having seen the battlefield, but knowing what I knew, prepared to build for a time of peace, where I

might live in the solitude I loved and needed, at due remove from
the busy centre where Arthur would be.

Meanwhile it would be wise to get hold of all the masons and
craftsmen I should require before Arthur's own great schemes for
his city began to burgeon. They came, shook their heads over my
plans, then set cheerfully to work to build what I wanted.

This was a small house, a cottage, if you will, set in the hollow of
the hillside, and facing south and west, away from Caer Camel,
towards the distant swell of the downs. The place was sheltered
from north and east, and, by a curve of the hill below, from the few
passers-by on the valley road. I had the tower rebuilt on its old
pattern, and the new house constructed against this, single
storeyed, with behind it a square courtyard or garth in the Roman
style. The tower formed a corner of this between my own dwelling
and the kitchen quarters. At the side opposite the house were
workshops and sheds for storage. On the north side of the garth was
a high wall coped with tiles, against which I hoped to set some of the
more delicate plants. I had long thought of doing what now the
masons shook their heads over; the wall was built double, and the
hypocaust led warm air into it. Not only in winter would the vines
and peaches be safe, but the whole garth would, I thought, benefit
from the warmth, as well as from the sunlight it would catch and
hold. This was the first time I had seen such an idea put into
practice, but later it was done at Camelot, and at Arthur's other
palace at Caerleon. A miniature aqueduct led water from the spring
into a well at the garth's centre.

The men, finding it a pleasant change from the years of military
building, worked quickly. We had an open winter that year. I rode
to Bryn Myrddin to oversee the moving of my books and certain of
the medical stores, then spent Christmas at Camelot with Arthur.
The carpenters went into my house early in the New Year, and the
work was done and the men free in time to start the permanent
building at Camelot in the spring.

I still had no servant of my own, and now had to set myself to find
one – not an easy task, for few men can settle happily in the kind of
solitude I crave, and my ways have never been those of the ordinary
master. The hours I keep are strange ones; I require little food or
sleep, and have great need of silence. I could have bought a slave

who would have had to put up with whatever I wanted, but I have never liked bought service. But this time, as always before, I was lucky. One of the local masons had an uncle who was a gardener; he had given him, he said, an account of the building of the heated wall, and the uncle had shaken his head and muttered something about new-fangled foreign nonsense, but had since evinced the liveliest curiosity about every stage of the building. His name was Varro. He would be glad to come, said the mason, and his daughter, who could cook and clean, would come with him.

So it was settled. Varro started the clearing and digging straight away, and the girl Mora began to scrub and air, and then, in one of those lucid and lovely spells of early weather, with primroses already showing under the budding hawthorns, and lambs couched warm beside the ewes in the hollows of flowering whin, I stabled my horse and unpacked my big harp, and was home.

★   ★   ★

Soon after, Arthur came to see me. I was in the garth, sitting in the sunshine on a bench between the pillars of the miniature colonnade. I was busy sorting seeds collected last summer and packed away in twists of parchment. Beyond the walls I heard the stamp and jingle of the King's escort, but he came in alone. Varro went past with a stare and a salute, carrying his spade. I got to my feet as Arthur raised a hand in greeting.

"It's very small," were his first words, as he looked about him.

"Enough. It's only for me."

"Only!" He laughed, then pivoted on his heel. "Mmm . . . if you like dog-kennels, and it seems you do, then I must say it's very pleasant. So that's the famous wall, is it? The masons were telling me about it. What are you planting there?"

I told him, and then took him on a tour of my little garth. Arthur, who knew as much about gardens as I about warfare, but who was always interested in making, looked and touched and questioned; he spent a lot of time at the heated wall, and on the construction of the small aqueduct that fed the well.

"Vervain, Camomile, Comfrey, Marigold . . ." He turned over the labelled packets of seed lying on the bench. "I remember

Drusilla used to grow marigolds. She gave me some concoction of them when I had the toothache." He looked round him again. "Do you know, there is already something of the same peace here that one had at Galava. If only for my sake, you were right in refusing to live in Camelot. I'll feel I have a refuge here, when things are pressing on me."

"I hope you will. Well, that's all here. I'll have my flowers here, and an orchard outside. There were a few old trees here already, and they seem to be doing well. Would you like to come in now and see the house?"

"A pleasure," he said, in a tone so suddenly formal that I glanced at him, to see that his attention was not on me at all, but on Mora, who had come out of a doorway and was shaking a cloth in the breeze. Her gown was blown close against her body, and her hair, which was pretty, flew in a bright tangle round her face. She stopped to push it back, saw Arthur, blushed and giggled, then ran indoors again. I saw a bright eye peep through a crack, then she caught me watching, and withdrew. The door shut. It was apparent that the girl had no idea who the young man was who had eyed her so boldly.

He was grinning at me. "I am to be married in a month, so you can stop watching me like that. I shall be the most model of married men."

"I am sure of it. Was I watching you? It's no concern of mine, but I should warn you that the gardener is her father."

"And a tough fellow he looks. All right, I'll keep my blood cool until May. God knows it's landed me in trouble before, and will again."

" 'A model married man?' "

"I was talking about my past. You warned me that it would reach into my future." He said it lightly; the past, I guessed, was well behind him now. I doubted if thoughts of Morgause still troubled his sleep. He followed me into the house and, while I found wine and poured it, went on another of his prowling tours of discovery.

There were only two rooms. The living-chamber took two-thirds of the length of the house, and its full width, with windows both ways, on garth and hill. The doorway opened on the colonnade that edged the garth. Today for the first time the door stood open to the mild air, and sunlight fell warmly across the terracotta tiles of the floor. At the end of the room was the place for the fire, with a wide chimney to take the smoke outside. In Britain we need fires as well as heated floors. The hearthstone was of slate, and the walls, of well finished stone, were hung with rich rugs I had brought back with me from my travels in the East. Table and stools were oak, from the same tree, but the great chair was of elm wood, as also the chest under the window, which held my books. A door at the end of the room led to my bedchamber, which was simply furnished with bed and clothes chest. With some memory, perhaps, of childhood, I had planted a pear tree outside the window.

All this I showed him, then took him to the tower. The door to this led off the colonnade in the corner of the garth. On the ground floor was the workroom or stillroom, where the herbs were dried, and medicines made up. There was no furniture but a big table, and stools and cupboards, and the small brick stove with its oven and charcoal burner. A stone stair against one wall led to the upper room. This was the chamber I meant to use as my private study. Here there was nothing as yet but a work-table and chair, a couple of stools and a cupboard with tablets and the mathematical instruments I had brought from Antioch. A brazier stood in one corner. I had had a window made looking out to the south, and this was covered with neither horn nor curtain. I do not readily feel the cold.

Arthur moved round the tiny room, stooping, peering, opening boxes and cupboards, leaning on his fists to gaze out of the window, filling the small space with his immense vitality, so that even the stout, Roman-built walls seemed barely to contain him.

In the main chamber once more, he took a goblet from me, and raised it. "To your new home. What will you call it?"

"Applegarth."

"I like that. It's right. To Applegarth then, and your long life here!"

"Thank you. And to my first guest."

"Am I? I'm glad. May there be many more, and may they all come in peace." He drank and set the goblet down, looking about him again. "Already it is full of peace. Yes, I begin to see why you chose it . . . but are you sure it is all you want? You know, and I know, that the whole of my kindom is yours by right, and I do assure you I'd let you have half of it for the asking."

"I'll let you keep it for the present. It's been too much trouble for me to envy you overmuch. Have you time to sit for a while? Will you eat? The very idea will frighten Mora into an epilepsy, because you can be sure she has been out to ask her father who the young stranger is, but I'm certain she can find something – "

"Thank you, no, I've eaten. Have you just the two servants? Who cooks for you?"

"The girl."

"Well?"

"Eh? Oh, well enough."

"Which means you haven't even noticed. For God's sake!" said Arthur. "Let me send you a cook. I don't like to think of you eating nothing but peasant messes."

"Please, no. The two of them round me by day are all I want, and even they go to their own home at night. I do very well, I assure you."

"All right. But I wish you would let me do something, give you something."

"When I find something I want, be sure I'll ask you for it. Now tell me how the building is going. I'm afraid I've been too occupied with my dog-kennel to pay much attention. Will it be ready for your wedding?"

He shook his head. "By summer, perhaps, it might be fit to bring a queen to. But for the wedding I'll go back to Caerleon. It will be in May. Will you be there?"

"Unless it's your wish that I should be there, I would prefer to stay here. I begin to feel I've had too much travelling in the past few years."

"As you wish. No, no more wine, thank you. One thing I wanted to ask you. You remember, when first the idea of my marriage was mooted – the first marriage – you seemed to have some doubts about it. I understood that you had had some sort of presentiment of disaster. If so, you were right. Tell me, please – this time, have you any such doubts?"

They tell me that when I guard my face, no man can read what is in my mind. I met his eyes level. "None. Need you ask me? Have you any doubts yourself?"

"None." The flash of a smile. "At least, not yet. How could I, when I am told that she is perfection itself? They all say she is lovely as a May morning, and they tell me this, that and the other thing. But then, they always do. It will suffice if she has a sweet breath and a compliant temper . . . Oh, and a pretty voice. I find that I care about voices. All this granted, it couldn't be a better match. As a Welshman, Merlin, you ought to agree."

"Oh, I do. I agree with everything Gwyl said, there in the hall. When do you go to Wales to bring her to Caerleon?"

"I can't go myself; I have to ride north in a week's time. I'm sending Bedwyr again, and Gereint with him, and – to do her honour, since I can't go myself – King Melwas of the Summer Country."

I nodded, and the conversation turned then on the reasons for his journey north. He was going, I knew, mainly to look at the defensive work in the north-east. Tydwal, Lot's kinsman, held Dunpeldyr now, ostensibly on behalf of Morgause and Lot's eldest son Gawain, though it was doubtful if the queen's family would ever leave Orkney.

"Which suits me very well," said the King indifferently. "But it creates certain difficulties in the north-east."

He went on to explain. The problem lay with Aguisel, who held the strong castle of Bremenium, in a nest of the Northumbrian hills, where Dere Street runs up into High Cheviot. While Lot had ruled to the north, Aguisel had been content to run with him, "as his jackal," said Arthur contemptuously, "along with Tydwal and Urien. But now that Tydwal sits in Lot's chair, Aguisel begins to be ambitious. I've heard a rumour – I have no proof of it – that when last the Angles sent their ships up the Alaunus River, Aguisel met them there, not in war, but to speak with their leader. And Urien follows him still, brother jackals, playing at being lions. They may think they are too far away from me, but I intend to pay them a visit and disillusion them. My excuse is to look at the work that has been done on the Black Dyke. From all I hear, I should like a pretext to remove Aguisel for good and all, but I must do it without rousing Tydwal and Urien to defend him. The last thing I can afford, until I am sure of the West Saxons, is a break-up of the allied kings in the north. If I have to remove Tydwal, it may mean bringing Morgause back to Dunpeldyr. A small thing, compared with the rest, but the day she sits in a mainland castle again cannot be a good day for me."

"Then let us hope the day will never come."

"As you say. I'll do my best to contrive it so." He looked round him again as he turned to go. "It's a pleasant place. I'm afraid I shan't have time to see you again before I ride, Merlin. I go before the week is out."

"Then all the gods go with you, my dear. May they be beside you, too, at your wedding. And some day, come and see me again."

He went. The room seemed to tremble and grow larger again, and the air to settle back into tranquillity.

2

And tranquillity was the sum of the months that followed. I went over to Camelot soon after Arthur's departure for the north, to see how the building work was going; then, satisfied, left Derwen to complete it, and retired to my new-made fastness with almost the same feeling of home-coming as I felt at Bryn Myrddin. The rest of that spring I spent about my own affairs, planting my garden, writing to Blaise, and, as the countryside burgeoned, collecting the herbs I needed for a renewal of my stores.

I did not see Arthur again before the wedding. A courier brought me news, which was brief but favourable. Arthur had found proof of Aguisel's villainy and had attacked him in Bremenium. The details I did not know, but the King had taken the place and put Aguisel to death; and this without rousing either Tydwal or Urien, or any of their kinsmen against him. In fact, Tydwal had fought beside Arthur in the final storming of the walls. How the King had achieved this, the report did not say, but with the death of Aguisel the world would be cleaner, and, since he died without sons, a man of Arthur's choosing could now hold the castle that commanded the Cheviot pass. Arthur chose Brewyn, a man he could be certain of, then went south to Caerleon well content.

The Lady Guinevere duly arrived in Caerleon, royally escorted by princes – Melwas and Bedwyr and a company of Arthur's knights. Cei had not gone with the party; as Arthur's seneschal his duty lay in the palace at Caerleon, where the wedding was celebrated with great splendour. I heard later that the bride's father had suggested May-Day, and that Arthur, after the briefest hesitation, had said, "No," so flatly that eyebrows were raised. But this was the only shadow. All else seemed set fair. The pair were married late in the month on a glorious day of sunshine, and Arthur took a bride to bed for the second time, with, now, days and nights to spare. They came to Camelot in early summer, and I had my first sight of the second Guinevere.

Queen Guinevere of Northgališ was more than "well enough and with a sweet breath"; she was a beauty. To describe her, one would have to rob the bards of all their old conventions; hair like golden corn, eyes like summer sky, a flower-fair skin and a lissom body – but add to all this the dazzle of personality, a sort of outgoing gaiety, and a way of communicating joy, and you will have some idea of her fascination. For fascinating she was; on the night she was brought to Camelot I watched her through the feasting, and saw other eyes than the King's fixed on her throughout the evening. It was obvious that she would be Queen, not only of Arthur, but of all the Companions. Except perhaps Bedwyr. His were the only eyes that did not seek hers constantly; he seemed quieter even than usual, lost in his own thoughts, and as for Guinevere, she barely glanced his way. I wondered if something had happened on the journey from Northgalis that stung his memory. But Melwas, who sat near her, hung on her every word, and watched her with the same eyes of worship as the younger men.

That was a beautiful summer, I remember. The sun shone blazing, but from time to time the sweet rains came and the soft wind, so that the fields bore crops such as few men could remember, and the cattle and sheep grew sleek, and the land ripened towards a great harvest. Everywhere, though the bells rang on Sundays in the Christian churches, and crosses were to be seen nowadays where once cairns of stone or statues had stood by the wayside, the countryfolk went about their tasks blessing the young King for giving them, not only the peace in which to grow their crops, but the wealth of the crops themselves. For them, both wealth and glory stemmed from their young ruler, as, during the last year of the sick Uther's life, the land had lain under the black blight. And the common folk waited confidently – as at Camelot the nobles waited – for the announcement that an heir was begotten. But the summer wore through, and autumn came, and, though the land yielded its great harvest, the Queen, riding out daily with her ladies, was as lissom and slender as ever, and no announcement was made.

And here in Camelot, the memory of the girl who had conceived the heir and died of him troubled no one. All was new and shining and building and making. The palace was completed, and now the carvers and gilders were at work, and women wove and stitched, and wares of pottery and silver and gold came into the new city daily, so that the roads seemed full of coming and going. It was the time of youth and laughter, and building after conquest; the grim years were forgotten. As for the "white shadow" of my foreboding, I began to wonder if it had indeed been the death of the other pretty Guenever that had cast that shadow across the light, and seemed to linger still in corners like a ghost. But I never saw her, and Arthur, if he once remembered her, said nothing.

So four winters passed, and Camelot's towers shone with new gilding, and the borders were quiet, the harvests good, and the people grew accustomed to peace and safety. Arthur was five and twenty, and rather more silent than of old; he seemed to be away from home more, and each time for longer. Cador of Cornwall married, and the High King rode down to his home country near Tintagel for the wedding, but Queen Guinevere did not go with him. For a few weeks there was whispered hope that she had a good reason for refusing the journey; but the King and his party went and returned, and then left again, by sea, for Gwynedd, and still the Queen at Camelot rode out and laughed and danced and held court, as slim as a maiden, and, it seemed, as free of care.

Then one raining day of early spring, just as dusk fell, a horseman came thudding to my gate with a message. The King was still away, and was not looked for yet for perhaps another week. And the Queen had vanished.

★   ★   ★

The messenger was Cei the seneschal, Arthur's foster-brother, the son of Ector of Galava. He was a big man, some three years older than the King, florid and broad-shouldered. He was a good fighter and a brave man, though not, like Bedwyr, a natural leader. Cei had neither nerves nor imagination, and, while this makes for bravery in war, it does not make for good leadership. Bedwyr, the poet and dreamer, who suffered ten times over for one grief, was the finer man.

But Cei was staunch, and now, since he was responsible for the ordering of the King's household, had come himself to see me, attended only by one servant. This, though he bore one arm in a rough sling, and looked tired and worried out of his slow mind. He told me the story, sitting in my room with the firelight flickering on the ceiling rafters. He accepted a cup of mulled wine, and talked quickly, while, at my insistence, he removed the sling and let me examine his injured arm.

"Bedwyr sent me to tell you. I was hurt, so he sent me back. No, I didn't see a doctor. Damn it, there hasn't been time! Anything could've happened, wait till I tell you . . . She's been gone since daybreak. You remember how fair it was this morning? She went out with her ladies, with only the grooms and a couple of men for escort. That was usual – you know it was."

"Yes." It was true. Sometimes one or more of the knights accompanied the Queen, but frequently they were occupied on affairs more important than squiring her on her daily rides. She had troopers and grooms, and nowadays there was no danger, so near Camelot, from the kind of wild outlaw who had frequented lonely places when I was a boy. So Guinevere had risen early on what promised to be a fine morning, mounted her grey mare, and set out with two of her ladies, and four men, of whom two were soldiers. They had ridden south, across a belt of dry moorland bordered, to the south, by thick forest. To their right hand lay the marshlands, where the rivers wound seaward through their deep, reedy channels, and to the east the land showed rolling and forested towards the high lift of the downs. The party had found game in plenty; the little greyhounds had run wild after it, and, said Cei, the grooms had their hands full riding after them to bring them back. Meantime, the Queen had flown her merlin after a hare, and had followed this herself, straight into the forest.

Cei grunted as my probing fingers found the injured muscle. "Well, but I told you that it was nothing much. Only a sprain, isn't it? A pulled muscle? Will it take long? Oh, well, it's not my sword arm . . . Well, she galloped the grey mare in, and the women stayed back. Her maid's no rider, and the other, the Lady Melissa, is not young. The grooms were coming back with the greyhounds on the saddle, and were still some way off. Nobody was worrying. She's a great horsewoman – you know she even rode Arthur's white stallion and managed it? – and besides, she's done it before, just to tease them. So they took it easy, while the two troopers rode after her."

The rest was easy to supply. It was true that this had happened before, with no chance of ill, so the troopers spurred after the Queen at no more than a hand-gallop. They could hear her mare thudding through the thick forest ahead of them, and the swish and crackling of the bushes and dead stuff underfoot. The forest thickened; the two soldiers slowed to a canter, ducking the boughs which still swung from the Queen's passing, and guiding their horses through the tangle of fallen wood and water-logged holes that made the forest floor such dangerous terrain. Half cursing, half laughing, and wholly occupied, it was some minutes before they realised that they could no longer hear the Queen's mare. The tangled underbrush showed no trace of a horse's passing. They pulled up to listen. Nothing but the distant scolding of a jay. They shouted, and got no answer. Annoyed, rather than alarmed, they separated, riding one in the direction of the jay's scolding, the other still deeper into the forest.

"I'll spare you the rest," said Cei. "You know how it is. After a bit they forgathered, and by then, of course, they were alarmed. They shouted some more, and the grooms heard them, and went in and joined the search. Then after a while they heard the mare again. She was going hard, they said, and they heard her whinnying. They struck their spurs in and went after her."

"Yes?" I settled the injured arm into the freshly tied sling, and he thanked me.

"That's better. I'm grateful. Well, they found the mare three miles off, lame, and trailing a broken rein, but no sign of the Queen. They sent the women back with one of the grooms, and they went on searching. Bedwyr and I took troops out, and for the rest of the day we've been quartering the forest as best we could, but nothing." He lifted his good hand. "You know what that country's like. Where it isn't a tangle of tree and scrub that would stop a fire-breathing dragon, it's marsh where a horse or a man would sink over their heads. And even in the forest there are ditches as deep as a man, and too wide to leap. That's where I came to grief. Dead fir boughs spread over a hole, for all the world like a wolf-trap. I'm lucky to have got away with just this. My horse got a spike in the belly, poor beast. It's doubtful if he'll be good for much again."

"The mare," I said. "Had she fallen? Was she mired?"

"To the eyeballs, but that means nothing. She must have galloped through marsh and mire for an hour. The saddle-cloth was torn, though. I think she must have fallen; I can't see the Queen falling off her, else – unless she was swept off by a bough. Believe me, we must have searched every brake and ditch in the forest. She'll be lying unconscious somewhere . . . if not worse. God, if she had to do such a thing, why couldn't she do it when the King was at home?"

"Of course you have sent to him?"

"Bedwyr sent a rider before we left Camelot. There are more men out there now. It's getting too dark to find her, but if she's been lying unconscious, and comes round, maybe they'll hear her calling. What else can we do? Bedwyr's got men down there now with dragnets. Some of those pools are deep, and there are currents in that river to the west . . ." He left it there. His rather stupid blue eyes stared at me, as if begging me to do a miracle. "After I took my toss he sent me back to you. Merlin, will you come with me now, and show us where to look for the Queen?"

I looked down at my hands, then at the fire, dying now to small flames that licked round a greying log. I had not put my powers to the test since Badon. And how long before that since I had dared to call on the least of them? Nor flames, nor dream, nor even the glimmer of Sight in the crystal or the water-drops: I would not importune God for the smallest breath of the great wind. If he came to me, he came. It was for him to choose the time, and for me to go with it.

"Or even just tell me, now?" Cei's voice cracked, imploring.

Time was, I thought, when I would only have had to look at the fire, like this, to lift a hand, like this . . .

The small flames hissed, and leaped a foot high, wrapping the grey log with blazing scarves of light, and throwing out a heat that seared the skin. Sparks jumped, stung, with the old welcome, quickening pain. The light, the fire, the whole living world flowed upwards, bright and dark, flame and smoke and trembling vision, carrying me with it.

A sound from Cei flicked my attention back to him. He was on his feet, backed away from the blaze. Through the ruddy light pouring over him I saw that he had gone pale. There was sweat on his face. He said hoarsely: "Merlin – "

He was already fading, drowned in flame and darkness. I heard myself say: "Go. Get my horse ready. And wait for me."

I did not hear him go. I was already far from the firelit room, borne on the cool and blazing river that dropped me, light as a leaf loosened by the wind, in the darkness at the gates of the Otherworld.

★   ★   ★

The caves went on and on for ever, their roofs lost in darkness, their walls lit with some strange subaqueous glow that outlined every ridge and boss of rock. From arches of stone hung stalactites, like moss from ancient trees, and pillars of rock rose from the stone floor to meet them. Water fell somewhere, echoing, and the swimming light rippled, reflecting it.

Then, distant and small, a light showed; the shape of a pillared doorway, formal and handsome. Beyond it something – someone – moved. In the moment when I wanted to go forward and see I was there without effort, a leaf on the wind, a ghost in a stormy night.

The door was the gateway to a great hall lighted as if for a feast. Whatever I had seen moving was no longer there; merely the great spaces of blazing light, the coloured pavement of a king's hall, the pillars gilded, the torches held in dragon-stands of gold. Golden seats I saw, ranged round the gleaming walls, and silver tables. On one of these lay a chessboard, of silver, dark and light, with pieces of silver gilt standing, as if half through an interrupted game. In the centre of the vast floor stood a great chair of ivory. In front of this was a golden chessboard, and on it a dozen or so gold chessmen, and one half-finished, lying with a rod of gold and a file where someone had been working to carve them.

I knew then that this was no true vision, but a dream of the legendary hall of Llud-Nuatha, King of the Otherworld. To this palace had they all come, the heroes of song and story. Here the sword had lain, and here the grail and the lance might one day be dreamed of and lifted. Here Macsen had seen his princess, the girl who in the world above he had married, and on whom he had begotten the line of rulers whose latest scion was Arthur . . .

Like a dream at morning, it had gone. But the great caves were still there, and in them, now, a throne with a dark king seated, and by him a queen, half visible in shadows. Somewhere a thrush was singing, and I saw her turn her head, and heard her sigh.

Then through it all I knew that I, Merlin, this time of all the times, did not want to see the truth. Knowing it already, perhaps, beneath the level of conscious thought, I had built for myself the palace of Llud, the hall of Dis and his prisoned Persephone. Behind them both lay the truth, and, as I was the god's servant and Arthur's, I had to find it. I looked again.

The sound of water, and a thrush singing. A dim room, but not lofty, nor furnished with silver and gold; a curtained room, well lighted, where a man and a woman sat at a little inlaid table and played at chess. She seemed to be winning. I saw him frown, and the tense set of his shoulders as he hunched over the board considering his move. She was laughing. He lifted his hand, hesitating, but withdrew it again and sat awhile, quite still. She said something, and he glanced aside, then turned to adjust the wick of one of the lamps near him. As he looked away from the board, her hand stole out and she moved a piece, neat as a thief in the market-place. When he looked back she was sitting, demure, hands in lap. He looked, stared, then laughed aloud and moved. His knight scooped her queen from the board. She looked surprised, and threw up her hands, pretty as a picture, then began to set the chessmen afresh. But he, suddenly all impatience, sprang to his feet and, reaching across the board, took her hands in his own and pulled her towards him. Between them the board fell over, and the chessmen spilled to the floor. I saw the white queen roll near his foot, with the red king over her. The white king lay apart, tumbled face downwards. He looked down, laughed again, and said something in her ear. His arms closed round her. Her robe scattered the chessmen, and his foot came down on the white king. The ivory smashed, splintering.

With it the vision splintered, broke in shadow that wisped, greying, back into lamplight, and the last glimmer from the dying fire.

I got stiffly to my feet. Horses were stamping outside, and somewhere in the garth a thrush was singing. I took my cloak from its hook and wrapped it round me. I went out. Cei was fidgeting by the horses, biting his nails. He hurried to meet me.

"You know?"

"A little. She is alive, and unhurt."

"Ah! Christ be thanked for this! Where, then?"

"I don't know yet, but I shall. A moment, Cei. Did you find the merlin?"

"What?" blankly.

"The Queen's falcon. The merlin she flew and followed into the forest."

"Not a sign. Why? Would it have helped?"

"I hardly know. Just a question. Now take me to Bedwyr."

3

Mercifully Cei asked no more questions, being fully occupied with his horse as we slithered and bounded, alternately, over the difficult ground. Though, in spite of the rain, there was still sufficient light to see the way, it was not easy to pick a quick and safe route across the tract of water-logged land which was the shortest way between Applegarth and the forest where the Queen had vanished.

For the last part of the way we were guided by distant torchlight, and men's voices, magnified and distorted by water and wind. We found Bedwyr up to the thighs in water, three or four paces out from the bank of a deep, still runnel edged with gnarled alders and the stumps of ancient oaks, some cut long ago for timber, and others blasted with time and storm, and growing again in the welter of smashed branches.

Near one of these the men were gathered. Torches had been tied to the dead boughs, and two other men with torches were out beside Bedwyr in the stream, lighting the work of dragging. On the bank, a short way along from the oak stump, lay a pile of sodden debris running with water, which glinted in the torchlight. Each time, one could guess, the nets would come up heavily weighted from the bottom, and each time all the men present would strain forward under the torchlight to see, with dread, if the net held the drowned body of the Queen.

One such load had just been tipped out as Cei and I approached, our horses slithering to a thankful stop on the very brink of the water. Bedwyr had not seen us. I heard his voice, rough with fatigue, as he showed the net-men where next to sink the drags. But the men on the bank called out, and he turned, then, seizing a torch from the man beside him, came splashing towards us.

"Cei?" He was too far gone with worry and exhaustion to see me there. "Did you see him? What did he say? Wait, I'll be with you in a moment." He turned to shout over his shoulder: "Carry on, there!"

"No need," I said. "Stop the work, Bedwyr. The Queen is safe."

He was just below the bank. His face, upturned in the torchlight, was swept with such a light of relief and joy that one could have sworn the torches burned suddenly brighter. "Merlin? Thank the gods for that! You found her, then?"

Someone had led our horses back. All around us now the men crowded, with eager questions. Someone put a hand down to Bedwyr, who came leaping up the bank, and stood there with the muddy water running off him.

"He had a vision." This was Cei, bluntly. The men went quiet at that, staring, and the questions died to an awed and uneasy muttering. But Bedwyr asked, simply:

"Where is she?"

"I can't tell you that yet, I'm afraid." I looked around me. To the left the muddy channel wound deeper into the darkness of the forest, but westward, to the right, a space of evening light could be seen through the trees where it opened out into a marshy lake. "Why were you dragging here? I understood the troopers didn't know where she fell."

"It's true they neither heard nor saw it, and she must have fallen some time before they got on the track of her mare again. But it looks very much as if the accident happened here. The ground's got trampled over now, so you can't see anything much, but there were signs of a fall, the horse shying, probably, and then bursting away through these branches. Bring the torch nearer, will you? There, Merlin, see? The marks on the boughs and a shred of cloth that must have come from her cloak . . . There was blood, too, smeared on one of the snags. But if you say she's safe . . ." He put up a weary hand to push the hair from his eyes. It left a streak of mud right down his cheek. He took no notice.

"The blood must have been the mare's," said someone, from behind me. "She was scratched about the legs."

"Yes, that would be it," said Bedwyr. "When we picked her up she was lame, and with a broken rein. Then when we found the marks here on the bank and among the branches, I thought I saw – I was afraid I knew what had happened. I thought the mare had shied and fallen, and thrown the Queen into the water. It's deep here, right under the bank. I reckoned she might have held on to the rein and tried to get the mare to pull her out, but the rein broke, and then the mare bolted. Or else the rein got caught on one of the snags, and it was only some time later that the mare could break loose and bolt. But now . . . What did happen?"

"That I can't tell you. What matters now is to find her, and quickly. And for that, we must have King Melwas' help. Is he here, or any of his people?"

"None of his men-at-arms, no. But we fell in with three or four of the marsh-dwellers, good fellows, who showed us some of the ways through the forest." He raised his voice, turning. "The Mere men, are they here still?"

It seemed that they were. They came forward, reluctant and over-awed, pushed by their companions. Two men, smallish and broad-shouldered, bearded and unkempt, and with them a stripling boy, the son, I guessed, of the younger man. I spoke to the eldest.

"You come from Mere, in the Summer Country?"

He nodded, his fingers twisting nervously in front of him at a fold of his sodden tunic.

"It was good of you to help the High King's men. You shall not be the losers by it, I promise you. Now, you know who I am?"

Another nod, more twisting of the hands. The boy swallowed, audibly.

"Then don't be afraid, but answer my questions if you can. Do you know where King Melwas is now?"

"Not rightly, my lord, no." The man spoke slowly, almost like one using a foreign language. These marsh-people are silent folk, and, when about their own business, use a dialect peculiar to themselves. "But you'll not find him at his palace on the Island, that I do know. Seen him away hunting, we did, two days gone. 'Tis a thing he does, now and again, just him and one of the lords, or maybe two."

"Hunting? In these forests?"

"Nay, master, he went fowling. Just himself, and one to row the boat."

"And you saw him go? Which way?"

"South-west again." The man pointed. "Down there where the causeway runs into the marsh. The land's dry in places thereabouts, and there be wild geese grazing in plenty. There's a lodge he has, a main beyond, but he won't be there now. It's empty since this winter past, and no servants in it. Besides, the news came up the water this dawning, that the young King was on his way home from Caer-y-n'a Von with a score of sail, so he would be putting in at the island, maybe with the next tide. And our King Melwas, surely, must be there to greet him?"

This was news to me, and, I could see, to Bedwyr. It is a constant mystery how these remote dwellers in the marshes get their news so quickly.

Bedwyr looked at me. "There was no beacon lighted on the Tor when news came about the Queen. Did you see it, Merlin?"

"No. Nor any other. The sails can't have been sighted yet. We should go now, Bedwyr. We'll ride for the Tor."

"You mean to speak with Melwas, even before we seek the Queen?"

"I think so. If you would give the orders? And see these men recompensed for their help?"

In the bustle that followed, I touched Bedwyr's arm, and took him aside. "I can't talk now, Bedwyr. This is a high matter, and dangerous. You and I must go alone to seek the Queen. Can you manage this without being questioned?"

He frowned, searching my face, but said immediately: "Of course. But Cei? Will he accept that?"

"He's injured. Besides, if Arthur is due, Cei should be back in Camelot."

"That's true. And the rest can ride for the Island, to wait for the tide. It'll be dark enough soon for us to slip away from them." The day's strain hacked abruptly through his voice. "Are you going to tell me what this is all about?"

"I'll explain as we ride. But I want no one else to hear, not even Cei."

A few minutes later we were on our way. I rode between Cei and Bedwyr, with the men clattering behind us. They were talking light-heartedly among themselves, wholly reassured, it seemed, by my word that all was well. I myself, though still knowing only what the dream allowed me, felt curiously light and easy, riding at the urgent pace Bedwyr set through the treacherous ground, without thought or care, not even feeling saddle or bridle-rein. It was not a new feeling, but it was many years since it had come to me; the god's will streaming past, and myself going with it, a spark blown between the lasting stars. I did not know what lay ahead of us in that watery dusk, but only that the Queen and her adventure were but a small part of the night's destiny, shadows already blown aside by this great forward surge of power.

My memory of that ride is all confusion now. Cei's party left us, and shortly afterwards we found boats, and Bedwyr embarked half the party by the short route across the Lake. The rest he divided, some by the shore road, others by the causeway that led directly to the wharf. The rain had stopped now, and mist lay everywhere with the night coming; above it the sky was filling with stars, as a net with flashing silver fish. More torches were lit, and the flat ferries crammed with men and horses were poled slowly through misty water that streamed with reflected light like smoke. As the troops on shore broke and re-formed, their horses shoulder deep in the rolling mist, we saw the glimmer of a distant torch mounting the Tor. Arthur's sails had been sighted.

It was easy then for Bedwyr and myself to slip away. Our horses plunged down from the hard road, cantered heavily through a league of wet meadow-land, and gained the fast going of the road that led south-west.

Soon the lights and sounds of the Island sank behind us and away. Mist curled from the water on either hand. The stars showed the way, but faintly, like lamps along a road for ghosts. Our horses settled into their stride, and soon the way widened, and we could ride knee to knee.

"This lodge to the south-west." His voice was breathless. "Is that where we go?"

"I hope so. Do you know it?"

"I can find it. Is that why you needed Melwas' help? Surely, when he knows of the Queen's accident, he'll let our troops search his land from end to end. And if he's not at the lodge now —"

Applegarth 265

"Let us hope he is not."

"Is that a riddle?" For the first time since I had known him, his voice was barely civil. "You said you'd explain. You said you knew where she was, and now you're looking for Melwas. Well, then –"

"Bedwyr, haven't you understood? I think Guinevere is at the lodge. Melwas took her."

The silence that followed was more stormy than any oath. When he spoke I could hardly hear him. "I don't have to ask you if you're sure. You always are. And if you did have a vision, I can only accept it. But tell me how, and why?"

"The why is obvious. The how I don't yet know. I suspect he has been planning this for some time. Her habits of riding out are known, and she often goes to the forest that edges the marsh. If she encountered him there, when she was riding ahead of her people, what more natural than that she should stop her mare and speak to him? That might account for the silence, while the troopers tried to find her at first."

"Yes . . . And if he gripped the rein and tried to seize her, and she spurred her mare on . . . That would account for the broken rein and the marks we found by the banks. By all the gods, Merlin! It's rape you're talking about! – And you said he must have been planning this for some time?"

"I can only guess at it," I said. "It seems likely that he must have made a few false casts before the chance came; the Queen unattended, and the boat ready nearby."

I did not pursue my own thoughts further. I was remembering that lamplit room, so carefully prepared for her; the chess game; the Queen's demure composure, and her smiling look. I was thinking, too, of the long hours of daylight and dusk that had passed since she had vanished.

So, obviously, was Bedwyr. "He must be mad! A petty king like Melwas to risk Arthur's anger? Is he out of his mind?"

"You could say so," I said drily. "It has happened before, where women are concerned."

Another silence, broken at length by a gesture, dimly seen, and a change in his horse's stride. "Slow here. We leave the roadway soon."

I obeyed him. Our horses slowed to a trot, a walk, as we peered around us in the mist. Then we saw it, a track leading, apparently, straight off into the marsh.

"This is it?"

"Yes. It's a bad track. We may have to swim the horses." I caught a glance back at me. "Will you be all right?"

Memory plucked at me; Bedwyr and Arthur in the Wild Forest, riding necks for sale, as boys will, but always with a care for myself, the poor horseman plodding at heel.

"I can manage."

"Then down here." His horse plunged down the narrow twist of mud between the reeds, then took the water like a boat launching; mine went after it, and we were forging, wet to the thigh, through the smooth water. It was a strange sort of progress, because the mist hid the water; hid, even, our horses' heads. I wondered how Bedwyr could see the way, then glimpsed, myself, far out across the gleam of water and banks of mist, and the black shapes of trees and bushes, the tiny glimmer of light that meant a dwelling. I watched it inching nearer, my mind racing this way and that with the possibilities of what must be done. Arthur, Bedwyr, Melwas, Guinevere . . . and all the time, like the deep humming that a harp builds up below an intricate web of music, was that other pressure of power which was driving me towards – what?

The horses heaved out of the water and stood, blowing and dripping, on a ridge of dry land. This stretched for some fifty paces ahead of us, and beyond it, some twenty paces further, was the house, across another channel of water. There was no bridge.

"And no boat, either." I heard him swear under his breath. "This is where we swim."

"Bedwyr, I'll have to let you do this last bit alone. But you – "

"Yes, by God!" His sword whispered loose in its scabbard.

I shot a hand out and gripped his horse's bridle above the bit. " – But you will do exactly as I tell you."

A silence. Then his voice, gentle and stubborn.

"I shall kill him, of course."

"You will do no such thing. You will save the High King's name and hers. This is Arthur's business, not yours. Let him deal with it."

Another silence, a long one. "Very well. I will be ruled by you."

"Good." I turned my horse quietly into the cover of a clump of alder. His, perforce, followed, with me still gripping the bit. "Now wait. Look yonder."

I pointed to the north-east, the way we had come. Far away in the night across the flat marshlands a cluster of lights showed, high up, like stars. Melwas' stronghold, alight with welcome. Unless the king himself was there, home from hunting, it could only mean one thing; Arthur had come back.

Then, the sound so magnified by the water that it made us start, came the click and creak of a door opening nearby, and the soft ripple of a boat moving through the water. The sounds came from behind the house, where something invisible to us took to the water and moved away into the mist. A man's voice spoke once, softly.

Bedwyr moved sharply, and his horse flung up its head against my restraining hand. His voice was strained. "Melwas. He's seen the lights. Damn it, Merlin, he's taking her –"

"No. Wait. Listen."

Light still showed from the house. A woman's voice called something. The cry had in it some kind of entreaty, but whether of fear, or longing, or sorrow at being left alone, it was impossible to tell. The boat's sound dwindled. The house door shut.

I still held Bedwyr's bridle. "Now, go across and bring the Queen, and we will take her home."

4

Almost before I had finished speaking he was off his horse, had dropped his heavy cloak across the saddle, and was in the water, swimming like an otter for the grassy slope before the door. He reached it, and began to draw himself up from the water. I saw him check, heard a grunt of pain, a stifled gasp, an oath.

"What is it?"

He made no reply. He got a knee to the bank, then pulled himself slowly, with the aid of a hanging willow, to his feet. He paused only to shake the wet from his shoulders, then trod up the slippery slope to the house door. He went slowly, as if with difficulty. I thought he was limping. As he went, his sword came rasping from the sheath.

He hammered on the door with the hilt. The sound echoed, as if from an empty house. There was no movement; no reply. (So much, I thought sourly, for the lady who waits for rescue.)

Bedwyr hammered again. "Melwas! Open to Bedwyr of Benoic! Open in the King's name!"

There was a long pause. It could be felt that someone within the house was waiting with held breath and beating heart. Then the door opened.

It was opened, not with a slam of defiance or bravery, but slowly, a crack only, which showed the small light of a taper, and the shadow of someone peering out. A slight figure, lissom and straight, with loose hair flowing, and a long gown of fine stuff with a creamy sheen.

Bedwyr said, and it came strangled: "Madam? Lady! Are you safe?"

"Prince Bedwyr." Her voice was breathless, but low, and

apparently composed. "I thank God for you. When I heard you coming I was afraid . . . But then, when I knew it was you . . . How did you come here? How did you find me?"

"Merlin guided me."

I heard the swift intake of her breath clear from where I stood holding the horses. The taper lit the pale shape of her face as she turned her head sharply, and saw me beyond the water. "*Merlin?*" Then her voice was once more soft and steady. "Then I thank God again for his art. I thought no one would ever come this way."

That, I thought, I can well believe. I said aloud: "Can you make ready, Madam? We have come to take you back to the King."

She did not answer me, but turned to go in, then paused, and said something to Bedwyr, too low for me to catch. He answered, and she pushed the door wide, and gestured him in after her. He went, leaving the door standing open. Inside the room I saw the pulsing ebb and flow of light that meant a fire. The room was softly lit by a lamp, and I caught glimpses through doorway and window of a room more richly furnished than any long-neglected hunting-lodge could have shown, with gilded stools and scarlet cushions, and, through another half-open doorway, the corner of a bed or couch, with a coverlet thrown across a tumble of bed-linen. Melwas had prepared the nest well for her, then. My vision of firelight and supper table and the friendly game of chess had been accurate enough. The words that would tell Arthur moved and raced and re-formed in my brain. The mist smoked up round the house like white ghosts, white shadows . . .

Bedwyr emerged from the house. His sword was back in its sheath, and in one hand he carried a lamp; the other held a pole such as marsh-men use to push their flat-bottomed craft through the reeds. He approached the water's edge, moving cautiously. "Merlin?"

"Yes? Do you want me to swim the horses over?"

"No!" sharply. "There are knives set below the water. I had forgotten that old trick, and drove a knee straight into them."

"I thought you were limping. Are you badly hurt?"

"No. Flesh wounds only. My lady has dressed them for me."

"All the more reason why you can't swim back, then. How do

you propose to get her over here? There must be some place where I can land the horses safely. Ask her."

"I have. She doesn't know. And there's no boat."

"So?" I said. "Has Melwas any gear that will float?"

"That's what I was thinking. There's sure to be something we can use; and the costlier the better." A shadow of amusement lightened the grim voice. But neither of us cared to comment on the situation across twenty feet of echoing water with Guinevere herself within earshot.

"She's dressing herself," he said shortly, as if in answer to my thought. He set the lamp down at the water's edge. We waited.

"Prince Bedwyr?"

The door opened again. She was in riding dress, and had braided her hair. Her cloak was over her arm.

Bedwyr limped up the bank. He held the cloak for her, and she drew it close and pulled the hood to cover the bright hair. He said something, then vanished indoors to reappear in a short while carrying a table.

I suppose the next few minutes, if anyone had been in the mood to appreciate it, would have been rich in comedy, but as it was, Queen Guinevere on one side of the water, and myself on the other, stood in silence and watched Bedwyr improvising his absurd raft, then, as an afterthought, pitching a couple of cushions into it, and inviting the Queen to board it.

This she did, and they came across, an undignified progress, with the Queen crouched low, holding on to one carved and gilded table leg, while the Prince of Benoic poled the contraption erratically across the channel.

The thing came to the bank, and I caught a leg and held it. Bedwyr scrambled ashore, and turned to help the Queen. She came gracefully enough, with a little gasp of thanks, and stood shaking out her stained and crumpled cloak. Like her riding dress, it had been soaked and roughly dried. I saw that it was torn. Something pale shook from the folds and fell to the muddy turf. I stooped to pick it up. It was a chessman of white ivory. The king, broken.

She had not noticed. Bedwyr pushed the table back into the water, and took his horse's bridle from me. I handed him his cloak and said formally to the Queen, so formally that my voice sounded stiff and cold: "I am glad to see you well and safe, lady. We have had a bad day, fearing for you."

"I am sorry." Her voice was low, her face hidden from me under the hood. "I took a heavy toss when my mare fell in the forest. I – I don't remember much after that, until I woke here, in this house . . ."

"And King Melwas with you?"

"Yes. Yes. He found me lying, and carried me here. I was fainting, I suppose. I don't remember. His servant tended me."

"He would have done better, perhaps, to have stayed by you till your own people came. They were searching the forest for you."

A movement of the hand that held the hood close about her face. I thought it was trembling. "Yes, I suppose so. But this place was near, just across the water, and he was afraid for me, he said, and indeed, the boat seemed best. I could not have ridden."

Bedwyr was in the saddle. I took the Queen's arm, to help her up in front of him. With surprise – nothing in that small composed voice had led me to suspect it – I felt her whole body shaking. I abandoned the questioning, and said, merely: "We'll take this ride easily, then. The King is back, did you know?"

I felt the shudder run through her, like an ague. She said nothing. Her body was light and slender, like a girl's, as I put her up in front of Bedwyr's saddle.

We went gently on the way back. As we neared the Island, it could be seen that the wharf was ablaze with lights, and milling with horsemen.

We were still some distance off when we saw, lit by their moving torches, a group of horsemen detach themselves from the crowd, and come at the gallop along the causeway. A man on a black horse was in the lead, pointing the way. Then they saw us. There were shouts. Soon they came up with us. In the lead, now, was Arthur, his white stallion black with mud to the withers. Beside him on the black horse, loud with relief and concern for the Queen, rode Melwas, King of the Summer Country.

★　　★　　★

I rode home alone. There was nothing to be gained, and too much to be lost, by confronting Arthur and Melwas now. So far, by Melwas' quick thinking in leaving the marsh house by the back way, and being present to greet Arthur as his ships put in to the wharf, the affair was saved from scandal, and Arthur would not be forced, whatever his private feelings when he found or guessed at the truth, into a hasty public quarrel with an ally. It was best left for the present. Melwas would take them all into his firelit palace and give them food and wine, and perhaps lodge them for the night, and by morning Guinevere would have told her story – some story – to her husband. I could not begin to guess what the story would be. There were elements in it which she would be hard put to it to explain away; the room so carefully ready for her; the loose robe she had worn; the tumbled bed; her lies to Bedwyr and myself about Melwas. And more than all, the broken chessman and its evidence of a true dream. But all this would have to wait until, at the very least, we were off Melwas' land, and no longer surrounded by his men-at-arms. As for Bedwyr, he had said nothing, and in the future, whatever his thoughts, his love for Arthur would keep his mouth shut.

And I? Arthur was High King, and I was his chief adviser. I owed him a truth. But I would not stay tonight, to face his questions, and perhaps evade them, or parry them with lies. Later, I thought wearily, as my tired horse plodded along the shore of the Lake, I would see more clearly what to do.

*   *   *

I went home the long way round, without troubling the ferryman. Even if he were willing to ply so late, I did not feel equal to his gossip, or that of the troops who might be making their way back. I wanted silence, and the night, and the soft veils of the mist.

The horse, scenting home and supper, pricked his ears and stepped out. Soon we had left the sounds and lights of the Island behind us, the Tor itself no more than a black shape of night, with stars behind its shoulder. Trees loomed, hung with mist, and below them lake water lapped on the flattened shingle. The smell of water and reeds and stirred mud, the steady plod of hoofs, the ripple of the

Lake, and through it all, faint and infinitely distant, but tingling like salt on the tongue, the breath of the sea-tide, turning to its ebb here at its languid limit. A bird called hoarsely, splashing somewhere, invisible. The horse shook his damp neck, and plodded on.

Silence and still air, and the calm of solitude. They drew a veil, as palpable as the mist, between the stresses of the day, and the night's tranquillity. The god's hand had withdrawn. No vision printed itself on the dark. About tomorrow, and my part in it, I would not think. I had been led to prevent trespass by a prophetic dream; but what "high matters" the sudden renewal of the god's power in me portended, I could not tell, and was too weary to guess at. I chirruped to the horse, and he quickened his pace. The moon's edge, above a shaw of elms, showed the night black and silver. In a short half mile we would leave the Lake shore, and make for home along the gravel of the road.

The horse stopped, so suddenly that I was jerked forward on his neck. If he had not been so far spent, he would have shied, and perhaps thrown me. As it was he balked, both forefeet thrust stiffly in front of him, jarring me to the bone.

Here the way ran along the crest of a bank which skirted the Lake. There was a sheer drop, half the height of a man, down to the water's surface. The mist lay thickly, but some movement of air – perhaps from the tide itself – stirred it faintly, so that it swirled and rose in peaks like cream in a tub, or flowed, itself like water, thickened and slow.

Then I heard a faint splashing, and saw what my horse had seen. A boat, being poled along a little way out from shore, and in it someone standing, balancing as delicately as a bird balances on a rocking twig. Only a glimpse I had, dim and shadow-like, of someone young-seeming and slight, in a cloak-like garment that hung to the thwarts and over the boat's edge to trail in the water. The boy stooped, and straightened again, wringing the stuff out. The mist coiled and broke round the movement, and its pallid drift reflected, briefly, the starlight. I saw his face. I felt shock thud under my heart like an arrow to its target.

"*Ninian!*"

He started, turned, stopped the boat expertly. The dark eyes looked enormous in the pale face.

"Yes? Who's that?"

"Merlin. Prince Merlin. Do you not remember me?" I caught at myself. Shock had made me stupid. I had forgotten that, when I fell in with the goldsmith and his assistant on the road to Dunpeldyr I had been in disguise. I said quickly: "You knew me as Emrys; that is my name. Myrddin Emrys from Dyfed. There were reasons why I couldn't travel under my own name. Do you remember now?"

The boat rocked. The mist thickened and hid it, and I knew a moment's blind panic. He had gone again. Then I saw him, still there, head on one side. He thought and then spoke, taking time about it, as always.

"Merlin? The enchanter? That is who you are?"

"Yes. I am sorry if I startled you. It was a shock seeing you like this. I thought you were drowned, that time at the Cor Bridge when you went swimming in the river with the other boys. What happened?"

I thought he hesitated. "I am a good swimmer, my lord."

There was some secret here. It did not matter. Nothing mattered. I had found him. This was what the night had been moving towards. This, not the Queen's trespass, was the "high matter" towards which the power had driven me. Here was the future. The stars flashed and sparkled as once they had flashed and sparkled on the hilt of the great sword.

I leaned forward over the horse's neck, speaking urgently. "Ninian, listen. If you don't want to answer questions, I'll ask none. All right, so you ran away from slavery; that doesn't matter to me. I can protect you, so don't be afraid. I want you to come to me. As soon as I saw you first, I knew what you were; you're like me, and by the Sight that God has given me, I think you will be capable of the same. You guessed it, too, didn't you? Will you come to me, and let me teach you? It won't be easy; you're young yet; but I was younger still when I went to my master, and you can learn it all, I know. Trust me. Will you come and serve me, and learn as much of my art as I can give you?"

This time there was no hesitation at all. It was as if the question had been asked and answered long ago. As perhaps it had. About some things there is this inevitability; they were in the stars from the last day of the Flood.

"Yes," he said, "I'll come. Give me a little time, though. There are things to – to arrange."

I straightened. My rib-cage hurt from the long breaths I drew. "You know where I live?"

"Everyone knows."

"Then come when you can. You will be welcome." I added, softly, as much to myself as to him: "By God himself, you will be welcome."

There was no reply. When I looked again, there was nothing but the white mist with the starlight on it, bitter-white, and from below, the lap of the lake-water on the shore.

★ ★ ★

Even so, it took me till I got to my own house to realise the very simple truth.

When I had seen the boy Ninian, and yearned to him as to the one human being I had known who could go with me wherever I had gone, it had been years ago. How many? Nine, ten? And he had been perhaps sixteen. Between a youth of sixteen and a man of twenty or more there is a world of change and growing: the boy I had just recognised with such a shock of joy, the face I had remembered a score of times with grief – this could not be the same boy, even had he escaped the river all those years ago, and lived.

As I lay that night in bed, wakeful, watching the stars through the black boughs of the pear tree, as I had done when a child, I went through the scene again. The mist, the ghostly mist; the upward starlight; the voice coming as an echo from the hidden water; the face so well remembered, dreamed over these ten years; these, combining suddenly to waken a forgotten and futile hope, had deceived me.

I knew then, with tears, that the boy Ninian was truly dead, and that this encounter in the ghostly dark had only mocked my weariness with a confused and cruel dream.

5

He did not come, of course. My next visitor was a courier from Arthur, bidding me to Camelot.

Four days had passed. I had half expected to be summoned before this, but, when no word came, assumed that Arthur had not yet decided what move to make, or that he was bent on hushing the affair up, and would not force a public discussion even in council.

Normally a courier passed between us three or four times a week, and any messenger whose commission took him past my house had long since formed the habit of calling at Applegarth to see if I had a letter ready, or to answer my questions. So I had kept myself informed.

I heard that, unbelievably, Guinevere was still on Ynys Witrin, where some of her ladies had joined her as guests of the old queen. Bedwyr, too, was still lodged in Melwas' palace; the knives had been rusty, and a couple of the wounds they made had become inflamed; added to this, he had taken a chill from wet and exposure, and was ill now with fever. Some of his own men were there with him, guests in Melwas' hall. Queen Guinevere herself, so said my informant, visited him daily, and had insisted on helping his nurses.

Another fragment of information I gathered for myself. The Queen's merlin had been found dead, hanging from its jesses in a high tree, near the place where Bedwyr had dragged the channel.

On the fifth day the summons came, a letter bidding me to confer with the High King about the new council hall, which had been finished while he was in Gwynedd. I saddled up and left immediately for Camelot.

Arthur was waiting for me on the western terrace of the palace. This was a wide paved walk, with formal garden beds wherein some of the Queen's roses bloomed, and pansies and the pretty summer flowers. Now, in the chilly spring afternoon, the only colour came from the daffodils, and the pale dwindling heads of the fair-maids.

Arthur stood by the terrace wall, looking out towards the distant, shining line that was the edge of the open sea. He did not turn to greet me, but waited until I was beside him. Then he glanced to make sure that the servant who had brought me to him had gone, and said abruptly:

"You will have guessed that it's nothing to do with the council hall. That was for the secretaries. I want to talk with you privately."

"Melwas?"

"Of course." He swung round with his back to the parapet, half leaning against it. He regarded me frowningly. "You were with Bedwyr when he found the Queen, and when he brought her back to Ynys Witrin. I saw you there, but when I turned to find you, you had gone. I am told, moreover, that it was you who told Bedwyr where to find her. If you knew anything about this affair that I do not, then why did you not wait and speak with me then?"

"There was nothing I could have told you then that would not have stirred up trouble that you could well do without. What was needed was time. Time for the Queen to rest; for you to talk with her; time to allay men's fears, not inflame them. Which you seem to have done. I am told that Bedwyr and the Queen are still on Ynys Witrin."

"Yes. Bedwyr is ill. He took straight to bed with a chill, and by morning was in a fever."

"So I heard. I blame myself. I should have stayed to dress those cuts. Have you talked with him?"

"No. He was not fit."

"And the Queen?"

"Is well."

"But not yet ready to make the journey home?"

"No," he said shortly. He turned away again, looking towards the distant gleam of the sea.

"I take it that Melwas must have offered some sort of explanation?" I said at length.

I expected the question to strike some kind of spark, but he merely looked tired, grey in a grey afternoon.

"Oh, yes. I talked with Melwas. He told me what had happened. He was fowling in the marshes, himself with one servant, a man called Berin. They had taken their boat into the edge of the forest, up the river that you saw. He heard the commotion in the forest, and then saw the Queen's mare plunge and slide in the mud of the bank. The Queen was thrown clear into the water. Her own people were nowhere to be seen. The two men rowed to her and pulled her out. She was unconscious as if she had struck her head in the fall. While they were doing this they heard her people go by at some distance, without coming near the river." A pause. "No doubt at this point Melwas should have sent his man after them, but he was on foot and they were mounted, and besides, the Queen was drenched and fainting, and very cold, and could hardly have been carried home, except by boat. So Melwas had the servant row to his lodge, and make a fire. He had food there, and wine. He had expected to go there himself to pass the night, so the place was ready."

"That was fortunate."

I kept the dryness from my voice, but he gave me a flick of a glance, sharp as a dagger. "Indeed. After a while she began to recover. He sent the servant with the boat to Ynys Witrin to bring help, and women to tend her, with either horses and a litter, or else a barge that could carry her in comfort. But before he had gone far the man returned to say that my sails were in sight, and that it looked as if I would land with the tide. Melwas judged it best to set off at once himself for the wharf to meet me, as his duty was, and to give me the news of her safety."

"Leaving her behind," I said, neutrally.

"Leaving her behind. The only craft he had was the light skin boat that he used for his fowling trips. It was not fit for her – certainly not in the state she was in. You must have seen that for yourself. When Bedwyr brought her to me, she could do nothing but weep and shiver. I had to let the women take her straight away and put her to bed."

He pushed himself away from the parapet, and, turning aside, took half a dozen rapid steps away and back again. He broke off a sprig of rosemary, and pulled it to and fro in his hands. I could smell its peppery, pungent scent from where I stood. I said nothing. After a while he stopped pacing and stood, feet apart, watching me, but still pulling the rosemary in and out between his fingers.

"So that is the story."

"I see." I regarded him thoughtfully. "And so you spent the night as Melwas' guest, and Bedwyr is still there, and the Queen is lodged there as well . . . until when?"

"I shall send for her tomorrow."

"And today you sent for me. Why? It seems that the affair is settled, and your decisions have been made."

"You must know very well why I sent for you." His voice had a sudden rough edge to it that belied his previous calm. "What do you know that 'would have stirred up trouble' if you had spoken to me that night? If you have something to say to me, Merlin, say it."

"Very well. But tell me first, have you spoken with the Queen at all?"

A lift of the brows. "What do you think? A man who has been away from his wife for the best part of a month? And a wife who was in need of comfort?"

"But if she was ill, being nursed by the women – "

"She was not ill. She was tired, and distressed, and she was very frightened."

I thought of Guinevere's composed, quiet voice, the careful poise, the shaking body.

"Not of my coming." He spoke sharply, answering what I had not said. "She feared Melwas, and she fears you. Are you surprised? Most people do. But she does not fear me. Why should she? I love her. But she was afraid that some evil tongue might poison me with lies . . . So until I went to her, and listened to her story, she could not rest."

"She was afraid of Melwas? Why? Was her story not the same as his?"

This time he did answer the implication. He sent the mangled sprig of rosemary spinning out over the terrace wall. "Merlin." It came quietly, but with a kind of hard-held finality. "Merlin, you do not have to tell me that Melwas lied to me, and that this was a rape. If Guinevere had been so badly hurt when she fell, that she lay fainting for most of the day, then she could hardly have ridden home with you, nor been as whole and sound as she was when I lay with her that night. She had sustained no hurt at all. Nothing but fear."

"She told you that his story was a lie?"

"Yes."

If Guinevere had told him a different tale, I thought I knew what she had not made clear. I said, slowly: "When she spoke with Bedwyr and myself, her story was the same as Melwas'. Now you say that *the Queen herself* told you it was a rape?"

"Yes." His brows twitched together. "You don't believe either story, do you? Is that what you are trying to tell me? You think — by God, Merlin, just what do you think?"

"I don't yet know the Queen's story. Tell me what she said."

He was so angry that I thought he would leave me then and there. But after a turn or two along the terrace he came back to where I waited. He had almost the air of a man approaching single combat.

"Very well. You are my counsellor, after all, and it seems I shall be in need of counsel." He drew in his breath. The story came in brief, expressionless sentences. "This is what she says. She did not take a fall at all. She saw her falcon stoop, and catch its jesses in a tree. She stopped her mare, and dismounted. Then she saw Melwas, in his boat by the bank. She called to him for help. He came up the bank to her, but did nothing about the merlin. He started to talk to her of love; how he had loved her since the time they had travelled up from Wales together. He would not listen when she tried to stop him, and when she made to mount again he took hold of her, and in the struggle the mare broke free and bolted. The Queen tried to call out for her people, but he put a hand over her mouth, and threw her down into the boat. The servant thrust it off from the bank, and rowed them away. The man was afraid, she says, and made some sort of protest, but he did as Melwas bade him. He took her to the lodge. It was all ready, as if he expected her . . . or some other woman. You saw it. Was it not so?"

I thought of the fire, the bed, the rich hangings, the robe Guinevere had worn. "I saw a little. Yes, it was prepared."

"He had had her in his mind so long . . . He had only been waiting his chance. He had followed her before — it was well known that she had a habit of outriding her people." There was a film of sweat on his face. He put the heel of his hand up to his brow and wiped it away.

"Did he lie with her, Arthur?"

"No. He held her there all day, pleading with her, she says, begging for her love . . . He began with sweet speeches and promises, but when they got him nowhere, he grew crazed, she says, and violent, and began to see his own danger. After he had sent his man away, she thinks he might have forced her, but the servant came quickly back to tell his master that my sails had been sighted, and Melwas left her in panic, and hurried to me to tell his lies. He threatened her that if she spoke the truth to me, he, Melwas, would say he had lain with her, so that I would kill her as well as him. She was to tell the same story as he would tell. Which you say she did, to you."

"Yes."

"And you knew it was not true?"

"Yes."

"I see." He was still watching me with that fierce but wary look. I was beginning to realise, but without much surprise, that even I could not keep secrets from him now. "And you thought she might have lied to me. That was the 'trouble' you foresaw?"

"Partly, yes."

"You thought she would lie to me? To me?" He repeated it as if it were unthinkable.

"If she were afraid, who could blame her for lying? Yes, I know you say she is not afraid of you. But she is only a woman, after all, and she might well be afraid of your anger. Any woman would lie to save herself. It would have been your right to kill her, and him, too."

"It is still my right to do that, whether there was a rape or not."

"Well, then – ? Could she have known that you would even listen to her, that you would be King and statesman before you allowed yourself to be the vengeful husband? Even I stand amazed, and I thought I knew you."

A flicker of grim amusement. 'With Bedwyr and the Queen on the Island as hostages, you might say my hands were tied . . . I shall kill him, of course. You know that, don't you? But

in my own time, and on some other cause, when all this is forgotten, and the Queen's honour cannot suffer from it." He swung
away, and put his two hands on the parapet, looking out again
across the darkening stretch of land towards the sea. Somewhere a
beam broke through the clouds, and a shaft of dusky light poured
down, lighting a distant stretch of water to a piercing gleam.

He spoke slowly, into the distance. "I've been thinking over the
story I shall put about. I shall take a tale midway between Melwas'
lie, and what the Queen told me. She was there all day with him,
after all, from dawn till dusking . . . I shall let it be given out that
she fell from her horse, as Melwas said, and was carried unconscious to the hunting-lodge, and there lay, shaken and fainting, for
most of the day. Bedwyr and you must bear this out. If it were
known that she was not hurt at all, there are those who would blame
her for not trying to escape. This, though the servant had the boat
under his eye all day, and even if she could have swum, there were
the knives . . . She could, of course, have threatened them with my
vengeance, but she saw that as the road only to her own end. He
could have kept her there, and had his pleasure and then killed her.
You know that her people had already accepted the fact of her
death. Except you. That was what saved her."

I said nothing. He turned.

"Yes. Except you. You told them she was alive, and you
took Bedwyr to her. Now, tell me how you knew. Was it a
'seeing'?"

I bent my head. "When Cei came for me, I called on the old
powers, and they responded. I saw her in the flame, and Melwas
too."

A moment of suddenly sharpening concentration. It was not
often that the High King searched me for truth as he was wont to
search lesser men. I could feel something of the quality that had
made him what he was. He had gone very still. "Yes. Now we
come to it, don't we? Tell me exactly what you saw."

"I saw a man and a woman in a rich room, and beyond the door a
bedchamber, with a bed that had been lain in. They were laughing
together, and playing chess. She was clad in a loose robe, as if
for night, and her hair was unbraided. When he took her in his arms
the chessboard spilled, and the man trod on the pieces." I held out a

hand to him, with the broken chessman. "When the Queen came out to us, this was caught in the fold of her cloak."

He took it, and bent his head over it, as if studying it. Then he sent it spinning after the sprig of rosemary. "So. It was a true dream. She said there was a table, and chessmen of ivory and ebony wood." To my surprise, he was smiling. "Is this all?"

"All? It is more than I would ever have told you, had I not owed it to you as your counsellor."

He nodded, still smiling. All the anger seemed to have gone. He looked out again over the dimming plain with its gleams of brightness and the shaft of wheeling light. "Merlin, a little while ago you said 'She is only a woman'. You have told me many times that you know nothing of women. Does it never occur to you that they lead lives of dependence so complete as to breed uncertainty and fear? That their lives are like those of slaves, or of animals that are used by creatures stronger than themselves, and sometimes cruel? Why, even royal ladies are bought and sold, and are bred to lead their lives far from their homes and their people, as the property of men unknown to them."

I waited, to see his drift. It was a thought I had had before, when I had seen women suffer from the whims of men; even those women who, like Morgause, were stronger and cleverer than most men. They were made, it seemed, for men's use, and suffered by it. The lucky ones found men they could rule, or who loved them. Like the Queen.

"This happened to Guinevere," he went on. "You yourself said just now that I must still be a stranger to her in some respects. She is not afraid of me, no, but sometimes I think that she is afraid of life itself, and of living. And most certainly she was afraid of Melwas. Don't you see? Your dream was true. She smiled, and spoke him fair, and hid her fear. What would you have had her do? Appeal to the servant? Threaten the two of them with my vengeance? She knew that was the road only to her own end. When he showed her the bedchamber, to let her change her wet clothing (he takes women to that house sometimes, it seems, out of sight of the old queen, his mother, and clothes are kept there, with things such as ladies like), she thanked him merely, then locked the door on him. Later, when he came to bid her to meat, she pretended faintness, but after a while he grew suspicious, then importunate, and she was afraid he would break the door, so she ate with him, and spoke him fair. And so, through the long day, till dusk. She let him think that, with nightfall, he would have his pleasure, while all the time she hoped for rescue still.''

"And then it came."

"Against all hope, and thanks to you, it came. Well, that is her story, and I believe it." That quick turn of the head again. "Do you?"

I did not answer straight away. He waited, showing neither anger nor impatience — nor any shadow of doubt.

When at length I spoke, it was with certainty. "Yes. She told the truth. Reason, instinct, 'Sight' or blind faith, you can be sure of it. I am sorry I doubted her. You were right to remind me that I don't understand women. I should have known she was afraid, and knowing that, I might have guessed that what poor weapons she had against Melwas, she would use . . . And for the rest — her silence until she could speak with you, her care for your honour and the safety of your kingdom — she has my admiration. And so, King, have you."

I saw him notice the form of address. Through his relief came a glint of laughter. "Why? Because I did not fly out in a high royal rage, and demand heads? If the Queen, in fear, could play-act for a day, surely I could do it for a few short hours, with her honour and my own at stake? But not for longer. By Hades, not for longer!" The force with which he brought his clenched fist down on the parapet showed just what he had held in check. He added, with an abrupt change of tone: "Merlin, you must be aware that the people do not — do not love the Queen."

"I have heard whispers, yes. But this is not for anything she is, or has done. It is only because they look daily for an heir, and she has been Queen for four years, without bearing. It's natural that there should be disappointed hopes, and some whispering."

"There will be no heir. She is barren. I am sure of it now, and so is she."

"I feared it. I am sorry."

"If I had not planted other seed here and there," he said with a wry smile, "I might share some of the blame with her; but there was the child I begot on my first queen, not to speak of Morgause's bastard by me. So the fault – if it is that – is known to be the Queen's, and because she is a queen, her grief at it cannot be kept private. And there will always be those who start whispers, in the hope that I will put her away. Which," he added with a kind of snap, "I shall not."

"It wouldn't occur to me to advise it," I said mildly. "What does occur to me is to wonder if this is the shadow that I saw once lie across your marriage bed . . . But enough of that. What we must do now is bring her back into the people's love."

"You make it sound easy. If you know how – "

"I think I do. Your swore just now by Hades, and it broke a dream I had. Will you let me go to Ynys Witrin, and bring her back to you myself?"

He started to ask why, then half laughed and shrugged. "Why not? Maybe to you it is as easy as it sounds . . . Go, then. I'll send word for them to prepare a royal escort. I'll receive her here. At least it saves me having to see Melwas again. Will you, with all your wise counsels, try to stop me from killing him?"

"As effectively as a mother hen calling the young swan out of the water. You will do as you think fit." I looked out across the water-logged plain, towards the Tor and the low-lying shape of its neighbour island, where the harbour lay. I added, thoughtfully: "It's a pity that he sees fit to charge harbour dues – exorbitant ones at that – to the war-leader who protects him."

His eyes widened, speculatively. A smile tugged at his mouth. He said slowly: "Yes, isn't it? And then there's the matter of the toll on the road along the ridge. If my captains should by any chance refuse to pay, then no doubt Melwas will bring the complaint here himself, and who knows, it may even be the first that comes to the new council chamber? Now, since that is what I told the scribe you were coming for, shall we go and see it? And tomorrow, at the third hour, I'll send the royal escort, to bring her home."

6

With Bedwyr still on Ynys Witrin, the royal escort was led by
Nentres, one of the western rulers who had fought under Uther, and
who now brought his allegiance and that of his sons to Arthur. He
was a grizzled veteran, spare of body, and as supple in the saddle as a
youth. He left the escort fidgeting under its Dragon banners on the
road below my house, and came riding himself up the curving track
by the stream, followed by a groom leading a chestnut horse
trapped with silver. Horse and trappings alike were burnished
to a glitter as bright as Nentres' shield, and jewels winked on the
breastband. The saddle-cloth was of murrey, worked with silver
thread.

"The King sent this for you," he said with a grin. "He reckons
your own would look like a dealer's throw-out among the rest.
Don't look at him like that, he's much quieter than he appears."

The groom gave me a hand to mount. The chestnut tossed his
head and mouthed the bit, but his stride was smooth and easy. After
my stolid old black gelding he was like a sailing-boat after a poled
barge.

The morning was cold, in the wake of the north wind that had
frozen the fields since mid-March. At dawn that day I had climbed
to the hilltop beyond Applegarth, and had felt against my skin that
indefinable difference that heralds a change of wind. The hilltop
thorns were no more than breaking into bud, but down in the valley
one could see the green haze on the distant woods, and the sheltered
banks nearby were thick with primroses and wild garlic. Rooks
cawed and tumbled about the ivied trees. Spring was here, waiting,
but held back by the cold winds, as the blackthorn flowers were
locked in the bud. But still the sky was overcast and heavy, almost

as if threatening snow, and I was glad of my cloak with all its regal splendours of fur and scarlet.

All was ready for us at Melwas' hall. The king himself was dressed in rich dark blue, and was, I noticed, fully armed. His handsome face wore a smile, easy and welcoming, but his eyes had a wary look, and there were altogether too many men-at-arms crowded in the hall, besides the full company outside, brought down at readiness from his hilltop fortress, to throng into the orchard-fields that served the palace for garden. Banners and bright trappings gave the welcome a festive air, but it was to be seen that every man wore both sword and dagger.

He had, of course, expected Arthur. When he saw me his look at first lightened with relief, then I saw the wariness deepen, and tight lines draw themselves around his mouth. He greeted me fairly, but very formally, like a man making the first move of a gambit at chess. I replied, with the long, studied speech of Arthur's deputy, then turned to the queen, his mother, who stood beside him at the end of the long hall. She showed no such caution as her son's. She greeted me with easy authority, and made a sign towards a door on the right of the hall. There was a stir as the crowd parted, and Queen Guinevere came in among her ladies.

She, too, had expected Arthur. She hesitated, looking for him in the glitter of the packed hall. Her gaze passed me, unseeing. I wondered what god had moved her to wear green, spring green, with flowers embroidered on the breast of her gown. Her mantle was green, too, with a collar of white marten, which framed her face and gave her a fragile look. She was very pale, but bore herself with rigid composure.

I remembered how, that night, I had found her shaking in my grasp; and on the thought, as if I had been dipped in cold water, I saw that Arthur had been right about her. She might be a queen in bearing and in courage, but under it all there was a timid girl, and one looking, all the time, for love. The gaiety, the ready laughter and high spirits of youth, had masked an exile's eager search for friendship among the strangers of a court vastly different from the homely hearth-stone of her father's kingdom. I would never, wrapped in Arthur as I had been for twenty years, even have troubled to think about her, except as his people thought; a vessel

for his seed, a partner for his pleasure, a glowing pillar of beauty to
shine, silver beside his gold, on the hilltop of his glory. Now I saw
her as if I had never seen her before. I saw a girl, tender of flesh and
simple enough of spirit, who had had the fortune to marry the
greatest man of the age. To be Arthur's Queen was no mean
burden, with all that it entailed of loneliness, and a life of banish-
ment in an alien country, with, as often as not, no husband near to
come between her and the flatterers, the power-hungry schemers,
those envious of her rank or beauty, or – perhaps most dangerous
of all – the young men ready to worship her. Then there would be
those (and you could trust them to be many) who would tell her,
over and over again, about the "other Guinevere", the pretty Queen
who had conceived from the King's first bedding of her, and for
whom he had grieved so bitterly. It would lose nothing in the
telling. But all this would have been nothing, would have passed
and been forgotten in the King's love, and her new, exciting power,
if only she had been able to conceive a child. That Arthur had not
used the Melwas affair to have her put aside, to take a fertile woman
to his bed, was proof indeed of his love; but I doubted if she had yet
had time to see it so. He had been right when he told me that she was
afraid of life, afraid of the people round her, afraid of Melwas;
and – I could see it now – more than any of them she was afraid of
me.

   She had seen me. The blue eyes widened, and her hands moved
up to clasp the fur at her throat. Her step checked momentarily,
then, once more held in that pale composure, she took her place
beside the queen, on the side away from Melwas. Neither she nor
the king had glanced at one another.

   There was a resounding silence. Someone's robe rustled, and it
sounded like a tree in the wind.

   I walked forward. As if Guinevere had been the only person
there, I bowed low, then straightened.

   "Greetings, Madam. It's good so see you recovered. I have
come, with others of your friends and servants, to escort you
home. The High King is waiting to receive you in your palace of
Camelot."

   The colour washed into her face. She only came up as high as my
throat. I have seen eyes like hers on a young deer pulled down and

waiting for the spear. She murmured something, and fell dumb. To cover it, and give her time, I turned to Melwas and his mother, and went smoothly into a courtly, over-elaborate speech, thanking them for their care of Arthur's Queen. It had become patent, while I was speaking, that Melwas' mother still had no idea that anything might be wrong. While her son watched me with a bold look glossing over that mixture of wariness and bravado, the old queen answered me with equally courtly thanks, messages for Arthur, compliments for Guinevere, and, finally, a pressing offer of hospitality. At that the young Queen looked up, briefly, then her eyelids hid her eyes again. As I declined, I saw her hands relax. I guessed that there had been no chance, since that parting in the marshes, for Melwas to speak with her and try to find out what she had told Arthur. I think, indeed, that he was going to insist on our staying, but something in my eyes stopped him, and then his mother, accepting the decision, came with obvious eagerness to the question that interested her.

"We looked for you that night, Prince Merlin. I understand that you were led by your vision to find the Queen, before even my son got back to the Island with the news. Will you not tell us, my lord, what this vision was?"

Melwas had jerked to attention. His bold look defied me to elaborate. I smiled, and my gaze bore his down. Without my prompting, the old woman had asked the very question that I wanted. I raised my voice.

"Willingly, lady. It is true that I had a vision, but whether it came from the gods of air and silence who have spoken to me in the past, or from the Mother Goddess to whose worship the shrine beyond those apple trees is sacred, I cannot tell. But I had a vision that led me straight through the marshland like a fledged arrow to its mark. It was a double vision, a bright dream through which the dreamer passes to a darker dream below; a reflection seen in deep water where the surface colour lies like glass over the dark world beneath. The visions were confused, but their meaning was clear. I would have followed them more quickly, but I think the gods willed it otherwise."

Guinevere's head came up at that, and her eyes widened. Again, in Melwas', that spark of doubt. It was the old queen who asked:

"How otherwise? They did not want the Queen found? What riddle is this, Prince Merlin?"

"I shall tell you. But first I will tell you about the dream that came to me. I saw a king's hall paved with marble, and pillared with silver and gold, where no servants waited, but where the lamps and tapers burned with scented smoke, bright as day . . ." I had let my voice take on the rhythm of the bard who sings in hall; its resonance filled the room and carried the words right out through the colonnade to the silent crowds outside. Fingers moved to make the sign against strong magic; even Guinevere's. The old queen listened with evident satisfaction and pleasure; it was to be remembered that she was the chief patroness of the Goddess's sacred shrine. As for Melwas, as I spoke I watched him move from suspicion and apprehension into bewilderment, and, finally, awe.

To everyone there, already, the dream had taken on a familiar pattern, the archetype of every man's journey into the world from which few travellers return.

". . . And on the precious table a set of gold chessmen, and nearby a great chair with arms curled like lions' heads, waiting for the King, and a stool of silver with doves' claws, waiting for the Lady. So I knew it for Llud's hall, where the sacred vessel is kept, and where once the great sword hung that now hangs on Arthur's wall in Camelot. And from overhead, in the sky beyond the hollow hill, I heard them galloping, the Wild Hunt, where the knights of the Otherworld course down their prey, and carry them deep, deep, into the jewelled halls of no return. But just as I began to wonder if the god was telling me the Queen was dead, the vision changed . . ."

To my right was a window, high in the wall. Outside was a prospect of sky, cloudy above the tops of the orchard trees. The budding apple-boughs showed lighter, in their young sorrel-and-green, than the slaty sky. The poplars stood pale like spears. But there had been that breath of change in the morning; I felt it still; I kept my eye on that indigo cloud, and spoke again, more slowly.

". . . And I was in an older hall, a deeper cavern. I was in the Underworld itself, and the dark King was there, who is older even than Llud, and by him sat the pale young Queen who was reft from the bright fields of Enna and carried out of the warm world to be the

Queen of Hell; Persephone, daughter of Demeter, the Mother of all that grows on the face of the earth . . ."

The cloud was moving slowly, slowly. Beyond the budding boughs I could see the edge of its shadow drawing its veil aside. From somewhere a breeze came wandering to shiver the tall poplars that edged the orchard.

Most of the people there would not know the story, so I told it, to the obvious satisfaction of the old queen, who must, like all devotees of the Mother's cult, be feeling the cold threat of change even here in this, its ancient stronghold. Once, when Melwas, doubting my drift, would have spoken, she silenced him with a gesture, and (herself perhaps with more instinctive understanding) put out a hand and drew the Queen closer to her side. I looked neither at the dark Melwas, nor at Guinevere, pale and wondering, but watched the high window out of the side of my eye, and told the old tale of Persephone's abduction by Hades, and the long, weary search for her that Demeter, the Mother Goddess, undertook, while the earth, robbed of its spring growth, languished in cold and darkness.

Beyond the window the poplars, brushed with the early light, bloomed suddenly golden.

"And when the vision died I knew what I had been told. Your Queen, your young and lovely Queen, was alive and safe, succoured by the Goddess and waiting only to be carried home. And with her coming, spring will come at last, and the cold rains will cease, and we shall have a land growing rich once again to harvest, in the peace brought by the High King's sword, and the joy brought by the Queen's love for him. This was the dream I had, and which I, Merlin, prince and prophet, interpret to you." I spoke straight past Melwas to the old queen. "So I beg you now, Madam, to let me take the Queen home, with honour and with joy."

And at that moment, the blessed sun came bursting out and laid a shaft of light clear across the floor to the Queen's feet, so that she stood, all gold and white and green, in a pool of sunshine.

★   ★   ★

We rode home through a brilliant day smelling of primroses. The clouds had packed away, and the Lake showed blue and glittering under its golden willows. An early swallow hawked for flies, close over the bright water. And the Spring Queen, refusing the litter we had brought for her, rode beside me.

She spoke only once, and then briefly.

"I lied to you that night. You knew?"

"Yes."

"You do see, then? You really do? You see all?"

"I see a great deal. If I set out to look, and if God wills it, I see."

The colour came into her face, and her look lightened, as if something had set her free. Before, I had believed her innocent: now I knew it. "So you, too, have told my lord the truth. When he did not come for me himself, I was afraid."

"You have no need to be, now or ever. I think you need never doubt that he loves you. And I can tell you too, Guinevere my cousin, that even if you never bear an heir for Britain, he will not put you aside. Your name will stand alongside his, as long as he is remembered."

"I will try," she said, so softly that I could hardly hear it. Then the towers of Camelot came in sight, and she was silent, bracing herself against what was to come.

★   ★   ★

So the seeds of legend were sown. During the golden weeks of spring that followed, I was more than once to hear men talking under their breaths of the "rape" of the Queen, and how she had been taken down almost to the dark halls of Llud, but brought back by Bedwyr, chiefest of Arthur's knights. So the sting of the truth was drawn; no shame attached to Arthur, none even to the Queen; and to Bedwyr was credited the first of his many glories, the story growing, and its hero gaining in stature, as his hurts healed and at last were well.

As for Melwas, in the way these things have, if the "Dark King" of the Underworld became linked in men's minds with the dark-avised king whose stronghold was the Tor, it was still without blame to Guinevere. What Melwas thought nobody knew. He must have realised that Guinevere had told Arthur the truth. He may have grown tired of being cast as the villain of the story, and of waiting (as everyone was waiting) for the High King to move against him. He may even have cherished hopes, still, that he might in some dim future come to possess the Queen.

Whatever the case, it was he who made the next move, and by doing so gave Arthur his way. One morning he rode to Camelot, and, perforce leaving his armed escort outside the council hall, took his seat in the Chair of Complaining.

*   *   *

The council hall had been built on the style of a smaller hall that Arthur had seen on one of the visits paid to the Queen's father in Wales. That had been merely a larger version of the daub-and-wattle round house of the Celts; this in Camelot was a big circular building, impressively built to last, with ribs of dressed stone, and between them walls of narrow Roman brick from the long-abandoned kilns nearby. There were vast double doors of oak, carved with the Dragon, and finely gilded. Inside, the place was open, with a fine floor of tiles laid out from the centre, like a spider's web. And, like the outer ring of a web, the walls were not curved, but sectioned off with flat panelling. These panels were covered with matting of a fine golden straw to keep out the draughts, but in time would be ablaze with needlework; Guinevere already had her maids set to it. Against each of these sections stood a tall chair, with its own footstool, and the King's was no higher than the next man's. This place was to be, he said, a hall for free discussion between the High King and his peers, and a place where any of the King's leaders could bring their problems. The only thing that marked Arthur's chair was the white shield that hung above it; in time, perhaps, the Dragon would shimmer there in gold and scarlet. Some of the other panels already showed the blazons of the Companions. The seat opposite the King's was blank. This was the one taken by anyone with a grievance to be settled by the Court. Arthur had called it the Chair of Complaining. But in later years I heard it called the Perilous Chair, and I think the name was coined after that day.

*   *   *

I was not present when Melwas tabled his complaint. Though I had at that time a place in the Round Hall (as it came to be called), I seldom took it. If his peers were equal there to the King, then the King must be seen to match them in knowledge, and to give his judgments without leaning on the advice of a mentor. Any discussions Arthur and I had were held in private.

We had talked over the Melwas affair for many hours before it came to the council table. To begin with Arthur seemed sure that I would try to stop him from fighting Melwas, but here was a case where the cold view and the hot coincided. To Arthur it would be satisfying, and to me expedient that Melwas should suffer publicly for his actions. The lapse of time, and Arthur's silence, with the legend I had invoked, ensured that Guinevere's honour would not be in question: the people had taken her once more into their loves, and wherever she went flowers strewed the way with blessings thrown like petals. She was their Queen – their darling's darling – who had almost been taken from them by death, and had been saved by Merlin's magic. So the story went among the common folk. But among the more worldly there were those who looked for the King to move against Melwas, and who would have been quick to despise him had he failed. He owed it to himself, as man and as King. The discipline he had imposed on himself over the Queen's rape had been severe. Now, when he found that I agreed with him, he turned, with a fierce joy, to planning.

He could, of course, have summoned King Melwas to the council hall on a trumped-up excuse, but this he would not do. "If we harass him until he makes a complaint himself, it comes to much the same thing in the sight of God," he said drily, "but in terms of my conscience – or my pride, if you like – I will not use a false charge in the Round Hall. It must be known as a place where no man need fear to come before me, unless he himself is false."

So harass him we did. Situated as the Island was, between the High King's stronghold and the sea, it was easy enough to find causes. Somehow or another there came to be constant arguments about harbour dues, rights of free way, levies and taxes arbitrarily imposed and hotly contested. Any of the petty kings would have grown restive under the constant stream of minor vexations, but Melwas was even quicker to protest than most. According to

Bedwyr (to whom I owed an account of the council meeting) it was apparent from the start that Melwas guessed he had been deliberately brought before the King to answer the older, more dangerous charge. He seemed eager to do so, but naturally enough allowed no hint of this to come into words: that must have meant his certain death for treason by the vote of the whole Council. So the grievances over dues and taxes, the arguments over the right levies for the protection offered by Camelot, took their long-drawn and tedious course, while the two men watched one another as swordsmen do, and at last came to the heart of the matter.

It was Melwas who suggested single combat. How he was brought towards this was not quite clear; my guess was that he took very little steering. Young, keen-tempered, a good swordsman, knowing himself to be in grave danger, he must have leaped at the chance of a quick, decisive solution that gave him a half-hope of success. He may have counted on more. His challenge came at last, hotly: "A meeting to settle these matters here and now, and man to man, if we are ever to agree as neighbours again! You are the law, King; then prove it with your sword!"

Uproar followed, arguments flying to and fro across the hall. The older of those present found it unthinkable that the King should risk himself, but all had by this time some inkling that there was more at stake than harbour dues, and the younger knights were quite frankly eager to see a fight. More than one of them (Bedwyr was the most insistent) offered himself as combatant in Arthur's place, until finally the King, judging his moment, got decisively to his feet. In the sudden silence he strode to the round table at the hall's centre, lifted the tablets where Melwas' grievances were listed, and sent them smashing to the floor.

"Now bring me my sword," he said.

*   *   *

It was midday when they faced one another on the level field in the north-east quarter of Caer Camel. The sky was cloudless, but a steady cool breeze tempered the warmth of the day. The light was high and even. The edge of the field was deep in people, the very ramparts furred with folk. At the top of one of Camelot's gilded towers I saw the cluster of azure and green and scarlet where the women had gathered to watch. The Queen, among them, was in white, Arthur's colour. I wondered how she was feeling, and could guess at the still composure with which she would hide her fear. Then the trumpet sounded, and silence fell.

The two combatants were armed with spears and shields, and each man had sword and dagger at his belt. Arthur was not using Caliburn, the royal sword. His armour – a light helmet and leather corselet – showed neither jewel nor device. Melwas' dress was more princely, and he was a shade the taller. He looked fierce and eager, and I saw him cast a look towards the palace tower where the Queen stood. Arthur had not glanced that way. He looked cool and infinitely experienced, listening apparently with grave attention to the herald's formal announcement.

There was a sycamore tree to one side of the field. Bedwyr, beside me in its shade, gave me a long look, and then drew a breath of relief.

"So. You're not worried. Thank God for that!"

"It had to come to this in the end. It's best. But if there had been danger for him, I would have stopped it."

"All the same, it's folly. Oh, I know that he wanted to, but he should never risk himself so. He should have let me do it."

"And what sort of showing would you make, do you suppose? You're still lame. You could have been cut down, if not worse, and then the legend would have had to start again. There are still simple folk who think that right is with the strongest sword."

"As it is today, or you'd not be standing idly by, I know. But I wish . . ." He fell silent.

"I know what you wish. I think you will have your wish, not once but many times, before your life's end."

He glanced sharply at me, started to say something more, but then the pennon fell, and the fight had begun.

For a long time the men circled one another, spears poised for the throw, shields ready. The light advantaged neither. It was Melwas who attacked first. He feinted once, then, with great speed and strength behind the throw, hurled the spear. Arthur's shield flashed up to deflect it. The blade slid screaming past the boss, and the spear buried itself harmlessly in the grass. Melwas, snatching for his sword-hilt, sprang back. But Arthur, in the same moment as he turned the spear aside, flung his own. By doing so he cancelled the advantage that Melwas' first throw had given him; but he did not draw his own sword; he reached for the other's spent spear, upright by him in the turf, pulled it up, and hefted it, just as Melwas, abandoning his sword-hilt, sent the King's spear also whizzing harmlessly from his shield, and turned, swift as a fox, to pick it up in the same way and face spear with spear once more.

But Arthur's weapon, harder flung, and more desperately parried, flew spinning to one side, to bounce level along the turf and skid away from Melwas' hand. There was no hope of snatching it up before Arthur could throw. Melwas, shield at the ready, feinted this way and that, hoping to draw the other's spear and so regain the advantage. He reached the fallen weapon; he stooped for it where it lay, the shaft half-propped to his hand by a clump of thistles. Arthur's arm moved, and the blade of his spear flashed in the light, drawing Melwas' eye. Melwas ducked, throwing his shield up into the line of the cast, at the same time swerving down to grab the fallen weapon. But the King's move had been a false one; in the unguarded moment when Melwas stooped sideways for the other spear, the King's, thrown straight and low, took him in the out-stretched arm. Arthur's sword whipped into his hand as he followed the spear.

Melwas staggered. As a great shout hit the walls and echoed round the field he recovered, grabbed the spear, and hurled it straight at the King.

Had he been any less fast, Arthur must have closed with him before he could use the spear. As it was, Melwas' weapon struck true when the King was halfway across the space between them. Arthur caught it on his shield, but at that short range the force was too great to turn. The long shaft whipped in a half circle, checking the King's rush. With the sword still held in his right hand, he tried to tear the spear-point from the leather, but it had gone in close by one of the metal stays, and jammed there, caught by its barbs. He flung the shield aside, spear and all, and ran it on Melwas, with nothing to guard his naked side but the dagger at his left hand.

The rush gave Melwas no time to recover himself and grab a

spear for a third cast. With the blood streaming down his arm, he dragged out his sword, and met the King's attack, body to body, with a slithering clash of metal. The exchange had left them still evenly matched, Melwas' wound, and the loss of strength in his sword-arm, against the King's unguarded side. Melwas was a good swordsman, fast and very strong, and for the first few minutes of the hand-to-hand struggle he aimed every stroke and slash at the King's left. But each one met iron. And step by step the King was pressing him; step by step Melwas was forced to give in front of the attack. The blood ran down, weakening him steadily. Arthur, as far as could be seen, was unhurt. He pressed forward, the ringing blows coming fast and hard, the whining whip and parry of the long dagger chiming between. Behind Melwas lay the fallen spear. Melwas knew it, but dared not glance to see where it lay. The dread of fouling it, and falling, made him slower. He was sweating freely, and beginning to breathe like a hard-ridden horse.

One of those moments came when, breast to breast, weapon to weapon, the men stood locked, totally still. Round the field the crowd was silent now, holding its breath.

The King spoke, softly and coldly. No one could hear what he said. Melwas did not reply. There was a moment's pause, then a swift movement, a sudden pressure, a grunt from Melwas, and some kind of growled answer. Then Arthur disengaged smoothly, and, with another low-spoken sentence, attacked afresh.

Melwas' right hand was a blur of glossy blood. His sword moved more slowly, as if too heavy for him. His breathing laboured, loud as a stag's in rut. With a great, grunting effort he brought his shield smashing down, like an axe, at the King. Arthur dodged, but slipped. The shield's edge took him on the right shoulder, and must have numbed the arm. His sword flew wide. There was a gasp and a great cry from the watching people. Melwas gave a shout, and swung his sword up for the kill.

But Arthur, now armed only with a dagger, did not spring back out of range. Before anyone could draw breath he had jumped forward, straight past the shield, and his long dagger bit into Melwas' throat.

And stayed still, followed only by a trickle of blood. No thrust followed. He spoke again, low and fierce. Melwas froze where he stood. The sword dropped from his lifted hand. The shield fell to the grass.

The dagger withdrew. The King stepped back. Slowly, in the sight of all that throng, the King's men and his own, and of the Queen watching from her tower, Melwas, King of the Summer Country, knelt on the bloody grass in front of Arthur, and made his surrender.

Now, there was no sound at all.

With a movement so slow as to be almost ceremonial, the King lifted his dagger, and cast it, point down, to quiver in the turf. Then he spoke again, more quietly even than before. This time Melwas, with bent head, answered him. They spoke for some time. Finally the King, still with that ceremony of gesture, reached a hand, and lifted Melwas to his feet. Then he beckoned the defeated man's escort to him, and, as his own people came crowding, turned away among them and walked back towards the palace.

*   *   *

In later years I heard several stories about this fight. Some said that it was Bedwyr who fought, not Arthur, but that is patently foolish. Others asserted that there was no fight, or Melwas would surely have been slain. Arthur and Melwas, they said, were brought by some mediator in the Council to agree on terms.

That is not true. It happened exactly as I have told it. Later I learned from the King what had passed between the two men on the field of combat; Melwas, expecting death, was brought to admit the truth of the Queen's accusation, and his own guilt. It is true that it would not have served for Arthur to kill him, but Arthur – and this on no advice from me – acted with both wisdom and restraint. It is a fact that after that day, Melwas was loyal to him, and Ynys Witrin was reckoned a jewel in the tally of Arthur's sovereignty.

It is a matter of public record that the King's ships paid no more harbour dues.

7

So the year went by, and the lovely month came, September, my birth-month, the wind's month, the month of the raven, and of Myrddin himself, that wayfarer between heaven and earth. The apple trees were heavy with fruit, and the herbs were gathered and drying; they hung in sheaves and bunches from the rafters in the outhouses at Applegarth, and the stillroom was full of ranked jars and boxes waiting to be filled. The whole house, garden, tower and living quarters, smelled sweetly of herbs and fruit, and of the honey that welled from the hives; even, at the end of the orchard, from the hollow oak where the wild bees lived. Applegarth, it seemed, reflected within its small boundaries the golden plenty of the kingdom's summer. The Queen's summer, men called it, as harvest followed hay-time, and still the land glowed with the Goddess-given plenty. A golden age, they said. For me, too, a golden age. But now, as never before, I had time to be lonely. And in the evenings, when the wind was in the south-west, I could feel it in my bones, and was grateful for the fire. Those weeks of nakedness and hunger, and exposure to the mountain weather in the Caledonian Forest, had left me a legacy that even a strong body could not shake off, and were pricking me forward into old age.

Another legacy that time had left me; whether as a lingering after-effect of Morgause's poison, or from some other cause, I had, from time to time, brief attacks of something that I might have called the falling sickness, save that this is not a malady that comes in later years if it has not been felt before. The symptoms, besides, were not like those in cases that I had seen or treated. The fit had come three times in all, and only when I was alone, so none knew of it but myself. What happened was this: resting quietly, I had drifted off, it seemed into sleep, only to wake, cold and stiff and weak with hunger – though not inclined to eat – many hours later. The first time it was a matter of twelve hours or so only, but I guessed from the giddiness, and the light, exhausted feeling, that it had not been normal sleep. On the second occasion the lapse of time was two nights and a day, and I was lucky that the malady had struck me when I was safely in my bed.

I told no one. When the third attack was imminent I recognised the signs; a light, half-hungry sensation, a slight giddiness, a wish to rest and be silent. So I sent Mora home, locked the doors, and took myself to my bedchamber. Afterwards I felt as I sometimes had after a time of prophecy, borne up like a creature ready for flight, with senses rinsed and clean as if new made, colours and sounds coming as fresh and brilliant as they must to a child. Of course I took to my books for enlightenment, but, finding no help there, I put the matter aside, accepting it, as I had learned to accept the pains of prophecy, and their withdrawal, as a touch of the god's hand. Perhaps now the hand was drawing me closer. There was no fear in the thought. I had done what he had required of me, and when the time came, would be ready to go.

But he did not, I reckoned, require me to sacrifice my pride. Let men remember the royal prophet and enchanter who retired from men's sight and his King's service in his own time; not a dotard who had waited overlong for his dismissal.

So I stayed solitary, busying myself with the garden and my medicine, writing and sending long letters to Blaise in Northumbria, and being cared for well enough by the girl Mora, whose cooking was from time to time enriched by some gift from Arthur's table. Gifts went back from me, too; a basket of some especially good apples from one of the young trees; cordials and medicines; perfumes, even, that I concocted for the Queen's pleasure; herbs for the King's kitchen. Simple stuff, after the fiery gifts of prophecy and victory, but somehow redolent of peace and the age of gold. Gifts of love and contentment; now, we had time for both. A golden time indeed, untroubled by foreboding; but with the prickling sense I recognised of some change to come; something undreaded, but ineluctable as the fall of the leaves and the coming of winter.

What it was, I would not allow myself to think. I was like a man alone in an empty room, contented enough, but listening for sounds beyond the shut door, and waiting with half a hope for someone to come, though knowing in his heart of hearts that he would not.

But he did.

He came on a golden evening, in about the middle of the month. There was a full moon, which had stolen, like a ghost, into the sky long before sunset. It hung behind the apple boughs like a great misty lantern, its light slowly waxing, as the sky around it darkened, to apricot and gold. I was in the stillroom, crumbling a pile of dried hyssop. The jars stood clean and ready. The room smelled of hyssop and of the racks of apples and plums laid on the shelves to ripen. A few late wasps droned, and a butterfly, snared by the room's warmth, flattened rich wings against the stone of the window-frame. I heard the light step behind me, and turned.

Magician they call me, and it is true. But I neither expected his coming, nor heard him until I saw him standing there in the dusk, lit by the deepening gold of the moon. He might have been a ghost, so did I stand and stare, transfixed. The meeting in the mist on the Island's shore had come back to me frequently, but never as something real; with every effort of recall it became more and more of a dream, something imagined, a hope only.

Now the real boy was here, flushed and breathing, smiling, but not quite at ease, as if unsure of his welcome. He held a bundle which, I supposed, must contain his goods. He was dressed in grey, with a cloak the colour of beech-buds. He had no ornaments, and no weapons.

He began: "I don't suppose you remember me, but – "

"Why should I not? You are the boy who is not Ninian."

"Oh, but I am. I mean, it is one of my names. Truly."

"I see. So when I called you – "

"Yes. When you spoke first, I thought you must know me; but then – when you said who you were – I knew you were mistaken, and – well, I was afraid. I'm sorry. I should have told you straight away, instead of running away like that. I'm sorry."

"But when I told you that I wanted to teach you my art, and asked you to come to me, you agreed to do so. Why?"

His hands, white on the bundle, clenched and twisted in the fold of the cloth. He hung still on the threshold, as if poised to run. "That was . . . When you said that he – this other boy – had been the – the kind of person who could learn from you . . . .You had felt it all along, you said, and he had known it, too. Well" – he swallowed – "I believe that I am, too. I have felt, all my life, that there were doors in the back of the mind that would open on light, if one could only find the key." He faltered, but his eyes did not waver from mine.

"Yes?" I gave him no help.

"Then when you spoke to me like that, suddenly, out of the mist, it was like a dream come true. Merlin himself, speaking to me by name, and offering me the very key . . , Even when I realised that you had mistaken me for someone else, who was dead, I had a wild thought that perhaps I could come to you and take his place . . . Then of course I saw how stupid that was, to think I could deceive you, of all people. So I did not dare to come."

"But now you have dared."

"I had to." He spoke simply, stating a fact. "I have thought of nothing else since that night. I was afraid, because . . . I was afraid, but there are things that you have to do, they won't let you alone, it's as if you were being driven. More than driven, hounded. Do you understand?"

"Very well." It was hard to keep my voice steady and grave. There must have been some note in it of what my heart felt, because, faint and sweet from the upper room, I heard the answer of my harp.

He had heard nothing. He was still braced, braving me, forcing himself into the role of suppliant. "Now you know the truth. I'm not the boy you knew. You know nothing about me. Whatever I feel, here in myself " – a hand moved as if to touch his breast, but clenched itself again on the bundle – "you may not think I'm worth teaching. I don't expect you to take me in, or spend any time on me. But if you would – if you would only let me stay here, sleep in the stable-place, anything, help you with – well, with work like that" – a glance at the pile of hyssop – "until perhaps you would come to know . . ." His voice wavered again, and this time died. He licked dry lips and stood mute, watching me.

It was my gaze that faltered, not his. I turned aside to hide the joy that I could feel mantling my cheeks. I plunged my hands wrist deep in the fragrant herbs, and rubbed the dry fragments between the fingertips. The scent of hyssop, clean and pungent, rose and steadied me.

I spoke slowly, to the herb jars. "When I called to you by the Lake, I took you for a boy with whom I travelled north many years ago, and who had a spirit that spoke to mine. He died, and ever since that day I have grieved for his death. When I saw you, I thought I had been mistaken, and that he still lived; but when I had time to think about it, I knew that now he would be a boy no longer, but a grown man. It was, you might say, a stupid error. I do not commonly make such errors, but at the time I told myself it was an error bred of weariness and grief, and of the hope that was still alive in me, that he, or such another spirit, would one day come to me again."

I paused. He said nothing. The moon had moved beyond the window-frame, and the door where the boy stood was almost in darkness. I turned back to him.

"I should have known it was no error. It was the hand of the god that crossed your path with mine, and now has driven you to me, in spite of your fear. You are not the boy I knew, but if you had not been just such another, you can be sure I would not have seen you, nor spoken to you. That night was full of strong magic. I should have remembered that, and trusted it."

He said eagerly: "I felt it, too. You could feel the stars like frost on the skin. I'd gone out to catch fish . . . but I let them be. It was no night for death, even for a fish." Dimly I saw that he smiled, but when he drew breath, it came unsteadily. "You mean I may stay? I will do?"

"You will do." I lifted my fingers from the hyssop, and let it trickle back onto the cloth, dusting my fingertips together. "Which of us, after this, will dare to ignore the god who drives us? Don't be afraid of me. You are very welcome. No doubt I'll warn you, when I have time to be cautious, of the heavy task you're undertaking, and all the thorns that lie in the way, but just at this moment I dare say nothing that will frighten you away from me again. Come in, and let me see you."

As he obeyed me, I lifted the unlit lamp from the shelf. The wick caught flame from the air, and flared high.

In full light, I knew that I could never have mistaken him for the goldsmith's boy, but he was very like. He was taller by a thumb's breadth, and his face was not quite so thin in outline. His skin was finer, and his hands, as fine boned and clever-looking as the other boy's, had never done slave's work. His hair was the same, a thick dark mane, roughly cut just short of his shoulders. His mouth was like, so like that I could have been deceived again; it had the gentle, dreaming lines that – I suspected – masked a firmness, even obstinacy of purpose. The boy Ninian had shown a quiet disregard of anything that he did not want to notice; his master's discourses had gone unheeded over his head while he took refuge in his own thoughts. Here was the same soft stubbornness, and in these eyes, too, the same half absent, dreaming look that could shut the world out as effectively as dropped eyelids. They were grey, the iris rimmed with black, and had the clarity of lake water. I was to find that like lake water they could reflect colour, and look green or blue or black-stormy as the mood came. Now they were watching me with what looked like a mixture of fascination and fear.

"The lamp?" I said. "You've not seen the fire called before? Well, that's one of the first things you'll learn; it was the first my own master taught me. Or is it the jars? You're looking at them as if you thought I was bottling poison. I was packing the garden herbs for winter's use."

"Hyssop," he said. I thought there was a glint of mischief, which in a girl I might have called demure. " 'To be burned with brimstone for inflammations of the throat; or boiled with honey to help pleurisy of the lungs.' "

I laughed. "Galen? Well, it seems we have a flying start. So you can read? Do you know – ? No, it must wait till morning. For the present, have you had supper?"

"Yes, thank you."

"You said that Ninian was 'one of your names'. What do you like to be called?"

" 'Ninian' will do . . . that is, unless you would rather not use it. What happened to him, the boy you knew? I think you said he was drowned?"

"Yes. We were at Corstopitum, and he went swimming with some other boys in the river beside the bridge where the Cor flows into the Tyne. They came running back to say he had been swept away."

"I'm sorry."

I smiled at him. "You will have to work very hard to make good his loss. Come, then, Ninian, we must find you a place to sleep."

⋆   ⋆   ⋆

That was how I acquired my assistant, and the god his servant. He had had his hand over both of us all that time. It seems to me now that the first Ninian was but a forerunner – a shadow cast before – of the real one who came to me later, from the Lake. From the start it was apparent that instinct had deceived neither of us; Ninian of the Lake, though knowing little of the arts I professed, proved a natural adept. He learned quickly, soaking up both knowledge and art as a cloth soaks up clear water. He could read and write fluently, and though he had not, as I in my youth had had, the gift of languages, he spoke a pure Latin as well as the vernacular, and had picked up enough Greek to be able to read a label or be accurate about a recipe. He had once, he told me, had access to a translation of Galen, but knew nothing of Hippocrates beyond hearsay. I set him to reading in the Latin version I had, and found myself, in some measure, sent back to school by the score of questions he asked, of which I had taken the answers so long for granted that I had forgotten how they were reached. Music he knew nothing of, and would not learn; this was the first time I came face to face with that gentle, immovable stubbornness of his. He would listen, his face full of dreaming light, when I played or sang; but sing himself, or even try to sing, he would not; and after a few attempts to teach him his notes on the big harp, I gave it up. I would have liked it if he had had a voice; I would not have wanted to sit by while another man made music with my harp, but now with age my own voice was not as good as it had once been, and I would have liked to hear a young voice singing the poems I made. But no. He smiled, shook his head, tuned the harp for me (that much he could and would do) and listened.

But in everything else he was eager and quick to learn. Recollecting as best I could the way old Galapas, my master, had inducted me into the skills of magic, I took him, step by step, into the strange and misty halls of art. The Sight he had already in some degree; but where I had surpassed my master from the start, Ninian would do well if in time he could equal me, and he was still a stranger to the flights of prophecy. If he went half as far as I, I would be content. Like all old men, I could not believe that that young brain and gentle body could withstand the stresses that I myself had withstood many times. I helped him, as Galapas had done me, with certain subtle yet safe drugs, and soon he could see in the fire or the lamp, and wake from the vision afterwards no more than weary, and, at times, disturbed by what he had seen. As yet he could not put truth together with vision. I did not help him to; and indeed, in those peaceful months of his apprenticeship there was little happening of enough moment to set prophecy stirring in the fire. Once or twice he spoke to me, in a kind of confusion, about the Queen, and Melwas and Bedwyr and the King, but I put the visions aside as obscure, and pursued them no further.

He steadfastly refused to tell me about himself or whence he came. He had lived most of his life, he said, on or near the Island, and allowed me to gather that his parents had been poor dwellers in one of the outlying Lake villages. Ninian of the Lake, he called himself, and said it was enough; so as such I accepted him. His past, after all, was nothing; whatever he was going to be, I would make. I did not press him; I had had enough, as a bastard and a child with no known father, of the shame of such questioning; so I respected the boy's silences, and asked no more than he would tell me.

All the practical side of healing, the study of anatomy, and the use of drugs, he was interested in, and good at. He could also, as I never could, draw with real skill. He began, that first winter, for sheer delight in the work, to compile a local herbal of his own, though most of the seeking and identifying of the plants, which is more than half the doctor's art, would have to wait till spring. But there was no hurry for it. He had, he told me, for ever.

So the winter passed in deep happiness, each day too short for all it could be filled with. To be with Ninian was to have everything; my own youth again, eager and quick to learn, with life unfolding full of bright promise; and at the same time the pleasures of quiet thought and of solitude. He seemed to sense when I needed to be alone, and either withdrew physically from my presence to his own room, or fell silent, and apparently into some deep abstraction, which left my thoughts free of him. He would not share the house with me, preferring, he said, to have rooms of his own where he need not disturb me, so I had Mora get ready the upper rooms that would have housed the servants, had any lived with me. The rooms were above the workshop and storeroom, facing west, and, though small and low under the rafters, were pleasant and airy. I did wonder at first if Mora and he had come to some sort of understanding; they spent a lot of time talking together in the kitchen, or down by the stream where the girl did some of the washing; I would hear them laughing, and could see that they were easy together; but there was no sign of intimacy, and in time I realised that Ninian, from things he let fall in talk, knew as little about love as I myself. Which, from the way the power grew in him, palpably week by week, I took to be only natural. The gods do not give two gifts at once, and they are jealous.

★   ★   ★

Spring came early the next year, with mild sunny days in March, and the wild geese going overhead daily, towards their nesting sites in the north. I caught some kind of chill, and kept to the house, but then one fine day went outside to sit in the little garth, where the doves were already busy about their love-making. The heated walls made the place as pleasant as a fireside; there were rosy cups of quince against the stone, and winter irises full out at the wall's base. In the gardens beyond the stable buildings I could hear the thud of Varro's spade, and thought idly of the planting I had planned. Nothing was in my mind beyond vague, pleasant plans of a domestic sort, and the sight of the pink sheen on the breast feathers of the doves, and the sleepy sound of their cooing . . .

Later, looking back, I wondered if for a brief hour my malady had blanketed me from consciousness of the present. It would have pleased me to think so. But it seems probable that the malady that overtook me was age, and the weakness left by the chill, and the lulling drug of contentment.

Quick footsteps on a stone stair startled me awake. I looked up. Ninian came hurrying down from his room, but with uncertain steps, as if it were he, not I, who was half drugged, or even ill. He kept a hand on the stone wall, as if without its guidance he would have stumbled. Still unsteadily, he crossed the colonnade, and came out into the sunshine. He paused there, with a hand to one of the pillars for support. His face was pale, his eyes enormous, the black pupils swimmingly overspreading the iris. His lips looked dry, but there was damp on his forehead, and two sharp lines of pain gouged down between his brows.

"What is it?" I began, in alarm, to get to my feet, but he put out a hand to calm me, then came forward. He sank down on the flags at my feet in the sun.

"I've had a dream," he said, and even his voice was unlike itself. "No, I wasn't asleep. I was reading by the window. There was a spider's web there, still full of drops from last night's rain. I was watching it as it shook in the sunlight . . ."

I understood then. I put a hand down to his shoulder and held it steadily. "Sit quiet for a moment. You will not forget the dream. Wait there. You can tell me later."

But as I got to my feet he shot a hand out and grabbed at my robe. "You don't understand! It was a warning! I am sure of that! There's some sort of danger —"

"I understand quite well. But until the headache goes, you will remember nothing clearly. Now wait. I'll be back soon."

I went into the stillroom. As I busied myself mixing the cordial I had only one thought in my mind. He, sitting reading and thinking, had had vision brought to him in a dewdrop's spark of light: I, waiting idly and with passive mind in full sunlight, had seen nothing. I found that my hand shook a little as I poured the cordial for him; it would take love, I thought, to stand peacefully aside and watch the god lift his wing from over me, and take another into its shadow. No matter that the power had brought pain and men's fear and sometimes hatred; no one who has known power like that has any wish to abdicate it to another. Not to anyone.

I carried the goblet out into the sunlight. Ninian, still curled on the flagstones, had his head down, a fist pressed tightly against his brow. He looked very slight and young. He raised his head at my step, and the grey eyes, swimming with tears of pain, looked at me blindly. I sat down, took his hand in mine, and guided the goblet to his mouth. "Drink this. It will make you feel better presently. No, don't try to talk yet."

He drank, then his head went down again, this time against my knee. I laid a hand on his hair. For some time we sat like that, while the doves, disturbed by his coming, flew down again onto the coping of the wall, and once more took up their gentle courtship. Beyond the stables the monotonous sound of Varro's spade went on and on.

Presently Ninian stirred.

I lifted my hand. "Better?"

He nodded and raised his head. The lines of pain had gone. "Yes. Yes, it's quite gone. It was more than a headache; it was like a sharp pain right through the brain. I've never felt anything like that before. Am I ill?"

"No. You are merely a seer, an eye and a voice for a most tyrannous god. You have had a waking dream, what men call a vision. Now tell me about it, and we shall see if it is a true one."

He drew his knees up, clasping them with both hands. He spoke, looking past me at the wall with the black branches and red cups of the quince. His eyes were still dark, dilated with vision, and his voice was low and even, as if reciting something learned by rote.

"I saw a stretch of grey sea, whipped with storm winds, breaking white over rocks like wolves' fangs. There was a beach of pebbles, grey too, and streaming with rain. The waves came in over the beach, and with them came broken spars and casks and torn sails – pieces of wreckage. And people; drowned bodies of men and women. One of the men's bodies rolled near me, and I saw he had not been drowned; there was a deep wound in his neck, but the blood had all been washed away by the sea. He looked like an animal that has been bled. There were dead children, too, three of them. One was naked, and had been speared. Then I saw, out beyond the breakers, another ship, a whole ship, with sails furled in the wind, and the oars out, holding her steady. She waited there, and I saw that she was low in the water as if heavily laden. She had a high, curved prow, with a pair of antlers fastened to it; I couldn't see if they were real, or carved in wood. I could see her name, though; it

was *King Stag*. The men in the ship were watching the bodies
tumbling on shore, and they were laughing. They were a long way
off across the sea, but I could hear what they said, quite clearly
. . . Can you believe that?"

"Yes. Go on."

"They were saying, 'You were guided, by God! Who could have
told that the old scow was so richly found? Luck like yours, and a
fair division of the spoils, and we'll all make our fortunes!' They
were speaking to the captain."

"Did you hear his name?"

"I think so. They called him 'Heuil'."

"Was that all?"

"No. There was a sort of darkness, like a mist. Then the *King Stag*
had gone, but near me on the shore there were horsemen, and some
of them had dismounted and were looking at the bodies. One man
lifted a piece of broken planking with something on it that might
have been the name of the wrecked ship, and carried it across to
where another was sitting on his horse. He was a dark man, carrying no device that I could see, but he was obviously their leader. He
looked angry. He said something, and the others got to their horses
again, and they all galloped up off the beach, through the dunes and
the long grasses. I was left there, and then even the dead bodies were
gone, and the wind was blowing into my eyes and making them
water . . . That was all. I was looking at the spider's web, and the
drops had melted in the sunlight. A fly was caught there, shaking
the web. I suppose that was what woke me. Merlin –"

He stopped abruptly, and cocked his head to listen. Now I could
catch, from the road below, the sounds of a troop of horsemen, and
a distant command to halt. A single rider detached himself, and
approached at a rapid canter.

"A messenger from Camelot?" I said. "Who knows, perhaps this
is your vision coming home."

The horse stopped. There was the jingle of the bridle being
thrown to Varro. Arthur came in through the archway.

"Merlin, I'm glad to see you about. They told me you had been
ill, and I came to see for myself." He paused, looking at Ninian. He
knew, of course, that the boy was with me, but they had not met
before. Ninian had refused to go with me to Camelot, and when–

ever the King had visited me, had made some excuse and retired to
his rooms. I did not press him, knowing the awe that the people of
the Lake villages felt for the High King.

I was on my feet, just beginning, "This is Ninian," when the boy
himself interrupted me. He came to his feet in one swift movement,
as fast as a snake uncurling, and cried out:

"That's the man! That's the one! It was a true dream, then, it was
true!"

Arthur's brows shot up, not, I knew, at the lack of ceremony, but
at the words. He looked from Ninian back to me. "A true dream?"
He said it softly. He knew the phrase of old.

I heard Ninian gasp, as, through the dregs of the vision, he
came back to the present. He stood there blinking, like someone
thrust suddenly into bright light. "It's the King. So it was the
King."

Arthur said, sharply now: "So what was the King?"

Ninian, flushing, began to stammer. "Nothing. That is, I was
just talking to Merlin. I didn't know you at first. I –"

"Never mind. You know me now. What is this about a true
dream?"

Ninian looked appealingly at me. Telling me his dream was one
thing; making his first prophecy to the King's face was quite
another. I said across him, to the King: "It seems that an old friend
of yours is indulging in piracy, or some villainy uncommonly like
it, somewhere in his home waters. Murder and robbery, and peaceful traders looted and then wrecked, and no one left alive to tell the
story."

He frowned. "An old friend of mine? Who, then?"

"Heuil."

"*Heuil*?" His face darkened. Then he stood for a few moments in
thought. "Yes, it fits. It fits. I had news a while back from Ector,
and he said Caw was failing, and that wild brood of his looking
around them like idle dogs for something to tear. Then three days
ago I heard from Urbgen, my sister's lord in Rheged, of a village on
the coast attacked and looted, and the folk killed or scattered. He
was inclined to blame the Irish, but I doubted that; the weather's
been too rough for anything but local raiding. Heuil, is it? You
don't surprise me. Shall I go?"

"It seems you had better. My guess is that Caw is dead, or dying. I can't believe that Heuil would dare, otherwise, to do anything to provoke Rheged."

"Your guess?"

"That is all."

He nodded. "It seems likely. In any case, it will answer very well. I had been almost ready to invent some pretext for a foray to the northward. With Caw's grip slackening, and that black dog Heuil collecting a following that could contest his brother's claim to the rulership of Strathclyde, I would like to be there to see things for myself. Piracy, eh? You did not see where?"

I glanced at Ninian. He shook his head. "No," I said, "but you'll find him. You will be there, on the shore, while the wreckage and the bodies still lie there. The raiders' ship is *King Stag*. That's all we know. You should be able to fasten the guilt where it belongs."

"I'll do that, never fear." He was grim. "I'll send north to Urbgen and Ector tonight to expect me, and I'll ride myself in the morning. I'm grateful. I've been looking for an excuse to cut my lord Heuil out of the pack, and now you give me this. It may be just the chance I need to get another agreement ratified between Strathclyde and Rheged, and throw my weight in behind the new king. I don't know how long I shall be away. And you, Merlin? All is really well with you?"

"All is very well."

He smiled. He had not missed the glance that had gone between Ninian and myself. "It seems you have someone to share your visions with, at last. Well, Ninian, I am glad to have met you." He smiled at the boy, and said something kind. Ninian, staring, made some sort of answer. I had been wrong, I saw, about him; he was not awed by the presence of the King. There was a quality in the way he looked at Arthur, something I could not quite put a name to; none of the worship that I was used to seeing in men's eyes, but a steady appraisal. Arthur saw it, looked amused, then dismissed the boy and turned back to me, asking for messages for Morgan and Ector. Then he said his goodbyes and went.

Ninian looked thoughtfully after him. "Yes, it was a true dream. The dark leader on the white horse, with the white shield shining, and no blazon on it but the light of the sky. It was Arthur beyond doubt. Who exactly is Heuil, and why does the King want an excuse to cut him down?"

"He's one of the sons of Caw of Strathclyde, who has been king on Dumbarton Rock since almost before I can remember. He's very old, and has sired nineteen sons on various women. There may be daughters, too, but those wild northern men make little of their girls. The youngest of the brood, Gildas, has recently been sent to my old friend Blaise, whom you know of, to learn to read and write. He, at least, will be a man of peace. But Heuil is the wildest of a wild breed. He and Arthur have always disliked one another. They fell out and fought, once, over a girl, when Arthur was a boy in the north country. Since then, with Caw's health failing, the King has seen Heuil as a danger to the balance of peace in the north. He would do anything, I think, to harm Arthur, even ally himself with the Saxons. Or so Arthur believes. But now that Heuil has taken to rapine and murder, he can be hunted down and destroyed, and the greater danger will be averted."

"And the King takes an army north, just like that, on your word?" There was awe in his face now, but not the awe of kings or their counsels. He was, for the first time, feeling the power in himself.

I smiled. "No, on yours. If I seemed to take the credit for the seeing I am sorry. But the matter was urgent, and he might not have believed you as readily."

"Of course not. But you saw it, too?"

"I saw nothing."

He looked startled. "But you believed me straight away."

"Of course. Because I did not share it, it doesn't mean it was not a true dream."

He looked worried, then rather scared. "But Merlin, do you mean that you knew nothing about this before I told you my dream? I mean, about Heuil's turning pirate . . . I should say, his intention to turn pirate? That you sent the King off to the north on my word alone?"

"That is what I mean, yes."

A silence, while worry, apprehension, excitement, and then joy, showed in his face as clearly as the reflection of light and cloud blowing across the waters of his native lake. He was still taking in the implications of power. But when he spoke he surprised me. Like Arthur, he saw straight past those implications to others that were my concern, not his. And his next words were an exact echo of Arthur's. "Merlin, do you mind?"

I answered him as simply. "Perhaps. A little, now. But soon, not at all. It's a harsh gift, and perhaps it is time that the god handed it on to you, and left me in peace to sit in the sun and watch the doves on the wall."

I smiled as I spoke, but there was no answering glimmer in his face. He did a strange thing then. He reached for my hand, lifted it to his cheek, then dropped it and went back upstairs to his room without another word or look. I was left standing there in the sun, remembering another, much younger boy, riding downhill from the cave of Galapas, with the visions swirling in his head, and tears on his face, and all the lonely pain and danger hanging in the clouds ahead of him. Then I went indoors to my own room, and read beside the fire till Mora brought the midday meal.

8

Arthur rode out next day for the north, and thereafter we got no more news. Ninian went about the place with a half dazed look, compounded, I think, of wonder at himself and the "true vision", and at me for not seeming distressed at the way it had passed me by. For myself, I admit I was divided; looking back on that day, I knew that I had been lingering in the edges of the poisoned dream that was my sickness; but even after Arthur's visit and acceptance of Ninian's prophecy, nothing had come to me out of the dark, either of proof or denial. For all that, I seemed to feel, in the rich quiet of the days, a tranquil approval. It was like watching a shadow that slowly, as the distant clouds move, withdraws from one field or forest, and passes on to shroud the next. I had been shown, gently enough, where happiness now lay; so I took it, preparing the boy Ninian to be as I had been, and myself for some future half seen and guessed at many times, but now seen more clearly and no longer dreaded, but moved towards, as a beast moves towards its winter sleep.

Ninian, more even than before, seemed to withdraw into himself. On one or two occasions, lying wakeful in the night, I heard him cross the garth soft-footed, and then run, like a young thing released, down the valley to the road. Twice, even, I sought to follow him in vision, but he must have taken care to cloud himself from me, for I saw no further than the roadway, then the slight figure running, running, into the mist that lay between Applegarth and the Island. It did not trouble me that he had secrets, any more than it troubled me to hear him and the girl Mora talking – sometimes at great length – in the stillroom or the kitchen. I had never counted myself lively company, and with age tended to be even more withdrawn. It only pleased me that the young people should find common interests, and keep each other contented in my service.

For service it was. I worked the boy harder than any slave. This is the way of love, I find; one longs so fervently for the beloved to achieve the best ends that he is spared nothing. And that I loved Ninian there could no longer be any doubt; the boy was myself, and through him I would go on living. As long as the King should need the vision and the power of a King's Prophet, he would find it, as ready to his hand as the royal sword.

One evening we built the fire up high against the chill wind of April, and sat beside it, watching the flames. Ninian settled straight down in his usual place, on the rug before the hearth, chin on fist, the grey eyes narrowed against the flames. Gradually, on the fine pale skin, the gleam of sweat showed, a film which caught the firelight and limned his face with a pure line, damping the edges of his hair, and fringing the black lashes with rainbows. I, as lately more and more often, found myself watching him, rather than reaching after my own power. It was a mixture of deep contentment, and a cruelly disturbing love that I made no attempt either to check or to understand. I had learned the lessons of the past; I went with the time, believing that I was master enough of myself and my thoughts to do the boy no harm.

There was a change in his face. Something moved there, a reflection of grief or distress or pain, like something seen faintly in a glass. Sweat was running into his eyes, but he neither blinked nor moved.

It was time I went with him. I stopped watching him, and turned my eyes to the fire.

I saw Arthur straight away. He was sitting his big white horse at the edge of the sea. It was a pebbled strand, and I recognised the crag-fast castle above; Rheged's sea-tower, which commands the Ituna Estuary. It was dusk, and the stormy sky piled indigo clouds behind a grey sea lighter than its own horizon. Foam-filled waves dashed down on the stones and raced hissing up the shore, to die in creamy froth and drag back through hissing pebbles. The white stallion stood fast, with the foam swirling round his fetlocks; his splashed and gleaming flanks, and Arthur's grey cloak blown with his horse's mane, looked part of the scene, as if the King had ridden out of the sea.

A man, a peasant by the look of him, was by Arthur's bridle, talking earnestly, and pointing seawards. The King followed the gesture, then sat straight in the saddle, his hand to his eyes. I saw what he was looking at; a light, far out towards the horizon, tossing with the tossing sea. The King asked a question, and the man pointed again, this time inland. The King nodded, something passed from hand to hand, then he turned his stallion's head and lifted an arm. The white horse went up the sea path at a gallop, and through the thickening mists of the vision I could see the troopers pressing after him. Just before the vision faded I saw, at the head of the cliff, lights pricking out in the tower.

I came back to the firelit room to find that Ninian was there before me. He was kneeling, or rather crouching, on the rug, with his head in his hands.

"Ninian?"

No movement but a slight shake of the head. I gave him a moment or two, then reached for the cordial I kept to hand.

"Come. Drink this."

He sipped, and his eyes thanked me, but still he did not speak.

I watched him for a few minutes in silence, then said: "So it seems that the King has reached the shores of the Ituna, and has found out about the pirates. He rests in Rheged's sea-tower, and with morning, I have no doubt, he will be hard on Heuil's tracks. So what is it? Arthur is safe, your vision was true, and he is doing what he set out to do."

Still nothing, but that look of white distress. I said quickly: "Come, Ninian, don't take it to heart so. For Arthur this is a small matter. The only hard thing about it is that he must punish Heuil without offending his brothers; and even that won't be too difficult. It's a long time since Heuil – metaphorically speaking – spat on his father's hearth-stone and went out to do his mischiefs in his own way. So even if old Caw is still alive, I doubt if he'll repine; and as for the elder sons, I've no doubt Heuil's death would come as a relief." I added, more sharply: "If it was tragedy you saw, or disaster, it's all the more important to speak of it. Caw's death we expected; whose, then? Morgan, the King's sister? Or Count Ector?"

"No." His voice sounded strange, like an instrument meant for music that is blown through by a gritty wind. "I did not see the King at all."

"You mean you saw nothing? Look, Ninian, this happens. You remember that it happened the other day, even to me. You must not let it distress you. There will be many times when nothing will come to you. I've told you before, you must wait for the god. He chooses the time, not you."

He shook his head. "It isn't that. I did see. But not the High King. Something else."

"Then tell me."

He gave me a desperate look. "I can't."

"Look, my dear, as you do not choose what you are shown, so neither do you choose what you will tell. There may come a time when you use your judgment in the halls of kings, but, with me, you tell me all that you see."

"I cannot!"

I waited a moment. "Now. You saw in the flames?"

"Yes."

"Did what you saw contradict what came before, or what I think I have just seen?"

"No."

"Then if you are keeping silent out of fear of me, or fear that I may be angry for some reason –"

"I have never been afraid of you."

"Then," I said patiently, "there can surely be no reason to keep silent, and every reason to tell me what you think you saw. It may not be the tragedy you so obviously think it is. You may be interpreting it wrongly. Has that not occurred to you?"

A flash of hope, soon shut out. He took a shaky breath, and I thought he would speak, then he bit his lip and remained silent. I wondered if he had foreseen my death.

I leaned forward and took his face in my hands and forced it up towards me. His eyes came reluctantly up to meet mine. "Ninian. Do you think I cannot go where you have just gone? Will you put me to that trouble and stress, or will you obey me now? What was it that you saw in the flame?"

His tongue came out to wet dry lips, and then he spoke, in a whisper, as if he was afraid of the sound. "Did you know that

Bedwyr is not with the High King? That he stayed behind in Camelot?"

"No, but I could have guessed it. It was obvious that the King must leave one of his chief captains to keep his stronghold and guard the Queen."

"Yes." He licked his lips again. "That's what I saw. Bedwyr in Camelot – with the Queen. They were – I think they are –"

He stopped. I took my hands away, and his eyes fell, how thankfully, away from mine.

There was only one way to interpret his distress. "Lovers?"

"I think so. Yes. I know they are." Then, in a rush now: "Merlin, how could she do this thing? After all that has happened – after all he has done for her! The Melwas affair – everyone knows what happened there! And Bedwyr, how could he so betray the King? The Queen – a woman to look aside from such a man, such a King . . . If only I could believe that this was no true dream! But I know it's true!" He stared at me, with eyes still dilated with the dream. "And Merlin, in God's name, what must we do?"

I said, slowly: "That I cannot tell you yet. But put it from you if you can. This is one burden that you must not be asked to share with me."

"Will you tell him?"

"I am his servant. What do you think?"

He bit his lip again, staring into the fire, but this time, I knew, seeing nothing. His face was white and wretched. I remember feeling vaguely surprised that he should, apparently, blame Guinevere more for her weakness than Bedwyr for his treachery. He said at length: "How could you tell him such a thing?"

"I don't know that yet. Time will show me."

He lifted his head. "You're not surprised." It sounded like an accusation.

"No. I think I knew, that night when he swam across to Melwas' lodge in the Lake. And afterwards, when she nursed him . . . And I remember how, when she first came to Caerleon for her wedding, Bedwyr was the only one of the knights who would not look at her, nor she at him. I think they had already felt it, on the journey from Northgalis, before ever she saw the King." I added: "And you might say that I was told clearly enough many years ago, when they were still boys together, and no woman had yet come, as women will, to disturb their lives.''

He got abruptly to his feet. "I'll go to bed," he said, and left me.

Alone, I went back into the flames. I saw them almost straight away. They were standing on the western terrace, where I had talked with Arthur. Now the palace was in darkness, but for the dispersed sparkle of the stars, and one shaft of lamplight that lay slanting over the tiles between the tubs of budding rose-trees.

They were standing silent and stock-still. Their hands were locked in each other's, and they were staring at one another with a kind of wildness. She looked afraid, and tears stood on her cheeks; his face was haunted, as if the white shadow sapped his spirit. Whatever kind of love had them in its claws, it was a cruel one, and, I knew, neither of them as yet had dared to let it kill their faithfulness.

I watched, and pitied, then turned from the smoking logs and left them to their privacy.

9

Eight weeks later the King came home. He had caught up with Heuil, beaten him in fair fight, burned his ships, and levied a fine which would keep him singing small for some time to come.

Once again he had crushed back his instincts in favour of policy. He had been met on his journey north with the tidings that Caw of Strathclyde had died, quietly in his bed. Quietly, that is, for Caw; he had spent the day hunting and half the night feasting, then, when the inevitable penalties struck his ninety-year-old body in the small hours of the dawning, had died, surrounded by such of his sons and their mothers as could get to the death-bed in time. He had also named his heir, the second son Gwarthegydd (the eldest had been badly maimed in fighting some years back). The messenger who brought Arthur the news also carried assurances of Gwarthegydd's friendship. So Arthur, till he had met and spoken with Gwarthegydd, and seen how he stood with his brother Heuil, would not put the friendship at risk.

He need not have been so careful. It was said that when Gwarthegydd heard the news of Heuil's defeat he let out a guffaw almost as hearty as his father's great bellow, and drank down a full horn of mead to Arthur's health. So the King rode north with Urbgen and Ector into Dumbarton and sat down with Gwarthegydd for nine days, and watched him crowned at the end of it. Then, well satisfied, he rode south again. He went by the east road to Elmet, found the Vale and the Saxon lands quiet, then crossed the country by the Pennine Gap to Caerleon. There he stayed for a month, and in the first days of June came home to Camelot.

It was time. Again and again in the fire I had seen the lovers, tossed between desire and faith, Bedwyr fine-drawn and silent, the

Queen with great eyes and nervous hands. They were never again alone: always with them her ladies sat and sewed, or his men rode in attendance. But they would sit or ride a little way apart from the rest, and talk and talk, as if, in speech, and now and again a light and desperate touch, there was comfort to be had.

And they watched day and night for Arthur's coming: Bedwyr, because he could not quit his post of torment without the King's leave; Guinevere with the forebodings of a lonely young woman who is half in awe of her husband, but has to depend on him for protection and comfort and what companionship he has time to give.

He was home in Camelot for ten days or so before he came to see me. It was a soft bright morning in June. I had risen soon after dawn, as was my habit, and went walking across the rolling hilltops above the house. I went alone; there was usually no sign of Ninian until Mora called him to breakfast. I had walked for an hour, thinking, and pausing from time to time to gather the plants I was looking for, when, beyond a fold of the downs, I heard hoof-beats, coming easily. Don't ask me how I knew it was Arthur; one hoof-beat is very like another, and there was no foresight in the air that day; but love has stronger wings than vision, and I merely turned and waited for him, in the lee of one of the groves of thorn that here and there break the pale sweep of the high downlands. The thorn trees crowned the edge of a little valley where ran a track as old as the land itself. Up this, presently, I saw him coming, sitting at ease on a pretty bay mare, and with his young hound, Cabal's successor, at heel.

He lifted a hand to me, turned the mare up the slope, then slid from the saddle, and greeted me with a smile.

"Well, so you were right. As if I had to tell you that! And now I suppose I don't even have to tell you what happened? Have you ever thought, Merlin, what a dull thing it is to have a prophet who knows everything before it has happened? Not only can I never lie to you, but I can hardly even come to you afterwards and boast about it."

"I'm sorry. But I assure you, this time, your prophet waited for your dispatches just as eagerly as anyone else. Thank you for sending the letters . . . How did you find me? Have you been to Applegarth?"

"I was on the way there, but a fellow with an ox cart – one of the sawyers – said he had seen you come this way. Are you going further? I'll walk with you if I may."

"Of course. I was just going to turn for home . . . Your letters were very welcome, but I still want to hear everything at first hand. It's strange to think that old Caw has gone at last. He's been sitting on that crag of his at Dumbarton for as long as I can remember. Do you think Gwarthegydd can hold his own now?"

"Against the Irish and the Saxons, yes, I wouldn't doubt him there. How he makes out with the seventeen other claimants to the kingdom is another matter." He grinned. "Sixteen, I suppose, since I clipped Heuil's wings for him."

"Make it fifteen. You can hardly count young Gildas, since he went to serve Blaise as his clerk."

"That's true. A clever boy, that, and was always Heuil's shadow. I fancy that when Blaise dies he'll be headed for a monastery. Perhaps it's as well. Like his brother, he has never loved me."

"Then it's to be hoped he can be trusted with his master's papers. You should get some of your own scribes to set your records down."

He cocked a brow at me. "What's this? A prophet's warning?"

"Nothing of the kind. A passing thought, merely. So Gwarthegydd is your man? There was a time when he threw Caw off and wooed the Irish kings."

"He was younger then, and Caw's hand was heavy. That's over. I think he will be well enough. What really matters at this stage is that he agrees with Urbgen . . ."

He talked on, telling me all the burden of the weeks away, while we walked slowly back across the downs, with the mare following, and the great hound coursing, nose down, in widening circles round our path.

In essence, I thought, listening, nothing had changed. Not yet. Less and less did he need to come to me for counsel, but, as always since his boyhood, he needed the chance to talk over – to himself as much as to me – the course of events, and the problems of the newly-built concourse of kingdoms as they arose. Usually, at the end of an hour or two, after a conversation to which I might have contributed much, or sometimes nothing at all, I could both hear and see that the knots were in a fair way to being unravelled. Then he would rise suddenly, stretch, give me farewell, and go; an abrupt disappearance with anyone else, but between us there was no need for more. I was the strong tree on which the eagle alighted in passing, for rest or thought. But now the oak showed a withered bough or two. How long would it take the sapling to be up to his weight?

He had come to the end of his narrative. Then, as if my thoughts had communicated themselves to him, he gave me a long look, with trouble in it. "Now, about you. How have you been during these last weeks? You look tired. Have you been ill again?"

"No. My health need not trouble you."

"I've thought more than once about my last visit to you. You said that it was this" – he hesitated over it – "your assistant who 'saw' Heuil and his rabble at their work."

"Ninian. Yes, it was."

"And you yourself saw nothing?"

"Yes," I said. "Nothing."

"So you told me. I still find that strange. Don't you?"

"I suppose so. But if you remember, I wasn't well that day. I suppose I had not fully recovered from that chill I caught."

"He's been with you – how long?"

"He came in September. That makes it, what? Nine months?"

"And you have taught him all you know?"

I smiled. "Hardly. But I have taught him a good deal. You need never lack a prophet, Arthur."

He did not smile in response. He was looking deeply troubled. He walked on across the flinty turf, with the mare's nose at his shoulder, and the hound running ahead. It was quartering the acres of furze with their loads of scented yellow blossom. Wherever it went it dislodged the tiny blue butterflies in clouds, and scattered the glossy scarlet of the ladybirds. There had been a plague of them that spring, and the furze bushes held them in their hundreds, like berries on the thorn.

Arthur was silent for a space, frowning at his thoughts. Then he came, apparently, to a sudden decision. "Do you trust him?"

"Ninian? Of course. Why not?"

"What do you know about him?"

"As much as I need to," I said, perhaps a little stiffly. "I told you how he came to me. I was certain then, and I am still certain, that it was the god who drew us together. And I could not have an apter pupil. Everything I have to teach him he is more than eager to learn. I don't have to drive him; I have to hold him back." I glanced at him. "Why? I would have thought you had seen the proof of his aptitude. His vision was true."

"Oh, I don't doubt his aptitude." He spoke drily. I caught the faintest of emphasis on the last word.

"What then? What are you trying to say?" Even I was not prepared for the degree of cold surprise in my voice.

He said quickly: "I'm sorry, Merlin. But I have to say this. I doubt his intentions towards you."

Though he had signalled the blow, it still struck with paralysing force. I felt the blood leave my heart. I stopped and faced him. Around us the scent of the gorse rose, sweet and strong. With it, unconsciously, I recognised thyme and sorrel and the crushed fescue as the bay mare put her head down and tore at a mouthful of grass.

I am not lightly made angry, least of all with Arthur. It was only a moment or two before I could say, levelly: "Whatever you have to say, you had certainly better say now. Ninian is more than my assistant, he bids fair to be my second self. If I have ever been a staff to your hand, Arthur, he will be such another when I am dead. Whether or not you like the boy – and why should you not, you hardly know him? – you may have to accept him so. I shall not live for ever, and he has the power. He has power already, and it will grow."

"I know. That is what troubles me." He looked away from me again. I could not judge if it was because he could not face me. "Don't you see, Merlin? He has the power. It was he who had the vision. And you did not. You say you were tired, you had been ill. But when did your god ever take that into account? This was no trivial "seeing"; it was not something that normally you would have missed. Because of it I was already there, on the borders of Rheged, when Caw died, and was able to support Gwarthegydd and prevent God knows how much trouble among those warring princes. So why did no vision come to you?"

"Must I keep repeating it? I – "

"Yes, you were ill. Why?"

Silence. A breeze came across the miles of downland, smelling of honey. Under it, through the immense stillness of the day, the grasses rustled. The mare cropped eagerly; the hound had come back to its master's feet and sat there, tongue lolling. Arthur stirred, and began to speak again, but I forestalled him.

"What are you saying? . . . No, don't answer. I know quite well what you are saying. That I have taken in this unknown boy, become infatuated, opened to him all the secret lore of drugs, and something of magic, and now he schemes to take my place and usurp my power. That he cannot be acquitted of using my own drugs against me. Is that it?"

Something of a smile touched his lips, though without lightening his grim look. "You never did deal in ambiguities, did you?"

"I never hid the truth, least of all from you."

"But then, my dear, you do not always see all the truth."

For some reason the very gentleness of the reply touched me with foreboding. I looked at him, frowning. "I am willing to accept that. So now, since I hardly imagine that all this springs from some vague suspicion, I must assume that you know something about Ninian that I don't. If that's so, why not tell me, and let me be the judge of its importance?"

"Very well. But –" Some change in his expression made me turn and follow his gaze. He was looking past me, away beyond the shoulder of the down, where a little valley held a stream fringed with birch and willow. Beyond this rose the green hill that sheltered Applegarth. Among the willows I caught a glint of blue, and then saw Ninian, who must have been up early after all, stooping over something at the edge of the stream. He straightened, and I saw that his hands were full of greenstuff. Watercress grew there, and wild mint among the king-cups. He stood for a moment, as if sorting the plants in his hands, then jumped the stream and ran away up the far slope, with his blue cloak flying out behind him like a sail.

"Well?" I said.

"I was going to say, let's go down there. We have to talk, and there must be more comfortable ways of doing it than standing face to face on top of the world. You unnerve me still, you know, Merlin, even when I know I'm right."

"That wasn't my intention. By all means let us go down."

He tugged the mare's head up from the grass, and led the way downhill to where the little wood crowded along the stream's edge. The trees were mostly birches, with here and there a twisted trunk of alder, overgrown with bramble and honeysuckle. One birch tree lay newly fallen, clean with silver bark. The King loosed a buckle from the mare's bit, tied one end of the rein to a sapling, then left her to graze, and came back to sit beside me on the birch trunk.

He came straight to the point. "Has Ninian ever told you anything about his parentage? His home?"

"No. I never pressed him. I suspected base origins, or at any rate bastardy – he hasn't the peasant look or way of speech. But both you and I know how little those questions can be welcomed."

"I have not had your scruples. I have wondered about him since that day when I met him with you at Applegarth. Since I came home I have asked about him."

"And found out what?"

"Enough to know that he has been deceiving you from the beginning." Then, striking a fist to his knee, with a sudden violence of exasperation: "Merlin, Merlin, are you so blind? I would swear that no man could be so deceived, except that I know you . . . Even now, a few minutes ago, watching him down here by the stream, you saw nothing?"

"What should I see? I imagine he had been collecting alder bark. He knew we needed more, and you can see where that tree has been stripped. And he was carrying watercress."

"You see? Your eyes are good enough for that, but not to see what any other man in the world would have seen – if not straight away, then within days of meeting him! I suspected it in those first few minutes there in your courtyard, while you told me the 'true dream', and then when I made inquiries I found that it was true. We both watched the same person running uphill just now. You saw a boy carrying watercress, but what I saw was a girl."

I cannot recall at what point during his speech I knew what he was going to tell me; before he got halfway it came like a truth already known; the heat before the lightning strikes, the silence after the lightning that is filled with the coming thunder. What the wise enchanter with his god-sent visions had not perceived, the young man, versed in the ways of women, had seen straight away. It was true. I could only marvel, dumbly, that I had been so easy to deceive. Ninian. The dim-seen figure in the mist, so like the lost boy that I had greeted her and put the words "boy" and "Ninian" into her head before she could even speak. Told her I was Merlin: offered her the gift of my power and magic, gifts that another girl – the witch Morgause – had tried in vain to prise from me, but which I had hastened eagerly to lay at this stranger's feet.

Small wonder that she had taken time to think, to arrange her affairs, to cut her hair and change her dress and gather her courage, before coming to me at Applegarth. That she had refused to share the house, preferring the rooms off the colonnade with their separate stair; that she had taken no interest in Mora, but that the two of them were so easy together. Mora had guessed, then? I swept the thought aside as others crowded. The speed with which she had learned from me; the power, with all its suffering, already accepted with dread, with resignation, and finally with willing joy. The grave, gentle look, the gestures of a worship carefully offered, and as carefully constrained. The way she had gone from me when I spoke so lightly of women disturbing men's lives. Her swift condemnation of Guinevere, rather than of Bedwyr, for giving way to a hurtful love. Then, with quickening memory, the feel of her dark hair under my hand, the sweet bones of her face, and the grey eyes watching in the firelight, and the disturbing love that had so troubled me, and now need trouble me no more. It came to me, like the sunlight breaking through the birch-trees on the forgotten bluebells of the copse where, long ago, a girl had offered me love, then mocked me for impotence, that this time no jealous god need come between us. At last I was free to give, along with all the rest of the power and effort and glory, the manhood that until now had been the god's alone. The abdication I had feared, and feared to grudge, would not be a loss, but rather a new joy gained.

I came back to the sunshine and a different birch-wood and the faded bluebells of June, to see Arthur staring.

"You don't even look surprised. Did you guess?"

"No. But I should have done; if not by any of the signs that were obvious to you, then by the way I felt . . . and feel now." I smiled at his look. "Oh, yes. An old fool if you like. But now I know for certain that my gods are merciful."

"Because you think you love this girl?"

"Because I love her."

"I thought you were a wise man," he said.

"And because I am a wise man, I know too well that love cannot be gainsaid. It's too late, Arthur. Whatever comes of it, it is too late. It has happened. No, listen. It has all come clear now, like sunlight on water. All the prophecies I have made, things in the future that I have foreseen with dread . . . I see them approaching me now, and the dread has gone. I have said often enough that prophecy is a two-edged sword; the gods are delphic; their threats, like their promises of fortune, turn in men's hands." I lifted my head and looked up through the gently moving leaves. "I told you that I had seen my own end. There was a dream I had once, a vision in the flame. I saw the cave in the Welsh hillside, and the girl my mother, whose name was Niniane, and the young prince my father, lying together. Then through and over the vision I saw myself, grey-haired, and a young girl with a cloud of dark hair, and closed eyes, and I thought that she, too, was Niniane. And so she was. So she is. Do you see? If she has any part in my end, then it will be merciful."

He got to his feet so abruptly that the hound, curled there, jumped aside, ridge-backed and looking round for danger. Arthur took three steps away from me, and three back to stand in front of me. He drove one fist into the other palm with such violence that the mare, a dozen paces away, started and then stood, ears erect, trembling. "How do you expect me to sit here and listen to you talking of your death? You told me once that you would end in a tomb, alive, you thought it would be in Bryn Myrddin. Now, I suppose, you will ask me to let you go back there so that this – this witch can leave you there entombed!"

"Not quite. You have not understood –"

"I understand as well as you do, and I think that I remember more! Have you forgotten Morgause's curse? That women's magic would snare you at the end? And what was promised you once by the Queen Ygraine, my mother? You told me what she said. That if Gorlois of Cornwall died, then she would spend the rest of her life praying to any gods there are that you would die betrayed by a woman."

"Well?" I said. "And have I not been snared? And have I not been betrayed? And this is all it is."

"Are you so sure? Forgive me for reminding you yet again that you don't know women. Remember Morgause. She tried to persuade you to teach her your magic, and when you would not, she took power another way . . . the way we know about. Now this girl has succeeded where Morgause failed. Tell me one thing: if she had come to you as herself, as a woman, would you have taken her in and taught her your skills?"

"I can't tell you that. Probably not. But the point is, surely, that she did not? The deception was not hers in the first instance; it was forced on her by my error, and that error in its turn was forced on me by the chance which led me first to meet and love the boy Ninian who was drowned. If you cannot see the god at work there, I am sorry."

"Yes, yes" – impatiently – "but you have just reminded me that this is a delphic god. What you see now as a joy may be the very death you have dreaded."

"No," I said. "You must take it the other way. That a fate long dreaded can prove, in the end, merciful, like this 'betrayal'. My long nightmare of entombment in the dark, alive, may prove to be such another. But whatever it is, I cannot avoid it. What will come, will come. The god chooses the time and the form. After all these years, if I did not trust in him, I would be the fool you think me."

"So you'll go back to this girl, keep her by you, and go on teaching her your art?"

"Just that. I could hardly stop now. I have sown the seeds of power in her, and, as surely as if it were a tree growing, or a child I had begotten, I cannot stop it. And the other seed has been sown, for good or ill. I love her dearly, and were she ten times an enchantress, I can only thank my god for it, and take her to me more nearly than before."

"I cannot bear to see you hurt."

"She will not hurt me."

"If she does," he said evenly, "witch or no witch, lover or no lover, I shall deal with her as she deserves. Well, it seems there is no

more to be said. We had better go back. That basket looks heavy.
Let me take it for you."

"No, a moment. There is one more thing."

"Yes?"

He was standing straight in front of me where I still sat on the
birch log. Against the delicate boughs of the birches and the shifting
of the leaves in the soft breeze he looked tall and powerful, the
jewels at shoulder and belt and sword-hilt glittering as if with their
own life. He looked, not young, but full of the richness of life, a
man in the flower of his strength; a leader among kings. His face
was contained. There was nothing to tell me what he would say,
what he might do, after I had spoken.

I said, slowly: "Since we have been talking of last things, there is
one thing I have to tell you. Another vision, which it is my duty to
bring to you. It's something that I have seen, not once, but several
times. Bedwyr your friend, and Guinevere your Queen, love one
another."

I had been looking away from him as I spoke, not wanting to see
how the wounding stroke went home. I suppose I had expected
anger, an outburst of violence, at the very least surprise and furious
disbelief. Instead there was silence, a silence so drawn out that at
length I looked up, to see in his face nothing of anger or even
surprise, but a kind of sternly-held calmness that tempered only
compassion and regret.

I said, not believing it: "You knew?"

"Yes," he said, quite simply. "I know." There was a pause, while
I looked for words and found none. He smiled. There was something in the smile that did not speak of youth and power at all, but of
a wisdom perhaps greater, because more purely human, than is
ascribed to me. "I do not have vision, Merlin, but I see what is
before my eyes. And do you not think that others, who guess and
whisper, have not been at pains to tell me? It sometimes seems to me
that the only ones who have given no hint by word or look have
been Bedwyr and the Queen themselves."

"How long have you known this?"

"Since the Melwas affair."

And I had never guessed. His kindness to the Queen, her relief
and growing happiness, had told me nothing. "Then why did you

leave Bedwyr with her when you went north?"

"To let them have something, however little." The sun was in his eyes, making him frown. He spoke slowly. "You have just been telling me that love cannot be ruled or stopped. If you are prepared to accept love, knowing that it may well bring you to your death, then how much more should I accept this, knowing that it cannot destroy friendship or faith?"

"You believe that?"

"Why not? Everything else you have ever told me has been true. Think back now over your prophecies about my marriage, the 'white shadow' that you saw when Bedwyr and I were boys, the *guenhwyvar* that touched us both. You said then that it would not blur or destroy the faith we had in one another."

"I remember."

"Very well. When I married my first Guenever you warned me that the marriage might be unwholesome for me. That little girl 'unwholesome'?" He laughed, without mirth. "Well, now we know the truth of the prophecy. Now we have seen the shadow. And now we see it falling across Bedwyr's life and mine. But if it is not to destroy our faith in one another, what would you have me do? I must give Bedwyr the trust and freedom to which he is entitled. Am I a cottager, with nothing in my life but a woman and a bed I am to be jealous of, like a cock on his dunghill? I am a king, and my life is a king's; she is a queen, and childless, so her life must be less than a woman's. Is she to wait year by year in an empty bed? To walk, to ride, to take her meals with an empty place beside her? She is young, and she has a girl's needs, of companionship and of love. By your god or any god, Merlin, if, during the years of days that my work takes me from court, she is ever to take a man to her bed, should I not be thankful it is Bedwyr? And what would you have me do, or say? Anything I say to Bedwyr would eat at the root of the very trust we have, and it would avail nothing against what has already happened. Love, you tell me, cannot be gainsaid. So I keep silent, and so will you, and by that token will faith and friendship stay unbroken. And we can count her barrenness a mercy." The smile again. "So the god works for us both in twisted ways, does he not?"

I got to my feet. The birches moved and the sun poured down.

The stream glittered against my eyes, so that they watered.

I said quietly: "You see? This is the final mercy. You no longer need either my strength or my counsel. Whatever you may need after this of warning or prophecy, you can still find at Applegarth. As for me, let your servant go in peace, back to my own home and my own hills, and whatever waits for me there." I picked the basket up and handed it to him. "But in the meantime, will you come back with me to Applegarth, and see her?"

10

When we reached Applegarth it seemed deserted. It was still very early. Varro had not yet come to start work, and I had seen Mora from a distance, making her way towards the village market, with her basket on her arm.

The mare knew the way to the stables, and trotted off, with a clap on the flank. We went into the house. The girl was there, sitting on her accustomed stool in the window embrasure, reading. Not far from her, on the stone sill, perched a redbreast, picking up the crumbs she had scattered.

She must have heard the horse, and assumed either that I had ridden that morning, instead of walking, or that a messenger had come very early from Camelot. She had obviously not expected the King himself. When I went into the room she looked up, with a smile and a "Good morning", and then, seeing Arthur's shadow fall across the doorway behind me, got to her feet and let the book roll together between her hands. "I'll leave you to talk, shall I?" she said, and turned, in no haste, to go.

I started to warn her. "Ninian –" I began, but then Arthur came quickly past me into the room, and stopped just inside the door, his eyes on her face.

Be sure that I was staring, too.

Now that I knew, I wondered how I had not always known. For eighteen, it was hardly a man's face; an immature eighteen might have had that smooth cheek and sweet mouth, and her body under the shapeless clothing was as slim as a boy's, but the hands were not a young man's hands, nor were the slender feet. I can only think that my own memory of the boy Ninian had kept me, blindly, to the image of him as he had been at sixteen: my desire to have him had been strong enough to let me recreate him, first in the dimly seen ghost of the Lake, then in this girl, so near to me, so closely watched, and yet not seen, through all the past long months. And then, perhaps (I thought), she had been able to use a little of my own magic against me, to keep me blind – and so to keep herself beside me, until her purposes were served.

She stood straight as a wand, facing us. I suppose it needed no magic for her to tell that we knew. The grey eyes met mine for the fraction of a moment, then she faced the King.

What happened then is difficult to describe. There was the quiet, everyday room, filled with the scents and sounds of the summer morning; sweet briar and early roses and the gillyflowers she had planted outside the window; last night's burned logs (the nights could still have a chill in them, and she had insisted on making a fire for me to sit by); the sweet sub-song of the redbreast as he flew up into the apple boughs outside. A summer room, where, to anyone of normal perceptions, nothing passed at all. Just three people, in a pause of silence.

But to me the air tingled suddenly over the skin, like water when lightning strikes. I felt the flesh creep on my bones, and the small hairs on my arms fur up; my nape stirred like the ruff of a dog in a thunder-storm. I do not think I moved. Neither the King nor the girl seemed to notice anything. She watched him gravely, un-alarmed, I might have thought unmoved and barely interested, if I had not been getting these fearsome currents washing over and through my flesh as the tide washes over a rock lying on the shore. Her grey eyes held his; his dark ones bored into her. I could feel the force as the two of them met. The air trembled.

Then he nodded, and put up a hand to loosen the cloak from his shoulder. I saw her mouth move with the shadow of a smile. The message had passed. For my sake, he would accept her. And for my sake, she would stand the trial. The room steadied, and I said, "Let me," and took his cloak from him to lay it down. The girl said: "Shall I bring you some breakfast? Mora left it ready, but you were late, so she went to market. She says the best things are taken if she is not there early."

She went. The platters were laid ready on the table, and we took our places. She brought bread, and the crock of honey, and a pitcher of milk along with one of mead. She set the latter down at the King's hand, then without a word took her usual place across from me. She had not looked at me again. When I poured a cup of milk for her she thanked me, but without lifting her eyes. Then she spread honey on her bread, and began to eat.

"Your name," said the King. "Is it Niniane?"

"Yes," she said, "but I was always called Nimuë."

"Your parentage?"

"My father was called Dyonas."

"Yes. King of the River Islands?"

"The same. He is dead now."

"I know that. He fought beside me at Viroconium. Why did you leave your home?"

"I was sent to the Lady's service, in the Isle of Glass. It was my father's wish." The glimmer of a smile. "My mother was a Christian, and when she lay dying she made him promise he would send me to the Island; I know she intended me for the service of the Church there. I was only six years old, but he promised her. He himself had never held with what he called the new God; he was an initiate of Mithras – his own father took him there in the time of Ambrosius. So when the time came for him to keep his promise to my mother, he did indeed take me to the Island, but to the service of the Good Goddess, in the shrine below the Tor."

"I see."

So did I. As one of the *ancillae* of the shrine she would have been there on the occasion of Arthur's thanksgiving after Caer Guinnion and Caerleon. Perhaps she had glimpsed me there, beside the King. She must have known that, for her, there was small chance of coming any nearer to the prince-enchanter, and learning any of the greater arts. Then on that misty night I had put the key into her hand. It had taken courage to grasp it, but God knew she had plenty of that.

The King was still questioning her. "And you wanted to study magic. Why?"

"Sir, I cannot say why. Why does a singer first want to learn music? Or a bird want to try the air? When I first went to the Island, I found some traces of it; and learned all they had to teach, but still I was hungry. Then one day I saw . . . ." She hesitated for the first time . . . "I saw Merlin in the shrine. You will remember the day. Later, I heard he had come to live here at Applegarth. I thought, if only I were a man I could go to him. He is wise, he would know that magic is in my blood, and he would teach me."

"Ah, yes. The day we gave thanks for our victories. But if you were there, how is it that you failed to recognise me, the first time you saw me here?"

She went scarlet. For the first time her gaze dropped from his. "I did not see you, sir. I told you, I was watching Merlin."

There was a flat pause of silence, as when a hand is laid across the harp-strings, killing the sound. I saw Arthur's mouth open and shut, then the flash of a vivid laughter in his face. She, looking steadfastly at the table, saw nothing of it. He shot me a look brimful of amusement, then drained his cup and sat back in the chair. His voice never altered, but the challenge had gone; he had lowered his sword.

"But you knew that Merlin was not likely to accept you as a pupil, even if the Lady could be persuaded to let you leave her cloisters."

"Yes. I knew that. I had no hope. But after that I settled even less easily into the life there among the other women. They seemed, oh, so contented to be penned there with the small magics and the prayers and spells, and looking backwards always towards the times of legend . . . It's hard to explain. If there is something within oneself, something burning to be free, one knows of it." A look straight at him, equal to equal. "You must have known it. I was still unborn, hammering at the egg, to get out into the air. But the only way I could have escaped from the Island would have been if some man had offered for me, and for that I would not have gone, nor would my father have made me."

He gave a brief nod of acceptance and, I thought, of understanding. "So?"

"It wasn't easy, even, to find time to be alone. I would watch and wait my chance, and slip out sometimes, only to be alone with my own thoughts, and with the water and sky . . . Then, on the night when Queen Guinevere was missing, and the Island was in uproar, I – I'm afraid all I thought of was my chance to get out without being missed . . . There was a boat I sometimes borrowed. I went out. I knew no one would see me in the mist. Then Merlin came along the Lake road, and spoke to me." She paused. "I think you must know the rest."

"Yes. So when chance – the god, you would say, if you are Merlin's pupil – made Merlin mistake you for the boy Ninian, and ask you to come and learn from him, you made the second chance for yourself."

She bent her head. "When he spoke first, I was confused. It was like a dream. Afterwards I realised what had happened, that he had mistaken me for some boy he had known."

"How did you get free of the shrine in the end? What did you tell the Lady?"

"That I had been called for higher service. I did not explain. I let her think I was going back to my father's house. I think she imagined that I had to go back to the River Isles, perhaps to be married to my cousin, who rules there now. She did not ask. She put no rub in my way."

No, I thought to myself; that imperious lady would be glad to rid herself of an adept who must have bidden fair to outshine her. Among those white-robed girls this young enchantress must have shone out like a diamond in white flax.

Behind me, the redbreast flew back to his perch on the window-sill, and tried a stave of song. I doubt if either Nimuë or Arthur heard it. His questions had changed direction: "Do you need fire for the vision, or can you see, like Merlin, in the small drops of dew?"

"It was in dew-drops that I saw the vision of Heuil."

"And that was a true one. So. It seems you already have some-thing of the greater power. Well, there is no fire, but will you look for me again, and tell me now if there is any other warning in the stars?"

"I can see nothing to order."

I bit my lip. It was my own voice as a young man, confident, perhaps a little pompous. He recognised it, too. He said gravely: "I am sorry. I should have known."

He got to his feet then, and reached for the cloak that I had laid across a chair. There was a perceptible flaw in her composure, as she hurried to help him with it. He was saying goodbye to me, but I hardly heard him. My own composure bade fair to be in ruins. I, who was never at a loss, had not had time to think what I must say.

The King was in the doorway. The sun caught him and sent his shadow streaming back between us. The great emeralds on Caliburn's hilt flashed in the light.

"King Arthur!" said Nimuë sharply.

He turned. If he found her tone peremptory he gave no sign of it.

She said: "If your sister, the Lady Morgan, comes to Camelot, lock up your sword and watch for treachery."

He looked startled, then said harshly: "What do you mean by that?"

She hesitated, looking in her turn surprised by what she had said. Then she lifted her palms out, in a gesture like a shrug. "My lord, I don't know. Only that. I am sorry."

"Well . . . " said Arthur. He looked across at me, lifted his brows, then shrugged in his turn, and went out.

Silence, so long that the robin hopped right into the room and onto the table where the breakfast lay, barely touched.

"Nimuë," I said.

She looked at me then, and I saw that, although she had stood in no awe of the King, she was afraid to meet my eyes. I smiled at her, and saw to my amazement the grey eyes fill with tears.

I put out both my hands. Hers met them. In the end there was no need of words. We did not hear the King's horse go down the hill, nor, much later, Mora come back from market to find the breakfast still uneaten.

BOOK 4

Bryn Myrddin

1

So, towards the end of my life, I found a new beginning. A beginning it was in love, for both of us. I had no skill, and she, vowed from childhood to be one of the Lake maidens, had hardly thought of love. But what we had was enough and more than enough: she, for all she was many years younger than I, seemed happy and satisfied; and I, calling myself in private dotard, old fool, wisdom dragged at mockery's chariot wheels, knew that I was none of these: between myself and Nimuë was a bond stronger than any between the best matched pair in the flower of their age and strength. We were the same person. We were part of each other as are night and daylight, dark and dawn, sun and shadow. When we lay together we lay at the edge of life where opposites fuse and make new entities, not of the flesh, but of the spirit, the issue as much of the ceaseless traffic of mind with mind, as of the body's pleasure.

We did not marry. Looking back now, I doubt if either of us even thought of cementing the relationship in this way; it was not clear what rites we could have used, nor what faster bond we could have hoped for. With the passing of the days and nights of that sweet summer, we found ourselves closer and yet more close, as if cast in a common mould: we would wake in the morning and know we had shared the same dream; meet at evening and each know what the other had learned and done that day. And all the time, as I believed, each of us harboured our own private and growing joy; I to watch her trying the wings of power like a strong young bird feeling for the first time the mastery of the air; she to receive this waxing strength, and to know, with love but without pity, that at the same time the power was leaving me.

So the month of June flew by, and then high summer was with

us. The cuckoo vanished from the brakes, the meadowsweet was out with its heavy honey smell, the bees droned all day in the blue borage and the lavender. Nimuë called to Varro to set a saddle on the chestnut – Arthur had made her a present of him – then she kissed me and rode off towards the Lake. It was, of course, known now that the former servant of the Goddess was with Merlin at Applegarth. There must have been speculation and gossip, some of it no doubt malicious – and (I was sure) all of it amazed at the impulse that had taken a young and lovely girl into the ageing enchanter's bed. But the High King had stated publicly, and had moreover made it clear by gifts and visits, that our relationship had his approval; so even the Lady of the shrine had not attempted to close her doors against Nimuë; she had, rather, made her welcome, in the hope (Nimuë suggested with amusement) that the shrine might fall heir to some of Merlin's secrets. Nimuë herself did not often leave Applegarth, either for the Island or the court at Camelot. But she was hardly to be blamed if she was a trifle flown with the power and excitement of these first months, and as a young bride enjoys showing off her new status among her maiden colleagues, so, I guessed, Nimuë was eager to revisit her friends among the Goddess's *ancillae*. She had not yet been to the court of Camelot without me; I guessed what she did not say; that, even with the King's support, she was doubtful of her reception there. But on three occasions she had been back to the Island, and this time, she told me, she would see about the promise of some plants from the garden near the holy well. She would be back at dusk. I saw her off, then checked over my bag of medicines, put on a straw hat against the sun, and set out across the hill to visit the house of a woman who was recovering from a bout of fever. I went blithely. The day was fine but fresh, and lark-song poured down from a clear sky like rillets of bright water. I reached the hilltop and followed the track between gorse bushes ablaze with flowers. A flock of goldfinches fluttered and dipped through a patch of tall, seeding thistles, making the sweet, plaintive call that the Saxons call "chirm", or "charm". The breeze smelled of thyme.

That is all I remember. Next – it seemed all in a moment – the world was dark, and the stars were out, with that clear sparkle that one can feel pricking down into the eyes and brain. I was lying on my back, flat on the turf, staring up at them. The gorse bushes were all round me, humped and dark, and gradually, as if sense were coming back from a limitless distance, I felt the stab of their prickles biting into hands and arms. Starlight sparked from the dew. Everywhere there was a great silence, like a held breath. Then above me, high in the black sky, another point of light began to grow. The darkness lit. Into this single, waxing point of light the smaller stars, like metal dust to a lodestone, like a swarm into the hive, fled, till in all the sky there was no other light. My eyes dazzled. I could not move, but lay there, it seemed alone on the curve of the world, watching the star. Then, intolerably bright, it started from its place, and swiftly, like a brand flung across the sky, it arched from the zenith to the earth's edge, trailing behind it a great train of light shaped like a dragon.

I heard someone call out: "The Dragon! The Dragon! See where the Dragon falls!" and knew the voice was my own.

Then lights, and hands, and Nimuë's face, white in the lantern light, with Varro behind her, and a youth I vaguely recognised as the shepherd who watched his flock on the down. Then voices. "Is he dead?" "No. Come, quickly, cover him. He's cold." "He's dead, mistress." "No! Never! I'll never believe it! Do as I say!" Then, with anguish, "Merlin, Merlin!" And a man's voice, fearfully, "Who will tell the King?"

After that a gap of time, and my own bed, and the taste of hot wine with herbs infused in it, and another long gap, this time of sleep.

* * *

Now we come to the part of my chronicle that is the most difficult to tell. Whether or not (as the popular belief went) the falling comet with the dragon's tail betokened the true end of Merlin's greater powers, I know that, looking back at the days and nights – more, the weeks and months – that followed, I cannot tell for certain whether what I remember was reality, or a dream. It was the year of my journeying with Nimuë. Looking back now, I see it, scene after scene, like reflections sliding past a boat, blurred and repeated, and broken, as the oars stir the water's glass. Or like the moments just before sleep, when scene after scene swims up into the mind's eye, the true memories like dreams, and the dreams as real as memory.

I still only have to close my eyes to see Applegarth, serene in the sun, with the silver lichen thick on the old trees, where the green fruit, slowly swelling, shone like lamps, and in the sheltered garth lavender and sage and sweet briar breathed their scent into the air as thickly as smoke. And on the hill behind the tower the thorn trees, those strange thorns that flower in winter and have small flowers with stamens like nails. And the doorway where the girl Nimuë first stood shyly, with the light behind her, like the gentle ghost of the drowned boy who might have been a greater enchanter than she. And the ghost itself; the "boy Ninian" who still haunts my memories of the garth, alongside the slender girl who sat at my feet in the sun.

For perhaps a week after my falling fit on the hilltop, I spent most of my time sitting on the carved seat in the garth. Not from weakness, but because Nimuë insisted, and I needed time to think.

Then one evening, in the warm dusk, I called her to me. She nestled down in her old place, on a cushion at my feet. Her head was against my knee, and my hand stroked the thick hair. This was growing now, and had reached her shoulderblades. I wondered daily at my old blindness that had not seen the curves of her body, and the sweet lines of throat and brow and wrist.

"You've been busy this week."

"Yes," she said. "Housewife's jobs. Cutting the herbs and bunching them to dry."

"Are they done?"

"Just about. Why?"

"I've been idle all this time while you have been working, but I have been thinking."

"About?"

"Among other things, Bryn Myrddin. You have never been there. So before the summer ends, I think we must leave Applegarth, you and I –"

"Leave Applegarth?" She started away from me, looking up in dismay. "Do you mean live at Bryn Myrddin again . . . both of us live there?"

I laughed. "No. Somehow I don't see that happening. Do you?"

She subsided against my knee, her head bent. She was silent for a while, then she said, muffled: "I don't know. I've never glimpsed even a dream of it. But you have told me that you will die there. Is that what you mean?"

I put out a hand again and touched her hair. "I know I have said that that will happen, but I've had no warning of it yet. I feel very well, better than for many months. But look at it like this: when my life does end, yours must begin. And for that to happen you must do one day as I did, and enter the crystal cave of vision. You know this. We've spoken of it before."

"Yes, I know." She did not sound reassured.

"Well," I told her cheerfully, "we shall go to Bryn Myrddin, but at the end of our journey. Before we get there we shall have travelled widely, and seen many places and many things. I want you to visit the places where I have passed my life, and see the things I have seen. I have told you as much as I can; now you must see as much as I am able to show you. Do you understand?"

"I think so. You are giving me the sum of your life, on which to build my own."

"Exactly that. For you, the stones on which to build the life you want; for me, the crown and harvest."

"And when I have it all?" she asked, subdued.

"Then we shall see." Amused, I caressed her hair again. "Don't look like that, child, take it lightly. It's a wedding journey, not a funeral procession. Our travels may have a purpose, but we'll take them for pleasure, that's for sure. I've had this in mind some time; it wasn't just suggested by this last sick turn of mine. We've been happy here in Applegarth, and no doubt we shall be happy here again, but you are too young to fold your wings here year after year. So we'll go travelling. I have a suspicion that my real object is just to show you the places I've known and loved, for no more serious reason than that I have known and loved them."

She sat up, looking easier. Her eyes began to sparkle. She was young. "A kind of pilgrimage?"

"You could call it that."

"Tintagel, you mean, and Rheged, and the place where you

found the sword, and the lake where you laid it to wait for the King?"

"More than that. God help us both, we must sail to Brittany. My story and the High King's has been bound up – as yours will be, too – in that great sword of his. I have to show you where the god himself first came to me, with the first sign of the sword. Which is why we should go soon. The seas are calm, but in another month or so the gales will start."

She shuddered. "Then by all means let us go now." Then, suddenly, all uncomplicated pleasure, a young woman setting out on an exciting journey, with no other thought in her head: "And you'll have to take me to Camelot. I really haven't got anything fit to wear . . ."

So next day I spoke with Arthur's courier, and not very long after that Arthur himself came to tell me that escort and ships were ready, and that we could go.

We set sail from the Island at the end of July, and Arthur and the Queen rode down to the harbour to see us on our way. Bedwyr was with us, his face a mixture of relief and misery: he had been sent to escort us across the sea, and he was like a man released from the torment of a drug which he knows will kill him, but for which, night and day, he craves. He was charged with dispatches from Arthur to his cousin King Hoel of Brittany, and would escort us as far as Hoel's court at Kerrec.

When we came to the quay the ship was still loading, but soon all was ready, and Arthur bade us farewell, with an admonition to Nimuë to "take care of him" which brought forcibly back to me memories of the voyage I had made with Arthur himself a squalling baby in his wet-nurse's arms, and King Hoel's escort scowling at the noise, and trying to give me due greeting through it all. Then he kissed Bedwyr, with nothing apparent in his look save warm affection, and Bedwyr muttered something, holding him, before turning to take his leave of the Queen. Smiling by the King's side, she had command of herself; her light touch of Bedwyr's hand, and the serene "Godspeed" she wished him showed barely more warmth than that given to Nimuë, and rather less than to me. (Since the Melwas affair, she had shown a pretty gratitude and liking, such as a girl might have for her elderly father.) I said my goodbyes, cast a wary eye at the smooth summer sea, and went on board. Nimuë, already pale, came with me. It needed no prophetic vision to foretell that we would see nothing of one another until the ship docked in the Small Sea.

It is no part of this tale to follow our travels league by league. Indeed, as I have explained, I cannot do so. We went to Brittany, that I know, and were welcomed there by King Hoel, and spent the autumn and winter in Kerrec, and I showed Nimuë the roads through the Perilous Forest, and the humble inn where Ralf, my page, guarded the child Arthur through the dangerous hidden years. But here already the memories are confused; as I write I can see them all, crossing each other like ghosts that crowd, century by century, into an old dwelling house. Each is as clear as the others. Arthur as a baby, asleep in the manger straw. My father watching me in the lamplight, asking, "What will come to Britain?" The druids at their murderous work in Nemet. Myself, a frightened boy, hiding in the cattle-shed. Ralf riding post-haste through the trees with messages for Hoel to send to me. Nimuë beside me in the budding woods of April, lying on green turf in a forest glade. The same glade, with the white doe fleeing like magic, to draw danger away from Arthur. And across this, confusedly, other memories or other dreams; a white stag with ruby eyes; the deer fleeing through the dusk under the oaks at Nodens' shrine; magic on magic. But through all, like a torch relit for another quest, the stars, the smiling god, the sword.

We stayed away till summer, this much I know for certain. I can even record the day of our arrival back in Britain. Cador, Duke of Cornwall, died that year, and we disembarked in a country deep in mourning for a great soldier and a good duke. What I cannot recall is which of us – Nimuë or myself – knew that it was time to be gone, or which harbour to sail for. We landed in a little bay a league or so from Tintagel, on Dumnonia's northern coast, two days after Cador's death, to find Arthur there already, with all his train. Having seen our sail, he came down to the wharf to meet us, and before ever we landed we saw the covered shields, the lowered pennons, and the unadorned white of mourning, and knew what had brought us home.

Scenes like these swim up, brightly lit with hardly a shadow. But then comes the candlelit chapel where Cador's body lay in state, with monks chanting; and the scene dislimns, and once again I am standing at the foot of his father's bier, waiting for the ghost of the man I had betrayed. Even Nimuë, when once I spoke to her of this, could be no help to me. For so long now we had shared thought and dream alike that she herself could not (she told me) separate the sight of Tintagel in the summer, with the gentle wind lifting the sea against the rocks, from my stormy tales of time past. Tintagel mourning for Duke Cador recently dead, seems less real to either of us than the storm-beaten stronghold where Uther, lying with Gorlois' wife Ygraine, begot Arthur for Britain.

And so it was with the rest of the time. After Tintagel we went north. Memory, or dream here in the long darkness, shows me the soft hills of Rheged, the hanging clouds of forest, the lakes ringing with fish, and, reflected in the glass of its own lake, Caer Bannog, where I hid the great sword for Arthur to find. Then the Green Chapel where later, on that legendary night, Arthur lifted it at last into his hand.

So, as I had done in earnest years ago, we lightly followed the sword, but something – some instinct I could no longer be sure was prophetic, or even wise – bade me keep silence about the other quest which, sometimes, I had glimpsed in the shadows. It would not be for me; it would come after me; and the time was not yet. So I said nothing of Segontium, or the place where still, deep in the ground, lay buried the other treasures that had come back with the sword to the West.

At last we came to Galava. It was a happy end to a pleasant journey. We were welcomed by Count Ector, an Ector grown stout with age and good living since the peace, who presented Nimuë to the Lady Drusilla (with a wink at me) as "Prince Merlin's wife, lass, at long last." And beside him was my faithful Ralf, flushed with pleasure, proud as a peacock of his pretty wife and four sturdy children, and avid for news of Arthur and the south.

Nimuë and I lay together in the tower room where I had once been carried to recover from Morgause's poison. It was some time after midnight, as we lay watching the moon touch the hilltops beyond the window, that she stirred, turning her cheek into the hollow of my shoulder, and said, softly:

"And what, after this? Bryn Myrddin and the crystal cave?"

"I think so."

"If your own hills are as beautiful as these, perhaps I shan't mind, after all, deserting Applegarth . . ." I heard a smile in her voice . . . "at least in summer."

"I promised you that it wouldn't come to that. Tell me this: for the last stage of your wedding journey, would you rather travel down the western roads, or take ship from Glannaventa, and go by sea to Maridunum? I'm told the seas are calm."

There was a short pause. Then she said: "But why ask me to choose? I thought –"

"You thought?"

Another pause. "I thought you had something still to show me."

It seemed that her instinct was as true as my own. I said: "What, then, my dear?"

"You have told me all the story of the sword, and you have shown me now all that happened to it, this wonderful Caliburn that is the symbol of the King's power, and by which he holds his kingdom. You have showed me the places of vision which led you to find it; where you hid it until Arthur should be ready to raise it, and where at last he did raise it. But you have never told me where you yourself found it. I had thought that this would be the last thing you would show me, before you took me home."

I did not reply. She raised herself in the bed, and lay on an elbow, looking down at me. The moonlight slid over her, making her a thing of silver and shadow, lighting the lovely lines of temple and cheek-bone, throat and breast.

I smiled, tracing the line of her shoulder with a gentle finger. "How can I think and answer you when you look like that?"

"Easily." She answered the smile, not moving. "Why have you never told me? It's because there's something else there, isn't it, that belongs to the future?"

So: instinct or vision, she knew. I said, slowly: "You spoke of a 'last thing'. Yes, there is still one mystery, the only one; and yes, it is for the future. I haven't seen it clearly myself, but once, before he was King, I made a prophecy for Arthur. It was between the finding and the raising of the sword, when the future was still hedged around with fire and vision. I remember what I said . . ."

"Yes?"

I quoted it. " 'I see a settled and shining land, with corn growing rich in the valleys, and farmers working their fields in peace as they did in the time of the Romans. I see a sword growing idle and discontented, and the days of peace stretching into bickering and division, and the need of a quest for the idle swords and the unfed spirits. Perhaps it was for this that the god took the grail and the spear back from me and hid them in the ground, so that one day you might set out to find the rest of Macsen's treasure. No, not you, but Bedwyr . . . it is his spirit, not yours, which will hunger and thirst, and slake itself in the wrong fountains.' "

A long silence. I could not see her eyes; they were full of moonlight. Then she whispered: "The grail and the spear? Macsen's treasure, hidden again in the ground, to be the objects of a quest as great as that of the sword? Where? Tell me where?"

She looked eager; not awed, but eager, like a runner in sight of the goal. When she does see the chalice and the spear, I thought, she will bend her head before their magic. But she is only a child, and still sees the things of power as weapons in her own hand. I did not say to her: "It is the same quest, because what use to anyone is the sword of power, without the fulfilment of the spirit? All the kings are now one King. It is time the gods became one God, and there in the grail is the oneness for which men will seek, and die, and dying, live."

I did not say it, but lay for a while in silence, while she watched me, unmoving. I could feel the power coming from her, my own power, stronger now in her than in my own hands. For myself, I felt nothing but weariness, and a kind of grief.

"Tell me, my darling," she said, whispering, intent.

So I told her. I smiled at her and said, gently: "I will do better than tell you. I shall take you there, and what there is to see, I shall show you. What is left of Macsen's treasure lies below the ground in the ruined temple of Mithras at Segontium, that is called Caer-y-n'a Von, below Y Wyddfa. And now that is all that I can give you, my dear, except my love."

I remember that she said, "And that would have been enough, even without the rest," as she stooped to put her mouth on mine.

After she slept I lay watching the moon, full and bright, becalmed, it seemed for hours, full in the centre of the window-frame. And I remembered how, long ago, as a child, I had believed that such a sight would bring me my heart's desire. What that had been in those days – power, prophecy, service, love – I could barely remember. Now all that was past, and my heart's desire lay here, sleeping in my arms. And the night, so full of light, was empty of the future, empty of vision; but still, like breathing ghosts from the past, came the voices.

Morgause's voice, the witch's voice spitting her curse at me: "Are you so sure you are proof against women's magic, Prince Merlin? It will snare you in the end."

And across it, Arthur's voice, vigorous, angry, full of love: "I cannot bear to see you hurt." And then: "Witch or no witch, lover or no lover, I shall deal with her as she deserves."

I held her young body close against my own, and kissed her sleeping eyelids, very gently. I said, to the ghosts, to the voices, to the empty moonlight: "It was time. Let me go in peace." Then, commending myself and my spirit to God who all these years had held me in his hand, I composed myself for sleep.

This was the last thing that I know to be truth, and not a dream in darkness.

2

When I was a small child at Maridunum I had slept with my nurse in a room in the servants' wing of my grandfather's palace. It was a ground-floor chamber, and outside the window grew a pear tree, where at evening a thrush would sing, and then afterwards the stars would come pricking out into the sky behind the branches, looking for all the world as if they were lights entangled in the tree. I used to lie watching them in the quiet of the night, and straining my ears to hear the music which, I had been told, the stars make as they move along the sky.

Now at last, it seemed, I heard it. I was lying, warmly shrouded, on – I thought – a litter, which must, from the swaying motion, be being borne along under a night sky. A great darkness wrapped me in, and far above me arched a night sky teeming and wheeling with stars, which rang like small bells as they moved. I was part of the ground that moved and echoed to my pulses, and a part of the enormous darkness that I could see above me. I was not even sure if my eyes were open. My last vision, I thought, feebly, and my heart's desire. My heart's desire was always this, to hear, before I died, the music of the stars . . .

Then I knew where I was. There must be people near me; I could hear voices talking softly, but seemingly at a great distance, like voices when one is sick with fever. Servants were carrying the litter; their arms brushed me with warmth, the beat in the ground was the soft tread of their sandals. This was no vision lighted by the singing spheres; I was only a sick old man, earth-bound, being carried home by stages, in the helpless silence of my malady. The music of the stars was no more than the bells on the harness of the mules.

How long it took I cannot tell. At length the litter levelled at the head of a long climb, and an archway of warm firelight met me, and more people, and voices everywhere, and someone weeping, and I knew that somehow, out of another falling-fit of the malady, I had been brought home to Bryn Myrddin.

More confusion after that. Sometimes I thought that Nimuë and I were still on our travels; I was showing her the streets of Byzantium, or walking with her on the heights above Berytus. She brought me the drugs she had made, and held them to my mouth. It was her own mouth that was on mine, tasting of strawberries, and her lips murmured sweet incantations above me, and the cave filled with smoke from handfuls of the precious frankincense. There were candles everywhere: in their mellow wavering light my merlin perched on the ledge by the cave's entrance, waiting for the god's breath on his feathers. Galapas sat by the brazier, drawing my first maps for me in the dust, and beside them, now, knelt the boy Ninian, poring over them with his grave and gentle eyes. Then he looked up, and I saw that it was Arthur, vivid and impatient, and ten years old . . . and then Ralf, young and sullen . . . and then at last the boy Merlin, going at his master's bidding up into the crystal cave. And so came the visions; I saw them again, the dreams that had first stormed into my child's brain here in this very cave. And this time Nimuë held my hand, and saw them with me, star for star, and held the cordial afterwards to my lips, while Galapas and the child Merlin, and Ralf and Arthur and the boy Ninian, faded and vanished like the ghosts they were. Only the memories remained, and they, now, were locked in her brain as they had been in mine, and would be hers for ever.

Through it all, though I had no sense of it, time was passing, and the days wore through, and still I lay in that strange limbo of helpless body and vividly working mind, while gradually, as a bee sips the honey from a flower, Nimuë the enchantress took from me, drop by drop, the distillation of all my days.

Then one early dawn, with the sound of birds singing outside, and the warm summer breeze bringing the scent of flowers and summer hay into the cave, I woke from a long sleep, and found that the malady had left me. Dream time was over, I was alive, and fully awake.

I was also alone, in darkness, save where a long quill of sunlight drilled through a gap left where they had pulled the tumble of rocks down across the cave-mouth, and had gone away, leaving me in my tomb.

★ ★ ★

I had no way of knowing how long I had lain in the waking death. We had been at Rheged in July, and it was still apparently high summer. Three weeks, or at most a month . . . ? If it had been longer, I would surely be weaker. As it was, until the last profound sleep, which must have been taken for death, I had been cared for and fed with my own cordials and medicines, so that, though stiff, and very weak, I had every chance of life. There was no hope of my being able to move any of the stones that sealed my tomb, but there was a good chance that I might be able to attract the attention of someone passing this way. The place had been a shrine, time out of mind, and the folk came regularly up the valley with offerings for the god who watched the sacred spring beside the cave. It was possible, now, that they would hold the place even more holy, knowing that Merlin, who had held the High King in his hand, but who had been their own enchanter, giving his time and skill to tend their hurts and those of their animals, was buried here. They had brought gifts daily, of food and wine, while he was alive; surely they would come with their offerings, to appease the dead?

So, stifling my fear, I raised myself and tried, through the swirling weakness of my new waking state, to judge what I must do.

They had laid me, not in the crystal cave, which was a small hollow high in the wall of the main cavern, but in the main cavern itself, on my own bed. This had been draped in some stuff that felt rich and stiff, and gave back, to the same probe of light, the glimmer of embroidery and precious gems. I fingered the pall that covered me; it was of some thick material, soft and warm, and beautifully woven. My fingers traced the pattern worked on it; the Dragon. And now I could see, at the four corners of the bed, the tall, heavily wrought candlesticks that gave off the gleam of gold. I had been left, apparently, with pomp and with royal honours. Had the King been here, then? I wished I could remember him. And Nimuë?

I supposed I had my own prophecies to thank that this was all the burial they had accorded me, and that they had not given me to the earth, or to the fire. The thought was a shiver over the skin, but it prompted me to action. I looked at the candles. Three of them had burned down almost to lumps of shapeless wax, and then died. The other, blown out perhaps by some chance draught, was still a foot or so tall. I put a finger to the nearest, where the wax had run down; it was still soft. Twelve hours, I calculated, or at most fifteen, since they had been lighted, and I had been left here. The place was still warm. If I was to keep alive, it must be kept that way. I leaned back against the stiff pillow, drew the pall with its golden dragon up over my body, fixed my eyes on the dead candle, and thought: we shall see. The simplest of magics, the first I ever learned here in this very place; let us see if this, too, has been taken from me. The effort sent me, exhausted, back into sleep.

I woke to see the sunlight, dim now and rosy, lighting a far corner of the cave, but the cave itself was full of light. The candle burned steadily, with a warm golden flame. It glimmered on two gold coins lying on the pall; I remembered, vaguely, the weight of them tumbling from my eyes as I woke and moved. It also showed me something more to the purpose; the ritual cakes and wine that had been left beside the bier as offerings to the dead. I spoke aloud to God who kept me, then, sitting on the bier, with the grave-clothes round me, ate and drank what had been left.

The cakes were dry, but tasted of honey, and the wine was strong, running into me like new life. The candle-light, dealing its own faint warmth, dispelled the last wisps of fear. "Emrys," I found myself whispering, "Emrys, child of the light, beloved of kings . . . you were told that you would be buried quick in dark-ness, your power gone; and look, here it has come to pass, and it is not fearful after all; you are buried, and quick, but you have light and air and – unless they have rifled the place – food and drink and warmth and medicines . . . ."

I lifted the candle from its heavy sconce and carried it into the inner caves which were the storerooms. Everything was just as I had left it. Stilicho had been a more than faithful steward. I thought of the wine and honey-cakes left beside the "bier", and wondered if, besides, the caverns had been scoured and garnished, then carefully furnished for the dead. Whatever the reason for leaving things as they were, there, row on row, box on box, were the precious stores, and in their places the flasks and jars of drugs and cordials, all that I had not taken with me to Applegarth. There was a real squirrel's hoard of food, dried fruit and nuts, honeycombs gently seeping into their jars, a barrel of olives in oil. No bread, of course, but in a crock I found, bone-hard, some thick oatcake made long ago by the shepherd's wife and given to me; it was still good, being dry as board, so I broke it up and put some of it to sop in wine. The meal garner was half full, and with oil from the olive-barrel I could make meal cakes of a sort. Water, of course, I had; soon after I had come to take up residence in the cave I had had my servant lead a pipe of water from the spring outside to fill a tank; this, kept covered, ensured clean water even through frost and storm. The overflow, channelled to run down to a fissured corner of a remote inner chamber, served as a privy. There were candles aplenty in store, and tinder with the flints on the ledge where I had always kept them. There was a sizeable pile of charcoal, but I hesitated, for fear of smoke or fumes, to light the brazier. Besides, I might need the warmth in the time ahead. If my reckoning of time were right, in a short month the summer would be over, and autumn setting in with its chill winds and its killing damp.

So at first, while the warm airs of summer still breathed through the cave, I used light only when I needed to see to prepare my food, and for comfort sometimes, when the hours dragged in darkness. I had no books, all having been taken to Applegarth. But writing materials were to hand, and as the days went by and I gained strength and began to fret in the idleness of captivity, I formed the idea of trying to set down in some kind of order the story of my boyhood and the times I had lived through and helped to mould. Music, too, would have been something to be made in darkness, but the standing harp had gone with my books to Applegarth, and my own small harp had not been brought with the other riches, to furnish the house of the dead.

Be sure that I had given thought to escaping from my grave. But those who had laid me there and given me, in honour, the sacred hill itself, with all that lay within it, had used the hill itself to seal me in; half the mountainside, seemingly, had been levered down to fall across the cave's entrance. Try as I would I could not shove or scrape a way through. No doubt someone with the right tools might have done it in time, but I had none. We kept spades and axes always in the stable below the cliff.

There was another possibility, which I considered time and again. As well as the caves which I used, there were other, smaller chambers which opened off one another, branching deep into the hill. One of these inner caves was little more than a chimney, a rounded shaft running up through the rock levels, to reach the air in a little corrie of the hill above. Here a low cliff, many years back, had, under the pressure from tree-roots and storms, split open to let light, and sometimes small rocks and rain-water, down into the hollow below. Through this fissure, now, the cave-dwelling bats made their daily flights. In time the pile of fallen stones in the cave had built up into a kind of buttress, reaching perhaps a third of the way up towards the "lantern", as I might term the hole above. When, hopefully, I looked to see if this rough stair had been extended, I was disappointed: above it, still, lay a sheer pitch three times the height of a man, and above that the same again, sloping at first steeply, and then more gently, to reach the gap of daylight. It was just possible that a fit and agile man could have climbed out unaided, though in places the rock was damp and slimy, and in others manifestly unsafe. But for an ageing man, recently in his sick-bed, it was impossible. The sole comfort of the discovery lay in the fact that here, literally, was a "chimney"; in the cold days to come I could light the brazier there with safety, and savour warmth and hot food and drink.

I did think, naturally, about making a fire of some kind, in the hope that the smoke might attract the attention of the curious, but there were two things against this. First, the country people who lived within sight of the hill were used to seeing the bats go up daily from the hillside, looking for all the world like plumes of smoke; the second was that I had little to spare of fuel. All I could do was conserve the precious stores I had, and wait for someone to make a way up the valley to visit the holy well.

But nobody came. Twenty days, thirty, forty, were notched on my tally stick. I recognised with reluctance that where the simple folk had come to pray to the spirit of the well, and offer gifts to the living man who healed them, they were afraid of the enchanter lately dead, and of the new haunting of the hollow hill. Since the valley led nowhere but to the cave and the spring, no travellers used it. Nothing came into the high valley, except the birds (which I heard) and, I supposed, the deer, and once a wolf or a fox that I heard snuffling in the night at the tumble of stones that blocked the cave's entrance.

So the tallied days dragged by, and I stayed alive, and – what was harder – kept fear at bay in every way I knew. I wrote, and wrestled with plans for escape, and did what domestic tasks the days demanded; and I am not ashamed to remember that I drugged the nights – and sometimes the desperate days – with wine, or with opiates that stupefied the senses and dulled time. Despair I would not feel; through all that long life in death, I held to one thing, as to a ladder let down from the light above me: throughout my life I had obeyed my god, had received power from him, and rendered it back again; now I had seen it pass to the young lover who had usurped me; but though my life was apparently done, my body had been kept – I could not tell how or why – from either earth or fire. I was alive, and had regained both strength and will, and, prison or no, this was the hollow hill of the god himself. I could not believe that there was not some purpose still to be fulfilled.

I think it was with this in mind that I nerved myself at length to climb into the crystal cave.

All this while, with my strength at low ebb and the power (I knew) gone from me, I had not been able to face the place of vision. But one evening when, with my store of candles running low, I had sat too long in darkness, I brought myself at last to climb the ledge at the back of the main cavern, and, bent double, to creep into the crystal-lined globe.

I went, I believe, for nothing more than the comfortable memories of past power, and of love. I took no light with me, and looked for no vision. I simply lay, as I had done when a boy, belly down on the rough crystals of the floor, letting the heavy silence enclose me, and filling it with my thoughts.

What they were I cannot now remember: I suppose I was praying. I do not think I spoke aloud. But in a while I became conscious – as, in a black night, a man realises, rather than sees, the coming dawn – of something that answered to my breathing. Not a sound, only the faintest echo of a breath, as if a ghost was waking, taking life from mine.

My heart began to thud; my breathing sharpened. Within the darkness the other rhythm quickened. The air of the cave hummed. Round the crystal walls ran, echoing, a whisper that I knew.

I felt the easy tears of weakness start into my eyes. I said aloud: "So, after all, they brought you back to your own place?" And, from the darkness, my harp answered me.

I groped forward towards the sound. My fingers met the live, silken feel of wood. The carved fore-pillar nestled into my hand as I had seen the hilt of the great sword slide into the King's grip. I backed out of the cave, silenced the harp's faint plaining against my breast, and picked my way carefully down again into my prison.

★ ★ ★

This was the song I made. I called it *Merlin's Song from the Grave.*

> *Where have they gone, the bright ones?*
> *I remember the sunlight*
> *And a great wind blowing;*
> *A god who answered me,*
> *Leaning out from the high stars;*
> *A star that shone for me,*
> *A voice that spoke to me,*
> *A hawk that guided me,*
> *A shield that sheltered me;*
> *And a clear way to the gate*
> *Where they wait for me,*
> *Where surely they wait for me?*
>
> *The day wanes,*
> *The wind dies.*
> *They are gone, the bright ones.*
> *Only I remain.*
>
> *What use to call to me*
> *Who have neither shield nor star?*

What use to kneel to me
Who am only the shadow
Of his shadow,
Only the shadow
Of a star that fell
Long ago.

★   ★   ★

No song comes brand-fire-new and finished from the first playing, so that now I cannot recall just on which occasion, as I was singing it, I became conscious of an unusual sound that had been, as it were, tapping at the door of my brain for several staves. I let the chords die, laid a hand along the strings, and listened.

The beating of my heart sounded loud in the still, dead air of the cave. Below it went another throbbing, a distant beat coming seemingly from the heart of the hill. I can hardly be blamed, shut as I had been for too long from the ordinary traffic of the world, if the first thoughts that came crowding were winged with instinct born of ancient beliefs – Llud of the Otherworld, the horses of the Wild Hunt, all the shadows dwelling in the hollow hills . . . Death for me at long last, on this still evening at the end of summer? Then, in less time than it takes for two short breaths, I had arrived at the truth – and it was already too late.

It was the traveller I had waited for, and at length despaired of; he had ridden up above the cave, and halted by the cliff where the "lantern" opened on the air, and had heard the music. There was a pause, broken only by the sharp strike of nervous hoofs on stone as the horse fretted, held and sidling. Then a man's voice, calling out:

"Is there anyone there?"

I had already laid the harp aside and, with what speed I could, was scrambling through the half dark towards the cave below him. As I went I tried to call out, but it was a moment or so before my thudding heart and dry throat would let me answer. Then I cried out:

"It is I, Merlin! Don't be afraid, I'm no ghost. I'm alive, and trapped here. Break a way out for me, in the King's name!"

My voice was drowned by the sudden confusion of noise from

above. I could guess what had happened. The horse, sensing, as beasts do, some strangeness – a man below ground, the unnatural sounds coming apparently from the fissure in the cliff, even my anxiety – gave a long, pealing whinny, and plunged, scattering stones and small gravel and setting other echoes rattling. I shouted again, but either the rider did not hear, or he took the horse's fear for an instinct truer than his own; there was another sharp clatter of hoofs and cascading stones, then the beating gallop retreated, faster than it had come. I could not blame the rider, whoever he was; even if he did not know whose tomb lay beneath him, he must have known the hill was sacred, and to hear music from the ground, at dusk, on the crest of such a hill . . .

I went back to pick up the harp. It was undamaged. I put it aside, and with it the hope of rescue, then set myself grimly to prepare what could, for want of a worse word, be called my supper.

3

It was perhaps two nights after this, or maybe three, when something woke me in the night. I opened my eyes on total darkness, wondering what had disturbed me. Then I heard the sound. Stealthy scrapings, rattlings of stone, the patter of earth falling. They came from the "lantern", high in the inner cave. Some beast, I thought, badger or fox or even wolf, scratching its way towards the smell of food. I drew the covers round me, and turned over and shut my eyes again.

But the sounds went on, stealthy, persistent, and now impatient, a fierce scrabbling among the stones that spoke of more than animal purpose. I sat up again, taut with sudden hope. Perhaps the horseman had come back? Or he had told his story, and some other, braver soul had come to investigate? I took breath to shout, then paused. I did not want to scare this one away like the first. I would wait for him to speak to me.

He did not; he was intent merely on scraping his way in through the opening in the cliff. More stuff fell, and I heard the chink of a crowbar, and then, unmistakably, a smothered curse. A man's voice, rough-spoken. There was a pause, as if he was listening, then once again the sounds began, and this time he was using some sort of heavy tool, a mattock or a spade, to dig his way in.

Not for worlds would I have shouted now. No one bent simply on investigating a strange story would do so in such stealthy secrecy; the obvious thing to do would be what the horseman had done, to call out first, or to wait quietly and listen, before attempting to force a way into the lantern. What was more, no innocent man would have come, for choice, alone and at night.

A few moments' reflection brought me the probable truth. This was a grave-robber; some outlaw, perhaps, who had heard rumours of a royal grave in Merlin's Hill, and who had doubtless had a look at the cave-mouth, decided it was too thoroughly blocked, and had settled on the shaft as being the easier and less conspicuous way of entry. Or perhaps a local man who had watched the rich procession pass, and who had known for years of the cliff and its precarious entry to the hill. Or even a soldier – one of those who, after the ceremonies, had helped to block the cave-mouth, and who had been haunted since by recollections of the riches there entombed.

Whoever he was, he must be a man of few nerves. He would be fully prepared to find a corpse laid here; to brave the stench and sight of a body some weeks dead; even to lay hands on it and rob it of its jewels before he tumbled it from the gem-encrusted pall and gold-fringed pillow. And if he should find, instead of a corpse, a living man? An old man, weakened by these long days underground; a man, moreover, whom the world believed to be dead? The answer was simple. He would kill me, and still rob my tomb. And I, stripped of my power, had no defences.

I rose silently from the bed, and made my way through to the shaft. The digging sounds went on, steadily now, and through the widened opening at the top of the shaft I could see light. He had some sort of lantern there, which dealt him light enough. It would also prevent him from noticing the faint glimmer of a rush-light from below. I went back to the main chamber, kindled a light carefully behind a screen, then set about the only preparations I could make.

If I lay in wait for him with a knife (I had no dagger, but there were knives for preparing food) or with some heavy implement, it was by no means certain that I would be quick enough, or powerful enough, to stun him; and such an attack would make my own end certain. I had to find another way. I considered it, coldly. The only weapon I had was one that in times past I had found to be more powerful than either dagger or cudgel. The man's own fear.

I took the blankets off the bed and folded them out of sight. I spread the jewelled pall over, smoothed it, and set the velvet pillow in place. The gold candlesticks still stood where they had been put, at the four corners of the bed. Beside the bed I set the gold goblet that had held the wine, and the silver platter studded with garnets. I took the gold coins, the ferryman's fee, from where I had laid them, wrapped myself in the king's mantle that they had left for me, blew out the light, and lay down on the pall.

A rending sound from the shaft, a scatter of rubble onto the cavern floor, and with it a rush of fresh night air, told me that he was through. I shut my eyes, placed the gold coins on the lids, smoothed the long folds of my mantle, then crossed my arms on my breast, controlled my breathing as best I could, and waited.

It was perhaps the hardest thing I have ever done. Often before I had faced danger, but never without knowing one way or the other what the risks were. Always before, in times of stress or terror – the fight with Brithael, the ambush in the Wild Forest – I had known there was pain to face, but in the end victory and safety and a cause won; now, I knew nothing. This stealthy murder in the dark, for a few jewels, might indeed be the ignominious end which the gods, with their sidelong smiles, had showed me in the stars as my "burial quick in the tomb". It was as they willed. But, I thought (not coolly at all), if I have ever served you, God my god, let me smell the sweet air once more before I die.

There was a soft thud as he landed in the shaft. He must have a rope with him, tied to one of the trees that grew from the cliff. I had been right; he was alone. Faintly, under the weight of the gold on my eyelids, I could see the warming of the dark that meant he had brought his lantern with him. Now he was feeling his way, carefully, across the uneven floor towards the chamber where I lay. I could smell his sweat, and the reek of the cheap lantern; which meant, I thought with satisfaction, that he would not catch the lingering odours of food and wine, or the smell of the recently doused rushlight. And his breathing gave him away; with even greater satisfaction I knew that, bravado or no, he was afraid.

He saw me, and stopped in his tracks. I heard his breath go in as harshly as a death-rattle. He had nerved himself, one would guess, to face a decaying corpse, but here was a body like that of a living, or newly-dead man. For seconds he stood, hesitating, breathing hard, then, remembering perhaps what he had heard of the embalmers' art, he cursed again softly under his breath, and tiptoed forward. The light shook and swung in his hand.

With the smell and sound of his fear my own calmness grew. I breathed smoothly and shallowly, trusting to the wavering of his lantern and its smoking light not to let him see that the corpse moved. For an age, it seemed, he stood there, but at last, with another sharp rattle of breath and an abrupt movement like a horse under the spur, he forced himself forward to my side. A hand, unsteady and damp with cold sweat, plucked the gold coins off my eyelids.

I opened my eyes.

In that one brief flash, before movement or blink or breath, I took it all in; the dark Celtic face lit by the horn lantern, the coarse clothing of some peasant levy, the pitted skin slithering with sweat, the greedy slack mouth and the stupid eyes, the knife in his belt, razor-sharp.

I said, calmly: "Welcome to the hall of the dead, soldier."

And from its dark corner, at the sound of my voice, the harp whispered something, on a sweet, fading note.

The gold coins fell, ringing, and rolled away into darkness. The lantern followed, to be smashed into smoking oil on the floor. He let out a yell of fear such as I have not often heard in my long life, and once again, from the darkness, came the mockery of the harp. Yelling again, he took to his heels and ran, stumbling blindly out of the cave and making for the shaft. He must have made a first vain attempt to climb his rope; he cried out again as he fell heavily back to the rock-strewn floor. Then fear lent him strength; I heard the sobbing breaths of effort receding upwards as he swarmed to the top. His footsteps ran and slipped down the hillside. Then the sounds died, and I was alone again, and safe.

Safe, in my grave. He had taken the rope. In fear, perhaps, that the enchanter's ghost could swarm after him and follow, he had dragged it up after him. The gap he had made showed a ragged window of sky, where a star shone, remote and pure and indifferent. Cool air blew in, and the cold, unmistakable smell of dawn coming. I heard a thrush from the cliff-top.

God had answered me. I had smelled the sweet air again, and heard the sweet bird. And life was as far from me as before.

I went back into the inner chamber and, as if nothing had happened, began my preparations for another day.

★   ★   ★

And another. And a third. On the third day, having eaten and rested and written and calmed my mind as far as I could, I once more examined the chimney shaft. The wretched grave-robber had left me a shred of new hope; the pile of fallen stones was higher by almost three feet, and, though he had pulled his rope up after him, he had left me another, which I found lying, loosely coiled, at the base of the shaft. But the hopes that this raised were soon proved false; the rope was of poor quality, a cord no more than four or five cubits in length. I could only assume that he had intended to tie his spoils together – he could never have hoped to carry even one of the candlesticks out with him on his climb – fasten them to the main rope's end, and draw them after him. I calculated that, even to bear away the four candlesticks, the thief must have made four journeys up and down the shaft. The cord would never, even had it been long enough to throw and loop over some rocky projection, have been strong enough to bear my weight. Nor could I – scanning yet again the damp and crumbling side of the chimney – see any such safe projection or foothold. It was possible that a young man or an agile boy might have managed the climb, but although I had been a strong man all my life, with a strong man's endurance, I had never been an athlete, and now, with age and illness and privation, the climb was quite beyond me.

One other thing the thief had done: where, before, I would have had to reach the high lantern and then set to work to dig and scrabble a way through – an impossible task without tools and ladder – now the way lay open. All I had to do was get to it. And I had a length of good cord. It would come hard, I thought, if I could not contrive some kind of scaffolding which would take me as far as the sloping section of the chimney, and from there, perhaps, I might be able to rig some kind of makeshift ladder. Much of the cave's furnishing had gone, but there was still the bed, a stool or two, and a table, the casks, and a stout bench forgotten in a corner. If I could find some way to break them up, fasten the pieces together with cord, or with torn strips of blanket, wedge them with sherds from the storage jars . . .

All the rest of that day, and the next following, working directly under the light thrown down from above, I toiled at my makeshift scaffold, bearing a wry thought for Tremorinus, my father's chief engineer, who had first taught me my craft. He would have laughed to see the great Merlin, the engineer-artificer who had outpaced his master, and had lifted the Hanging Stones of the Giants' Dance, cobbling together a structure of which the sorriest apprentice would have been ashamed. All I needed to do, he would have said, was to take my harp like Orpheus, and play to the fragments of the broken furniture, and watch it build itself like the walls of Troy. This had been his theory, stoutly held in public, about the way I had managed the lifting of the great trilithons of the Dance.

By nightfall of the second day I had rigged a sort of rough scaffolding roofed with the stout plank of the bench, which might serve as a base for a ladder. It was nine feet high, and fixed firmly enough with a pile of stones holding it in place. I had only, I reckoned, another twenty-five feet to build.

I worked until dusk, then lighted the lantern and made my wretched meal. Then, as a man turns to the comfort of a lover, I lifted the harp into my arms and, without thoughts of Orpheus or Troy, played until my eyelids drooped, and a false chord warned me that it was time to sleep. Tomorrow would be another day.

★   ★   ★

Who could have guessed what kind of day? Tired from my labours, I slept deeply, and woke later than usual to the light of a bright thread of sunshine, and the sound of someone calling my name.

For a moment I lay still, thinking myself still caught in the mists of a dream that had mocked me so often before, but then I came fully awake to the discomfort of the cavern floor (I had broken my bed up for use) and the voice again. It came from the lantern, a man's voice, overpitched with nerves, but with something familiar about the queerly accented Latin.

"My lord? My lord Merlin? Are you there, my lord?"

"Here! Coming!"

In spite of aching joints, I was on my feet as swiftly as any boy, and ran to the foot of the shaft.

Sunshine was pouring down from above. I picked my way, stumbling, to the foot of the rude structure that almost filled the base of the shaft. I craned upwards.

Framed in the gap of brilliant sky was a man's head and shoulders. At first I could distinguish little against the brightness. Me, he must be able to see clearly, unkempt, bearded, no doubt pale as the ghost he must have feared to see. I heard his shivering gasp of breath, and the head drew back.

I cried out: "Stay for me, for God's sake! I'm no ghost! Stay! Help me out of here! Stilicho, stay!"

Almost without thinking, I had identified his accent, and him with it. My old servant, the Sicilian, Stilicho, who had married Mai, the miller's daughter, and kept the mill on the Tywy at the valley's foot. I knew his kind, credulous, superstitious, easily afraid of what they did not understand. I leaned against the upright of the scaffolding, gripped it with shaking hands, and fought for a composure that would reassure him. His head came cautiously back. I saw the black eyes staring, the sallow pallor of his face, the open mouth. With a self-control that shook me with another wave of weakness I spoke in his own language, slowly and with apparent calm:

"Don't be afraid, Stilicho. I was not dead when they left me here in error, and all these weeks I have been trapped here in the hill. I am not a ghost, boy; it truly is Merlin, alive, and very much in need of your help."

He leaned nearer. "Then the King – all those others who were here – ?" He stopped, swallowing painfully.

"Do you think that a ghost could have built this scaffolding?" I asked him. "I hadn't despaired of escaping. I've lived here in hope, all through these weeks, but by the God of all gods, Stilicho, if you leave me now without helping me from here, I swear I shall be dead before the day is out." I stopped, ashamed.

He cleared his throat. He sounded shaken, as well he might, but scared no longer. "Then it really is you, lord? They said you were dead and buried, and we have been mourning you . . . but we should have known that your magic would keep you from death."

I shook my head. I forced myself to go on talking, knowing that with every word he was coming nearer to accepting my survival as true, and nerving himself to approach the tomb and its living ghost.

"Not magic," I said, "it was the malady that deceived you all. I am no longer an enchanter, Stilicho, but I have God to thank that I am still a strong man. Otherwise these weeks below the earth would surely have killed me. Now, my dear, can you get me out? Later we can talk, and decide what's to be done, but now, for God's sake, help me out of here and into the air . . ."

It was a grim business, and it took a long time, not least because, when he would have left me to go for help, I begged him, in terms of which I am now ashamed, not to leave me. He did not argue, but set himself to knotting the long, stout rope which he had found still attached to an ash sapling in the rock above the lantern. He finished it with a loop for my foot, then lowered it carefully. It reached the platform, with some length to spare. Then he let himself down into the shaft, and in a short space of time was beside me at the foot of the scaffolding. I think he would have gone on his knees, as his habit had been, to kiss my hands, but I gripped him so tightly that instead he held me, supporting me with his young strength, and then helped me back into the main cavern.

He found the one remaining stool for me, then lit the lantern and brought me wine, and after a while I was able to say, with a smile: "So now you know that I am a solid body, and no ghost? It was brave of you to come at all, and braver still to stay. What on earth brought you to this place? You're the last person who I'd have thought would go visiting a tomb."

"I wouldn't have come at all," he said frankly, "but that something I heard made me wonder if you were not dead after all, but living here alone. I knew you were a great magician, and thought that perhaps your magic would not let you die like other men."

"Something you heard? What was that?"

"You know the man I have to help me at the mill, Bran, he's called? Well, he was in the town yesterday, and brought home some tale of a fellow who'd drunk himself silly in one of the taverns, and the story was going about that he had been up to Bryn Myrddin, and that the enchanter had come out of the tomb and spoken to him. People were standing him drinks and asking for more, and of course the tale as he told it was plainly lies, but there was enough to make me wonder . . ." He hesitated. "What did happen, lord? I knew someone had been here, because of the rope on the tree."

"It happened twice," I told him. "The first time it was a horseman riding over the hill . . . you can see how long ago, I marked it on the tally yonder. He must have heard me playing; the sound would carry up through the hole in the cliff. The second time was four – five? – days since, when some ruffian came to rob the tomb, and opened the cliff as you saw it, and let himself down with the rope." I told him what had happened. "He must have been too scared to stop and untie his rope. It's a mercy you heard his story, and came up before he got his courage back, and came back for it – and perhaps dared the tomb again."

He gave me a sidelong, shamefaced look. "I'll not pretend to you, lord. It's not right you praising me for courage. I came up yesterday evening. I didn't want to come alone, but I was ashamed to bring Bran, and Mai wouldn't go within a mile of the place . . . Well, I saw the mouth of the cave was just as it had been, and then I heard the harp. I – I turned and ran home. I'm sorry."

I said, gently: "But you came back."

"Yes. I couldn't sleep all night. You remember when you left me once to guard the cave, and you showed me your harp, and how it played sometimes by itself, just with the air moving? And how you gave me courage, and showed me the crystal cave and told me I would be safe there? Well, I thought of all that, and I thought of the times you were good to me, how you took me out of slavery and gave me freedom and the life I have now. And I thought, even if it is my lord's ghost, or the harp playing by magic, alone in the hollow hill, he would never harm me . . . So I came again, but this time I came by daylight. I thought, if it is a ghost, then in sunlight it will be sleeping."

"And so I was." The thought touched me, like a cold dagger's point, that if I had drugged myself last night, as I had so often done, I might have heard nothing.

He was going on: "I walked over the hill this time, and I saw the new broken stone showing white in the corrie where the little air-shaft comes out. I went to look. I saw the rope then, tied to the ash tree, and the big gap in the cliff, and when I looked down the shaft, I saw the" – he hesitated – "the thing you built there."

I had not thought to feel amusement ever again. "That is a builder's scaffold, Stilicho."

"Yes, of course. Well, I thought, no ghost made that. So I shouted. That's all."

"Stilicho," I said, "if ever I did anything for you, be sure you have paid me a thousand times over. In fact, you have saved me twice over. Not only today; if you hadn't left the place the way I found it, I should have died weeks back, from starvation and cold. I shall not forget it."

"We've got to get you out of here now. But how?" He looked around him at the stripped cave and the broken furnishings. "Now we've spoken, and you're feeling stronger, lord, shall I not go and bring men and tools, and open the doorway for you? It would be the best way, truly it would."

"I know that, but I think not. I've had time now to consider. Until I know how things stand in the kingdoms, I can't suddenly 'come to life'. That is how the common people will see it, if Prince Merlin comes back from the tomb. No part of the story must be told until the King knows. So, until we can get a private message to him –"

"He's gone to Brittany, they say."

"So?" I thought for a moment. "Who is Regent?"

"The Queen, with Bedwyr."

A pause, while I looked down at my hands. Stilicho was sitting cross-legged on the floor. In the lantern's light he looked still much like the boy I had known. The dark Byzantine eyes watched me.

I wetted my lips. "The Lady Nimuë? Do you know who I mean? She –"

"Oh, yes, all the world knows her. She has magic, as you used to – as you have, lord. She is always near the King. She lives near Camelot."

"Yes," I said. "Well, I am sorry, my dear, but I cannot have it known before the King comes back from Brittany. Somehow, between us, we shall have to get me out of the shaft. I have no doubt that, if you will bring the tools up out of the stable, we'll manage something."

And so we did. He was back in something under half an hour

with nails and tools and the small stock of timber that had been left in the stable. It was a bad half hour for me: I had no doubts that he would return, but the reaction was so intense that, left alone again, I sat there on the stool, sweating and shaking like a fool. But by the time the stuff was pitched down the shaft, with himself following it, I had myself in hand, and we set to work, and, with me sitting idly on the stool watching and directing, he put together a ladder of a sort and fixed it to the platform I had made. This reached the sloping section of the chimney. Here, as an adjunct to the knotted rope, he cut pieces of wood which, with the help of cracks and protuberances of rock he wedged at intervals against the side of the chimney to act, if not as steps, then as resting-places where one could set a knee.

When all was done he tested it, and while he did so I wrapped the harp in the remaining blanket, and with it my manuscripts and a few of the drugs that I might need to restore my strength fully. He climbed out with them. Finally I took a knife and cut the best of the jewels off the pall, and dropped them, together with the gold coins, into a leather bag which had held herbs. I slipped the thong of the bag over my wrist, and was waiting at the scaffold's foot when at last Stilicho reappeared at the top, laid hold of the rope, and called for me to begin my climb.

4

I stayed a month with Stilicho at the mill. Mai, who had held me
formerly in trembling awe, once she saw that this was no terrifying
wizard, but a man sick and in need of care, looked after me
devotedly. I saw no one beside these two. I kept to the upper
chamber they gave me – it was their own, the best, they would hear
of nothing else. The hired man slept out in the granary sheds, and
knew only that some ageing relative of the miller's was staying
there. The children were told the same, and accepted me without
question, as children will.

At first I kept to my bed. The reaction from the recent weeks was
a severe one; I found daylight trying, and the noises of every day
hard to bear – the men's voices in the yard as the grain barges came
in to the wharf, hoofs on the roadway, the shouts of the children
playing. At first the very act of talking to Mai or Stilicho came hard,
but they showed all the gentleness and understanding of simple
folk, so things gradually became easier, and I began to feel myself
again. Soon I left my bed, and began to spend time with my
writing, and, calling the elder of the children to me, began to teach
them their letters. In time I even came to welcome Stilicho's ebulli-
ence, and questioned him eagerly about what had happened since I
had been shut away.

Of Nimuë he knew little beyond what he had already told me. I
gathered that her reputation for magic, in the weeks since my
going, had grown so quickly that the mantle of the King's
enchanter had fallen naturally upon her shoulders. She spent some
of her time at Applegarth, but since the Lady's death had gone back
to the Island shrine, to be accepted without question as the new
Lady of the place. One rumour seemed to indicate that the status of

the Lady would change with her; she did not remain on the Island, a maiden among maidens: she paid frequent visits to the court at Camelot, and there was talk of a probable marriage. Stilicho could not tell me who the man was said to be, "But of course," he said, "he will be a king."

With this I had to be content. There was little other news. Most of the men who came up-river to the mill were simple workmen, or barge-masters, whose knowledge was only local, and who cared for little beyond getting a good price for the goods they carried. All I could gather was that the times were still prosperous; the kingdom was at peace; the Saxons kept to their treaties. And the High King, in consequence, had felt free to go abroad.

Why, Stilicho did not know. And this did not, for the moment, matter to me, except that it must mean my own continued secrecy. I thought the matter over again, after my return to health, and the conclusions I came to were the same. No purpose could be served by my public return to affairs. Even the "miracle" of a return from the grave would do no more for the kingdom and its High King than my "death" and the transfer of power had done. I had no power or vision to bring him; it would be wrong to indulge in a return that would tend to discredit Nimuë as my successor, without bringing anything fresh or even valid to Arthur's service. I had made my farewells, and my legend, such as it was, had already begun to gather way. So much I could understand from the tales that, according to Stilicho, had already added themselves to the grave-robber's tale of the enchanter's ghost.

As for Nimuë, the same arguments applied. With what wisdom I could command in the matter, I saw that the love we had had together was already a thing of the past. I could not go back, expecting to claim again the place I had had with her, and to tie jesses to the feet of a falcon already in flight. Something else held me back, something I would not recognise in daylight, but which mocked me in dreams with old prophecies buzzing around like stinging flies. What did I know of women, even now? When I remembered the steady draining of my power, the last, desperate weakness, the trance-like state in which I had lain before the final desertion in darkness, I asked myself what that love had been but the bond that held me to her, and bade me give her all I owned? And even when I recalled her sweetness, her generous worship, her words of love, I knew (and it took no vision to do so) that she would not lay her power down now, even to have me back again.

It was hard to make Stilicho understand my reluctance to re-appear, but he did accept my desire to wait for Arthur's return before making plans. From his references to Nimuë he was obviously not yet aware that she had been more to me than a pupil who had taken up the master's charge.

At length, feeling myself again, and not wanting to impose any longer on Stilicho's little household, I prepared to set off for Northumbria, and set Stilicho to make arrangements for me. I decided to go north by sea. A sea voyage is something I never willingly undertake, but by road it would be a long, hard journey, with no guarantee of continued fine weather, and besides, I could hardly have gone alone; Stilicho would have insisted upon accompanying me, even though at this time of year he could ill be spared from the mill. Indeed, he tried to insist on going with me by ship, but in the end let himself be overruled; this not only by expedience, but because I think he believed me still to be the "great enchanter" whom he had served in the past with such awe and pride. In the end I had my way, and one morning early I went quietly downstream on one of the barges, and embarked at Maridunum on a north-bound coastal ship.

I had sent no message to Blaise in Northumbria, because there was no courier I could trust with the news of "Merlin's return from the dead". I would think of some way to prepare him when I came near the place. It was even possible that he had not yet heard news of my death; he lived so retired from the world – held to the times only by my dispatches – that it was conceivable that he had only just unrolled my last letter from Applegarth.

This, as it turned out, was the fact; but I did not find out yet for a while. I did not get to Northumbria, but travelled no further north than Segontium.

The ship put in there, on a fine, still morning. The little town sunned itself at the edge of the shining strait, its clustered houses dwarfed by the great walls of the Roman-built fortress that had been the headquarters of the Emperor Maximus. Across the strait the fields of Mona's Isle showed golden in the sun. Behind the town, a little way beyond the fortress walls, stood the remains of the tower that was known as Macsen's Tower. Near by was the site of the ruined temple of Mithras, where years ago I had found the King's sword of Britain, and where, deep under the rubble of the floor and the ruined altar of the god, I had left the rest of Macsen's treasure, the lance and the grail. This was the place I had promised to show Nimuë on our way home from Galava. Beyond the tower the great Snow Hill, Y Wyddfa, reared against the sky. The first white of winter was on its crest, and its cloud-haunted sides, even on that golden day, showed purple-black with scree and dead heather.

We nosed in to the wharf. There were goods to unload, and this would take time, so I went thankfully ashore, and, after a word at the harbour-master's office, made for the wharfside inn. There I could have a meal, and watch the loading and unloading of my ship.

I was hungry, and likely to get hungrier. My idea of any sea voyage, however calm, is to get below and stay below, without food or drink, until it is over. The harbour-master had told me that the ship would not sail before the evening tide, so there was ample time to rest and make ready for the next dreaded stage of the journey. It did cross my mind to wish I might have time to make my way up once again to the temple of Mithras, but I put the thought aside. Even if I were to revisit the place, I would not disturb the treasure. It was not for me. Besides, the privations of the journey had tired me, and I needed food. I made for the inn.

This was built round three sides of a court, the fourth being open to the wharf, for the convenience, I suppose, of carrying goods straight from the ships into the inn's storerooms, which served as warehouses for the town. There were benches and stout wooden tables under the overhanging eaves of the open courtyard, but, fine though the weather was, it was not warm enough to persuade me to eat out of doors. I found my way into the main room, where a log fire burned, and ordered food and wine. (I had paid my passage with – appropriately – one of the gold coins which had been the "ferryman's fee"; this had left me change besides, and caused the ship's master to accord me a respect which my apparent style hardly called for.) Now, the servant hastened to serve me with a good meal, of mutton and fresh bread, with a flask of rough red wine such as seamen like, then left me in peace to enjoy the warmth of the fire and watch through the open door the scene at the quay-side.

The day wore through. I was more tired than I had realised. I dozed, then woke, and dozed again. Over at the wharf the work went on, with creak of windlass and rattle of chain and straining of ropes as the cranes swung the bales and sacks inboard. Overhead the gulls wheeled and cried. Now and again an ox-cart creaked by on clumsy wheels.

There was little coming and going in the inn itself. Once, a woman crossed the courtyard with a basket of washing on her head, and a boy hurried through with a batch of bread. There was another party staying, it seemed, in chambers to the right of the court. A fellow in slave's dress hurried in from the town, carrying a flat basket covered with a linen cloth. He vanished through a doorway, and a short while later some children came running out, boys, well dressed but noisy, and with some kind of outlandish accent I could not place. Two of them – twins by their look – settled down on the sunlit flagstones for a game of knuckle-bones, while the other two, though ill matched for age and size, started some kind of mock fight with sticks for swords, and old box-lids for shields. Presently a decent-looking woman, whom I took to be their nurse, came out of the same doorway and sat down on a bench in the sun to watch them. From the way the boys, now and then, ran to gaze towards the wharf, I guessed that their party was perhaps waiting to join my ship, or continue its voyage on another vessel that was tied up a few lengths away along the quay.

From where I was sitting I could see the master of my ship, and at his elbow some sort of tallyman with stilus and wax. The latter had written nothing for some time, and on board the activity seemed to have ceased. It would soon be time to get back to my uneasy bed below decks, and wait miserably until the light breezes carried us northward on the next stage of the journey.

I got to my feet. As I did so I saw the master raise his head, with a movement like that of a dog sniffing the air. Then he swung round to look upwards at the inn roof. Straight above my head I heard the long creak of the weather vane swinging round, then whining to and fro in small uneasy arcs as the suddenly rising breeze of evening caught it. To and fro it went, then settled into silence in front of a steady wind. The wind went across the harbour like a grey shadow over the water, and in its wake the moored ships swayed, and ropes sang and rattled against the masts like drumsticks. Beside me the fire flickered and then roared up the open chimney. The master, with a gesture of impatient anger, strode for the ship's gangway, calling out orders. Mingled with my own annoyance was relief; the seas would roughen quickly in this wind, but I would not be on them. With the fickle violence of autumn, the wind had veered. The ship could not sail. The fresh wind was blowing straight from the north.

I walked across to speak to the master, who, watching the sailors stow and rope the cargo against the new weather, glumly confirmed that there was no question of sailing until the wind blew our way again. I sent a boy to bring up my gear, and went back to bespeak a room at the inn. That there would be one vacant I knew, for the ill wind had apparently blown good for the other lodgers in the place. I could see sailors making ready on the other ship, and back at the inn there was a rush and bustle of preparation. The children had vanished from the courtyard, and presently reappeared, cloaked and warmly shod, the smallest boy holding his nurse's hand, the others frolicking around her, lively and noisy and obviously excited at the prospect of the voyage. They waited, skipping with impatience, while the slave I had seen, with another to help him, came out loaded with baggage, followed by a man in the livery of a chamber-groom, sharp-voiced and authoritative. They must be people of consequence, in spite of their strange speech. About the tallest of the boys, I thought, there was something vaguely familiar. I stood in the shadow of the inn's main doorway, watching them. The innkeeper had bustled up now, to be paid by the chamber-groom, and then a woman, his wife, perhaps, came running with a package. I heard the word "laundry", then the two of them backed away from the doorway with bow and curtsy, as the principal guest at length emerged from the chamber.

It was a woman, cloaked from head to foot in green. She was slightly built, but bore herself proudly. I caught the gleam of gold at her wrist, and there were jewels at her throat. Her cloak was lined and edged with red fox fur, deep and rich, and the hood, too. This was thrown back on her shoulders, but I could not see her face; she was turned away, speaking to someone behind her in the room.

Another woman came out carefully, carrying a box. This was wrapped in linen, and seemed heavy. She was plainly dressed, like a waiting woman. If the box contained her mistress's jewels, these were persons of consequence indeed.

Then the lady turned, and I knew her. It was Morgause, Queen of Lothian and Orkney. There could be no mistake. The lovely hair had lost its rose-gold glimmer, and had darkened to rose-brown, and her body had thickened with child-bearing, but the voice was the same, and the long slant of the eyes, and the pretty, folded mouth. So the four sturdy boys, ruddy and clamorous with the outlandish accent of the north, were her children by Lot of Lothian, Arthur's enemy.

I had no eyes for them now. I was watching the doorway. I wondered if, at last, I was going to see her eldest son, her child by Arthur himself.

He came swiftly out of the doorway. He was taller than his mother, a slim youth who, though I had never seen him before, I would have known anywhere. *Dark hair, dark eyes, and the body of a dancer.* Someone had once said that of me, and he was like me, was Arthur's son Mordred. He paused beside Morgause, saying something to her. His voice was light and pleasant, an echo of his mother's. I caught the words "ship" and "reckoning", and saw her nod. She laid her pretty hand on his, and the party started to move off. Mordred glanced at the sky, and spoke again, with what looked like a hint of anxiety. They went by within feet of where I was standing.

I drew back. The movement must have caught her attention, for she glanced up, and for the merest fraction of a moment, her eyes met mine. There was no recognition in them. But as she turned to hurry for the ship I saw her shiver, and draw the furred cloak about her as if she felt the wind suddenly cold.

The train of servants followed, and Lot's children; Gawain, Agravaine, Gaheris, Gareth. They trod over the gang-plank of the waiting ship.

They were going south, all of them. What Morgause purposed there I could not guess at, but it could be nothing but evil. And I was powerless to stop them, or even to send a message ahead of them, for who would believe a message from the dead?

Then the innkeeper and his wife were beside me, wanting to know my pleasure.

I did not, after all, ask to sleep in the rooms that the Queen of Orkney and her train had just vacated.

*   *   *

The wind still blew from the north next day, cold, strong, and steady. There was no question of my own ship's continuing north. I thought again of sending some message of warning to Camelot, but Morgause's ship would easily outpace a horseman, and to whom, in any case, could I send? To Nimuë? To Bedwyr or the Queen? I could do nothing until the High King was back in Britain. And, by the same token, while Arthur was still abroad, Morgause could do him no evil. I thought about it as I made my way out of the town, and set off along the track that led below the fortress walls towards Macsen's Tower. It would be an ill wind indeed if I could get no good of it at all. Yesterday's rest had refreshed me, and I had the day in hand. So I would use it.

When I had last been in Segontium, that great military city built and fortified by Maximus whom the Welsh call Macsen, it had been all but a ruin. Since then, Cador of Cornwall had repaired and re-fortified it against attackers from Ireland. That had been many years ago, but more recently Arthur had seen to it that Maelgon, his commander in the West, kept it in repair. I was interested to see what had been done, and how; and this, as much as anything else, took me along the valley track. Soon I was well above the town. It was a day of sunshine and chilly wind, and the city lay bright and washed with colour below me in the arm of the dark-blue sea. Beside the track the fortress walls rose stout and well-kept, and within them I could hear the clash and bustle of an alert and well-maintained garrison. As if I had still been Arthur's engineer, proposing to report to him, I marked all that I saw. Then I came to the south side of the fortress, where ruin and the four winds had been allowed their way, and paused to look up the valley slope towards Macsen's Tower.

There was the track, once trodden by the faithful legionaries, but probably now only used by sheep or goats and their herds. It led up the steep hillside to the swell of stony turf that hid the ancient, underground shrine of Mithras. For more than a hundred years the place had been ruinous, but when I had been there before, the steps that led down to the entrance had still been passable, and the temple itself, though patently unsafe, still recognisable. I started slowly up the track, wondering why, after all, I had come to see it again.

I need not have wondered. It was not there. There was no sign, either of the mound that had hidden the roof, or of the steps that had led downwards. I did not need to look far to find the cause. At the head of the slope where the temple had lain, the restorers of Segontium, levering away the great stones of the fortress wall for their rebuilding, and quarrying here and there for smaller metal, had set half the hillside rolling in a long slope of scree. In this had seeded and grown half a hundred small trees – thorn and ash and blackberry – so that even the track of the fallen scree was hard to trace. And everywhere, like the weft of a loom, the narrow sheep-trods, white with summer dust, criss-crossed the hillside.

I seemed to hear again, faintly, the receding voice of the god.

"Throw down my altar. It is time to throw it down."

Altar, shrine and all, had vanished into the locked depths of the hill.

* * *

There is something not quite believable about any change of this kind. I stood there for some time, casting about for the bearings I knew. There was no question of the accuracy of my memory; a line straight from Macsen's Tower on the hill above, to the south-west corner of the old fortress, and another, from the Commandant's house to the distant peak of Y Wyddfa, would intersect one another right over the site of the shrine. Now, they intersected one another right in the middle of the scree. I could see where, almost at that very point, the bushes were sparse, and the boulders showed gaps between, as of a space below.

"Lost something?" asked a voice.

I looked round. A boy was sitting perched above me, on a fallen block of stone. He was very young, perhaps ten years old, and very dirty. He was tousled and half-naked, and was chewing a hunk of barley bread. A hazel stick lay near him, and his sheep grazed placidly a little way up the hill.

"A treasure, it seems," I said.

"What kind of treasure? Gold?"

"It might be. Why?"

He swallowed the last bit of bread. "What's it worth to you?"

"Oh, half my kingdom. Were you going to help me find it?"

"I've found gold here before."

"You have?"

"Aye. And once a silver penny. And once a belt buckle. Bronze, that was."

"It seems your pasture is richer than it looks," I said, smiling. This had once been a busy road between fortress and temple. The place must be full of such trove. I looked at the boy. His eyes were clear and lively in the dirty face. "Well," I added, "I don't actually want to dig for gold, but if you can help me with some information, there's a copper penny in this for you. Tell me, have you lived here all your life?"

"Aye."

"Kept sheep in this valley?"

"Aye. Used to come with my brother. Then he got sold to a trader and went on a ship. I keep the sheep now. They're not mine. Master's a big man over to the hill."

"Do you remember –" I asked it without hope; some of the saplings were surely ten years grown – "do you remember when this landslide came? When they were rebuilding the fort, perhaps?"

A shake of the tousled head. "It's always been like this."

"No. It wasn't always like this. When I was here before, many years ago, there was a good track along the hillside here, and deep in the side of the hill, just over yonder, was an underground building. It had once been a temple. In old times the soldiers used to worship Mithras there. Have you never heard tell of it?"

Another shake.

"From your father, perhaps?"

He grinned. "Tell me who that is, I'll tell you what he said."

"Your master, then?"

"No. But if it's under there," a jerk of the head towards the scree,

"I know where. There's water under. Where the water is, that'll be the place, surely?"

"There was no water when I –" I stopped. A prickling ran over my flesh, like a cold draught. "Water under where?"

"Under the stones. There. Way under. Twice a man's height, by the feel of it."

I took in the small dirty figure, the bright grey eyes, the hazel stick at his feet. "You can find water under the ground? With the hazel?"

"It's easiest wi' that. But I get the feeling sometimes, just the same, on my own."

"And metal? Is that the way you found gold here before?"

"Once. It was a nice bit of a statue or something. A dog, sort of. The master took it off me. If I found some more now I wouldn't tell him. But mostly it's copper, copper coins. Up there in the old buildings."

"I see." I was thinking that when I found the shrine it had already been a deserted ruin for a century or more. But when it was built, no doubt it would have been beside a spring. "If you will show me where the water lies below the stones, there will be silver in it for you."

He did not move. I thought he looked wary. "That's where it is, this treasure you're looking for?"

"I hope so." I smiled at him. "But it's nothing that you could find for yourself, child. It would take men with crowbars to shift those stones, and even if you led them to the place, you would get nothing of what they found. If you show me now, I promise that you will be paid."

He sat still for a moment or two, scuffling his bare feet in the dirt. Then, groping inside the skin kilt that was his only garment, he produced, flat on a dirty palm, a silver coin. "I was paid, master. There's others knew about the treasure. How was I to know it was yours? I showed them where to dig, and they lifted the stones and took the box away."

Silence. Here in the lee of the hill the wind had no way. The bright world seemed to spin far away, then steady, and come back. I sat down on a boulder.

"Master?" The boy slipped from his perch and padded downhill.

He stopped near me, peering, but still poised warily, as if for flight.
"Master? If I did wrong –"
"You did no wrong. How could you know? No, stay, please,
and tell me about it. I shan't hurt you. How could I? Who were
they, and how long ago did they take the box away?"
He gave me another doubtful look, then appeared to take me at
my word. He spoke eagerly. "Only two days since. It was two
men, I don't know them, slaves they were, and they came with the
lady."
"*The lady?*"
At something in my face he stepped back half a pace, then stood
his ground. "Aye. Came two days ago, she did. She must have had
magic, I think. Went straight to it, like a bitch to the porridge-pot.
Pointed almost to the very place, and said 'Try there'. The two
fellows started shifting the rocks. I was sitting up there. When
they'd been at it for a bit, they were moving the wrong way, so I
went down. Told her what I told you, that I could find things.
'Well,' she says, 'there's metal hid somewhere hereabout. I've lost
the map,' she says, 'but I know it's here. The owner sent me. If you
can show us where to dig, there's a silver coin in it for you.' So I
found it. Metal! It took the hazel clean from my hand, like a big dog
snatching a bone. A powerful kind of gold there must have been
there?"
"Indeed," I said. "You saw them find it?"
"Aye. I waited for my pay, see?"
"Of course. What was it like?"
"A box, so by so." Gestures sketched the size. "It looked heavy.
They never opened it. She made them lay it down, then she laid her
hands right across it, like this. I told you she had magic. She looked
right up there, right into Y Wyddfa, as if she was talking to the
spirit. You know, the one that lives there. It made a sword once,
they say. The King has it now. Merlin got it for him from the King
of the hills."
"Yes," I said. "Then?"
"They took it away."
"Did you see where they went?"
"Well, yes. Down towards the town." He shuffled his toes in the
dirt, regarding me with clouded eyes. "She did say the owner sent

her. Was that a lie? She was very sweet spoken, and the slaves had badges with a crown on. I thought she was a queen."

"So she was," I said. I straightened my back. "Don't look like that, child, you have done nothing wrong. In fact, you have done more than most men would have done in your place; you told me the truth. You could have earned another silver coin if you had kept your mouth shut, showed me the place, and gone on your way. So I shall pay you, as I promised. Here."

"But this is silver, master. And for nothing."

"Not for nothing. You gave me news that must be worth half the kingdom, or even more. A king's ransom, don't they call it?" I got to my feet. "Don't try to understand me. Stay here in peace, and watch your sheep and find your fortune, and the gods be with you."

"And with you too, master," said he, staring.

"It may be," I said, "that they still are. All they have to do now is to send another ship in the wake of the first one, and take me south."

I left him looking wonderingly after me, with the silver coin clutched tightly in the dirty hand.

A south-bound ship docked next day at noon, and sailed again with the evening tide. I was on board, and stayed prostrate and suffering until she came, five days later, safely into the Severn Channel.

5

The winds stayed strong, but variable. By the time we reached the Channel, the weather had settled to fair, so we did not put in at Maridunum, but held straight on up the estuary.

Enquiries had told me that the *Orc,* Morgause's ship, had been bound for Ynys Witrin, putting in at least twice on the way. It was possible, since by good luck mine was a fast ship, that Morgause and her party might not be too far ahead of me. I suppose I might have bribed the master of my ship to put in at the Island also, but nothing could have saved me there from recognition, with the consequent uproar that I had striven to avoid. Had I known when I saw Morgause that she had the things of power with her from the Mithraeum, and had still (since the boy's judgment seemed good) some magic in her hands, I would have felt bound, whatever the risks, to sail with her in the *Orc,* though I might never have survived the voyage.

I had no means of knowing when Arthur was expected home, and, if I had to stay in hiding until he came, Morgause would probably be able to reach him before I did. What I was hoping for, as I travelled south so closely in her wake, was that I could somehow reach Nimuë. I had faced what might be the result of that. A return from the dead is rarely a success. It was very possible that she might herself want to stop me from reaching Arthur again, and reclaiming my place in his affection and his service. But she had my power. The grail was for the future, and the future was hers. Warn her I must, that another witch was on the way. The rape of Macsen's treasure had sounded some note of danger which I could not ignore.

To my relief my ship passed the mouth of the estuary that led to the Island's harbour, and held on up into the narrowing Severn channel. We put in at length at a small wharf at the mouth of the Frome River, from which there is a good road leading straight to Aquae Sulis in the Summer Country. I had paid my passage this time with one of the jewels from my grave-clothes, and with the change from this I bought myself a good horse, filled the saddle-bags with food and a change of clothing, and set off at once along the road towards the city.

Except in those places where I was very well known, I thought there was small chance now of my being recognised. I had grown thinner since my entombment, my hair was now quite grey, and I had not shaved my beard. For all that, I planned to skirt towns and villages if I could, and lie at country taverns. I could not lie out; the weather was turning colder every day, and, not much to my surprise, I found the ride exhausting. By the evening of the first day I was very ready to rest, and put up thankfully at a small, decent-looking tavern still four or five miles short of Aquae Sulis.

Before I even asked for food, I sought news, and was told that Arthur was home, and at Camelot. When I spoke of Nimuë they answered readily, but more vaguely. "Merlin's lady", they called her, "the King's enchantress", and elaborated with one or two fanciful tales, but they were not sure of her movements. One man said she was at Camelot with the King, but another was sure she had left the place a month back; there had been, he said, some trouble in Rheged; some tale about Queen Morgan, and the King's great sword.

So Nimuë, it seemed, was out of touch; and Arthur was home. Even if Morgause did land on the Island, she might not hasten straight to confront the King. If I made all haste, I might reach him before she did. I hurried with my meal, then paid my shot, had them saddle up once more, and took again to the road. Though I was tired, I had come a scant ten miles, and my good horse was still fresh. If I did not press him, I knew that he could go all night.

There was a moon, and the road was in repair, so we made good time, reaching Aquae Sulis well before midnight. The gates were locked, so I skirted the walls. I was stopped twice, once by a gate guard calling to know my business, and once by a troop of soldiers wearing Melwas' badge. Each time I showed my brooch with its

Dragon jewel, and said curtly, "King's business", and each time the brooch, or my assurance, told, and they let me by. A mile or so after that the road forked, and I turned south by south-east.

The sun came up, small and red in an icy sky. Ahead, the road led straight across the bleak hill land, where the limestone shows white as bone, and the trees are all racked north-eastwards away from the gales. My horse dropped to a walk, then to a plod. Myself, I was riding in a dream, gone in exhaustion beyond either stiffness or soreness. Out of mercy to both weary animals, I drew rein by the next water-trough we passed, tossed hay down from the net that hung at the saddle bow, and myself sat down on the trough's edge and took out my breakfast of raisins and black bread and mead.

The light broadened, flashing on the frosty grass. It was very cold. I broke the cat-ice on the trough, and laved my face and hands. It refreshed me, but made me shiver. If the horse and I were to stay alive we must soon move on. Presently I bitted up again, and led him to where I might mount from the edge of the trough. The horse threw up his head and pricked his ears, and then I heard it, too; hoofs approaching from the direction of the city, and at a fast gallop. Someone who had left the city as soon as the gates had opened, and was coming in a hurry, on a fresh horse.

He came in sight; a young man riding hard, on a big blue roan. When he was a hundred paces off, I recognised the insignia of the royal courier, and, clambering stiffly down from the trough's edge, moved into the road and held up a hand.

He would not have stopped for me, but here the road was edged on the one side by a low ridge of rock, and on the other by a steep drop, with the trough blocking the narrow verge. And I had turned my horse so that he stood across the way.

The rider drew rein, holding the restless roan, and saying impatiently: "What is it? If you're fain for company, my good man, I can't provide it. Can't you see who I am?"

"A King's messenger. Yes. Where are you bound?"

"Camelot." He was young, with russet hair and a high colour, and (as his kind have) a kind of prideful arrogance in his calling. But he spoke civilly enough. "The King's there, and I must be there myself tomorrow. What is it, old man, is your horse gone lame? Your best plan is –"

"No. I shall manage. Thank you. I would not have stopped you
for a triviality, but this is important. I want you to take a message
for me, please. It is to go to the King."

He stared, then laughed, his breath like a cloud on the icy air.
"For the King, he says! Good sir, forgive me, but a King's messenger has better things to do than take tales from every passer-by. If
it's a petition, then I suggest you trot back to Caerleon yourself.
The King's to be there for Christmas, and you might get there in
time, if you hurry." His heels moved as if he would set spurs to
his horse, and ride on. "So by your leave, stand aside and let me
by."

I did not move. I said, quietly: "You would do well to listen, I
think."

He swung back, angry now, and shook his whip free. I thought
he would ride over me. Then he met my eyes. He bit back what he
had been going to say. The roan, anticipating the whip, bounded
forward, and was curbed sharply. It subsided, fretting, its breath
puffing white like a dragon's. The man cleared his throat, looked
me up and down doubtfully, then fixed his eyes on my face again. I
saw his doubt growing. He made a concession and a face-saver at
the same time.

"Well – sir – I can listen. And be sure I'll take any message that
seems up to my weight. But we're not supposed to act as common
carriers, and I have a schedule to keep."

"I know. I would not trouble you, except that it is urgent that I
reach the King, and as you have pointed out, you will get there
rather more quickly than I. The message is this: that you met an old
man on the road who gave you a token, and told you that he is on his
way to Camelot to see the King. But he can only make his way
slowly, so if the King wishes to see him he must come to him by the
way. Tell him which road I am taking, and say that I paid you with
the ferryman's guerdon. Repeat it, please."

These men are practised at remembering word for word. Often
the messages they take are from men who cannot write. He began
to obey me, without thought: "I met an old man on the road who
gave me a token, and told me that he is on his way to Camelot to see
the King. But he can only make his way slowly, so if the King
wishes to see him, he must – hey, now, what sort of a message is

that? Are you out of your mind? The way you put it, it sounds as if you're sending for the King, just like that."

I smiled. "I suppose it does. Perhaps I might phrase it better, if it will make a more comfortable message to deliver? In any case, I suggest you deliver it in private."

"I'll say it had better be in private! Look, I don't know who you are, sir – and it's my guess you're somebody, in spite of, well, not looking it – but by the god of going, it had better be a powerful token, and a good guerdon, too, if I'm to take a summons to King Arthur, however privately."

"Oh, it is." I had wrapped my Dragon brooch in linen, and fastened it into a small package. I handed him this, and with it the second of the gold coins that had sealed my eyelids in the tomb. He stared at the gold coin, then at me, then turned the package over in his hand, eyeing it. He said, doubtfully: "What's in it?"

"Only the token I spoke of. And let me repeat, this is important, and it's urgent that you should give it to the King in private. If Bedwyr is there with him, no matter, but no other person. Do you understand?"

"Ye-es, but . . . ." With a movement of knees and wrist he wheeled the roan horse half away from me, and with another movement too fast for me to prevent, he broke open the package. My brooch, with the royal Dragon glinting on the gold ground, fell into his hand. "This? This is the royal cypher."

"Yes."

He said, abruptly: "Who are you?"

"I am the King's cousin. So have no fear of delivering the message."

"The King has no cousin, other than Hoel of Brittany. And Hoel doesn't rate the Dragon. Only the . . ." His voice trailed away. I saw the blood begin to drain from his face.

"The King will know who I am," I said. "Don't think I blame you for doubting me, or for opening the package. The King is well served. I shall tell him so."

"You're Merlin." It came out in a whisper. He had to lick his lips and try twice before he could make a sound.

"Yes. Now you see why you must see the King alone. It will be a shock to him, too. Don't be afraid of me."

"But . . . Merlin died and was buried." He was perfectly white now. The reins ran slack through his fingers, and the roan, deciding to take advantage of the respite, lowered its head and began to graze.

I said quickly: "Don't drop the brooch. Look, man, I'm no ghost. It is not every grave that is the gate of death."

I had meant that as a reassurance, but he went, if possible, more ashen than before. "My lord, we thought . . . Everybody knew . . ."

"It was thought that I had died, yes." I spoke briskly, keeping it matter-of-fact. "But all that happened was that I fell into a sickness like death, and I recovered. That is all. Now I am well, and will re-enter the King's service . . . but secretly. No one must know until the King himself has had the news, and spoken with me. I would have told no one but one of the King's own couriers. Do you understand?"

This had the effect, as I had hoped, of bringing back his self-assurance. The red came back into his cheeks, and he straightened his back. "Yes, my lord. The King will be – very happy, my lord. When you died – that is, when you – well, when it happened, he shut himself up alone for three days, and would speak to no one, not even to Prince Bedwyr. Or so they say."

His voice came back to normal while he was speaking, warming, I could see, with pleasurable excitement at the thought of the good news he would have to carry to the King. Gold was the least of it. As he came to an end of telling me how Merlin had been missed and mourned "the length and breadth of the kingdom, I promise you, sir," he pulled the roan's head up from the frosty grass, and set it dancing. The colour was back bright in his face, and he looked excited and eager. "Then I'll be on my way."

"When do you expect to reach Camelot?"

"Tomorrow noon, with good fortune, and a good change of horses. More probably, tomorrow at lamplighting. You couldn't give my horse a pair of wings while you're about it, could you?"

I laughed. "I should have to recover a little further before I could manage that. One moment more, before you go . . . There's another message that should go straight to the King. Perhaps you bear it already? Did you get any news in Aquae Sulis of the Queen of

Orkney? I heard that she was travelling south by ship to Ynys Witrin, no doubt on her way to court."

"Yes, it's true. She's arrived. Landed, I mean, and on her way now to Camelot. There were those who said she wouldn't obey the summons –"

"Summons? Do you mean that the High King *sent* for her?"

"Yes, sir. That's common knowledge, so I'm not talking out of turn. As a matter of fact I won a small wager on it: they were saying she wouldn't come, even with the safe conduct for the boys. I said she would. With Tydwal sitting tight in Lot's other castle, and Arthur's sworn man, where could she look for refuge if the High King chose to smoke her out?"

"Where, indeed?" I said it absently, almost blankly. This, I had not foreseen, and could not understand. "Forgive me for detaining you, but I have been a long time without news. Can you tell me why the High King should summon her – and apparently under threat?"

He opened his lips, shut them again, then, obviously deciding that telling the King's cousin and erstwhile chief adviser was no breach of his code, nodded. "I understand it's a matter of the boys, sir. One in particular, the eldest of the five. The queen was to bring them all to Camelot."

The eldest of the five. So Nimuë had found Mordred for him . . . where I had failed. Nimuë, who had gone north on "some business for the King".

I thanked the man, and stood back, moving my horse out of his way. "Now, on your way, Bellerophon, as best you can, and 'ware dragons."

"I've got all the dragons I need, thanks." He gathered the reins, and raised a hand in salute. "But that's not my name."

"What is it, then?"

"Perseus," he said, and looked puzzled when I laughed. Then he laughed with me, flourished his whip, and sent the roan past me at a gallop.

6

The need for hurry was over. It was likely that Morgause would reach Arthur before the courier, but about that I could do nothing. Though it still disturbed me to know that she had with her the things of power, the sharpest of my worries was gone: Arthur was forearmed; she was there by his orders, and her hostages with her. It was also probable that I myself would be able to see and talk with him before he had dealt with Morgause and Mordred. I had no doubt at all that Arthur, the moment he saw my token and heard the message, would be on the road to find me. Meeting the courier had been a stroke of excellent fortune; even in my prime I could not have ridden as these men ride.

Nor was it urgent, now, that I should get in touch with Nimuë. Of this, in an obscure way, I was glad. There are some tests that one shrinks from making, and some truths that one would rather not hear. I think that if I could have concealed my existence from her I would have done so. I wanted to remember her words of love and grief at my passing, not see in fresh daylight her face of dismay when she saw me living.

For the rest of that day I went slowly, and, well before sunset on a still, cold afternoon, came to a wayside inn, and stopped there. There were no other travellers staying, for which I was glad. I saw my horse stabled and fed, then ate the good supper provided by the innkeeper's wife, and went early to bed, and a dreamless sleep.

All the next day I stayed indoors, glad of the rest. One or two folk passed that way; a drover with his flock, a farmer with his wife on their way home from market, a courier going north-west. But again, at nightfall, I was the only guest, and had the fire to myself. After supper, when the host and his wife withdrew to their own place, I was left alone in the small, raftered room, with my pallet of straw drawn near the fire, and a stack of logs nearby to keep the place warm.

That night I made no attempt to seek sleep. Once the inn was sunk in silence, I pulled a chair near to the hearth and fed fresh wood to the flames. The goodwife had left a pot of water simmering at the edge of the fire, so I mixed hot water with the remains of the supper's wine, and drank it, while around me the small sounds of the night took over; the settling of the logs in the fire, the rustle of the flames, the scuttle of rats in the thatch, the sound, far away, of an owl hunting in the icy night. Then I set the wine aside and closed my eyes. How long I sat there I have no idea, nor what form the prayers took that brought the sweat to my skin and set the night noises whirling and receding into a limitless and stinging silence. Then at last, the light of the flames against my eyeballs, and through the light the darkness, and through the darkness, light . . .

★   ★   ★

It was a long time since I had seen the great hall at Camelot. Now it was lit against the dark of an autumn evening. An extravagance of waxlight glittered on the gay dresses of the women, and the jewels and weapons of the men. Supper was just over. Guinevere sat in her place at the centre of the high table, lovely in her gold-backed chair. Bedwyr was on her left. They looked happier, I thought, high of heart and smiling. On the Queen's right, the King's great chair was empty.

But just as the chill had touched me, of not seeing him who was all I desired to see, I saw him. He was walking down the hall, pausing here and there to speak to a man as he passed. He was calm, and smiling, and once or twice set them laughing. A page led him; some message, then, had been sent up to the high table, and the King was answering it himself. He reached the great door, and, with a word to the sentries, dismissed the boy and stepped outside. Two soldiers – guards from the gatehouse – waited for him there, with, between them, a man I had seen before; Morgause's chamber-groom.

The latter started forward as soon as the King appeared, then

stopped, apparently disconcerted. It was obvious that he had not
expected to see Arthur himself. Then, mastering his surprise, he
went down on a knee. He started to speak, in that strange northern
accent, but Arthur cut across it.

"Where are they?"

"Why, at the gate, my lord. Your lady sister sent me to beg an
audience of you tonight, there in the hall."

"My orders were that she should come tomorrow to the Round
Hall. Did she not receive the message?"

"Indeed, my lord. But she has travelled far, and is weary, and in
some anxiety of mind about your summons. She and her children
cannot rest until she knows your will. She has brought them – all –
with her tonight, and begs you of your grace that you and the
Queen will receive them –"

"I will receive them, yes, but not in the hall. At the gate. Go back
and tell her to wait there."

"But, my lord –" Against the King's silence, the man's protests
died. He got to his feet with a kind of dignity, bowed to Arthur,
then withdrew into the darkness with the two guards. More
slowly, Arthur followed them.

The night was dry and still, and frost furred the small clipped
trees that lined the terraces. The King's robe brushed them as he
passed. He was walking slowly, head down, frowning as he had not
let himself frown in the hall full of men and women. No one was
about except the guards. A sergeant saluted him and asked a
question. He shook his head. So, with neither escort nor company,
he walked alone through the palace gardens, past the chapel wall,
and down the steps by the silent fountain. Then through another
gate with its saluting sentries, and on to the roadway which led
down through the fortress to the south-west gate.

And, sitting by the blaze in the faraway tavern, with the vision
driving its nails of pain through my eyes, I cried out to him with a
warning as plain as I could make it:

*Arthur. Arthur. This is the fate you begot on that night at Luguvallium.
This is the woman who took your seed to make your enemy. Destroy them.
Destroy them now. They are your fate. She has in her hand the things of
power, and I am afraid. Destroy them now. They are in your hand.*

He had stopped in the middle of the way. He raised his head as if he could hear something in the night sky. A lantern hanging from a pole threw light on his face. I scarcely knew it. It was sombre, hard, cold, the face of a judge, or an executioner. He stood for a few minutes, quite still, then moved as suddenly as a horse under the spur, and strode down towards the main gate of the fortress.

They were there, the whole party. They had changed and robed themselves, and their horses were fresh and richly caparisoned. Torchlight showed the glint of gold tassels and green and scarlet harness. Morgause wore white, a robe trimmed with silver and small pearls, and a long scarlet cloak lined with white fur. The four younger boys were to the rear, with a pair of servants, but Mordred was beside his mother, on a handsome black horse, its bridle ringing with silver. He was looking around him curiously. He does not know, I thought; she has not told him. The black brows, tipped like wings, were smooth; the mouth, a still mouth, folded like Morgause's, kept its secrets. The eyes were Arthur's, and my own.

Morgause sat her mare, still and upright, waiting. Her hood was thrown back, and the light caught her face. It was expressionless and rather pale; but the eyes glittered green under the long lids, and I saw the kitten's teeth savaging her underlip. I knew that, under the cool exterior, she was disconcerted, even afraid. She had ignored Arthur's messenger, and deliberately brought her little train to Camelot at this late hour, when all would be assembled in the great hall. She must have reckoned on bringing her royal brood to the steps of the high throne, and perhaps even presenting Arthur's son in public, so forcing the King's hand before his Queen and all the assembled nobles and their ladies. These, she could be sure, would have stood the allies of a lonely queen with a brood of innocents. But she had been stopped at the gate, and now, against all precedent, the King had come out alone to see her, with no witness but his soldiers.

He came down now under the torchlight. He stopped a few paces away, full in the light, and said to the guards: "Let them come."

Mordred slid from his horse's back, and handed his mother down. The servants took the horses and withdrew to the gatehouse. Then Morgause, with a boy to either side of her, and the three younger ones behind, went forward to meet the King.

It was the first time they had met since the night in Luguvallium when she sent her maid to lead him to her bed. Then he had been a stripling, a prince after his first battle, gay and young and full of fire; the woman had been twenty years old, subtle and experienced, with her double web of sex and magic to entrance the boy. Now, in spite of the years of child-bearing, there was still something left of whatever had drawn men's eyes and sent them mad for her. But she was not now facing a green and eager boy; this was a man in the flower of his strength, with the judgment that makes a King, and the power to enforce it, and with it all something formidable, dangerous, like a fire banked down that needs only a breath of air to set it blazing.

Morgause went down to the frosty ground in front of him, not in the deep curtsy that one might have expected from a suppliant who had need of his forgiveness and grace; but kneeling. Her right hand went out and forced the young Mordred, likewise, to his knees. Gawain, on her other side, stood, with the other children, looking wonderingly from his mother to the King. She left them so; they were Lot's, self-confessed, big boned and high-coloured, with the fair skin and hair bequeathed by their mother. Whatever Lot had done in the past, Arthur would visit none of it on his children. But the other, the changeling with the thin face and the dark eyes that had come down through the royal house from Macsen himself . . . she forced him to his knees, where he stayed, but with his head up, and those dark eyes darting round him, looking, it seemed, all ways at once.

Morgause was speaking, in the light, pretty voice that had not changed. I could not catch what she said. Arthur stood like stone. I doubt if he heard a word. He had hardly glanced at her; his eyes were all for his son. Her voice took an edge of urgency. I caught the word "brother", and then "son". Arthur listened, still-faced, but I could feel the words flying like darts between them. Then he took a step forward, and put out a hand. She laid hers in it, and he raised her. I saw among the boys, and in the men who waited at the gate, a subtle relaxation. Her servants' hands did not drop from their hilts – they had studiously not been near them – but the effect was the same. The two older boys, Gawain and Mordred, exchanged a look as their mother rose, and I saw Mordred smile. They waited now for the King to give her the kiss of peace and friendship.

He did not give it. He raised her, and said something, then, turning, led her a little way aside. I saw Mordred's head go round like a hunting dog's. Then the King spoke to the boys:

"Be welcome here. Now go back to the gatehouse, and wait."

They went, Mordred with a backward look at his mother. For a moment I saw terror in her face, then the mask of calm came down again. Some message must have passed, for now the chamber-groom came forward, in a hurry, from the gatehouse, bearing in his hands the box that they had brought from Segontium. The things of power . . . unbelievably, she had brought them for the King. Unbelievably, she hoped to buy her way to his favour with the treasure of Macsen . . .

The man knelt at the King's feet. He opened the box. The light shone down on the treasure that lay within. I saw it all, as clearly as if it lay at my feet. Silver, all silver; cups and bracelets, and a necklet made of silver plaques, designed with those fluid and interlocking lines with which the northern silversmiths invoke their magic. There was no sign of Macsen's emblems of power, no grail studded with emeralds, no lance-head, no dish crusted with sapphire and amethyst. Arthur gave it barely a glance. As the chamber-groom scuttled back into the shelter of the gatehouse, the King turned again to Morgause, leaving the gift lying on the frosty ground. And as he had ignored the gift, so he ignored all that, until now, she had been saying. I heard his voice quite clearly.

"I sent for you, Morgause, for reasons which may not be clear to you. You were wise to obey me. One of my reasons concerns your children; you must have guessed this; but you need not fear for them. I promised you that none of them should be harmed, and I shall keep my promise. But for yourself, no such promise was made. You do well to kneel and sue for mercy. And what mercy can you expect? You killed Merlin. It was you who fed him the poison that in the end brought him to his death."

She had not expected this. I saw her gasp. The white hands fluttered, as if she would have put them to her throat. But she held them still. "Who has told you this lie?"

"It is no lie. When he lay dying, he himself accused you."

"He was always my enemy!" she cried.

"And who is to say he was wrong? You know what you have done. Do you deny it?"

"Of course I deny it! He hated me, always! And you know why. He wanted no one to have power over you but himself. We sinned, yes, you and I, but we sinned in innocence —"

"If you are wise, you will not speak of that." His voice was dry and icy. "You know, as well as I do, what sins were committed, and why. If you hope for any mercy now, or ever, you will not speak of it."

She bowed her head. Her fingers twisted together. Her pose was humble. When she spoke, she spoke quietly. "You are right, my lord. I should not have spoken so. I will not encumber you with memories. I have obeyed you, and brought your son to you, and I leave your heart and conscience to deal rightly with him. You will not deny that *he* is innocent."

He said nothing. She tried again, with the hint of her old sideways, glinting look.

"For myself, I admit that I stand accused of folly. I come to you, Arthur, as a sister, who —"

"I have two sisters," he said stonily. "The other one has just now tried to betray me. Do not speak to me of sisters."

Her head went up. The thin disguise of suppliant was shed. She faced him, a queen to his king. "Then what can I say, except that I come to you as the mother of your son?"

"You have come to me as the murderer of the man who was more to me than my own father. And as nothing else. You are no more to me, and no less. This is why I sent for you, and what I shall judge you for."

"He would have killed me. He would have had you kill your own son."

"That is not true," said the King. "He prevented me from killing you both. Yes, I see that shakes you. When I heard of the child's birth, my first thought was to send someone up to kill him. But, if you remember, Lot was before me . . . And Merlin, of all men, would have saved the child, because he is mine." For the first time passion showed through a crack in his composure. "But he is not here now, Morgause. He will not protect you again. Why do you think I refused to receive you in the open hall tonight, in the presence of the Queen and the knights? That is what you hoped for, is it not? You, with your pretty face and voice, your four fine boys by Lot, and this youth here with those dark eyes, and the look of his royal kindred . . ."

"He has done you no harm!" she cried.

"No, he has done me no harm. Now listen to me. Your four sons by Lot I will take from you, and have them trained here at Camelot. I will not have them left in your care, to be brought up as traitors, to hate their King. As for Mordred, he has done me no wrong, though I have wronged him sorely, and so have you.. I will not add sin to sin. I have been warned of him, but a man must do right, even to his own hurt. And who can read the gods accurately? You will leave him with me also."

"And have you murder him as soon as I am gone?"

"And if I do, what choice have you but to let me?"

"You've changed, brother," she said, spitefully.

For the first time, something like a smile touched his mouth. "You might say so. For what comfort it is to you now, I shall not kill him. But you, Morgause, because you slew Merlin, who was the best man in all this realm –"

He was interrupted. From the gatehouse came a clatter of hoofs, the quick challenge from the sentries, a breathless word, then the creak and crash of the gates opening. A horse, tagged with foam, clattered through, and came to a halt beside the King and stood. Its head went down to its knees. Its limbs trembled. The courier slid down from the saddle, grabbed at the girth to keep his own limbs from folding under him, then went carefully on one knee, and saluted the King.

It was hardly a comfortable interruption. Arthur faced about, his brows drawn, and anger in his face. "Well?" he asked. His voice was even. He knew that no courier would have got through to him at such a moment, and in such a state, unless his business drove him. "Wait, I remember you, don't I? Perseus, is it not? What news can you possibly bring from Glevum that makes it worth your while to kill a good horse, and break in on my private councils?"

"My lord –" The man cleared his throat, with a glance at Morgause. "My lord, it is urgent news, most urgent, that I must deliver privately. Forgive me." This half to Morgause, who was standing like a statue, hands to her throat. Some wisp of forgotten magic, trailing, may have warned her what the news might be.

The King regarded him in silence for a moment, then nodded. He called out an order, and two of the guards came forward, halting one on either side of Morgause. Then he turned, with a sign to the courier, and walked back up the roadway with the man following him.

At the foot of the palace steps he paused and turned.

"Your message?"

Perseus held out the package I had given him. "I met an old man on the road who gave me this token, and told me that he is on his way to Camelot to see the King. But he can only make his way slowly, so if the King wishes to see him, he must come to him. He is travelling by the road that runs over the hills between Aquae Sulis and Camelot. He told me –"

"*He gave you this?*" The brooch lay in the King's hand. The Dragon winked and glittered. Arthur looked up from it, his face colourless.

"Yes, my lord." The clipped recital hurried. "I was to tell you that he paid me for my service with the ferryman's guerdon." He held out his hand with the gold coin in the palm.

The King took it like a man in a dream, glanced at it, and handed it back. In his other hand he was turning the brooch this way and that, so that the Dragon flashed in the torchlight. "You know what this is?"

"Indeed, my lord. It's the Dragon. When I saw it first I asked what his right to it was, but then I knew him. My lord, yes . . ." The King, his face quite bloodless now, was staring. The man licked his lips, and somehow got the rest of the message out. "When he stopped me, yesterday, he was near the thirteenth milestone. He – he didn't look too good, my lord. If you do ride to meet him, it's my guess he won't have got much beyond the next inn. It stands back from the road, on the south side, and the sign's a bush of holly."

"A bush of holly." Arthur repeated it with no expression at all, like a man talking in his sleep. Then, suddenly, the trance that held him shattered. Colour flooded his face. He threw the brooch up in the air, flashing and turning, and caught it again. He laughed aloud.

"I might have known! I might have known . . . This is real, at any rate!"

"He told me," said Perseus, "he told me he was no ghost. And that it wasn't every tomb that was the gate of death."

"Even his ghost," said Arthur. "Even his ghost . . ." He whirled and shouted. Men came running. Orders were flung at them. "My grey stallion. My cloak and sword. I give you four minutes." He put out a hand to the courier. "You will stay here in Camelot till my return. You have done more than well, Perseus. I'll remember it. Now go and rest . . . Ah, Ulfin. Tell Bedwyr to bring twenty of the knights and follow me. This man will direct them. Give him food, and tend his horse and keep him till I come again."

"And the lady?" asked someone.

"Who?" It was plain that the King had forgotten all about Morgause. He said, indifferently: "Hold her until I have time for her, and let her speak to no one. No one, do you understand me?"

The stallion was brought, with two grooms clinging to the bit. Someone came running with cloak and sword. The gates crashed open. Arthur was in the saddle. The grey stallion screamed and climbed the torchlit air, then leapéd forward under the spur, and was out of the gate with the speed of a thrown spear. It went down the steep, winding causeway as if it had been a level plain in daylight. It was the way the boy Arthur had once ridden through the Wild Forest, and to the same assignation . . .

Morgause, her virgin white spattered with thrown turf and sods, stood stiffly between her guards, as men-at-arms clattered past her. The boys were in their midst, and Mordred among them. They vanished towards the palace without a backward look.

For the first time since I had known her, I saw her, no more than a frightened woman, making the sign against strong enchantment.

7

Next morning the innkeeper and his wife, to their alarm and distress, found me lying on the cooling hearth, apparently in a faint. They got me into bed, wrapped winter-stones to warm me, piled blankets around me, and got the fire going once more. When, in time, I wakened, the good folk looked after me with the anxious care they might have accorded their own father. I was not much the worse. Moments of vision have always to be paid for; first with the pain of the vision itself, then afterwards in the long trance of exhausted sleep.

Reckoning out the distances, I let myself rest quietly for the remainder of that day, then next morning, putting my hosts' protests aside, had them saddle my horse. They were reasssured when I told them I would not ride far, but only a mile or so down the road, where a friend could be expected to meet me. I further allayed their fears by asking them to prepare a dinner "for myself and my friend".

"For," I said, "he loves good food, and the goodwife's cooking is as tasty as any, I'll swear, at the King's court of Camelot."

At that the innkeeper's wife laughed and bridled, and began to talk of capons, so I left money to pay for the food, and went my way.

After the spell of hard frost, the weather had slackened. The sun was up, and dealing some warmth. The air was mild enough, but still everywhere was the hint of winter's coming; in the bare trees of the heights, the fieldfares busy in the berried holly, redwings flocking on the bushes, nuts ripe in the hazel coppices. The bracken was fading gold, and there were still flowers out on the gorse.

My horse, after his long rest, was fresh and eager, and we covered the first stretch of road at a fast canter. We met no one. Soon the road left the high crest of the limestone hills, and slanted downwards along a valley side. All along the lower reaches of the valley the slopes were crowded with trees in the flaming colours of autumn; beech, oak and chestnut, birch in its yellow gold, with everywhere the dark spires of the pine trees and the glossy green of holly. Through the trees I caught the glint of moving water. Down by the river, the innkeeper had told me, the way forked. The road itself held straight across the river, which here was paved in a shallow ford, and just beyond the water another way led off to the right, through the forest. This was a little-used track, and a rough one, which cut off a corner to rejoin the gravelled road some miles further towards the east.

This was the place I was making for. It was a full mile since I had seen any sort of dwelling; the ford was as private for our meeting as a midnight bedchamber. I dared not to go further to meet him. Whenever Arthur had to ride, he made all speed, and cut all corners. Not knowing the forest track, I could not count on his using it, so might miss him if I took one way or the other.

It was a good place to wait. Down in the hollow the sun shone warmly, and the air was mild but fresh. It smelled of pines. Two jays wrestled and scolded in a shaw of hollies, then flew low across the road with a flash of sky-blue in their wings. Distantly, in the woods to the south-east, I heard the long rasping noise that meant a woodpecker at work. The river whispered across the road, running gently, no more than a foot deep across the Roman setts of the ford.

I unsaddled my horse and slacked his bit, then unbuckled an end of the rein, tied it to a hazel stem, and left him to graze. There was a fallen pine a few paces from the river's edge, full in the sun. I set the saddle down by the tree trunk, then sat down beside it to wait.

My timing had been good. I had waited there barely an hour when I caught the sound of hoofs on the gravel road. So, he had kept to the high road, not cutting the corner through the forest. He was not hurrying, but riding easily, no doubt resting his horse. Nor was he alone. Bedwyr, hard on his heels, had perhaps been allowed to come up with him.

I walked out into the road and stood waiting for him.

Three horsemen came trotting through the forest, and down the gentle slope leading to the far side of the ford. They were all strangers; moreover, they were a kind of man who nowadays was rare enough. In times past the roads, especially those in the wilder lands to the north and west, were rife with danger for the lonely traveller, but Ambrosius, and Arthur after him, had swept the main posting-roads clear of outlaws and masterless men. But not quite, it seemed. These three had been soldiers; they still wore the leather armour of their calling, and two of them sported battered metal caps. The youngest of them, sprucer than the others, had stuck a sprig of scarlet berries behind one ear. All three were unshaven, and armed with knives and short-swords. The oldest of them, with streaks of grey in a heavy brown beard, had an ugly-looking cudgel strapped to his saddle. Their horses were sturdy mountain cobs, cream, brown and black, their hides thick with dirt and damp, but well fed, and powerful. It did not need any prophet's instinct to know that here were three dangerous men.

They halted their horses at the river's brink and looked me over. I stood my ground and returned the look. I had the knife at my belt, but my sword was with the saddle-bags. And flight, with my horse stripped and tethered, was out of the question. If truth be told, I was still no more than faintly apprehensive; there had been a time when no one, however wild and desperate, would have dared lay a finger on Merlin; and I suppose that the confidence of power was still with me.

They looked at one another, and a message passed. It was danger, then. The leader, he with the greying beard and the black horse, walked the beast forward a pace, so that the water swirled past its fetlocks. Then he turned, grinning, to his fellows.

"Why, look you, here's a brave fellow, disputing the ford with us. Or are you the Hermes, come to wish us godspeed? I must say, you're not what one expects of the Herm." This with a guffaw in which his fellows joined.

I moved aside from the centre of the road. "I'm afraid I can't claim any of his talents, gentlemen. Nor do I mean to dispute the way with you. When I heard you coming I took you for the outriders of the troop that is due this way very soon. Did you see any sign of troopers on the road?"

Another glance. The youngest – he of the cream cob and the woodbine spray – set his horse at the water and came splashing out beside me. "There was no one on the road," he said. "Troopers? What troopers would you be expecting? The High King himself, maybe?" He winked at his companions.

"The High King," I said, equably, "will be riding this way soon, by all accounts, and he likes the law of the roads looked to. So go your ways in peace, gentlemen, and let me go mine."

They were all through the ford now, ranged round me. They looked relaxed and pleasant enough, good-tempered, even. Brown-beard said: "Oh, we'll let you go, won't we, Red? Free as air to go, you'll be, good sir, free as air, and travelling light."

"Light as a feather," said Red, with a laugh. He was the one with the brown horse. He shifted the belt round from his thick thighs, so that the haft of his knife lay nearer to his hand. The youngest of the three was already moving towards the fallen pine where the saddle-bags lay.

I began to speak, but the leader kicked his horse in closer, dropped the reins on its withers, then suddenly reached down, catching hold of me by the neck of my robe. He gathered the stuff in a choking grip, and half lifted me towards him. He was immensely strong.

"So, who were you waiting for, eh? A troop, was it? Was that the truth, or were you lying to scare us off?"

The second man, Red, thrust his horse near on the other side. There was no faintest chance of escaping them. The third one had dismounted, and, without troubling to undo them, had a long knife out and was slitting the leather of the saddle-bags. He had not even glanced over his shoulder to see what his fellows did.

Red had his knife in his hand. "Of course he was lying," he said roughly. "There were no troops on the road. Nor any sign of them. And they wouldn't be coming by the forest track, Erec, you can be sure of that."

Erec reached back with his free hand and slipped the knobbed cudgel from its moorings. "Well, so it was a lie," he said. "You can do better than that, old man. Tell us who you are and where you're bound for. This troop you're talking about, where are they coming from?"

"If you let me go." I said with difficulty, for he was half choking me, "I will tell you. And tell your fellow to leave my things alone."

"Why, here's high crowing from an old rooster!" But he relaxed his hold, and let me stand again. "Give us the truth, then, and maybe do yourself a bit of good. Which way did you come, and where's this troop you were talking about? Who are you, and where are you bound?"

I began to straighten my clothes. My hands were shaking, but I managed to make my voice steady enough. I said: "You will do well to loose me, and save yourselves. I am Merlinus Ambrosius, called Merlin, the King's cousin, and I am bound for Camelot. A message has gone before me, and a troop of knights is riding this way to meet me. They should be close behind you. If you go west now, quickly –"

A great guffaw of laughter cut me off. Erec rocked in his saddle. "Hear that, Red? Balin, did you get it? This is Merlin, Merlin himself, and he's bound for the court at Camelot!"

"Well, he might be, at that," said Red, shaking with mirth. "Looks a proper skeleton, don't he? Straight from the tomb, he is, and that's for sure."

"And straight back to it." Suddenly savage, Erec seized me again and shook me violently.

A shout from Balin gave him pause. "Hey! Look here!"

Both men turned. "What have you got?"

"Enough gold to get us a month's food and good beds, and something to go in them, forby," called Balin, cheerfully. He threw the saddle-bag down to the ground, and held up his hand. Two of the jewels glinted.

Erec drew in his breath. "Well, whoever you are, our luck's in, it seems! Look in the other one, Balin. Come on, Red, let's see what he's got on him."

"If you harm me," I said, "be sure that the King –"

I stopped, as if a hand had been laid across my mouth. I had been standing there, perforce, hemmed between the two horses, staring up at the bearded face bent down over me, with the high bright sky behind him. Now, across that sky, with the sun striking bronze from its black gloss, went a raven. Flying low, silent for once, tilting and sidling on the air, went the bird of Hermes the messenger, the bird of death.

It told me what I had to do. Till now, instinctively, I had been playing for time, as any man will play, to ward off death. But if I succeeded, if I made the murderers pause and hold their hands, then Arthur, riding alone, and on a weary horse, with nothing in his heart but the thought of meeting me, would come on them there, three to one, in this lonely place. In a fight, I could not help him. But I could still serve him. I owed God a death, and I could give Arthur another life. I must send these brutes on their way, and quickly. If he came across my murdered body here, he would go after them, no doubt of that; but he would know what he was doing, and he would have help.

So I said nothing. Balin started on the other saddle-bag. Erec seized me again, dragging me close. Red came behind me, tearing at the belt that held my wallet, with the rest of my gold stitched into its lining. Above me the knotted bludgeon swung high.

If I reached for my own weapon, they might kill me sooner. My hand went back for the knife in my belt. From behind Red's hard hand caught and held my wrist, and the knife spun to the ground. The bones of my hand ground together. He thrust his sweating face over my shoulder. He was grinning. "Merlin, eh? A great enchanter like you could show us a thing or two, I'm sure. Go on then, save yourself, why don't you? Cast a spell and strike us dead."

The horses broke apart. Something flashed and drove like a light across the sky. The cudgel flew wide and fell. Erec's hand loosed me, so suddenly that I staggered, and fell forward against his horse. Bending above me still, the brown-bearded face wore a look of surprise. The eyes stared, fixed. The head, severed cleanly by that terrible, slashing blow, bounced on the horse's neck in a splatter of blood, then thudded to the ground. The body slumped slowly, almost gracefully, onto the cob's withers. A gush of blood, bright and steaming, flooded over the beast's shoulder and splashed down over me where I reeled, clinging to the breast-band. The horse screamed once, in terror, then reared and slashed out at the air, tore itself free, and bolted. The headless body bobbed and swayed for a bound or two before it pitched from the saddle to the road, still spouting blood.

I was thrown hard down on the grass. The cool dampness struck up through my hands, steadying me. My heart thumped; the treacherous blackness threatened, then withdrew. The ground was thudding and shaking to the beat of hoofs. I looked up.

He was fighting the two of them. He had come alone, on his big grey horse. He had outstripped Bedwyr and the knights, but neither he nor the stallion showed any trace of weariness. It was a wonder to me that the three murderers had not broken and fled at the very sight of him. He was lightly armed only – no shield, but a leather tunic stitched with metal phalerae, and a thick cloak twisted round his left arm. His head was bare. He had dropped the reins on the stallion's neck, and controlled him with knee and voice. The great horse reared and wheeled and struck like another battle-arm. And all around horse and King, like a shield of impenetrable light, whirled the flashing blade of the great sword that was mine and his; Caliburn, the King's sword of Britain.

Balin flung himself on his horse, and spurred, yelling, to his fellow's aid. A ribbon of leather flying from Arthur's tunic showed where one of them had slashed him from behind – while he was killing Brown-Beard, probably – but now, try as they might, they could not pass that deadly ring of shining metal, nor close in past the stallion's lashing hoofs.

"Out of the way," said the King, curtly, to me. The horses plunged and circled. I started to drag myself to my feet. It seemed to take a long time. My hands were slimy with blood, and my body shook. I found that I could not stand, but crawled instead to the fallen pine, and sat there. The air shook and clashed with battle, and I sat there, helpless, shaking, old, while my boy fought for his life and mine, and I could not summon even the mortal strength of a man to help him.

Something glinted near my foot. My knife, lying where Red had struck it from my hand. I reached for it. I still could not stand, but threw it as hard as I could at Red's back. It was a feeble throw, and missed him. But the flash of its passing made the brown horse flinch and swerve, and sent its rider's blow wide. With the slither and whine of metal, Caliburn caught the blade and flung it wider, then Arthur drove the great stallion in and killed Red with a blow through the heart.

There was a moment when the sword jammed and could not be withdrawn, and the body, falling, made a dead weight on the King's sword-arm. But the grey stallion knew about that, too. Balin, trying to wheel the cream cob to take the King in the rear, met teeth and armed hoofs. An upward slash laid the cream's shoulder open. It swerved, screaming, and turned against rein and spur to flee. But Balin – brave ruffian that he was – wrenched its head back by main force, just as the King dragged his sword clear of Red's body and wheeled back, right-handed, into fighting range.

I believe that, in that last moment, Balin recognised the King. But he was given no time to speak, much less beg for mercy. There was one more vicious, brief flurry, and Balin took Caliburn's point in his throat, and fell to the trampled and bloody grass. He writhed once, gasped, and drowned on a gush of blood. The cob, instead of running, now that it was no longer constrained, simply stood with head hanging and shaking legs, while the blood ran down its shoulder. The other horses had gone.

Arthur leaped down, wiped his sword on Balin's body, shook the folds of his cloak from his left arm, and came across to me, leading the grey. He touched my bloodstained shoulder.

"This blood. Is any of it yours?"

"No. And you?"

"Not a scratch," he said, cheerfully. He was breathing only a little faster than usual. "Though it wasn't quite a massacre. They were trained men, or so it seemed to me, when there was time to notice . . . Sit quietly for a moment; I'll get you some water."

He dropped the stallion's reins into my hand, reached to the pommel for the silver-mounted horn he carried there, then trod lightly towards the river. I heard his foot strike something. The quick stride stopped short, and he exclaimed. I turned my head. He was staring down at the wreck of one of my saddle-bags, where, in the scatter of spilled food and slashed leather, lay a strip of torn velvet, heavily stitched with gold. One of the jewels that Balin had torn from it lay winking beside it in the grass.

Arthur swung round. He had gone quite white.

"By the Light! It's you!"

"Who else? I thought you knew."

"*Merlin!*" Now he really was trying for breath. He came back to stand over me. "I thought – I hardly had time to look – just those murdering rascals butchering an old man – unarmed, I thought, and poor, by the look of the horse and trappings . . ." He went on both knees beside me. "Ah, Merlin, Merlin . . ."

And the High King of all Britain laid his head down on my knee, and was silent.

After a while he stirred and lifted his head.

"I got your token, and the message from the courier. But I don't think I really quite believed him. When he first spoke and showed me the Dragon it seemed right . . . I suppose I'd never thought you could really die, like mortal men . . . but on the way here, riding alone, with nothing to do but think – well, it ceased to be real. I don't know what I pictured; myself ending up again, perhaps, in front of that blocked cave-mouth, where we buried you alive." I felt a shiver go through him. "Merlin, what has happened? When we left you for dead, sealed in the cave, it was the malady, of course, giving the appearance of death: I realise that now. But afterwards? When you woke, alone and weighed down with your own grave-clothes? God knows, that would be enough to bring another death! What did you do? How survive, locked alone in the hill? How escape? And when? You must have known how sorely I was bereft. Where have you been all this while?"

"Not so great a while. When I escaped, you were abroad. They told me you had gone to Brittany. So I said nothing, and lodged with Stilicho, my old servant, who keeps the mill near Maridunum, and waited for your return. I'll tell you everything soon – if you will get me that drink of water."

"Fool that I am, I was forgetting!" He jumped up and ran to the river. He filled the horn and brought it, then went down on one knee to hold it for me.

I shook my head and took it from him. "Thank you, but I'm quite steady now. It's nothing. I was not hurt. I am ashamed to have been of so little help."

"You gave me all I needed."

"Which was not much," I said, half laughing. "I could almost feel sorry for those wretches, thinking they had an easy kill, and bringing Arthur himself down on them like a thunderbolt. I did warn them, but who could blame them for not believing me?"

"You mean to tell me they knew who you were? And still used you like that?"

"I told you, they didn't believe me. Why should they? Merlin was dead. And the only power I have now is in your name – and they didn't believe that, either. 'An old man, unarmed and poor.' " I quoted him, smiling. "Why, you didn't know me yourself. Am I so much changed?"

He considered me. "It's the beard, and, yes, you are quite grey now. But if I had once looked at your eyes . . ." He took the horn from me and got to his feet. "Oh, yes, it is you. In all that ever mattered, you are unchanged. Old? Yes, we must all grow old. Age is nothing but the sum of life. And you are alive, and back with me here. By the great God of heaven, I have you back with me. What should I fear now?"

He drained the horn, replaced it, and looked around him. "I suppose I had better tidy up this mess. Are you really all right now? Could you tend my horse for me? I think he could be watered now."

I led the stallion down to the water, and with it the cream cob, which was grazing quietly, and made no attempt to escape me. When they had drunk I tethered them, then got some salve from my pack and doctored the cut on the cob's shoulder. It rolled an eye back at me, and the skin of its shoulder flickered, but it showed no sign of pain. The cut bled still, but sluggishly, and the beast was not walking lame. I loosed the girths of both horses, and left them grazing while I retrieved the scattered contents of my saddle-bag.

Arthur's way of clearing up the "mess" – three men violently dead – was to haul the bodies by their heels to a decent hiding-place at the forest's edge. The severed head he picked up by the beard and slung it after. He was whistling while he did it, a gay little tune I recognised as one of the soldiers' marching songs, which was frank, not to say over-explicit, about the sexual prowess of their leader. Then he looked around him.

"The next rain will clear some of the blood away. And even if I had a spade or mattock, I'm damned if I'd spend the time and trouble in digging that carrion in. Let the ravens have them. Meanwhile, we might as well impound their horses; I see they've stopped to graze away up the road there. I'll have to wash the blood off first, or I'll never get near them. You'd better abandon that cloak of yours, it'll never be the same again. Here, you can wear mine. No, I insist. It's an order. Here."

He dropped it over the pine log, then went down to the river and washed. While he remounted and went cantering up the road after the other horses, I stripped off my cloak, which was already stiffening with blood, and washed myself, then shook out Arthur's cloak of royal purple, and put it on. My own I rolled up and pitched after the dead men into the undergrowth.

Arthur came back at a trot, leading the thieves' horses.

"Now, where is this inn with the bush of holly?"

8

The innkeeper's boy was out in the road watching for me. I suppose he had been posted there to give the goodwife warning of when the "meal fit for the King's court" would be wanted. When he saw us coming, two men and five horses, he stood staring awhile, then went with a skip and a jump back into the inn. When we were still seventy paces short of the place, the innkeeper himself came out to see.

He recognised Arthur almost straight away. What drew his eye first was the quality of the King's horse. Then came a long, summing look at the rider, and the man was on his knee out on the road.

"Get up, man," said the King, cheerfully. "I've been hearing good things of the house you keep here, and I'm looking forward to trying your hospitality. There's been a little skirmish down by the ford – nothing deadly, just enough to get up a bit of an appetite. But that will have to wait a little. Look after my friend here first, will you, and if your goodwife can clean his clothes, and someone can tend to the horses, we'll cheerfully wait for the meal." Then, as the man began to stammer something about the poverty of his house, and the lack of accommodation, "As to that, man, I'm a soldier, and there've been times when any shelter from the weather could be counted a luxury. From what I've heard of your tavern, it's a haven indeed. And now, may we come in? Wine we cannot wait for, nor fire . . ."

We had both in a very short time. The innkeeper, once he had recovered himself, came to terms quickly with the royal invasion, and very sensibly set all aside except the immediate service that was needed. The boy came running to take the horses, and the innkeeper himself piled logs on the fire and brought wine, then helped me out of my soiled and blood-splashed robes, and brought hot water, and fresh clothes from my baggage roll. Then, at Arthur's bidding, he locked the inn door against casual passers-by, and got himself off to the kitchen, there, one imagined, to instil a panic frenzy into his excellent wife.

When I had changed, and Arthur had washed, and spread his cloak to the blaze, he poured wine for me, and took his place at the other side of the hearth. Though he had travelled fast and far, and with a fight at the end of it, he looked as fresh as if he had newly risen from his bed. His eyes were bright as a boy's, and colour sprang red in his cheeks. Between the joy of seeing me again, and the stimulus of the danger past, he seemed a youth again. When at length the goodwife and her husband came in with the food, making some ado about setting the board and carving the capons, he received them with gay affability, so easily that, by the time we had done, and they had withdrawn, the woman had so far forgotten his rank as to scream with laughter at one of his jests, and cap it herself. Then her husband pulled at her gown, and she ran out, but laughing still.

At last we were alone. The short afternoon drew in. Soon it would be lamp-lighting. We went back to our places one on either side of the blaze. I think we both felt tired, and sleepy, but neither of us could have rested until we had exchanged such news as could not be spoken of in front of our hosts. The King had, he told me, ridden the whole way with only a few hours' respite for sleep, and to rest his horse.

"For," he said, "if the courier's message, and the token he brought, told a true tale, then you were safe, and would wait for me. Bedwyr and the others came up with me, but they, too, stopped to rest. I told them to stay back, and give me a few hours' grace."

"That could have cost you dear."

"With that carrion?" He spoke contemptuously. "If they hadn't caught you unarmed and unawares, you could have dealt with them yourself."

And time was, I thought, when, without even a dagger in my hand, I could have dealt with them. If Arthur was thinking the same, he gave no sign of it. I said: "It's true that they were hardly worth your sword. And talking of that, what have I been hearing about the theft of Caliburn? Some tale about your sister Morgan?"

He shook his head. "That's over, so let it wait. What's more to the point now is that I should know what has been happening to you. Tell me. Tell me everything. Don't leave anything out."

So I told my story. The day drew in, and beyond the small, deep-set windows the sky darkened to indigo, then to slate. The room was quiet, but for the crack and flutter of the flames. A cat crept from some corner and curled on the hearth, purring. It was a strange setting for the tale I had to tell, of death and costly burial, of fear and loneliness and desperate survival, of murder foiled and rescue finally accomplished. He listened as so many times before, intent, lost in the tale, frowning over some parts of it, but relaxed into the warmth and contentment of the evening. This was another of the times that comes vividly back to me in memory whenever I think of him; the quiet room, the King listening, the firelight moving red on his cheek and lighting the thick fall of dark hair, and the dark watching eyes, intent on the story I was telling him. But with a difference now: this was a man listening with a purpose; summing up what he was told, and judging, ready to act.

At the end he stirred. "That fellow, the grave-robber – we must find him. It shouldn't be hard, if he's cadging drinks from that story all over Maridunum . . . I wonder who it was who heard you the first time? And the miller, Stilicho; I've no doubt you'll want me to leave that to you?"

"Yes. But if you could ride over that way some time, perhaps when you're next in Caerleon? Mai will die of terror and ecstasy, but Stilicho will take it as no more than his due, who served the great enchanter . . . and then boast about it for the rest of his days."

"Of course," he said. "I was thinking, while I was on the road; we'll go straight on from here to Caerleon now. I imagine you're not yet ready to go back to court –"

"Not now, or ever. Or to Applegarth. I have left that for good." I did not add "to Nimuë"; her name had not been mentioned by either of us. So carefully had we avoided it that it seemed to ring through every sentence that was spoken. I went on: "I've no doubt you'll fight me to the death over this, but I want to go back to Bryn Myrddin. I'll be more than glad to stay with you in Caerleon until it can be made ready again."

Of course he objected, and we argued for a while, but in the end he let me have my way, on the (very reasonable) condition that I did not live there alone, but was cared for by servants. "And if you must have your precious solitude, then you shall have it. I shall build a place for the servants, out of your sight and below the cliff; but they must be there."

" 'And that is an order?' " I quoted, smiling.

"Certainly . . . There'll be time enough to see about it; I'll spend Christmas at Caerleon, and you with me. I take it you won't insist on going back there till the winter is past?"

"No."

"Good. Now, there's something in your story that doesn't agree with the facts . . . that business you described in Segontium." He glanced up, smiling. "So that was where you found Caliburn? In the soldiers' shrine of the Light? Well, it tallies. I remember that you told me, years ago, just before we left the Forest, that there were other treasures there still. You spoke of a grail. I still remember what you said. But the gift Morgause brought to me was no treasure of Macsen's. It was silver goods – cups and brooches and torques, the sort of thing they fashion in the far north. Very handsome, but not as you described the treasure to me."

"No. I did catch a glimpse of it, there in the vision. It was not Macsen's treasure. But the shepherd boy was certain that it was taken, and I believe him."

"You don't know?"

"No. How could I, without power?"

"But you had this vision. You watched Morgause and the boys accost me at Camelot. You saw the silver treasure she gave me. You knew the courier had come, and that I was on my way to you."

I shook my head. "That was not power, not as you and I have known it. That is Sight only, and that, I think, I shall have until I die. Every village sibyl has it, in some degree or another. Power is more than that; it is doing and speaking with knowledge; it is bidding without thought, and knowing that one will be obeyed. That has gone. I don't repine now." I hesitated. "Nor, I hope, do you? I have heard tales of Nimuë, how she is the new Lady of the Lake, the mistress of the Island's shrine. I am told that men call her the King's enchantress, and that she has done you service?"

"Indeed, yes." He looked away from me, leaning forward to adjust a log on the burning pile. "It was she who dealt with the theft of Caliburn."

I waited, but he left it there. I said at length: "I understood she was still in the north. She is well?"

"Very well." The log was burning to his satisfaction. He set his chin on a fist, and stared at the fire. "So. If Morgause had the treasure with her when she embarked, it will be somewhere on the Island. My people saw to it that she did not go ashore between Segontium and her landing there. She lodged with Melwas, so it should not be beyond me to have it traced. Morgause is being held under guard until I get back. If she refuses to speak, the children will hardly be proof against questioning. The younger ones are too innocent to see any harm in telling the truth. Children see everything; they will know where she left the treasure."

"I understand that you're going to keep them?"

"You saw that? Yes. You would also see that your courier came just in time to save Morgause."

I thought of my own effort to reach him with my dreaming will, when I thought she would use the stolen grail against him. "You were going to kill her?"

"Certainly, for killing you."

"Without proof?"

"I don't need proof to have a witch put to death."

I raised a brow at him, and quoted what had been said at the opening of the Round Hall: " 'No man nor woman shall be harmed unjustly, or punished without trial or manifest proof of their trespass.' "

He smiled. "Well, all right. I did have proof. I had your own word that she tried to kill you."

"So you said. I thought you said it to frighten her. I told you nothing."

"I know. And why not? Why did you keep it secret from me that it was her poison that sent you to your death in the Wild Forest, and then left you with the sickness that was almost your death again?"

"You've answered that yourself. You would have killed her, after the Wild Forest. But she was the mother of those young sons, and heavy with another, and I knew that one day they would come to

you, and become, in time, your faithful servants. So, I did not tell
you. Who did?"

"Nimuë."

"I see. And she knew, how? By divination?"

"No. From you. Something you said in your delirium."

Everything, she had taken from me; every last secret. I said
merely: "Ah, yes . . . And do I take it that she also found Mordred
for you? Or did Morgause bring him into the open, once Lot and I
were dead?"

"No. He was still hidden. I understand that he was lodged
somewhere in the Orkney Islands. Nimuë had nothing to do with
that. It was by the purest chance that I heard of him. I got a letter. A
goldsmith from York, who had done work for Morgause before,
travelled that way with some jewels he hoped to sell her. These
fellows, as you know, get into every corner of the kingdom, and see
everything."

"Not Beltane."

His head came up, surprised. "You know him?"

"Yes. He's as good as blind. He has to travel with a servant –"

"Casso," said the King, then, as I stared: "I told you I got a
letter."

"From *Casso?*"

"Yes. It seems he was in Dunpeldyr when – ah, I see, that was
when you met them? Then you will know they were there on the
night of the massacre. Casso, it appears, saw and heard a good deal
of what went on; people talk in front of a slave, and he must have
understood more than he was meant to. His master could never be
brought to believe that Morgause had anything to do with events so
dreadful, so went up to Orkney to try his luck again. Casso, being
less credulous, watched and listened, and managed at length to
locate the child who went missing on the night of the massacre. He
sent a message straight to me. As it happened, I had just heard from
Nimuë that it was Morgause who caused your death. I sent for her,
and saw to it that she brought Mordred with her. Why are you
looking so dumbfounded?"

"On two counts. What should make a slave – Casso was a
quarryman's labourer when I first found him – write 'straight to'
the High King?"

"I forgot I had not told you; he served me once before. Do you remember when I went north into Lothian to attack Aguisel? And how hard it was to find some way of destroying that dirty jackal without bringing Tydwal and Urien down on my head, swearing vengeance? Some word of this must have got around, because I got a message from this same slave, evidence – with facts that could be proved – of something he had seen when he was in Aguisel's service. Aguisel had misused a page, one of Tydwal's young sons, and then murdered him. Casso told us where to find the body. We found it; and others besides. The child had been killed just as Casso had told us."

"And afterwards," I said drily, "Aguisel cut out the tongues of the slaves who had witnessed it."

"You mean the man is dumb? Well, that might account for the free way men seem to talk in front of him. Aguisel paid dearly for failing to make sure he could not read or write."

"Neither he could. When I knew him in Dunpeldyr he was both dumb and helpless. It was I who, for a service he had done me – or rather, for no reason that I remember, except perhaps the prompting of the god – arranged to have him taught."

Arthur, smiling, raised his cup to me. "Did I call it 'pure chance'? I should have remembered who I was talking to. I rewarded Casso after the Aguisel affair, of course, and told him where to send any other information. I believe he has been useful once or twice. Then, over this last thing, he sent straight to me."

We spoke of it for a while longer, then I came back to present matters. "What will you do with Morgause now?"

"I shall have to settle that, with your help, when I get back. Meanwhile I shall send orders that she is to be kept under guard, at the nunnery at Amesbury. The boys will stay with me, and I'll have them brought down to Caerleon for Christmas. Lot's sons will be no problem; they're young enough to find life at court exciting, and old enough now to do without Morgause. As for Mordred, he shall have his chance. I will do the same for him."

I said nothing. In the pause, the cat purred, suddenly loud, and then stopped short on a sighing breath, and slept.

"Well," said Arthur, "what would you have me do? He is in my protection now, so – even if I could ever have harmed him –

I cannot kill him. I haven't had time to think this thing through, and there'll be time enough later to discuss it with you. But it has always seemed to me that, once the boy had survived Lot's murderous purge, I would sooner have him near me, and under my eye, than hidden somewhere in the kingdom, with the threat that that might entail. Say you agree with me."

"I do. Yes."

"So, if I keep him by me, and grant him the birthright that he must have thought he would never see –"

"I doubt if that has crossed his mind," I said. "I don't think she has told him who he is."

"So? Then I shall tell him myself. Better still. He'll know that I needn't have accepted him. Merlin, it might be well. You and I both remember what it was like to live our youth out as unfathered bastards, and then to be told we were of Ambrosius' blood. And who am I to take on me yet again the wish for my son's death? Once was too much. God knows I paid for it." He looked away again into the flames. There was a bitter line to his mouth. After a while he lifted a shoulder. "You asked about Caliburn. It seems that my sister Morgan took herself a lover; he was one of my knights, a man called Accolon, a good fighter and a fine man – but one who could never say no to a woman. When King Urbgen was here with Morgan, she cast her eyes on Accolon, and soon had him at her girdle, like a greyhound fawning. Before she came south she had got some northern smith to make a copy of Caliburn, and while she was here in Camelot she managed to get Accolon to exchange this for the sword itself. She must have reckoned, in a time of peace, on getting herself free of the court and back to the north before the loss was discovered. I don't know what favours she granted Accolon, but certainly when she went north again with King Urbgen, Accolon took leave and went with them."

"But why did she do this?"

His quick, surprised look made me realise how rarely I had had to ask such a question. "Oh, the usual reason: ambition. She had some idea of putting her husband on the high throne of Britain with herself as his queen. As for Accolon, I'm not sure what she promised him, but whatever it was, it cost him his life. It should have cost hers, too, but there was no proof, and she is Urbgen's wife. Her being my sister should not have helped her, but he knew nothing of the plot, and I cannot afford to have him as my enemy."

"How did she hope to get away with it?"

"You had gone," he said simply. "She must have had word from Morgause that you were ailing, and she was making ready for her time of greatness. She reckoned that any man who held the sword could command a following, and if the King of Rheged were to raise it . . . Before that, of course, I was to have been killed. Accolon tried. He picked a quarrel and fought me. It was the substitute sword, of course; the metal was brittle as glass. As soon as I tested it for use, I knew there was something wrong, but it was too late. At the first clash it broke off short below the hilt."

"And?"

"Bedwyr and the rest were shouting 'treachery', but they hardly needed to. I could see from Accolon's face that treachery was there. For all that his sword was still whole, and mine was broken, I think he was afraid. I drove the hilt into his face, and killed him with my dagger. I don't think he made any resistance. Perhaps he was a true man, after all. I like to think so."

"And the true sword? How did you know where it was?"

"Nimuë," he said. "It was she who told me what had happened. Do you remember that day, at Applegarth, when she told me to beware Morgan and the sword?"

"Yes. I thought she must mean Morgause."

"So did I. But she was right. All the time Morgan was at court, Nimuë hardly left her side. I wondered why, because it was obvious there was no love lost between them." He gave a rueful little laugh. "I'm afraid I took it as a women's quarrel . . . she's not overly fond of Guinevere, either . . . but she was right about Morgan. The witch corrupted her when she was no more than a girl. How Nimuë got the sword back I don't know. She sent it down from Rheged with an armed escort. I haven't seen her since she went north."

I started to ask something more, but he suddenly raised his head, listening.

"And here comes Bedwyr, if I'm not mistaken. We've had little enough time together, Merlin, but there will be other times. As God is good, there will be other times." He got to his feet, put his hands down, and raised me. "Now we have talked enough. You look exhausted. Will you go to your rest now, and leave me to face Bedwyr and the others, and give them the news? I warn you, it won't be a quiet party. They're likely to clean our good host out of anything drinkable he has in his cellars, and take the night to drink it . . ."

But I stayed with him to receive the knights, and afterwards to drink with them. Nobody, all through the long, noisy celebration, mentioned Nimuë to me, and I did not ask again.

9

We spent another full day resting at the "Bush of Holly". A party went back to the ford to bury the dead men, and from there on to Camelot with messages from the King. Another party was sent to Caerleon to give warning of the King's approach. Then, while I rested, the young men went hunting. Their day's sport provided an excellent dinner, and their servants and pages, who came up with us that day, helped the innkeeper and his wife cook and serve it. Where everyone slept that night, I have no idea; I suspect that the horses were turned out, and that the stable was even fuller than the inn. On the following day, to our hosts' evident regret, the royal party moved off for Caerleon.

Even after the building of Camelot, Caerleon had kept its status as Arthur's western stronghold. We rode in on a bright, windy day, with the Dragon standards snapping and rippling from the roofs, and the streets leading up to the fortress gates crowded with people. At my own insistence, I rode cloaked and hooded, and to the rear of the party, rather than beside the King. Arthur had finally been brought to accept my decision not to take my place near him again; one cannot go back on an abdication, and mine had been complete. He still had not mentioned Nimuë's part in that, though he must have been wondering (along with others, who also avoided mentioning her name to me) just how much of my power she had managed to assume. Of all people, she should have "seen" that I was above ground again, and with the King; should have known, in fact, that I had been put still living into my tomb . . .

But no one asked questions, and I was not prepared to supply what I believed to be the answers.

In Caerleon they had allotted royal chambers to me, next to

Arthur's own. Two young pages, eyeing me with the liveliest curiosity, conducted me to the rooms through corridors crowded with bustling servants. Many of them knew me, and all had obviously heard some version of the strange story; some merely hurried past, making the sign against strong enchantment, but others came forward with greetings and offers of service. At last we reached my rooms, sumptuous apartments where a chamberlain awaited me, and showed me a splendid array of clothing sent by the King for me to choose from, with jewels from the royal coffers. A little to his disappointment I set aside the cloth of gold and silver, the peacock and the scarlet and the azure, and chose a warm robe of dark red wool, with a girdle of gilded leather, and sandals of the same. Then, saying, "I will send light, my lord, and water for your washing," he withdrew. A little to my surprise he signed to the two boys to leave the chamber with him, and left me there unattended.

It was already past the time of lamp-lighting. I went over to the window, where the sky was deepening slowly from red to purple, and sat down to wait for the pages to bring light.

I did not look round when the door opened. The flickering light of a cresset stole into the chamber, sending the evening sky receding, darkening beyond its weak young stars. The page moved softly round the room, touching lamp after lamp with flame, until the chamber glowed.

I felt tired after the ride, and heavy with reaction. It was time I roused myself, and let myself be made ready for the feasting tonight. The boy had gone out to set the cresset back in its iron bracket on the corridor wall. The chamber door was ajar.

I got to my feet. "Thank you," I began. "Now, if of your goodness –"

I stopped. It was no page. It was Nimuë who came swiftly in, then stood backed against the door, watching me. She was clad in a long gown of grey, stitched with silver, and there was silver in her hair, which was loose, and flowing down over her shoulders. Her face was white, and her eyes wide and dark, and while I stood gazing, they suddenly brimmed over with tears.

Then she was across the room and had me fast in her arms, and was laughing and crying and kissing me, with words tumbling out that made no sense at all except the one, that I was alive, and that all the time she had been grieving for me as dead.

"Magic," she kept saying, in a wondering, half-scared voice, "it's magic, stronger than any I could ever know. And you told me you had given it all to me. I should have known. I should have known. Ah, Merlin, Merlin . . ."

Whatever had passed, whatever had kept her from me, or blinded her to the truth, none of it mattered. I found myself holding her close, with her head pressed against my breast, and my cheek on her hair, while she repeated over and over, like a child: "It's you. It's really you. You've come back. It is magic. You must still be the greatest enchanter in all the world."

"It was only the malady, Nimuë. It deceived you all. It was not magic. I gave all that to you."

She lifted her head. Her face was tragic. "Yes, and how you gave it! I only pray that you cannot remember! You had told me to learn all that you had to tell me. You had said that I must build on every detail of your life; that after your death I must be Merlin . . . And you were leaving me, slipping from me in sleep . . . I had to do it, hadn't I? Force the last of your power from you, even though with it I took the last of your strength? I did it by every means I knew – cajoled, stormed, threatened, gave you cordials and brought you back to answer me again and again – when what I should have done, had you been any other man, was to let you sleep, and go in peace. And because you were Merlin, and no other man, you roused yourself in pain and answered me, and gave me all you had. So minute by minute I weakened you, when it seems to me now that I might have saved you." She slid her hands up to my breast, and lifted swimming grey eyes. "Will you tell me something truthfully? Swear by the god?"

"What is it?"

"Do you remember it, when I hung about you and tormented you to your death, like a spider sucking the life from a honey-bee?"

I put my hands up to cover hers. I looked straight into the beautiful eyes, and lied. "My darling girl, I remember nothing of that time but words of love, and God taking me peacefully into his hand. I will swear it if you like."

Relief swept into her face. But still she shook her head, refusing to be comforted. "But then, even all the power and knowledge you gave me could not show me that we had buried you living, and send me back to get you out. Merlin, I should have known, I should have known! I dreamed again and again, but the dreams were full of confusion. I went back once to Bryn Myrddin, did you know? I went to the cave, but the door was blocked still, and I called and called, but there was no sound —"

"Hush, hush." She was shivering. I pulled her closer, and bent my head and kissed her hair. "It's over. I am here. When you came back for me, I must have been still in the trance. Nimuë, what happened was the will of the god. If he had wanted to save me from the tomb, he would have spoken to you. Now, he has brought me back in his own time, and for that, he saved me from being put quick into the ground, or given to the flames. You must accept it all, and thank him, as I do."

She shivered again. "That was what the High King wanted. He would give you, he said, a pyre as high as an emperor's, so that your death would be a beacon to the living the length and breadth of the land. He was wild with grief, Merlin. I could hardly make him listen to me. But I told him I had had a dream, and that you yourself had said that you wished to be laid in your own hollow hill, and left in peace to become part of the land you loved." She put a hand up to brush tears from her face. "And it was true. I did have such a dream, one of many. But even so, I failed you. Who did what I should have done, and helped you to escape? What happened?"

"Come over here, to the fire, and I'll tell you. Your hands are cold. Come, we have a little time, I think, before we need go into the hall."

"The King will stay for us," she said. "He knows I am here. He sent me to you."

"Did he?" But I put that aside for the present. In a corner of the room a brazier burned red in front of a low couch covered with rugs and skins. We sat side by side in the warm glow, and, to her eager questions, I told my story yet again.

By the time I had finished her distress was gone, and a little colour had crept back into her cheeks. She sat close in my arm, with one of my hands held tightly in both her own. Magician or mortal man, there was no shadow of doubt in my mind that the joy she showed was as real as the glow of the brazier that warmed us both. Time had run back. But not quite: mortal man or magician, I could sense secrets still.

Meantime she listened and exclaimed, and held my hand tightly, and presently, when I had done, she took up the story.

"I told you about the dream I had. It made me uneasy; I began to wonder, even, if you had been truly dead when we left you in the cave. But there had seemed no doubt; you had lain so long without movement, and seemingly without breath, and then all the doctors declared you dead. So in the end we left you there. Then, when the dreams drove me back to the cave, all seemed normal. Then other dreams, other visions, came, which crowded that one out and confused it. . ."

She had moved away from me while she was speaking, though she still held my hand between her own. She lay back against the cushions at the end of the couch, looking away from me, into the heart of the glowing charcoal.

"Morgan," I suggested, "and the theft of the sword?"

She gave me a quick glance. "I suppose the King told you about that? Yes. You heard how the sword was stolen. I had to leave Camelot, and follow Morgan, and take back the sword. Even there, the god was with me. While I was in Rheged a knight came there from the south; he was travelling to visit the queen, and at night, in Urbgen's hall, he told a strange tale. He was Bagdemagus – Morgan's kinsman, and Arthur's. You remember him?"

"Yes. His son was sick two summers back, and I treated him. He lived, but was left with an inflammation of the eyes."

She nodded. "You gave him some salve, and told him to use the same if the eyes troubled him again. You said it was blended with some herb you had at Bryn Myrddin."

"Yes. It was wild clary, that I brought back from Italy. I had a supply at Bryn Myrddin. But how did he think he was going to get it?"

"He thought you meant that it grew there. He may have thought you had planted a garden, as we did at Applegarth. Of course he knew that you were buried there in the hill. He didn't admit to us that he was afraid, but I think he must have been. Well, he told us his story, how he had ridden across the hilltop, and heard music coming seemingly up out of the earth. But then his horse bolted in terror, and he didn't dare go back. He said he hadn't told anyone his story, because he was ashamed of his flight, and afraid of being laughed at; but then, he said, just before he came north, he had heard some tale in Maridunum about a fellow who had seen and spoken with your ghost . . . Well, you know who that was, your grave-robber. Taken both together, and along with my persistent dreams, the story spoke aloud to me. You were alive, and in the cave. I would have left Luguvallium that night, but something else happened that forced me to stay."

She glanced across at me, as if waiting for me to nod, knowing what was to come. But I said merely: "Yes?"

There was the same brief flash of surprise that Arthur had shown, then she bit her lip, and explained.

· "Morgause arrived, with the boys. All five. I was hardly a welcome guest, as you may guess, but Urbgen was civility itself, and Morgan was afraid of what she had done, and almost clung to me. I believe she thought, as long as I was there, that Urbgen's anger wouldn't be vented on her. And of course, I suppose she hoped that I might intercede with Arthur. But Morgause . . ." She lifted her shoulders as if with cold.

"Did you see her?"

"Briefly. I could not stay there with her. I took my leave, and let them think I was going south, but I did not leave Luguvallium. I sent my page, secretly, to speak with Bagdemagus, and he came to see me at my lodgings. He's a good man, and he owed you his son's life. I did not tell him that I believed you were still living. I told him merely that Morgause had been your enemy, and your bane, and that Morgan had showed herself a witch also, and the enemy of the King. I begged him to spy, if he could, on their counsels, and report to me. You can be sure that I had already tried to reach Morgause's mind myself, and had failed. All I could hope for was that the sisters might talk together, and something could be learned from that about the drug that had been used on you. If my dream was right, and you still lived, the knowledge might help me save you yet. If not, I would have more evidence to give the King, and procure Morgause's death." She lifted her hand to my cheek. Her eyes were sombre. "I sat there in my lodgings waiting for him to come back, and knowing all the time that you might be dying, alone in the tomb. I tried to reach you, or even just to see, but whenever I tried to see you, and the hill, and the tomb, light would break across the vision and dash it aside, and there, moving down the light, floated a grail, clouded like a moon hidden in storm or mist. Then it would vanish, and pain and loss would break through the dream till I woke distracted, and crying, through the longing and the sorrow, to dream again."

"So you were warned of that? My poor child, left to guard such a treasure . . . Did Bagdemagus warn you that Morgause had heard of it, and meant to steal it?"

"What?" She looked at me blankly. "What do you mean? What had Morgause to do with the grail? It would have soiled the god himself if she had even looked at it. How was she to know where to find it?"

"I don't know. But she took it. I was told so, by someone who watched her do it."

"Then you were told a lie," said Nimuë roundly. "I took it myself."

"*It was you who took Macsen's treasure?*"

"Indeed it was." She sat up, glowing. In her eyes two little braziers, reflected, shone and glittered. The candid grey eyes looked, with the red points of light, like cat's eyes, or witch's. "You told me yourself where it lay buried; do you remember that? Or were you already gone into your own mists, my dear?"

"I remember."

She said soberly: "You told me that power was a hard master. It was the hardest thing I have ever done, to go to Segontium, instead of travelling south again to Bryn Myrddin. But in the end I knew I had been bidden to do it, so I went. I took two of my servants, men I could trust, and found the place. It had changed. The shrine had gone, under a landslip, but I took the bearings you had given me, and we dug there. It might have taken a long time, but we had help."

"A dirty little shepherd boy, who could hold a hazel stick over the earth, and tell you where the treasure was hidden."

Her eyes danced. "So, why do I trouble to tell you my story? Yes. He came and showed us, and we dug down, and took the box away. I went up into the fortress then, and spoke with the Commandant, and slept there that night, with a guard on my room. And during the night as I lay in my bed, with that box beneath it, the visions came teeming. I knew that you were alive, and free, and that you would soon be with the King. So in the morning I asked for an escort to take the treasure south, and set off for Caerleon."

"And so missed me by two days," I said.

"Missed you? Where?"

"Did you think I 'saw' the shepherd boy in the fire? No, I was there." I told her then, briefly, about my stay in Segontium, and my visit to the vanished shrine. "So when the boy told me about you and your two servants, like a fool I assumed it was Morgause. He didn't describe the woman, except that she —" I paused, and looked across at her with raised brows. "He said she was a queen, and the servants had royal badges. That was why I assumed —"

I stopped. Her hand, holding mine, had clenched suddenly. The laughter in her eyes died; she looked at me fixedly, with a strange mixture of appeal and dread. It did not need the Sight to guess the part of the story that she had not told me, nor why Arthur and the rest had avoided speaking of her to me. She had not usurped my power, or had a hand in trying to destroy me: all she had done, once the old enchanter had gone, was to take a young man to her bed.

I seemed to have been expecting this moment for a very long time. I smiled, and asked her, gently: "Who is he, the king of yours?"

The red rushed into her cheeks. I saw the tears sting her eyes again. "I should have told you straight away. They said they hadn't told you. Merlin, I didn't dare."

"Don't look like that, my dear. What we had, we had, and one cannot drink the same draught of elixir twice. If I had still been half a magician, I should have known long ago. Who is he?"

"Pelleas."

I knew him, a young prince, handsome and kind, with a sort of gaiety about him that would help to offset the haunted sombreness that sometimes hung around her. I spoke of him, commending him, and in a while she grew calmer, and began, with growing ease, to tell me about her marriage. I listened, and watched, and had time, now, to mark the changes in her; changes, I thought, due to the power that she had had so drastically to assume. My gentle Ninian had gone, with me into the mists. There was an edge to this Nimuë that had not been there before; something quietly formidable, a kind of honed brightness, like a weapon's edge. And in her voice, at times, sounded a subtle echo of the deeper tones that the god used, when, with authority and power, he descends to mortal speech. These attributes had once been mine. But I, accepting them, had taken no lover. I found myself hoping, for Pelleas' sake, that he was a strong-minded young man.

"Yes," said Nimuë, "he is."

I started out of my thoughts. She was watching me, her head on one side, her eyes alight once more with laughter.

I laughed with her, then put out my arms. She came into them, and lifted her mouth. I kissed her, once with passion, and once with love, and then I let her go.

10

Christmas at Caerleon. Pictures come crowding back to me, sun and snow and torchlight, full of youth and laughter, of bravery and fulfilment and time won back from oblivion. I have only to shut my eyes; no, not even that; I need only glance into the fire and they are here with me, all of them.

Nimuë, bringing Pelleas, who treated me with deference, and her with love, but who was a king and a man. "She belongs to the King," he said, "and then to me. And I – well, it's the same, isn't it? I am his before ever I was hers. Which of us, in the sight of God and King, is ever his own man?"

Bedwyr, coming on me one evening down beside the river, which slipped along, swollen and slate-grey, between its winter banks. A fleet of swans were proving the mud at the water's edge among the reeds. Snow had begun to fall, small and light, floating like swansdown through the still air. "They told me you had come this way," said Bedwyr. "I came to take you back. The King stays for you. Will you come now? It's cold, and will get colder." Then, as we walked back together: "There's news of Morgause," he said. "She has been sent north into Lothian, to the nunnery at Caer Eidyn. Tydwal will see to it that she's kept fast there. And there's talk of Queen Morgan's being sent to join her. They say that King Urbgen finds it hard to forgive her attempt to embroil him in treachery, and he's afraid that if he keeps her by him the taint will cling, to him and to his sons. Besides, Accolon was her lover. So the talk goes that Urbgen will put her away. He has sent to Arthur for permission. He'll get it, too. I think Arthur will feel more comfortable with both his loving sisters safely shut up, and a good long way away. It was Nimuë's suggestion." He laughed, looking at me sideways. "Forgive me, Merlin, but now that the King's enemies are women, perhaps it is better that he has a woman to deal with them. And if you ask me, you'll be well out of it . . ."

Guinevere, sitting at her loom one bright morning, with sun on the snow outside, and a caged bird singing on the sill beside her. Her hands lay idle among the coloured threads, and the lovely head turned to watch, down beside the moat, the boys at play. "They might be my own sons," she said. But I saw that her eyes did not follow the bright heads of Lot's children, but only the dark boy Mordred, who stood a little way apart from the others, watching them, not as an outcast might watch his more favoured brothers, but as a prince might watch his subjects.

Mordred himself. I never spoke with him. Mostly the boys were on the children's side of the palace, or in the care of the master-at-arms or those set to train them. But one afternoon, on a dark day drawing to dusk, I came on him, standing beside the arch of a garden gateway, as if waiting for someone. I paused, wondering how to greet him, and how he might receive his mother's enemy, when I saw his head turn, and he started forward. Arthur and Guinevere came together through the dead roses of the garden, and out through the archway. It was too far away for me to hear what was said, but I saw the Queen smile and reach out a hand, and the King spoke, with a kind look. Mordred answered him, then, in obedience to a gesture from Arthur, went with them as they moved off, walking between them.

And, finally, Arthur, one evening in the King's private chamber, when Nimuë brought the box to show him the treasure from Segontium.

The box lay on top of the big marble table that had been my father's. It was of metal, and heavy, its lid scored and dented with the weight of the stuff that had fallen on it when the shrine crumbled to ruin. The King laid hands to it. For a few moments it resisted him, then suddenly, light as a leaf, it lifted.

Inside were the things just as I remembered them. Rotten canvas wrappings, and, gleaming through them, the head of a lance. He drew it out, trying the edge with a thumb, a gesture as natural as breathing.

"For ornament, I think," he said, rubbing the jewels of the

binding with his hand, and laying it aside. Then came a flattish dish, gold, with the rim crusted with gems. And finally, out of a tumble of greyed linen fallen to dust, the bowl. It was the type of bowl they call sometimes a cauldron, or a grail of the Greek fashion, wide and deep. It was of gold, and from the way he handled it, very heavy. There was chasing of some sort round the outside of the bowl, and on the foot. The two handles were shaped like birds' wings. On a band round it, out of the way of the drinker's lips, were emeralds and sapphires. He turned and held it out to me with both hands.

"Take it and see. It is the most precious thing I have ever seen." I shook my head. "It is not for me to touch."

"Nor for me," said Nimuë.

He looked at it for a moment longer, then he put it back in the box with the lance and the dish, gently wrapping the things away in the linen which was worn thin, like a veil. "And you won't even tell me where to keep such splendour, or what I am to do with it?"

Nimuë looked across at me, and was silent. When I spoke, it was only a gentle echo of what I had said before, long ago. "It is not for you, either, Arthur. You do not need it. You yourself will be the grail for your people, and they will drink from you and be satisfied. You will never fail them, nor ever leave them quite. You do not need the grail. Leave it for those who come after."

"Then since it is neither mine nor yours," said Arthur, "Nimuë must take it, and with her enchantments hide it so that no one can find it except that they are fitted."

"No one shall," she said, and shut the lid on the treasure.

★   ★   ★

After that, another year dawned cold, and drew slowly into spring. I went home at April's end, with the wind turning warm, and the young lambs crying on the hill, and catkins shivering yellow in the copses.

The cave was swept and warm again, a place for living, and there was food there, with fresh bread and a crock of milk and a jar of honey. Outside, by the spring, were offerings left by the folk I knew, and all my belongings, with my books and medicines, my instruments and the great standing harp, had been brought from Applegarth.

My return to life had been easier than I had anticipated. It seems that, to the simple folk, as indeed to the people in distant parts of Britain, the tale of my return from death was accepted, not as plain truth, but as a legend. The Merlin they had known and feared was dead; a Merlin lived on in the "holy cave", working his minor magics, but only a ghost, as it were, of the enchanter they had known. It may be they thought that I, like so many pretenders of the past, was some small magician merely claiming Merlin's reputation and his place. In the court, and in the cities and the great places of the earth, people looked now to Nimuë for power and help. To me the local folk came to have their sores or their aches healed; to me Ban the shepherd brought the sickly lambs, and the children from the village their pet puppies.

So the year wore on, but so lightly that it seemed only like the evening of a quiet day. The days were golden, tranquil and sweet. There was no call of power, no great high clean wind, no pain in the heart or pricking of the flesh. The great doings of the kingdom seemed no longer to trouble me. I did not hunger or ask after news, for when it came, it was brought by the King himself. Just as the boy Arthur, racing up to see me in the shrine of the Wild Forest, had poured out all the doings of every day at my feet, so did the High King of Britain bring me all his acts, his problems and his troubles, and spread them out there on the cave floor in the firelight, and talk to me. What I did for him I do not know; but always, after he had gone, I found myself sitting, drained and silent, in the stillness of complete content.

The god, who was God, had indeed dismissed his servant, and was letting him go in peace.

★　★　★

One day I drew the small harp to me, and set myself to make a new verse for a song sung many years ago.

Rest here, enchanter, while the fire dies.
In a breath, in an eyelid's fall,

You will see them, the dreams;
The sword and the young king,
The white horse and the running water,
The lit lamp and the boy smiling.

Dreams, dreams, enchanter! Gone
With the harp's echo when the strings
Fall mute; with the flame's shadow when the fire
Dies. Be still, and listen.

Far on the black air
Blows the great wind, rises
The running tide, flows the clear river.
Listen, enchanter, hear
Through the black air and the singing air
The music . . .

I had to leave the song there because a string broke. He had
promised to bring me new ones, next time he came.

★   ★   ★

He came again yesterday. Something had called him down to
Caerleon, he said, so he had ridden up, just for an hour. When I
asked him what the business was in Caerleon, he put the question
aside, till I wondered – then dismissed it as absurd – if the journey
had been made merely to see me. He brought gifts with him – he
never came empty-handed – wine, a basket of cooked meats from
his own kitchen, the promised harp-strings, and a blanket of soft
new wool, woven, he told me, by the Queen's own women. He
carried them in himself, like a servant, and put them away for me.
He seemed in spirits. He told me of some young man who had
recently come to court, a noble fighter, and a cousin of March of
Cornwall. Then he spoke of a meeting he was planning with the
Saxon "king", Eosa's successor, Cerdic. We talked till the dark
drew in, and his escort came jingling up the valley track for him.
Then he rose, lightly, and, as always now when he left me,
stooped to kiss me. Usually he made me stay there, by the fire,

while he went out into the night, but this time I got up and followed him to the cave entrance, and waited there to watch him go. The light was behind me, and my shadow stretched, thin and long, like the tall shadow of old, across the little lawn and almost to the grove of thorn trees where the escort waited below the cliff.

It was almost night, but over beyond Maridunum in the west, a lingering bar of light hinted at the dying sun. It threw a glint on the river skirting the palace wall where I was born, and touched a jewel spark on the distant sea. Near at hand the trees were bare with winter, and the ground crisp with the first frost. Arthur trod away from me across the grass, leaving ghost-prints in the frost. He reached the place where the track led down to the grove, and half turned. I saw him raise a hand.

"Wait for me." It was the same farewell always. "Wait for me. I shall come back."

And, as ever, I made the same reply:

"What else have I to do but wait for you? I shall be here, when you come again."

The sound of the horses dwindled, faded, was gone. The winter's silence came back to the valley. The dark drew down.

A breath of the night slid, like a sigh, through the frost-hung trees. In its wake, faintly, like no sound but the ghost of a sound, came a faint, sweet ringing from the air. I lifted my head, remembering, once more, the child who had listened nightly for the music of the spheres, but had never heard it. Now here it was, all around me, a sweet, disembodied music, as if the hill itself was a harp to the high air.

Dark fell. Behind me the fire dimmed, and my shadow vanished. Still I stood listening, with the calmness over me of a great contentment. The sky, heavy with night, drew nearer the earth. The glimmer on the far sea moved, light and following shadow, like the slow arc of a sword sliding back to its sheath, or a barge dwindling under sail across the distant water.

It was quite dark. Quite still. A chill brushed my skin, like the cold touch of crystal.

I left the night, with its remote and singing stars, and came in, to the glow of the fire, and the chair where he had been sitting, and the unstrung harp.

The Legend

When King Uther Pendragon lay close to death, Merlin approached him in the sight of all the lords and made him acknowledge his son Arthur as the new king. Which he did, and afterwards died, and was buried by the side of his brother Aurelius Ambrosius within the Giants' Dance.

Then Merlin had a great sword fashioned, and fixed by his magic art into a great stone shaped like an altar. There were gold letters on the sword which said: "Whoso pulleth out this sword of this stone, is rightwise king born of all England." When at length it was seen by all men that only Arthur could pull the sword from the stone, the people cried out: "We will have Arthur unto our king, we will put him no more in delay, for we all see that it is God's will that he should be our king, and who that holdeth against it, we will slay him." So Arthur was accepted by the people, high and low, and raised to be king. When he was crowned, he made Sir Kay the seneschal of England, and Sir Ulfius was made his chamberlain.

After this were many years of wars, and battles, but then came Merlin on a great black horse, and said to Arthur, "Thou hast never done, hast thou not done enough? It is time to say Ho! And therefore withdraw you unto your lodging and rest you as soon as ye may, and reward your good knights with gold and with silver, for they have well deserved it." "It is well said," quoth Arthur, "and as thou hast devised, so it shall be done." Then Merlin took his leave of Arthur, and travelled to see his master Blaise, that dwelt in Northumberland. So Blaise wrote the battles word by word, as Merlin told him.

Then one day King Arthur said to Merlin, "My barons will let me have no rest, but needs I must take a wife." "It is well done," said Merlin, "that ye take a wife. Now is there any that ye love more than another?" "Yea," said King Arthur, "I love Guinevere, the king's daughter, Leodegrance of the land of Cameliard, the which holdeth in his house the Table Round that *ye told he had of my father Uther."* Then Merlin advised the King that Guinevere was not wholesome for him to take to wife, and warned him that Lancelot should love her, and she him again. In spite of this the King determined to wed Guinevere, and sent Sir Lancelot, the chief of his knights and his trusted friend, to bring her from her home.

On this journey Merlin's prophecy came to pass, and Lancelot and Guinevere loved one another. But they were helpless to realise their love, and in time Guinevere was married to the King. Her father, King Leodegrance, sent the Round Table to Arthur as a wedding gift.

Meanwhile Arthur's half-sister Morgause had borne her bastard son by the King. His name was Mordred. Merlin had prophesied that great danger should come to Arthur and his kingdom through this child, so when the King heard of the birth he sent for all the children born upon May-day, and they were put into a ship and set adrift. Some were four weeks old, some less. By chance the ship drove against a rock where stood a castle. The ship was destroyed, and all in it died except Mordred, who was found by a good man, and reared until he was fourteen years of age, when he was brought to the King.

Soon after the wedding of Arthur and Guinevere the King had to leave the court, and in his absence King Meleagant (Melwas) carried the Queen off into his kingdom from which, as men said, no traveller ever returned. The only way into her moated prison was by two very perilous paths. One of these was called "the water bridge" because the bridge lay under water, invisible and very narrow. The other bridge was much more perilous, and had never been crossed by a man, made as it was of a sharp sword. No one dared go after her but Lancelot, and he made his way through unknown country, until he came near Meleagant's lodge that had been built for the Queen. Then he crossed the sword bridge, and sustained grievous wounds therefrom, but he rescued the Queen, and later, in the presence of King Arthur and the court, he fought and killed Meleagant.

Then it befell that Merlin fell in a dotage on one of the damosels of the Lake, whose name was Nimuë, and Merlin would let her have no rest, but always he would be with her. He warned King Arthur that he should not be long above earth, but for all his craft he would be put alive into the earth, and he warned him also to keep his sword and the scabbard safely, for it would be stolen from him by a woman that he most trusted. "Ah," said the King, "since ye know of your adventure, why do you not put it away by your magic arts, and prevent it?" "That cannot be," said Merlin. "It is

*ordained that ye shall die a worshipful death, and I a shameful death."
Then he left the King. Shortly after this Nimuë, the damosel of the Lake,
departed, and Merlin went with her wherever she went. They went over
the sea to the land of Benwick, in Brittany, where King Ban was king, and
Elaine his wife had with her the young child called Galahad. Merlin
prophesied that one day Galahad should be the most man of worship in the
world. Then after this Nimuë and Merlin left Benwick, and came into
Cornwall. And the lady was afraid of him because he was a devil's son, and
she did not know how to make away with him. Then it happened that
Merlin showed her a cave in a rock which could be sealed with a great stone.
So by her subtle working she made Merlin go under that stone to show her
the magic that dwelt there, but she cast a spell on him so that he could not
ever come out again. And she went away and left him there in the cave.*

*And anon a knight, a cousin of the King's called Bagdemagus, rode out
from the court, to find a branch of an holy herb for healing. It happened that
he rode by the rock where the Lady of the Lake had put Merlin under the
stone, and there he heard him lamenting. Sir Bagdemagus would have
helped him, but when he went to the stone to lift it, it was so heavy that an
hundred men could not have moved it. When Merlin knew he was there, he
told him to save his labour, for all was in vain. So Bagdemagus went, and
left him there.*

*Meantime it had happened as Merlin had foretold, and Arthur's sister
Morgan le Fay had stolen the sword Excalibur and its sheath. She gave
these to Sir Accolon with which to fight the King himself. And when the
King was armed for the fight there came a maiden from Morgan le Fay, and
brought to Arthur a sword like Excalibur, with its scabbard, and he thanked
her. But she was false, for the sword and the scabbard were counterfeits, and
brittle. So there was a battle between King Arthur and Accolon. The Lady
of the Lake came to this battle, for she knew that Morgan le Fay wished ill
to the King, and she wanted to save him. King Arthur's sword broke in his
hand, and only after a grievous fight did he get his own sword Excalibur
back from Sir Accolon and defeat him. Then Accolon confessed the treason
of Morgan le Fay, King Urien's wife, and the King granted mercy to him.*

*And after this the Lady of the Lake became the friend and guardian of
King Arthur, in the stead of Merlin the enchanter.*

Author's Note

According to legend, of which the main source is Malory's Morte
d'Arthur, *Merlin stayed above ground only a short while after Arthur was
crowned. The period of battles and tournaments that follows the coronation
can surely be taken to represent the actual battles fought by the historic
Arthur. All that we know of the real war-leader, Arthur the Soldier (dux
bellorum), is that he fought twelve major battles before he could count
Britain safe from the Saxon enemy, and that eventually he died, and
Mordred with him, at the battle of Camlann. The much-quoted account of
the twelve battles occurs in the* Historia Brittonum *written by the Welsh
monk Nennius in the ninth century.*

*Then Arthur fought against them in those days, with the kings of the
Britons, but he himself was the leader of battles. The first battle was at
the mouth of the river which is called Glein. The second, third, fourth
and fifth, on another river, which is called Dubglas, and is in the region
of Linnuis. The sixth battle was on the river which is called Bassas. The
seventh was a battle in the wood of Celidon, that is Cat Coit Celidon.
The eighth was the battle at Castellum Guinnion, in which Arthur
carried the image of Saint Mary, ever Virgin, on his shoulders, and the
pagans were put to flight on that day and there was a great slaughter of
them through the power of our Lord Jesus Christ and through the power
of Saint Mary the Virgin, his mother. The ninth battle was fought
at the City of the Legions. The tenth battle he fought on the river,
which is called Tribuit. The eleventh occurred on the mountain,
which is called Agned. The twelfth was the battle of Mount Badon, in
which there fell together in one day 960 men in one onset of Arthur,
and no one laid them low save himself alone. And in all the battles he
remained victor.*

Only two of these battles can be located with any kind of certainty; that in the Caledonian Forest – the Old Caledonian Forest that stretched down from Strathclyde into the modern Lake District – and the one at the City of Legions, which could be either Chester or Caerleon. I have contented myself with using Nennius' own place-names, and identifying only one other, the battle of the River Tribuit. It has been suggested that this is an early name of the River Ribble. There is a place where the old Roman road crosses the Ribble and heads towards the Aire Gap (the "Pennine Gap"). This is called Nappa or Nappay Ford, and local tradition remembers a battle there. The nearby camp that I have called "Tribuit" was at Long Preston; the other two in the Gap were of course Elslack and Ilkley. I also made use of a tradition that Arthur fought at High Rochester (Bremenium) in the Cheviots. Apart from these two "battle sites" I have inserted none in the map.

Blaise. According to Malory, Blaise "wrote down Arthur's battles word for word", a chronicle which, if it ever existed, has vanished utterly. I took the liberty of building in a destructive agent in the person of Gildas, the young son of Caw of Strathclyde and brother of Heuil. These are historic personages. We are told that Arthur and Heuil hated one another. Gildas the monk, writing in about 540 A.D., refers to the victory of "Mount Badon", but without mentioning Arthur by name. This has been interpreted as a sign, at the least, of disapproval of a leader who had shown himself no friend to the Church.

Merlin's illness. The episode in the Wild Forest is taken from the story of Merlin's madness as told in the Vita Merlini, *a twelfth century Latin poem commonly ascribed to Geoffrey of Monmouth. This is in part a retelling of the older Celtic "Lailoken" tale of the madman who roamed the Caledonian Forest. Merlin-Lailoken was present at the battle of Arfderydd (the modern Arthuret, near Carlisle) where his friend, the king, was killed. Driven mad by grief, he fled into the forest, where he eked out a wretched existence.*

There are two poems in The Black Book of Carmarthen *which are attributed to him. In one he describes the apple-tree that shelters and feeds him in the forest; in the other he addresses the piglet which is his sole companion.*

Guenever and Guinevere. Tradition asserts that Arthur had two wives of the same name, or even three – though this was probably only a con-

veniently poetic round number. The rape of Guinevere by Melwas (or Meleagant) occurs in the mediæval romance Lancelot *of Chrétien de Troyes. In Chrétien's story Lancelot has to cross a sword bridge leading to the hollow hill of faery — a version of the ancient rape fantasy that we find in the tales of Dis and Persephone, or Orpheus and Eurydice.*

Guinevere, according to the mediæval legends, suffered abduction from time to time as a matter of course, and equally as a matter of course was rescued by Lancelot. A modern reader can see how the stories rose around "the much-abducted queen". Mediæval singers found in "King Arthur and his Court" a rich source of story-telling, and in time a long series of tales came to be hung around the central figures, much as the television series-writers hang their scripts today. Gradually, in the legends, Arthur himself fades into the background, and various new "heroes" take the centre of the stage; Lancelot, Tristram, Gawain, Gereint. Lancelot, being purely fictional (and an invention some centuries later than the "Arthurian fact"), is made to fill the role of the Queen's lover so essential to the mediæval romancers and their convention of courtly love.

But it is tempting to believe that the first of the "rape stories", the Queen's abduction by Melwas, was founded on fact. Certainly Melwas existed, and remains have been found of the right period that indicate strongholds on and near Glastonbury Tor. In my tale Bedwyr, whose name is linked with Arthur's long before "Lancelot" ever appears, takes the Lancelot role. In the character of Guinevere, as here drawn, I believe I was influenced by Chaucer's treatment of the "false" Criseyde.

Nimuë *(Niniane, Vivien). Nor is there any necessity to attribute the same sort of "falseness" to Merlin's lover Nimuë. The "betrayal" theme of this legend springs from the need to explain the death or disappearance of an all-powerful enchanter. My version of Merlin's end is based on a tradition which obtains still in parts of the "Summer Country". It was sent me many years ago by a Wiltshire correspondent. This version of the tale is that Merlin, with age drawing on, desired to hand on his magic powers to someone who could be Arthur's adviser after his death. For this he chose his pupil Nimuë, who showed herself adept. This tale not only allows the "great enchanter" his dignity, and a measure of common sense, but also explains Nimuë's subsequent influence over Arthur. The King would hardly otherwise have kept her near him, or accepted her help against his enemies.*

Ninian. *The "boy Ninian" episode was suggested by another incident found in the* Vita Merlini. *Here Merlin sees a youth buying shoes, and pieces of leather to repair them with to make them last longer. Merlin knows that the youth will have no need of the new shoes, as he will be drowned the same day.*

Cerdic Elesing. *The Anglo-Saxon Chronicle records that Cerdic and Cynric his son landed at Cerdices-ora with five ships. Cerdic was Elesing (the son of Elesa, or Eosa). The date given is 494 A.D.*

Whatever doubt there may be about the dates of Cerdic's battles, or the locations of his first conquests (Cerdices-ora is thought to be Netley, near Southampton), all the chroniclers seem to agree that he was the founder of the first West Saxon monarchy from which Alfred was to claim descent. For Cerdic, and for the changing of the burial customs that Gereint suggests on page 99, see Hodgkin's History of the Anglo-Saxons, *Vol. 1, Section IV.*

Llud-Nuatha, or Nodens. *The shrine of Nodens is still to be seen, at Lydney in Gloucestershire.*

Merlin's song. *"He who is companionless" is based on the Anglo-Saxon poem "The Wanderer".*

Finally, for the many gaps in my knowledge of this enormous subject I can only beg forgiveness, and paraphrase what H. M. and N. K. Chadwick wrote in the preface to their Growth of English Literature: *"If I had read more widely I should never have completed this book." More: if I had even known how much there was to read, I would never have dared to start to write at all. By the same token I cannot list all the authorities I have followed. But I can hope, in all humility, that my Merlin trilogy may be, for some new enthusiast, a beginning.*

Mary Stewart
Edinburgh 1975 – 1979

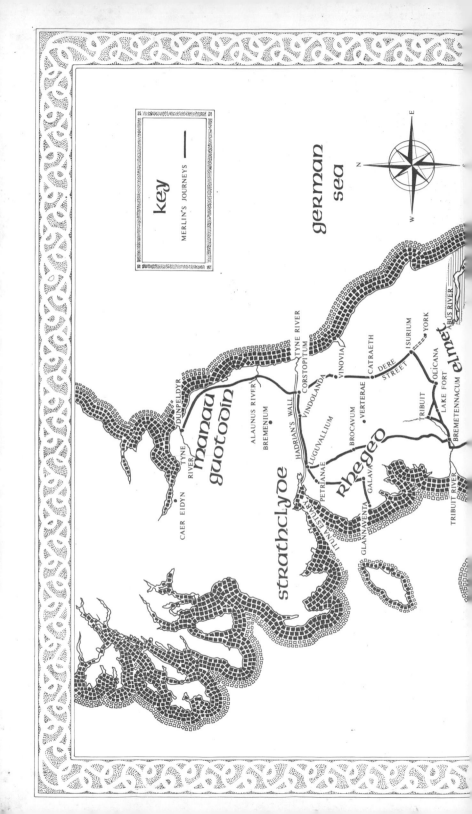